Fodor's 04

ALASKA

Where to Stay and Eat
for All Budgets

Must-See Sights
and Local Secrets

Ratings You Can Trust

Fodor's Travel Publications   New York, Toronto, London, Sydney, Auckland
www.fodors.com

FODOR'S ALASKA 2004

Editor: Mary Beth Bohman

Editorial Production: Stacey Kulig

Editorial Contributors: Mary Engel, Robin Mackey Hill, Satu Hummasti, Sue Kernaghan, Melissa Klurman, Dr. Charles Lane, Mike Miller, Stanton H. Patty, Don Pitcher, Tom Reale, Melissa Rivers, Helayne Schiff, M. T. Schwartzman, Bill Sherwonit, Sarah Sper, Kent Sturgis, William Travis, Eric Troyer, Peggy Wayburn, Howard C. Weaver

Maps: David Lindroth, *cartographer*; Bob Blake and Rebecca Baer, *map editors*

Design: Fabrizio La Rocca, *creative director*; Guido Caroti, *art director*; Melanie Marin, *senior picture editor*

Production/Manufacturing: Colleen Ziemba

Cover Photo (Denali National Park): Larry Ulrich/Stone/Getty Images

COPYRIGHT

ISBN 1–4000–1305–4

ISSN 0271–2776

SPECIAL SALES

Fodor's Travel Publications are available at special discounts for bulk purchases for sales promotions or premiums. Special editions, including personalized covers, excerpts of existing guides, and corporate imprints, can be created in large quantities for special needs. For more information, contact your local bookseller or write to Special Markets, Fodor's Travel Publications, 1745 Broadway, New York, NY 10019. Inquiries from Canada should be directed to your local Canadian bookseller or sent to Random House of Canada, Ltd., Marketing Department, 2775 Matheson Boulevard East, Mississauga, Ontario L4W 4P7. Inquiries from the United Kingdom should be sent to Fodor's Travel Publications, 20 Vauxhall Bridge Road, London SW1V 2SA, England.

AN IMPORTANT TIP & AN INVITATION

Although all prices, opening times, and other details in this book are based on information supplied to us at press time, changes occur all the time in the travel world, and Fodor's cannot accept responsibility for facts that become outdated or for inadvertent errors or omissions. So **always confirm information when it matters,** especially if you're making a detour to visit a specific place. Your experiences—positive and negative—matter to us. If we have missed or misstated something, **please write to us.** We follow up on all suggestions. Contact the Alaska editor at editors@fodors.com or c/o Fodor's at 1745 Broadway, New York, NY 10019.

PRINTED IN THE UNITED STATES OF AMERICA

10 9 8 7 6 5 4 3 2 1

DESTINATION ALASKA

Alaska's otherworldly beauty is common but never ordinary. Awe-inspiring works of nature fill the state's vast breadth, from the fjord-laced Southeast to the majestic peaks of expansive mountain ranges. For lovers of the outdoors, few places parallel Alaska. Most people aren't used to having wilderness, colossal in scale, just outside town. Skiers at Mendenhall Glacier are only a dozen miles from downtown Juneau, the state's charming vest-pocket capital. Other cities and towns punctuate the breathtaking landscape. In places such as Skagway, Fairbanks, and Anchorage, you can eat well, celebrate until the sun sets (well after midnight in summer), and learn about Alaska's vibrant cultural heritage, forged by early Native settlers and 19th-century gold-prospecting pioneers, among others. You won't run out of things to see and do in this last American frontier; you will only run out of time.

Karen Cure, Editorial Director

CONTENTS

ABOUT THIS BOOK

There's no doubt that the best source for travel advice is a like-minded friend who's just been where you're headed. But with or without that friend, you'll have a better trip with a Fodor's guide in hand. Once you've learned to find your way around its pages, you'll be in great shape to find your way around your destination.

SELECTION Our goal is to cover the best properties, sights, and activities in their category, as well as the most interesting communities to visit. We make a point of including local food lovers' hot spots as well as neighborhood options, and we avoid all that's touristy unless it's really worth your time. You can go on the assumption that everything you read about in this book is recommended wholeheartedly by our writers and editors. Flip to On the Road with Fodor's to learn more about who they are. It goes without saying that no property mentioned in the book has paid to be included.

RATINGS Orange stars ★ denote sights and properties that our editors and writers consider the very best in the area covered by the entire book. These, the best of the best, are listed in the Fodor's Choice section in the front of the book. Black stars ★ highlight the sights and properties we deem Highly Recommended, the don't-miss sights within any region. Fodor's Choice and Highly Recommended options in each region are usually listed on the title page of the chapter covering that region. Use the index to find complete descriptions. In cities, sights pinpointed with numbered map bullets ❶ in the margins tend to be more important than those without bullets.

SPECIAL SPOTS Pleasures & Pastimes focuses on types of experiences that reveal the spirit of the destination. Watch for Off the Beaten Path sights. Some are out of the way, some are quirky, and all are worth your while. If the munchies hit while you're exploring, look for Need a Break? suggestions.

TIME IT RIGHT Wondering when to go? Check On the Calendar up front and chapters' Timing sections for weather and crowd overviews and best days and times to visit.

SEE IT ALL Use Fodor's exclusive Great Itineraries as a model for your trip. (For a good overview of the entire destination, follow those that begin the book, or mix regional itineraries from several chapters.) In cities, Good Walks guide you to important sights in each neighborhood; ▶ indicates the starting points of walks and itineraries in the text and on the map.

BUDGET WELL Hotel and restaurant price categories from ¢ to $$$$ are defined in the opening pages of each chapter. Expect to find a balanced selection for every budget. For attractions, we always give standard adult admission fees; reductions are usually available for children, students, and senior citizens. Look in Discounts & Deals in Smart Travel Tips for information on destination-wide ticket schemes. Want to pay with plastic? AE, D, DC, MC, V following restaurant and hotel listings indicate whether American Express, Discover, Diners Club, MasterCard, or Visa are accepted.

BASIC INFO Smart Travel Tips lists travel essentials for the entire area covered by the book; city- and region-specific basics end each chapter. To find the best way to get around, see the transportation section; see individual modes of travel ("By Car," "By Train") for details. We assume you'll check Web sites or call for particulars.

ON THE MAPS   Maps throughout the book show you what's where and help you find your way around. Black and orange numbered bullets ❶ ① in the text correlate to bullets on maps.

BACKGROUND   In general, we give background information within the chapters in the course of explaining sights as well as in CloseUp boxes and in Understanding Alaska at the end of the book.

FIND IT FAST   The book begins with chapters on cruising and wilderness adventures to help you decide how you will see Alaska. Then it's on to the Great Land itself. Anchorage as well as Vancouver and Victoria in British Columbia—the gateway cities—come first. The regional chapters that follow are divided into small territories, within which towns are covered in logical geographical order; attractive routes and interesting places between towns are flagged as En Route. Heads at the top of each page help you find what you need within a chapter.

DON'T FORGET   Restaurants are open for lunch and dinner daily unless we state otherwise; we mention dress only when there's a specific requirement and reservations only when they're essential or not accepted—it's always best to book ahead. Hotels have private baths, phones, TVs, and air-conditioning and operate on the European Plan (a.k.a. EP, meaning without meals). We always list facilities but not whether you'll be charged extra to use them, so when pricing accommodations, find out what's included.

SYMBOLS

Many Listings
- ★ Fodor's Choice
- ★ Highly recommended
- ⊠ Physical address
- ✛ Directions
- ⌖ Mailing address
- ☎ Telephone
- 🖷 Fax
- ⊕ On the Web
- ✉ E-mail
- 🎟 Admission fee
- ☉ Open/closed times
- ► Start of walk/itinerary
- ⊟ Credit cards

Outdoors
- ⚲ Golf
- ⛺ Camping

Hotels & Restaurants
- 🏨 Hotel
- ➷ Number of rooms
- ♿ Facilities
- ❘❍❘ Meal plans
- ✕ Restaurant
- ✍ Reservations
- 🎩 Dress code
- ❘ Smoking
- 🍸 BYOB
- ✕🏨 Hotel with restaurant that warrants a visit

Other
- ♨ Family-friendly
- ✦ Contact information
- ⇨ See also
- ⊠ Branch address
- ☞ Take note

ON THE ROAD WITH FODOR'S

A trip takes you out of yourself. Concerns of life at home completely disappear, driven away by more immediate thoughts—about, say, what marvels will beguile the next day or where you'll have dinner. That's where Fodor's comes in. We make sure that you know all your options, so that you don't miss something that's around the next bend just because you didn't know it was there. Because the best memories of your trip might well have nothing to do with what you came to Alaska to see, we guide you to sights large and small all over the region. You might set out to see Mt. McKinley or wildlife in Denali National Park, but back at home you find yourself unable to forget sea kayaking in Glacier Bay National Park. With Fodor's at your side, serendipitous discoveries are never far away.

Our success in showing you every corner of Alaska is a credit to our extraordinary writers. Although there's no substitute for travel advice from a good friend who knows your style, our contributors are the next best thing—the kind of people you would poll for travel advice if you knew them.

Vancouver-born freelance writer Sue Kernaghan is a fourth-generation British Columbian. Between Fodor's assignments, Sue writes travel feature articles and management books.

Don Pitcher's knowledge of Alaska comes from a dozen seasons spent guiding visitors to brown-bear viewing areas, counting salmon at fish weirs, studying fires in Wrangell–St. Elias National Park, and building trails in rainy Southeast Alaska. He is the author of guidebooks on Alaska, Wyoming, Washington, and Berkeley, California.

A midwesterner who moved to Alaska in 1984, Tom Reale has traveled extensively throughout the state, writing about it and about wilderness adventures for a variety of publications. He and his wife hunt, fish, camp, backpack, ski, and hike at every opportunity.

An Anchorage resident since 1982, writer Bill Sherwonit has contributed stories about Alaska to a variety of newspapers, magazines, and books and is the author of four books on Alaska. He also teaches a class on wilderness writing at the University of Alaska.

Time Zones

Numbers below vertical bands relate each zone
to Greenwich Mean Time (0 hrs.).
Local times frequently differ from these general indications,
as indicated by light-face numbers on map.

F 10 <

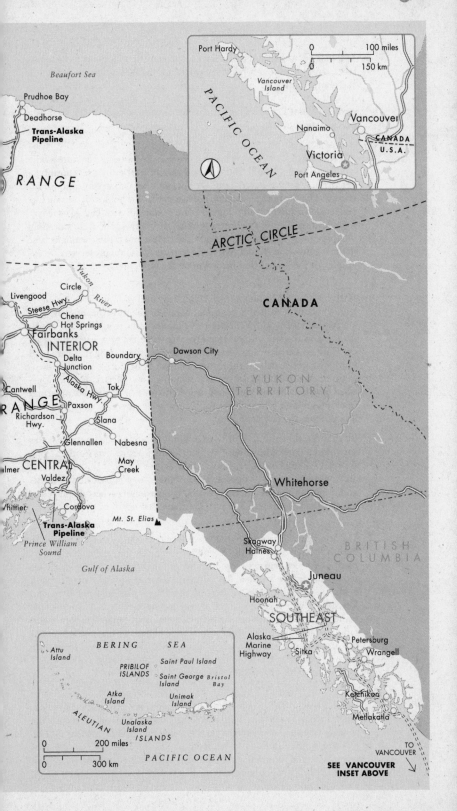

Beaufort Sea

Prudhoe Bay

Deadhorse

Trans-Alaska Pipeline

RANGE

Port Hardy

PACIFIC OCEAN

Vancouver Island

0   100 miles

0   150 km

Nanaimo

Vancouver

CANADA

U.S.A.

Victoria

Port Angeles

ARCTIC CIRCLE

Yukon River

Circle

Livengood

Steese Hwy.

Chena Hot Springs

Fairbanks

INTERIOR

Delta Junction

Boundary

Dawson City

CANADA

YUKON TERRITORY

Cantwell

RANGE

Paxson

Richardson Hwy.

Slana

Alaska Hwy.

Tok

Glennallen

Nabesna

CENTRAL

May Creek

lmer

Valdez

Cordova

Whittier

Trans-Alaska Pipeline

Prince William Sound

Mt. St. Elias

Gulf of Alaska

Whitehorse

Skagway

Haines

BRITISH COLUMBIA

Juneau

Hoonah

SOUTHEAST

Alaska Marine Highway

Sitka

Petersburg

Wrangell

Ketchikan

Metlakatla

Attu Island

BERING SEA

PRIBILOF ISLANDS

Saint Paul Island

Saint George Island

Bristol Bay

Atka Island

Unimak Island

Unalaska Island

ALEUTIAN

ISLANDS

0   200 miles

0   300 km

PACIFIC OCEAN

TO VANCOUVER

SEE VANCOUVER INSET ABOVE

In a place as big as Alaska, it's no surprise to find incredible variations of geography, topography, and climate. Of the 20 highest mountains in the United States, 17 are in Alaska: the state has 19 peaks higher than 14,000 feet. And nearly all of the Southeast lies in a rain forest, the Tongass National Forest, whereas the northernmost part of the state is a precipitation desert.

③ Anchorage

Alaska's biggest city (population more than 261,000) is the state's only true metropolis. You'll find a varied selection of ethnic restaurants, a performing arts center, theater groups, an opera company, and an orchestra. The Anchorage Museum of History and Art houses an outstanding collection of historic and contemporary Alaskan art. The Alaska Native Heritage Center celebrates the rich diversity of the state's original inhabitants. At nearby Lake Hood—the largest and busiest seaplane base in the world—the Alaska Aviation Heritage Museum preserves rare examples of the planes that helped tame the wilderness.

④ Vancouver & Victoria, British Columbia

With the Coast Mountains as its backdrop and the Pacific Ocean at its feet, Vancouver, British Columbia, is one of the most beautifully situated cities in the world. Vancouver's Chinatown, the third largest in North America, is the site of the Ming Dynasty–style Dr. Sun Yat-Sen Classical Chinese Garden. On Granville Island, buskers, bright colors, and outdoor eateries delight the senses. Half an hour's drive west, the Museum of Anthropology serves as a window on civilizations that flourished here long before the British sailed into port. A celebrated aquarium celebrates nature's work in the trail-laced wilderness of Stanley Park just blocks from the city center.

In Victoria, the capital of British Columbia, stately Victorian structures surround a harbor alive with sailboats, street performers, and hanging flower baskets. Once an outpost of the British Empire, this city retains an Anglophile air in its double decker buses, cozy pubs, afternoon teas and, especially, in its citizens' passion for gardening—best displayed at the spectacular 55-acre Butchart Gardens, just north of town.

⑤ Southeast Alaska

The Southeast encompasses the Inside Passage—more than a century ago the traditional route to the Klondike goldfields and today the centerpiece of Alaska cruises. Here are glacier-filled fjords and the justly famous Glacier Bay National Park. Juneau, the state's water-locked capital, is also in the Southeast, as are fishing villages such as Petersburg and Ketchikan, which is known for its totem-pole carving. An onion-dome cathedral accents Sitka, the onetime capital of Russian America. Each fall up to 4,000 eagles gather just outside Haines to feast on salmon at the Alaska Chilkat Bald Eagle Preserve. Nearby Skagway is filled with historic buildings from the heyday of the Klondike gold rush and is a favorite stop for cruise-ship passengers.

⑥ South Central Alaska

Beyond Anchorage, South Central is an outdoor playground for fishing, hiking, wildlife watching, and rafting. Especially well visited are the towns of Seward and Homer on the Kenai Peninsula. Kodiak, 100 mi offshore in the Gulf of Alaska, is known as the Emerald Island for its green-carpeted mountains. The famous Kodiak brown bear, which can weigh up to 1,500 pounds and is the biggest terrestrial carnivore on Earth, makes its home here.

7 The Interior

Bounded by the Brooks Range to the north and the Alaska Range to the south, the Interior is home to Mt. McKinley, the highest peak in North America, and to Denali National Park. Fairbanks, founded in 1901 by a merchant and a prospector who together struck it rich in their respective endeavors, is today Alaska's second-largest city. Fairbanks is the gateway to the Far North—the towns of the Arctic and the Bering Coast that are connected mainly by air—and to Canada's Yukon Territory, whose gold-rush history is preserved in towns such as Dawson City and Whitehorse.

8 The Bush

The Bush, more a spirit than a place, is the last frontier of the Last Frontier. From Nome to Barrow, much of the ground is permanently frozen, and for months at a time the sun never sets—or never rises. In the Arctic are the hardy Eskimo people and the Prudhoe Bay oil fields, near Barrow, America's northernmost community. Prospectors still pan for gold on the beach in Nome, where they are occasionally joined by a wandering polar bear. Only one road leads up to the Arctic, the Dalton Highway. Otherwise, the only link between these outposts of civilization is by air or sea—unless you happen to have a sled-dog team, a snowmobile, or a Rollagon (a vehicle specially designed for crossing tundra).

The Alaska Peninsula and Aleutian Islands have steaming volcanoes and fast-changing weather. Katmai National Park's Novarupta and Mt. Katmai have kept things steamy through the years, and the park is also a prime brown-bear viewing ground. The Bering seacoast, a watery wilderness of more than 100,000 square mi, arcs from Bristol Bay to the Arctic Circle.

Planning a trip to Alaska requires a careful look at both your interests and finances. Those who prefer luxury travel in organized groups will probably choose a cruise-ship vacation. For independent travelers visiting Alaska, endless options appear. The state is far too big and undeveloped to see it all in a short period, so unless you have all summer—and are able to print your own money—you'll need to be very selective.

Highlights of Alaska
8 to 11 days

Sprawling national parks of unspoiled wilderness, wildlife viewing in Kenai Peninsula, breathtaking views from the overlooks of the Chugach Mountains outside Anchorage: Alaska begs to be experienced. Besides seeing many natural wonders, you can gain a sense of the state's culture from the communities that dot its limited highway system. Start or end this survey with two or three days in Anchorage.

SEWARD
2 or 3 days. Surrounded by lush mountains at the head of Resurrection Bay, Seward is the primary gateway to Kenai Fjords National Park. Here you can spot whales, sea otters, and puffins on coastal wildlife tours; walk to the icy snout of Exit Glacier; or explore the massive cold-water tanks at Alaska SeaLife Center, a research and visitor facility with examples of many of Alaska's marine mammals and seabirds.

KENAI & SOLDOTNA
1 or 2 days. The sportfishing hubs of South Central Alaska, these sister cities lie along the world-famous Kenai River, a clear-flowing, aqua-color stream. Five species of Pacific salmon spawn here each sum-

mer, including the mighty king, which may weigh 80 to 90 pounds or more. When not watching the salmon runs, you can take a stroll through Kenai's old town, which includes the Holy Assumption Russian Orthodox Church, or dig some clams at Clam Gulch, 24 mi south of Soldotna.

HOMER
2 or 3 days. This end-of-the-road coastal town proclaims itself the halibut capital of the world, but it also has a thriving community of artists and writers. Take a water taxi to nearby Kachemak Bay State and Wilderness Park, a rugged coastal wilderness of rain forest, jagged mountains, sheltered bays, pale blue glaciers, and abundant wildlife. A fishing charter includes an opportunity to view whales, seals, and porpoises close up. Before or after a wilderness excursion, visit the Pratt Museum, which has a saltwater aquarium, wildflower garden, and cultural and natural history displays. The Bunnell Street Gallery showcases work by local artists.

TALKEETNA
1 day. This small, rural community is the gateway to Denali. Mountaineers congregate here before flying into the Alaska Range; flightseers fly above it—sometimes even landing on glaciers. Denali National Park's entrance area is another 140 mi up the highway. You can also take sportfishing charters or join locals for libations and a game of pool in the historic Fairview Inn.

FAIRBANKS
2 days. Born as a gold-mining camp at the start of the 20th century, the Golden Heart of Alaska's Interior is the starting point for trips into much of northern Bush Alaska, including several remote wilderness parks accessible only by air. Near town, you

can hike the nature trails in Creamer's Field Migratory Waterfowl Refuge, where you might spot waterfowl, cranes, songbirds, or even a moose or bear. Or visit Pioneer Park, a theme park with museums, an art gallery, Native displays, and a gold-rush exhibit.

Wilderness Alaska
10 to 16 days

Grizzly bears and herds of caribou, placid bays and white-water rapids, the colorful dance of the northern lights: Alaska's wildlands are an outdoor playground for nature lovers. Though some areas are remote and expensive to visit, you can access several of the state's premier parks, refuges, and other public lands from the highway system and nearby gateway communities.

DENALI NATIONAL PARK & PRESERVE
3 or 4 days. Larger than the state of Massachusetts, Alaska's oldest and most famous parkland is a wilderness of high mountains, glacial rivers, northern forest, and expansive tundra plains. Mt. McKinley, also popularly known as Denali ("the High One"), rises 20,320 feet into the heavens, while grizzly bears roam alpine meadows and lowland valleys and wolves hunt caribou, moose, and Dall sheep. You'll find plentiful opportunities for camping, hiking, and river rafting in one of the country's most beautiful landscapes.

DENALI STATE PARK
1 or 2 days. Little Denali, as it is sometimes called, has some of South Central Alaska's best tundra hikes, along the Curry-Kesugi Ridge. The park's spectacular views of Mt. McKinley, North America's highest peak, are among the finest anywhere. At Byers Lake, just off the busy George

Yukon River

Fairbanks

3

265 mi.

Denali National Park and Preserve

Denali State Park

237 mi.

▲ **Mt. McKinley**

3

Talkeetna

113 mi.

3

Wasilla • Palmer

1 · 27 mi.

Anchorage •

1

Chugach State Park

Kenai

150 mi.

1

Soldotna

KENAI NAT'L WILDLIFE REFUGE

108 mi.

175 mi.

40 mi.

9

Chugach National Forest

24 mi.

Seward

Kenai National Wildlife Refuge

Kenai Fjords National Park

Resurrection Bay

84 mi.

1

Homer

Cook Inlet

KENAI FJORDS NAT'L PARK

KACHEMAK BAY STATE AND WILDERNESS PARK

Prince William Sound

---

can hike, climb mountains, ride horses, and fish. The park's major access points are all within a short drive of Alaska's largest city.

CHUGACH NATIONAL FOREST

1 or 2 days. Sprawling across much of the Kenai Peninsula and Prince William Sound, this 6-million-acre national forest has vast wooded lowlands, glacially carved mountains, and pristine coastal areas. While visiting, you can stay in campgrounds or the public-use cabins that dot the trails, saltwater beaches, and alpine lakes.

KENAI NATIONAL WILDLIFE REFUGE

1 or 2 days. Covering nearly 2 million acres, the Kenai refuge encompasses part of the vast Harding Icefield as well as rugged peaks and forested lowlands inhabited by moose, black bears, and grizzlies. You can set up camp in one of its 14 road-accessible campgrounds and spend your time canoeing or kayaking its myriad rivers and lakes.

KENAI FJORDS NATIONAL PARK

2 or 3 days. Tidewater glaciers, rugged fjords, and a variety of ocean life are highlights of this spectacular coastal parkland. Explore the park's perimeters on coastal wildlife tours based in Seward. Sea otters, sea lions, porpoises, and tens of thousands of seabirds—maybe even a whale or two—can be spotted from a tour boat. You can also fly in, stay in public-use cabins, and travel by kayaks in bays devoid of other humans. After a short hike on a trail at the end of the park road, you'll be face to face with the heavily crevassed Exit Glacier.

CHUGACH STATE PARK

2 or 3 days. Anchorage's ½-million-acre backyard wilderness includes 3,350-foot Flattop Mountain, Alaska's most-climbed peak. Dozens of glaciers, jagged spires, tundra meadows, forested valleys, grizzlies, moose, and a couple of wolf packs populate this natural expanse. You can camp, picnic, view wildlife, or pick berries. The more active

Parks Highway, you can camp or stay in public-use cabins. Popular activities are picnicking, boating, fishing, and watching for moose, loons, beavers, or the black bears that fish for spawning salmon.

Because Alaska is so big, each region experiences a different climate, and seasons come and go at different times of the year. In summer, the sun does not set for more than 2½ months in Barrow, north of the Arctic Circle. Even as far south as Juneau, you can see a glow of twilight in the sky at midnight. In winter, the situation is reversed, and the sun does not rise for more than two months in Alaska's northernmost regions. Anchorage gets about 5½–6 hours of daylight in mid-December.

Alaska is not a land of perpetual ice and snow—97% of the state is snow-free during those long summer days. With fair weather comes an onslaught of tourists and peak season prices. Summer, particularly late June through July, brings on plagues of mosquitoes. July and August are also the rainiest months throughout South Central and Interior Alaska. Fortunately, in perpetually wet Southeast Alaska, these months are the driest portion of the year. To avoid the summer crowds and prices, go during spring or fall.

Winter is the season for skiing, sledding, ice-skating, dog mushing, ice-fishing, and other sports. The long nights are also ideal for viewing the northern lights.

Climate

The chart below lists the average daily maximum and minimum temperatures for several Alaskan cities.

🔲 Forecasts **Weather Channel Connection** ☎ 900/932-8437, 95¢ per minute from a Touch-Tone phone 🌐 www.weather.com.

ANCHORAGE

Jan.	22F	– 6C	May	55F	13C	Sept.	55F	13C
	7	–14		38	3		40	4
Feb.	25F	4C	June	62F	17C	Oct.	41F	5C
	9	13		47	8		27	– 3
Mar.	31F	– 1C	July	65F	18C	Nov.	27F	– 3C
	14	–10		50	10		14	–10
Apr.	43F	6C	Aug.	63F	17C	Dec.	20F	– 7C
	27	– 3		49	9		6	–14

BARROW

Jan.	– 9F	–23C	May	24F	– 4C	Sept.	34F	1C
	–22	–30		13	–11		27	– 3
Feb.	–12F	–24C	June	39F	4C	Oct.	22F	– 6C
	–25	–32		29	– 2		12	–11
Mar.	– 8F	–22C	July	46F	8C	Nov.	7F	–14C
	–22	–30		33	1		– 5	–21
Apr.	7F	–14C	Aug.	44F	7C	Dec.	– 4F	–20C
	– 8	–22		33	1		–17	–27

FAIRBANKS

Jan.	– 2F	–19C	May	59F	15C	Sept.	54F	12C
	–20	–29		35	2		33	1
Feb.	11F	–12C	June	71F	22C	Oct.	35F	2C
	–10	–23		46	8		18	– 8
Mar.	23F	– 5C	July	72F	22C	Nov.	12F	–11C
	– 4	–20		48	9		– 5	–21
Apr.	42F	6C	Aug.	66F	19C	Dec.	1F	–17C
	17	– 8		44	7		–16	–27

ON THE CALENDAR

Top seasonal events include the Anchorage Fur Rendezvous in February, the Iditarod Trail Sled Dog Race in March, Juneau's Alaska Folk Festival in April, Sitka's Alaska Day Celebration in October, and Fairbanks's Oktoberfest in fall.

WINTER

Dec.	The offbeat Talkeetna Winterfest (☎ 907/733–2330) combines competitive athletic events for women in the Wilderness Women Contest, with competitive bidding for eligible mountain-man bachelors at the Bachelor Society Ball.
Jan.	Bethel's Kuskokwim 300 (☎ 907/543–3300 ⊕ www.k300.org) is one of the state's premier sled-dog races.
	At Seward's Polar Bear Jump Off (☎ 907/224–5230 ⊕ www.sewardak.org) bare skin meets barely above-freezing water.
	Spread over two weekends, the Anchorage Folk Festival (☎ 907/566–2334 ⊕ www.anchoragefolkfestival.org) at the University of Alaska Anchorage features hundreds of performers and musical workshops.
Mid-Jan.–Feb.	Sled-Dog Racing (☎ 907/562–2235) season in Anchorage begins with sprints every weekend.
Feb.	Tent City Winter Festival (☎ 800/367–9745 ⊕ www.wrangellchamber.org) in Wrangell captures the flavor of Alaska's early days.
	At the Cordova Iceworm Festival (☎ 907/424–7260 ⊕ www.iceworm.org) a 140-foot ice worm parades through city streets. Other events include a talent show and fun fair.
	Participants in the Yukon Quest International Sled Dog Race (☎ 907/452–7954 ⊕ www.yukonquest.com) mush their way between Whitehorse, the Yukon Territory, and Fairbanks.
	Anchorage's Fur Rendezvous (☎ 907/277–8615 ⊕ www.furrondy.net) delivers more than 150 events—from snowshoe softball to the Open World Championship Sled Dog Races.

SPRING

Mar.	The World Ice Art Championships and Winter Carnival (☎ 907/452–1105 ⊕ www.icealaska.com) brings the finest ice artists to downtown Fairbanks.
	The Iditarod Trail Sled Dog Race (☎ 907/376–5155 or 800/545–6874 ⊕ www.iditarod.com) stretches 1,049 mi from Anchorage to Nome. More than 70 dog teams compete in the world's premier sled-dog race.
	The Bering Sea Ice Golf Classic (☎ 907/443–5535 ⊕ www.nomealaska.org) is played with orange golf balls on the pack ice of the Bering Sea near Nome during the Iditarod. The seasonal "Nome National Forest" (150 or so abandoned Christmas trees) provides forest cover.

Apr.	The three-day Camai Dance Festival (☎ 907/543–1977 ⊕ www. bethelarts.com) in Bethel attracts dance groups from throughout Alaska and also from outside the state.
	The Alaska Folk Festival (☎ 907/463–3316 ⊕ www.juneau.com/aff) in Juneau is a laid-back mix of music, handmade crafts, and foods.
	The Alyeska Spring Carnival (☎ 907/754–2259 or 800/880–3880 ⊕ www.alyeskaresort.com) holds court at the Alyeska Resort & Ski Area, 40 mi southeast of Anchorage. The featured event is the Slush Cup, in which skiers and snowboarders attempt to ski across a slushy pond at the base of the mountain.
	The World Free Skiing Championship (☎ 206/933–2809 ⊕ www. cmfvaldez.com) lures the world's top daredevil skiers to snowy Thompson Pass near Valdez. It's part of the Chugach Mountain Festival, which also includes a mountain-bike race, backcountry ski race, and film festival.
Late Apr.– early May	During the Copper River Delta Shorebird Festival (☎ 907/424–7260 ⊕ www.ptialaska.net/~midtown) in Cordova, there are tours to beaches to witness the migration of millions of shorebirds.
May	The Little Norway Festival (☎ 907/772–4636 ⊕ www.petersburg. org) in picturesque Petersburg salutes the town's Scandinavian heritage.
	The Kodiak Crab Festival (☎ 907/486–5557 ⊕ www.kodiak.org) brings good food, a parade, a footrace, a survival-suit race, and the blessing of the fleet.
	Juneau Jazz 'n Classics (☎ 907/463–3378 ⊕ www.juneau.com/ music) features performances by regionally and nationally known classical and jazz musicians over a 10-day period.
SUMMER	
June	The Sitka Summer Music Festival (☎ 907/747–6774 ⊕ www. sitkamusicfestival.org) is a monthlong series of chamber music performances.
	The Midnight Sun Baseball Game (☎ 907/451–0095 ⊕ www. goldpanners.com) celebrates the longest day of the year, in Fairbanks. The game begins at 10:30 PM with no need for stadium lights.
July	The Mt. Marathon Race (☎ 907/224–8051 ⊕ www.sewardak.org) in Seward is a rugged and often bloody race up the 3,000-foot mountain. The best vantage point is right below the trail's starting line.
	The World Eskimo–Indian Olympics (☎ 907/452–6646 ⊕ www.weio. org) in Fairbanks tests participants in such skills as ear pulling, the knuckle hop, and the blanket toss.
	The popular KBBI Concert on the Lawn (☎ 907/235–7721 ⊕ www. kbbi.org) transforms Homer with a mini-Woodstock mélange of live bands and good food.

Aug.	Southeast Alaska State Fair (☎ 907/766–2476 ⊕ www.seakfair.org) brings exhibits, music, and other fun-filled activities to the Haines Fairgrounds.
Late Aug.–early Sept.	The Alaska State Fair (☎ 907/745–4827 or 800/850–3247 ⊕ www.alaskastatefair.org) in Palmer is the state's big end-of-summer blowout. Don't miss the famous 90-pound cabbages and other gargantuan vegetables.

FALL

Oct.	The Alaska Day Celebration (☎ 907/747–5940 ⊕ www.sitka.com) brings out the whole town of Sitka to celebrate October 18, the day the United States acquired Alaska from Russia. The weeklong festival includes a period costume ball and a parade.
	Held in conjunction with the annual Alaska Federation of Natives convention, the Quyana Alaska Native Dance Festival (☎ 907/274–3611 ⊕ www.nativefederation.org) in Anchorage provides a taste of the state's Native culture.
Nov.	The Athabascan Old Time Fiddling Festival (☎ 907/452–1825) enlivens Fairbanks with traditional Native music.
	The Carrs Great Alaska Shoot-out (☎ 907/786–1230 ⊕ www.shootout.net) takes place at Sullivan Arena in Anchorage, where some of the best college basketball teams in the country compete.

PLEASURES & PASTIMES

Bicycling

Biking can be a rewarding adventure in accessible parts of the state. The paved-road system is straightforward, and automobile traffic is usually light on most Alaska roads. However, the road shoulders can be narrow, and people tend to drive fast in rural areas. Unpaved highways are bikable but are tougher going; expect dust, ruts, and flying gravel.

Anchorage has an excellent bike-trail system—one along the coast and several others inland. You can take your bike on the Alaska Railroad and bike in Denali National Park. Although the park road is largely unpaved, it has a good dirt surface and only light traffic. You can also bring your bike on Alaska's ferry system for an extra charge. Use it to explore the Southeast's charming communities and surrounding forests, but come prepared for heavy rain. Companies that rent bicycles in the Southeast seem to cycle in and out of business faster than you can shift gears. Your best bet, if you don't bring your own, is to call local bike shops, parks and recreation departments, or visitor information centers for rental information.

Many Interior residents are avid bikers, and mountain biking has become a hot sport here. Fairbanks has miles of scenic bike paths along the Chena River and into the city's outskirts. Most roads have wide shoulders and, of course, those incredible Alaska views. Trails used in winter by mushers, snow-mobilers, and cross-country skiers are taken over by mountain bikers when the snow melts.

Dogsledding

Alaskans are dog crazy. With more and more mushers conducting wintertime tours, you can try anything from a half-hour jaunt outside Anchorage to a two-week outing in the Brooks Range or an expedition along the Iditarod Trail. You can participate as much or as little as you like, riding in the basket and being pampered at an overnight lodge or helping harness the dogs and taking a turn on the back of the sled. When choosing a tour, make sure your musher has the experience to handle the unpredictable blizzard, moose encounter, or runaway team. In the summer, some mushers put wheels on their sleds, giving you a taste of dogsledding without the snow and cold.

Fishing

With more than 3 million lakes and more coastline than the rest of the United States combined, Alaska has no shortage of fishing spots. People from all over the world come to Alaska for a chance to land a trophy salmon (the record is 97 pounds) or a 200-pound-plus halibut. If you're driving through Alaska, you can fish from the roadside in the Interior and on the Kenai Peninsula. In the Southeast you can sink a line right off the docks. If you're a truly serious fisherman, though, a guided boat charter or a stay at a fly-in fishing lodge is the ultimate Alaska fishing adventure. Many companies assemble sportfishing packages that include everything you'll need, from transportation to tackle. Bag limits and special provisions vary throughout the state's 12 sportfishing-management areas.

Flightseeing

The magnitude of Alaska can perhaps best be comprehended from the air. Every major destination from the Southeast to the Arctic has flightseeing services that will show you Alaska from a bird's-eye view. It's an experience not to be missed.

Gardens & Parks
Alaska has a short growing season, but the days of midnight sun produce some of the biggest blooms you'll ever see. Anchorage beautifies its downtown parks each summer with spectacular plantings, and every August the Alaska State Fair (⇨ On the Calendar) in Palmer is a showcase for 90-pound cabbages and other oversize vegetables.

Alaska has 15 national parks, preserves, and monuments; two national forests; and 16 national wildlife refuges. The most visited of all is Denali National Park, site of Mt. McKinley, at 20,320 feet the tallest peak in North America. Wrangell–St. Elias National Park, east of Anchorage, is the largest national park in the United States—six times the size of Yellowstone.

Kayaking
Sea kayaking is big among Alaskans. It was the Aleuts who invented the kayak (or *bidarka*) to fish and hunt sea mammals. When early explorers encountered the Aleuts, they compared them to sea creatures, so at home did they appear on their small ocean crafts. Kayaks have the great advantage of portability, and some models can be broken down and carried on a ferry or small aircraft. Less practical but perhaps more important advantages are that they give the boater a feel for the water and a view from water level. They are also more stable than canoes. Oceangoing kayakers will find offshore adventures, especially in the protected waters of the Southeast, Prince William Sound, or out of Kenai Fjords National Park.

Seafood & Sourdough
Alaska's primary claim to gastronomic fame is seafood. The rich coastal waters produce prodigious quantities of halibut, salmon, crab, and shrimp, along with such specialties as abalone, sea urchin, herring roe, and sea cucumbers (a favorite in Japan). If you haven't yet tasted fresh Alaskan salmon, do so here—there's nothing quite like a barbecued Copper River king salmon. Alaska, unlike Norway, Chile, or British Columbia, does not allow salmon farming, so you are guaranteed to have wild fish from the ocean. Be sure, however, to ask whether the seafood is fresh or frozen, particularly during the off-season.

Sourdough bread, pastries, and pancakes are a local tradition, dating back to the gold-rush days. Prospectors and pioneers carried a stash of sourdough starter so that they could always whip up a batch of dough in short order. The old-timers became known as sourdoughs, a title that latter-day Alaskans earn by living here for 20 years.

In general, the quality of Alaskan restaurants is directly proportional to the population. In the smallest villages you may be hard pressed to find a shop selling even greasy burgers and fries. Most larger towns have the requisite McDonald's, Burger Kings, and Subways, along with standard all-American restaurants serving bacon-and-egg breakfasts, iceberg lettuce salads, and fresh-from-the-freezer pizza dough. Fortunately, not everything is this bad. In towns with a significant tourist presence—such as Haines, Homer, Ketchikan, Petersburg, Seward, Sitka, or Skagway—you'll always find cafés serving espresso and baked goods, plus at least one restaurant where the food is fresh and delicious. Anchorage, Juneau, and Fairbanks all have a range of eateries, with something to please everybody. Not surprisingly, Anchorage—

with almost half the state's population—has the best selection, including ethnic food from all corners of the globe, creative seafood restaurants, half a dozen brewpubs, vegetarian cafés, and European-style bakeries and delis.

Shopping

Among the most prized items sought by souvenir hunters are Native crafts. Each of the Native groups is noted for particular skills; their wares are sold throughout the state. Eskimo art, native to the Arctic and other areas of the Bush, includes animal carvings of walrus ivory, spirit masks, dance fans, baskets made of baleen (a fibrous material found in the mouths of bowhead whales), and jewelry fashioned from walrus ivory, jade, baleen, or a combination of the three. Also be on the lookout for mukluks (seal- or reindeer-skin Eskimo boots). The Tlingit of Southeast Alaska are known for their totems and other wood carvings, as well as for baskets and hats woven from spruce root and cedar bark. Tsimshian Indians also work with spruce root and cedar bark, and Haida Indians are noted basket makers and totem and slate carvers. Athabascans specialize in skin sewing, fur garments, and beadwork. The Aleuts' grass basketry is considered among the best in the world.

The state has adopted two symbols that guarantee the authenticity of crafts made by Alaskans: a hand symbol indicates the item was made by one of Alaska's Native peoples; a polar bear marks an item as made in Alaska. Better prices are found in the more remote villages where you buy directly from the artisan or at crafts fairs such as Anchorage's downtown Saturday Market.

Your shopping trip need not end at the crafts fair, however. In communities with a Russian past, such as Kodiak and Sitka, check out the Russian nesting dolls in the local shops. Bringing home smoked and canned salmon allows you to transport a taste of Alaska even if you aren't an angler. Also look for birch syrup, a distinctively flavorful Alaska-only product found in local shops. One of the best is Kahiltna Birchworks, a family operation based in the wilderness west of Talkeetna.

Skiing & Snowboarding

Although it has no lack of snow or mountains, Alaska is not a big ski destination. Numerous opportunities, however, exist for both downhill and cross-country adventures. You can charter a helicopter to go backcountry skiing in the Valdez area or visit one of the downhill areas near Anchorage, Fairbanks, or Juneau. Ski in the summer by chartering a plane to a glacier in Denali National Park. At Juneau, Eaglecrest is across from the city on the slopes of Douglas Island. Skiing is also done on the glaciers of the Juneau Ice Field, reached by helicopter. Turnagain Pass, 59 mi from Anchorage on the Seward Highway, is often trafficked with backcountry skiers and snowmobilers. Hilltop Ski Area and Alpenglow are small alpine ski areas within 10 mi of downtown Anchorage. The World Extreme Skiing Championships are held at Valdez every April. Cross-country skiers will find many miles of groomed trails in Anchorage. Additional cross-country ski trails can be found around Fairbanks, Homer, and Palmer. Snowboarding has more than caught on in South Central Alaska, and boarders are welcome at all three Anchorage ski areas. Rentals are available at the various ski areas and outdoor equipment shops.

FODOR'S CHOICE

The sights, restaurants, hotels, and other travel experiences on these pages are our editors' top picks—our Fodor's Choices. They're the best of their type in the area covered by the book—not to be missed and always worth your time. In the destination chapters that follow, you will find all the details.

LODGING

$$$$ **Alyeska Prince Hotel**, Girdwood. In the ski resort settlement of Girdwood (an hour south of Anchorage), this luxurious hotel is perfect for winter skiers or summer visitors in search of an escape from city life. Take the aerial tram to Seven Glaciers Restaurant for dining with unparalleled views.

$$$$ **Brooks Lodge**, Katmai National Park and Preserve. Within walking distance of Katmai's Brooks River and Falls, the lodge provides easy access to bear-viewing platforms and fly-fishing for salmon and rainbow trout, in the midst of the Alaskan wilderness.

$$$$ **Denali Backcountry Lodge**, Kantishna. Here you'll get the chance to stay deep within Denali National Park without having to live out of a tent. Enjoy guided hikes and excellent food—and there's a bar, too.

$$$$ **Kenai Princess Wilderness Lodge**, Cooper Landing. Charming bungalows with fireplaces and vaulted ceilings of natural-finish wood make up this sprawling complex on a bluff overlooking the Kenai River.

$$$$ **Pan Pacific Hotel**, Vancouver. This luxury hotel is part of the eye-catching Canada Place complex, which mimics the design of an ocean liner. Spacious, modern rooms and spectacular views are also worth a second look.

$$$$ **Waterfall Resort**, Prince of Wales Island. This former cannery in a remote part of Prince of Wales Island has been lovingly transformed into an upscale fishing resort with custom-built fishing boats, bountiful meals, and cozy cabins for the guests.

$$–$$$$ **Alaska's Capital Inn**, Juneau. Luxury meets history in this gracious hilltop bed-and-breakfast with upscale services, delicious breakfasts, and period furnishings from the early 1900s.

$$ **Chena Hot Springs Resort**, Chena Hot Springs. There are enough activities at this full-service, year-round resort to keep you busy all day, but be sure to save some time for a soak in the hot-springs-warmed hot tubs.

$$ **Wedgewood Resort**, Fairbanks. Enjoy large, comfortable suites on a landscaped campus in close proximity to the Creamer's Field wildlife refuge.

$ **Teddy's Inn the Woods**, Seward. Set back from the road in a forest of spruce trees in parklike surroundings, this B&B has prime sun-lounging spots on two decks. The breakfast of fresh homemade pastries just might be complemented with freshly smoked salmon.

BUDGET LODGING

¢ | **U.S. Forest Service Cabins,** Tongass National Forest. Nearly 150 public recreation cabins, scattered throughout the forest, provide a rustic and totally authentic way to experience the wild places. Access is generally by floatplane or boat.

RESTAURANTS

$$$$ | **Gustavus Inn,** Gustavus. You'll think you're on an old New England farm when you stay at this comfortable 1928 homestead just a few miles from Glacier Bay National Park. Dinners are served family style and always include fresh seafood and vegetables from the organic garden.

$$$–$$$$ | **C Restaurant,** Vancouver. Innovative dishes, such as octopus-bacon-wrapped scallops, and dramatic presentations, such as a four-tier display Taster Box, have won C a place among Vancouver's best seafood restaurants.

$$$–$$$$ | **Marx Brothers' Cafe,** Anchorage. A regional legend—it's been here since 1979—this cozy little café delivers gourmet dining with an Alaskan twist. In addition to made-at-your-table Caesar salads, fresh seafood, and luscious desserts, there's an outstanding wine list.

$$–$$$$ | **The Fiddlehead,** Juneau. In existence since 1978, this always-popular restaurant offers eclectic entrées in a casual dining space downstairs and in a more formal setting upstairs.

$–$$$$ | **Pump House Restaurant,** Fairbanks. A restaurant in a former mining pump station might not sound promising, but this local institution is actually one of the Interior's finest dining establishments, perfecting such local specialties as Alaskan reindeer stew.

$–$$$$ | **Sackett's Kenai Grill,** Cooper Landing. Enjoy the specialty of the house, the smoked prime rib, and the views of Kenai Lake and the surrounding Kenai Mountains, at an outdoor table on a sunny day.

$$–$$$ | **Liliget Feast House,** Vancouver. Sample alder-grilled salmon and steamed fern shoots at one of the few places in the world serving the original Northwest Coast First Nations cuisine.

$–$$$ | **Saltry in Halibut Cove,** Homer. Curries and pastas showcase the local seafood at this intimate spot in Halibut Cove.

BUDGET RESTAURANTS

¢–$$$ | **Lynx Creek Pizza,** near Denali National Park. In the opinion of many Alaskans, Lynx Creek offers up the state's best pizza, an unexpected treat in a nonurban environment.

CRUISE SHIPS

Norwegian Star, Norwegian Cruise Lines. Ten restaurants, a 24-hour fitness center, a lavish spa, great kids' programs, and the longest indoor lap pool afloat should keep everyone happily occupied, even on the rainiest Alaskan days.

Seven Seas Mariner, Seven Seas Cruises. Cordon Bleu cuisine, a luxurious spa, and impeccable service make this all-suites, all-balcony ship a top choice among luxury cruisers.

Spirit of Oceanus, Cruise West. Cruise West's flagship vessel is small enough to get up close and personal with Alaskan scenery, but big enough for a comfortable, even luxurious cruise experience.

MARKETS

Granville Island Public Market, Vancouver. Dozens of unique stalls sell chocolates, cheeses, fish, meat, and locally grown fruits and vegetables. Plus, there are crafts vendors and loads of fresh flowers.

Saturday Market, Anchorage. Vendors serve Alaskan art and crafts and deliciously fattening finger food at this all-summer event in the heart of downtown at 3rd Avenue and E Street.

MUSEUMS

Alaska Native Heritage Center, Anchorage. A large central facility provides an introduction to the diverse Native cultural groups that populate Alaska. Five village exhibits encircle a small lake.

Anchorage Museum of History and Art, Anchorage. In addition to a fine collection of historical items, this museum features contemporary Alaskan art, guided tours, great meals (courtesy of Marx Brothers' Cafe), and a classy gift shop.

Living Museum of the Arctic, Kotzebue. You can experience Eskimo culture firsthand at this unique museum. Listen to a storyteller, watch a ceremonial dance, and bounce high on a blanket toss—an ancient practice whereby hunters were launched high in the air from blankets of walrus or seal hide to scan the seas for game.

Royal British Columbia Museum, Victoria. A genuine Kwakwaka'wakw longhouse; a replica of Captain Vancouver's ship, the HMCS *Discovery*; and a rain-forest exhibit are just a few of the attractions here.

University of Alaska Museum, Fairbanks. A must-see for all visitors to the Interior, the museum gives an excellent overview of Alaska's human and natural history.

OUTDOOR ACTIVITIES

Dogsledding. Traveling through Alaska's winter landscape behind a dog team is both a grand adventure and a part of a tradition reaching back to Alaska's first peoples.

Sea Kayaking. Explore Alaska's vast, wild coastline and encounter seabirds and mammals with minimal disturbance. Sea kayaking offers solitude, quiet, and an intimate connection to the ocean waters through which you travel.

Strolling the Tony Knowles Coastal Trail, Anchorage. A favorite of locals and visitors, this 11-mi paved path follows Cook Inlet from downtown, past Westchester Lagoon (a good picnic spot), and all the way to wooded Kincaid Park.

Whale-Watching. There are few sights as stirring as a breaching humpback whale or a pod of orcas on the hunt, and there are few places that offer the prime whale-viewing opportunities of Alaska, which is the seasonal home to 15 species of whales.

PARKS & GARDENS

Denali National Park. This is Alaska's premier tourist destination, and for good reasons—excellent opportunities to see free-roaming mega-fauna and a decent chance to gaze at Mt. McKinley, North America's highest peak.

Dr. Sun Yat-Sen Garden, Vancouver. Artisans from Suzhou, China, incorporated traditional design elements and materials in the construction of the first authentic Ming dynasty–style garden outside of China.

Glacier Bay National Park and Preserve. Most visitors to this jewel of a park arrive by cruise ship or small tour boat, but to really see it right join one of Alaska Discovery's multiday sea kayaking trips into the heart of the wilderness.

Misty Fiords National Monument, Ketchikan. Alaska Cruises arranges half-day adventures that provide the perfect introduction to the towering cliffs, deep fjords, and abundant wildlife within Misty Fiords National Monument.

Stanley Park, Vancouver. A morning or afternoon in Stanley Park gives you a capsule tour of Vancouver that includes beaches, the ocean, Douglas fir and cedar forests, and a view of the North Shore mountains.

UNIQUELY ALASKA

Chilkoot Charlie's, Anchorage. Alaska's most infamous party spot, this rambling building features nine bars, three dance floors, and loud rock music nightly. Their motto says it all: "We cheat the other guy and pass the savings on to you."

Iditarod Trail Sled Dog Race. Alaska's biggest annual event, this grueling thousand-mile trip takes mushers and their dogs from Anchorage to Nome each March.

WILDLIFE

Alaska SeaLife Center, Seward. Dive into Alaska's fascinating marine ecosystem at this facility—part marine research lab, part rehabilitation center for injured animals, and part classroom.

McNeil River State Game Sanctuary, Alaska Peninsula. As many as 100 or more brown bears, the coastal subspecies of grizzlies, come to this Alaska Peninsula stream each summer to feed on salmon, making this the largest gathering of brown bears in Alaska—and the world.

St. Paul Island, Pribilof Islands. The largest northern fur-seal herd in the world and more than 180 varieties of birds shelter on these remote shores.

SMART TRAVEL TIPS

Finding out about your destination before you leave home means you won't squander time organizing everyday minutiae once you've arrived. You'll be more streetwise when you hit the ground as well, better prepared to explore the aspects of Alaska that drew you here in the first place. The organizations in this section can provide information to supplement this guide; contact them for up-to-the-minute details, and consult the A to Z sections that end each chapter for facts on the various topics as they relate to Alaska's many regions. Happy landings!

AIR TRAVEL

Alaska Airlines is the flagship carrier to Alaska, with year-round service from Seattle to Anchorage, Juneau, Fairbanks, Ketchikan, and towns around the state. In addition, the airline has nonstop flights linking Anchorage with Chicago, Los Angeles, and Portland, Oregon. Alaska Air and its subsidiary, Horizon Air, fly to many other North American cities from their Seattle hub, with nonstop Alaska flights to Boston, Denver, Washington D.C., Miami, Newark, Orlando, and various Mexican cities. Continental and United have year-round flights to Anchorage from Seattle. Other year-round nonstop flights to Anchorage are aboard Northwest from Minneapolis–St. Paul and Detroit, and Delta from Cincinnati and Salt Lake. Hawaiian Vacations has year-round charters between Anchorage and Honolulu.

Several airlines provide summer-only nonstop Anchorage flights from Lower 48 cities: Alaska from San Francisco; American from Dallas and St. Louis; Continental from Houston, Newark, and Cleveland; Delta from Seattle and Atlanta; and United from Chicago, Denver, and San Francisco. Sun Country Airlines has seasonal charters connecting Anchorage with Minneapolis.

International travel connections to Anchorage include nonstop flights from a number of cities in Asia and Europe. Year-round service is offered from Seoul on Korean Air and from Petropavlovsk in Russia on Magadan Airlines. In summer Alaska Air and Air Canada have flights from Vancouver, China Airlines from Taipei, and Thomas Cook Airlines from Frankfurt. Both Japan Airlines and Alaskan Vacations have summer service between Anchorage and Tokyo.

Alaska Airlines has nonstop flights into Fairbanks from Seattle year-round, and Northwest has seasonal nonstops from Minneapolis–St. Paul. Thomas Cook Airlines flies into Fairbanks in summer from Frankfurt with a stop in Whitehorse, Yukon. Air North connects Whitehorse, Canada, with Juneau and Fairbanks year-round. Other Fairbanks air connections include a stop in Anchorage.

If you are traveling from Britain, Continental Airlines flies from Gatwick, Birmingham, or Manchester via Newark and Seattle; Delta from Gatwick to Cincinnati or Salt Lake City; and United from Heathrow via San Francisco or Chicago. Travelers from Australia and New Zealand can take Qantas into Los Angeles out of Sydney, Melbourne, or Auckland. Air New Zealand flies from Sydney and Auckland to Los Angeles. United flies from Sydney to Los Angeles and San Francisco and to Los Angeles from Melbourne and Auckland.

Commercial air travel to major towns in Alaska is usually by jet or turboprop. Scheduled air-taxi and air-charter services provide access to smaller towns and remote locales, using propeller-driven Bush aircraft that land on wheels, on floats, or on skis. Helicopters are increasingly popular for flightseeing and fast transport.

Most of Alaska's wild places can be reached only by air, but don't consider that a drawback. Small planes have played a legendary part in the state's history: Bush pilots have helped explore Alaska and have been responsible for many dramatic rescue missions. But be aware that small planes cannot transport more than a limited amount of gear and cannot fly safely in poor weather. Your drop-off and pickup flights are therefore subject to delays, which are sometimes counted in days, not hours. When traveling in remote areas away from any towns or villages, be sure to carry extra food. Although most villages have general stores, fresh produce tends to be expensive and sometimes unavailable. Note also that some items are not allowed on commercial aircraft. This includes camp-stove fuel and the so-called "bear mace" (pepper spray) sold in camping-goods stores.

Contact the following airlines for flights within Alaska: Bering Air for flights from Nome or Kotzebue to smaller communities of the Far North; ERA Aviation for flights to Cordova, Homer, Iliamna, Kenai, Kodiak, Valdez, and 17 western Alaska villages; and Frontier Flying Service from Anchorage to Fairbanks, along with many Bush villages. Contact Warbelow's Air Ventures and Larry's Flying Service for flights out of Fairbanks to Interior destinations and Peninsula Airways (PenAir) for flights to western Alaska, including Aniak, Dutch Harbor, McGrath, Dillingham, King Salmon, Sand Point, St. Paul, and St. George.

BOOKING

When you book, **look for nonstop flights** and remember that "direct" flights stop at least once. Try to avoid connecting flights, which require a change of plane. Two airlines may operate a connecting flight jointly, so ask whether your airline operates every segment of the trip; you may find that the carrier you prefer flies you only part of the way. To find more booking tips and to check prices and make online flight reservations, log on to www.fodors.com.

CARRIERS

Major Airlines Air Canada ☎ 888/247-2262 ⊕ www.aircanada.ca. **Air New Zealand** ☎ 800/262-1234, 800/063-385 in Australia, 0800/737-000 in New Zealand ⊕ www.airnz.com. **Alaska Airlines** ☎ 800/426-0333 ⊕ www.alaskaair.com. **American** ☎ 800/433-7300 ⊕ www.aa.com. **China Airlines** ☎ 800/227-5118 ⊕ www.china-airlines.com. **Continental** ☎ 800/525-0280, 0800/776-464, 01293/776-464 in U.K. ⊕ www.continental.com. **Delta** ☎ 800/221-1212, 0800/414-767 in U.K. ⊕ www.delta.com. **Japan Airlines** ☎ 800/525-3663 ⊕ www.jal.com. **Korean Air** ☎ 800/438-5000 ⊕ www.koreanair.com. **Northwest** ☎ 800/225-2525 ⊕ www.nwa.com. **Qantas** ☎ 800/227-4500, 800/112-121 in Australia, 800/808-767 in New Zealand ⊕ www.qantas.com. **Thomas Cook Airlines** ☎ 800/524-6975 ⊕ www.thomascook.us. **United** ☎ 800/241-6522, 800/722-5243 in Canada, 0800/888-555 in U.K., 131-777 in Australia ⊕ www.ual.com.

Smaller Airlines Air North ☎ 867/668-228, 800/764-0407 in U.S., 800/661-0407 in Canada ⊕ www.flyairnorth.com. **Bering Air** ☎ 907/443-5464 or 800/478-4111 ⊕ www.beringair.com. **ERA Aviation** ☎ 907/266-8394 or 800/866-8394 ⊕ www.eraaviation.com. **Frontier Flying Service** ☎ 907/474-0014 or 800/478-6779 ⊕ www.frontierflying.com. **Hawaiian Vacations** ☎ 907/243-

2323 or 800/969-2700 ⊕ www.hawaiianvacations. com. **Ketchum Air Service** ☎ 907/243-5525 or 800/ 433-9114 ⊕ www.ketchumair.com. **Larry's Flying Service** ☎ 907/474-9169 ⊕ www.larrysflying.com. **Magadan Air** ☎ 907/248-2994. **PenAir** ☎ 907/243-2323 or 800/448-4226 ⊕ www.penair.com. **Regal Air** ☎ 907/243-8535 ⊕ www.alaska.net/~regalair. **Rust's Flying Service** ☎ 907/243-1595 or 800/544-2299 ⊕ www.flyrusts.com. **Sun Country Airlines** ☎ 800/359-6786 ⊕ www.suncountry.com. **Warbelow's Air Ventures** ☎ 907/474-0518 or 800/478-0812 ⊕ www.warbelows.com.

CHECK-IN & BOARDING

Always ask your carrier about its check-in policy. Plan to arrive at the airport about 2 hours before your scheduled departure time for domestic flights and 2½ to 3 hours before international flights. You may need to arrive earlier if you're flying from one of the busier airports or during peak air-traffic times. To avoid delays at airport-security checkpoints, try not to wear any metal. Jewelry, belt and other buckles, steel-toe shoes, barrettes, and underwire bras are among the items that can set off detectors.

Assuming that not everyone with a ticket will show up, airlines routinely overbook planes. When everyone does, airlines ask for volunteers to give up their seats. In return, these volunteers usually get a several-hundred-dollar flight voucher, which can be used toward the purchase of another ticket, and are rebooked on the next flight out. If there are not enough volunteers, the airline must choose who will be denied boarding. The first to get bumped are passengers who checked in late and those flying on discounted tickets, so get to the gate and check in as early as possible, especially during peak periods.

Always **bring a government-issued photo ID to the airport;** even when it's not required, a passport is best.

CUTTING COSTS

The least expensive airfares to Alaska are priced for round-trip travel and must usually be purchased in advance. Airlines generally allow you to change your return date for a fee; most low-fare tickets, however, are nonrefundable. It's smart to call a number of airlines and check the Internet; when you are quoted a good price, book it on the spot—the same fare may not be

available the next day, or even the next hour. Always check different routings and look into using alternate airports. Also, price off-peak flights, which may be significantly less expensive than others. Travel agents, especially low-fare specialists (⇨ Discounts & Deals), are helpful.

Consolidators are another good source. They buy tickets for scheduled flights at reduced rates from the airlines, then sell them at prices that beat the best fare available directly from the airlines. Sometimes you can even get your money back if you need to return the ticket. Carefully read the fine print detailing penalties for changes and cancellations, purchase the ticket with a credit card, and **confirm your consolidator reservation with the airline.**

The Internet is an increasingly important source for discount travel information. Three helpful sites are **Travelocity, Expedia,** and **Orbitz.** If you have flexibility in your travel dates, check airline Internet sites for special last-minute deals. **Alaska Airlines** (⊕ www.alaskaair.com) and some other carriers have specials to and from Alaska. These generally allow only a maximum one-week stay but sometimes cost less than half the going rate.

🖪 **Consolidators Best Fares** ☎ 800/576-8255 or 800/576-1600 ⊕ www.bestfares.com; $59.90 annual membership. **Cheap Tickets** ☎ 800/377-1000 or 888/922-8849 ⊕ www.cheaptickets.com. **Expedia** ☎ 800/397-3342 or 404/728-8787 ⊕ www.expedia. com. **Hotwire** ☎ 866/468-9473 or 920/330-9418 ⊕ www.hotwire.com. **Now Voyager Travel** ✉ 45 W. 21st St., 5th floor, New York, NY 10010 ☎ 212/459-1616 🖷 212/243-2711 ⊕ www.nowvoyagertravel.com. **Onetravel.com** ⊕ www.onetravel.com. **Orbitz** ☎ 888/656-4546 ⊕ www.orbitz.com. **Priceline.com** ⊕ www.priceline.com. **Travelocity** ☎ 888/709-5983, 877/282-2925 in Canada, 0870/111-7060 in U.K. ⊕ www.travelocity.com.

ENJOYING THE FLIGHT

State your seat preference when purchasing your ticket, and then repeat it when you confirm and when you check in. For more legroom, you can request one of the few emergency-aisle seats at check-in, if you are capable of lifting at least 50 pounds—a Federal Aviation Administration requirement of passengers in these seats. Seats behind a bulkhead also offer more legroom, but they don't have underseat storage. Don't sit in the row in front of the emergency aisle or in front of a bulkhead, where seats may not recline.

Ask the airline whether a snack or meal is served on the flight. If you have dietary concerns, request special meals when booking. These can be vegetarian, low-cholesterol, or kosher, for example. It's a good idea to pack some healthful snacks and a small (plastic) bottle of water in your carry-on bag. On long flights, try to maintain a normal routine, to help fight jet lag. At night, get some sleep. By day, eat light meals, drink water (not alcohol), and **move around the cabin** to stretch your legs. For additional jet-lag tips consult *Fodor's FYI: Travel Fit & Healthy* (available at bookstores everywhere).

All flights to and within Alaska are smoke-free, including charter flights and flights into the Bush.

FLYING TIMES

Average travel time is 3½ hours from Seattle to Anchorage, 8 hours from Chicago, 7 hours from Dallas, and 6 hours from Los Angeles. Travel times from other destinations depend on your connection, since you'll need to route through other cities to get to Anchorage.

HOW TO COMPLAIN

If your baggage goes astray or your flight goes awry, complain right away. Most carriers require that you **file a claim immediately.** The Aviation Consumer Protection Division of the Department of Transportation publishes *Fly-Rights,* which discusses airlines and consumer issues and is available on-line. You can also find articles and information on mytravelrights.com, the Web site of the nonprofit Consumer Travel Rights Center.

Airline Complaints Aviation Consumer Protection Division ⊠ U.S. Department of Transportation, C-75, Room 4107, 400 7th St. SW, Washington, DC 20590 ☎ 202/366-2220 ⊕ airconsumer.ost.dot.gov. **Federal Aviation Administration Consumer Hotline** ⊠ For inquiries: FAA, 800 Independence Ave. SW, Washington, DC 20591 ☎ 800/322-7873 ⊕ www.faa.gov.

RECONFIRMING

Check the status of your flight before you leave for the airport. You can do this on your carrier's Web site, by linking to a flight-status checker (many Web booking services offer these), or by calling your carrier or travel agent.

AIRPORTS

Ted Stevens Anchorage International Airport (ANC) ☎ 907/266-2525 ⊕ www.dot.state.ak.us. **Vancouver International Airport (YVR)** ☎ 604/303-3603.

ALASKA PUBLIC LANDS OFFICES

Get details on Alaska's vast public lands from Alaska Public Lands Information centers in Ketchikan, Tok, Anchorage, and Fairbanks or on the Internet at ⊕ www.nps.gov/aplic.

Alaska Public Lands Information Center ⊠ 605 W. 4th Ave., Anchorage 99501 ☎ 907/271-2737 ⊠ 250 Cushman St., Suite 1A, Fairbanks 99701 ☎ 907/456-0527 🖷 907/456-0154 ⊠ 50 Main St., Ketchikan 99901 ☎ 907/228-6214 ⊠ Mile 1314, Alaska Hwy., Tok 99780 ☎ 907/883-5667. **Southeast Alaska Discovery Center** ⊠ 50 Main St., Ketchikan 99901 ☎ 907/228-6220 🖷 907/228-6234.

BEARS

If you're lucky—and careful—the sight of one of these magnificent creatures in the wild can be a highlight of your visit. By respecting bears and exercising care in bear country, neither you nor the bear will suffer from the experience. Remember that bears don't like surprises. Make your presence known by talking, singing, rattling a can full of gravel, or tying a bell to your pack, especially when terrain or vegetation obscures views. Travel with a group, which is noisier and easier for bears to detect. If possible, walk with the wind at your back so your scent will warn bears of your presence. And avoid bushy, low-visibility areas whenever possible.

Give bears the right-of-way—lots of it—especially sows with cubs. Don't camp on animal trails; they're likely to be used by bears. If you come across a carcass of an animal or detect its odor, avoid the area entirely; it's likely a bear's food cache. Store all food and garbage away from your campsite in airtight or specially designed bear-proof containers. The Park Service supplies these for hikers in Denali and Glacier Bay national parks and requires that backcountry travelers use them. If a bear approaches you while you are fishing, stop. If you have a fish on your line, cut your line.

If you do encounter a bear at close range, don't panic, and, above all, don't run. You can't outrun a bear, and by fleeing you could trigger a chase response from the bear. Talk in a normal voice to help identify yourself as a human. If traveling with others, stand close together to "increase your size." If the bear charges, it could be a bluff; as terrifying as this may sound, the experts advise standing your ground. If a brown bear actually touches you, then drop to the ground and play dead, either flat on your stomach or curled in a ball with your hands behind your neck. If you don't move, a brown bear will typically break off its attack once it feels the threat is gone. If you are attacked by a black bear, you are probably better off fighting back with rocks, sticks, or anything else you find, since black bears are more likely to attack a person intentionally. Polar bears can be found in remote parts of the Arctic, but tourists are highly unlikely to encounter them in summer.

For more information on bears, ask for the brochure "Bear Facts: The Essentials for Traveling in Bear Country" from any of the Alaska Public Lands offices. Bear safety information is also available on the Internet at ⊕ www.state.ak.us/adfg.

BIKE TRAVEL

Cyclists will find a wide variety of conditions in Alaska. The main highways are heavily trafficked in the summer, and the shoulders are often not particularly wide. Bikers traveling between such crowded routes as Anchorage to Seward are risking their lives. A better bet would probably be to choose less-traveled roads and trails. Mountain bikes are available for rent in the larger Alaskan towns, or you can bring your own. Ferry travelers pay a small extra charge to transport bikes. Pick up an Alaska cycling guidebook, such as *Alaska Bicycle Touring Guide* by Pete Praetorius (Denali Press) and *Mountain Bike Alaska* by Richard Larson (Glacier House Publications), for further details. Mountain-bike rentals are available in most larger Alaskan towns for around $30 per day or $15 for three hours.

🚲 Bike Rentals & Tours **Downtown Bicycle Rental** ✉ 245 W. 5th Ave., Suite 212, Anchorage ☎ 907/279-5293 ⊕ www.alaska-bike-rentals.com.

Mountain Bike Alaska ☐ Box 6754, Palmer 99645 ☎ 907/745-5014 or 866/354-2453 ⊕ www. mountainbikealaska.com.

BIKES IN FLIGHT

Most airlines accommodate bikes as luggage, provided they are dismantled and boxed; check with individual airlines about packing requirements. Some airlines sell bike boxes, which are often free at bike shops, for about $15 (bike bags can be considerably more expensive). International travelers often can substitute a bike for a piece of checked luggage at no charge; otherwise, the cost is about $100. U.S. and Canadian airlines charge $40–$80 each way.

BOAT & FERRY TRAVEL

If you are looking for a casual alternative to a luxury cruise, **travel as Alaskans do, aboard the ferries of the Alaska Marine Highway System.** When planning your trip, ask about special onboard programming. Forest Service naturalists ride the larger ferries in summer, providing a running commentary on sights. In addition, the Arts-on-Board Program presents educators and entertainers on selected summer sailings. The Alaska Marine Highway ferries travel within Alaska and between Bellingham, Washington, and the towns of the Inside Passage. The Marine Highway also links up with British Columbia Ferries in Prince Rupert, and as of 2004, a speedy catamaran ferry offers vehicle and passenger service connecting Juneau with Sitka and Petersburg. In addition, the Inter-Island Ferry Authority serves Southeast Alaska's Prince of Wales Island with the towns of Ketchikan, Wrangell, and Petersburg.

CUTTING COSTS

The AlaskaPass allows unlimited travel on bus, ferry, and rail lines in Alaska, along with bus and ferry travel in British Columbia and the Yukon. Passes are available for 15 or 22 consecutive days of travel ($729 and $899 respectively), as well as for 8 days of travel in a 12-day period ($599) or 12 days of travel in a 21-day period ($749).
🚌 **AlaskaPass** ☎ 206/463-6550 or 800/248-7598 🖨 206/463-6777 ⊕ www.alaskapass.com.

FARES & SCHEDULES

Make reservations for ferry travel by calling the Alaska Marine Highway System, which will mail the tickets, or you can pick them up from the ferry office at your starting point. Request a copy of its printed schedule over the phone, or find it on the Internet at ⊕ www.alaska.gov/ferry. Online reservations are also available.

PAYING

You can pay for ferry travel by cash, credit card (American Express, Discover, Master-Card, or Visa), cashier's check, money order, certified check, or personal check from an Alaskan bank.

🄵 **Alaska Marine Highway** ⌂ 6858 Glacier Hwy., Juneau 99801-7909 ☎ 907/465-3941 or 800/642-0066 ⎙ 907/277-4829 ⊕ www.alaska.gov/ferry. **B. C. Ferries** ✉ 1112 Fort St., Victoria, British Columbia V8V 4V2 ☎ 250/386-3431, 888/223-3779 in B.C. ⎙ 250/381-5452 ⊕ www.bcferries.bc.ca. **Inter-Island Ferry Authority** ⌂ Box 495, Craig 99921 ☎ 907/826-4848 or 866/308-4848 ⎙ 907/826-2829 ⊕ www.interislandferry.com.

BUSINESS HOURS

Most Alaskan stores are open weekdays from 9 AM to 5 PM, though many have longer hours and remain open on weekends. All the larger towns have at least one convenience store that stays open all the time. In small Bush villages, the general store may be open just a few hours per day and closed on Sunday, whereas in larger cities the grocery stores remain open 24 hours a day, seven days a week.

BANKS & OFFICES

Banks and credit unions are typically open weekdays 10–5, and some have limited Saturday hours, particularly in Anchorage, Fairbanks, and Juneau. Most government and other offices are open weekdays 9–5, though some close at 4:30.

GAS STATIONS

Many Alaskan gas stations remain open until 10 PM, and in the larger towns and cities, some stay open 24 hours a day. Most are also open on weekends, particularly along the main highways. In the smallest villages gas may be available only on weekdays, but these settlements typically have only a few miles of roads.

MUSEUMS & SIGHTS

Hours of sights and attractions are denoted in the book by the clock icon, ☉. Museums in smaller Southeast Alaska

towns typically open whenever a cruise ship or ferry is in port, even if it is late on a Sunday evening. *See* specific town descriptions for more information.

PHARMACIES

Pharmacy hours vary across Alaska, but most local hospitals have a pharmacy that provides service at any hour. The Carrs store at 1650 West Northern Lights Boulevard in Anchorage has a 24-hour pharmacy.

SHOPS

Alaskan gift shops are typically open weekdays or whenever cruise ships are in port. Gift shops in Anchorage are generally open year-round, but in other towns many places close in October and reopen in May.

BUS TRAVEL

A number of companies provide bus or van service connecting towns in South Central and Interior Alaska. Alaska Direct Bus Lines operates year-round van service between Anchorage, Fairbanks, Glennallen, Delta Junction, Skagway, and Tok in Alaska, along with Whitehorse in the Canadian Yukon. It also offers summer-only service to Haines. The Parks Highway Express also provides year-round bus service between Anchorage and Fairbanks, plus seasonal service between Fairbanks and Valdez and from Fairbanks to Dawson City in the Yukon. The Alaska Park Connection has summertime service between Seward and Anchorage, continuing north to Denali National Park. Homer Stage Lines provides year-round service between Anchorage and Homer, plus summertime service between Homer and Seward. Greyhound Lines of Canada serves Vancouver, with service as far north as Whitehorse in the Yukon. Quick Shuttle bus service runs between Vancouver and Seattle. Smoking is prohibited on all buses or vans. Contact the individual companies for their scheduled service.

CUTTING COSTS

The AlaskaPass allows unlimited travel on bus, ferry, and rail lines in Alaska (*see* Cutting Costs *in* Boat & Ferry Travel).

PAYING

Accepted forms of payment vary among the bus companies, but all accept MasterCard and Visa, along with traveler's checks.

RESERVATIONS

Reservations are generally not needed for bus transportation around Alaska, but it is always a good idea to call ahead if your travel dates are not flexible.

Alaska Direct Bus Lines Box 100501, Anchorage 99510 907/277-6652 or 800/770-6652. **Alaska Park Connection** Box 22-1011, Anchorage 99522 907/245-0200 or 800/266-8625 www.alaskacoach.com. **Greyhound Lines of Canada** 604/482-8747 or 800/661-8747 www.greyhound.ca. **Homer Stage Line** Box 1912, Homer 99603 907/868-3914 or 907/235-2252 907/235-0565 www.homerstagelines.com. **Parks Highway Express** Box 84278, Fairbanks 99708 907/457-2034 or 888/600-6001 www.alaskashuttle.com. **Quick Shuttle** 604/244-3744 or 800/665-2122 www.quickcoach.com.

CAMERAS & PHOTOGRAPHY

Alaska is one of the world's premier spots for nature and wildlife photography. Because of the high latitude, the light remains at a low angle for many hours during long summer days, creating extraordinary photographic conditions. For most amateur purposes, an ISO 200-speed print film is sufficient, though ISO 400 is better for low-light situations and for action shots. Many professional photographers shoot color slides, using Fuji's Sensia II or Velvia, along with Kodak's Ektachrome 100SW. Digital cameras are increasingly used by both amateurs and professional photographers, and the proliferation of Internet cafés has made it possible to e-mail digital photos to friends easily as you travel. Larger towns generally have at least one business where you can transfer these photos to CDs. If you're shooting digital, be sure to carry extra rechargeable batteries (and a charger), along with additional memory cards or other ways to store your images.

A zoom lens covering 28–105 mm is adequate for most Alaskan scenes, but longer telephoto lenses (200 mm and up) are useful for wildlife photos. A tripod is essential in dimly lighted situations and highly recommended for photographing wildlife with a telephoto lens.

Not everyone in Alaska appreciates being photographed, particularly in smaller Native villages where locals have sometimes been exploited by photographers.

Ask for permission before taking a photograph of someone. Many museums do not allow flash or tripods, and photography is restricted or prohibited inside Russian Orthodox churches and certain Native cemeteries.

The *Kodak Guide to Shooting Great Travel Pictures* (available at bookstores everywhere) is loaded with tips.

Photo Help **Kodak Information Center** 800/242-2424 www.kodak.com.

EQUIPMENT PRECAUTIONS

A plastic bag or umbrella will help keep your camera dry during wet weather. Winter travelers may need to contend with extremely cold conditions, which can greatly reduce battery life, fog lenses, and even cause complete mechanical failure. Be sure to pack extra batteries for your camera, especially when heading into remote areas. Lens fogging can be lessened by storing the camera and lenses in a cool place.

Don't pack film and equipment in checked luggage, where it is much more susceptible to damage. X-ray machines used to view checked luggage are extremely powerful and therefore are likely to ruin your film. Try to ask for hand inspection of film, which becomes clouded after repeated exposure to airport X-ray machines, and keep videotapes and computer disks away from metal detectors. Always keep film, tape, and computer disks out of the sun. Carry an extra supply of batteries, and be prepared to turn on your camera, camcorder, or laptop to prove to airport security personnel that the device is real.

FILM & DEVELOPING

Print film is available almost everywhere in Alaska, but slide film is often not available outside the larger towns and cities. Both types tend to be expensive (up to $8 for a 24-exposure roll), so carry plenty. All the larger towns have film developing and printing available, and many also have one-hour photo labs.

CAR RENTAL

Rates in the larger towns begin around $45 a day and $280 a week for an economy car with air-conditioning (not needed in Alaska), an automatic transmission, and unlimited mileage. You're likely to pay at least $50 per day and $300 per week from the major companies, more for four-wheel drives. **Reserve well ahead for the summer season, particularly for the popular minivans and sport utility vehicles.** Be sure to ask in advance about discounts if you have a AAA or Costco card.

⬚ Major Agencies Alamo ☎ 800/327-9633 ⊕ www.alamo.com. **Avis** ☎ 800/331-1212, 800/879-2847 or 800/272-5871 in Canada, 0870/606-0100 in U.K., 02/9353-9000 in Australia, 09/526-2847 in New Zealand ⊕ www.avis.com. **Budget** ☎ 800/527-0700, 0870/156-5656 in U.K. ⊕ www.budget.com. **Dollar** ☎ 800/800-4000; 0124/622-0111 in U.K., where it's affiliated with Sixt; 02/9223-1444 in Australia ⊕ www.dollar.com. **Hertz** ☎ 800/654-3131, 800/263-0600 in Canada, 0870/844-8844 in U.K., 02/9669-2444 in Australia, 09/256-8690 in New Zealand ⊕ www.hertz.com. **National Car Rental** ☎ 800/227-7368, 0870/600-6666 in U.K. ⊕ www.nationalcar.com.
⬚ Smaller Agencies Payless ☎ 800/729-5377 ⊕ www.paylesscarental.com. **Thrifty** ☎ 907/276-2855 or 800/367-2277 ⊕ www.thrifty.com.

CUTTING COSTS

For a good deal, book through a travel agent who will shop around. Also, price local car-rental companies—whose prices may be lower still, although their service and maintenance may not be as good as those of major rental agencies—and research rates on the Internet. Remember to ask about required deposits, cancellation penalties, and drop-off charges if you're planning to pick up the car in one city and leave it in another. If you're traveling during a holiday period, also make sure that a confirmed reservation guarantees you a car.

⬚ Local Agencies Affordable New Car Rentals ☎ 907/243-3370, 800/248-3765 in Anchorage, 907/452-7341 in Fairbanks ⊕ www.ancr.com. **Arctic Rent-A-Car** ☎ 800/478-8696, 907/561-2990 in Anchorage, 907/479-8044 in Fairbanks ⊕ www.arcticrentacar.com. **Denali Car Rental** ☎ 907/276-1230, 800/757-1230 in Anchorage. **U-Save Auto Rental** ☎ 907/272-8728 or 800/254-8728 in Anchorage, 907/479-7060 or 877/979-7060 in Fairbanks ⊕ www.usaveak.com.

INSURANCE

When driving a rented car you are generally responsible for any damage to or loss of the vehicle. You also may be liable for any property damage or personal injury that you may cause while driving. Before you rent, see what coverage you already

have under the terms of your personal auto-insurance policy and credit cards.

For about $10 to $25 a day, rental companies sell protection, known as a collision- or loss-damage waiver (CDW or LDW), that eliminates your liability for damage to the car; it's always optional and should never be automatically added to your bill. In most states you don't need a CDW if you have personal auto insurance or other liability insurance. However, **make sure you have enough coverage to pay for the car.** If you do not have auto insurance or an umbrella policy that covers damage to third parties, purchasing liability insurance and a CDW or LDW is highly recommended.

REQUIREMENTS & RESTRICTIONS

In Alaska you must be 21 (and no older than 99) to rent a car, and rates may be higher if you're under 25. When picking up a car, non-U.S. residents will need a reservation voucher, a passport, a driver's license (written in English), and a travel policy that covers each driver.

SURCHARGES

Before you pick up a car in one city and leave it in another, ask about drop-off charges or one-way service fees, which can be substantial. Note, too, that some rental agencies charge extra if you return the car before the time specified in your contract. To avoid a hefty refueling fee, **fill the tank just before you turn in the car,** but be aware that gas stations near the rental outlet may overcharge. It's almost never a deal to buy the tank of gas that's in the car when you rent it; the understanding is that you'll return it empty, but some fuel usually remains. Surcharges may apply if you're under 25 or if you take the car outside the area approved by the rental agency. You'll pay extra for child seats (about $6 a day), which are compulsory for children under five, and usually for additional drivers (about $10 per day).

CAR TRAVEL

Driving to Alaska is a popular alternative to flying or cruising, especially for RVers, but you'll need to **set aside plenty of time.** Though journeying through Canada on the Alaska Highway can be exciting, the trek from the Lower 48 states is a long one. It's a seven-day trip from Seattle to

Anchorage or Fairbanks, covering close to 2,500 mi. From Bellingham, Washington, and the Canadian ports of Prince Rupert and Stewart, you can link up with ferry service along the Marine Highway to reach southeastern Alaska.

The Alaska Highway begins at Dawson Creek, British Columbia, and stretches 1,442 mi through Canada's Yukon to Delta Junction; it enters Alaska at Tok. The two-lane highway is paved for its entire length and is open year-round. Highway services are available about every 50 to 100 mi (sometimes at shorter intervals).

The rest of the state's roads are found almost exclusively in the South Central and Interior regions. They lie mainly between Anchorage, Fairbanks, and the Canadian border. Only one highway extends north of Fairbanks, and a couple run south of Anchorage to the Kenai Peninsula. These roads vary from four-lane freeways to nameless two-lane gravel roads and are generally open and maintained year-round. The Glenn Highway begins at Tok and travels south to Anchorage. The Richardson Highway parallels the Alaska pipeline from Fairbanks south to the port city of Valdez.

The Seward Highway heads south from Anchorage through the Kenai Mountains to Seward, with the Sterling Highway branch heading southwest to Kenai and Homer. The George Parks Highway connects Anchorage and Fairbanks, passing Denali National Park en route. The Steese Highway runs northwest of Fairbanks to the gold-rush town of Circle. The Dalton Highway begins at the end of the Elliott Highway, 73 mi north of Fairbanks, and leads 414 mi to Deadhorse, the supply center for the Prudhoe Bay oil fields. This gravel truck route presents unique challenges; **contact the Alaska Public Lands Information centers in Fairbanks, Tok, or Anchorage if you plan to drive the Dalton Highway.**

If you plan extensive driving in Alaska, join an automobile club such as AAA that offers towing and other benefits. Because of the long distances involved, you should seriously consider a plan (such as AAA Plus) that extends towing benefits to 100 mi in any direction.

The Milepost, available in bookstores or from Morris Communications, is a mile-

by-mile guide to sights and services along Alaska's highways. **Alaska Public Lands Information Center** ⊠ 605 W. 4th Ave., Anchorage ☎ 907/271-2737 ⊕ www.ak. blm.gov ⊠ 250 Cushman St., Suite 1A, Fairbanks 99701 ☎ 907/456-0527 ⊠ 907/456-0154 ⊠ 50 Main St., Ketchikan ☎ 907/228-6214 ⊠ Mile 1314, Alaska Hwy., Tok ☎ 907/883-5667. *The Milepost* ⊠ Morris Communications, 735 Broad St., Augusta, GA 30901 ☎ 907/272-6070 or 800/726-4707 ⊠ 907/ 258-5360 ⊕ www.themilepost.com.

GASOLINE

Gas prices in the Anchorage area are comparable with those in the Lower 48, but expect to pay more elsewhere. You will probably pay around 30¢ per gallon more in towns such as Juneau or Ketchikan and far more in remote areas, particularly small villages off the road network, where fuel must be flown in. Fuel prices in Canada along the Alaska Highway are also very high. Most gas stations take Visa and MasterCard, and many also accept other credit cards and debit cards.

ROAD CONDITIONS

If you are planning to drive to Alaska, come armed with patience. Road construction sometimes creates long delays on the Canadian side of the border, so don't plan a tight schedule. Also, frost damage creates dips in the road that require slower driving.

Driving in Alaska is much less rigorous than it used to be, although it still presents some unusual obstacles. Moose often wander onto roads and highways. If you come across one while you're driving, it's best to **stop your car, pull off the road, and wait for the moose to cross.** The moose will usually move on its own. Be especially vigilant when driving at dusk or night, since moose can be active at all hours. In addition, keep your eyes open for other moose in the area, since a mother will often cross the road followed by one or two calves.

Flying gravel is a hazard to watch for along the Alaska and Dalton highways, especially in summer. A bug screen will help keep gravel and kamikaze insects off the windshield, but few travelers use them. Some travelers use clear, hard plastic guards to cover their headlights. (These are inexpensive and are available from almost any garage or service station along the major access routes.) Don't cover headlights with cardboard or plywood, because you'll need your lights often, even in daytime, as dust is thrown up by traffic passing in both directions. (Headlights must be used at all times on the Seward Highway south of Anchorage.)

Unless you plan to undertake one of the remote highways (especially the Dalton Highway to Prudhoe Bay), you won't need any special equipment. But be sure that the equipment you do have is in working condition, from tires and spare to brakes and engine. Carrying spare fuses, spark plugs, jumper cables, a flashlight with extra batteries, a tool kit, and an extra fan belt is recommended.

If you get stuck on any kind of road, be careful about pulling off; the shoulder can be soft. In summer it stays light late, and though traffic is also light, one of Alaska's many good Samaritans is likely to stop to help and send for aid (which may be many miles away). In winter, pack emergency equipment—a shovel, tire chains, such high-energy food as nuts or chocolate, and extra-warm clothing and blankets to help you through the wait for aid should you need it. Never head out onto unplowed roads unless you are prepared to walk back.

Cellular phones are an excellent idea for travel in Alaska, particularly on the main roads, but check with your service provider for coverage. AAA members may also want to upgrade to the "Plus" policy, which allows for towing of up to 100 mi if you break down. Road maps are available at gas stations and grocery stores throughout Alaska.

RULES OF THE ROAD

Alaska honors valid driver's licenses from any state or country, and the speed limit on most state highways is 55 mph, but much of the Parks Highway (between Wasilla and Fairbanks) and the Seward Highway (between Anchorage and Seward) is 65 mph. Unless otherwise posted, you may make a right turn on a red light after coming to a complete stop. Seat belts are required on all passengers in Alaska, and children under age five must be in child safety seats. State troopers rigorously enforce speed limits along the main highways.

State law requires that slow-moving vehicles pull off the road at the first opportunity if leading more than five cars. This is particularly true on the highway between Anchorage and Seward, where RV drivers have a bad reputation for not pulling over. Alaskans don't take kindly to being held up en route to their favorite Kenai River fishing spot.

RVS

The secret to a successful RV trip to Alaska is preparation. Expect to drive on more gravel and rougher roads than you're accustomed to. **Batten down everything**; tighten every nut and bolt in and out of sight, and don't leave anything to bounce around inside. Travel light, and your tires and suspension system will take less of a beating. Protect your headlights and the grille area in front of the radiator. Make sure you carry adequate insurance to cover the replacement of your windshield.

Most of Alaska's public campgrounds accommodate trailers, but hookups are available only in private RV parks. Water can be found at most stopping points, but it may be limited for trailer use. Think twice before deciding to drive an RV or pull a trailer during the spring thaw. The rough roadbed can be a trial.

CHILDREN IN ALASKA

Be sure to plan ahead and involve your youngsters as you outline your trip. When packing, include things to keep them busy en route. On sightseeing days try to schedule activities of special interest to your children. Many families travel to Alaska with children in tow, and most tourist facilities—including restaurants, museums, and hotels—go out of their way to accommodate them. Note, however, that some bed-and-breakfasts cater to couples looking to escape their own or other people's children and do not allow kids, particularly those under 12. Young children may easily become bored on long bus or plane trips, and many of the more adventurous activities in Alaska such as sea kayaking, river rafting, and bear viewing are potentially dangerous for youngsters. If you are considering an adventure trip, ask about taking kids. Baby-sitting agencies do not exist in Alaska, but short-term care may be available at local day-care centers in the larger towns.

If you are renting a car, don't forget to **arrange for a car seat** when you reserve. For general advice about traveling with children, consult *Fodor's FYI: Travel with Your Baby* (available in bookstores everywhere).

FLYING

If your children are two or older, ask about children's airfares. As a general rule, infants under two not occupying a seat fly at greatly reduced fares or even for free. But if you want to guarantee a seat for an infant, you have to pay full fare. Consider flying during off-peak days and times; most airlines will grant an infant a seat without a ticket if there are available seats.

Experts agree that it's a good idea to use safety seats aloft for children weighing less than 40 pounds. Airlines set their own policies; if you use a safety seat, U.S. carriers usually require that the child be ticketed, even if he or she is young enough to ride free, because the seats must be strapped into regular seats. And even if you pay the full adult fare for the seat, it may be worth it, especially on longer trips. Do **check your airline's policy about using safety seats during takeoff and landing.** Safety seats are not allowed everywhere in the plane, so get your seat assignments as early as possible.

When reserving, request children's meals or a freestanding bassinet (not available at all airlines) if you need them. But note that bulkhead seats, where you must sit to use the bassinet, may lack an overhead bin or storage space on the floor.

LODGING

Most hotels in Alaska allow children under a certain age to stay in their parents' room at no extra charge, but others charge for them as extra adults; be sure to **find out the cutoff age for children's discounts.** **Best Choices** **Comfort Inn Ship Creek** ✉ 111 Ship Creek Ave., Anchorage 99501 ☎ 907/277-6887 or 800/228-5150 🖷 907/274-9830. **Frontier Suites Airport Hotel** ✉ 9400 Glacier Hwy., Juneau 99801 ☎ 907/790-6600 or 800/544-2250 🖷 907/790-6612 ⊕ www.frontiersuites.com. **Merrill Field Inn** ✉ 420 Sitka St., East Anchorage 99501 ☎ 907/276-4547 or 800/898-4547 🖷 907/276-5064 ⊕ www.merrillfieldinn.com. **SpringHill Suites by Marriott** ✉ 3401 A St., Anchorage 99503 ☎ 907/562-3247 or 888/287-9400 🖷 907/562-3250 ⊕ www.springhillsuites.com.

SIGHTS & ATTRACTIONS

Places that are especially appealing to children are indicated by a rubber-duckie icon (🦆) in the margin.

CONSUMER PROTECTION

Whether you're shopping for gifts or purchasing travel services, **pay with a major credit card** whenever possible, so you can cancel payment or get reimbursed if there's a problem (and you can provide documentation). If you're doing business with a particular company for the first time, contact your local Better Business Bureau and the attorney general's offices in your state and (for U.S. businesses) the company's home state as well. Have any complaints been filed? Finally, if you're buying a package or tour, always consider travel insurance that includes default coverage (⇨ Insurance).
BBBs Council of Better Business Bureaus ✉ 4200 Wilson Blvd., Suite 800, Arlington, VA 22203 ☎ 703/276-0100 🖷 703/525-8277 ⊕ www.bbb.org.

CUSTOMS & DUTIES

When shopping abroad, **keep receipts** for all purchases. Upon reentering the country, be ready to show customs officials what you've bought. Pack purchases together in an easily accessible place. If you think a duty is incorrect, appeal the assessment. If you object to the way your clearance was handled, note the inspector's badge number. In either case, first ask to see a supervisor. If the problem isn't resolved, write to the appropriate authorities, beginning with the port director at your point of entry.

IN AUSTRALIA

Australian residents who are 18 or older may bring home A$400 worth of souvenirs and gifts (including jewelry), 250 cigarettes or 250 grams of cigars or other tobacco products, and 1,125 ml of alcohol (including wine, beer, and spirits). Residents under 18 may bring back A$200 worth of goods. Members of the same family traveling together may pool their allowances. Prohibited items include meat products. Seeds, plants, and fruits need to be declared upon arrival.
Australian Customs Service ⊕ Regional Director, Box 8, Sydney, NSW 2001 ☎ 02/9213-2000 or 1300/363263, 02/9364-7222 or 1800/803-006 quar-

antine-inquiry line ☎ 02/9213-4043 ⊕ www. customs.gov.au.

IN CANADA

Canadian residents who have been out of Canada for at least seven days may bring in C$750 worth of goods duty-free. If you've been away fewer than seven days but more than 48 hours, the duty-free allowance drops to C$200. If your trip lasts 24 to 48 hours, the allowance is C$50. You may not pool allowances with family members. Goods claimed under the C$750 exemption may follow you by mail; those claimed under the lesser exemptions must accompany you. Alcohol and tobacco products may be included in the seven-day and 48-hour exemptions but not in the 24-hour exemption. If you meet the age requirements of the province or territory through which you reenter Canada, you may bring in, duty-free, 1.5 liters of wine *or* 1.14 liters (40 imperial ounces) of liquor *or* 24 12-ounce cans or bottles of beer or ale. Also, if you meet the local age requirement for tobacco products, you may bring in, duty-free, 200 cigarettes and 50 cigars. Check ahead of time with the Canada Customs and Revenue Agency or the Department of Agriculture for policies regarding meat products, seeds, plants, and fruits.

You may send an unlimited number of gifts (only one gift per recipient, however) worth up to C$60 each duty-free to Canada. Label the package UNSOLICITED GIFT—VALUE UNDER $60. Alcohol and tobacco are excluded.

F **Canada Customs and Revenue Agency** ⊠ 2265 St. Laurent Blvd., Ottawa, Ontario K1G 4K3 ☎ 800/461-9999, 204/983-3500, 506/636-5064 ⊕ www. ccra.gc.ca.

IN NEW ZEALAND

All homeward-bound residents may bring back NZ$700 worth of souvenirs and gifts; passengers may not pool their allowances, and children can claim only the concession on goods intended for their own use. For those 17 or older, the duty-free allowance also includes 4.5 liters of wine or beer; one 1,125-ml bottle of spirits; and either 200 cigarettes, 250 grams of tobacco, 50 cigars, *or* a combination of the three up to 250 grams. Meat products, seeds, plants, and fruits must be declared upon arrival to the Agricultural Services Department.

F **New Zealand Customs** ⊠ Head office: The Customhouse, 17-21 Whitmore St. ☎ Box 2218, Wellington ☎ 09/300-5399 or 0800/428-786 ⊕ www.customs.govt.nz.

IN THE U.K.

From countries outside the European Union, including the United States, you may bring home, duty-free, 200 cigarettes or 50 cigars; 1 liter of spirits or 2 liters of fortified or sparkling wine or liqueurs; 2 liters of still table wine; 60 ml of perfume; 250 ml of toilet water; plus £145 worth of other goods, including gifts and souvenirs. Prohibited items include meat products, seeds, plants, and fruits.

F **HM Customs and Excise** ⊠ Portcullis House, 21 Cowbridge Rd. E, Cardiff CF11 9SS ☎ 0845/010-9000 or 0208/929-0152, 0208/929-6731 or 0208/910-3602 complaints ⊕ www.hmce.gov.uk.

IN THE U.S.

U.S. residents who have been out of the country for at least 48 hours may bring home, for personal use, $800 worth of foreign goods duty-free, as long as they haven't used the $800 allowance or any part of it in the past 30 days. This exemption may include 1 liter of alcohol (for travelers 21 and older), 200 cigarettes, and 100 non-Cuban cigars. Family members from the same household who are traveling together may pool their $800 personal exemptions. For fewer than 48 hours, the duty-free allowance drops to $200, which may include 50 cigarettes, 10 non-Cuban cigars, and 150 ml of alcohol (or 150 ml of perfume containing alcohol). The $200 allowance cannot be combined with other individuals' exemptions, and if you exceed it, the full value of all the goods will be taxed. Antiques, which the U.S. Bureau of Customs and Border Protection defines as objects more than 100 years old, enter duty-free, as do original works of art done entirely by hand, including paintings, drawings, and sculptures. This doesn't apply to folk art or handicrafts, which are in general dutiable.

You may also send packages home duty-free, with a limit of one parcel per addressee per day (except alcohol or tobacco products or perfume worth more than $5). You can mail up to $200 worth of goods for personal use; label the package PERSONAL USE and attach a list of its contents and their retail value. If the package contains your used personal belongings, mark it AMERICAN GOODS RETURNED to avoid paying duties. You may send up to $100 worth of goods as a gift; mark the package UNSOLICITED GIFT. Mailed items do not affect your duty-free allowance on your return.

To avoid paying duty on foreign-made high-ticket items you already own and will take on your trip, register them with Customs before you leave the country. Consider filing a Certificate of Registration for laptops, cameras, watches, and other digital devices identified with serial numbers or other permanent markings; you can keep the certificate for other trips. Otherwise, bring a sales receipt or insurance form to show that you owned the item before you left the United States.

U.S. Bureau of Customs and Border Protection ✉ For inquiries and equipment registration, 1300 Pennsylvania Ave. NW, Washington, DC 20229 ⊕ www.customs.gov ☎ 877/287-8667, 202/354-1000 ✉ For complaints, Customer Satisfaction Unit, 1300 Pennsylvania Ave. NW, Room 5.5D, Washington, DC 20229.

DISABILITIES & ACCESSIBILITY

Travelers with disabilities will find good facilities at the most popular tourist areas, particularly places that deal with large numbers of elderly cruise-ship passengers. Some Forest Service cabins are wheelchair accessible, and the state ferries and trains are well set up to accommodate passengers with disabilities.

In general, Bush Alaskan villages are not at all wheelchair friendly, with rough gravel roads and minimal facilities. Travelers with disabilities may also have difficulties getting into and out of the small aircraft used to reach these villages.

Access Alaska is a nonprofit independent-living center in Anchorage. It posts a helpful listing of accessible hotels and restaurants, car and van rental information, tour companies, and other details for travelers with disabilities on its Web site. Individuals with disabilities can contact the center for more specialized details about Alaska facilities and support. Keith Carpenter of AKcess Eco-Tours is a Juneau-based biologist who sets up accessible van tours, along with boating and backcountry trips. Alaska Welcomes You!

has a complete database of accessible accommodations, attractions, and tours. It also books tours, cruises, and other trips customized to personal abilities.

Local Resources Access Alaska ✉ 121 W. Fireweed La., Suite 105, Anchorage 99503 ☎ 907/248-4777, 800/770-4488 in Alaska, 907/248-8799 TTY 🖶 907/248-0639 ⊕ www.accessalaska.org. **AKcess Eco-Tours** ✉ 4208 Taku, Juneau 99801-9221 ☎ 907/789-2090 ⊕ www.akcess.org. **Alaska Welcomes You!** 🖅 Box 91333, Anchorage 99509 ☎ 907/349-6301 or 800/349-6301 🖶 907/344-3259 ⊕ www.accessiblealaska.com.

LODGING

Despite the Americans with Disabilities Act, the definition of accessibility seems to differ from hotel to hotel. Some properties may be accessible by ADA standards for people with mobility problems but not for people with hearing or vision impairments, for example.

If you have mobility problems, ask for the lowest floor on which accessible services are offered. If you have a hearing impairment, check whether the hotel has devices to alert you visually to the ring of the telephone, a knock at the door, and a fire/emergency alarm. Some hotels provide these devices without charge. Discuss your needs with hotel personnel if this equipment isn't available, so that a staff member can personally alert you in the event of an emergency.

If you're bringing a guide dog, get authorization ahead of time and write down the name of the person with whom you spoke.

All larger hotels in Alaska have at least one wheelchair-accessible room, and those built since the mid-1990s often have several such rooms. Most bed-and-breakfasts are not as wheelchair-friendly; contact B&B referral agencies for those with accessible facilities. Alaska Welcomes You! can set up accessible lodging throughout the state.

RESERVATIONS

When discussing accessibility with an operator or reservations agent, ask hard questions. Are there any stairs, inside *or* out? Are there grab bars next to the toilet *and* in the shower/tub? How wide is the doorway to the room? To the bathroom? For the most extensive facilities meeting the latest legal specifications, **opt for**

newer accommodations. If you reserve through a toll-free number, consider also calling the hotel's local number to confirm the information from the central reservations office. Get confirmation in writing when you can.

TRANSPORTATION

Alaska Direct Bus Lines offers a 10% discount to passengers with disabilities for intercity travel. AnchorRIDES provides transportation for senior citizens and those with disabilities within the Anchorage area. You do not need to be an Alaska resident to use this service, but you should contact AnchorRIDES at least a day in advance. Hertz has hand-controlled rental cars in Anchorage. The Alaska Marine Highway System has elevators on eight of its nine vessels and wheelchair-accessible cabins on its six vessels equipped with staterooms. ERA Helicopters has wheelchair lifts at its Juneau and Denali National Park locations, and Alaska Cab offers lift-equipped van service in Anchorage. The Alaska Railroad has cars that are accessible for people who use wheelchairs; cars also have wheelchair locks and lifts. Seward, Portage, Whittier, Anchorage, Talkeetna, Denali National Park, and Fairbanks stations all have lifts, with at least one lock-down for service on all trains.

Bus Travel **Alaska Direct Bus Lines** ✈ Box 501, Anchorage 99501 ☎ 907/277-6652 or 800/770-6652 🌐 www.tokalaska.com/dirctbus.shtml. **Anchor-RIDES** ☎ 907/562-8444.

Car Rental **Hertz** ☎ 800/654-3131, 800/654-2280 TTY.

Ferry Travel **Alaska Marine Highway** ☎ 907/465-3941 or 800/642-0066 🖨 907/277-4829 🌐 www.alaska.gov/ferry.

Flightseeing **ERA Helicopters** ☎ 907/266-8351 or 800/843-1947 🌐 www.eraaviation.com.

Taxis **Alaska Cab** ☎ 907/563-5353 🌐 www.alaskacabs.com.

Train Travel **Alaska Railroad** ☎ 907/265-2494 in Anchorage, 907/458-6025 in Fairbanks, 800/544-0552 🖨 907/265-2323 🌐 www.akrr.com.

Complaints **Aviation Consumer Protection Division** (⇨ Air Travel) for airline-related problems. **Departmental Office of Civil Rights** ☒ For general inquiries, U.S. Department of Transportation, S-30, 400 7th St. SW, Room 10215, Washington, DC 20590 ☎ 202/366-4648 🖨 202/366-9371 🌐 www.dot.gov/ost/docr/index.htm. **Disability Rights Section** ☒ NYAV, U.S. Department of Justice, Civil Rights Division, 950 Pennsylvania Ave. NW, Washington, DC 20530 ☎ ADA information line 202/514-0301, 800/

514-0301, 202/514-0383 TTY, 800/514-0383 TTY 🌐 www.ada.gov. **U.S. Department of Transportation Hotline** ☎ For disability-related air-travel problems, 800/778-4838 or 800/455-9880 TTY.

TRAVEL AGENCIES

In the United States, the Americans with Disabilities Act requires that travel firms serve the needs of all travelers. Some agencies specialize in working with people with disabilities.

Travelers with Mobility Problems **Access Adventures** ☒ 206 Chestnut Ridge Rd., Scottsville, NY 14624 ☎ 585/889-9096 ✐ dltravel@prodigy.net, run by a former physical-rehabilitation counselor.

Accessible Vans of America ☒ 9 Spielman Rd., Fairfield, NJ 07004 ☎ 877/282-8267, 973/808-9709 reservations 🖨 973/808-9713 🌐 www.accessiblevans.com.

CareVacations ☒ No. 5, 5110-50 Ave., Leduc, Alberta T9E 6V4, Canada ☎ 780/986-6404 or 877/478-7827 🖨 780/986-8332 🌐 www.carevacations.com, for group tours and cruise vacations.

Flying Wheels Travel ☒ 143 W. Bridge St. ✈ Box 382, Owatonna, MN 55060 ☎ 507/451-5005 🖨 507/451-1685 🌐 www.flyingwheelstravel.com.

Travelers with Developmental Disabilities **New Directions** ☒ 5276 Hollister Ave., Suite 207, Santa Barbara, CA 93111 ☎ 805/967-2841 or 888/967-2841 🖨 805/964-7344 🌐 www.newdirectionstravel.com.

DISCOUNTS & DEALS

Be a smart shopper and compare all your options before making decisions. A plane ticket bought with a promotional coupon from travel clubs, coupon books, and direct-mail offers or purchased on the Internet may not be cheaper than the least expensive fare from a discount ticket agency. And always keep in mind that what you get is just as important as what you save. The AlaskaPass allows unlimited travel on bus, ferry, and rail lines in Alaska (see Cutting Costs in Boat & Ferry Travel).

DISCOUNT RESERVATIONS

To save money, look into discount reservations services with Web sites and toll-free numbers, which use their buying power to get a better price on hotels, airline tickets (⇨ Air Travel), even car rentals. When booking a room, always **call the hotel's local toll-free number** (if one is available) rather than the central reservations number—you'll often get a better price. Always ask about special packages or corporate rates.

🏷 Airline Tickets **Air 4 Less** ☏ 800/AIR4LESS, low-fare specialist.

🏷 Hotel Rooms **Accommodations Express** ☏ 800/444-7666 or 800/277-1064 ⊕ www. accommodationsexpress.com. **Hotels.com** ☏ 800/ 246-8357 or 214/369-1246 ⊕ www.hotels.com. **RMC Travel** ☏ 800/245-5738 ⊕ www.rmcwebtravel. com. **Turbotrip.com** ☏ 800/473-7829 ⊕ www. turbotrip.com.

PACKAGE DEALS

Don't confuse packages and guided tours. When you buy a package, you travel on your own, just as though you had planned the trip yourself. Fly/drive packages, which combine airfare and car rental, are often a good deal. In cities, ask the local visitor's bureau about hotel packages that include tickets to major museum exhibits or other special events.

EATING & DRINKING

The restaurants we list are the cream of the crop in each price category. Restaurants are indicated in the text by a knife-and-fork icon, ✕. Establishments denoted by both a knife-and-fork icon and a lodging icon, ✕🏠, stand out equally for their restaurants and rooms.

For restaurants:

CATEGORY	ALASKA*	VANCOUVER & VICTORIA*
$$$$	over $25	over C$30
$$$	$20–$25	C$20–C$30
$$	$15–$20	C$12–C$20
$	$10–$15	C$8–C$12
¢	under $10	under C$8

*per person for a main course at dinner

MEALTIMES

Alaskan restaurants typically serve breakfast until 10 or 11, lunch from 11 to 2, and dinner starting around 4. Unless otherwise noted, the restaurants listed in this guide are open daily for lunch and dinner.

RESERVATIONS & DRESS

Reservations are always a good idea; we mention them only when they're essential or not accepted. Book as far ahead as you can, and reconfirm as soon as you arrive. (Large parties should always call ahead to check the reservations policy.) We mention dress only when men are required to wear a jacket or a jacket and tie.

SPECIALTIES

Alaska is best known for its seafood, particularly such stars as king salmon, halibut, king crab, and shrimp. Anchorage and Juneau have superb restaurants specializing in fresh seafood, but you will also discover seafood on the menu in virtually any coastal Alaskan town. The open-air salmon bakes in Juneau, Tok, Denali National Park, and Fairbanks serve excellent, all-you-can-eat grilled salmon and halibut. Anchorage has the greatest diversity of restaurants, including classy steak houses, noisy brewpubs, authentic Thai and Mexican eateries, and a wide variety of other ethnic places.

WINE, BEER & SPIRITS

Alcohol is sold at liquor stores in most Alaskan towns and cities along the road system, as well as in settlements along the Inside Passage. Alcoholism is a devastating problem in Native villages, and because of this many of these Bush communities are "dry" (no alcohol allowed) or "damp" (limited amounts allowed for personal use, but alcohol cannot be sold). Be sure to check the rules before flying into a Bush community with alcohol, or you might find yourself charged with illegally importing alcohol.

Alaska's best-known microbrew is made by Alaskan Brewing Company in Juneau. Its Alaskan Amber is available in six-packs or on draft throughout the Pacific Northwest. Anchorage is home to several popular brew pubs, and their beers are sold in local liquor stores. Homer Brewing Company in the town of Homer sells its beers in local bars or in take-away bottles. You'll also find brewpubs in Fairbanks, Haines, Ketchikan, Skagway, and Wasilla.

ECOTOURISM

Concern for the environment has spawned a worldwide movement called ecotourism, or green tourism. Ecotourists aim to travel responsibly, taking care to conserve the environment and respect indigenous populations. The **Alaska Wilderness Recreation and Tourism Association** (⊕ www.awrta. org) includes many of the state's wilderness-dependent businesses and promotes eco-friendly activities across the state. For information about environmental concerns peculiar to Alaska as well as a list of resources and ecotour operators, *see* Planning a Wilderness Adventure *in* Chapter 3.

GAY & LESBIAN TRAVEL

Alaska is a politically conservative state, and openly gay and lesbian travelers may not be well accepted in some towns. Although Fairbanks and Juneau both have active gay and lesbian communities, Anchorage is the real center for Alaska, with a Gay and Lesbian Community Center, two gay bars (Mad Myrna's and the Raven), along with gay-oriented travel agencies, stores, and a theater company (Out North Contemporary Art House) that sometimes presents related plays. For gay and lesbian information, Identity Inc. produces a monthly magazine, operates a gay and lesbian help line, and runs the above-mentioned community center.

▶ Gay- & Lesbian-Friendly Travel Agencies **Different Roads Travel** ⊠ 8383 Wilshire Blvd., Suite 520, Beverly Hills, CA 90211 ☎ 323/651-5557 or 800/429-8747 Ext. 14 for both 🖶 323/651-3678 ✉ lgernert@tzell.com. **Kennedy Travel** ⊠ 130 W. 42nd St., Suite 401, New York, NY 10036 ☎ 212/840-8659, 800/237-7433 🖶 212/730-2269 ⊕ www.kennedytravel.com. **Now, Voyager** ⊠ 4406 18th St., San Francisco, CA 94114 ☎ 415/626-1169 or 800/255-6951 🖶 415/626-1169 ⊕ www.nowvoyager.com. **Skylink Travel and Tour** ⊠ 1455 N. Dutton Ave., Suite A, Santa Rosa, CA 95401 ☎ 707/546-9888 or 800/225-5759 🖶 707/636-0951, serving lesbian travelers.

▶ Gay & Lesbian Resources **Gay and Lesbian Community Center** ⊠ 2110 E. Northern Lights Blvd. ☎ 907/929-4528 **Identity Inc.** ☎ 907/258-4777 ⊕ www.alaska.net/~identity

HEALTH

PESTS & OTHER HAZARDS

During the summer months Alaska is infamous for its sometimes-dense clouds of mosquitoes and other biting insects. They are generally the worst in Interior Alaska but can be an annoyance throughout the state. **Be sure to bring mosquito repellents containing DEET.** Also popular (but less effective) is the Avon product Skin So Soft. Mosquito coils may be of some help if you are camping out or staying in remote cabins. Headnets are sold in local sporting-goods stores and are a wise purchase if you plan to spend extended time outdoors.

HOLIDAYS

Major national holidays are New Year's Day (January 1); Martin Luther King Day (third Monday in January); Presidents' Day (third Monday in February); Memorial Day (last Monday in May); Independence Day (July 4); Labor Day (first Monday in September); Columbus Day (second Monday in October); Thanksgiving Day (fourth Thursday in November); Christmas Eve and Christmas Day (December 24 and 25); and New Year's Eve (December 31).

INSURANCE

The most useful travel-insurance plan is a comprehensive policy that includes coverage for trip cancellation and interruption, default, trip delay, and medical expenses (with a waiver for preexisting conditions).

Without insurance you'll lose all or most of your money if you cancel your trip, regardless of the reason. Default insurance covers you if your tour operator, airline, or cruise line goes out of business. Trip-delay covers expenses that arise because of bad weather or mechanical delays. Study the fine print when comparing policies.

U.K. residents can buy a travel-insurance policy valid for most vacations taken during the year in which it's purchased (but check preexisting-condition coverage). Always **buy travel policies directly from the insurance company;** if you buy them from a cruise line, airline, or tour operator that goes out of business, you probably won't be covered for the agency or operator's default, a major risk. Before making any purchase, review your existing health and home-owner's policies to find what they cover away from home.

▶ Travel Insurers In the U.S.: **Access America** ⊠ 6600 W. Broad St., Richmond, VA 23230 ☎ 800/284-8300 🖶 804/673-1491 or 800/346-9265 ⊕ www.accessamerica.com. **Travel Guard International** ⊠ 1145 Clark St., Stevens Point, WI 54481 ☎ 715/345-0505 or 800/826-1300 🖶 800/955-8785 ⊕ www.travelguard.com.

FOR INTERNATIONAL TRAVELERS

For information on customs restrictions, *see* Customs & Duties.

CAR RENTAL

When picking up a rental car, non-U.S. residents need a reservation voucher for any prepaid reservations that were made in the traveler's home country, a passport, a driver's license, and a travel policy that covers each driver.

CURRENCY

The dollar is the basic unit of U.S. currency. It has 100 cents. Coins include the copper penny (1¢); the silvery nickel (5¢), dime (10¢), quarter (25¢), and half-dollar (50¢); and the golden $1 coin, replacing a now-rare silver dollar. Bills are denominated $1, $5, $10, $20, $50, and $100, all green and identical in size; designs vary.

ELECTRICITY

The U.S. standard is AC, 110 volts/60 cycles. Plugs have two flat pins set parallel to each other.

EMERGENCIES

For police, fire, or ambulance, **dial 911** (0 in rural areas).

INSURANCE

Britons and Australians need extra medical coverage when traveling overseas.
🛈 Insurance Information In the U.K.: **Association of British Insurers** ✉ 51 Gresham St., London EC2V 7HQ ☎ 020/7600-3333 🖷 020/7696-8999 ⊕ www.abi.org.uk. In Australia: **Insurance Council of Australia** ✉ Insurance Enquiries and Complaints, Level 3, 56 Pitt St., Sydney, NSW 2000 ☎ 1300/363683 or 02/9251-4456 🖷 02/9251-4453 ⊕ www.iecltd.com.au. In Canada: **RBC Insurance** ✉ 6880 Financial Dr., Mississauga, Ontario L5N 7Y5 ☎ 800/565-3129 🖷 905/813-4704 ⊕ www.rbcinsurance.com. In New Zealand: **Insurance Council of New Zealand** ✉ Level 7, 111-115 Customhouse Quay 🕮 Box 474, Wellington ☎ 04/472-5230 🖷 04/473-3011 ⊕ www.icnz.org.nz.

MAIL & SHIPPING

You can buy stamps and aerograms and send letters and parcels in post offices. Stamp-dispensing machines can occasionally be found in airports, bus and train stations, office buildings, drugstores, and the like. You can also deposit mail in the stout, dark blue steel bins at strategic locations everywhere and in the mail chutes of large buildings; pickup schedules are posted.

For mail sent within the United States, you need a 37¢ stamp for first-class letters weighing up to 1 ounce (23¢ for each additional ounce) and 23¢ for postcards. You pay 80¢ for 1-ounce airmail letters and 70¢ for airmail postcards to most other countries; to Canada and Mexico, you need a 60¢ stamp for a 1-ounce letter and 50¢ for a postcard. An aerogram—a single sheet of lightweight blue paper that folds into its own envelope, stamped for overseas airmail—costs 70¢.

To receive mail on the road, have it sent c/o General Delivery at your destination's main post office (use the correct five-digit ZIP code). You must pick up mail in person within 30 days and show a driver's license or passport.

PASSPORTS & VISAS

When traveling internationally, carry your passport even if you don't need one (it's always the best form of ID) and **make two photocopies of the data page** (one for someone at home and another for you, carried separately from your passport). If you lose your passport, promptly call the nearest embassy or consulate and the local police.

Visitor visas aren't necessary for Canadian or European Union citizens, or for citizens of Australia who are staying fewer than 90 days.
🛈 Australian Citizens **Passports Australia** ☎ 131-232 ⊕ www.passports.gov.au. **United States Consulate General** ✉ MLC Centre, Level 59, 19-29 Martin Pl., Sydney, NSW 2000 ☎ 02/9373-9200, 1902/941-641 fee-based visa-inquiry line ⊕ usembassy-australia.state.gov/sydney.
🛈 Canadian Citizens **Passport Office** ✉ To mail in applications: 200 Promenade du Portage, Hull, Québec J8X 4B7 ☎ 819/994-3500 or 800/567-6868 ⊕ www.ppt.gc.ca.
🛈 New Zealand Citizens **New Zealand Passports Office** ✉ For applications and information, Level 3, Boulcott House, 47 Boulcott St., Wellington ☎ 0800/22-5050 or 04/474-8100 ⊕ www.passports.govt.nz. **Embassy of the United States** ✉ 29 Fitzherbert Terr., Thorndon, Wellington ☎ 04/462-6000 ⊕ usembassy.org.nz. **U.S. Consulate General** ✉ Citibank Bldg., 3rd floor, 23 Customs St. E, Auckland ☎ 09/303-2724 ⊕ usembassy.org.nz.
🛈 U.K. Citizens **U.K. Passport Service** ☎ 0870/521-0410 ⊕ www.passport.gov.uk. **American Consulate General** ✉ Queen's House, 14 Queen St., Belfast BT1 6EQ, Northern Ireland ☎ 028/9032-8239 🖷 028/9024-8482 ⊕ www.usembassy.org.uk. **American Embassy** ✉ For visa and immi-

gration information [enclose an SASE], Consular Information Unit, 24 Grosvenor Sq., London W1 1AE ✉ To submit an application via mail, Visa Branch, 5 Upper Grosvenor St., London W1A 2JB ☎ 09068/ 200-290 recorded visa information or 09055/444- 546 operator service, both with per-minute charges, 0207/499-9000 main switchboard ⊕ www. usembassy.org.uk.

TELEPHONES

All U.S. telephone numbers consist of a three-digit area code and a seven-digit local number. Within many local calling areas, you dial only the seven-digit number. Within some area codes, you must dial "1" first for calls outside the local area. To call between area-code regions, dial "1" then all 10 digits; the same goes for calls to numbers prefixed by "800," "888," "866," and "877"—all toll free. For calls to numbers preceded by "900" you must pay—usually dearly.

For international calls, dial "011" followed by the country code and the local number. For help, dial "0" and ask for an overseas operator. The country code is 61 for Australia, 64 for New Zealand, 44 for the United Kingdom. Calling Canada is the same as calling within the United States. Most local phone books list country codes and U.S. area codes. The country code for the United States is 1.

For operator assistance, dial "0." To obtain someone's phone number, call directory assistance at 555–1212 or occasionally 411 (free at public phones). To have the person you're calling foot the bill, phone collect; dial "0" instead of "1" before the 10-digit number.

At pay phones, instructions often are posted. Usually you insert coins in a slot (usually 25¢–50¢ for local calls) and wait for a steady tone before dialing. When you call long-distance, the operator tells you how much to insert; prepaid phone cards, widely available in various denominations, are easier. Call the number on the back, punch in the card's personal identification number when prompted, then dial your number.

LODGING

The lodgings we list are the cream of the crop in each price category. We always list the facilities that are available—but we don't specify whether they cost extra:

when pricing accommodations, always ask what's included and what costs extra.

For hotels:

CATEGORY	ANCHORAGE*	ELSEWHERE IN ALASKA*
$$$$	over $250	over $225
$$$	$200–$250	$175–$225
$$	$150–$200	$125–$175
$	$100–$150	$75–$125
¢	under $100	under $75

All prices are for a standard double room in high season, excluding tax and service.

CATEGORY	VANCOUVER & VICTORIA*
$$$$	over C$250
$$$	C$175–C$250
$$	C$125–C$175
$	C$75–C$125
¢	under C$75

All prices are for two people in a standard double room in high season, excluding 10% provincial accommodation tax, service charge, and 7% GST.

Assume that hotels operate on the **European Plan** (EP, with no meals) unless we specify that they use the **Continental Plan** (CP, with a Continental breakfast), **Modified American Plan** (MAP, with breakfast and dinner), or the **Full American Plan** (FAP, with all meals).

BED & BREAKFASTS

Bed-and-breakfasts are common across Alaska and provide a fine way to learn about the area while staying with a local. Nearly every Alaskan town has at least one B&B, and dozens of choices are available in the larger cities. At last count, Anchorage had more than 175 B&Bs, including modest suburban apartments, elaborate showcase homes with dramatic vistas, and everything in between.

🔲 Reservation Services **Alaska Private Lodgings/ Stay with a Friend** ⌕ Box 3552, Homer 99603- 3552 ☎ 907/235-2148 or 888/235-2148 🖷 907/235- 3773 ⊕ www.alaskabandb.com. **Alaska Sourdough Bed & Breakfast Association** ✉ 889 Cardigan Cir., Anchorage 99503 ☎ 907/563-6244 🖷 907/563- 6073. **Alaska's Mat-Su Bed & Breakfast Association** ⌕ Box 873507, Wasilla 99687 ⊕ www. alaskabnbhosts.com. **Alaska Tour & Travel** ⌕ Box 221011, Anchorage 99522-1011 ☎ 907/245-0200 or 800/208-0200 ⊕ www.alaskatravel.com. **Anchorage Alaska Bed & Breakfast Association** ⌕ Box 242623, Anchorage 99524-2623 ☎ 907/272-5909 or 888/584-5147 ⊕ www.anchorage-bnb.com. **Bed & Breakfast Association of Alaska** ⊕ www.

alaskabba.com. **Bed & Breakfast Association of Alaska Innside Passage Chapter** ⬦ Box 22800, Juneau 99802 ☎ 907/789-8822 🖷 907/780-4673 ⊕ www.accommodations-alaska.com.

CAMPING

Camping in Alaska needn't be a daunting experience: think of it as camping elsewhere in the Lower 48, except that the mosquitoes are worse and there's a greater likelihood of a nighttime bear visit. Some newcomers to bear country are uneasy sleeping in a tent, but encounters are rare. **Store food inside your vehicle** where it's less likely to tempt bears. The midnight sun can also keep tent campers awake. Whether you're in a tent or an RV, you'll need warm bedding, insect repellent, rain protection, and tight containers for food storage.

Public campgrounds in Alaska are operated by the U.S. Forest Service, State Division of Parks and Outdoor Recreation, National Park Service, and Bureau of Land Management. Of the national parks, only Denali has developed car-camping facilities, and these campsites fill quickly. Several other Alaskan national parks have walk-in campgrounds, and all parks allow backcountry camping. In addition to the public campgrounds, private RV parks can be found in Alaska's larger towns.

HOME EXCHANGES

If you would like to exchange your home for someone else's, join a home-exchange organization, which will send you its updated listings of available exchanges for a year and will include your own listing in at least one of them. It's up to you to make specific arrangements.
🖪 Exchange Clubs **HomeLink International** ⬦ Box 47747, Tampa, FL 33647 ☎ 813/975-9825 or 800/638-3841 🖷 813/910-8144 ⊕ www.homelink. org; $110 yearly for a listing, on-line access, and catalog; $40 without catalog. **Intervac U.S.** ✉ 30 Corte San Fernando, Tiburon, CA 94920 ☎ 800/ 756-4663 🖷 415/435-7440 ⊕ www.intervacus.com; $105 yearly for a listing, on-line access, and a catalog; $50 without catalog.

HOSTELS

No matter what your age, you can **save on lodging costs by staying at hostels.** In some 4,500 locations in more than 70 countries around the world, Hostelling International (HI), the umbrella group for a number of national youth-hostel associations, offers single-sex, dorm-style beds and, at many hostels, rooms for couples and family accommodations. Membership in any HI national hostel association, open to travelers of all ages, allows you to stay in HI-affiliated hostels at member rates; one-year membership is about $28 for adults (C$35 for a two-year minimum membership in Canada, £13.50 in the U.K., A$52 in Australia, and NZ$40 in New Zealand); hostels in Alaska run about $15 per night. Members have priority if the hostel is full; they're also eligible for discounts around the world, even on rail and bus travel in some countries.

Alaska has four official Hostelling International (HI) hostels: Anchorage, Ketchikan, Ninilchik, and Sitka, but of these, only the Anchorage hostel is open year-round. Quite a few private hostels are not affiliated with HI, including ones in Anchorage, Circle, Denali, Fairbanks, Girdwood, Haines, Homer, Juneau, McCarthy, Palmer, Petersburg, Seward, Slana, Skagway, Sterling, Talkeetna, Tok, Valdez, Wasilla, and Wrangell. **Hostels.com** (⊕ www.hostels.com) has contact information for all of these.
🖪 **Hostelling International–USA** ✉ 8401 Colesville Rd., Suite 600, Silver Spring, MD 20910 ☎ 301/495-1240 🖷 301/495-6697 ⊕ www.hiayh. org. **Hostelling International–Canada** ✉ 400-205 Catherine St., Ottawa, Ontario K2P 1C3 ☎ 613/237-7884 or 800/663-5777 🖷 613/237-7868 ⊕ www. hihostels.ca. **YHA England and Wales** ✉ Trevelyan House, Dimple Rd., Matlock, Derbyshire DE4 3YH, U.K. ☎ 0870/870-8808 🖷 0870/770-6127 ⊕ www. yha.org.uk. **YHA Australia** ✉ 422 Kent St., Sydney, NSW 2001 ☎ 02/9261-1111 🖷 02/9261-1969 ⊕ www. yha.com.au. **YHA New Zealand** ✉ Level 3, 193 Cashel St. ⬦ Box 436, Christchurch ☎ 03/379-9970 or 0800/278-299 🖷 03/365-4476 ⊕ www.yha. org.nz.

HOTELS

Alaskan motels and hotels are similar in quality to those in the Lower 48 states. Most Alaskan motels are independent, but you'll find the familiar chains (including Best Western, Comfort Inn, Days Inn, Hampton Inn, Hilton, Holiday Inn, Marriott, Super 8, and Sheraton) in Anchorage. Westmark Hotels is a regional chain, owned by cruise-tour operator Holland America Westours, with 15 locations, including hotels in Anchorage, Fairbanks,

Kenai, Kodiak, Sitka, and Valdez in Alaska, plus Beaver Creek and Whitehorse in Canada's Yukon Territory. Princess Tours owns a luxury hotel in Fairbanks and lodges outside Denali National Park, near Denali State Park, near Wrangell–St. Elias National Park, and on the Kenai Peninsula. All hotels listed have private bath unless otherwise noted.

⧉ Toll-Free Numbers Best Western ☎ 800/528-1234 ⊕ www.bestwestern.com. **Choice** ☎ 800/424-6423 ⊕ www.choicehotels.com. **Comfort Inn** ☎ 800/424-6423 ⊕ www.choicehotels.com. **Days Inn** ☎ 800/325-2525 ⊕ www.daysinn.com. **Doubletree Hotels** ☎ 800/222-8733 ⊕ www.doubletree.com. **Embassy Suites** ☎ 800/362-2779 ⊕ www.embassysuites.com. **Fairfield Inn** ☎ 800/228-2800 ⊕ www.marriott.com. **Hilton** ☎ 800/445-8667 ⊕ www.hilton.com. **Holiday Inn** ☎ 800/465-4329 ⊕ www.sixcontinentshotels.com. **Howard Johnson** ☎ 800/446-4656 ⊕ www.hojo.com. **La Quinta** ☎ 800/531-5900 ⊕ www.laquinta.com. **Marriott** ☎ 800/228-9290 ⊕ www.marriott.com. **Quality Inn** ☎ 800/424-6423 ⊕ www.choicehotels.com. **Radisson** ☎ 800/333-3333 ⊕ www.radisson.com. **Red Lion and WestCoast Hotels and Inns** ☎ 800/733-5466 ⊕ www.redlion.com. **Sheraton** ☎ 800/325-3535 ⊕ www.starwood.com/sheraton. **Sleep Inn** ☎ 800/424-6423 ⊕ www.choicehotels.com. **Westin Hotels & Resorts** ☎ 800/228-3000 ⊕ www.starwood.com/westin.

WILDERNESS LODGES

To really get away from it all, book a remote lodge with rustic accommodations in the middle of breathtaking Alaskan wilderness. Some of the most popular are in the river drainages of Bristol Bay, in Southeast Alaska, and along the Susitna River north of Anchorage. Most of these lodges place a heavy emphasis on fishing; a stay generally includes daily guided fishing trips as well as all meals. They can be astronomically expensive (daily rates of $250–$600 per person), so if you're not interested in fishing, you won't want to seek these out. Lodges in and near Denali National Park emphasize the great outdoors, and some even include wintertime dogsledding. Activities focus on hiking, rafting, flightseeing, horseback riding, and natural-history walks. For getting deep into the wilderness, these lodges are an excellent alternative to the hotels and cabins outside the park entrance.

MEDIA

INTERNET ACCESS

Alaska is one of the most "wired" places in America. Internet access is available in all the larger towns and cities and even in many remote Bush communities. Most Alaska public libraries have computer terminals where you can check e-mail or surf the Web for free, and many towns also have businesses that rent computer access by the hour. In addition, hotel rooms are increasingly set up with data ports on their phones for those traveling with laptop computers. The larger and newer hotels typically have a business center with computers for Internet access, along with fax and copy machines.

NEWSPAPERS & MAGAZINES

Alaska's primary statewide newspaper is the *Anchorage Daily News* (⊕ www.adn.com). Other papers with substantial regional coverage are the *Fairbanks Daily News-Miner* (⊕ www.news-miner.com) and the *Juneau Empire* (⊕ www.juneauempire.com). *Alaska Magazine* (⊕ www.alaskamagazine.com) covers the state on a monthly basis and is distributed nationally.

RADIO & TELEVISION

Most larger Alaskan communities have their own commercial AM or FM radio stations. Alaska also has an extensive network of public stations, with **National Public Radio/Alaska Public Radio** (⊕ www.aprn.org) affiliates based in 20 different towns. The flagship station is KSKA 91.1 FM in Anchorage, but public radio can also be heard in many of the smallest villages around the state. Native-owned KNBA 90.3 FM, in Anchorage, broadcasts a mix of music and programming (without ads) aimed at the state's large Native community.

Most Alaskan hotels and motels have cable or satellite television reception, providing a wide selection of channels. The primary Anchorage TV stations are KIMO channel 13 (ABC), KTVA channel 11 (CBS), KTUU channel 2 (NBC), KTBY channel 4 (Fox), and KAKM channel 7 (PBS). In Fairbanks they are KATN channel 2 (ABC), KTVF channel 11 (CBS and NBC), K07UU channel 7 (Fox), and KUAC channel 9 (PBS). In Juneau they are KJUD channel 8 (ABC) and KTOO channel 3 (PBS).

MONEY MATTERS

Because of its off-the-beaten-path location, Alaska has always been an expensive travel destination. Major roads link Anchorage with Fairbanks and other cities and towns in South Central and Interior Alaska, but most other parts of the state are accessible only by air or water. This is even true of Alaska's state capital, Juneau. Costs in Anchorage and Fairbanks are only slightly higher than for Lower 48 cities, and you will find discount stores such as Wal-Mart and Fred Meyers, but as you head to more remote parts of the state, prices escalate. In Bush communities food, lodging, and transportation costs can be far higher than in Anchorage, since nearly everything must be brought in by air.

Prices throughout this guide are given for adults. Substantially reduced fees are almost always available for children, students, and senior citizens. For information on taxes, *see* Taxes.

ATMS

All the larger towns (and most places with a bank) in Alaska now have ATMs, but **don't expect to find an ATM in the remote Bush villages.** Nearly all ATMs in Alaska charge a fee (typically $1.50) if you don't have an account. Grocery stores typically accept ATM cards and will give you cash back with no surcharge.

CREDIT CARDS

🔳 Reporting Lost Cards **American Express** ☎ 800/441-0519. **Diners Club** ☎ 800/234-6377. **Discover** ☎ 800/347-2683. **MasterCard** ☎ 800/622-7747. **Visa** ☎ 800/847-2911.

NATIONAL PARKS

Look into discount passes to save money on park entrance fees. For $50, the National Parks Pass admits you (and any passengers in your private vehicle) to all national parks, monuments, and recreation areas, as well as other sites run by the National Park Service, for a year. (In parks that charge per person, the pass admits you, your spouse and children, and your parents, when you arrive together.) Camping and parking are extra. The $15 Golden Eagle Pass, a hologram you affix

to your National Parks Pass, functions as an upgrade, granting entry to all sites run by the NPS, the U.S. Fish and Wildlife Service, the U.S. Forest Service, and the Bureau of Land Management. The upgrade, which expires with the parks pass, is sold by most national-park, Fish and Wildlife, and BLM fee stations. A percentage of the proceeds from pass sales funds National Parks projects.

Both the Golden Age Passport ($10), for U.S. citizens or permanent residents who are 62 and older, and the Golden Access Passport (free), for those with disabilities, entitle holders (and any passengers in their private vehicles) to lifetime free entry to all national parks, plus 50% off fees for the use of many park facilities and services. (The discount doesn't always apply to companions.) To obtain them, you must show proof of age and of U.S. citizenship or permanent residency—such as a U.S. passport, driver's license, or birth certificate—and, if requesting Golden Access, proof of disability. The Golden Age and Golden Access passes are available only at NPS-run sites that charge an entrance fee. The National Parks Pass is also available by mail and via the Internet.

🔳 **National Park Foundation** ✉ 11 Dupont Cir. NW, 6th floor, Washington, DC 20036 ☎ 202/238-4200 ⊕ www.nationalparks.org. **National Park Service** ✉ National Park Service/Department of Interior, 1849 C St. NW, Washington, DC 20240 ☎ 202/208-6843 ⊕ www.nps.gov. **National Parks Conservation Association** ✉ 1300 19th St. NW, Suite 300, Washington, DC 20036 ☎ 202/223-6722 ⊕ www.npca.org.

🔳 Passes by Mail and On-Line **National Park Foundation** ⊕ www.nationalparks.org. **National Parks Pass** 🖅 Box 34108, Washington, DC 20043 ☎ 888/467-2757 ⊕ www.nationalparks.org; include a check or money order payable to the National Park Service, plus $3.95 for shipping and handling, or call for passes by phone.

PACKING

Not all of Alaska has the fierce winters that are usually associated with the state. Winter in the Southeast and South Central coastal regions is relatively mild—Chicago and Minneapolis experience harsher weather than Juneau. It's a different story in the Interior, where temperatures in the subzero range and biting winds keep most visitors indoors.

The best way to keep warm under colder conditions is to **wear layers of clothing, starting with thermal underwear and socks.** The outermost layer should be lightweight, windproof, rainproof, and hooded. Down jackets (and sleeping bags) have the disadvantage of becoming soggy when wet; the newer synthetics (particularly wind-block fabrics) are the materials of choice, though wool is still used. Footgear needs to be sturdy, and if you're going into the backcountry, be sure it's waterproof. Rubber boots are often a necessity in coastal areas. When wearing snow boots, be certain they are not too tight. Restricting your circulation will only make you colder.

Wherever you go in Alaska (and especially in the Southeast), **be prepared for rain.** To keep yourself dry, pack a collapsible umbrella or bring a rain slicker, as sudden storms are common. Although Alaskan summers are mild, an extra sweater or jacket for cool evenings will come in handy. UVA/UVB sunscreen, insect repellent, and sunglasses are necessities. A pair of binoculars will help you track any wildlife you encounter.

Befitting the frontier image, dress is mostly casual day and night. Bring along one outfit that is appropriate for "dress-up," if you enjoy doing so, though it's not necessary.

In your carry-on luggage, pack an extra pair of eyeglasses or contact lenses and enough of any medication you take to last a few days longer than the entire trip. You may also ask your doctor to write a spare prescription using the drug's generic name, as brand names may vary from country to country. In luggage to be checked, **never pack prescription drugs, valuables, or undeveloped film.** And don't forget to carry with you the addresses of offices that handle refunds of lost traveler's checks. Check *Fodor's How to Pack* (available at on-line retailers and bookstores everywhere) for more tips.

To avoid customs and security delays, carry medications in their original packaging. Don't pack any sharp objects in your carry-on luggage, including knives of any size or material, scissors, and corkscrews, or anything else that might arouse suspicion.

To avoid having your checked luggage chosen for hand inspection, don't cram bags full. The U.S. Transportation Security Administration suggests packing shoes on top and placing personal items you don't want touched in clear plastic bags.

CHECKING LUGGAGE

You're allowed to carry aboard one bag and one personal article, such as a purse or a laptop computer. Make sure what you carry on fits under your seat or in the overhead bin. Get to the gate early, so you can board as soon as possible, before the overhead bins fill up.

Baggage allowances vary by carrier, destination, and ticket class. On international flights, you're usually allowed to check two bags weighing up to 70 pounds (32 kilograms) each, although a few airlines allow checked bags of up to 88 pounds (40 kilograms) in first class. Some international carriers don't allow more than 66 pounds (30 kilograms) per bag in business class and 44 pounds (20 kilograms) in economy. On domestic flights, the limit may be 50 pounds (23 kilograms) per bag. Most airlines won't accept bags that weigh more than 100 pounds (45 kilograms) on domestic or international flights. Check baggage restrictions with your carrier before you pack.

Airline liability for baggage is limited to $2,500 per person on flights within the United States. On international flights it amounts to $9.07 per pound or $20 per kilogram for checked baggage (roughly $640 per 70-pound bag) and $400 per passenger for unchecked baggage. You can buy additional coverage at check-in for about $10 per $1,000 of coverage, but it often excludes a rather extensive list of items, shown on your airline ticket.

Before departure, **itemize your bags' contents** and their worth, and label the bags with your name, address, and phone number. (If you use your home address, cover it so potential thieves can't see it readily.) Include a label inside each bag and pack a copy of your itinerary. At check-in, make sure each bag is correctly tagged with the destination airport's three-letter code. Because some checked bags will be opened for hand inspection, the U.S. Transportation Security Administration recommends that you leave luggage unlocked or use the plastic locks offered at check-in. TSA screeners place an inspection notice inside searched bags, which are resealed with a special lock.

If your bag has been searched and contents are missing or damaged, file a claim with the TSA Consumer Response Center as soon as possible. If your bags arrive damaged or fail to arrive at all, file a written report with the airline before leaving the airport.

🔳 Complaints **U.S. Transportation Security Administration Consumer Response Center** ☎ 866/289-9673 ⊕ www.tsa.gov.

SAFETY

Alaska is big, wild, and not particularly forgiving, so travelers lacking outdoor experience need to take precautions when venturing away from the beaten path. If you lack backcountry skills or feel uncomfortable handling yourself if a bear should approach (⇨ Bears), take a guided trip instead or join a class at the **National Outdoor Leadership School** (☎ 907/745-4047 ⊕ www.nols.edu), which is based in Palmer (an hour north of Anchorage).

SENIOR-CITIZEN TRAVEL

The Alaska Railroad offers senior citizens a 50% discount during off-peak months (late September–early May). The Alaska Marine Highway offers discounted fares year-round. Alaska Direct Bus Lines offers a 10% discount for intercity travel.

To qualify for age-related discounts, **mention your senior-citizen status up front** when booking hotel reservations (not when checking out) and before you're seated in restaurants (not when paying the bill). Be sure to have identification on hand. When renting a car, ask about promotional car-rental discounts, which can be cheaper than senior-citizen rates.

🔳 Educational Programs **Elderhostel** ✉ 11 Ave. de Lafayette, Boston, MA 02111-1746 ☎ 877/426-8056, 978/323-4141 international callers, 877/426-2167 TTY 🖶 877/426-2166 ⊕ www.elderhostel.org. **Interhostel** ✉ University of New Hampshire, 6 Garrison Ave., Durham, NH 03824 ☎ 603/862-1147 or 800/733-9753 🖶 603/862-1113 ⊕ www.learn.unh.edu.

SHOPPING

The best buys in Alaska are products of local materials made by Native peoples and other artists and craftspeople living in the state. Before you buy, **make sure the local crafts are genuine.** The state has adopted two symbols that guarantee the authenticity of crafts made by Alaskans. A hand symbol indicates the item was made by one of **Alaska's Native peoples** (☎ 907/269-6610 or 888/278-7424 ⊕ www.eed.state.ak.us/aksca). A polar bear verifies the item was **Made in Alaska** (⊕ www.madeinalaska.org). If some items with these tags seem more expensive than you expected, examine them closely and you'll probably find that they are handmade, one-of-a-kind pieces.

Although these symbols are designed to ensure authentic Alaskan and Native-made products, it doesn't mean that items lacking them are not authentic. This applies in particular to Native artists who may or may not go through the necessary paperwork to obtain the silver hand labels. They often come to town and sell items directly to shop owners for cash. It pays to shop around, ask questions, and learn about the different types of Native crafts from around the state.

Some Alaskan shops sell carved items made in Southeast Asia, primarily Bali, and not all of these crafts are labeled as such. When some clerks are asked about these items' origins, they may say, "We got it in Anchorage." Unfortunately, this may just mean that they picked it up at the Anchorage airport after the items were flown in from Asia. Before buying something—particularly an expensive piece—ask questions to make sure it is authentic. You can protect yourself by visiting a number of shops first to learn the differences between Alaskan handcrafted items and those that are mass-produced.

Carved walrus ivory pieces are sold in many Alaskan shops. Some of these are pieces of raw ivory carved by Native Alaskan artists, and others are fossilized ivory, which can be legally used by other carvers. Although walrus ivory is legal to own in the United States, transporting it through other countries—including Canada—requires a **Convention on Trade in Endangered Species (CITES)** permit (⊕ www.cites.org).

SMART SOUVENIRS

Authentic Native art is always worth looking over, even if you cannot afford the finest pieces. Alaska has an abundance of artists whose works fill local galleries. Some, such as Rie Muñoz and Barbara Lavalle, are nationally known, but you should also check out prints by Ray Troll and Evon Zerbetz in Ketchikan, unique and colorful pins by William Spear in Juneau, and the paintings of Nancy Yaki and Erik Behnke in Homer. Also look for items made from musk-ox wool (qiviut) in Anchorage and Palmer, along with birch syrup from **Kahiltna Birchworks** (www.alaskabirchsyrup.com); it's sold in many Alaskan gift shops and at the Anchorage Saturday Market.

SIGHTSEEING GUIDES

A couple of companies operate sightseeing tours statewide. For local sightseeing outfits in individual cities and towns, *see* Tours *in* the chapter A to Z sections.
Sightseeing-Tour Companies **Alaska Sightseeing/Cruise West** ☎ 206/441-8687 or 800/580-0072 www.cruisewest.com. **Glacier Bay Cruiseline** ☎ 206/623-7110 or 800/451-5952 www.glacierbaytours.com. **Gray Line of Alaska** ☎ 907/277-5581 or 800/544-2206 🖶 907/225-9386 www.graylineofalaska.com.

SPORTS & THE OUTDOORS

FISHING

License fees for nonresidents are $10 for a 1-day permit, $20 for 3 days, $30 for 7 days, $50 for 14 days, and $100 for an annual license. If you're going to be fishing for king salmon, an additional stamp that doubles these costs is required. Licenses are available from the Fish and Game Web site or, in-state, from sporting-goods stores, charter-boat operators, and fishing lodges.
Information & Licenses **Alaska Department of Fish and Game** 🖃 Box 25525, Juneau 99802-5525 ☎ 907/465-4180 seasons and regulations, 907/465-2376 licenses www.state.ak.us/adfg.

STUDENTS IN ALASKA

Student discounts are available at many Alaskan museums and other attractions.
IDs & Services **STA Travel** 🖃 10 Downing St., New York, NY 10014 ☎ 212/627-3111 or 800/777-0112 🖶 212/627-3387 www.sta.com. **Travel Cuts** 🖃 187 College St., Toronto, Ontario M5T 1P7, Canada ☎ 416/979-2406, 800/592-2887, 866/246-9762 in Canada 🖶 416/979-8167 www.travelcuts.com.

TAXES

SALES TAX

Alaska does not impose a state sales tax, but individual cities and boroughs have their own. Anchorage has no sales tax.

TIME

Nearly all of Alaska lies within the Alaska time zone, 20 hours behind Sydney, 9 hours behind London, 4 hours behind New York City, 3 hours behind Chicago, and 1 hour behind Los Angeles. The nearly unpopulated Aleutian Islands are in the same time zone as Hawaii, 5 hours behind the East Coast.

TIPPING

In addition to tipping waiters and waitresses, taxi drivers, and baggage handlers, tipping others who provide personalized services is common in Alaska. Tour-bus drivers who offer a particularly informative trip generally receive a tip from passengers at the end of the tour. A small amount left in your hotel room is also much appreciated by the cleaning staff. Fishing guides are commonly tipped around 10% by their clients, particularly if the guide helped them land a big one. In addition, gratuities may also be given to pilots following a particularly good flight-seeing or bear-viewing trip, but the amount is up to your own discretion.

TOURS & PACKAGES

Because everything is prearranged on a prepackaged tour or independent vacation, you spend less time planning—and often get it all at a good price.

BOOKING WITH AN AGENT

Travel agents are excellent resources. But it's a good idea to collect brochures from several agencies, as some agents' suggestions may be influenced by relationships with tour and package firms that reward them for volume sales. If you have a special interest, **find an agent with expertise in that area**; the American Society of Travel Agents (ASTA; ⇨ Travel Agencies) has a database of specialists worldwide.

Make sure your travel agent knows the accommodations and other services of the place being recommended. Ask about the hotel's location, room size, and beds and whether it has a pool, room service, or programs for children, if you care about these. Has your agent been there in person or sent others whom you can contact?

Do some homework on your own, too: local tourism boards can provide information about lesser-known and small-niche operators, some of which may sell only direct.

BUYER BEWARE

Each year consumers are stranded or lose their money when tour operators—even large ones with excellent reputations—go out of business. So check out the operator. Ask several travel agents about its reputation, and try to **book with a company that has a consumer-protection program.** (Look for) information in the company's brochure.) In the United States, members of the National Tour Association and the United States Tour Operators Association are required to set aside funds to cover payments and travel arrangements in the event that the company defaults. It's also a good idea to choose a company that participates in the American Society of Travel Agents' Tour Operator Program; ASTA will act as mediator in any disputes between you and your tour operator.

Remember that the more your package or tour includes, the better you can predict the ultimate cost of your vacation. Make sure you know exactly what is covered, and beware of hidden costs. Are taxes, tips, and transfers included? Entertainment and excursions? These can add up.

🔢 Tour-Operator Recommendations **American Society of Travel Agents** (⇨ Travel Agencies). **National Tour Association** (NTA) ✉ 546 E. Main St., Lexington, KY 40508 ☎ 859/226-4444 or 800/682-8886 🖷 859/226-4404 ⊕ www.ntaonline.com. **United States Tour Operators Association** (USTOA) ✉ 275 Madison Ave., Suite 2014, New York, NY 10016 ☎ 212/599-6599 🖷 212/599-6744 ⊕ www.ustoa.com.

FLIGHTSEEING

Although flightseeing is expensive, it's not only the best way to grasp the expansiveness and grandeur of the land but also the only way to reach remote parts of Alaska. However, it can be dangerous. Before your flight, contact the air tour operator to check how long the company has been in service, its accident/incident statistics, and its safety procedures. If possible, try to meet with and talk to your pilot before the trip. Know where you're going and how long the trip will take. Avoid trips with long stopovers in remote areas—drastic weather changes can result in the cancellation or complication of your return flight. Pay attention to the safety message at the start of the flight, especially noting the location of emergency survival gear. The long distances, mountainous terrain, and challenging weather conditions are all hazardous factors, but pilot error, due sometimes to passenger interference, is often involved. Never push a pilot to do something he or she is reluctant to do, such as circle low over a bear, and never pressure the pilot to hurry up. Missing your scheduled landing or ship departure is much better than pushing a pilot to fly in unsafe weather conditions.

For flightseeing operators, *see* regional A to Z sections.

GROUP TOURS

Among companies that sell tours to Alaska, the following are nationally known, have a proven reputation, and offer plenty of options. The classifications used below represent different price categories, and you'll probably encounter these terms when talking to a travel agent or tour operator. The key difference is usually in accommodations, which run from budget to better, and better-yet to best.

🔢 Super-Deluxe **Abercrombie & Kent** ✉ 1520 Kensington Rd., Suite 212, Oak Brook, IL 60521-2141 ☎ 630/954-2944 or 800/323-7308 🖷 630/954-3324 ⊕ www.abercrombiekent.com.

🔢 Deluxe **Maupintour** ✉ 10650 W. Charleston Blvd., Summerlin, NV 89135-1014 ☎ 800/255-4266 🖷 702/260-3787 ⊕ www.maupintour.com. **Tauck World Discovery** ✉ 276 Post Rd. W 🖅 Box 5027, Westport, CT 06881-5027 ☎ 203/226-6911 or 800/788-7885 🖷 203/222-7702 ⊕ www.tauck.com.

🔢 Deluxe/First-Class **Globus** ✉ 5301 S. Federal Cir., Littleton, CO 80123-2980 ☎ 303/797-2800 or 866/755-8581 🖷 303/347-2080 ⊕ www.globusjourneys.com.

🔢 First-Class & Tourist-Range **Collette Vacations** ✉ 162 Middle St., Pawtucket, RI 02860 ☎ 401/728-3805 or 800/340-5158 🖷 401/728-4745 ⊕ www.collettevacations.com. **Gadabout Tours** ✉ 700 E. Tahquitz Canyon Way, Palm Springs, CA 92262-6767 ☎ 760/325-5556 or 800/952-5068 🖷 760/325-5127 ⊕ www.gadabouttours.com. **Mayflower Tours** ✉ 1225 Warren Ave. 🖅 Box 490, Downers Grove, IL 60515 ☎ 630/435-8500 or 800/323-7604 🖷 630/960-3575 ⊕ www.mayflowertours.com. **Trafalgar**

Tours ✉ 11 E. 26th St., Suite 1300, New York, NY 10010 ☎ 212/689-8977 or 800/854-0103 📠 800/457-6644 ⊕ www.trafalgartours.com.
🛇 Budget **Cosmos** (⇨ Globus).

PACKAGES

Like group tours, independent vacation packages are available from major tour operators and airlines. Packages may include fly/drive itineraries with bed-and-breakfast accommodations or ferry-liner tours. The companies listed below offer vacation packages in a broad price range.

🛇 Independent Vacation Packages **Alaska Airlines Vacations** ✇ Box 69677, Seattle, WA 98168 ☎ 800/468-2248 ⊕ www.alaskaair.com. **Alaska Bound** ✉ 116 Cass St., Traverse City, MI 49684 ☎ 231/947-0880 or 888/252-7527 📠 231/439-3004 ⊕ www.alaskabound.com. **Alaska Rainforest Tours** ✉ 1873 Shell Simmons Dr., Juneau 99801-9398 ☎ 907/463-3466 📠 907/463-4453 ⊕ www.alaskarainforesttours.com. **Alaska Tour & Travel** ✇ Box 221011, Anchorage 99522-1011 ☎ 907/245-0200 or 800/208-0200 ⊕ www.alaskatravel.com. **Gorp Travel** ✉ 6707 Winchester Cir., Suite 101, Boulder, CO 80301 ☎ 303/516-1153 or 877/440-4677 📠 303/440-8576 ⊕ www.gorptravel.com. **Gray Line of Alaska** ☎ 907/277-5581 or 800/544-2206 ⊕ www.graylineofalaska.com. **Knightly Tours** ✇ Box 16366, Seattle, WA 98116 ☎ 206/938-8567 or 800/426-2123 📠 206/938-8498 ⊕ www.knightlytours.com. **Viking Travel** ✇ Box 787, Petersburg 99833 ☎ 907/772-3818 or 800/327-2571 📠 907/772-3940 ⊕ www.alaskaferry.com.
🛇 From the U.K. **Arctic Experience Ltd.** ✉ 29 Nork Way, Banstead SM7 1PB ☎ 01737/218-800 ⊕ www.arctic-discover.co.uk. **Kuoni Travel** ✉ Kuoni House, Dorking RH5 4AZ ☎ 01306/744-445 ⊕ www.kuoni.co.uk. **Vacation Canada** ✉ Cambridge House, 8 Cambridge St., Glasgow G2 3DZ ☎ 0870/707-0444.

THEME TRIPS

🛇 Bicycling **Alaska Bicycle Adventures** ✉ 907 E. Dowling Rd., Suite 29, Anchorage 99518 ☎ 907/243-2329 or 800/770-7242 📠 907/243-4985 ⊕ www.alaskabike.com. **Backroads** ✉ 801 Cedar St., Berkeley, CA 94710-1800 ☎ 510/527-1555 or 800/462-2848 📠 510/527-1444 ⊕ www.backroads.com.
🛇 Bird-Watching **Alaska Birding and Wildlife Tours** ✉ 4300 B St., Suite 402, Anchorage 99503 ☎ 877/424-5637 📠 907/278-2316 ⊕ www.alaskabirding.com. **Bird Watching Tours of Anchorage, Alaska** ✉ 4030 Galatica Dr., Anchorage 99517 ☎ 907/248-7282 or 888/334-7282 📠 907/248-7285 ⊕ www.anchoragebirding.com. **Victor Emanuel Nature Tours** ✉ 2525 Wallingwood Dr., Suite 1003, Austin TX 787646 ☎ 512/328-5221 or 800/328-8368 📠 512/328-2919 ⊕ www.ventbird.com. **Wilderness Birding Adventures** ✉ 5515 Wild Mountain Rd., Eagle River 99577 ☎📠 907/694-7442 ⊕ www.wildernessbirding.com. **Wings Birding Tours** ✉ 1643 N. Alvernon Way, Suite 105, Tucson, AZ 85712 ☎ 520/320-9868 or 888/293-6443 📠 520/320-9373 ⊕ www.wingsbirds.com.
🛇 Camping **Alaska Wildland Adventures** ✇ Box 389, Girdwood 99587 ☎ 907/783-2928 or 800/334-8730 📠 907/783-2130 ⊕ www.alaskawildland.com. **CampAlaska Tours** ✇ Box 872247, Wasilla 99687 ☎ 907/376-9438 or 800/376-9438 📠 907/376-2353 ⊕ www.campalaska.com.
🛇 Canoeing, Kayaking & Rafting **Alaska Discovery** ✉ 5310 Glacier Hwy., Juneau 99801 ☎ 907/780-6226 or 800/586-1911 📠 907/780-4220 ⊕ www.akdiscovery.com. **Alaska Outdoor Adventures** ✉ 9400 Vanguard Dr., Anchorage 99507 ☎ 907/276-2628 or 877/408-2628 📠 907/222-1898 ⊕ www.akadventures.com. **Alaska River Adventures** ✇ Box 725, Cooper Landing 99572 ☎ 907/595-2000 or 800/836-9027 📠 907/595-3454 ⊕ www.alaskariveradventures.com. **Alaska Wildland Adventures** (⇨ Camping). **Alaska Worldwide Adventures** ✇ Box 220204, Anchorage 99522 ☎ 907/349-2964 or 888/842-2964 📠 907/344-6877. **Anadyr Adventures** ✇ Box 1821, Valdez 99572 ☎ 907/835-2814 or 800/865-2925 ⊕ www.anadyradventures.com. **CampAlaska Tours** (⇨ Camping). **James Henry River Journeys** ✇ Box 807, Bolinas, CA 94924 ☎ 415/868-1836 or 800/786-1830 📠 415/868-9033 ⊕ www.riverjourneys.com. **OARS** ✇ Box 67, Angels Camp, CA 95222 ☎ 209/736-4677 or 800/346-6277 📠 209/736-2902 ⊕ www.oars.com. **REI Adventures** ✇ Box 1938, Sumner, WA 98390-0800 ☎ 253/437-1100 or 800/622-2236 📠 253/395-8160 ⊕ www.rei.com. **TrekAmerica** ✇ Box 189, Rockaway, NJ 07866 ☎ 973/983-1144 or 800/221-0596 📠 973/983-8551 ⊕ www.trekamerica.com.
🛇 Dogsledding/Iditarod **Alaska Trails and Tails Dog Sled Tours** ✇ Box 874293, Wasilla 99687-4293 ☎ 907/373-1408 or 800/300-6874 📠 907/383-1408. **Chugach Express Dog Sled Tours** ✇ Box 1396, Girdwood 99587 ☎ 907/783-2266 📠 907/783-2625. **Godwin Glacier Dog Sled Tours** ✇ Box 28038, Scottsdale, AZ 85255 ☎ 907/224-8239 or 888/989-8239 📠 907/224-2398 ⊕ www.alaskadogsled.com. **IdidaRide Sled Dog Tours** ✇ Box 2906, Seward 99664-2906 ☎ 907/224-8607 or 800/478-3139 📠 907/224-8608 ⊕ www.ididaride.com. **Plettner Sled Dog Kennels** ✇ Box 878586, Wasilla 99687-8586 ☎ 907/892-6944 or 877/892-6944 📠 907/892-6945 ⊕ www.home.gci.net/~plettner. **Sourdough Outfitters** ✇ Box 90, Bettles 99726 ☎ 907/692-5252 📠 907/692-5557 ⊕ www.sourdoughoutfitters.com.
🛇 Ferry Tours **Knightly Tours** (⇨ Packages). **Viking Travel** (⇨ Packages).

Hiking Alaskan Gourmet Adventures ✉ 11090 Hideaway Lake Dr., Anchorage, AK 99516 ☎ 907/346-1087 ⊕ www.alaskan.com/akadventures. **Alaska Wilderness Experience** (⇨ Canoeing, Kayaking & Rafting). **Mountain Travel-Sobek** ✉ 6420 Fairmount Ave., El Cerrito, CA 94530 ☎ 510/527-8100 or 888/687-6235 🖶 510/525-7710 ⊕ www.mtsobek.com. **Sourdough Outfitters** (⇨ Dogsledding/Iditarod).

Learning Vacations Earthwatch Institute ✉ 3 Clock Tower Pl., Suite 100 ⬧ Box 75, Maynard, MA 01754 ☎ 978/461-0081 or 800/776-0188 🖶 978/461-2332 ⊕ www.earthwatch.org. **National Audubon Society** ✉ 700 Broadway, New York, NY 10003 ☎ 212/979-3066 🖶 212/353-0190 ⊕ www. audubon.org. **Natural Habitat Adventures** ✉ 2945 Center Green Ct., Boulder, CO 80301 ☎ 303/449-3711 or 800/543-8917 🖶 303/449-3712 ⊕ www.nathab. com. **Nature Expeditions International** ✉ 7860 Peters Rd., Suite F-103, Plantation, FL 33324 ☎ 954/693-8852 or 800/869-0639 🖶 954/693-8854 ⊕ www.naturexp.com. **Naturequest** ✉ 30872 South Coast Hwy., Suite 185, Laguna Beach, CA 92651 ☎ 949/499-9561 or 800/369-3033 🖶 949/499-0812 ⊕ www.naturequesttours.com. **Oceanic Society Expeditions** ✉ Fort Mason Center, Bldg. E, San Francisco, CA 94123-1394 ☎ 415/441-1106 or 800/326-7491 🖶 415/474-3395 ⊕ www.oceanic-society.org. **Questers Worldwide Nature Tours** ✉ 381 Park Ave. S, New York, NY 10016 ☎ 212/251-0444 or 800/468-8668 🖶 212/251-0890 ⊕ www. questers.com. **Sierra Club** ✉ 85 2nd St., 2nd floor, San Francisco, CA 94105 ☎ 415/977-5522 🖶 415/977-5795 ⊕ www.sierraclub.org. **Smithsonian Journeys** ⬧ Box 23293, Washington, DC 20026-3293 ☎ 202/357-4700 or 877/338-8687 🖶 202/633-9250 ⊕ www.smithsonianjourneys.org.

Native Tours A.L.E.U.T. Tours ⬧ Box 156, Unalaska 99685 ☎ 907/581-6001. **Alexander's River Adventure** ⬧ Box 62, Nenana 99760 ☎ 907/474-3924. **Athabasca Cultural Journeys** ☎ 907/829-2261 or 800/423-0094. **Cape Fox Tours** ⬧ Box 6656, Ketchikan 99901 ☎ 907/225-4846 ⊕ www. capefoxtours.com. **Dig Afognak** ✉ Afognak Native Corporation, 215 Mission Rd., Suite 212, Kodiak 99615 ☎ 907/486-6014 or 800/770-6014 ⊕ www. afognak.com/dig. **Kiana Lodge** ⬧ Box 210269, Anchorage 99521 ☎ 907/333-5866 🖶 907/338-8447 ⊕ www.alaskaoutdoors.com/Kiana. **Northern Alaska Tour Company** ⬧ Box 82991, Fairbanks 99708 ☎ 907/474-8600 or 800/474-1986 🖶 907/474-4767 ⊕ www.northernalaska.com. **Tour Arctic** ✉ 1001 E. Benson Blvd., Anchorage 99508 ☎ 907/265-4157 or 800/523-7405 🖶 907/265-4123 ⊕ www.tour-arctic.com. **Tundra Tours** ⬧ Box 189, Barrow 99723 ☎ 907/852-3900 or 800/478-8520 ⊕ www.topoftheworldhotel.com.

Natural History Alaska Wildland Adventures

(⇨ Camping). **Great Alaska Adventure Lodge** ✉ 33881 Sterling Hwy., Sterling 99672 ☎ 907/262-4515 or 800/544-2261 🖶 907/262-8797 in summer ⊕ www.greatalaska.com. **Hallo Bay Wilderness Camp** ⬧ Box 2904, Homer 99603 ☎ 907/235-2237 ⊕ www.hallobay.com. **Wilderness Birding Adventures** (⇨ Bird-Watching).

Photography Colors of Nature Photo Tours ⬧ Box 1086, Ojai, CA 93024 ☎ 888/385-5595 🖶 805/649-0701 ⊕ www.colorsofnature.com. **Hallo Bay Wilderness Camp** (⇨ Natural History). **Joseph Van Os Photo Safaris** ⬧ Box 655, Vashon Island, WA 99070 ☎ 206/463-5383 ⊕ www.photosafaris. com. **Alaska Photo Tours** ⬧ Box 141, Talkeetna 99676 ☎ 907/733-3051 or 800/799-3051 🖶 907/733-3052 ⊕ www.alaskaphototours.com.

RV Tours Alaska Highway Cruises ✉ 18384 Redmond Way, Redmond, WA 98052 ☎ 425/497-1212 or 800/323-5757 🖶 425/882-2479 ⊕ www. alaskarv.com.

Sportfishing Alaska River Adventures (⇨ Canoeing, Kayaking & Rafting). **Alaska Wildland Adventures** (⇨ Camping). **Fishing International** ✉ 1825 4th St., Santa Rosa, CA 95404 ☎ 707/542-4242 or 800/950-4242 🖶 707/526-3474 ⊕ www. fishinginternational.com. **Great Alaska Adventure Lodge** (⇨ Natural History). **Rod & Reel Adventures** ✉ 32617 Skyhawk Way, Eugene, OR 97405 ☎ 541/349-0777 or 800/356-6982 🖶 541/338-0367 ⊕ www.rodreeladventures.com. **Sport Fishing Alaska** ✉ 9310 Shorecrest Dr., Anchorage 99515 ☎ 907/344-8674 or 888/552-8674 🖶 907/243-9447 ⊕ www.alaskatripplanners.com.

Wilderness High Adventures Alaska Mountaineering School ⬧ Box 566, Talkeetna 99676 ☎ 907/733-2649 🖶 907/733-1362 ⊕ www. climbalaska.org. **Brooks Range Aviation** ⬧ Box 10, Bettles 99726 ☎ 907/692-5444 or 800/692-5443 🖶 907/692-2185 ⊕ www.brooksrange.com. **Ketchum Air Service** ⬧ Box 190588, Anchorage 99519 ☎ 907/243-5525 or 800/433-9114 🖶 907/243-8311 ⊕ www.ketchumair.com. **Rust's Flying Service** ⬧ Box 190867, Anchorage 99519 ☎ 907/243-1595 or 800/544-2299 ⊕ www.flyrusts.com. **Sourdough Outfitters** (⇨ Dogsledding).

TRAIN TRAVEL

The state-owned Alaska Railroad has service connecting Seward, Anchorage, Denali National Park, and Fairbanks. Amtrak serves Seattle and Vancouver; VIA Rail Canada serves Vancouver and Prince Rupert, British Columbia.

Travel aboard the Alaska Railroad is leisurely (Anchorage to Fairbanks is an all-day trip), so you can enjoy spectacular scenery along the way. Some cars have narration, and food is available on board in the dining car and at the café. And unlike bus travel, train travel allows you to get up and stretch your legs. Some private tour companies that offer a more glitzy trip between Anchorage and Fairbanks hook their luxury railcars to the train. For a less expensive alternative, ride one of the public dome cars, owned and operated by the railroad. Seating in the public cars is unassigned, and passengers take turns under the observation dome. The railroad's public cars are a great place to meet resident Alaskans.

Except for the Seward–Anchorage leg, all service operates year-round. Trains run daily in summer; service is reduced from September to late May. Dining cars are available on all trains.

For a scenic and historic trip between Skagway and Fraser, British Columbia, take the White Pass & Yukon Route, which follows the treacherous path taken by prospectors during the Klondike gold rush of 1897–98. A bus links the terminal at Fraser with Whitehorse, capital of the Yukon Territory.

CUTTING COSTS

The **AlaskaPass** allows unlimited travel on bus, ferry, and rail lines in Alaska; *see* Cutting Costs *in* Boat and Ferry Travel.

FARES & SCHEDULES

Tickets can be purchased in advance over the phone using a credit card. If your reservation is a month or more ahead of time, the company will mail you the ticket; otherwise travelers can pick them up at the departure station. Travel agents also sell tickets for travel aboard the Alaska Railroad.

🚆 **Alaska Railroad** ⬧ Box 107500, Anchorage 99510 ☎ 907/265-2494 in Anchorage, 907/458-6025 in Fairbanks, 800/544-0552 🖷 907/265-2323 ⊕ www.akrr.com. **Amtrak** ☎ 800/872-7245 ⊕ www.amtrak.com. **VIA Rail Canada** ☎ 800/561-3949 ⊕ www.viarail.com. **White Pass & Yukon Route** ⬧ Box 435, Skagway 99840 ☎ 907/983-2217, 800/343-7373 in U.S. and Canada ⊕ www.whitepassrailroad.com.

PAYING

Cash, Discover, Visa, and MasterCard are accepted.

RESERVATIONS

Advance reservations are highly recommended for midsummer train travel, particularly between Seward and Anchorage and between Anchorage and Denali National Park.

TRANSPORTATION AROUND ALASKA

Visitors to Alaska arrive by air and highway, and aboard ships and ferries. Cruise ships are a particularly popular way to travel, especially in Southeast Alaska, where many towns (including the state capital of Juneau) are not accessible by road. The Alaska Marine Highway ferry system provides car and passenger service throughout Southeast Alaska, as well as a number of towns in South Central Alaska and out to the Aleutian Islands.

The famous Alaska Highway is the primary road access into the state, starting in Dawson Creek, British Columbia, and continuing 1,390 mi to Delta Junction, Alaska. A network of two-lane highways connects the main towns and cities in South Central and Interior Alaska, including Anchorage and Fairbanks. Jet service is available to Alaska's cities and larger towns. Smaller Bush planes (sometimes on floats) are the lifeblood of more remote parts of Alaska.

TRAVEL AGENCIES

A good travel agent puts your needs first. Look for an agency that has been in business at least five years, emphasizes customer service, and has someone on staff who specializes in your destination. In addition, **make sure the agency belongs to a professional trade organization.** The American Society of Travel Agents (ASTA)—the largest and most influential in the field with more than 20,000 members in some 140 countries—maintains and enforces a strict code of ethics and will step in to help mediate any agent-client disputes involving ASTA members if necessary. ASTA (whose motto is "Without a travel agent, you're on your own") also maintains a Web site that includes a directory of agents. (If a travel agency is also acting as your tour operator, *see* Buyer Beware *in* Tours & Packages.)

Travel agents are found in all of Alaska's cities and larger towns, and some of the state's larger travel agencies are listed below.

Local Agent Referrals American Society of Travel Agents (ASTA) ✉ 1101 King St., Suite 200, Alexandria, VA 22314 ☎ 703/739-2782, 800/965-2782 24-hr hot line ♨ 703/739-3268 ⊕ www.astanet.com. **Association of British Travel Agents** ✉ 68-71 Newman St., London W1T 3AH ☎ 020/7637-2444 ♨ 020/7637-0713 ⊕ www.abtanet.com. **Association of Canadian Travel Agents** ✉ 130 Albert St., Suite 1705, Ottawa, Ontario K1P 5G4 ☎ 613/237-3657 ♨ 613/237-7052 ⊕ www.acta.ca. **Australian Federation of Travel Agents** ✉ Level 3, 309 Pitt St., Sydney, NSW 2000 ☎ 02/9264-3299 ♨ 02/9264-1085 ⊕ www.afta.com.au. **Travel Agents' Association of New Zealand** ✉ Level 5, Tourism and Travel House, 79 Boulcott St. ⌂ Box 1888, Wellington 6001 ☎ 04/499-0104 ♨ 04/499-0786 ⊕ www.taanz.org.nz.

Alaska Travel Agencies Alaska Tours ✉ 413 G St., 2nd floor, Anchorage 99501 ☎ 907/277-3000 ♨ 907/272-2532 ⊕ www.alaskatours.com. **All Ways Travel** ✉ 302 G St., Anchorage 99501-2186 ☎ 907/276-3644 ♨ 907/258-2211 ⊕ www.alaskatripshop.com. **Arctic Travel** ✉ 423 E. 5th Ave., Anchorage 99501-2634 ☎ 907/272-6789 or 888/838-5678 ♨ 907/272-6787. **Easy Travel** ✉ 3120 Denali St., Suite 1, Anchorage 99503-4029 ☎ 907/562-3279 or 800/383-3279 ♨ 907/273-1998 ⊕ www.alaskaeasytravel.com. **Navigant International/Alaska** ✉ 206 W. 34th Ave., Anchorage 99503 ☎ 907/786-3200 or 800/478-2829 ♨ 907/786-3298 ⊕ www.navigant.com. **One Stop Travel** ✉ 1501 Huffman Rd., Suite 197, Anchorage 99515 ☎ 907/278-7006 or 800/770-4440 ♨ 907/565-7888 ⊕ www.onestoptravel.net. **USTravel** ✉ 1415 E. Tudor Rd., Anchorage 99507-1033 ☎ 907/561-2434 or 800/478-2434 ♨ 907/786-0180 ⊕ www.ustravelak.com.

VISITOR INFORMATION

The Alaska Travel Industry Association (a partnership between the state and private businesses) publishes the *Alaska Vacation Planner*, a free, comprehensive information source for statewide travel year-round. Alaska's regional tourism councils distribute vacation planners highlighting their local attractions. The official State of Alaska Web site contains additional information and links.

Statewide Information Alaska Internet Travel Guide ⊕ www.alaskaone.com. **Alaska Travel Industry Association** ⌂ 2600 Cordova St., Suite 201, Anchorage 99503 ☎ 907/929-2200 or 800/862-5275 to order Alaska Vacation Planners ⊕ www.travelalaska.com. **Alaska Marine Highway System** ☎ 800/642-0066 ⊕ www.alaska.gov/ferry. **Alaska**

Public Lands Information Center ⊕ www.nps.gov/aplic. **AlaskaGuidebook.com** ⊕ www.alaskaguidebook.com. **State of Alaska Tourism Info** ⌂ Box 110809, Juneau 99811-0809 ☎ 907/465-2012 ♨ 907/465-3767 ⊕ www.state.ak.us/tourism.

Regional Information Kenai Peninsula Tourism Marketing Council ✉ 14896 Kenai Spur Hwy., Suite 106A, Kenai 99611 ☎ 907/283-3850 or 800/535-3624 ♨ 907/283-2838 ⊕ www.kenaipeninsula.org. **Southeast Alaska Tourism Council** ⌂ Box 20710, Juneau 99802-0710 ☎ 907/225-6166 or 888/287-9055 ♨ 907/225-4250 ⊕ www.alaskainfo.org. **Southwest Alaska Municipal Conference** ✉ 3300 Arctic Blvd., Suite 203, Anchorage 99503 ☎ 907/562-7380 ♨ 907/562-0438 ⊕ www.swamc.org.

City Information Alaska Anchorage ⊕ www.anchorage.net. **Fairbanks** ⊕ www.explorefairbanks.com. **Juneau** ⊕ www.juneau.org.

British Columbia & Yukon Tourism British Columbia ⌂ Box 9830, Victoria, British Columbia V8W 9W5 ☎ 604/435-5622 or 800/435-5622 ⊕ www.hellobc.com. **Tourism Yukon** ⌂ Box 2745, Whitehorse, Yukon Territory Y1A 5B9 ☎ 867/667-5340 ♨ 867/667-3546 ⊕ www.touryukon.com. **Tourism Victoria** ✉ 812 Wharf St., Victoria, British Columbia V8W 1T3 ☎ 250/953-2033 or 800/663-3883 ♨ 250/382-6539 ⊕ www.tourismvictoria.com. **Tourism Vancouver** ✉ 200 Burrard St., Vancouver, British Columbia V6C 3L6 ☎ 604/683-2000 ♨ 604/682-6839 ⊕ www.tourism-vancouver.org.

Government Advisories Consular Affairs Bureau of Canada ☎ 800/267-6788 or 613/944-6788 ⊕ www.voyage.gc.ca. **U.K. Foreign and Commonwealth Office** ✉ Travel Advice Unit, Consular Division, Old Admiralty Bldg., London SW1A 2PA ☎ 020/7008-0232 or 020/7008-0233 ⊕ www.fco.gov.uk/travel. **Australian Department of Foreign Affairs and Trade** ☎ 02/6261-1299 Consular Travel Advice Faxback Service ⊕ www.dfat.gov.au. **New Zealand Ministry of Foreign Affairs and Trade** ☎ 04/439-8000 ⊕ www.mft.govt.nz.

WEB SITES

Do check out the World Wide Web when planning your trip. You'll find everything from weather forecasts to virtual tours of famous cities. Be sure to visit Fodors.com (⊕ www.fodors.com), a complete travel-planning site. You can research prices and book plane tickets, hotel rooms, rental cars, vacation packages, and more. In addition, you can post your pressing questions in the Travel Talk section. Other planning tools include a currency converter and weather reports, and there are loads of links to travel resources.

CRUISING IN ALASKA

FODOR'S CHOICE

Norwegian Star, Norwegian Cruise Line

Seven Seas Mariner, Seven Seas Cruises

Spirit of Oceanus, Cruise West

HIGHLY RECOMMENDED

Coral Princess & Island Princess, Princess Cruise Line

Clipper Odyssey, Clipper Cruise Lines

Crystal Harmony, Crystal Cruise Line

Mercury, Celebrity Cruises

Oosterdam, Holland America Line

Radiance of the Seas, Royal Caribbean Cruise Line

Safari Quest, American Safari Cruises

By M. T.
Schwartzman

Updated by
Sue Kernaghan

ALASKA, IT WOULD SEEM, was made for cruising. The traditional route to the state is by sea, through a 1,000-mi-long protected waterway known as the Inside Passage. From Vancouver, B.C., in the south to Skagway in the north, it winds around islands large and small, past glacier-carved fjords and hemlock-blanketed mountains. This great land is home to breaching whales, nesting eagles, spawning salmon, and calving glaciers. The towns here can be reached only by air or sea; there are no roads between them. Juneau, in fact, is the only water-locked state capital in the United States. Beyond the Inside Passage, the Gulf of Alaska leads to Prince William Sound—famous for its marine life and more fjords and glaciers—and Anchorage, Alaska's largest city.

Alaska is one of cruising's showcase destinations, so the lines are sailing their grandest ships in these waters. Itineraries give passengers more choices than ever before—from traditional loop cruises of the Inside Passage, round-trips from Vancouver, B.C., Seattle, or San Francisco, to one-way Inside Passage–Gulf of Alaska cruises. A few smaller boats sail only in Prince William Sound, away from big-ship traffic.

CHOOSING YOUR CRUISE

Types of Ships

The type of ship you choose is the most important factor in your Alaska cruise vacation because it will determine how you see Alaska. Ocean liners sail farther from land and visit major ports of call such as Juneau, Skagway, and Ketchikan. Small ships spend much of their time hugging the coastline, looking for wildlife, waterfalls, and other natural and scenic attractions. For more independent types, there's no better way to see Alaska than aboard the ferries of the Alaska Marine Highway System, which allow you to travel with your car or RV and explore at your own pace.

Ocean Liners

Alaska's ocean-liner fleet represents the very best that today's cruise industry has to offer. Nearly all the ships were built within the last two decades and have atrium lobbies, state-of-the-art health spas, high-tech show lounges, elaborate dining rooms, and a variety of alternative restaurants. By night they come alive with Vegas-style revues, pulsating discos, and somewhat more sedate cabaret or comedy acts. Most of the latest liners have cabins with verandas—a great bonus in Alaska for watching the scenery go by from the privacy of your own stateroom. The newest cruise ships are lined with glass throughout their corridors and public rooms, so you're never far from the sea or a great view.

Small Ships

Unlike ocean liners, the smaller vessels cruising in Alaska are designed to reach into the most remote corners of the world. Shallow drafts allow them to navigate up rivers, close to coastlines, and into shallow coves. Hulls may be hardened for sailing in Arctic ice. Motorized rubber landing craft, known as Zodiacs, are usually kept on board, making it possible for passengers to put ashore almost anywhere. Alaska, not casinos or spa treatments, is the focus of these cruises. Lectures and talks—conducted daily by naturalists, Native Alaskans, and other experts in the Great Land's natural history and native cultures—are the norm. But in comparison with those on ocean liners, cabins on expedition ships can be quite tiny, usually with no phone or TV, and sometimes with bathrooms no bigger than cubbyholes. Often, the dining room and the lounge are the only common public areas on these vessels.

Ferry Liners

The state ferry system is known as the Alaska Marine Highway because its vessels carry vehicles as well as passengers. Each ferry has a car deck that can accommodate every-size vehicle from the family car to a Winnebago. You can take your vehicle ashore, drive around, even live in it, and then transport it with you to the next port of call. From Skagway or Haines (the only Inside Passage towns connected to a road system), you can drive farther north to Fairbanks and Anchorage by way of the Alaska Highway. Each ferry also has a main, or "weather," deck to accommodate passengers, and onboard camping is allowed year-round.

Itineraries

You'll want to give some consideration to your ship's Alaskan itinerary when you are choosing your cruise. The length of the cruise will determine the variety and number of ports you visit, but so will the type of itinerary and the point of departure. **Loop cruises** start and end at the same point and usually explore ports close to one another; **one-way cruises** start at one point and end at another and range farther afield.

Ocean liners typically follow one of two itineraries: round-trip Inside Passage loops starting and finishing in Vancouver, B.C., or Seattle; and one-way Inside Passage–Gulf of Alaska cruises sailing between Vancouver or Seattle and Anchorage. Both itineraries are usually seven days, though some lines offer longer trips. A few lines also schedule one-way or round-trip sailings from San Francisco or Los Angeles. Small ships typically sail within Alaska, setting out from Juneau, Sitka, or other Alaskan ports.

Whether you sail through the Inside Passage or along it will depend on the size of your vessel. Smaller ships can navigate narrow channels, straits, and fjords. Larger vessels must sail farther from land, so don't expect to see much wildlife from the deck of a megaship.

Cruise Tours

Most cruise lines give you the option of an independent, hosted, or fully escorted land tour before or after your cruise. Independent tours allow maximum flexibility. You have a preplanned itinerary with confirmed hotel reservations and transportation arrangements, but you're free to follow your interests and whims in each town. A hosted tour is similar, but tour-company representatives are available along the route to help out should you need assistance. On fully escorted tours, you travel with a group, led by a tour director. Activities are preplanned (and typically prepaid), so you have a good idea of how much your trip will cost (not counting incidentals) before you depart.

Most cruise-tour itineraries include a ride aboard the Alaska Railroad in a glass-dome railcar. Running between Anchorage, Denali National Park and Preserve, and Fairbanks are Holland America Westours' *McKinley Explorer,* Princess Tours' *Midnight Sun Express,* and the Royal Caribbean *Wilderness Express,* which offer unobstructed views of the passing land and wildlife from private railcars. If you choose to travel by rail independently, the Alaska Railroad cars are clean and comfortable and make the trip between Anchorage and Fairbanks hooked up to the same engines as the cruise-line cars.

Of the ocean-liner fleets, only Carnival Cruise Lines, Crystal Cruises, Norwegian Cruise Lines, and World Explorer Cruises are not currently offering cruise-tour packages with land segments in Alaska; they may, however, have tours in the Canadian Rockies. In addition to full-length cruise tours, many cruise lines have pre- or post-cruise hotel and sightseeing packages in Vancouver, B.C., Seattle, or Anchorage lasting one to three days.

Also popular among cruise passengers is independent travel by rental car or RV before or after the cruise segment. Generally passengers will plan to begin or end their cruise in Anchorage, the most practical port city to use as a base for exploring the state. Almost any type of car or recreational vehicle, from a small, two-person RV to a large, luxurious motor home, can be rented, and there are few restrictions on where you can park it to spend the night.

Shore Excursions

Shore excursions arranged by the cruise line are a convenient way to see the sights, although you pay extra for this convenience. Before your cruise, you'll receive a booklet describing the shore excursions your cruise line offers. A few lines let you book excursions in advance; all sell them on board during the cruise. If you cancel your excursion, you may incur penalties, the amount varying with the number of days remaining until the tour. Because these trips are specialized, many have limited capacity and are sold on a first-come, first-served basis.

Among the many options available, some are "musts." At least once during your cruise, try flightseeing—it's the only way you'll grasp the expansiveness and grandeur of the land. Go to an evening salmon feast, where you'll savor freshly caught fish cooked over an open fire. And experience an outdoor adventure—you don't have to be athletically inclined to raft down a river or paddle a sea kayak along the coastline.

Cruise Costs

Cruise costs can vary enormously. If you shop around and book early, you will undoubtedly pay less. Your cruise fare typically includes accommodation and all onboard meals, snacks, and activities. It does not normally include airfare to the port city, shore excursions, tips, alcoholic drinks, or spa treatments. Only the most expensive Alaska cruises include airfare. Virtually all lines offer air add-ons, which may or may not be less expensive than the latest discounted fare from the airlines.

Shore excursions can be a substantial expense; the best in Alaska are not cheap. But, skimp too much on your excursion budget and you'll deprive yourself of an important part of the Alaska experience.

Tipping is another extra. At the end of the cruise, it's customary to tip your room steward, server, and the person who buses your table, though some lines include the tips in the fare. If tips are not included, expect to pay an average of $7.50 to $10 per day in tips. Each ship offers guidelines.

Single travelers should be aware that there are few single cabins on most ships; taking a double cabin for yourself can cost as much as twice the advertised per-person rates (which are based on two people sharing a room). Some cruise lines will find roommates of the same sex for singles so that each can travel at the regular per-person, double-occupancy rate.

When to Go

Cruise season runs from mid-May to late September; the most popular sailing dates are from late June through August. May and June are the driest months to cruise. Daytime temperatures along the cruise routes in May, June, and September are in the 50s and 60s. July and August averages are in the 60s and 70s, with occasional days in the 80s. Bargains can be found both early and late in the season. Cruising in the low seasons provides plenty of advantages besides discounted fares. Availability of ships and particular cabins is greater in the low and shoulder seasons, and the ports are almost completely free of tourists.

November is the best month for off-season ferry travel, after the stormy month of October and while it's still relatively warm on the Inside Passage (temperatures will average about 40°F). It's a good month for wildlife watching as well. Some animals show themselves in greater numbers during November. In particular, humpback whales are abundant off Sitka, and bald eagles congregate by the thousands near Haines.

BEFORE YOU GO

Tickets & Vouchers

After you make the final payment to your travel agent, the cruise line will issue your cruise tickets and vouchers for airport–ship transfers. Depending on the airline, and whether you have purchased an air-sea package, you may receive your plane tickets or charter-flight vouchers at the same time; you may also receive vouchers for any shore excursions, although most cruise lines issue these aboard ship. Should your travel documents not arrive when promised, contact your travel agent or cruise line. If you book late, tickets may be delivered directly to the ship.

Passports & Visas

For Alaska cruises, whether they begin in the U.S. or in Canada, American and Canadian citizens require proof of citizenship. A valid passport, though not required, is the best document to carry. If you do not have a passport, take a certified copy of your birth certificate, which must have a raised seal, and some form of photo identification. Permanent residents of the U.S. who are not citizens should carry their green card.

If you are a citizen of another country, you may be required to obtain visas in advance. It is always the responsibility of the person traveling to obtain the necessary travel documents, including visas. Check with your travel agent or cruise line about specific requirements. If you do need a visa for your cruise, your travel agent should be able to help you obtain it, but there may be a charge for this service, in addition to the visa charge. Read your cruise documents carefully to see what documents you'll need for embarkation. You don't want to be turned away at the pier.

Immigration regulations require every passenger boarding a cruise ship from a U.S. port to provide additional personal data, such as your current mailing address and telephone number, to the cruise operator in advance of embarkation. Failure to provide this information required by the U.S. government may result in denial ofboarding.

Disabilities & Accessibility

The latest cruise ships have been built with the needs of travelers with disabilities in mind, and many older ships have been modified to accommodate them. But several cruise lines operate older ships that have not been modified or do not have elevators: explorer-type vessels are not the easiest ships to navigate if you are in a wheelchair. If you need a specially equipped cabin, book as far in advance as possible and ask specific questions of your travel agent or a cruise-line representative.

The best cruise ship for passengers who use wheelchairs is one that ties up right at the dock at every port, at which time a ramp or even an elevator is always made available. Unfortunately, it's hard to ascertain this in advance, since a ship may tie up at the dock at one port on one voyage and, on the next, anchor in the harbor and have passengers transported to shore via tender. Ask your travel agent to find out which ships are capable of docking. If a tender is used, some ships will have crew members carry the wheelchair and passenger from the ship to the tender. Unfortunately, other ships will refuse to take wheelchairs on tenders, especially if the water is choppy.

What to Pack

Certain packing rules apply to all cruises. Always take along a sweater to counter cool evening ocean breezes or overactive air-conditioning. A rain slicker is essential—many travelers who plan on indulging in some of the more active shore excursions pack a complete rain suit. Be prepared to dress in layers, since temperatures can vary considerably during the day. Make sure you take at least one pair of comfortable walking shoes for exploring port towns. Waterproof footwear will be useful as well. Ankle-high rubber boots are ideal for many shore trips.

Generally speaking, plan on one outfit for every two days of cruising, especially if your wardrobe contains many interchangeable pieces. Ships often have laundry facilities. No two cruises have quite the same dress policy, but evening dress on Alaskan cruises tends to fall into two categories: semiformal on the ocean liners and casual on the smaller ships. On semiformal cruises men generally wear a jacket and tie to dinner. Women should pack one gown or cocktail dress for every two or three formal evenings on board. On smaller cruises, shipboard dress is usually informal.

Outlets in cabin bathrooms are usually compatible with U.S.-purchased appliances. This may not be the case on older ships or those with European registries; call ahead if this is a concern for you. Most cabin bathrooms are equipped with low-voltage outlets for electric shavers, and many newer ships have built-in hair dryers.

ARRIVING & DEPARTING

If you have purchased an air-sea package, you will be met by a cruise-company representative when your plane lands at the port city and then shuttled directly to the ship in a bus or minivan. Some cruise lines arrange to transport luggage between airport and ship so passengers don't have to deal with baggage claim at the start of the cruise or with baggage check-in at the end. If you decide not to buy the air-sea package but still plan to fly, ask your travel agent if you can use the ship's transfer bus. Otherwise, you will have to take a taxi to the ship.

If you live close to the port of embarkation, bus transportation may be available. Another option for those who live close to their point of departure is to drive to the ship, an increasingly popular option. Major U.S. cruise ports all have parking facilities.

Embarkation

Check-In

On arrival at the dock, you must check in before boarding your ship. An officer will collect or stamp your ticket, inspect or even retain your passport or other official identification, ask you to fill out a tourist card, check that you have the correct visas, and collect any unpaid port or departure tax. Seating assignments for the dining room are often handed out at this time, too. You may also register your credit card to open a shipboard account, or that may be done later at the purser's office.

After this, you will be required to go through a security check and to pass your hand baggage through an x-ray inspection. These are the same machines in use at airports, so ask to have your photographic film inspected by hand.

Although it takes only 5 or 10 minutes per family to check in, lines are often long, so aim for off-peak hours. The worst time tends to be immediately after the ship begins boarding; the later it is, the less crowded. For example, if boarding is from 2 to 4:30, lines are shorter after 3:30.

Boarding the Ship
You will either be escorted to your cabin by a steward or, on a smaller ship, given your key—now usually a plastic card—by a ship's officer and directed to your cabin. Some elevators are unavailable to passengers during boarding, since they are used to transport luggage. You may arrive to find your luggage outside your cabin or just inside the door; if it hasn't arrived a half hour before sailing, contact the purser. If your luggage doesn't make it to the ship in time, the purser will have it flown to the next port.

Disembarkation

The last night of your cruise is full of business. On most ships you must place everything except your hand luggage outside your door, ready to be picked up by midnight or early in the morning. Color-coded tags, distributed to your cabin in a disembarkation packet, should be placed on your luggage before the crew collects it. The color of your tag will determine when you leave the ship and help you retrieve your luggage on the pier.

Your shipboard bill is left in your room during the last day of a cruise or on the morning of your departure from the ship. To pay the bill (if you haven't already put it on your credit card) or to settle any questions, you must stand in line at the purser's office. Tips to the cabin steward and dining staff are distributed on the last night of the cruise or are automatically added to your onboard account. On many ships, you can review your account on your in-cabin television and change those tips in any way you like, up or down. You may also make changes to or discuss your bill at the purser's office at any time during the cruise. Some ships will deliver your account to your room the morning of your departure. If you have not already paid it by credit card or wish to dispute any charges on it, go to the purser immediately to settle or discuss your account. Do not wait until you're ready to get off the ship, as lines may be long and the wait could delay your departure and fray your nerves. Some lines close down their computer files for the cruise by 9 AM or 10 AM to prepare for the next cruise and may be unable to credit your account with any disputed charges, requiring you to contact your credit-card company or the cruise line later for a refund.

On the morning the cruise ends, in-room breakfast service may not be available because stewards are too busy, but you will usually find breakfast being served in both the formal dining room and at the ship's buffet dining area. Most passengers clear out of their cabins as soon as possible, gather their hand luggage, and stake out a chair in one of the public lounges to await the ship's clearance through customs. Be patient— it takes a long time to unload and sort thousands of pieces of luggage.

Passengers are disembarked in groups according to color-coded luggage tags; those with the earliest flights get off first. If you have a tight connection, notify the purser before the last day, and he or she may be able to arrange faster pre-clearing and disembarkation.

SAFETY AT SEA

Health Care

High-quality medical care at sea is an important safety issue. All big ships are equipped with medical infirmaries to handle minor emergencies. However, these should not be confused with hospitals. There are no international standards governing medical facilities or personnel aboard cruise ships, although the American Medical Association has recommended that such standards be adopted. If you have a preexisting medical condition, discuss your upcoming cruise with your doctor. Pack an extra supply of any medicines you might need. Once aboard, see the ship's doctor and alert him or her to your condition, and discuss treatments or emergency procedures before any problem arises. Passengers with potentially life-threatening conditions should consider signing up with a medical evacuation service, and all passengers should review their health insurance to make sure they are covered while on a cruise.

If you become seriously ill or injured and happen to be near a major city, you may be taken to a medical facility shoreside. But if you're farther afield, you may have to be airlifted off the ship by helicopter and flown either to the nearest American port or to an airport where you can be taken by charter jet to the United States. Many standard health insurance policies, including Medicare plans, do not cover these or other medical expenses incurred outside the United States. You can, however, buy supplemental health insurance that is in effect only when you travel.

The most common minor medical problems confronting cruise passengers are seasickness and gastrointestinal distress. Modern cruise ships, unlike their transatlantic predecessors, are relatively motion-free vessels outfitted with computer-controlled stabilizers, and they usually sail in relatively calm waters. If you do feel queasy, you can get seasickness pills aboard ship. (Many ships give them out for free at the front desk.)

Outbreaks of food poisoning occasionally occur aboard cruise ships. Episodes are random; they can occur on ships old and new, big and small, budget and luxury. The Centers for Disease Control and Prevention (CDC) monitors cruise-ship hygiene and sanitation procedures, conducting voluntary inspections twice a year of all ships that sail regularly from U.S. ports (this program does not include ships that never visit the United States). A high score on the CDC report doesn't mean you won't get sick. Outbreaks have taken place on ships that consistently score very highly; conversely, some ships score very poorly yet passengers never get sick.

For a free listing of the latest cruise-ship sanitation scores, write to the CDC's **National Center for Environmental Health** (✆ Vessel Sanitation Program, 1015 North America Way, Room 107, Miami, FL 33132 ☏ 888/232–3299 for fax-back service ⊕ www.cdc.gov). If you use the fax-back service, request publication 510051.

Crime on Ships

Crime aboard cruise ships has occasionally become headline news, thanks in large part to a few well-publicized cases. Most people never have any type of problem, but you should exercise the same precautions aboard ship that you would at home. Keep your valuables out of sight—on big ships virtually every cabin has a small safe in the closet. Don't carry too much cash ashore, use your credit card whenever possible, and keep your money in a secure place, such as a front pocket that's harder to pick. Single women traveling with friends should stick together, especially when returning to their cabins late at night. Be careful about whom you befriend, as you would anywhere, whether it's a fellow passenger or a member of the crew. Don't be paranoid, but do be prudent.

THE CRUISE FLEET

For each cruise line, we list only the ships (grouped by similar configurations) that regularly cruise in Alaska. When two or more ships are substantially similar, their names are given at the beginning of a review and separated by commas. Within each cruise line, ships are listed from largest to smallest.

Passenger-capacity figures are given on the basis of two people sharing a cabin (basis-2); however, many of the larger ships have 3- and 4-berth cabins, which can increase the total number of passengers tremendously when all berths are occupied. When total occupancy figures differ from basis-2 occupancy, we give them in parentheses.

Ocean Liners

Carnival Cruise Lines

Carnival Cruise Lines is the largest and most successful cruise line in the world, carrying more passengers than any other. Brash and sometimes rowdy, Carnival throws a great party. Activities and entertainment are nonstop, beginning just after sunrise and continuing well into the night. Under Carnival's "Total Choice Dining" plan, all ships serve food at all hours, including 24-hour room service. Carnival cruises are popular with young, single cruisers as well as with those older than 55. The line's offerings also appeal to parents cruising with their children.

Gratuities are customarily given on the last evening of the cruise, but they may be prepaid at a rate of $9.75 per passenger per day. Carnival recommends the following tips: cabin steward, $3.50 per day; dining-room team service, $5.50 per day; alternative dining service, 75¢ per day. A 15% gratuity is automatically added to bar and beverage tabs.

🖰 *Carnival Cruise Lines, 3655 N.W. 87th Ave., Miami, FL 33178-2428* ☎ *305/599–2600, 800/438–6744, or 800/327–9501* ⊕ *www.carnival.com.*

THE SHIPS OF
CARNIVAL
CRUISE LINES
🐌

Spirit. The first of Carnival's Spirit-class ships entered service in 2001 with notable design improvements over previous lines. For example, all staterooms aboard these superliners are above ocean level, making for a more comfortable cruise. Cabins have ample drawer and closet space, and in-cabin TVs show first-run films. Other innovations include eye-popping, 11-story atriums, two-level promenades (partially glass enclosed to create a protected viewing perch), wide decks, shopping malls, and reservations-only supper clubs. Greater speed allows Spirit-class ships to visit destinations in a week that would take other ships 10 days or more. Most staterooms have ocean views, and of those, 80% have balconies. Terrific children's programs and a pool with a retractable roof for all-weather swimming make this a good ship for any family vacation. ⥤ *1,062 cabins, 2,124 passengers (2,667 at full occupancy), 13 passenger decks* ⅋ *Dining room, 3 restaurants, pizzeria, in-room safes, 4 pools, fitness classes, gym, hair salon, 5 outdoor hot tubs, spa, 16 bars,* *casino, cinema, dance club, showroom, video game room, children's programs (ages 2–15), laundry facilities, laundry service, computer room, no-smoking rooms* 🚬 *AE, D, MC, V.*

Celebrity Cruises

Celebrity Cruises has made a name for itself based on sleek ships and superior food. Celebrity has risen above typical mass-market cruise cuisine by hiring Chef Michel Roux as a consultant. All food is prepared from scratch, using only fresh produce and herbs, aged beef, and fresh fish—even the ice cream on board is homemade. In just a short time Celebrity has won the admiration of its passengers and its competitors—who have copied its nouvelle cuisine, occasional adults-only cruises, and cigar clubs, and hired its personnel (a true compliment). Celebrity attracts everyone from older couples to honeymooners.

Tip your cabin steward/butlers $3.50 per day; chief housekeeper 50¢ per day; dining-room waiter $3.50 per day; assistant waiter $2 per day; and restaurant manager 75¢ per day, for a total of $10.25 per day. A 15% service charge is added to all beverage checks. Gratuities are typically handed out on the last night of the cruise, or they may be charged to your shipboard account.

🗑 *Celebrity Cruises, 1050 Caribbean Way, Miami, FL 33132-2096* ☎ *305/539–6000 or 800/646–1456* 🖶 *800/437–5111* ⊕ *www. celebritycruises.com.*

THE SHIPS OF **Infinity, Summit.** Dramatic, exterior glass elevators, a glass-dome pool area,
CELEBRITY and a window-wrapped ship-top observation lounge keep the magnif-
CRUISES icence of Alaska well within the passenger's view. These are the newest
and largest in Celebrity's fleet, and each stocks plenty of premium amenities, including a flower-filled conservatory, music library, expansive spa, Internet café with 18 workstations, golf simulator, and brand-name boutiques. Cabins are bright, spacious, and well appointed, and 80% have an ocean view (74% of those have private verandas). There is also in-cabin Internet access. With a staff member for every two passengers, service is especially attentive. 🔗 *975 cabins, 1,950 passengers, 11 passenger decks ⚓ Dining room, restaurant, food court, ice cream parlor, pizzeria, in-room safes, minibars, in-room VCRs, 3 pools, fitness classes, gym, hair salon, 3 outdoor hot tubs, sauna, spa, steam room, 6 bars, casino, cinema, dance club, showroom, video game room, children's programs (ages 3–17), dry cleaning, laundry service, computer room, Internet in some rooms, no-smoking rooms* 🚬 *AE, MC, V.*

★ 🌙 **Mercury.** With features such as a golf simulator, video walls, and interactive television systems in cabins, this ship is a high-tech pioneer, yet it is elegant and warm. Many large windows—including a dramatic two-story wall of glass in the dining room and wraparound windows in the Stratosphere Lounge, in the gym, and in the beauty salon—bathe the ship in natural light and afford excellent views of Alaska's natural beauty. Plus there are retractable glass sunroofs over the pools. The elaborate Elemis spas have enormous Thalassotherapy pools and the latest in treatments. Standard cabins are intelligently appointed and apportioned, with few frills; space is well used, making for maximum elbow room in the bathrooms and good storage space in the closets. 🔗 *935 cabins, 1,870 passengers, 10 passenger decks ⚓ Dining room, 2 restaurants, food court, ice cream parlor, pizzeria, in-room safes, minibars, 3 pools, fitness classes, gym, hair salon, 4 outdoor hot tubs, sauna, spa, steam room, 6 bars, casino, cinema, dance club, showroom, video game room, children's programs (ages 3–17), dry cleaning, laundry service, computer room, no-smoking rooms* 🚬 *AE, MC, V.*

Crystal Cruise Line

Crystal ships have long set standards for onboard pampering. White-glove service, stellar cuisine, and even air-conditioned tenders complete the effect of total luxury and comfort. To the typical litany of ocean-liner diversions, Crystal adds destination-oriented lectures and talks by scholars, political figures, and diplomats, plus luxe theme cruises emphasizing such topics as food and wine or the arts. On select cruises highly trained and experienced youth counselors are brought in to oversee activities for kids and teens. The staff is well trained, friendly, highly motivated, and thoroughly professional. However, unlike Seven Seas Cruises, the other luxury line sailing Alaskan waters, Crystal's fares do not include tips, so the crew can be noticeably solicitous of gratuities. Crystal's target clientele is affluent and older but still active.

Suggested tipping guidelines are as follows: stewardess, $4 per day (single travelers, $5 per day); waiter, $4 per day ($6 per day in alternative restaurants); assistant waiter, $2.50 per day; butler penthouse, $4 per day; 15% added to bar bills. Gratuities may be charged to a shipboard account.

⌖ *Crystal Cruise Line, 2049 Century Park East, Suite 1400, Los Angeles, CA 90067* ☎ *800/446–6620 or 310/785–9300* 🖷 *310/785–9201* ⊕ *www.crystalcruises.com.*

THE SHIPS OF
CRYSTAL
CRUISE LINE
★ ☾

Crystal Harmony. The only Alaska-bound liner offering 12-day round-trip sailings from San Francisco, Crystal's sleek ship is uncluttered, with classy, understated interiors. *Harmony* has plenty of open deck space for watching the scenery, plus the forward observation lounge, set high above the bridge, has oversize windows. Best of all, it is roomy, with one of the highest ratios of passenger to space of any ship. Staterooms deliver space in abundance—the smallest measuring 183 square feet—and more than half have private verandas. Even the lowest-category staterooms have a separate sitting area (love seat with coffee table), a desk/vanity, and queen or twin beds—with space left over to comfortably move about. Large closets, ample drawer space, and bathtubs are standard. Cabins are equipped with voice mail, goose-down pillows, fine linens, and thick towels. Onboard amenities include grand lounges and Broadway-style entertainment. ⇝ *408 cabins, 940 passengers, 8 passenger decks* ⚓ *Dining room, 2 restaurants, café, grill, ice cream parlor, in-room safes, minibars, in-room VCRs, 2 swimming pools, 1 lap pool, fitness classes, gym, hair salon, 2 outdoor hot tubs, sauna, spa, steam room, 7 bars, casino, cinema, dance club, showroom, video game room, children's program (ages 3–16), dry cleaning, laundry facilities, laundry service, computer room, Internet, no-smoking rooms; no kids under 3 months* ▭ *AE, D, MC, V.*

Holland America Line

Founded in 1873, Holland America (HAL) is one of the oldest names in cruising. Steeped in the traditions of the transatlantic crossing, its cruises are classic, conservative affairs renowned for their grace and gentility. Service is taken seriously: the line maintains a school in Indonesia to train staff members, rather than hiring out of a union hall. The staff on the line's Alaska cruises includes a naturalist and Native artist-in-residence. HAL passengers tend to be older and less active than those traveling on the ships of its parent line, Carnival, although the age difference is getting narrower. As its ships attract a more youthful clientele, HAL has taken steps to shed its "old folks" image, now offering trendier cuisine and a "Club Hal" children's program.

HAL has a no-tips-required policy. Passengers don't feel the pressure or the discomfort of having crew members solicit tips. On the other hand, this is not a no-tipping policy, and most passengers give tips comparable to those recommended on other lines—entirely at their own discretion.

⌂ *Holland America Line, 300 Elliott Ave., Seattle, WA 98119* ☎ *206/281–3535 or 877/932–4259* 🖷 *206/281–7110* ⊕ *www.hollandamerica. com.*

THE SHIPS OF
HOLLAND
AMERICA LINE
★ ☺

Oosterdam. Panoramic views from exterior elevators are a dramatic addition to this new Vista-class ship. Launched in 2003, the *Oosterdam* boasts more space per passenger—in both public rooms and cabins—than any other ship in the Holland America fleet. All the HAL trademarks, including lush traditional decor, white-gloved stewards, and a multimillion-dollar art collection are here, as are such up-to-date touches as in-cabin Internet access, a golf simulator, extensive spa facilities, and an alternative restaurant with a Pacific Northwest menu. A retractable dome over the pool means you can enjoy a swim, even in Alaska. ⤴ *924 cabins, 1,848 passengers, 11 decks ☼ Dining room, 2 restaurants, café, some in-room VCRs, 3 pools, fitness classes, gym, hair salon, sauna, spa, 4 bars, casino, cinema, dance club, showroom, children's programs (ages 5–17), dry-cleaning, laundry service, computer room, Internet, no-smoking rooms ⊟ AE, D, MC, V.*

☺ **Volendam, Zaandam.** These ships are structurally similar to HAL's other vessels, with the signature two-tier dining room and retractable roof over the main pool, but they are newer, entering service in 1999 and 2000, respectively. They are also slightly larger than the line's other ships and have Internet cafés and practice-size tennis courts. Priceless antiques and artwork line the halls; huge bouquets of fresh, fragrant flowers are everywhere (a Holland America trademark); and each ship has a teak promenade completely encircling the ship, which means there will always be room for you at the rail to watch the sunset. All standard outside cabins come with a bathtub, and all suites and minisuites have private verandas. The "Passport to Fitness" encourages a healthful diet and exercise. ⤴ *658/720 cabins (Volendam/Zaandam), 1,316/1,440 passengers (1,378/1,848 at full occupancy), 10/10 passenger decks ☼ Dining room, 2 restaurants, food court, in-room safes, refrigerators, in-room VCRs, 2 pools (1 indoor), fitness classes, gym, hair salon, 2 outdoor hot tubs, sauna, spa, steam room, 6 bars, casino, cinema, dance club, showroom, video game room, children's programs (ages 5–17), dry cleaning, laundry facilities, laundry service, computer room, Internet, no-smoking rooms ⊟ AE, D, MC, V.*

Amsterdam. Holland America Lines is known for its old-world elegance, and the *Amsterdam* delivers with antiques, original art, brass fixtures, and teak deck chairs. It is a new ship, however, with such up-to-date amenities as practice-size tennis courts, a pool with a retractable roof, and an Internet café. The promenade that completely encircles the ship ensures plenty of viewing space. ⤴ *690 cabins, 1,380 passengers, 10 decks ☼ Dining room, 2 restaurants, café, pool, fitness classes, gym, hair salon, hot tub, sauna, spa, 6 bars, casino, dance club, showroom, children's programs (ages 5–17), dry cleaning, laundry facilities, laundry service, computer room, Internet ⊟ AE, D, MC, V.*

Maasdam, Ryndam, Statendam, Veendam. An abundance of glass, outdoor deck space, and a retractable roof over the main pool make these good ships for Alaska cruising. Great views can be found along the wraparound promenade. From bow to stern, these ships are full of lounges and restaurants—14 in all—some cozy, some grand, and most with expansive floor-to-ceiling windows. The Crow's Nest is a combined observation lounge and nightclub overlooking the bow, and the Lido Restaurant, the hallmark of every Holland America Line ship, has an adjoining outdoor terrace. A three-deck atrium and a two-tier dining room, replete with dual grand staircases framing an orchestra balcony, are among the welcoming public spaces. Antiques and artwork line the halls; staterooms are restful, with understated elegance. ⊅ *633 cabins, 1,266 passengers (1,590 at full occupancy), 10 passenger decks ♿ Dining room, 3 restaurants, food court, ice cream parlor, in-room safes, 2 pools, fitness classes, gym, hair salon, 2 hot tubs, sauna, spa, steam room, 9 bars, casino, cinema, dance club, showroom, video game room, children's programs (ages 5–17), dry cleaning, laundry facilities, laundry service, computer room, Internet, no-smoking rooms* ⊟ *AE, D, MC, V.*

Prinsendam. Teak decks, antiques, and specially commissioned artworks grace Holland America's smallest vessel. New to Alaska in 2003, the *Prinsendam* offers a high crew-to-passenger ratio and a more intimate feel than some of the newer megaships. The cabins are roomy, and 40 percent have private verandas. ⊅ *398 cabins, 793 passengers (837 full occupancy), 9 decks ♿ Dining room, 2 restaurants, café, 2 pools, fitness classes, gym, hair salon, hot tub, sauna, spa, 4 bars, casino, dance club, showroom, children's programs (ages 5–17), dry cleaning, laundry facilities, laundry service, computer room, Internet, no-smoking rooms* ⊟ *AE, D, MC, V.*

Norwegian Cruise Line

In 1966, Norwegian Cruise Line (NCL) launched a new concept in cruising: regularly scheduled cruises on a single-class ship. No longer simply a means of transportation, the ship became a destination unto itself. NCL continues to innovate. It offers "Freestyle Cruising," which eliminates dinner table and time assignments and dress codes. The line has even loosened the rules on disembarkation, which means passengers can relax in their cabins until it's time to leave the ship (instead of gathering in a lounge to wait for their numbers to be called). Most of NCL's Alaska fleet is based in Seattle rather than Vancouver, B.C., which can be a more convenient departure point for many U.S.-based passengers. The line's passenger list usually includes seniors, families, and younger couples, mostly from the United States and Canada.

NCL applies a service charge to passengers' shipboard accounts: $10 per passenger per day for those 13 and older, and $5 per day for children (ages 3–12). These automatic tips can be increased, decreased, or removed. A 15% gratuity is added to bar tabs and spa bills.

🖃 *Norwegian Cruise Line, 7665 Corporate Center Dr., Miami, FL 33126* ☎ *305/436–4000 or 800/327–7030* ⊕ *www.ncl.com.*

THE SHIPS OF
NORWEGIAN
CRUISE LINE
☾
Fodor'sChoice
★

Norwegian Star. NCL's newest and, at 25 knots, its fastest, Alaska-bound ship was built specifically to accommodate the line's Freestyle Cruising concept. Offering more dining choices than any other ship in Alaska, *Star* has 10 different eateries, with everything from French, Italian, contemporary, and spa cuisine to tapas and sushi. The ship also has a two-deck, 24-hour fitness center; a Balinese-theme spa; a golf driving range; and an indoor pool. Garden Villas, the top-of-the-line staterooms, have private rooftop terraces. Standard cabins take their cue from high-end hotel rooms, with rich cherrywood, tea- and coffeemakers, and large bathrooms. Most staterooms can accommodate a third guest, and many cabins can be linked to create suites for larger groups. ⊅ *1,120 cabins, 2,240 passengers, 11 passenger decks ♿ 2 dining rooms, 6 restaurants, 2 cafés, food court, ice cream parlor, in-room safes, refrigerators, 2 pools (1 indoor), fitness classes, gym, hair salon, 2 hot tubs, spa, 9 bars, cinema, 2 dance clubs, showroom, video game room, chil-*

*dren's programs (ages 2–17), dry cleaning, laundry service, computer
room, Internet* ⊟ *AE, D, MC, V.*

☺ **Norwegian Sky, Norwegian Sun.** These ships come with all the bells and
whistles, including a variety of dining options, specialty bars, and Internet access—both in a café and in cabins. A 24-hour health club has
expansive ocean views, and the presence of the full-service Mandara Spa
means you can turn your cruise into a spa vacation. Cabins are adequately
laid out, with large circular windows and sitting areas, sufficient (but
not generous) shelf and drawer space, and two lower beds that convert
to a queen. But what makes Norwegian Cruise Line's ships different from
other large ships is their relaxed onboard atmosphere and Free-Style Dining concept, which means main dining rooms are smaller but there are
more dining venues (some with an additional cost). ⇔ *1,001/1,001 cabins (Sky/Sun), 2,002/2,002 passengers (2,400/2,400 at full occupancy),
12/11 passenger decks ⚓ 2 dining rooms, 8/7 restaurants, food court,
in-room safes, refrigerators, 2 pools, fitness classes, gym, hair salon, 4
hot tubs, sauna, spa, steam room, 13/11 bars, casino, cinema, dance club,
showroom, video game room, children's programs (ages 2–17), dry
cleaning, laundry facilities, computer room, Internet; no kids under 6
months* ⊟ *AE, D, MC, V.*

Princess Cruise Line

Princess was catapulted to stardom in 1977, when it became the star of
The Love Boat television series, which introduced millions of viewers to
the still-new concept of a seagoing vacation. The name and famous "sea-
witch" logo have remained synonymous with cruising ever since. Nearly
everything about Princess is big, but the line doesn't sacrifice quality for
quantity when it comes to building beautiful vessels. Service, especially
in the dining rooms, is of a high standard. In short, Princess is refined
without being pretentious. Many Princess ships offer the line's innovative "Personal Choice Cruising" program, an individualized, unstructured
style of cruising that gives passengers choice and flexibility in customiz-
ing their cruise experience—multiple dining locations, flexible entertainment, and affordable private balconies. Princess passengers' average
age is 45; you see a mix of younger and older couples on board.

Princess suggests tipping $10 per person, per day. On ships with Personal
Choice Cruising, gratuities are automatically added to accounts, which
passengers can adjust at the purser's desk; 15% is added to bar bills.

🖉 *Princess Cruise Line, 24305 Town Center Dr., Santa Clarita, CA
91355-4999* ☎ *661/753–0000 or 800/774–6237* ⊕ *www.princess.com.*

THE SHIPS OF   **Coral Princess, Island Princess.** Launched in 2003, these sister ships offer
PRINCESS   a wealth of high-tech amenities. The two-story Universe Lounge has full
CRUISE LINE   TV production capabilities and three revolving stages; the wedding
★   chapel is complete with video cameras; plus there's an Internet café and
a golf simulator. Also on board are a 9-hole putting green, a '60s-theme
martini bar, and a Cajun-style restaurant with live jazz. The retractable
dome roof on the pool allows for all-weather swimming. Ninety percent of cabins are outside staterooms, and most of those have balconies.
Princess's Personal Choice Cruising allows you to choose between traditional fixed seating in the dining room or dining when you like in any
of the onboard restaurants. ⇔ *987 cabins, 1,970 passengers, 11 passenger decks ⚓ 2 dining rooms, 2 restaurants, 2 cafés, ice cream parlor, pizzeria, in-room safes, 4 pools, fitness classes, gym, hair salon, 5
hot tubs, sauna, spa, 5 bars, casino, cinema, dance club, 3 showrooms,
video game room, children's programs (ages 3–17), dry cleaning, laun-*

dry facilities, laundry service, computer room, Internet; no kids under 6 months ▤ *AE, D, MC, V.*

🐾 **Sun Princess, Dawn Princess.** More than 70% of outside cabins in these sister ships have private balconies. All standard cabins are decorated in light colors, and have a queen-size bed convertible to two singles, ample closet and bath space (with shower only), terry robes, and hair dryers. Several cabins on each ship are deemed fully accessible. A wraparound teak promenade lined with canopied steamer chairs provides a peaceful setting for reading, napping, or daydreaming, and a pool with a retractable glass roof allows for all-weather swimming. ↪ *975 cabins, 1,950 passengers, 14 passenger decks* ♿ *3 dining rooms, 5 restaurants, café, food court, ice cream parlor, pizzeria, in-room safes, refrigerators, 5 pools, fitness classes, gym, hair salon, 9 hot tubs, sauna, spa, steam room, 12 bars, casino, cinema, dance club, showroom, video game room, children's programs (ages 3–17), dry cleaning, laundry facilities, laundry service, computer room, no-smoking rooms; no kids under 6 months* ▤ *AE, D, MC, V.*

Royal Caribbean Cruise Line

Imagine if the Mall of America were sent to sea. That's a fair approximation of what the megaships of Royal Caribbean Cruise Line (RCL) are all about. These mammoth vessels are indoor/outdoor wonders, with every conceivable activity in a resortlike atmosphere, including atrium lobbies, shopping arcades, large spas, and expansive sundecks. The main problem with these otherwise well-conceived vessels is that the line packs too many people aboard, making for an exasperating experience at embarkation, while tendering, and at disembarkation. Nevertheless, Royal Caribbean is one of the best-run and most popular cruise lines. Although the line competes directly with Carnival for passengers—active couples and singles in their thirties to fifties, as well as a large family contingent—there are distinct differences of ambience and energy. Royal Caribbean is a bit more sophisticated and subdued than Carnival, even while delivering a good time on a grand scale.

Royal Caribbean suggests the following tips per passenger: dining-room waiter, $3.50 a day; stateroom attendant, $3.50 a day, assistant waiter, $2 a day. Gratuities for headwaiters and other service personnel are at your discretion. A 15% gratuity is automatically added to beverage and bar bills. All gratuities may be charged to your onboard account.

🖫 *Royal Caribbean International, 1050 Caribbean Way, Miami, FL 33132* ☎ *305/539–600 or 800/327–6700* ⊕ *www.royalcaribbean.com.*

THE SHIPS OF
ROYAL
CARIBBEAN
CRUISE LINE
★ 🐾

Radiance of the Seas. Speed (which allows for longer itineraries) and the line's highest percentage of outside cabins are the selling points here. More than 80% of all cabins have ocean views, and more than 70% of those include private verandas. All cabins have two twin beds convertible into a queen, computer jack, vanity table with an extendable working surface, and bedside reading lights. The central atrium spans 10 decks, and sea-facing elevators give you a view of the ocean. The coffeehouse/bookstore combination, the rock-climbing wall, and the self-leveling pool tables are novel touches. The African-theme solarium, with its retractable glass roof, pool, hot tubs, palm trees, and waterfalls, provides a pleasant escape from inclement Alaskan weather. ↪ *1,056 cabins, 2,100 passengers (2,501 at full occupancy), 12 passenger decks* ♿ *3 dining rooms, 5 restaurants, food court, in-room data ports, in-room safes, refrigerators, 3 pools, fitness classes, gym, hair salon, 3 hot tubs, sauna, spa, steam room, 9 bars, casino, cinema, dance club, showroom, video* *game room, children's programs (ages 3–17), dry cleaning, laundry service, computer room, no-smoking rooms.* ⊟ *AE, D, MC, V.*

Legend of the Seas, Vision of the Seas. These sister ships are among the fastest on the Alaska run. Both ships have large windows throughout and, on the uppermost deck, a viewing lounge with wraparound glass. The covered pool and indoor-outdoor deck area of the Solarium Spa are especially well suited to cruising in often rainy Alaska. Among the bright, spacious cabins are connecting staterooms, cabins with private balconies, and family suites with separate bedrooms for parents and children. ↝ *900/1,200 cabins (Legend/Vision), 1,800/2,400 passengers, 9/10 passenger decks* ⚓ *Dining rooms, 2 restaurants, 2 pools, fitness classes, gym, hair salon, 4/6 hot tubs, sauna, spa, steam room, 8/6 bars, casino, dance club, showroom, children's programs (ages 3–17), computer room, Internet* ⊟ *AE, D, MC, V.*

Seven Seas Cruises

Seven Seas Cruises (formerly Radisson Seven Seas Cruises) is the world's largest luxury line, with more than 2,000 berths in this category. The line's spacious, ocean-view cabins have the industry's highest percentage of private balconies; there's open seating and complimentary wine at dinner; and activities are oriented toward exploring the destinations on the itinerary. SSC provides a high level of service and a sense of intimacy on midsize ships that have the stability of larger vessels. Passengers are older, affluent, and active.

Seven Seas has a strict no-tipping policy.

🖫 *Seven Seas Cruises, 600 Corporate Dr., Suite 410, Fort Lauderdale, FL 33334* ☎ *954/776–6123, 800/477–7500, or 800/285–1835* 🖷 *954/772–3763* ⊕ *www.rssc.com.*

THE SHIPS OF
SEVEN SEAS
☾
Fodor'sChoice
★

Seven Seas Mariner. The world's first and only all-suite, all-balcony ship is also Seven Seas' largest, with the highest space-per-passenger ratio in the fleet. All cabins are outside suites ranging from 301 square feet to 1,580 square feet including the veranda. The ship's dining rooms include Signatures, the only restaurant at sea staffed by chefs wearing the Blue Riband of Le Cordon Bleu of Paris, the famed culinary institute. On certain voyages the chefs offer Le Cordon Bleu "Classe Culinare des Croisiers," workshops that offer a hands-on introduction to the art of French cooking. Passengers on SSC ships have consistently placed the Judith Jackson spas among their favorites on land or sea. ↝ *328 cabins, 700 passengers, 8 passenger decks* ⚓ *Dining room, 3 restaurants, in-room safes, minibars, in-room VCRs, pool, fitness classes, gym, hair salon, outdoor hot tub, sauna, spa, steam room, 4 bars, casino, cinema, dance club, showroom, children's programs (ages 6–17), dry cleaning, laundry service, no-smoking rooms; no kids under age 1* ⊟ *AE, D, MC, V.*

Small Ships

American Safari Cruises

Unlike most yachts, which have to be chartered, American Safari's vessels sail on a regular schedule and sell tickets to individuals: there's no need to charter the whole boat, though that is an option. With just 12 to 21 passengers and such decadent amenities as ocean-view hot tubs, American Safari's yachts are among the most comfortable small ships cruising Alaska. The chefs serve a choice of individually prepared dinner entreés, and breads and desserts are made fresh on board. Itineraries are usually flexible; there's no rush to move on if the group spots a pod of whales or a family of bears. All sailing is in daylight, with nights spent at anchor in secluded coves, and the yachts stop daily to let you kayak, hike, or beachcomb. An onboard naturalist offers informal lectures and guides you on shore expeditions. All three ships carry exercise equipment, kayaks, mountain bikes, Zodiac landing crafts, and insulated Mustang suits for Zodiac excursions. All shore excursions—even a flightseeing trip—and alcoholic drinks are included in the fare.

Tips are discretionary, but 5%–10% of the fare is suggested. A lump sum is pooled among the crew at the end of the cruise.

⌂ *American Safari Cruises, 19101 36th Ave. W, Suite 201, Lynnwood, WA 98036* ☏ *425/776–4700 or 888/862–8881* 🖷 *425/776–8889* ⊕ *www.amsafari.com.*

THE SHIPS OF
AMERICAN
SAFARI CRUISES

★

Safari Quest. American Safari's largest vessel, this luxurious yacht has warm wood trim throughout. Four cabins have small balconies accessed by sliding glass doors, and a single cabin is available. There's plenty of outer deck space for taking in the views, and a reading lounge on the top deck is a pleasant hideaway. ⇨ *11 cabins, 21 passengers, 4 passenger decks* ⚓ *Dining room, in-room VCRs, outdoor hot tub, bar; no smoking.*

Safari Escape. Although *Escape* is one of Alaska's smallest cruise ships, it comes with all kinds of creature comforts usually associated with bigger ships, including exercise equipment, mountain bikes, and, in one cabin, a private sauna. Everyone dines together at one grand table; lunch might be a gourmet picnic on a secluded beach. Standard staterooms have queen or twin beds, and port lights rather than windows. The higher-end staterooms have a king-size bed and a window. All have rich fabrics and wood paneling. ⇨ *6 cabins, 12 passengers, 3 passenger decks* ⚓ *Dining room, in-room VCRs, outdoor hot tub, bar; no smoking.*

Safari Spirit. A comfortable lounge and an open bar are part of the pampering, as are the excellent meals, served at one grand table. Every bright and cheerful cabin has a private bath with a Jacuzzi tub; the high-end cabins have king beds; and one has a small balcony. ⇨ *6 cabins, 12 passengers, 4 decks* ⚓ *Dining room, in-room VCRs, outdoor hot tub, bar; no smoking.*

American West Steamboat Company

In the 19th century, paddle wheelers were a key part of Alaska's coastal transport, taking adventurers and gold seekers north. In 2003, American West Steamboat Company launched the *Empress of the North,* the first overnight stern-wheeler to ply these waters in 100 years. A naturalist and historian gives lectures on local history and culture, and gold-rush follies, Russian-American dances, and Native American songs and dances bring the region's past to life. A shore excursion is included at each port of call, including a trip on the White Pass & Yukon Railroad. This novel small ship is expected to attract primarily North American passengers, with an average age of about 55.

Tips are pooled by the crew at the end of the cruise. A tip of $12 to $14 per person per night is suggested.

⌂ *American West Steamboat Company, 2101 4th Ave., Suite 1150, Seattle, WA 98121* ☏ *206/621–0913 or 800/434–1232* 🖷 *206/340–0975* ⊕ *www.americanweststeamboat.com.*

THE SHIPS OF
AMERICAN WEST
STEAMBOAT
COMPANY

Empress of the North. Alaskan art and historical artifacts enrich the public areas, and the staterooms mimic Victorian opulence, with lush fabrics and rich colors. All cabins have big picture windows, and most have balconies. Lavish two-room suites, as well as single, triple, and wheelchair-accessible cabins are available. The chandelier-lighted dining room looks formal, but it is actually small-ship casual, with open seating and no need to dress up. Variety shows, ranging from golden oldies and big band to country and western, play nightly. ☞ *112 cabins, 235 passengers, 4 passenger decks ⚓ Dining room, café, minibars, in-room DVD players, 3 bars, showroom; no smoking.*

Clipper Cruise Lines

Clipper Cruise Lines keeps the focus on fully experiencing each destination. A fleet of motorized Zodiacs is on hand to take passengers to isolated beaches and, on every voyage, onboard experts share their knowledge of the region's cultures, wildlife, history, and geography. Clipper chefs take pride in their healthful American cuisine. Each dish is made to order, and almost everything served is made from scratch on board. There's little formality on board these relaxed yacht-size cruisers. Casual attire is the norm, and sports coats and dresses don't usually appear until the captain's farewell party. Passengers are typically active and well-traveled older adults.

Tips are pooled together at the end of the cruise. Ten dollars per day per passenger is suggested.

🖈 *Clipper Cruise Lines, 11969 Westline Industrial Dr., St. Louis, MO 63146-3220 ☎ 314/655–6700 or 800/325–0010 ⊕ www.clippercruise. com.*

THE SHIPS OF CLIPPER CRUISE LINES

Yorktown Clipper. Although deck space is limited on this coastal cruiser, floor-to-ceiling windows in the forward observation lounge and large windows in the dining room allow sightseeing in all weather. Cabins are all outside, with twin lower berths and a private bathroom with a shower. Most have large windows. ☞ *69 cabins, 138 passengers, 4 passenger decks ⚓ Dining room, in-room safes, bar; no smoking.*

★ *Clipper Odyssey.* The *Odyssey* brings elements of a luxury yacht experience to small-ship cruising in Alaska. Window-lined dining rooms and lounges keep the scenery in sight. Each cabin also has an ocean view, as well as a sitting area with a sofa and a bathroom with a shower and tub. Other amenities include exercise equipment, a jogging track, and a library. ☞ *64 cabins, 128 passengers, 5 passenger decks ⚓ Dining room, in-room safes, refrigerators, gym, hair salon, outdoor hot tub, bar, laundry service; no smoking.*

Cruise West

A big player in small ships, Seattle-based Cruise West sends seven coastal cruisers to Alaska each summer. As with other smaller vessels, Alaskan wilderness, wildlife, and culture take precedence over shipboard diversions. An exploration leader, who is both naturalist and cruise coordinator, offers evening lectures and joins passengers on many of the shore excursions—at least one of which is included at each port of call. Binoculars in every cabin, a library stocked with books of local interest, and crew members as keen to explore Alaska as the passengers all enhance the experience. The lounge feels like a living room, wholesome meals include bread baked on board, and jeans are as formal as it gets. The passengers, who inevitably get to know one another during the cruise, are typically active, well-traveled, over-fifties. They come from all regions of the United States, as well as from Australia, Canada, and the United Kingdom.

Suggested tips are $10 per person per day; these are pooled for all the crew and staff at the end of the cruise.

🖈 *Cruise West, 2401 4th Ave., Suite 700, Seattle, WA 98121 ☎ 206/ 441–8687 or 800/888–9378 ⊕ www.cruisewest.com.*

Spirit of Oceanus. Cruise West's largest vessel is also its most luxurious, with marble and polished wood in the dining room, lounges, library, and cabins. All the staterooms are outside, and 12 of them have teak-floor private balconies. The ship, equipped with stabilizers for open ocean cruising, also carries a fleet of Zodiacs for close-up visits to glaciers, waterfalls, and icebergs. Breakfast and lunch are served on deck when the weather permits. ➦ *57 cabins, 114 passengers, 5 decks ⚓ Dining room, in-room safes, refrigerators, in-room VCRs, gym, outdoor hot tub, bar; no smoking.*

Spirit of Endeavour. One of Cruise West's largest and fastest ships, the *Endeavour* provides ample deck space and a roomy lounge with large picture windows for superb views. Most of the cabins also have picture windows, and some have connecting doors, which make them convenient for families traveling together. The ship's speed allows for more flexibility: the captain can linger to let passengers watch a group of whales, and still make the next stop on time. Exercise equipment is available. ➦ *51 cabins, 102 passengers, 4 passenger decks ⚓ Dining room, some refrigerators, in-room VCRs, bar; no smoking.*

Spirit of '98. With rounded stern and wheelhouse, old-fashioned smokestack, and Victorian decor, the *Spirit of '98* evokes a turn-of-the-20th-century steamer although she is actually a modern ship, built in 1984. Mahogany trim inside and out, overstuffed chairs with plush floral upholstery, and a player piano in the salon add to the gold rush–era motif. For private moments, you'll find plenty of nooks and crannies aboard the ship, including the cozy Soapy's Parlor bar at the stern. All cabins, including the two single cabins on board, have picture windows. The owner's suite has a living room and a whirlpool tub. Exercise equipment is available. ➦ *48 cabins, 96 passengers, 4 passenger decks ⚓ Dining room, some refrigerators, in-room VCRs, bar; no smoking.*

Spirit of Discovery. Floor-to-ceiling windows in the main lounge provide stunning views aboard this snazzy cruiser. From here, passengers have direct access to a large outdoor viewing deck, one of two aboard. Every cabin has windows; toilets and showers are a combined unit. Two cabins are reserved for single travelers, and exercise equipment is available on board. ➦ *43 cabins, 84 passengers, 3 decks ⚓ Dining room, some refrigerators, some in-room VCRs, bar; no smoking.*

Spirit of Alaska. The sleek *Spirit of Alaska* carries a fleet of Zodiacs for impromptu stops at isolated beaches and close-up looks at glaciers. Most cabins are small but cheerfully decorated. Toilets and showers are a combined unit (the toilet is inside the shower). Top-deck cabins have windows on two sides, so you can sample both port and starboard views. Solo travelers can book a lower-deck cabin with no single supplement. Exercise equipment is available. ➦ *39 cabins, 78 passengers, 4 passenger decks ⚓ Dining room, some in-room refrigerators, some in-room VCRs, bar; no TV in some rooms, no smoking.*

Spirit of Columbia. The *Columbia's* interior is inspired by the national park lodges of the American West, with muted shades of evergreen, rust, and sand. Cabins range from windowless inside units (which solo travelers can book with no single supplement), to comfortable staterooms with chairs and picture windows. The Columbia Deluxe cabin stretches the width of the vessel; just under the bridge, its row of forward-facing windows gives a captain's-eye view of the ship's progress. Exercise equipment is available on board. ➦ *39 cabins, 78 passengers, 4 passenger decks ⚓ Dining room, some refrigerators, some in-room VCRs, bar; no smoking.*

Sheltered Seas. Passengers on this daylight touring yacht cruise the Inside Passage by day and spend each night ashore at hotels at Ketchikan, Petersburg, and Juneau. The *Sheltered Seas* has all the amenities of other small ships, including full meal service, an onboard naturalist, lounges on two levels, and large viewing decks both fore and aft. This unique style of cruising is popular with Alaskan residents and with visitors who like a chance to see coastal towns when other visitors have returned to their ships for the night. ⤵ *No cabins, 70 passengers, 2 passenger decks* ☖ *Dining room, bar; no smoking.*

Glacier Bay Cruiseline

Owned in part by Tlingit people, descendants of those who settled the Glacier Bay area thousands of years ago, this cruise line has something of an inside scoop on the history, culture, and wildlife of the Great Land. Designed for soft adventure cruising, each ship has a fleet of kayaks, a floating kayak launch, and landing craft to take passengers ashore for beachcombing and hiking expeditions. Glacier Bay offers three different cruise styles: Low, Medium, and High Adventure. Low Adventure cruises focus on scenic cruising and port calls; Medium Adventure trips alternate days of cruising, landing craft excursions, and port visits with days of moderate-intensity hiking and kayaking; High Adventure voyages bypass towns altogether and take passengers on hiking and kayaking trips in remote areas each day of the cruise. Add-ons include stays at Glacier Bay Lodge, the only overnight accommodation in Glacier Bay National Park. Fleece and outdoor gear, not jackets and ties, are the norm on board, and food is hearty and home style. Glacier Bay cruises attract active, adventurous 30-to-60-year-olds, though, of course, the High Adventure cruises call for a greater level of physical fitness than the Low Adventure trips. Adventure gear and training are included in the fare, and single supplements are waived in May and September.

Tipping is discretionary, but $15 to $20 per person per day is suggested. Tips are pooled among the staff and crew at the end of the cruise.

⌂ *Glacier Bay Cruiseline, Seattle, WA 98119* ☎ *206/623–2417 or 800/451–5952* ⊕ *www.glacierbaycruiseline.com.*

THE SHIPS OF GLACIER BAY CRUISELINE

Wilderness Discoverer. Glacier Bay's largest ship has plenty of viewing space on two decks. The surroundings are simple and decorated with Alaskan art. Most cabins have picture windows, and several can accommodate three passengers. Four outside staterooms on the top deck have queen beds and large picture windows. Only the pricier cabins have TVs, but there is a communal TV and VCR in the main lounge. ⤵ *44 cabins, 96 passengers, 4 passenger decks* ☖ *Dining room, some in-room VCRs, bar; no TV in some rooms, no smoking.*

Wilderness Adventurer. This friendly ship has the casual comforts of home. The coffee's always on and you'll never need a jacket and tie for dinner. A full wrap deck makes the most of sunny days; Alaskan art and varnished wood enhances the otherwise simple interior. Some cabins are triples. A library of books and videos has a nice selection of Alaska titles. There are no TVs, but you can watch the library tapes—or your own wildlife footage—on the VCR in the main lounge. ⤵ *34 cabins, 76 passengers, 3 passenger decks* ☖ *Dining room, bar; no room TVs, no smoking.*

Wilderness Explorer. The *Wilderness Explorer* is billed as a "floating base camp" for "active adventure," and that's no exaggeration. Sea-kayak outings may last more than three hours (a 5-mi paddle). Discovery hikes cross dense thickets and climb rocky creek beds. You'll spend most of your time off the ship—a good thing, since you wouldn't want to spend much time on it. The ship is pleasant enough, but it's strictly utilitarian. Public spaces are limited and the cabins are positively tiny; all but one have bunk beds. This ship should be considered only by the serious outdoor enthusiast. ⚓ *16 cabins, 32 passengers, 3 passenger decks* ♿ *Dining room, bar; no room TVs, no smoking.*

Lindblad Expeditions

The ships of Lindblad Expeditions forgo port calls at larger, busier towns and instead spend time looking for wildlife, exploring out-of-the way inlets, and making Zodiac landings at isolated beaches. Each ship has a video-microphone, a hydrophone, and an underwater camera so passengers can listen to whale songs and watch live video of what's going on beneath the waves. In the evening, the ships' naturalists recap the day's sights and adventures over cocktails in the lounge. A video chronicler captures the whole cruise on tape. All shore excursions except flightseeing are included, and Lindblad charges one of the industry's lowest single supplements. Lindblad attracts active, adventurous, well-traveled over-forties, with quite a few singles.

Tips of $12 per person per day are suggested; these are pooled among the crew at journey's end.

📬 *Lindblad Expeditions, 720 5th Ave., New York, NY 10019* ☎ *212/765–7740 or 800/397–3348* 🌐 *www.expeditions.com.*

THE SHIPS OF LINDBLAD EXPEDITIONS **Sea Bird, Sea Lion.** These small, shallow-draft sister ships can tuck into nooks and crannies that big ships can't reach. An open-top sundeck, forward observation lounge, and viewing deck at the bow offer plenty of room to take in the scenery. These ships are comfortable, but public spaces and cabins are small. All staterooms are outside, but the lower-category cabins have portholes rather than windows. ⚓ *37 cabins, 70 passengers, 4 passenger decks* ♿ *Dining room, bar; no smoking.*

Ferry Liners

Alaska Marine Highway System

Serving 32 ports of call in Alaska as well as Bellingham, Washington, and Prince Rupert, B.C., Alaskan ferries are a scenic option for getting to and around Alaska. Ferry travel is generally slow: maximum speed is 16.5 knots, compared with 21 knots or better for the typical large cruise ship. However, two fast ferries, the *M.V. Fairweather,* which, at press time, was due to start service between Juneau and Sitka in 2004, and the *M.V. Chenega,* planned for the Cordova, Whittier, and Valdez route in 2005, will motor at twice that speed.

Ferries are a great way to take in the landscape, meet local people, and maybe see a whale or two. The ferry system also affords freedom of movement. Unlike the big cruise ships, which follow a set itinerary, ferries come and go frequently. You can get on and off whenever you wish, and stay as long as you want. Ferries serve major towns daily and call at smaller centers every two to three days, though some exotic routes, including the Cross-Gulf and Aleutian Chain ferries, see service only once a month. Stops are often made at smaller communities, such as Angoon and Tenakee Springs—just a strip of houses on stilts huddled along the shoreline. Another advantage of ferry travel is affordable fares.

The ferries are less than luxurious, but comfortable enough. Each has a glass-lined observation lounge and all but the smallest ferries have a bar. Onboard cafeterias serve hearty, inexpensive meals. Cabins are simple and serviceable, and camping in the solarium is an option. Cabins book up almost instantly for cruises during the summer season; it's essential to book in advance if you're traveling with a vehicle. A number of tour operators sell packages that include shipboard accommodations. **Knightly Tours** (✉ Box 16366, Seattle, WA 98116 ☎ 206/938–8567 or 800/426–2123 🖷 206/938–8498 ⊕ www.knightlytours.com) is one of the most established of these.

⌖ *Alaska Marine Highway System, 6858 Glacier Hwy., Juneau, AK 99801-7909* ☎ *907/465–3941 or 800/642–0066* 🖷 *907/277–4829* ⊕ *www.state.ak.us/ferry.*

British Columbia Ferries

British Columbia Ferries, or BC Ferries, take vehicles and passengers from Port Hardy, on the northern tip of Vancouver Island, to Prince Rupert, B.C., where you can pick up an Alaskan ferry to continue your journey north. The ferries have cabins and cafeterias on board, and the journey takes 15 hours in summer, somewhat longer in winter. Reservations are required for vehicles and recommended for foot passengers. BC Ferries also provide service to Vancouver Island from the British Columbia mainland.

⌖ *1112 Fort St., Victoria, BC V8V 4V2* ☎ *250/386–3431 or 888/223–3779 (in B.C. and Alberta only)* 🖷 *250/381–5452* ⊕ *www.bcferries.com.*

PARKS &
WILDERNESS
ADVENTURES

2

FODOR'S CHOICE

Dogsledding

Sea Kayaking

Whale-Watching Cruises

HIGHLY RECOMMENDED

OUTFITTERS   Alaska Discovery for Sea Kayaking

Arctic Treks for Hiking and Backpacking

Kenai Fjords Tours for Whale-Watching

Nova for River Rafting

Sourdough Outfitters for Dogsledding

St. Elias Alpine Guides for Glacier Trekking

Ultima Thule Outfitters for Skiing

By Peggy
Wayburn and
Mary Engel

Updated by
Bill Sherwonit

IN THE ALEUT LANGUAGE, the word *Alaska* means "the Great Land"—an appropriate name for the 49th of the United States, the one with more land in parks, wilderness areas, and wildlife refuges than all the other states combined. In fact, about one-third of Alaska's 375 million acres is set aside in protected public lands.

These are lands not only of prodigious scale but of prodigious beauty. Four great mountain ranges—and more than 30 lesser chains—sweep through Alaska: the St. Elias, Alaska, Brooks, and Chugach ranges. One is the highest coastal range in the world; another includes the highest point of the North American continent (Mt. McKinley, 20,320 feet); the third lies north of and roughly defines the Arctic Circle; and the fourth arcs through Alaska's most populous region. In between the mountains are rugged canyons, treeless valleys, flower-filled meadows, limpid lakes, blue-iced glaciers, waterfalls, deep-shadowed rain forests, and spacious tundras. Adding to this wealth are some 47,000 mi of spectacular tidal coastline.

Because of its relative inaccessibility and frequently demanding climate, most of this extraordinary area has remained largely undeveloped since it was acquired by the United States in 1867. (The United States paid Russia all of $7.2 million for this treasure.) First called Indian Country and then made a district, Alaska became a proper territory in 1912. However, except for military and federal reservations and a handful of homesites, the first extensive subdivision of Alaska did not occur until 1959, when the territory achieved statehood.

At that time Congress granted the new state 104 million acres to be selected out of more than 300 million acres of "vacant, unappropriated public land," which up to that time had been administered in Alaska by the Bureau of Land Management (or BLM, the federal agency that is charged with caring for the country's uncommitted public lands). Of that total, 90.6 million acres have so far been conveyed to the state. In 1970 another congressional act—the Alaska Native Claims Settlement Act (ANCSA)—gave to Alaska's Native people an additional 44 million acres to be chosen from the remaining unappropriated lands; so far, about 37.5 million acres have actually been selected and transferred to Native ownership. And in 1980, the Alaska National Interest Lands Conservation Act (ANILCA) established federal protection for about 104 million acres of outstanding Alaska land for the use and enjoyment of all the American people—and indeed of people throughout the world. Gaining passage of this legislation is considered by many to be the most extraordinary environmental achievement in the country's history.

Alaska's protected federal lands now include nearly 53 million acres of national parks (administered by the National Park Service), 73 million acres of national wildlife refuges (administered by the United States Fish and Wildlife Service), 25 wild and scenic rivers totaling nearly 2 million acres (administered by federal agencies), and 5.8 million acres of land administered by the United States Forest Service as wilderness areas. (Forest Service "multiple use" lands total nearly 17 million acres.) Alaska's remaining vacant and unappropriated public land still administered by the BLM now totals just under 86 million acres and will continue to decline as land is allotted. Along with the federally protected lands established in Alaska by the passage of ANILCA in 1980, approximately 3.2 million acres of superb lands are set aside as state parks.

Because Alaska's public lands are as varied as they are magnificent, recreational opportunities within them are likewise varied. They range from such spectator activities as wildlife viewing to rigorous participatory sports such as mountaineering (there are still many unclimbed peaks for intrepid climbers to scale) and extreme skiing. Many of these lands are only partially accessible: although you can drive to some, you will more often have to go by air—usually air taxi—or boat to the area of your choice.

Thousands of mountains in this state not only haven't been climbed but also haven't been named. The state's most-visited parks are Denali National Park and Preserve, Glacier Bay National Park and Preserve, Kenai Fjords National Park, and Chugach State Park; however, this doesn't mean a backpacker or kayaker can't have a remote wilderness experience there. Parks closer to roads, and closer to Anchorage and Fairbanks, are likely to have more visitors, but that doesn't necessarily translate into the numbers encountered in parks in the Lower 48. On the other hand, if you're after a truly remote and out-of-the-way experience, you may want to try some of the least-visited places in the state, such as Wood-Tikchik State Park, where one lonely ranger patrols 1.55 million acres, or Aniakchak National Monument and Preserve, south of Katmai, where a ranger can go days or sometimes weeks without seeing a visitor.

PLANNING A WILDERNESS ADVENTURE

Camping

Hundreds of campgrounds—both public and private—exist along Alaska's road system. But if you wish to explore Alaska's vast backcountry, you will almost certainly have to establish your own campsites (though some park units do have remote tent sites). Before heading into the backcountry, contact the appropriate management agency for any advice or restrictions. Several variables must be considered whenever camping in the backcountry, including water sources, good drainage (you don't want to end up swamped in heavy rains), protection from high winds, and the presence of any game trails (which should be avoided, particularly if bears are known to inhabit the area). Campers are also advised to practice "low-impact" camping techniques to minimize damage to the environment. For example: carry out *all* garbage; avoid camping on fragile vegetation, which can be easily trampled; if possible, camp on already established sites; never cut standing trees; wash yourself, your clothes, and your dishes at least 100 feet from water sources; bring a trowel and dig "cat-hole" latrines for human waste at least 100 feet from your camp, water sources, and trails; burn or carry out toilet paper. When traveling in trail-less areas (particularly tundra), fan out instead of walking single file, again to avoid trampling vegetation. Alaska's weather is unpredictable: anticipate delays, especially when traveling to backcountry areas by plane, and bring more food and fuel than you think you'll need.

Ecotourism

Concern for the environment has spawned a worldwide movement called ecotourism, or green tourism. Ecotourists aim to travel responsibly, taking care to conserve natural environments and show respect for local, indigenous populations. Ecotourism typically is smaller scale and involves more education than traditional tourism; often, you are led by guides who know the local natural history of plants, animals, and landscape and are familiar with local cultures. It is also slower paced and therefore allows you to have a closer connection to the areas explored. Ecotourists are encouraged to experience the landscape and its wildlife on its own terms, instead of rushing from one destination to another. As one Alaskan guide says, "Slow down, take a deep breath, feel where you are."

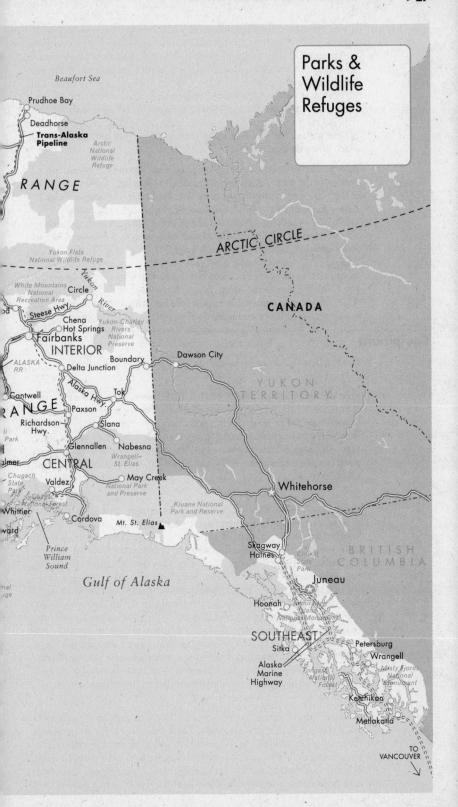

Parks & Wildlife Refuges

Beaufort Sea

Prudhoe Bay
Deadhorse
Trans-Alaska Pipeline

Arctic National Wildlife Refuge

RANGE

ARCTIC CIRCLE

Yukon Flats National Wildlife Refuge

CANADA

White Mountains National Recreation Area
Circle
Steese Hwy.
Chena Hot Springs
Fairbanks
INTERIOR
ALASKA RR
Delta Junction
Boundary
Dawson City

Yukon-Charley Rivers National Preserve

Yukon River

YUKON TERRITORY

Cantwell
RANGE
Paxson
Richardson Hwy.
Park
Slana
Glennallen
Nabesna
CENTRAL
Valdez
May Creek
Whitier
Cordova
ward

Alaska Hwy.
Tok

Wrangell–St. Elias National Park and Preserve

Kluane National Park and Reserve

Whitehorse

Chugach State Park
Chugach National Forest
Prince William Sound

Mt. St. Elias

Gulf of Alaska

BRITISH COLUMBIA

Skagway
Haines

Chilkat State Park

Juneau

Hoonah

Admiralty Island National Monument

SOUTHEAST
Sitka
Alaska Marine Highway

Petersburg
Wrangell

Tongass National Forest

Misty Fjords National Monument

Ketchikan

Metlakatla

TO VANCOUVER

If you want to enjoy the wilderness while limiting your impact on it, the Ecotourism Society, a nonprofit research and advocacy group based in Alexandria, Virginia, gives these tips: know what type of adventure you want (for example, remote wilderness backpacking or wilderness lodge with heated cabins and meals); choose a local guide or a well-trained naturalist as your guided-tour operator; learn about local customs and pertinent facts about the nature of your destination before starting your trip; get clear instructions on how to approach wildlife and how to dispose of wastes; choose low-impact transportation and guided outfits that place limits on group size.

A large and still-growing number of ecotour companies operate in all regions of the state. A state-produced *Alaska Vacation Planner* containing information on ecotourism can be obtained from the **Alaska Travel Industry Association** (✉ 2600 Cordova St., Suite 201, Anchorage 99503 ☎ 907/929–2200 or 800/862–5275 to order Alaska Vacation Planners ⊕ www.travelalaska.com). The **Alaska Wilderness Recreation and Tourism Association** (✉ 2207 Spenard Road, Suite 201, Anchorage 99503 ☎ 907/258–3171 ⊕ www.awrta) can provide information on many eco-friendly businesses and activities across the state. **Recreational Equipment Inc.** (✉ 1200 W. Northern Lights Blvd., Anchorage 99503 ☎ 907/272–4565 ⊕ www.rei.com) has a helpful brochure titled "Minimum Impact Camping" as well as a useful handout on backpacking equipment needs.

Equipment

Get the best equipment you can afford; it's a must in Alaska.

Backpacking

First decide whether to get a pack with an internal or external frame. If you choose the latter, pick one that balances the pack upright when you set it on the ground; this is a great help in the many areas of Alaska that don't have trees. Internal frames are an advantage when going through brush, which is common in Alaska. A rainproof cover for your pack is a good idea, even if it's just a heavy plastic garbage bag (bring along extras).

Camping

Because winterlike storms can occur at almost any time of year, a four-season tent is highly recommended—one that can withstand strong winds and persistent rainfall (or even snow squalls). There are few things worse than being stuck in a battered, leaky tent with a storm raging outside. Tie-down ropes and tent flies are essential items, and mosquito netting is another must. For sleeping comfort, bring a sleeping pad to add cushioning and insulation beneath your sleeping bag. Be sure your bag is warm enough for the changing conditions; even in mid-summer, nighttime temperatures may fall to the freezing mark, especially in the mountains. You should also carry a lightweight stove with fuel; if nothing else, you'll need to boil your water to protect against *Giardia* (an intestinal parasite). Firewood is often a scarce item in Alaska, and what there is may be wet. The burning of wood in many parklands is now frowned upon or prohibited in order to protect the habitat.

Day Pack

When setting out for a day hike from a base camp, it's wise to carry a pack stocked with a few essentials. These include a knife, preferably a multifunction pocketknife; a first-aid kit, including bandages and moleskin; a cup and spoon, on which you may wish to bang to alert bears; a bottle of drinking water; extra candy bars or gorp (nuts, chocolate, and raisins); a warm sweater or jacket and windproof rain gear, in case the weather suddenly changes (be sure to avoid cotton clothing; cotton does not retain body warmth when wet); waterproof matches (you can make these by coating kitchen matches with wax) and other fire starters, such as a candle or heat tab; a flare or flashlight; a topographical map; toilet paper; sunglasses; bug repellent; duct tape, for all kinds of emergencies; and a compass.

A note about compasses: the farther north you travel, the more the compass needle will be skewed upward and to the east of north by several degrees. U.S. Geological Survey maps show this difference between magnetic and true north—called magnetic declination—at the bottom. With these maps, you can use your compass accordingly; otherwise, allow for this deviation as you do your compass reading.

Terrain

Forests

Forest trails are often wet, especially in coastal lowlands, and they may be soggy or potholed—sometimes they're even blocked with beaver dams. Trails through forested lands are difficult to maintain. The ground stays wet much of the time, and brush grows back quickly after it is cut. Especially nasty is devil's club, a large, attractive plant that is armored thickly with stinging needles. Virtually all hiking country in the Southeast is part of the 17-million-acre Tongass National Forest, administered by the U.S. Forest Service. Several popular trails have also been built within Chugach National Forest and Chugach State Park in South Central Alaska. Although the Forest Service does not consider trail maintenance a top priority, it is a good source for checking the latest condition of backcountry roads and paths.

Rivers

Crossing Alaska's rivers requires care. Many are swift, glacial, silty streams that are harder to read than clear-water streams. Many flow over impermeable bottoms (either rock or permafrost), which means a good rain can raise water levels a matter of feet, not inches, in just a short time. Warm days can also dramatically increase the meltwater from glaciers. Be aware of weather changes that might affect the ease of river crossings. Look for the widest, shallowest place you can find, with many channels. This may entail traveling up- or downstream. A guide who knows the region is invaluable at such times.

A sturdy staff—your own or made from a handy branch—is useful to help you keep your balance and measure the depths of silty water. You may find it easier to uncinch your pack when crossing a swift stream; you can then shed it if you need to. Avoid wearing a long rain poncho; it can catch the water like a sail catches wind and tip you off your feet. For added stability it may help for two or more people to link arms when crossing. Hikers debate the best footwear for crossing Alaskan rivers. Some take along sneakers and wear them through the water; others take off their socks so they will remain dry and can comfort cold feet on the opposite shore. But bear in mind that Alaskan waters are probably frigid, and the bottom is usually rough; bare feet are not advised. One school even advocates wearing your boots—socks and all—and continuing your hike with wet feet.

Tundra

Tundra hiking—especially in higher alpine country—can be a great pleasure. In places, the ground is so springy you feel like you're walking on a trampoline. In the Arctic, however, where the ground is underlaid with permafrost, you will probably find the going as wet as it is in the Southeast, particularly at lower elevations. The summer sun melts the top, often a thin layer above the permafrost, leaving puddles, small lakes, and marshy spots behind. Comfortable waterproof footgear can help when traversing such wet landscapes. Tundra travel can require the skill of a ballet dancer if the ground is tufted with tussocks (mushroom-shape clumps of grass, making slippery, unstable hummocks). This can quickly tire those not used to it.

Wilderness Safety

Alaska's terrain is rugged, demanding care and strength. Its weather is often wet and cold, even in summer. Always be prepared for storms and winterlike conditions, particularly when traveling through the state's mountain ranges or along its jagged coastline, where the weather can change dramatically with little warning.

Be sure you're in good shape before venturing into backcountry—or travel with an experienced guide. Do your homework and prepare yourself for the type of landscape you'll be visiting. If you are traveling by boat along the coast, bring a tide book; some of Alaska's coastal areas have tidal swings of 30 feet–40 feet. If hiking or backpacking overland, know in advance whether you'll have to cross large glacial rivers. Pay attention to the weather, which can greatly influence the ease or difficulty of crossing those streams.

Bring the essentials you'll need to follow your chosen route and keep track of your location. Use maps (preferably 1 inch:1 mi maps published by the U.S. Geological Survey) and a compass at the very minimum. Some adventurers now carry cell phones, though they might not always be useful in remote wilderness areas. Other options for emergency use are electronic locator devices and handheld aviation radios.

When you're hiking in a national park, national forest, wildlife refuge, state park, or any other kind of protected, administered land, plan to check in and out with a ranger or person staffing the reserve. Be sure to leave plans and an itinerary with at least one trustworthy person before you go. Be as specific as you can about your destination and estimated date of return, and leave the names of people to call in case of an emergency. Be prepared for unexpected delays; Alaska's weather can play havoc with air and water transportation. One of the most common phrases used by wilderness explorers in Alaska is "weather permitting." Never "push" the weather, even if it means being late or missing connections; over the years, many people have died in aviation, boating, and overland accidents because they wanted to get home on schedule despite dangerously stormy conditions.

Hypothermia—the lowering of the body's core temperature—is an ever-present threat in Alaska's wilderness. To help avoid it, be sure to wear warm clothing (in layers) when the weather is cool and/or wet; this includes a good wind- and waterproof parka or shell, warm head- and hand gear, and waterproof or water-resistant boots. Be sure to eat regularly and drink enough liquids to stay properly hydrated.

The onset of hypothermia can be recognized by the following symptoms: shivering, accelerated heartbeat, and goose bumps; this may be followed by loss of judgment, clumsiness, loss of control over bodily functions, slurred speech, disorientation, and unconsciousness and, in the extreme, can result in death. If you notice any of these symptoms in yourself—whether from overexertion, sweating (which can act as a refrigerating agent), or improper clothing—stop, add layers of clothing, light a fire or camp stove, and warm yourself, using your sleeping bag if necessary; a cup of hot tea or another warm drink also helps. Avoid alcohol, which will only speed hypothermia and impair judgment. If your clothes are wet, change immediately. And be sure to put on a warm hat (most of the body's heat is lost through the head). If the weather is wet and/or windy, it may be necessary to set up a tent and curl up in a sleeping bag to get out of the weather. If you notice these symptoms in a traveling companion, follow the same procedure. The most important thing is to stop heat loss. If there are only two of you, stay together: a person with hypothermia should never be left alone.

Finally, Alaska's waters, even its wild rivers, often carry *Giardia,* a parasite that can cause diarrhea and sap your strength. Boil your drinking water in the Bush.

Wildlife Viewing

Alaska is one of the few places in the country where you can easily view wildlife in its natural state. It's unique among the 50 United States for its vast resource of protected wilderness and is rich in birds, animals, and fish. Alaska's wild beauty adds a powerful dimension to any wildlife-viewing experience.

Alaska's 375 million acres support more than 800 species of animals—mammals, birds, and fish. The 105 different mammals range from whales to shrews (Alaska's shrews are the smallest of North America's land mammals, weighing 1/10 ounce). The nearly 300 species of birds range from hummingbirds to bald eagles, including species found nowhere else in North America. Migrant birds come here annually from every continent and many islands to take advantage of Alaska's rich breeding and rearing grounds: its wetlands, its rivers, its shores, and its tundras. Among the 430 different kinds of fish—including five different kinds of salmon—some weigh more than 300 pounds (halibut) and others weigh often less than a pound (arctic grayling).

The most prodigious numbers of animals can be seen during periods of migration. The state is strategically positioned for creatures that migrate vast distances. Some birds, for instance, fly from the southern tip of South America to nest and rear their young on sandbars in Alaska's wild rivers. Others travel from parts of Asia to enjoy an Alaskan summer. The arctic tern is the greatest of these long-distance voyagers, coming here all the way from Antarctica. Sea mammals congregate in great numbers in the waters of Prince William Sound, the Panhandle, the Gulf of Alaska, and the Bering, Beaufort, and Chukchi seas. Tens of thousands of caribou move between Canada and Alaska across the Arctic slope. Anadromous fish by the millions swim up Alaska's rivers, returning unerringly to the place where they were born.

Bears live in virtually every part of the state, and though they are often solitary, it is not unusual to see a mother bear with cubs. In some areas the bears gather in large numbers to feed upon rich runs of salmon. Several world-class bear-viewing areas from Southeast to Southwest Alaska attract visitors. Moose abound in the wetter country of the Southeast, as well as in South Central and Interior Alaska. Caribou wander over the tundra country of the Arctic, sub-Arctic, and even South Central, although there are fewer in this part of the state. The coastal mountains of the Southeast and South Central harbor wild goats, and the mountains of the South Central, Interior, and Arctic regions are home to snow-white Dall sheep, which sometimes come down to the streams in the summer. Wolves and lynx, though not so easily seen, live in many parts of the Southeast, South Central, Interior, and Arctic regions, and if you're lucky, a wolf may dash across the road in front of you, or a smaller mammal, such as the arctic fox, may watch you when you're rafting or even when you're traveling on wheels.

Strategies for Spotting Wildlife

Know what you're looking for. Have some idea of the habitat the wildlife you seek thrives in. Season and time of day are critical. You may want to view during twilight, which during summer in certain parts of Alaska can last all night. Interestingly, winter may be the best time to look for wolves because they stand out against the snow (not true for the arctic fox, which turns white in winter). You may have only a few hours out of the day during which you can look, and in northern Alaska, there won't be any daylight at all during the winter months.

Be careful. Keep a good distance, especially with animals that can be dangerous (⇨ The Bear Facts box). Whether you're on foot or in a vehicle, don't get too close. A pair of good binoculars or a scope is well worth the extra weight. Don't get too close to or touch a fox (if you're traveling with pets, keep them leashed). The fox you admire may be carrying rabies. **Move slowly,** stop often, look, and listen. The exception is when you see a bear; you may want to let the animal know you're there. Avoid startling an animal and risking a dangerous confrontation, especially with a mother bear with cubs or a mother moose with calf.

Keep your hat on if you are in territory where arctic terns or pomarine jaegers nest. Both species are highly protective of their nests and young, and they are skillful dive-bombers. Occasionally, they connect with human heads, and the results can be painful.

Be prepared to wait; patience often pays off. And if you're an enthusiastic birder or animal watcher, **be prepared to hike over some rough terrain**—Alaska is full of it—to reach the best viewing vantage. **Respect and protect** both the animal you're watching and its habitat. Don't chase or harass the animals. The willful act of harassing an animal is punishable in Alaska by a $1,000 fine. This includes flushing birds from their nests and purposely frightening animals with loud noises.

Don't disturb or surprise the animals, which also applies to birds' eggs, the young, the nests, and such habitats as beaver dams. It's best to let the animal discover your presence quietly, if at all, by keeping still or moving slowly (except when viewing bears or moose). If the animal should be disturbed, limit your viewing time and leave as quietly as possible. **Don't use a tape recorder** to call a bird or to attract other animals if you're in bear country, as you might call an angry bear. And **don't feed the animals,** as any creature that comes to depend on humans for food almost always comes to a sorry end. Both state and federal laws prohibit the feeding of wild animals.

Best Viewing

Even those traveling by car in Alaska have abundant opportunity to spot wildlife. For those traveling by boat, the **Alaska Marine Highway**—the route plied by Alaska's state ferries—passes through waters rich with fish, sea mammals, and birds. Throughout the Southeast, ferries often provide sightings of whales and sea otters and virtually always of bald eagles. In **Kenai Fjords National Park,** tour boats enable you to view sea mammals and seabirds. Smaller boats and touring vessels are found in such places as **Glacier Bay National Park and Preserve,** an especially good place to spot humpback whales, puffins, seals, shorebirds, and perhaps a black or brown bear. **Denali National Park and Preserve** is known worldwide for its wildlife; you are likely to see grizzlies, moose, Dall sheep, caribou, foxes, golden eagles, and perhaps even wolves. The

THE BEAR FACTS

ALASKA IS SOMETIMES CALLED "bear country," and for good reason. It is the only one of the nation's 50 states to be inhabited by all three North American ursine species: the polar bear, black bear, and brown bear (also known as grizzly). The statewide population of each species thrives, thanks largely to Alaska's abundance of wild, remote, and undeveloped regions.

You'll find few places in Alaska where bears don't inhabit the landscape. Even Anchorage, with its urban developments and large human population, is visited by black and brown bears. Wherever you venture in Alaska, keep in mind these tips for travel in bear country:

Avoid sudden encounters. Whenever possible, travel in open country, during daylight hours, and in groups. Make noise—talking or singing is preferable to carrying "bear bells"—and leave your dog at home. Most attacks occur when a bear is surprised at close quarters or feels threatened.

Stay alert. Look for signs of bears, such as fresh tracks, scat, matted vegetation, or partially consumed salmon.

Choose your tent site carefully. Pitch the tent away from trails, streams with spawning salmon, and berry patches. Avoid areas that have a rotten smell or where scavengers have gathered; these may indicate the presence of a nearby bear cache, and bears aggressively defend their food supplies.

Keep food away from campsites. Cook meals at least 100 feet from tents, and store food and other odorous items away from campsites. Hang them in trees where possible, or store your food in bear-resistant food containers. Avoid strong-smelling foods, and clean up after cooking and eating. Store garbage in airtight containers or burn it, and pack up the remains.

If you encounter a bear:

Identify yourself. Talk to the bear, to identify yourself as a human. Don't yell. And don't run. Running will trigger a bear's predatory instincts, and a bear can easily outrun you. Back away slowly, and give the bear an escape route. Don't ever get between a mother and her cubs.

Bigger is better. Bears are less likely to attack a larger target. Therefore, increase your apparent size. Raise your arms above your head to appear larger and wave them slowly, to better identify yourself as a human. With two or more people, it helps to stand side by side. In a forested area it may be appropriate to climb a tree, but remember that black bears and young grizzlies are agile tree climbers.

As a last resort, play dead. If a bear charges and makes contact with you, fall to the ground, lie flat on your stomach or curl into a ball, hands behind your neck, and remain passive. If you are wearing a pack, leave it on. Once a bear no longer feels threatened, it will usually end its attack. Wait for the bear to leave before you move. The exception to this rule is when a bear displays predatory behavior. Instead of simply charging, a bear hunting for prey will show intense interest while approaching at a walk or run and it may circle, as if stalking you. But remember that such circumstances are exceedingly rare and most often involve black bears, which are much smaller and less aggressive than grizzlies.

2

Alaska Chilkat Bald Eagle Preserve hosts the world's largest gathering of bald eagles each fall and winter.

BEARS   You can't be absolutely sure you'll spot a grizzly bear in **Denali National Park** (⌂ Box 9, Denali National Park 99755 ☎ 907/683–2294 ⊕ www. nps.gov/dena), but your chances are better than 50-50 that you'll see grizzlies digging in the tundra or eating berries. Sometimes females even nurse their cubs within sight of the park road. Talk with the staff at the visitor center near the park entrance when you arrive.

Katmai National Park (⌂ Box 7, King Salmon 99613 ☎ 907/246–3305 ⊕ www.nps.gov/katm), on the Alaska Peninsula, has an abundance of bears—on average more than one brown bear per square mile, among the highest densities of any region in North America. In July, when the salmon are running up Brooks River, bears concentrate around Brooks River Falls, resulting in a great view of these animals as they fish, and the spectacle of hundreds of salmon leaping the falls.

Kodiak National Wildlife Refuge (✉ 1390 Buskin Rd., Kodiak 99615 ☎ 907/487–2600 ⊕ www.r7.fws.gov), on Kodiak Island, is an excellent place to see brown bears, particularly along salmon-spawning streams.

The **McNeil River State Game Sanctuary,** on the Alaska Peninsula, hosts the world's largest gathering of brown bears—as many as 70 have been counted at one time at McNeil Falls—and thus affords unsurpassed photographic opportunities. Peak season, when the local salmon are running, is early June through mid-August. Much-sought-after reservations are available by a lottery conducted in March by the **Alaska Department of Fish and Game** (✉ 333 Raspberry Rd., Anchorage 99518 ☎ 907/267–2182 ⊕ www.wc.adfg.state.ak.us/mcneil).

At **Pack Creek,** on Admiralty Island, you'll see brown bears (the coastal equivalents of grizzlies) fishing for spawning salmon—pink, chum, and silver. To get here, you can fly (air charter) or take a boat from Juneau. If you time your visit to coincide with the salmon runs in July and August, you will almost surely see bald eagles and flocks of gulls, too. Permits are required to visit during the peak bear-viewing period; contact **Admiralty Island National Monument** (✉ 8465 Old Dairy Rd., Juneau 99801 ☎ 907/586–8800 ⊕ www.fs.fed.us/r10/tongass/districts/admiralty/packweb/packhome.html).

The **Silver Salmon Creek Lodge** (⌂ Box 3234, Soldotna 99669 ☎ 888/872–5666 ⊕ www.silversalmoncreek.com) conducts a bear-viewing program along the shores of western Cook Inlet, near Lake Clark National Park, with lodging, meals, and guide services for both bear viewing and sportfishing.

BIRDS   If you come on your own, try the following sure and easily accessed bets for bird spotting. In **Anchorage,** walk around Potter Marsh or Westchester Lagoon or along the Coastal Trail for shorebirds, waterfowl, and the occasional bald eagle. Songbird enthusiasts are likely to see many species in town or neighboring Chugach State Park. The **Anchorage Audubon Society** (☎ 907/338–2473) has a bird-report recording. In **Juneau,** visit the Mendenhall Wetlands State Game Refuge, next to the airport, for ducks, geese, and swans (there are trails and interpretive signs). In **Fairbanks,** head for the Creamer's Field Migratory Waterfowl Refuge on College Road. Here, if you're lucky, you might see sandhill cranes in summer and spectacular shows of ducks and geese in spring.

Great crowds of bald eagles visit the Chilkat River, near **Haines** in Southeast Alaska, each November and December. In the summer, rafting on almost any Alaskan river brings the near certainty of sighting nesting shorebirds, arctic terns, and merganser mothers trailed by chicks. Approximately 200 species of birds have been sighted on the **Pribilof Islands,** but you will almost certainly need to be part of a guided tour to get there.

CARIBOU The migrations of caribou across Alaska's Arctic regions are wonderful to watch, but they are not always easy to time because of annual variations in weather and routes that the herds follow. The U.S. Fish and Wildlife Service and Alaska Department of Fish and Game will have the best guess as to where you should be and when. Or you can settle for seeing a few caribou in places such as Denali National Park.

MARINE At **Round Island,** outside Dillingham in the Southwest, bull walruses by
ANIMALS the thousands haul out during the summer. Part of the Walrus Islands State Game Sanctuary, Round Island can be visited by permit only. For details, contact the **Alaska Department of Fish and Game** (⌖ Box 1030, Dillingham 99576 ☎ 907/842–2334 ⊕ www.state.ak.us/adfg/wildlife/region2/refuge2/rnd-isl.htm). Access is by floatplane or, more commonly, by boat. Expect rain, winds, and the possibility of being weathered in. Rubber boots are essential, as are a four-season tent, high-quality rain gear, and plenty of food.

It's easier, but still expensive, to visit the remote **Pribilof Islands**—where about 80% of the world's northern fur seals and 200 species of birds can be seen—but you may also encounter fog and Bering Sea storms. Tours to the Pribilofs leave from Anchorage. Contact the **Alaska Maritime National Wildlife Refuge** (✉ 2355 Kachemak Bay Dr., Suite 101, Homer 99603-8021 ☎ 907/235–6546 or 907/235–6961 ⊕ www.r7fws.gov) for information about wildlife-viewing.

WILDERNESS ADVENTURES

Vacationing in Alaska can be a lot more than viewing glaciers. An increasing number of trips and tours now make it possible for you to spend a week or two (or more) learning—and performing—feats from horsepacking within sight of Mt. McKinley to mushing through some of the state's most challenging landscapes, including Gates of the Arctic National Park, far above the Arctic Circle. Below you'll find some recommended trips, questions to consider, and suggestions to help you choose the right program. When comparing offerings, be sure to consider the following.

To reserve a spot, most operators require you to put down a deposit by a particular day and then pay the rest sometime before the starting date. In most cases, if you cancel your reservation, you get at least a partial refund, but policies vary widely. **Find out how far in advance you must cancel to get a full refund,** and ask whether any allowances are made for cancellations due to medical emergencies. If cancellation insurance is available, you may want to take it. You'll receive a full refund regardless of why you don't show up as planned.

Taxes are generally not included in the quoted price, and they can add substantially to the cost of your trip. Depending on the program, you should also **ask about gratuities**—inquire about which members of the tour personnel customarily get tipped and what the average rate is.

Dogsledding

Fodor'sChoice "Hike!" commands a musher as he releases a brake. They don't call it
★ "mushing" for nothing. The word is from the French *moucher,* which means "to go fast." And the dogs do. On command, a team of surprisingly small but amazingly strong huskies charges off, howling and yowling excitedly. Of all the wild sporting adventures out there, dogsledding

may be the wildest—not only because it's exotic but also because you're literally out in the wilds with pack animals, just like a polar explorer.

Dogsledding is not for everyone. For one thing, you have to like the cold. You also have to like roughing it. Even the nicest accommodations are only a step or two removed from camping, and with camping out comes cooking out. Most important, you have to like dogs—a lot. Contrary to the romantic image you may have of sled dogs, they're not all cuddly, clean Siberian huskies. They're often mutts—that is, mixed-breed Alaskan huskies—and often not particularly well groomed. Most mushers, including the people who run dogsled tours, take very good care of their dogs, but the dogs are working dogs, not show dogs or pets.

Here are some facts to consider when choosing your trip: on some mushing trips, participants travel by cross-country skiing or snowshoeing, rather than actually mushing, for at least part of the trip; some introduction to these sports is usually included in your orientation. If you're not interested in skiing or snowshoeing, make sure you'll be given a sled. It's always smart to **get a good idea of how strenuous the outfitter's pace is.** If you're expecting a relaxing vacation, make sure you **don't pick an outfitter who'll have you doing everything** from hitching up the dogs to pitching tents.

Outfitters

Chugach Express Dog Sled Tours. Year-round mushing tours pass through a valley surrounded by the Chugach Mountains, about an hour's drive south of Anchorage. The one- and two-hour tours include a visit to the kennel of the owner, a former Iditarod musher, and you can learn about dog care, feeding, breeding, and equipment. You can also drive the team. ✎ *Box 1396, Girdwood 99587* ☎ *907/783-2266.*

Redington Sled Dog Rides. Raymie Redington, son of the Iditarod Trail Sled Dog Race's founding father, Joe Redington Sr., leads half-hour to overnight mushing trips along the historic Iditarod Trail in the Susitna Valley north of Anchorage. ✉ *Mile 12.5, Knik Rd.* ✎ *Box 877653, Wasilla 99687* ☎ *907/376-6730.*

★ **Sourdough Outfitters.** Seven- to 11-day sledding expeditions are organized from January through April within the Gates of the Arctic National Park and the Arctic National Wildlife Refuge, two of the last great wilderness areas in the world. Sourdough Outfitters also leads day trips in and around the community of Bettles, where the outfit is based. The owners provide all camping gear plus special boots, heavy-hooded parkas, insulated windproof mittens, and snowshoes. ✎ *Box 26066, Bettles Field 99726* ☎ *907/692-5252* 🖨 *907/692-5557* ⊕ *www.sourdoughoutfitters. com.*

Glacier Trekking

An estimated 100,000 glaciers flow out of Alaska's mountains, covering 29,000 square mi—or 5% of the state. These slow-moving "rivers of ice" concentrate in the Alaska Range, Wrangell Mountains, and the state's major coastal mountain chains: the Chugach, St. Elias, Coast, and Kenai ranges. Alaska's largest glacier, the Bering, covers 2,250 square mi—twice the size of Rhode Island.

Glaciers are formed where annual snowfall exceeds melting. As it accumulates, snow is buried and recrystallized. Eventually it becomes compacted into dense, airless ice, sometimes thousands of feet thick. Where glaciers reach tidewater, as at Glacier Bay and Kenai Fjords National Parks, they may calve immense icebergs.

Many glaciers can be approached from Alaska's road system or coastal waters—but don't try to walk on them, or even get too close, without the proper gear and training. Large chunks of ice sometimes fall from a glacier's snout with no forewarning; unwitting sightseers have been killed by such ice blocks when standing too close. Unprepared trekkers have also slipped and fallen to their deaths in the glacier's crevasses. If you're an adventurous backcountry traveler, glaciers present icy avenues into the remote corners of several premier mountain wilderness areas, including Denali, Wrangell–St. Elias, and Kenai Fjords national parks and Chugach and Kachemak Bay state parks.

Glacier travel, however, should be attempted only after you've been properly trained. Glacier terrain includes a mix of ice, rock debris, and often-deep surface snow; sometimes frigid pools of meltwater collect on the surface or icy rivulets flow across the glacier. Most dangerous are glacier crevasses. Sometimes hidden by snow, especially in spring and early summer (a popular time for glacier trekking), these cracks in the ice may present life-threatening traps for unwary travelers. Though some are only inches wide, others may be several yards across and hundreds of feet deep. If you haven't been taught proper glacial travel and crevasse-rescue techniques, **hire a backcountry guide** to provide the necessary gear and expertise.

The staffs of parks and other public lands can provide a list of guides who operate on their lands. When contacting guides, **determine how well they know the mountains and glaciers you wish to explore.** Explain your own goals and abilities and be sure to **ask what sort of training you'll receive** as well as the length of trips and the amount of gear you'll be required to carry, especially for longer treks. Guides normally provide group gear, such as tents and tarps, and specialized glacier-travel equipment, such as ice axes, helmets, ropes, and crampons. However, they will expect you to provide your own personal equipment. In some cases, guides will rent gear such as sleeping bags or packs. On day hikes, a guide may bring along lunch or snack food. On longer expeditions, because of weight considerations, the food is more likely to be lightweight, such as freeze-dried meals.

Because you'll be in the mountains, always be prepared for cool, wet weather, even in summer. April through June are considered the prime months for glacial travel; but even then, conditions can be wintry in the mountains, with subfreezing temperatures and occasional blizzards. Beyond June, glacial crevasses tend to "open up" as snow melts, making travel more difficult and dangerous; plus the weather is often stormier in July and August. Most guides plan their trips so that hikers and backpackers will have time to relax and enjoy the landscape, but as with hiking and ski trips, it's a good idea to **ask about the travel schedule and number of miles to be covered daily.**

Outfitters

Alaska Mountaineering School and Alaska-Denali Guiding. Whether it's on mountaineering expeditions to 20,320-foot Mt. McKinley or less extreme treks into the Alaska Range or other mountains, this company takes wilderness explorers on glacier treks through pristine backcountry. You can also learn the region's natural and human history while exploring rugged mountain landscapes. The mountaineering school can provide training before you go. ✆ *Box 566, Talkeetna 99676* ☎ *907/733–1016* 🖷 *907/733–1362* ⊕ *www.climbalaska.org.*

★ **St. Elias Alpine Guides.** Based in the town of McCarthy, within Wrangell–St. Elias National Park, St. Elias Alpine Guides conducts day hikes to nearby glaciers and also leads extended glacier treks into the wild back-country of this "mountain kingdom." ⬠ *Box 111241, Anchorage 99511* ☏ *907/345–9048, 888/933–5427 year-round, 907/554–4445 summer only* ⬠ *907/345–9049* ⬢ *www.steliasguides.com.*

Ultima Thule Outfitters. Based at a fly-in-only lodge on the Chitina River within Wrangell–St. Elias National Park, Ultima Thule leads guided ac-tivities in the surrounding mountains, including glacier treks, moun-taineering, and Nordic and telemark skiing. Other adventures include mushing, wildlife viewing, and rafting. A longtime presence in the St. Elias Mountains, Ultima Thule is known as much for its family-style hospitality as its scenic backcountry adventures. ⬠ *Box 109, Chitina 99566* ☏ *907/258–0636* ⬠ *907/278–2292* ⬢ *www.ultimathulelodge. com.*

Hiking & Backpacking

From Southeast coastal rain forest to Interior mountain meadows with spectacular views of Mt. McKinley and alpine tundra in the high Arc-tic, Alaska presents some of the continent's finest landscape for wilder-ness hiking and backpacking. Or, if remote backcountry is not your preference, it's possible to travel well-maintained and well-marked trails on the edges of Alaska's largest city and still get a taste of the wild.

Chugach State Park, along Anchorage's eastern edge, has dozens of trails, many of them suited for "frontcountry" explorers. And though it is best known for its "trail-less wilderness," Denali National Park has several easy-to-hike trails near the park entrance. These, however, are excep-tions to the rule. Most of Alaska remains pristine wilderness, with few or no trails. In such areas it's best to **be an experienced backcountry trav-eler** who understands the dangers and challenges of trail-less wilderness terrain: how to behave in bear country, how to navigate using map and compass techniques, and how to cross glacial streams.

For those without such experience, **hire a backcountry guide** to provide the necessary expertise. The staffs of refuges, forests, and parks can pro-vide a list of outfitters and guides who operate on their lands. When contacting guides, determine how well they know the place you wish to explore. Explain your own goals and abilities and be sure to **ask about the difficulty of the terrain** you'll be traveling as well as the amount of gear you'll be required to carry. Guides normally provide group gear, such as tents and tarps, and expect you to **provide your own personal equip-ment.** In some cases, guides can rent you gear such as sleeping bags or packs. On day hikes, a guide may bring along lunch or snack food. On longer expeditions, because of weight considerations, the food is more likely to be lightweight, such as freeze-dried meals. It's best to go with a small group to minimize the impact on the landscape and wildlife—fewer than 10 people, with 6 or fewer being ideal. The weather varies greatly throughout the state, but hikers and backpackers should always be prepared for cool, wet weather, even in midsummer. The best time to visit also varies greatly. In most parts of the state, June through Au-gust are considered the prime months for summer backcountry trips. July is usually the warmest month but also the buggiest. Most guides plan their trips so that you'll have time to relax and enjoy the landscape or look for wildlife, but it's a good idea to **ask about the travel schedule and number of miles to be covered daily.**

Outfitters

Alaska Mountaineering School and Alaska-Denali Guiding. Though perhaps best known for its mountaineering expeditions on Mt. McKinley, this company also leads custom-designed backcountry expeditions in the Alaska Range and other mountain chains around the state. The company emphasizes a "holistic" approach to its trips. You have a chance to learn the area's natural and human history while exploring the wild landscape and watching wildlife. ✍ *Box 566, Talkeetna 99676* ☎ *907/733–1016* 🖷 *907/733–1362* ⊕ *www.climbalaska.org.*

Alaska Nature Tours and Backcountry Outfitters. This company in Southeast Alaska leads hiking trips into the Alaska Chilkat Bald Eagle Preserve near Haines from May through September, with an emphasis on the area's natural history. ✍ *Box 491, Haines 99827* ☎ *907/766–2876* 🖷 *907/766–2844* ⊕ *www.kcd.com/aknature.*

★ **Arctic Treks.** Wilderness hiking and backpacking trips, sometimes combined with river trips, explore areas throughout the Arctic region's Brooks Range, including two of North America's most remote and ruggedly beautiful wildlands: Gates of the Arctic National Park and the Arctic National Wildlife Refuge. ✍ *Box 73452, Fairbanks 99707* ☎ *907/455–6502* 🖷 *907/455–6522* ⊕ *www.arctictreksadventures. com.*

St. Elias Alpine Guides. For more than two decades, this outfitter has been taking people into a part of Alaska that some people call North America's mountain kingdom: the St. Elias and Wrangell mountain ranges. Based in the town of McCarthy, within Wrangell–St. Elias National Park, St. Elias Alpine Guides leads a full spectrum of day activities, including ghost-town tours of the Kennicott Mine, glacier walks, mountain hikes, and nature tours. The company also guides mountain ascents and extended backpacking expeditions. ✍ *Box 111241, Anchorage 99511* ☎ *907/345–9048, 888/933–5427 year-round, 907/554–4445 summer only* 🖷 *907/345–9049* ⊕ *www.steliasguides.com.*

Horsepacking

There are no traffic jams and no overcrowded campgrounds on horsepacking vacations. The farther into the wilderness you go, the more untouched and spectacular the landscape. You can also cover a lot more ground with less effort than you can while backpacking. All outfitters who operate on federal lands are required to have a permit.

To minimize a horsepacking group's impact on the environment, most are limited to 12 riders. Some go down to just three or four. Most outfits post at least two wranglers for 12 guests, and some bring along another person who serves as cook and/or assistant wrangler.

It's a good idea to **find out how much time is spent in the saddle** each day and how difficult the riding is. Six hours is a long day in the saddle, and although some outfitters schedule that much, most keep the riding time to about four hours. Most trips move at a walk, but some trot, lope, and even gallop. As with the other guided adventures, special expertise is not required for horsepacking.

On trips into the wilderness, expect the food to be generally straightforward cowboy fare, cooked over a campfire or cookstove. Although a cook goes along on some trips, guides often pull double duty in the kitchen, and often a little help from group members is willingly accepted. If you have any dietary restrictions, make arrangements beforehand. For lodging, don't allow yourself to be surprised: **find out what the rooms are like** if you're going to be staying in motels or cabins, and if the trip involves camping, **ask about the campsites** and about shower and latrine arrangements.

Castle Mountain Outfitters. Based in the Matanuska Valley below towering mountains, this outfitter conducts a variety of trips ranging from guided hour-long horseback rides to one-week horsepacking expeditions. 🖃 *Box 115, Chickaloon 99674* ☎ *907/745–6427* 🖷 *907/745–6428* 🌐 *www.cmoride.com.*

North Country Outfitters. Horsepacking trips of varying lengths are organized in the community of Tok, near the Alaska-Canada border, and run through parts of South Central and Interior Alaska. 🖃 *Box 453, Tok 99780* ☎ *907/883–5506* 🖷 *907/883–5500.*

River Rafting

From the Southeast Panhandle to the far reaches of the Arctic, Alaska is blessed with an abundance of wild, pristine rivers. The federal government has officially designated more than two dozen of Alaskan streams as "wild and scenic rivers," but hundreds more would easily qualify for that description. Some meander gently through forests or tundra. Others, fed by glacier runoff, rush wildly through mountains and canyons.

Because so much of Alaska is roadless wilderness, rivers often serve as the best avenues to explore the landscape and view wildlife. This is especially true in several of Alaska's premier parklands and refuges. Here, as elsewhere, rivers are ranked according to their degrees of difficulty. Class I rivers are considered to be "easy" floats with minimal rapids; at the other extreme, Class VI rivers are extremely dangerous to nearly impossible to navigate. Generally only very experienced river runners should attempt anything above Class II on their own. Also be aware that river conditions change considerably from season to season and sometimes day to day. Always check ahead to determine a river's current condition. Do-it-yourselfers would be wise to consult two books on Alaska's rivers: *Fast & Cold: A Guide to Alaska Whitewater* (Skyhouse), by Andrew Embick (though intended primarily for white-water kayakers, it has good information for rafters as well), and *The Alaska River Guide: Canoeing, Kayaking, and Rafting in the Last Frontier* (Alaska Northwest Books), by Karen Jettmar.

Fortunately you don't have to be an expert river runner to explore many of Alaska's premier waterways. Experienced rafting companies operate throughout the state. Some outfits emphasize extended wilderness trips and natural-history observations, whereas others specialize in thrilling one-day (or shorter) floats through Class III and IV white water that will get your adrenaline pumping. And some combine a little of both.

As with other guided activities, it always pays to do your homework. If you'll be traveling in a park or refuge, request a list of commercial operators from park staff. It is always essential to **find out how long a guide has been operating** on the river of your choice. **Ask about the dangers,** and the river's degree of difficulty. Be certain that the guide gives you a safety talk before going on the water. It's important to know what you should do if you do get flipped out of the raft or if the boat overturns. Also find out what gear and clothing are required. Ask if you'll be paddling or simply riding as a passenger. Reputable rafting companies will discuss all of this, but it never hurts to ask.

Alaska Discovery. This outfitter leads 10- to 12-day trips down two of North America's wildest rivers, the Tatshenshini and Alsek. The river trips begin in Canada and end in one of Alaska's premier parklands, Glacier Bay, as rafters float between peaks nearly 3 mi high and through valleys inhabited by grizzlies, moose, and sometimes wolves. The company also does combined rafting and hiking trips in the Arctic National Wildlife Refuge and on the Noatak River, which runs through Gates of the Arctic National Park. ⊠ *5310 Glacier Hwy., Juneau 99801* ☎ *907/ 780–6226 or 800/586–1911* 🖷 *907/780–4220* ⊕ *www.akdiscovery. com.*

Denali Raft Adventures. River trips are conducted on the glacially fed, whitewater Nenana River, which skirts the eastern boundary of Denali National Park. Trips vary from two-hour Class I–II scenic floats to all-day white-water canyon trips with big rapids and overnight outings. The two-hour scenic and canyon trips can also be combined. ⌂ *Drawer 190 DRA, Denali Park 99755* ☎ *907/683–2234 or 888/ 683–2234* 🖷 *907/683–1281* ⊕ *www.deniliraft.com.*

★ **Nova.** This outfitter has been rafting Alaska's rivers since 1975. For most of that time, the company has specialized in full-, part-, or multiday whitewater trips down the Matanuska, Chickaloon, and Talkeetna rivers in South Central Alaska. Over the past decade, Nova has expanded its reach and now also leads float trips in Wrangell–St. Elias National Park and on the Kenai Peninsula's Six-Mile River. White-water ratings range from Class I to Class V. ⊠ *Mile 76, Glenn Hwy.* ⌂ *Box 1129, Chickaloon 99674* ☎ *907/745–5753 or 800/746–5753* 🖷 *907/745–5754* ⊕ *www.novalaska.com.*

Wilderness Birding Adventures. The owners are both experienced river runners and expert birders. Among their trips is a rafting, hiking, and birding expedition through one of the world's last great wilderness areas, the Arctic National Wildlife Refuge. ⌂ *5515 Wild Mountain Rd., Eagle River 99577* ☎🖷 *907/694–7442* ⊕ *www.wildernessbirding.com.*

Sea Kayaking

Fodor'sChoice Sea kayaking can be as thrilling or as peaceful as you make it. More
★ stable than a white-water kayak and more comfortable than a canoe, a sea kayak—even one loaded with a week's worth of gear—is maneuverable enough to poke into hidden crevices, explore side bays, and beach on deserted spits of sand.

Anyone who doesn't mind getting a little wet and has an average degree of fitness can be a sea kayaker. The basic stroke is performed in a circular motion with a double-bladed paddle: you pull one blade through the water while pushing forward with the other through the air. Most people pick it up with a minimal amount of instruction. Don't assume, though, that if you've done 10 minutes without tipping over you'll be adequately prepared to circumnavigate Glacier Bay National Park. There's a lot to learn, and until you know your way around tides, currents, and nautical charts, you should go with an experienced guide who also knows what and how to pack and where to pitch a tent. A reputable outfitter can supply such a guide.

In choosing an outfitter, you should be concerned primarily with safety. An outfitter should be equipped with both the proper technical and first-aid gear and should know what to do with it. Question every outfitter carefully so that you know what you're getting into.

It is essential to **find out how long the guides have been leading trips** and how long they have been leading in the area where you want to go. Generally it is best to have a guide who knows an area very well. A qualified guide's first visit to an area can also be exciting, but *only if* that guide has had extensive experience elsewhere.

It is important for you to **honestly evaluate your own tolerance for cold, dampness, and high winds.** Nothing can ruin a trip faster than pervasive discomfort.

Always **ask whether the outfitter stocks a variety of boats,** so you can experiment until you find the kayak that best fits your weight, strength, ability, and paddling style.

Outfitters

★ **Alaska Discovery.** One of Alaska's oldest outfitters, this company has been running low-impact, nature-oriented adventure trips since 1972. Experienced guides know Southeast Alaska intimately, and they emphasize both sea-kayaking skills and safety in their instruction. Destinations include Glacier Bay, Icy Bay, Point Adolphus (an excellent spot for whale-watching), Admiralty Island (with bear viewing at Pack Creek), and Granite Fjord. ✉ *5310 Glacier Hwy., Juneau 99801* ☎ *907/780–6226 or 800/586–1911* 🖶 *907/780–4220* ⊕ *www.akdiscovery.com.*

Spirit Walker Expeditions, Inc. This veteran Southeast company offers guided wilderness sea-kayaking trips that combine a mix of scenery, wildlife, solitude, and paddling within the Inside Passage. Guides prepare meals, offer instruction, and provide all needed paddling gear. Beginners are welcome. ✇ *Box 240, Gustavus 99826* ☎ *907/697–2266 or 800/529–2537* 🖶 *907/697–2701* ⊕ *www.seakayakalaska.com.*

Sunny Cove Sea Kayaking Company. Extended trips in and around Kenai Fjords National Park in South Central Alaska include five nights of camping at Northwestern Fjord or three nights in Aialik Bay; at both locales kayakers can paddle among icebergs, seals, and seabirds as tidewater glaciers calve in the distance. Day and overnight trips navigate within Resurrection Bay, near Seward. Tours include kayaking equipment and instruction, meals, and lots of chances to see wildlife. Combination tours with Kenai Fjords Cruises are also offered. ✇ *Box 3332, Seward 99664* ☎ *907/224–8810, 800/770–9119 reservations* 🖶 *907/224–881* ⊕ *www. sunnycove.com.*

Skiing

It may not have the reputation of several other western states, but Alaska offers plenty of skiing terrain for both Nordic skiers and downhill racers. Three of Alaska's largest cities—Anchorage, Fairbanks, and Juneau—have nearby alpine ski areas, complete with equipment rentals, ski schools, and other amenities. Many of Alaska's towns, both large and small, have regularly maintained trails for cross-country skiers. Anchorage's trail system is considered among the nation's finest and has hosted world-class races.

For those who are more ambitious, Alaska's wilderness areas present unlimited opportunities—and lots of challenges. Unless you are knowledgeable in winter backcountry travel, camping techniques, and avalanche dangers, the best strategy is to **hire a guide when exploring Alaska's backcountry on skis.** Given the extremes of Alaska's winters, your primary concern should be safety: **be sure your guide has had avalanche-awareness and winter-survival training.** Conditions can change quickly, especially in mountainous areas, and what began as an easy cross-country ski trip can suddenly become a survival saga if you're not prepared for the challenges of an Alaska winter.

As with other backcountry activities, **verify that your guide is familiar with the region you'll be visiting.** Know what specialized equipment is necessary for the conditions you'll face and be clear about your own limitations. If you're a novice, you don't want to start out on difficult terrain or travel long distances without proper preparation. When you are prepared, the rewards of backcountry skiing are well worth the hardships and challenges: immense solitude and quiet, sparkling skies; fantastic landscapes; and, if you're lucky, a display of northern lights or perhaps the distant howling of wolves.

Outfitters

Alaska Mountaineering School and Alaska-Denali Guiding. Custom cross-country ski trips of varying lengths and degrees of difficulty can be arranged, primarily through Denali national and state parks, with an emphasis on natural history as well as backcountry exploration and the challenges of winter travel. ✑ Box 566, Talkeetna 99676 ☎ 907/733–1016 🖷 907/733–1362 ⊕ www.climbalaska.org.

Alaska Nature Tours and Backcountry Outfitters. This company in Southeast Alaska rents ski gear and, from December through March, leads Nordic ski trips into the Alaska Chilkat Bald Eagle Preserve near Haines. If you visit in early winter, you are likely to see many of the bald eagles that visit the preserve annually. ✑ Box 491, Haines 99827 ☎ 907/766–2876 🖷 907/766–2844 ⊕ www.kcd.com/aknature.

★ **Ultima Thule Outfitters.** Based at a fly-in-only lodge on the Chitina River within Wrangell–St. Elias National Park, Ultima Thule leads guided activities in the surrounding mountains, including alpine treks and Nordic and telemark skiing. Other adventures include mushing, wildlife viewing, rafting, and mountain climbing. A longtime presence in the St. Elias Mountains, Ultima Thule is known as much for its family-style hospitality as its scenic backcountry adventures. ✑ Box 109, Chitina 99566 ☎ 907/258–0636 🖷 907/278–2292 ⊕ www.ultimathulelodge.com.

Sportfishing

Filled with hundreds of species of fish, including many highly prized catches, Alaska's more than 3 million lakes, innumerable streams, and thousands of miles of coastal waters are an angler's paradise. All five species of Pacific salmon (king, silver, sockeye, pink, and chum) spawn in Alaska's waters, alongside ample quantities of rainbow trout, steelhead, arctic char, Dolly Varden char, arctic grayling, northern pike, and halibut.

A few fish reach huge proportions: for example, a world-record king salmon weighing 97¼ pounds was caught in Alaska's Kenai River, and halibut exceeding 300—and occasionally 400—pounds are annually caught in Pacific Ocean waters. But some anglers will tell you that bigger isn't necessarily better. Sockeye, among the smallest salmon, are considered by many to be both the best tasting and best fighting, pound for pound, of any fish. And though the arctic grayling commonly weighs a pound or less, it is a favorite among fly fishermen.

Roadside fishing for salmon, trout, char, and grayling is possible in South Central and Interior Alaska. In fact, Alaska's best-known salmon stream, the Kenai River, is road accessible. But in most of the state, prime fishing waters can be reached only by boat or air. Not surprisingly, hundreds of fishing charters and dozens of sportfishing lodges operate statewide, attracting anglers from around the world. Southwest Alaska, in particular, is known for its fishing, but many of its prime spots are remote and expensive to reach.

You should be aware that sportfishing regulations vary widely from area to area. Licenses are required for both fresh- and saltwater fishing. To learn more about regulations, contact the **Alaska Department of Fish and Game** (⌂ Box 25526, Juneau 99802-5526 ☎ 907/465–4180 sportfishing seasons and regulations, 907/465–2376 licenses ⊕ www.state.ak.us).

Information on local fishing guides and/or sportfishing lodges can be obtained from parks and refuges around the state as well as the chamber of commerce offices in many communities. When hiring a guide, **find out how long a company has worked in the area.** The guide can also tell you what species are likely to be caught, catch limits, and any equipment or special clothing needs. Normally, all necessary fishing gear is provided and the guides will teach you the appropriate fishing techniques. In some cases, catch-and-release ethics may be emphasized.

Outfitters & Charters

Alaskan Fishing Adventures. Anglers are guided in several areas of the Kenai Peninsula south of Anchorage, including Resurrection Bay, Cook Inlet, and the Kenai River, home of the famous "Kenai Kings," salmon that may reach 90 pounds or more. Among the other species they catch are halibut, sockeye and silver salmon, and rainbow trout. Boats have a four-person limit on rivers, six-person limit on salt water. ⌂ *Box 2457, Soldotna 99669 ☎ 800/548–3474 or 907/262–9683 ⊟ 907/262–0827 ⊕ www.alaskanfishing.com.*

Central Charter Booking Agency. In Homer, this company can arrange fishing trips in outer Kachemak Bay and Lower Cook Inlet, areas known for excellent halibut fishing. Though most charters focus on halibut, some also fish for salmon. Boat sizes vary considerably; some have a 6-person limit, whereas others can take up to 25 passengers. ✉ *4241 Homer Spit, Homer 99603 ☎ 907/235–7847, 800/478–7847 ⊟ 907/235–2895 ⊕ www.centralcharter.com.*

Great Alaska Adventure Lodge. Fishing packages are among the adventure trips run out of this Kenai River lodge. Trips include fly-in fish camps, river floats, and saltwater charters. Expert guides can get you into king, silver, and pink salmon; halibut; rainbow trout; and grayling. Stories are traded at happy hour and during dinner in the lodge. ✉ *33881 Sterling Hwy., Sterling 99672 ☎ 907/262–4515 in summer, 360/697–6454 in winter, 800/544–2261 year-round ⊟ 907/262–8797 ⊕ www.greatalaska.com.*

Alaska's Top Fish & Their Sources

SPECIES	COMMON NAME	WHERE FOUND
Arctic Char (F, S)	Char	SC, SW, NW, I, A
Arctic Grayling (F)	Grayling	SE, SC, SW, NW, I, A
Brook Trout (F)	Brookie	SE
Burbot (F)	Lingcod	SC, SW, NW, A
Chinook (F, S)	King Salmon	SE, SC, SW, I
Chum Salmon (F, S)	Dog Salmon	SE, SC, SW, NW, I
Coho Salmon (F, S)	Silver Salmon	SE, SC, SW, NW, I
Cutthroat Trout (F, S)	Cutthroat	SE, SC
Dolly Varden (F, S)	Dolly	SE, SC, SW, NW, I, A
Lake Trout (F)	Laker	SC, SW, NW, I, A

Northern Pike (F)	Northern	SC, SW, NW, I
Hammerhandle Pacific Halibut (S)	Halibut	SE, SC, SW, NW
Pink Salmon (F, S)	Humpie	SE, SC, SW, NW, I
Smelt (F, S)	Smelt	SE, SC, SW, NW, I, A
Rainbow Trout (F)	Rainbow	SE, SC, SW, I
Sheefish (F)	Shee, Inconnu	NW, I
Sockeye Salmon (F, S)	Red Salmon	SE, SC, SW, NW, I
Steelhead (F, S)	Steelie	SE, SC, SW

(F) = Freshwater	A = Arctic	SC = South Central
(S) = Saltwater	I = Interior	SE = Southeast
(F, S) = Freshwater and Saltwater	NW = Northwest	SW = Southwest

Whale-Watching Cruises

Fodor's Choice
★

A close encounter with whales in their natural environment can be a thrilling experience. Hearing the resonant whoosh of a cetacean exhaling and witnessing such acrobatics as "spy-hopping" (a whale poking its head straight out of the water for a look around), breaching, and skimming, you can't help but feel their awesome presence.

It's possible to see migrating whales along much of Alaska's coast from June through August: from the Southeast region's Inside Passage to South Central's Prince William Sound, Kodiak Archipelago, and Kenai Fjords National Park, and then north through the Bering, Chukchi, and Beaufort seas in Arctic waters. The whales most commonly seen on whale-watching trips are killer whales, or orcas, and humpbacks.

Whale-watching is not the average spectator sport. It's more like a seagoing game of hide-and-seek. Whales are unpredictable, so be prepared to wait and watch patiently, scanning the water for signs. Sometimes it seems that the whales don't want to be watched; other times they might rub up against the boat. Also unpredictable are the weather and sea conditions. You can get wet and chilled, and possibly seasick.

Most cruises travel in or through waters that attract several species, although some focus on a particular type of whale. If you **ask when the best time to take a specific trip is,** you may find out that the sighting record is better during some months than others. You have to **weigh the pros and cons of traveling on small versus large boats.** Make sure you know what kind of boat is used for the trip you are considering. A trip with 15 people is certain to be quite different from one with 150. The larger boats can handle stormy seas much better than the smaller boats and offer much better indoor accommodations when the weather turns nasty. The smaller boats should appeal to those who want to steer clear of crowds; plus you feel closer to the surrounding seascape. More flexible itineraries are another benefit of small boats.

Tour Companies

Glacier Bay Cruiselines. Multiday tours through the Inside Passage provide opportunities to view whales and other marine life, such as sea otters, porpoises, seals, and seabirds. Trips into Glacier Bay National Park run from the dock at Bartlett Cove, near Glacier Bay Lodge. Watching for whales, as well as calving glaciers, is part of the daily routine. The uniformed Park Service naturalists on board provide local expertise. ⌐ *9097 Glacier Hwy, Suite 100, Juneau 99801* ☎ *907/789–4183 or 800/478–3610* ⎙ *206/789–9383* ⊕ *www.goldbelttours.com.*

Mariah Tours. Seward's small-boat trips offer whale-watching and glacier tours into Kenai Fjords National Park. Its two boats carry no more than 22 passengers each. Mariah runs 9½- to 10-hour tours into the park, including a "captain's choice" that goes where the wildlife action is. Tours run from mid-May through early September. Besides killer and humpback whales, you're likely to see bald eagles, sea otters, sea lions, seals, and thousands of seabirds. ⌐ *2525 C St., Suite 405, Anchorage 99503* ☎ *907/276–6249 or 800/478–8068* ⎙ *907/263–5559* ⊕ *www. kenaifjords.com.*

★ **Kenai Fjords Tours.** This company leads a variety of tours, including those that explore Resurrection Bay and Kenai Fjords National Park in South Central Alaska. They range from three-hour natural-history tours to five-hour gray-whale-watching tours (late March to early May only) and full-day cruises to Aialik Bay or Northwestern Fjord. Prime whale-watching time for orcas and humpbacks is June through August. Most of the company's boats are 75 feet–95 feet long, with room for 90–150 passengers, but it also has a smaller vessel with a 22-passenger limit. ⌐ *2525 C St., Suite 405, Anchorage 99503* ☎ *907/276–6249 or 800/478–8068* ⎙ *907/263–5559* ⊕ *www.kenaifjords.com.*

ANCHORAGE

3

FODOR'S CHOICE

Alaska Native Heritage Center, *East Anchorage*

Alyeska Prince Hotel, *Girdwood*

Anchorage Museum of History and Art, *Downtown*

Chilkoot Charlie's, *Midtown*

Iditarod Trail Sled Dog Race

Marx Brothers' Cafe, *Downtown*

Saturday Market, *Downtown*

Tony Knowles Coastal Trail, *Downtown*

HIGHLY RECOMMENDED

RESTAURANTS Jens', *Midtown*

Moose's Tooth Pub & Pizzeria, *Midtown*

New Sagaya's City Market, *Downtown*

Ristorante Orso, *Downtown*

Sacks Café, *Downtown*

Seven Glaciers, *Girdwood*

HOTELS Anchorage Hotel, *Downtown*

Aurora Winds Bed & Breakfast, *Anchorage*

Hotel Captain Cook, *Downtown*

Millennium Anchorage Hotel, *Midtown*

SIGHTS Alaska Heritage Library and Museum, *Midtown*

Alaska Public Lands Information Center, *Downtown*

NIGHTLIFE Fly by Night Club, *Midtown*

By Robin
Mackey Hill
and Howard
C. Weaver

Updated by
Don Pitcher

AMID THE WILD COUNTRYSIDE that crowds around it on all sides, Anchorage has grown into a vigorous, spirited, cosmopolitan city—by far Alaska's largest and most sophisticated. The relative affluence of this white-collar city—with a sprinkling of olive drab from nearby military bases—attracts fine restaurants and pricey shops, first-rate entertainment, and world-class sporting events. Flashy modern towers stab the skyline, and colorful flowers spill from hundreds of baskets on downtown lampposts. Traffic from the city's busy international airport, served by more than 15 international and domestic airlines, lends Anchorage more diversity than you might expect from a city with a population of more than 261,000, nearly half the people in the state. You'll also discover some development you may not have come to Alaska to see—14 McDonald's, 2 Wal-Marts, a 16-plex movie theater, and dozens of espresso bars. Those who live in the Bush joke about "being able to see Alaska" by visiting Anchorage, but the city has not entirely lost touch with its frontier spirit. Sled-dog races are still among the most revered events held here, moose often roam along city bike trails, and spectacular country is just a short drive away.

First incorporated in 1920, Anchorage is still a young city. Nearly everything was built in the last few decades—an Anchorage home dating from the 1950s almost merits historic status. In addition to acting as the center for oil development in the state, Anchorage hustles its living as a government, banking, transportation, and communications hub. The median age of 30 years and an aggressive style make it—not the capital city of Juneau—the state's power center.

Anchorage residents are primarily from elsewhere in America—including oil workers from such conservative oil-patch states as Oklahoma and Texas—and the attitudes they bring have added fuel to the fire of the pro-development mentality that characterizes the city, and Alaska, as a whole. Although representing less than 8% of the population, Alaskan Native peoples add an important cultural dimension, along with rapidly growing Asian and Hispanic populations.

Anchorage got its start with the construction of the federally built Alaska Railroad, completed in 1917, and traces of the railroad heritage remain today. Once the tracks were laid, the town grew because its pioneer forerunners actively sought growth by hook and—not infrequently—by crook. City officials used to delight in telling how they tricked a visiting member of Congress into dedicating a site for a not-yet-approved federal hospital.

Boom and bust periods followed major events: an influx of military bases during World War II; a massive buildup of Arctic missile-warning stations during the cold war; reconstruction following the devastating Good Friday earthquake of 1964; and in the late 1960s the biggest jackpot of all—the discovery of oil at Prudhoe Bay and the construction of the trans-Alaska pipeline. Not surprisingly, Anchorage positioned itself as the perfect home for the Trans-Alaska pipeline administrators and support industries, and it continues to attract a large share of the state's oil-tax dollars.

In the last decade, Anchorage has become an increasingly important focus of travelers to Alaska. The central location, relatively mild climate, and excellent transportation system make it a natural place to begin or end a trip.

Before you put on your comfortable shoes and grab your camera, take a few minutes to figure out what you're most interested in—seeing wildlife, shopping, taking a hike in the surrounding Chugach Mountains, or soaking up some of Alaska's rich Native culture.

If you have 1 day

Take a stroll through downtown Anchorage to acquaint yourself with the fine shops and galleries, historic sites, museums, and parks. Walk along the Tony Knowles Coastal Trail if the weather's cooperating. If you have a car, explore the city highlights, including the Alaska Aviation Heritage Museum and the Alaska Native Heritage Center. End the day with some window-shopping downtown or dinner and a walk along the Delaney Park Strip. Several places are open late if coffee and dessert—or beer and nachos, for that matter—sound like the perfect nightcap.

If you have 3 days

Follow the one-day itinerary; then head south along the Seward Highway for views of Potter Marsh and Turnagain Arm. Drive 40 mi to the community of Girdwood, with its several good restaurants, scenic hiking trails, and inviting shops. Continue farther down the highway to Alyeska Resort at Girdwood, where you can ride the tram to the 2,300-foot level for lunch with a view. Head south of Girdwood to Portage Glacier and the Begich-Boggs Visitor Center, all the while looking for Dall sheep and beluga whales. Back in Anchorage on Day 3, consider visiting some of the special-interest museums or, if it's the season, taking in a baseball game at Mulcahy Stadium. A hike along one of the city's many bike trails or in the neighboring Chugach Mountains lets you see the role nature plays in the lives of those who make Anchorage their home. Bears and moose roam the park, which has trails from 2 mi to 30 mi in length.

EXPLORING ANCHORAGE

Navigating downtown Anchorage's flower-lined streets is simple. The grid plan was laid out with military precision by the Army Corps of Engineers, and streets and avenues run exactly east–west and north–south, with numbers in the first direction and letters of the alphabet or Alaska place-names (Barrow, Cordova, Denali, etc.) in the other. The only aberration is the absence of a J Street—a concession, some say, to the city's early Swedish settlers, who had difficulty pronouncing the letter.

Outside of downtown, Anchorage is considerably less pedestrian friendly, with widely scattered neighborhoods and large shopping malls clustered along busy thoroughfares. Fortunately, the city has a decent local bus system.

You'll find plenty to do year-round in Anchorage, though most visitors, particularly first-timers, might be happiest in June, July, or August, when the days are longer and the temperatures warmer. Locals embrace the 18-plus hours of daylight. Dog walkers, bikers, golfers, and softball players are out until it gets dark, which in late June can be nearly midnight. Spring comes late and fall early to Anchorage. These are less desirable times to visit, because weather can be cool and rainy and some attractions might be closed. But you'll also encounter fewer fellow travelers during the shoulder seasons.

Numbers in the text correspond to numbers in the margin and on the Anchorage map.

Downtown Anchorage

Downtown Anchorage is nearly flat, making for a delightful stroll. Throughout the summer, hanging floral baskets line the streets. Start at the **Log Cabin Visitor Information Center** ❶ ▶, where friendly volunteers answer questions and racks of brochures line the walls. The marble statue in front of **Old City Hall** ❷ next door honors William Seward. Along 4th Avenue are some of Anchorage's original buildings. They date from 1920, when Anchorage was incorporated. Catercorner from the Old City Hall is the **Alaska Public Lands Information Center** ❸, one of four in the state that provide information on all of Alaska's public lands.

Take F Street north downhill to 2nd Avenue, the site of original townsite homes built by the Alaska Engineering Commission, which also built the Alaska Railroad in the early 1900s. A neighborhood marker at the intersection of F Street and 2nd Avenue tells of Anchorage's first mayor, Leopold David, and the start of the Anchorage Women's Club.

Walk east along 2nd Avenue past the Eisenhower Memorial to a set of stairs leading down to the **Alaska Railroad depot** ❹. Salmon run up **Ship Creek** ❺, north of the depot, all summer, attracting anglers and gawkers alike. It's easy to watch the action from the banks of the creek, where you'll also find photographs from the city's early days.

Ask Anchorage residents what the best thing about living in the city is, and many will say that it's the **Tony Knowles Coastal Trail** ❻, a recreational trail that begins west of 2nd Avenue and curls along Cook Inlet. Follow 2nd Avenue to K Street, go south a block to 3rd Avenue, and follow 3rd Avenue westward to **Resolution Park** ❼, with its statue of Captain Cook. From here you can admire the grand vistas over Cook Inlet to Mt. McKinley and other peaks in the Alaska Range. The **Oscar Anderson House Museum** ❽, off the coastal trail at the north end of Elderberry Park, was Anchorage's first permanent frame house, built in 1915 by city butcher Oscar Anderson. Elderberry Park, just in front of the house, is a good place for children to run off steam, watch passing trains, and look for whales off the coastline. If young travelers are getting restless, head back up the 5th Avenue hill to the **Imaginarium** ❾, an experiential science museum with a great gift shop.

Walk down 5th Avenue past the **Egan Convention Center** (✉ 555 W. 5th Ave. ☎ 907/263–2800), whose lobby has several modern Native Alaskan sculptures and a beaded curtain that evokes the northern lights. Across the street is a park (Town Square) that's packed with flowers in the summer, and just southwest of it is the **Alaska Center for the Performing Arts** ❿. Continue on to A Street and 7th Avenue for the entrance to the **Anchorage Museum of History and Art** ⓫, which occupies the whole block between 6th and 7th avenues. The red metal sculpture out front is a favorite hide-and-seek site for children.

TIMING This walking tour should take two to three hours, or longer if you get caught up in shopping and museum-hopping. Volunteers from **Anchorage Historic Properties** (☎ 907/274–3600 ⊕ www.anchoragehistoricproperties. org) lead historic walking tours on weekdays in the summer. These depart from Old City Hall at 524 West 4th Avenue and cost $5.

Hiking & Walking

Anchorage is a hiker's paradise, laced with rugged dirt paths through the Chugach Mountains and more than 120 mi of paved urban trails that meander through wooded greenbelts and quiet neighborhoods. Easiest of these is the Tony Knowles Coastal Trail, an 11-mi ribbon of asphalt beginning downtown and stretching west to Kincaid Park. Pick up a guide to local hiking trails at the Alaska Public Lands Information Center (⇨ What to See *in* Exploring Anchorage) or at area bookstores. A note of caution: when hiking in the hills, be sure to wear hiking boots and to take plenty of water, rain gear, and a light jacket—the weather can change with little warning. And although bear encounters are rare, be alert and make noise when walking in thick brush.

3

Shopping

Anchorage's shopping matches any taste and price range. Souvenir shops selling everything from painted gold pans to plastic totem poles can be found on nearly every downtown block. Native Alaskan handicrafts of all kinds are sold at many of the gift shops downtown—the best selection is at the downtown outdoor Saturday Market in the parking lot at 3rd Avenue and E Street. Check for the official polar bear symbol, which means the item was made in Alaska; a hand symbol indicates an article was made locally by Native artisans. Tlingit and Haida traditional arts and crafts include button blankets, wood carvings, and silver jewelry. Athabascan craftspeople are known for their beadwork, which adorns slippers, headbands, and jewelry. Eskimo handicrafts include ivory and soapstone carvings and baleen baskets. Aleut grass baskets are so fine and tightly woven that some can hold water.

What to See

❿ Alaska Center for the Performing Arts. The distinctive stone-and-glass building fronts on an expansive park filled with brilliant flowers all summer. Take a look inside for upcoming events, or just relax amid the blossoms on a sunny afternoon. You can watch IMAX films or slide shows on the northern lights. Hour-long tours are available. ⊠ *621 W. 6th Ave., at G St., Downtown* ☎ *907/263–2900, 800/478–7328 tickets* ⊕ *www.alaskapac.org* ⊗ *Daily 8–5 Free tours Wed. at 1 PM.*

★ ☺ ❸ Alaska Public Lands Information Center. Stop here for information on all of Alaska's public lands, including national and state parks, national forests, and wildlife refuges. You can make reservations for a state ferry; watch nature videos; plan a hiking, sea-kayaking, bear-viewing, or fishing trip; find out about public-use cabins; learn about Alaska's plants and animals; or head to the theater for films highlighting different parts of the state. The bookstore sells maps and nature books. Guided walks to historic downtown sights depart daily. ⊠ *605 W. 4th Ave., at F St., Downtown* ☎ *907/271–2737* ⊕ *www.nps.gov/aplic* ⊗ *Memorial Day–Labor Day, daily 9–5:30; Labor Day–Memorial Day, weekdays 10–5:30.*

❹ Alaska Railroad depot. Totem poles and a locomotive built in 1907 are outside the station, the headquarters of the Alaska Railroad since 1915. A monument in front of the depot relates the history of the railroad,

Anchorage

which brought an influx of people into the city during the early 1900s. During February's Fur Rendezvous festival, model-train buffs set up their displays here. ✉ *411 W. 1st Ave., Downtown* ☎ *907/265–2494* ⊕ *www. akrr.com* ☾ *Daily, depending on train schedules.*

Anchorage Museum of History and Art. An impressive collection of historic and contemporary Alaskan art is exhibited along with dioramas and displays on Alaskan history and village life. The first-floor atrium is often the site of free daily presentations, which occur in July, by local artists and authors. You can join an informative 45-minute tour (given several times daily) or step into the theater to watch a film on Alaska. A café spills out into the atrium, serving delicious lunches from the Marx Brothers' Cafe, and the gift shop sells classy souvenirs. ✉ *121 W. 7th Ave., Downtown* ☎ *907/343–4326, 907/343–6173 recorded information* ⊕ *www. anchoragemuseum.org* ✉ *$6.50* ☾ *Mid-May–mid-Sept., Fri.–Wed. 9–6, Thurs. 9–9; mid-Sept.–mid-May, Tues.–Sat. 10–6, Sun. 1–5.*

Imaginarium. Children can stand inside a giant soap bubble at the bubble lab, hold a starfish in the marine exhibit, learn about the northern lights, or take a galaxy tour in the planetarium at this experiential science museum. Other attractions include such "radical reptiles" as an iguana, an alligator, and even a 19-foot python. It's a fun house for children and adults alike. ✉ *737 W. 5th Ave., Downtown* ☎ *907/276–3179* ⊕ *www.imaginarium.org* ✉ *$5* ☾ *Mon.–Sat. 10–6, Sun. noon–5.*

Log Cabin Visitor Information Center. A giant jade boulder stands outside this Bush-style log cabin, whose sod roof is festooned with huge hanging baskets of flowers. Anchorage calls itself the "Air Crossroads of the World" (it's a major stopping point for cargo jets en route to Asia), and a signpost out front marks the mileage to many international destinations. After a stop in the visitor-center cabin, step out the back door to a more spacious visitor center stocked with brochures. ✉ *4th Ave. and F St., Downtown* ☎ *907/274–3531* ⊕ *www.anchorage.net* ☾ *June–Aug., daily 7:30–7; May and Sept., daily 8–6; Oct.–Apr., daily 9–4.*

Old City Hall. Offices of the Anchorage Convention and Visitors Bureau now occupy this 1936 building. A few exhibits and historic photos are right inside the lobby. Out front, take a look at the marble sculpture of William Seward, the secretary of state who engineered the purchase of Alaska from Russia. ✉ *524 W. 4th Ave., Downtown.*

Oscar Anderson House Museum. City butcher Oscar Anderson built Anchorage's first permanent frame house in 1915 at a time when most of Anchorage consisted of tents. A Swedish Christmas open house is held the first two weekends of December. Guided 45-minute tours are available whenever the museum is open. ✉ *420 M St., Downtown* ☎ *907/ 274–2336* ⊕ *www.anchoragehistoricproperties.org* ✉ *$3* ☾ *June–mid-Sept., Mon.–Sat. noon–5; mid-Sept.–May, by appointment.*

Resolution Park. A cantilevered viewing platform dominated by a monument to Captain Cook is found in this tiny park. Mt. Susitna, known as the Sleeping Lady, is the prominent low mountain to the northwest. Mt. McKinley—referred to by most Alaskans by its traditional name, Denali—is often visible 125 mi away. ✉ *3rd Ave. at L St., Downtown.*

Ship Creek. The creek is dammed here, with a footbridge across the dam. You'll see a waterfall; salmon running upstream; anglers; and, above it all, the tall buildings of downtown. ✉ *Whitney Rd., Downtown.*

Tony Knowles Coastal Trail. Strollers, runners, bikers, dog walkers, and in-line skaters cram this recreation trail on sunny summer evenings, particularly around Westchester Lagoon. In winter, cross-country skiers take to it by storm. The trail begins off 2nd Avenue, west of Christensen Drive, and curls along Cook Inlet for approximately 11 mi to Kincaid Park, beyond the airport. In summer, you might spot beluga whales offshore in Cook Inlet. Access points are on the waterfront at the ends of 2nd, 5th, and 9th avenues and at Westchester Lagoon.

Midtown & Beyond

a good drive

Head west on Northern Lights Boulevard past Earthquake Park, 2 mi after Minnesota Drive. Signs describe the devastating power of the 1964 earthquake, the largest ever recorded in Alaska, with a magnitude of 9.2 on the Richter scale. Another 1¾ mi west on Northern Lights Boulevard is Point Woronzof, great for scenic views of Cook Inlet, Mt. Susitna (Sleeping Lady), the Alaska Range, and Mt. McKinley.

Turn left out of the parking lot at Point Woronzof and go back east along Northern Lights Boulevard 1½ mi to Aircraft Drive. Turn right and continue south and east along roads skirting the edge of two large lakes, Lakes Spenard and Hood. Lake Spenard has a beach where hardy souls may take a dip. Along Lake Hood—the world's largest and busiest seaplane base—you'll see planes (and geese) take off and land. The **Alaska Aviation Heritage Museum** ⑫ ▶, overlooking the south end of the lake and 1½ mi from the intersection with Aircraft Drive, has more than 30 vintage aircraft.

Take the first left out of the parking lot at the aviation museum and head 2 mi east on International Airport Boulevard to Minnesota Drive. Take Minnesota south about 9 mi (it becomes O'Malley Road and crosses Seward Highway) and continue uphill to the **Alaska Zoo** ⑬. From the zoo, take a right on O'Malley and head back 2 mi to Seward Highway. Three miles south on the highway is the turnoff to **Potter Marsh** ⑭, where Canada geese, arctic terns, and other migratory birds make their home in summer.

From Potter Marsh, head north on Old Seward Highway for 8 mi and turn left (west) on Northern Lights Boulevard to C Street, where you will find the **Alaska Heritage Library and Museum** ⑮. This outstanding small museum displays Native artifacts and photos. From here, take Benson Boulevard (a one-way street just south of Northern Lights) back to Old Seward Highway. Go left (north) and make a right (east) on 15th Avenue, which becomes DeBarr Road, and a left (north) on Muldoon Road to the Glenn Highway. The entrance to the **Alaska Native Heritage Center** ⑯ is on the north side of this intersection. The center is a must-see for anyone interested in Native peoples. End your Anchorage tour at the **Alaska Botanical Garden** ⑰, off Tudor Road. Head south from the base on Boniface Parkway, and turn left onto Tudor Road. Follow it ½ mi, turn right on Campbell Airstrip Road, and continue a block to the floral gardens.

TIMING Driving the route without stopping will take about two hours. You should allow from a half day to a full day, depending on the amount of time you'd like to spend at the sights.

What to See

👏 ▶ ⑫ **Alaska Aviation Heritage Museum.** The state's unique aviation history is presented here with 25 vintage aircraft—7 of which have been completely restored—a theater, an observation deck along **Lake Hood,** and a gift shop. Highlights include a historic Fairchild American Pilgrim and a Stearman C2B, the first plane to land on Mt. McKinley, back in the early 1930s. Volunteers are working to restore many of the planes and are eager to talk shop. ✉ *4721 Aircraft Dr.* ☎ *907/248–5325* ⊕ *www.*

alaskaairmuseum.com ✉ $5 ⊙ *June–Sept., Wed.–Mon. 10–6; Oct.–May, Fri.–Sat. 10–4, Sun. noon–4.*

👋 ⑰ **Alaska Botanical Garden.** A pleasant 1-mi nature trail leads through the 110-acre garden, where you'll find some 480 varieties of plants. Other trails crisscross the grounds, which include perennial, rock, and herb gardens. An information kiosk is at the entrance. ✉ *Campbell Airstrip Rd. off Tudor Rd. (park at Benny Benson School), East Anchorage* ☎ *907/ 770–3692* ⊕ *www.alaskabg.org* ✉ *Donation* ⊙ *Daily 9–9.*

★ ⑮ **Alaska Heritage Library and Museum.** Alaskan Native artifacts are the main draw in the quiet, unassuming lobby of a large midtown bank. You'll also find paintings by Alaskan artists and a library of rare books. ✉ *Wells Fargo Bank, 301 W. Northern Lights Blvd., at C St., Midtown* ☎ *907/265–2834* ⊕ *www.wellsfargohistory.com/museums* ✉ *Free* ⊙ *Late May–early Sept., weekdays noon–5; early Sept.–late May, weekdays noon–4.*

👋 ⑯ **Alaska Native Heritage Center.** Situated on a 26-acre site facing the Chugach Mountains, this facility provides an introduction to Alaska's Native peoples. The spacious Welcome House has interpretive displays, artifacts, photographs, demonstrations, performances, and films, along with a café and gift shop. Step outside for a stroll around the adjacent lake, where you will pass five village exhibits representing Native cultural groups through traditional structures and exhibitions. The Heritage Center provides a free shuttle from the Log Cabin Visitor Information Center (⇨ What to See in Downtown Anchorage) several times a day in summer. You can also hop a bus at the downtown transit center; Route 4 will take you to the Heritage Center front door. ✉ *8800 Heritage Center Dr. (Glenn Hwy. at Muldoon Rd.), East Anchorage* ☎ *907/330–8000 or 800/315–6608* ⊕ *www.alaskanative. net* ✉ *$21 in summer, $9 in winter* ⊙ *Mid-May–Sept., daily 9–6; Oct.–mid-May, Sat. noon–5.*

FodorsChoice ★

👋 ⑬ **Alaska Zoo.** Caribou, Dall sheep, reindeer, Siberian tigers, musk ox, seals, moose, and various Alaskan birds call this home—you'll even find the state's only elephant. The star attractions are Oreo, a brown bear, and Ahpun, a polar bear; the two were orphaned as cubs and grew up together at the zoo. You can hop a city bus here from downtown. ✉ *4731 O'Malley Rd., South Anchorage, 2 mi east of New Seward Hwy.* ☎ *907/ 346–3242* ⊕ *www.alaskazoo.org* ✉ *$8* ⊙ *May–Labor Day, daily 9–6; Labor Day–Apr., daily 10–5.*

⑭ **Potter Marsh.** Canada geese and other migratory birds as well as the occasional moose or beaver frequent this marsh about 10 mi south of downtown on the Seward Highway. An elevated boardwalk makes viewing easy. The **Potter Section House,** an old railroad service building just south of the marsh, operates as a state-park office. Out front is an old engine with a rotary snowplow that was used to clear avalanches. ✉ *Seward Hwy., South Anchorage* ☎ *907/345–5014* ⊕ *www.dnr.state.ak.us/parks* ⊙ *Weekdays 8–noon, 1–4:30.*

off the beaten path

EKLUTNA NATIVE VILLAGE – A small indigenous community in a tiny cluster of homes 26 mi north of Anchorage on the Glenn Highway is the oldest continually inhabited Athabascan Indian site in the area. At the village cemetery, note the hand-built Siberian-style prayer chapel, traditional Russian Orthodox crosses, and 80 colorful Native spirit houses. Admission includes an informative 30-minute tour. A gift shop sells Native crafts. ☎ *907/688–6026* ⊕ *www.eklutna.com* ✉ *Tours $6* ⊙ *Mid-May–mid-Sept., daily 8–6.*

GIRDWOOD – A ski resort, summer vacation spot, and home to an eclectic collection of locals, the town of Girdwood, 40 mi southeast of Anchorage near the head of Turnagain Arm, sits in the trees within a deep valley and is backdropped by tall mountains on three sides. The main attraction is the Mt. Alyeska Ski Resort, the largest ski area in Alaska. Besides enjoying the obvious winter attractions, you can mountain hike or visit several restaurants and gift shops open all year. Girdwood is wetter than Anchorage; it often rains (or snows) here while the sun shines 40 mi to the north. ⊕ *www. girdwoodalaska.com.*

WHERE TO EAT

Fishing in Alaska is a multimillion-dollar industry employing thousands of people. For those eager to sample the fruits of those labors, dining out in Anchorage is a pleasure. Several restaurants—from formal dining rooms to casual pubs—serve such favorites as halibut, salmon, Alaskan king crab legs, scallops, oysters, and mussels.

Ethnic restaurants, especially Thai and other Asian styles, and a growing number of places with extensive vegetarian menus, veer off from traditional seafood fare. In the last few years, half a dozen microbreweries with adjoining restaurants have opened, two of them downtown, giving the area a convivial spirit. Espresso bars have also taken root all over town. For a quick lunch downtown, track down one of the 4th Avenue vendors for a reindeer sausage with grilled onions.

Smoking has been banned in all Anchorage restaurants, except for bars that also serve meals. Most local restaurants are open daily in summer, with reduced hours in winter. Only a few places require reservations, but it's always best to call ahead, especially for dinner.

	WHAT IT COSTS				
	$$$$	$$$	$$	$	¢
AT DINNER	over $25	$20–$25	$15–$20	$10–$15	under $10

Prices are for a main course.

Downtown

American/Casual

$–$$$$ ✕ **Glacier BrewHouse.** Always packed with locals, the cavernous, wood-beam BrewHouse serves a dozen or so ales, stouts, lagers, and pilsners. Dinner selections range from thin-crust, 10-inch pizzas to seafood chowder, barbecue pork ribs to jambalaya fettuccine. For dessert, don't miss the wood-oven roasted bread pudding. You can watch the hardworking chefs in the open kitchen. The brewery sits behind a glass wall, and the same owners operate Ristorante Orso, next door. ✉ *737 W. 5th Ave., Downtown* ☎ *907/274–2739* ⊕ *www.glacierbrewhouse.com* ⊟ *AE, D, DC, MC, V.*

¢–$ ✕ **Downtown Deli.** Although you can choose from familiar sandwiches, like the French dip or the chicken teriyaki, this deli—owned by Alaska's former governor Tony Knowles—also has Alaskan favorites, like grilled halibut and reindeer stew. The dark, rich chicken soup comes with either noodles or homemade matzo balls, and breakfasts range from omelets to cheese blintzes. You can sit in one of the wooden booths for some privacy or out front at the sidewalk tables for some people-watch-

Where to Stay & Eat in Anchorage

Restaurants ▼

Hotels ▼

ing. ✉ *525 W. 4th Ave., Downtown* ☎ *907/276–7116* ⚔ *Reservations not accepted* ▭ *AE, D, DC, MC, V.*

¢ ✕ **Sweet Basil Cafe.** Lunchtime sandwiches (hot or cold) on freshly baked sweet basil bread are a hit at this small, friendly café. Try the spicy andouille sausage with cheese, peppers, and onions. Fresh pastas, salads, wraps, fish tacos, pastries, and light breakfasts fill out the menu. The juice bar is one of a handful in Anchorage, and the lattes may be the best downtown. ✉ *335 E St., Downtown* ☎ *907/274–0070* 🖷 *907/274–2434* ▭ *AE, MC, V* ✆ *Closed Sun. No dinner.*

Contemporary

$$$$ ✕ **Crow's Nest Restaurant.** Elegant cuisine is the order of the day, along with the best view in Anchorage—the Chugach Mountains to the east, the Alaska Range to the north, and the sprawling city of Anchorage 20 stories below. Equally impressive are the 10,000-bottle wine cellar and hefty portions. The expert waitstaff presents a menu of seafood, along with game and other meats, in an elegant atmosphere, with plenty of starched linen, brass, and teak. It's best known for a leisurely five-course set menu: $60 per person or $90 with wine pairings. ✉ *Hotel Captain Cook, 20th floor, 5th Ave. and K St., Downtown* ☎ *907/343–2217* 🖷 *907/343–2211* ⊕ *www.captaincook.com* ⚔ *Reservations essential* ▭ *AE, D, DC, MC, V* ✆ *Closed Sun. No lunch.*

$$$–$$$$ ✕ **Marx Brothers' Cafe.** Inside a little frame house built in 1916, this na-
Fodor's Choice tionally recognized café opened in 1979 and is still going strong. For
★ an appetizer, try the king crab–stuffed squash blossoms. The outstanding made-at-your-table Caesar salad is a superb opener for the baked halibut with a macadamia crust served with coconut curry sauce and fresh mango chutney. The wine list includes more than 400 international choices. A second Marx Brothers' Cafe is housed in the Anchorage Museum of History and Arts. ✉ *627 W. 3rd Ave., Downtown* ☎ *907/278–2133* ⊕ *www.marxcafe.com* ⚔ *Reservations essential* ▭ *AE, DC, MC, V* ✆ *Closed Mon. Sept.–May. No lunch.*

★ $$–$$$$ ✕ **Sacks Café.** This bright and colorful restaurant serves light American cuisine such as butternut squash ravioli with a shallot saffron sauce; rack of New Zealand lamb; and free-range chicken stuffed with prosciutto, spinach, caramelized onion, and Romano. Be sure to ask about the daily specials. Fresh flowers adorn all tables, and singles congregate in the friendly separate bar area. The café is especially crowded during lunch, served 11–2:30. Sacks Saturday and Sunday brunch menu includes eggs Benedict, a Mexican scrambled egg dish called *migas,* and various salads and sandwiches. ✉ *328 G St., Downtown* ☎ *907/276–3546 or 907/274–4022* ⊕ *www.sackscafe.com* ⚔ *Reservations essential* ▭ *AE, MC, V.*

$$–$$$$ ✕ **Simon and Seafort's Saloon & Grill.** Big windows overlooking Cook Inlet vistas, high ceilings, and a brass-and-wood interior have made this an Anchorage favorite since 1978. The diverse menu includes prime rib (aged 28 days), pasta, and sesame chicken salads, but the main attraction here is seafood—fish is blackened, grilled, fried, or prepared any other way you like it. Try the crab legs or grilled Alaskan salmon with orange-ginger sauce. The Brandy Ice—vanilla ice cream whipped with brandy, Kahlúa, and crème de cacao—is always a deliciously decadent affair here. The bar is a great spot for microbrews and appetizers, and validated parking is available at the nearby Hotel Captain Cook garage. ✉ *420 L St., Downtown* ☎ *907/274–3502* ⊕ *www.r-u-i.com/sim* ⚔ *Reservations essential* ▭ *AE, DC, MC, V* ✆ *No lunch weekends.*

Eclectic

¢ ✕ **Snow City Cafe.** At this unassuming café along "lawyer row" you'll find dependably good and reasonably priced breakfasts and lunches. Formica tables, mismatched chairs, and fluorescent lights fill its interior. Snow City's lunch menu consists of hot or cold sandwiches, fresh soups, and salads. Breakfast is served all day, but arrive early on the weekend or be prepared to wait. The café closes at 4 most afternoons but stays open (with limited food service) 'til 11 on Sunday night for an open-mike session and Wednesday night, when Irish musicians invade the space. ⊠ *4th Ave. at L St., Downtown* ☎ *907/272–2489* 🖶 *907/272–6338* ⊙ *No dinner* ⊟ *AE, D, DC, MC, V.*

Italian

★ $–$$$$ ✕ **Ristorante Orso.** One of Anchorage's current culinary stars, Ristorante Orso ("bear" in Italian) evokes the earthiness of a Tuscany villa. Alaskan touches flavor rustic Italian dishes, including traditional pastas, fresh seafood, wood-grilled meats, and locally famous desserts—most notably a delicious molten chocolate cake. Be sure to ask about the daily specials. The large, open bar serves the same menu, and upstairs you'll find a cozier, quieter space. ⊠ *737 W. 5th Ave., Downtown* ☎ *907/222–3232* 🖶 *907/277–1033* ⊕ *www.orsoalaska.com* ⊟ *AE, D, DC, MC, V.*

Japanese

$$–$$$$ ✕ **Kumagoro.** A favorite of the suit-and-tie lunch crowd, Kumagoro has Japanese-style lunches, a take-out deli with such specialties as herring roe on kelp, and a sleek sushi bar (open evenings only). The best items on the dinner menu are the sizzling salmon or beef teriyaki, both served with miso (soybean) soup and salad. With the *shabu-shabu* dinner ($26 per person), you cook your own meats and vegetables in a stockpot of boiling broth. Inexpensive homemade *ramen* (deep-fried Japanese-style noodles) soups are also available. All entrée prices include a 10% gratuity. ⊠ *533 W. 4th Ave., Downtown* ☎ *907/272–9905* ⊟ *AE, D, DC, MC, V.*

Steak

$$$–$$$$ ✕ **Club Paris.** Alaska's oldest steak house has barely changed since opening in 1957, and many of the friendly staff members have been here since the 1980s. The restaurant has dark woods and an old-fashioned feel and serves tender, flavorful steaks of all kinds, including a 4-inch-thick filet mignon. If you have to wait for a table, have a martini at the bar and order the hors d'oeuvres platter ($26)—a sampler of top sirloin steak, cheese, and prawns that could be a meal for two. For dessert, try a tart key lime pie or triple-chocolate cheesecake. ⊠ *417 W. 5th Ave., Downtown* ☎ *907/277–6332* ⊕ *www.clubparisrestaurant.com* ⊟ *AE, D, DC, MC, V* ⊙ *No lunch Sun.*

Greater Anchorage

American

$–$$$$ ✕ **Gwennie's Old Alaskan Restaurant.** Historic Alaskan photos, stuffed animals, and memorabilia adorn this old family favorite, just south of city center toward the airport. Lunch and dinners are available—including an all-you-can-eat beef barbecue for $16—but the restaurant is best known for its old-fashioned breakfasts, available all day. Try the sourdough pancakes, reindeer sausage and eggs, or crab omelets. Start the morning the right way with Anchorage's best Bloody Mary. ⊠ *4333 Spenard Rd., Midtown* ☎ *907/243–2090* ⊟ *AE, D, DC, MC, V.*

Cajun/Creole

$$–$$$$ ✕ **Double Musky Inn.** Anchorage residents say eating here is worth the one-hour drive south to Girdwood and the inevitable wait for dinner. It's quite noisy, and the interior consists of tacky art and Mardi Gras souvenirs, but the windows frame views of huge Sitka spruce trees. The diverse menu mixes Cajun-style meals with such favorites as garlic

seafood pasta, rack of lamb, French pepper steak, and lobster kebabs. For dessert lovers, the biggest attraction here is the gooey, chocolate-rich Double Musky pie. The restaurant and lounge are both smoke-free. ⊠ *Crow Creek Rd., Girdwood* ☎ *907/783–2822* ⚞ *Reservations not accepted* ⊟ *AE, D, DC, MC, V* ⊘ *Closed Mon. and Nov. No lunch.*

Chinese

¢–$ ✕ **Fu Du.** Alaska isn't known for its Chinese restaurants, but this is one of the oldest and best. Although it's surrounded by fast-food spots and gas stations, when you step inside Fu Du, the flame-red Chinese wallpaper and lanterns, ultrafriendly staff, and Asian music take you to another continent. All the standards are available, including beef with oyster sauce, kung pao chicken, sweet-and-sour pork, and various vegetable entrées. Portions are enormous and always include soup, kimchee, rice, egg roll, and tea. Lunch specials are an even better deal, and free delivery is offered if you don't want to leave your hotel. ⊠ *2600 E. Tudor Rd., Midtown* ☎ *907/561–6610* ⊟ *AE, MC, V.*

Contemporary

★ **$$$$** ✕ **Seven Glaciers.** A 60-passenger aerial tram (free with dinner reservations, otherwise $19 round-trip) carries you to this refined yet relaxing mountainside restaurant, perched at the 2,300-foot level of Mt. Alyeska. The comfortable dining room overlooks seven glaciers. Try the artfully presented smoked and grilled salmon or mesquite-grilled strip loin of buffalo. Appetizers—particularly the peppered crab cakes—are extraordinary. Prices are high, but a four-course menu ($70 per person, including a matched wine) is available nightly in summer. Both tram and restaurant are wheelchair-accessible. ⊠ *Alyeska Prince Hotel, 1000 Arlberg Rd., Girdwood* ☎ *907/754–2237* ⊕ *www.alyeskaresort.com* ⊟ *AE, D, MC, V* ⊘ *Closed Sun.–Thurs. Nov.–mid-Apr. No lunch.*

★ **$$–$$$$** ✕ **Jens'.** Despite its location in a midtown strip mall, Jens' is tastefully decorated with Alaskan art and serves fine food. The dinner menu changes daily and almost always includes Alaskan salmon, halibut, and rockfish. Other specialties are rack of lamb, tenderloin of veal, and the justly famous pepper steak. Head chef Jens Haagen Hansen's heritage shows through at lunch when the Danish specials appear, along with soups, salads, pastas, and vegetarian meals. For a lighter evening meal, sample the appetizers in the wine bar. ⊠ *701 W. 36th Ave., Midtown* ☎ *907/561–5367* ⊕ *www.jensrestaurant.com* ⊟ *AE, D, DC, MC, V* ⊘ *Closed Sun. and Jan. No lunch Sat., no dinner Mon.*

Eclectic

★ **¢–$** ✕ **New Sagaya's City Market.** Stop here for quick lunches and Kaladi Brothers espresso. The in-house bakery (L'Aroma) cranks out specialty breads and pastries of all types, and the international deli and grocery serves California-style pizzas, Chinese food, lasagna, rotisserie chicken, salads, and even stuffed cabbage. You can eat inside on the sheltered patio or grab an outside table on a summer afternoon. New Sagaya's has one of the best seafood counters in town and will even box and ship your fish. ⊠ *900 W. 13th Ave., Downtown* ☎ *907/274–6173 or 800/764–1001* ⊟ *907/274–2042* ⊠ *3700 Old Seward Hwy., Midtown* ☎ *907/562–9797* ⊟ *907/274–2042* ⊕ *www.newsagaya.com* ⊟ *AE, D, DC, MC, V.*

Italian

$$–$$$ ✕ **CampoBello Bistro.** Tucked into a midtown mall, CampoBello has surprisingly sophisticated Italian entrées and sinful desserts. Step inside for a romantic lunch or dinner surrounded by splashes of modern art on the walls and candles on the tables. Specialties include ample servings of seafood crepes, veal saltimbocca, house-made four-cheese ravioli, and scampi Florentine (a rich blend of shrimp, sun-dried tomatoes, fresh basil, spinach, shallots, and garlic, over fettuccine). Service is attentive, and the wine list—particularly the Italian choices—is impressive. ⊠ *601 W. 36th Ave., Midtown* ☎ *907/563–2040* ▤ *DC, MC, V* ⊘ *Closed Sun., no lunch Sat., no dinner Mon.*

Mexican

$$ ✕ **Mexico in Alaska.** Since 1972 the most authentic Mexican food in town, and maybe even in Alaska, has been served here. Owner Maria Elena Ball befriends everyone, particularly young children. Favorite dishes—all are subtle and not greasy—include lime-marinated fried chicken, *chilaquiles* (tortilla casserole with mole sauce), and *entremesa de queso* (melted cheese, jalapeños, and onions with homemade tortillas). Weekday lunch buffets ($10) and Sunday dinner buffets ($12) are popular, and a vegetarian menu is available. The restaurant is several miles south of downtown, so you'll need to drive or catch the city bus. ⊠ *7305 Old Seward Hwy., South Anchorage* ☎ *907/349–1528* ▤ *AE, D, MC, V* ⊘ *No lunch Sun.*

Pizza

★ **$–$$$** ✕ **Moose's Tooth Pub & Pizzeria.** Jovial locals pack this down-home brewpub and pizzeria. Pizzas and handcrafted beers, including more than a dozen ales, ambers, porters, and stouts, are the order of the day, and the homemade root beers, cream sodas, and ginger ales are also delicious. You can match these unique brews with one of the 40 different pizzas with such varied toppings as roasted red peppers, jalapeños, cream cheese, halibut, and capers. Weekday lunches are a real bargain, starting at just $5 for a slice of pizza and a salad. The owners also run **Moose's Tooth Theatre Pub** (⊠ 1220 W. 27th Ave., Midtown ☎ 907/ 276–4200), a popular theater that screens second-run and art films for only $3 and also serves tasty pizzas, sandwiches, burritos, salads, and beer while you watch. ⊠ *3300 Old Seward Hwy., Midtown* ☎ *907/258– 2537* ⊕ *www.moosestooth.net* ▤ *D, DC, MC, V.*

Thai

¢–$ ✕ **Thai House Restaurant.** Among the Thai restaurants scattered around Anchorage, this is one of the best, with authentic Thai cooking and quick and friendly service; it's housed in an old Dairy Queen on a busy street corner. You will find fare such as fresh rolls (a house specialty), pad thai (spicy cooked noodles with shrimp, chicken, and eggs), and *tom khar gai* (a flavorful soup of coconut milk, chicken, lemongrass, and ginger). Vegetarians have a number of meatless choices. The restaurant closes at 9, so get there early. ⊠ *830 E. 36th Ave., Midtown* ☎ *907/563–8616* 🖷 *907/562–9490* ▤ *AE, MC, V.*

Vegetarian

¢ ✕ **Middle Way Cafe & Coffee House.** Vegetarian and nonvegetarian dishes are served at this cramped little lunchtime niche, including gussied-up grain-and-soy burgers, turkey cranberry sandwiches, avocado melts, vegan baked goods, and jumbo whole-grain tortillas wrapped around combinations of organic veggies, falafel, brown rice, and beans. You can get a fruit smoothie at the juice bar, choose from 35 different teas, or enjoy an espresso. Be sure to check out the daily specials. A kids' menu has smaller portions. ⊠ *1200 W. Northern Lights Blvd., Midtown* ☎ *907/ 272–6433* ⌔ *Reservations not accepted* ▤ *No credit cards* ⊘ *Kitchen closed Sun.*

WHERE TO STAY

Several hotels in Anchorage have top-drawer amenities, with summertime rates to match. Smaller inns and 175 or so bed-and-breakfasts offer character and quaint amenities at more modest prices. Most hotels in Anchorage are downtown, in midtown, or along Spenard Avenue. Girdwood, 40 mi south of downtown along the Seward and Alyeska highways, has ski-resort amenities and a picturesque mountain setting. For a listing of hotels, inns, and B&Bs, contact the Anchorage Convention and Visitors Bureau. For campgrounds in and around town, contact the Alaska Public Lands Information Center (⇨ What to See *in* Exploring Anchorage). In summer, reservations are a must for the major hotels; many places fill up months in advance. A good option for budget travelers is Priceline.com, where you can often find rooms in Anchorage hotels for half off the going rate.

WHAT IT COSTS				
	$$$$	$$$	$$	$	¢
FOR 2 PEOPLE	over $250	$200–$250	$150–$200	$100–$150	under $100

Prices are for two people in a standard double room in high season, excluding tax and service.

Downtown

$$$$ 🏨 **Anchorage Hilton.** Alaska's largest hotel is just a block from city center and fills with cruise-ship tourists all summer long. An inviting and ample lobby includes Alaskan touches and is flanked by a café and a classy sports bar. The hotel's premier restaurant, Top of the World, occupies the 15th floor. Well-maintained rooms, decorated in a contemporary style with oak and maple furnishings, are in two towers, one of which is 22 floors. Request a corner north-facing suite on the upper levels for Mt. McKinley vistas. ⊠ *500 W. 3rd Ave., Downtown, 99501* ☎ *907/272–7411 or 800/245–2527* 🖨 *907/265–7044* ⊕ *www.anchoragehilton.com* ⤴ *572 rooms, 23 suites* ⑃ *2 restaurants, cable TV with movies and video games, indoor pool, health club, 2 lounges, Internet, meeting rooms* ⊟ *AE, D, DC, MC, V.*

$$$$ 🏨 **Anchorage Marriott Downtown.** One of Anchorage's largest lodging places, the brightly decorated Marriott appeals to business travelers, tourists, and corporate clients. The hotel's Cafe Promenade serves American cuisine with an Alaskan flair. All guest rooms have huge windows; views are breathtaking from the top floors. Well-designed furnishings include workstation desks with two-line phones and voice mail. If you stay on one of the top three levels of this 20-story hotel, you have access to a concierge lounge and are served a light breakfast as well as evening hors d'oeuvres and desserts. ⊠ *820 W. 7th Ave., Downtown, 99501* ☎ *907/279–8000 or 800/228–9290* 🖨 *907/279–8005* ⊕ *www.marriott.com* ⤴ *392 rooms, 3 suites* ⑃ *Restaurant, room service, some microwaves, cable TV with movies, indoor pool, gym, hot tub, bar, shops, concierge, Internet, business services, meeting rooms* ⊟ *AE, D, DC, MC, V.*

★ **$$$$** 🏨 **Hotel Captain Cook.** Dark teak paneling and a nautical theme throughout this classy hotel recall Captain James Cook, an explorer who canvassed Alaskan waters in 1778 in an attempt to find the Northwest Passage. The hotel occupies an entire city block with three towers, the tallest of which is capped by the Crow's Nest Restaurant. The most luxurious accommodation is found on the 19th floor of Tower III—a sprawling, 1,600-square-foot two-bedroom suite, which costs a mere $1,500 per night. ⊠ *5th Ave. and K St., Downtown, 99501* ☎ *907/276–6000 or 800/843–1950* 🖨 *907/343–2298* ⊕ *www.captaincook.com* ⤴ *451 rooms, 96 suites* ⑃ *3 restaurants, room service, fans, cable TV with movies and video games, indoor pool, gym, health club, hair salon,* *hot tub, sauna, racquetball, shops, concierge, Internet, business services, meeting rooms; no a/c* ▤ *AE, D, DC, MC, V.*

$$$$ ▣ **Sheraton Anchorage.** A glass-canopy lobby with a jade-tile staircase, acres of cream-color marble, and guest rooms that include voice mail, an iron and ironing board, and a coffeemaker make this 16-story hotel one of the city's best, despite its marginal neighborhood. Get a room high up on the north side to watch F-16s and other jets flying tight patterns over nearby Elmendorf Air Force Base. A downstairs restaurant (Ptarmigan Bar & Grill) serves three meals a day, and a 15th-floor restaurant (Josephine's) serves a daily seafood buffet and Sunday brunch-with-a-view all summer. ✉ *401 E. 6th Ave., Downtown, 99501* ☎ *907/276–8700 or 800/325–3535* 🖷 *907/276–7561* ⊕ *www.sheraton.com* ⇨ *375 rooms, 5 suites* ♨ *Restaurant, room service, cable TV with movies and video games, health club, hot tub, sauna, bar, Internet, meeting rooms* ▤ *AE, D, DC, MC, V.*

$$$–$$$$ ▣ **Anchorage Westmark Hotel.** Each comfortable room in this 13-story hotel has a small private balcony and dark teak furnishings. Reserve a room or suite on the higher floors for the best mountain views. (Do not confuse the Westmark Hotel with the reasonably priced but far more basic Westmark Inn.) ✉ *720 W. 5th Ave., Downtown, 99501* ☎ *907/276–7676 or 800/544–0970* 🖷 *907/276–3615* ⊕ *www.westmarkhotels.com* ⇨ *182 rooms, 18 suites* ♨ *Restaurant, coffee shop, room service, cable TV with movies, Internet, meeting room* ▤ *AE, D, DC, MC, V.*

★ $$$ ▣ **Anchorage Hotel.** The little Anchorage Hotel building has been around since 1916. Experienced travelers call it the only hotel in Anchorage with charm: the original sinks and tubs have been restored, and upstairs hallways are lined with old Anchorage photos. The rooms are nicely updated with dark cherrywood furnishings and stocked minibars. The small lobby, its fireplace crackling in chilly weather, has a quaint European feel, and the staff is adept at meeting your needs. Request a corner room if possible; rooms facing the street may have some traffic noise. The junior suites include comfortable sitting areas. ✉ *330 E St., Downtown, 99501* ☎ *907/272–4553 or 800/544–0988* 🖷 *907/277–4483* ⊕ *www.historicanchoragehotel.com* ⇨ *16 rooms, 10 junior suites* ♨ *Some kitchenettes, minibars, cable TV, Internet, meeting rooms; no a/c, no smoking* ▤ *AE, D, DC, MC, V* ⏁ *CP.*

$$–$$$ ▣ **Comfort Inn Ship Creek.** Ship Creek gurgles past this popular family hotel, a short walk northeast of the Alaska Railroad depot. Rooms, which can be a bit noisy at times, come in a variety of configurations. A substantial Continental breakfast is served each morning. The hotel stocks a limited number of fishing poles for those who want to try their luck catching salmon in Ship Creek. ✉ *111 Ship Creek Ave., Downtown, 99501* ☎ *907/277–6887 or 800/362–6887* 🖷 *907/274–9830* ⊕ *www.comfortinn.com* ⇨ *88 rooms, 12 suites* ♨ *Some kitchens, microwaves, refrigerators, cable TV with movies and video games, pool, gym, hot tub, Internet, business services, some pets allowed (fee)* ▤ *AE, D, DC, MC, V* ⏁ *CP.*

$$ ▣ **Inlet TowerHote and Suites.** Windows overlook either the Chugach Mountain Range, the Cook Inlet, or downtown Anchorage in the 14-story Inlet Tower, built in 1953 in a residential area south of downtown and remodeled in 2003. Rooms and suites are spacious and have contemporary furnishings. Corner rooms, particularly those on the northeast side, provide expansive views. ✉ *1200 L St., Downtown, 99501* ☎ *907/276–0110 or 800/544–0786* 🖷 *907/258–4914* ⊕ *www.inlettower.com* ⇨ *154 rooms, 26 suites* ♨ *Restaurant, some kitchens, microwaves, refrigerators, cable TV, laundry facilities, meeting room, airport shuttle, free parking; no a/c* ▤ *AE, D, DC, MC, V.*

$$ ▨ **Sleeping Lady Bed & Breakfast.** The Tony Knowles Coastal Trail is steps away from this attractive B&B. Unwind on the large back deck and take in the lengthy summer sunsets over Cook Inlet. Four spacious and private guest rooms are attractively furnished, with three facing the water. The largest contains high arched windows and a fireplace. Downtown restaurants and shopping are within easy walking distance. ⊠ *545 M St., Downtown, 99501* ☎ *907/258–4455* 🖷 *907/258–4955* ⊕ *www. anchsleepingladybnb.com* ⇗ *4 rooms* ⌂ *Cable TV; no a/c, no smoking* ⊟ *MC, V* ⦿ *CP.*

$$ ▨ **Voyager Hotel.** Both business and leisure travelers stay here for the complete kitchens, sofa beds, coffeemakers, irons and ironing boards, quality linens, voice mail, and cable modems in the rooms. Upstairs, westside rooms have views of the inlet. ⊠ *501 K St., Downtown, 99501* ☎ *907/277–9501 or 800/247–9070* 🖷 *907/274–0333* ⊕ *www. voyagerhotel.com* ⇗ *40 rooms* ⌂ *In-room data ports, kitchens, microwaves, refrigerators, cable TV; no smoking* ⊟ *AE, D, DC, MC, V.*

$–$$ ▨ **Copper Whale Inn.** A view across Cook Inlet to Sleeping Lady and other mountains, rooms furnished with cherrywood beds, and a little backyard graced with a pleasant flower garden make this small inn on the edge of downtown cozy. Great food is available just a few steps away at Simon and Seafort's or Snow City Cafe. Owner Tony Carter, a marine biologist, leads an excellent all-day wildlife ecotour for $75. ⊠ *440 L St., Downtown, 99501* ☎ *907/258–7999* 🖷 *907/258–6213 or 888/ 942–5346* ⊕ *www.copperwhale.com* ⇗ *15 rooms* ⌂ *Dining room, Internet; no a/c, no room TVs, no smoking* ⊟ *AE, D, DC, MC, V* ⦿ *CP.*

$ ▨ **Merrill Field Inn.** Reasonable prices and surprisingly large rooms make this well-maintained motel, 1 mi east of downtown and across from Anchorage's small-plane airfield, a favorite with families. ⊠ *420 Sitka St., East Anchorage, 99501* ☎ *907/276–4547 or 800/898–4547* 🖷 *907/276– 5064* ⊕ *www.merrillfieldinn.com* ⇗ *39 rooms, 1 suite* ⌂ *Microwaves, refrigerators, cable TV, airport shuttle, some pets allowed (fee); no a/c* ⊟ *AE, D, DC, MC, V.*

¢–$ ▨ **Oscar Gill House.** Gill originally built his home in the settlement of Knik (north of Anchorage) in 1913. Three years later, he floated it by boat to Anchorage, where he later served as the mayor for three terms and then Speaker of the Territorial House. The home has been transformed into a comfortable B&B in a quiet neighborhood along Delaney Park Strip, with downtown attractions a short walk away. Two rooms share a bath with a classic claw-foot tub, and the third contains a private bath and Jacuzzi tub. Little touches include down comforters, bicycles, and a delicious breakfast. ⊠ *1344 W. 10th Ave., Downtown, 99501* ☎ *907/279–1344* ⊕ *www.oscargill.com* ⇗ *3 rooms* ⌂ *Cable TV, Internet; no a/c, no smoking* ⊟ *AE, MC, V* ⦿ *CP.*

$ ▨ **Anchorage Guesthouse.** Popular with young outdoorsy travelers, this hostel in a residential neighborhood near downtown has shared and private rooms. All rooms share three bathrooms, and there's a complimentary Continental breakfast. You can rent bikes here, then head out for the Tony Knowles Coastal Trail. On-site storage keeps your stuff safe. ⊠ *826 K St., Midtown, 99517* ☎ *907/274–0408* ⊕ *www.akhouse. com* ⇗ *1 shared room, 3 private rooms* ⌂ *Kitchen, bicycles, library, laundry facilities, Internet; no room phones, no room TVs, no smoking* ⊟ *AE, MC, V* ⦿ *CP.*

Greater Anchorage

$$$$ ▨ **Alyeska Prince Hotel.** Lush forests surround this large and luxurious hotel at the base of Mt. Alyeska Ski Resort, an hour south of Anchorage. Some rooms have views of the Chugach Mountains. Rooms are on the small side, but all have heated towel racks, ski-boot storage, bathrobes,

FodorsChoice
★

and slippers, plus phones are in both the bathrooms and bedrooms. A spectacular aerial tram (free if you have dinner reservations) transports diners to the Seven Glaciers restaurant at the 2,300-foot level of the mountain. ⊠ *1000 Arlberg Rd.* ⌖ *Box 249, Girdwood 99587* ☎ *907/754–1111 or 800/880–3880* 🖷 *907/754–2200* ⊕ *www.alyeskaresort.com* ⇆ *296 rooms, 12 suites* ⚲ *2 restaurants, room service, in-room safes, refrigerators, cable TV with movies, indoor pool, gym, hot tub, massage, sauna, cross-country skiing, downhill skiing, ice-skating, bar, shop, Internet, business services, meeting room, no-smoking rooms* ▭ *AE, D, DC, MC, V.*

★ **$$$$** ▦ **Millennium Anchorage Hotel.** Perched on the shore of Lake Hood, the Millennium Anchorage Hotel is one of the city's best spots to watch planes come and go. The lobby resembles a hunting lodge with its stone fireplace, trophy heads, and mounted fish on every wall. The luxuriously appointed guest rooms continue the inviting Alaskan theme. Most have colorful Native Alaskan–style bedding and moose-shape cast-iron lamps. All rooms have coffeemakers and hair dryers. The Flying Machine Restaurant here is locally famous for its enormous Sunday brunch buffets ($29). ⊠ *4800 Spenard Rd., Midtown, 99517* ☎ *907/243–2300 or 800/544–0553* 🖷 *907/243–8815* ⊕ *www.millennium-hotels.com* ⇆ *243 rooms, 5 suites* ⚲ *Restaurant, room service, refrigerators, cable TV with movies and video games, gym, hot tub, sauna, steam room, lobby lounge, laundry service, airport shuttle, some pets allowed* ▭ *AE, D, DC, MC, V.*

$$–$$$$ ▦ **Mahogany Manor.** Escape from city life at this rambling B&B, hidden behind a tall fence along busy 15th Avenue and decorated with Native Alaskan art throughout. Unwind with the expansive decks, large picture windows, indoor waterfall, fireplaces, and big-screen television. An unusual 19-foot hot tub and jetted lap pool occupies a lower deck. The spacious three-room suite is perfect for families and small groups. A generous Continental breakfast is served anytime, and you have access to a separate kitchen. ⊠ *204 E. 15th Ave., Midtown, 99501* ☎ *907/278–1111 or 888/777–0346* 🖷 *907/258–7877* ⊕ *www.mahoganymanor. com* ⇆ *5 rooms* ⚲ *Dining room, cable TV, 2 pools, hot tub, Internet; no a/c, no smoking* ▭ *AE, D, MC, V* ⏣ *CP.*

$$$ ▦ **Hampton Inn.** Midway between the airport and downtown, the Hampton has all the now-standard room features: designer furnishings, coffeemakers, hair dryers, and voice mail. The same management also runs **Hilton Garden Inn,** directly across A Street. ⊠ *4301 Credit Union Dr., Midtown, 99503* ☎ *907/550–7000 or 800/426–7866* 🖷 *907/561–7330* ⊕ *www.stonebridgecompanies.com* ⇆ *101 rooms* ⚲ *In-room data ports, microwaves, refrigerators, cable TV with movies and video games, indoor pool, exercise equipment, hot tub, laundry service, Internet, business services, meeting room* ▭ *AE, D, DC, MC, V* ⏣ *CP.*

★ **$$–$$$** ▦ **Aurora Winds Bed & Breakfast.** Anchorage's largest B&B—it sprawls across a lavish 12,000-square-foot Hillside home—exudes a quiet elegance. Rooms are filled with classic pieces, including one with a cherrywood sleigh bed, fireplace, private sitting area, and Jacuzzi tub. All rooms have amenities expected in a fine hotel, and co-owner James Montgomery's gourmet breakfasts are always a hit. The home also features a library, theater, billiards room, and full gym. Kids are welcome. ⊠ *7501 Upper O'Malley, 99516* ☎ *907/346–2533* 🖷 *907/346–3192* ⊕ *www.aurorawinds.com* ⇆ *5 suites* ⚲ *Dining room, cable TV, gym, indoor pool, hot tub, sauna, billiards, Internet; no smoking* ▭ *AE, MC, V* ⏣ *CP.*

$$–$$$ ▦ **Courtyard by Marriott.** Business travelers pack this modern hotel near the airport. The restaurant serves breakfast and dinner but only limited room service in the evening. Some rooms have a whirlpool bath and king-size bed; all have two phones, coffeemakers, and hair dryers. ⊠ *4901 Spenard Rd., Midtown, 99517* ☎ *907/245–0322 or 800/321–2211* 🖷 *907/248–1886* ⊕ *www.marriott.com* ⇆ *148 rooms, 6 suites* ⚐ *Restaurant, room service, some in-room hot tubs, cable TV with movies, pool, exercise equipment, hot tub, sauna, laundry service, meeting room, airport shuttle, no-smoking rooms* ⊟ *AE, D, DC, MC, V.*

$$ ▣ **SpringHill Suites by Marriott.** The city's main public library and a 16-plex movie theater are near this midtown Anchorage hotel. Spacious suites have separate living and sleeping areas and either a king bed or two double beds with a pull-out sofa. Up to five people can stay in these suites for the same price. ⊠ *3401 A St., Downtown, 99503* ☎ *907/562–3247 or 888/287–9400* 🖷 *907/562–3250* ⊕ *www.springhillsuites.com* ⇆ *102 suites* ⚐ *Microwaves, refrigerators, cable TV with movies, indoor pool, gym, meeting rooms, airport shuttle* ⊟ *AE, D, DC, MC, V* ⦿| *CP.*

¢ ▣ **Qupqugiaq Inn.** A bland, boxy exterior disguises this cross between a motel and a hostel with an unpronounceable name. The interior architecture of "Q Inn" is distinctive, with curved walls and bright pine accents. This is a good option for budget travelers who tolerate small quarters and the lack of in-room phones but appreciate clean and well-maintained facilities. You have access to a communal kitchen and sitting room. ⊠ *640 W. 36th Ave., Midtown, 99503* ☎ *907/562–5681* ⊕ *www.qupq.com* ⇆ *16 rooms, 4 with shared bath* ⚐ *Café, Internet, meeting rooms; no a/c, no room phones, no TV in some rooms, no smoking* ⊟ *AE, MC, V.*

NIGHTLIFE & THE ARTS

Nightlife

Anchorage does not shut down when it gets dark. Bars here—and throughout Alaska—open early (in the morning) and close as late as 3 AM on weekends. The *Anchorage Daily News* entertainment section, published on Friday, has a complete listing of entertainment options, ranging from concerts and theater to movies and a roundup of nightspots featuring live music.

Bars & Nightclubs

FodorsChoice **Chilkoot Charlie's** (⊠ 2435 Spenard Rd., Midtown ☎ 907/272–1010
★ ⊕ www.koots.com), a rambling timber building with sawdust floors, nine bars, three dance floors, loud music (rock or swing bands and DJs) nightly, and rowdy customers, is where young Alaskans go to get crazy. This legendary bar has all sorts of unusual nooks and crannies, including a room filled with Russian artifacts and serving the finest vodka drinks, plus a reconstructed version of Alaska's infamous Birdhouse Bar. "Koots" even made *Playboy*'s list as the number one bar in America in 2000. If you haven't been to Koots, you haven't seen Anchorage nightlife at its most insane.

Lots of old-timers favor the dark bar of **Club Paris** (⊠ 417 W. 5th Ave., Downtown ☎ 907/277–6332 ⊕ www.clubparisrestaurant.com). Once the classiest place in downtown Anchorage, with its Paris mural and French street lamps hanging behind the bar, it has lost the glamour but not the faithful clientele. There's mostly swing on the jukebox.

F Street Station (⊠ 325 F St., Downtown ☎ 907/272–5196), a crowded little downtown bar, is a delightful spot for a perfectly prepared and reasonably priced lunch or dinner. Check the board for the day's specials, or just enjoy a beer and appetizers with the suit-and-tie crowd. A half-dozen small tables are available, or you can eat at the bar and chat with the chefs as they work.

A trendy place for the dressy "in" crowd, the bar at **Simon and Seafort's Saloon and Grill** (✉ 420 L St., Downtown ☎ 907/274–3502 ⊕ www.r-u-i.com/sim) has stunning views of Cook Inlet, a special single-malt Scotch menu, and a wide selection of imported beers.

Snowgoose Restaurant (✉ 717 W. 3rd Ave., Downtown ☎ 907/277–7727 ⊕ www.alaskabeers.com) is a good place to unwind with beer inside or on the airy outside deck overlooking Cook Inlet. There's excellent food, too.

Anchorage's gay nightlife centers on a pair of bars, both of which attract a mixed crowd that includes straights, gays, and lesbians. **Mad Myrna's** (✉ 530 E. 5th Ave., Downtown ☎ 907/276–9762 ⊕ www.alaska.net//~madmyrna) has karaoke on Wednesday, country dancing (with lessons) on Thursday, and drag shows every Friday. The **Raven** (✉ 708 E. 4th Ave., Downtown ☎ 907/276–9672) is a smoky neighborhood hangout where you'll meet regulars over a game of billiards or darts. In addition to the bars, Anchorage also has a popular alcohol-free **Gay and Lesbian Community Center** (✉ 2110 E. Northern Lights Blvd., Midtown ☎ 907/929–4528). It's open daily.

Comedy

★ Mr. Whitekeys is the proprietor of **Fly by Night Club** (✉ 3300 Spenard Rd., Midtown ☎ 907/279–7726 ⊕ www.flybynightclub.com), a self-proclaimed "sleazy Spenard nightclub." Every summer, the "Whale Fat Follies" revue has tacky Alaska jokes, a witty skewering of the state's politicians, accomplished singing, and the boogie-woogie piano of Mr. Whitekeys himself. Go with a local to really appreciate all the inside jokes. Shows start at 8; reserving several days in advance is a good idea. The club is smoke-free Tuesday, Wednesday, and Thursday night; it's closed Sunday–Monday and January–March.

Live Music

See the "8" section in Friday editions of the *Anchorage Daily News* for complete listings of upcoming concerts and other musical performances, or get the same entertainment info on-line at ⊕ www.adn.com. On most summertime Fridays, open-air concerts are performed at noon on the stage in front of the **Old City Hall** (✉ 524 W. 4th Ave., Downtown). A range of performers plays at the **Saturday Market** (✉ 3rd Ave. and E St., Downtown ☎ 907/272–5634 ⊕ www.anchoragemarkets.com) every Saturday from late May to mid-September. The music includes everything from family bands (with daughter on violin and dad on guitar and vocals) to Peruvian pan-pipe musicians.

Chilkoot Charlie's (⇨ Bars & Nightclubs) is an exceptionally popular party place, with live music every night of the week. One of Anchorage's favorite singles bars, **Humpy's Great Alaskan Alehouse** (✉ 610 W. 6th Ave., Downtown ☎ 907/276–2337 ⊕ www.humpys.com), serves up rock, blues, and folk seven nights a week, along with dozens of microbrews (including more than 40 beers on tap) and surprisingly tasty pub grub. It's noisy, smoky, and always packed.

Blues Central/Chef's Inn (✉ 825 W. Northern Lights Blvd., Midtown ☎ 907/272–1341 ⊕ www.bluescentralproductions.com), a modest and smoky eatery, is also a blues mecca that stages bands on weekend nights. Tony Lamas and Wranglers are the uniform of choice at South Anchorage's country venue, **Long Branch Saloon** (✉ 1737 E. Dimond Blvd., South Anchorage ☎ 907/349–4142).

Fans of salsa, merengue, and other music crowd the dance floor at the downtown **Club Soraya** (⊠ 333 W. 4th Ave., Downtown ☎ 907/276–0670). There are free Latin dance classes at 8 PM on Saturday, followed by live bands. **Hot Rods** (⊠ 4848 Old Seward Hwy., Midtown ☎ 907/562–5701) has dance tunes from the '70s and '80s most nights, with karaoke on Thursday, and has a retro look from a time when Elvis ruled the charts. Downstairs, 16 antique billiards tables attract pool sharks. Downtown's **Snow City Cafe** (⊠ 4th Ave. at L St., Downtown ☎ 907/272–2489) has open-mike sessions on Sunday evening along with Wednesday-evening Irish jam sessions.

The Arts

Anchorage often surprises by the variety—and high quality—of cultural activities in this town of ¼ million people. In addition to top-name touring groups and performers, a sampling of local productions, including provocative theater, children's shows, improvisational troupes, Buddhist lectures, photography exhibits, poetry readings, and Native Alaskan dance performances, are always going on around town. The Friday entertainment section of the *Anchorage Daily News* is packed with events and activities. Tickets for many cultural events can be purchased at any Carrs grocery store. **Carrs Tix** (☎ 907/263–2787 or 800/478–7328 ⊕ www.tickets.com) has recorded information on cultural events of the week and the option to buy tickets by phone or from the Web site.

The **Alaska Center for the Performing Arts** (⊠ 621 W. 6th Ave., Downtown ☎ 907/263–2787 or 907/263–2900 ⊕ www.alaskapac.org) has three theaters and hosts local performing groups as well as traveling production companies that in the last few years have brought *Rent, Les Misérables,* and *Cabaret* to the Anchorage stage. The lobby box office, open Monday–Saturday 10–6, sells tickets to the productions and is a good all-around source of cultural information. During the summer, you can watch IMAX movies at the Center for the Performing Arts, along with a special northern lights show.

Opera & Classical Music

The **Anchorage Opera** (☎ 907/279–2557 ⊕ www.anchorageopera.org) produces three operas during its November–March season. The **Anchorage Symphony Orchestra** (☎ 907/274–8668 ⊕ www.anchoragesymphony.org) performs classical concerts October through April. The box office of the Alaska Center for the Performing Arts sells tickets for both.

Theater

The **Alaska Center for the Performing Arts** hosts the Anchorage Opera and the Anchorage Symphony Orchestra among other major performances. **Cyrano's Off-Center Playhouse** (⊠ 4th Ave. and D St., Downtown ☎ 907/274–2599 ⊕ www.cyranos.org) mounts innovative productions in a cozy theater connected to a namesake café and bookstore. **Out North Contemporary Art House** (⊠ 1325 Primrose St., just west of Bragaw Rd. off DeBarr Rd., East Anchorage ☎ 907/279–8200 ⊕ www.outnorth.org), whose productions are thought-provoking and, at times, controversial, often earns critical acclaim from local reviewers. Student productions from the **University of Alaska Anchorage Theater** (⊠ 3211 Providence Dr., East Anchorage ☎ 907/786–4721) are timely and well done. The theater is intimate, with seating on three sides.

SPORTS & THE OUTDOORS

Anchorage is an active city, with a blend of spectator and do-it-yourself fun. Wintertime brings hockey, dog mushing, and ski races, and the long summer days provide the chance to watch a semipro baseball game, bike the Coastal Trail, and still have time to watch the sun go down at midnight.

Baseball

Two semiprofessional baseball teams, made up of college players, play at Mulcahy Stadium next to the Sullivan Arena. The games played here are intense—many players have gone on to star in the major leagues. The **Anchorage Bucs** (☎ 907/561–2827 ⊕ www.anchoragebucs.com) have a dozen or so former players who went on to the majors, including standouts Wally Joyner, Jeff Kent, and Bobby Jones. The most famous player on the **Glacier Pilots** (☎ 907/274–3627 ⊕ www.glacierpilots.com) was Mark McGwire, but many other pre–major leaguers have played for them over the years.

Basketball

The University of Alaska Anchorage hosts the **Great Alaska Shootout** (⊕ www.shootout.net) at the Sullivan Arena over Thanksgiving weekend. In addition, the UAA Seawolves men's and women's basketball teams play on campus during the winter months.

Bicycling, Running & Walking

Anchorage has more than 120 mi of paved bicycle trails, and many streets have marked bike lanes. Although busy during the day, downtown streets are uncrowded and safe for cyclists in the evening. The **Tony Knowles Coastal Trail** (⊕ www.trailsofanchorage.com) and other bike trails in Anchorage are used by runners, cyclists, in-line skaters, and walkers. It begins downtown off 2nd Avenue and is also easily accessible from Westchester Lagoon near the west end of 15th Avenue. The trail runs from the lagoon 2 mi to Earthquake Park and then continues an additional 7 mi to Kincaid Park.

A number of running events are held annually in Anchorage: the **Alaska Run for Women** (⊕ www.akrfw.org) in early June, the late-April **Heart Run**, and the **Mayor's Midnight Sun Marathon** (⊕ www.mayorsmarathon.com) on the summer solstice in late June.

Downtown Bicycle Rental (✉ 245 W. 5th Ave., Downtown ☎ 907/279–5293 ⊕ www.alaska-bike-rentals.com) rents mountain bikes and provides trail recommendations.

Bird-Watching

Popular bird-watching places include the Tony Knowles Coastal Trail, which provides access to Westchester Lagoon and nearby tide flats, along with Potter Marsh on the south end of Anchorage. The local chapter of the **Audubon Society** (☎ 907/276–7034 ⊕ www.audubon.org/chapter/ak) refers you to local birders who will advise you on the best bird-watching spots. You can also sign up for bird-watching classes and field trips. A **bird hot line** (☎ 907/338–2473) tracks the latest sightings in town. For guided bird-watching, contact **Bird Watching Tours of Anchorage, Alaska** (☎ 907/248–7282 or 888/334–7282 ⊕ www.anchoragebirding.com) or **Wilderness Birding Adventures** (☎ 907/694–7442 ⊕ www.wildernessbirding.com).

Canoeing & Kayaking

Local lakes and lagoons, such as Westchester Lagoon, Goose Lake, and Jewel Lake, have favorable conditions for boating. More adventurous paddlers will want to head to Whittier or Seward for sea kayaking. Rent sea kayaks from **Kayak and Custom Adventures Worldwide** (✉ 328 3rd Ave., Seward 99664 ☎ 907/258–3866 or 800/288–3134 ⊕ www.kayakak.com), which also leads day trips in the Seward area. Better known as REI, **Recreational Equipment Inc.** (✉ 1200 W. Northern Lights Blvd., Midtown ☎ 907/272–4565 ⊕ www.rei.com) sells and rents all sorts of outdoor gear, including canoes and sea kayaks.

Dogsled Races

World-championship races are run in mid-February, with three consecutive 25-mi heats through downtown Anchorage, out into the foothills, and back. People line the route with cups of coffee in hand to cheer on their favorite mushers. The three-day races are part of the annual **Fur Rendezvous,** one of the largest winter festivals in the United States; other attractions include a snow-sculpture competition, car races, the Miners and Trappers Ball, a carnival, and even snowshoe softball. The **festival office** (✉ 400 D St., No. 200, Downtown, 99501 ☎ 907/277–8615 ⊕ www.furrondy.net) has a guide to the events.

FodorsChoice
★

In March, mushers and their dogs compete in the 1,100-mi **Iditarod Trail Sled Dog Race** (☎ 907/376–5155 or 800/545–6874 Iditarod Trail Headquarters ⊕ www.iditarod.com). The race commemorates the delivery of serum to Nome by dog mushers during the diphtheria epidemic of 1925. The serum run was the inspiration for the animated family film *Balto*. Dog teams leave downtown Anchorage and wind through the Alaska Range, across the Interior, out to the Bering Sea coast, and on to Nome. Depending on weather and trail conditions, winners can complete the race in nine days (⇨ The Last Great Race on Earth box).

Fishing

Nearly 30 local lakes are stocked with trout. You must have a valid Alaska sportfishing license. Jewel Lake in South Anchorage and Mirror and Fire lakes near Eagle River all hold fish. Coho salmon return to Ship Creek (downtown) in August, and king salmon are caught between late May and early July. Campbell Creek and Bird Creek just south of town are also good spots. Fishing licenses may be purchased at any Carrs grocery or local sporting goods store. Contact the **Alaska Department of Fish and Game** (☎ 907/267–2218 ⊕ www.state.ak.us/adfg) for licensing information.

Golf

Anchorage is Alaska's golfing capital, with several public courses. They won't compare to offerings in Phoenix or San Diego, but courses are open until 10 PM on long summer days.

Anchorage Golf Course (☎ 907/522–3363) on O'Malley Road has 18 holes with greens. Golf carts and clubs are available for rent. **Russian Jack Springs** (☎ 907/333–8338) is run by the city and generally open May–September. It has 9 holes, synthetic greens, and clubs for rent. **Tanglewood Lakes Golf Club** (☎ 907/345–4600) is a 9-hole course in South Anchorage.

Hockey

Hockey is in the blood of any true Alaskan, and kids as young as four years crowd local ice rinks in hopes of becoming the next Scott Gomez (who still lives in Anchorage when he's not playing for the New Jersey Devils).

The West Coast Hockey League's **Anchorage Aces** (☎ 907/258–2237 ⊕ www.anchorageaces.com) play minor-league professional hockey in the arena. The **University of Alaska Anchorage** has a Division I NCAA hockey team that draws several thousand loyal fans to home games at the Sullivan Arena.

Ice-Skating

Ice-skating is a favorite wintertime activity in Anchorage, with several indoor ice arenas, outdoor hockey rinks, and local ponds opening when temperatures drop.

Ben Boeke (⌧ 334 E. 16th Ave., Midtown ☎ 907/274–5715 ⊕ www. benboeke.com) is a city-run indoor ice arena with open skating and skate rentals year-round. The **Dimond Ice Chalet** (⌧ 800 E. Dimond Blvd., South Anchorage ☎ 907/344–1212 ⊕ www.dimondcenter.com) has an indoor ice rink at Dimond Mall that is open to the public daily, with lessons and skate rentals. In winter, **Westchester Lagoon**, 1 mi south of downtown, is a favorite outdoor family (and competitive) skating area, with smooth ice and piles of firewood next to the warming barrels.

Racquet Sports & Fitness Club

The park strip at 9th Avenue and C Street has several tennis courts. On the south side of Anchorage, the **Dimond Athletic Club** (⌧ 800 E. Dimond Blvd., at Old Seward, South Anchorage ☎ 907/344–7788) has a lap pool, Nautilus equipment, free weights, saunas, hot tubs, steam rooms, and racquetball courts, plus various exercise classes. You can buy a daily guest pass for $15.

Rafting

Based in Girdwood, **Class V Whitewater** (⌼ Box 591, Girdwood 99587 ☎ 907/783–2004 ⊕ www.alaskanrafting.com) leads scenic floats on the Twenty Mile and Portage rivers, along with white-water trips on the Talkeetna and Sixmile rivers. Alaska's oldest adventure and wilderness guiding company (in business since 1975), **Nova** (⌼ Box 1129, Chickaloon 99674 ☎ 907/745–5753 or 800/746–5753 🖷 907/745–5754 ⊕ www.novalaska.com) provides both scenic and white-water wilderness rafting trips statewide.

Skiing

Cross-country skiing is extremely popular in Anchorage. Locals ski on trails in town at Kincaid Park or Hillside and farther away at Girdwood Valley, Turnagain Pass, and Chugach State Park. Downhill skiing is convenient to downtown. A number of cross-country ski events are held annually in Anchorage. The **Alaska Ski for Women** (⊕ www. alaskaskiforwomen.org), held in February, is the biggest women's ski race in North America, attracting more than 1,500 skiers. The **Nordic Skiing Association of Anchorage** (⊕ www.alaska.net/~nsaa) sponsors many other ski races and events throughout the winter. The **Tour of Anchorage** (⊕ www.tourofanchorage.com) comes to town in March.

Alyeska Ski Resort (☎ 907/754–1111, 800/880–3880, 907/754–7669 recorded information ⊕ www.alyeskaresort.com), at Girdwood, 40 mi south of the city, is a full-service resort with a day lodge, hotel, restaurants, six chairlifts, a tram, a vertical drop of 2,500 feet, and runs for all abilities. The tram ($19) is open during the summer, providing access to the Seven Glaciers restaurant and hiking trails. **Alyeska Accommodations** (☎ 907/783–2000 or 888/783–2001 🖷 907/783–2425 ⊕ www. alyeskaaccommodations.com) can set you up in a privately owned cabin or condo. **Alpenglow at Arctic Valley** (☎ 907/428–1208, 907/249–9292 recorded information ⊕ www.skialpenglow.com) is a small ski area just north of Anchorage. On the edge of town, **Hilltop Ski Area** (☎ 907/346–1446 ⊕ www.hilltopskiarea.org) is a favorite ski area with families.

The locally owned **Alaska Mountaineering and Hiking** (⌧ 2633 Spenard Rd., Midtown ☎ 907/272–1811 ⊕ www.alaskan.com/amh) outdoors shop has a highly experienced staff and plenty of cross-country skis for

CloseUp

THE LAST GREAT RACE ON EARTH

SINCE 1973, mushers and their sled-dog teams have raced more than 1,100 mi across Alaska in a marathon vision quest unlike any other: the Iditarod Trail Sled Dog Race, the longest sled-dog race in the world. After a ceremonial start in downtown Anchorage on the first Saturday in March, dog teams wind through Alaska, battling almost every imaginable winter challenge. Ten days later, the "Last Great Race on Earth" ends with spectacular fanfare in Nome, on the Bering Sea coast.

The Iditarod's origins can be traced to two events: an early 1900s long-distance race called the All-Alaska Sweepstakes and the delivery of a lifesaving serum to Nome by dog mushers during a diphtheria outbreak in 1925. Fascinated with the trail's history, Alaskan sled-dog enthusiasts Dorothy Page and Joe Redington Sr. staged the first race in 1967 to celebrate the role of mushing in Alaska's history. Only 50 mi long and with a purse of $25,000—no small amount at that time—it attracted the best of Alaska's competitive mushers. Enthusiasm waned in 1969, however, when the available winnings fell to $1,000. Instead of giving up, Redington enlarged it.

In 1973, after three years without a race, he organized a 1,000-mi race from Anchorage to Nome, with a then-outrageous purse of $50,000. Critics scoffed, but 34 racers entered. First place went to a little-known musher named Dick Wilmarth, who finished in 20 days. Redington then billed the Iditarod as a 1,049-mi race to symbolize Alaska, the 49th state (still the official distance, even though the race really covers 1,100 mi).

The race actually begins in Wasilla, home of the Iditarod headquarters, a few miles from Anchorage. The first few hundred miles take mushers and dogs through wooded lowlands and flat hills, including a stretch known as Moose Alley. Teams then cross the Alaska Range, where they travel through a narrow, boulder-filled canyon known as the Dalzell Gorge. Beyond the Alaska Range, they enter Interior Alaska, with Athabascan villages and gold-rush ghost towns, including

Iditarod. Only a few abandoned and weather-beaten buildings now mark the site of the race's namesake. Next, the trail follows the frozen Yukon River, then cuts over to the Bering Sea coast for the final 270-mi "sprint" to Nome. It was here, in 1985, that Libby Riddles drove her team into a blinding blizzard, en route to a victory that made her the first woman to win the race. After that, Susan Butcher (now retired) won the race four times, but the all-time record holder is Rick Swenson, with five victories. The fastest time was recorded in 2002, when Swiss-born musher Martin Buser completed the race in just under nine days.

In any given year, both Iditarod mushers and dogs may have to endure extreme cold, deep snow, gale-force winds, whiteouts, river overflow, and moose attacks, not to mention fraying tempers. Racers contending for the challenge also face exhaustion and hallucinations that result from their sleep deprivation. As for the dogs, the race has sparked harsh criticism from animal rights supporters, who claim the animals are mistreated. Indeed, this remains a sensitive issue, and Iditarod policy continues to enforce humane care and treatment of dogs.

More than three decades after its establishment, Redington's long-distance dream has gained international acclaim. The Iditarod race purse tops $600,000, with more than $60,000 to the champion. Dozens of journalists from around the world report from the trail, and entrants have come from more than a dozen countries. Though racers such as Swenson, Dee Dee Jonrowe, Martin Buser, and Jeff King draw the biggest crowds and the most media attention, all mushers—and dogs—who reach Nome are appropriately treated like champions after surviving their 1,100-mi run across Alaska's wilderness.

sale or rent. Ski sales and rentals are available from **Recreational Equipment Inc.** (REI; ✉ 1200 W. Northern Lights Blvd., Midtown ☎ 907/272–4565 ⊕ www.rei.com).

Water Sports

H2Oasis Water Park (✉ 11030 Chelea St., South Anchorage, 99516 ☎ 907/344–8610 or 888/426–2747 ⊕ www.h2oasiswaterpark.com) is Alaska's first—and only—water park. Housed within a medieval castle-shape structure, this large indoor facility opened in 2003 and is a favorite of kids of all ages. Attractions include a pool that generates 3-foot bodysurfing waves, a 475-foot-long water-powered roller coaster, a 150-foot slide, plus a pirate ship with water cannons and slides, a children's lagoon and lazy river, a splash pool, and more. All told, the park has pools filled with more than 350,000 gallons of water. H2Oasis is open year-round and costs adults $20 for all day; kids pay $15.

For something simple, head to the **West High School Pool,** where a spiral water slide is available, along with diving boards and lap lanes. The large pool and high ceilings at the **University of Alaska Anchorage** (☎ 907/786–1231 ⊕ www.uaa.alaska.edu) are geared toward fitness swimmers. Your $5 admission to the UAA pool also provides access to the ice rink, weight room, saunas, racquetball courts, and gym.

SHOPPING

Stock up for your travels around Alaska in Anchorage, where prices are reasonable and there's no sales tax. It's a good choice for souvenirs as well; downtown gift shops sell trinkets and artwork. The Saturday market is packed with Alaskan-made products of all types, and you're likely to meet local artisans.

Malls & Department Stores

Anchorage's **5th Avenue Mall** occupies a city block at 5th Avenue and A Street and contains dozens of stores spread over several levels, including a JCPenney. The top level houses a food court for quick, inexpensive meals. Just across 6th Avenue, and connected by a skywalk to the 5th Avenue Mall, is Alaska's only **Nordstrom.** The city's largest shopping mall, **Dimond Center,** is on the south end of town at Dimond Boulevard and Old Seward Highway. In addition to dozens of shops, Dimond Center houses a movie theater. Nearby are several big-box discount stores, including Costco, Best Buy, and Wal-Mart.

Market

Fodor'sChoice During the summer, Anchorage's **Saturday Market** (☎ 907/272–5634
★ ⊕ www.anchoragemarkets.com) is open in the parking lot at 3rd Avenue and E Street. Browse here for Alaskan-made crafts, ethnic imports, and deliciously fattening food. It's open from mid-May to mid-September, Saturday 10–6. A smaller market sells local produce and crafts June–August, Wednesday 11–5, at Northway Mall in East Anchorage.

Specialty Shops

Art

Anchorage's **First Friday** art openings have become a popular monthly event, with 15 or so galleries offering a chance to sample hors d'oeuvres while looking over the latest works by regional artists. Alaska's oldest gallery, **Artique** (✉ 314 G St., Downtown ☎ 907/277–1663 ⊕ www.artiqueltd.com), sells paintings, prints, and jewelry by prominent Alaskan artists. **Decker/Morris Gallery** (✉ 621 W. 6th Ave., south side of Alaska Center for the Performing Arts, Downtown ☎ 907/272–1489 ⊕ www. deckermorrisgallery.com) carries works by better-known Alaskan artists—both Native and non-Native—contemporary originals and prints, jewelry, and sculpture. The **International Gallery of Contemporary Art** (✉ 427 D St., Downtown ☎ 907/258–0307 ⊕ www.igcaalaska.org) is Anchorage's premier fine arts gallery, with changing exhibits monthly. Right next door is **One People** (✉ 425 D St., Downtown ☎ 907/274–4063) with the works of Alaskan artists and crafts workers, including an excellent selection of Native pieces.

Books

Barnes & Noble Booksellers (✉ 200 E. Northern Lights Blvd., at A St., Midtown ☎ 907/279–7323 ⊕ www.bn.com) is Alaska's largest bookstore, with books and magazines plus a Starbucks. **Borders Books & Music** (✉ 1100 E. Dimond Blvd., west of Seward Hwy., South Anchorage ☎ 907/344–4099 ⊕ www.borders.com) stocks a diverse selection of titles and has a café. **Cook Inlet Book Company** (✉ 415 W. 5th Ave., Downtown ☎ 907/258–4544 or 800/240–4148 ⊕ www.cookinlet. com) has the largest collection of Alaskan titles in the state and a substantial newspaper and magazine section. **Metro Music & Book Store** (✉ 530 E. Benson Blvd., Midtown ☎ 907/279–8622) is great for browsing and carries a well-thought-out inventory of fiction and nonfiction. The collection of CDs is easily the best in Alaska, and you're welcome to listen to any of them before buying.

Gift Ideas

Tundra Arts (✉ 425 D St., Downtown ☎ 907/276–0190) is one of the best downtown spots to find Alaska Native pieces. Several downtown shops sell quality Native Alaskan artwork, but the best buys can be found in the gift shop at the **Alaska Native Medical Center** (✉ 4315 Diplomacy Dr., at Tudor and Bragaw Rds., East Anchorage ☎ 907/729–1122), which is open weekdays 10–2 and 11–2 on the first and third Saturday of the month. Also of note is **Alaska Native Heritage Center** (✉ 8800 Heritage Center Dr. [Glenn Hwy. at Muldoon Rd.], East Anchorage ☎ 907/ 330–8000 or 800/315–6608 ⊕ www.alaskanative.net), with a gift shop that sells Native crafts.

Laura Wright Alaskan Parkys sells distinctive Eskimo-style "parkys" (parkas) and will custom-sew one for you. They're available at Moose Hollow Gifts (✉ 720 D St., Downtown ☎ 907/274–4215 ⊕ www. alaskan.com/parkys). **Oomingmak** (✉ 6th Ave. and H St., Downtown ☎ 907/272–9225 or 888/360–9665 ⊕ www.qiviut.com), a Native-owned cooperative, sells items made of qiviut, the warm undercoat of the musk ox. Scarves, shawls, and tunics are knitted in traditional patterns.

Frozen seafood and smoked fish are available from **10th and M Seafoods** (✉ 1020 M St., Downtown ☎ 907/272–3474 or 800/770–2722 ⊕ www.10thandmseafoods.com ✉ 301 Muldoon Rd. ☎ 907/337–8831). **New Sagaya's City Market** sells an excellent selection of fresh seafood. If you don't want to carry the fish with you, the market will pack and ship it home. Get smoked reindeer meat and salmon products at **Alaska Sausage Company** (✉ 2914 Arctic Blvd., Midtown ☎ 907/562–3636 or 800/798–3636 ⊕ www.alaskasausage.com).

Although furs may not be to everyone's taste or ethics, a number of Alaska fur companies have stores and factories in Anchorage. One of the city's largest and best-known furriers is **David Green Master Furrier** (✉ 130 W. 4th Ave., Downtown ☎ 907/277–9595). **Alaska Fur Exchange**

(✉ 4417 Old Seward Hwy., Midtown ☎ 907/563–3877 ⊕ www.
alaskafurexchange.com) has a large midtown store that sells both furs
and Native artwork.

Jewelry

The **Kobuk Valley Jade Co.** (✉ Olympic Cir., Girdwood ☎ 907/783–2764),
at the base of Mt. Alyeska, sells hand-polished jade pieces as well as Native masks, baskets, and jewelry.

ANCHORAGE A TO Z

*To research prices, get advice from other travelers, and book travel ar-
rangements, visit www.fodors.com.*

AIRPORTS & TRANSFERS

Ted Stevens Anchorage International Airport is 6 mi from downtown
Anchorage on International Airport Road. It is served by Alaska, American, Continental, Delta, Northwest, and United airlines, along with a
number of international carriers. Several carriers, including ERA and
PenAir, connect Anchorage with smaller Alaskan communities. Floatplane operators and helicopters serve the area from Lake Hood, which
is adjacent to and part of Anchorage International Airport. There are
also a number of smaller air taxis and air-charter operations at Merrill
Field, 2 mi east of downtown on 5th Avenue.

A major redevelopment project at Ted Stevens Anchorage International
Airport has brought a new air terminal and Alaska Railroad station with
direct service to downtown.
🔐 **Ted Stevens Anchorage International Airport** ☎ 907/266-2529 ⊕ www.
anchorageairport.com.

AIRPORT   Taxis queue up at the lower level of the airport terminal outside the bag-
TRANSFERS   gage-claim area. Alaska Cab, Borealis Shuttle, Checker Cab, Yellow Cab,
and Anchorage Taxi Cab (⇨ Taxis) all operate here; you'll get whichever
cab is next in line. Most charge about $17, not including tip, for the
ride to downtown hotels.

BOAT & FERRY TRAVEL

Cruise ships sailing the Gulf of Alaska and the Alaska Marine ferries
call in Seward, several hours by train or bus south of Anchorage. The
South Central route of the Alaska Marine Highway connects Kodiak,
Port Lions, Homer, Seldovia, Seward, Valdez, Cordova, and Whittier.
🔐 **Alaska Marine Highway System** ✉ 605 W. 4th Ave., inside Alaska Public Lands
Information Center, Downtown ☎ 907/272-7116 or 800/642-0066 🖷 907/277-4829
⊕ www.state.ak.us/ferry.

BUS TRAVEL

The municipal People Mover covers the whole Anchorage bowl. Get schedules and information from the central bus depot at 6th Avenue and G
Street. The one-way fare is $1.25 for rides outside the downtown area;
rides within downtown are free.
🔐 **People Mover** ☎ 907/343-6543 ⊕ www.peoplemover.org.

CAR TRAVEL

The Glenn Highway enters Anchorage from the north and becomes 5th
Avenue near Merrill Field; this route will lead you directly into down-
town. Gambell Street leads out of town to the south, becoming New
Seward Highway at about 20th Avenue. South of town, it becomes the
Seward Highway.

EMERGENCIES

Doctors & Dentists Physician-referral service ☎ 800/265-8624 Alaska Regional Hospital, 907/261-4900 Providence Alaska Medical Center.

Emergency Services Police, fire, and ambulance ☎ 911. **Poison Control Center** ☎ 800/222-1222.

Hospitals Alaska Regional Hospital ✉ 2801 DeBarr Rd., East Anchorage ☎ 907/276-1131 ⊕ www.alaskaregional.com. **First Care** ✉ 3710 Woodland Dr., East Anchorage ☎ 907/248-1122 ✉ 1301 Huffman Rd. ☎ 907/345-1199. **Providence Alaska Medical Center** ✉ 3200 Providence Dr., East Anchorage ☎ 907/562-2211 ⊕ www.providence.org.

24-hour Pharmacy Carrs ✉ 1650 W. Northern Lights Blvd., at Minnesota Dr., Midtown ☎ 907/297-0560.

LODGING

BED &
BREAKFASTS

Local Agents Alaska Sourdough Bed & Breakfast Association ✉ 889 Cardigan Cir., Anchorage 99503 ☎ 907/563-6244 ☎ 907/563-6073. **Anchorage Alaska Bed & Breakfast Association** ✉ Box 242623, Anchorage 99524-2623 ☎ 907/272-5909 or 888/584-5147 ⊕ www.anchorage-bnb.com.

TAXIS

Prices for taxis are $2 for pickup, plus an additional $2 for each mile. Most people in Anchorage telephone for a cab; it is not common to hail one. Allow 20 minutes for arrival of the cab during morning and evening rush hours. Alaska Cab has taxis with wheelchair lifts. Borealis Shuttle has lower rates if you are willing to share the ride.

Taxi Companies Alaska Cab ☎ 907/563-5353 ⊕ www.alaskacabs.com. **Anchorage Taxi Cab** ☎ 907/245-2207. **Borealis Shuttle** ☎ 907/276-3600 or 888/436-3600 ⊕ www.borealisshuttle.com. **Checker Cab** ☎ 907/276-1234. **Yellow Cab** ☎ 907/272-2422.

TOURS

FLIGHTSEEING

Any air-taxi company (check the Anchorage Yellow Pages) can arrange for a flightseeing trip over Anchorage and environs. The fee will be determined by the length of time you are airborne and the size of the plane. Tours of about an hour and a half generally cost around $200 per person. Three-hour flights over Mt. McKinley, including a landing on a remote backcountry lake, run about $250 per person.

ERA Helicopters offers a 50-minute trip over Anchorage and the Chugach Mountains as well as a two-hour glacier expedition that includes a landing on the ice. ERA Classic Airlines offers travelers a nostalgic air cruise aboard elegantly restored DC-3s from the 1940s. These 90-minute flights vary in destination, depending upon the weather, flying over Mt. McKinley or the mountains of South Central Alaska. Ketchum Air Service on Lake Hood has a number of flightseeing tours, including one to Mt. McKinley, as well as fly-in service to remote lake cabins for hunting and fishing, and houseboat rentals. Also at Lake Hood, Rust's Flying Service flies ski-planes over Mt. McKinley that include a landing on Ruth Glacier—a spectacular alpine amphitheater high on the mountain.

ERA Classic Airlines ☎ 907/266-8394 or 800/866-8394 ☎ 907/266-8483. **ERA Helicopters** ☎ 907/266-8351 or 800/843-1947 ☎ 907/266-8349 ⊕ www.eraaviation. com. **Ketchum Air Service** ☎ 907/243-5525 or 800/433-9114 ⊕ www.ketchumair.com. **Regal Air** ☎ 907/243-8535 ⊕ www.alaska.net/~regalair. **Rust's Flying Service** ☎ 907/243-1595 or 800/544-2299 ⊕ www.flyrusts.com.

ORIENTATION
TOURS

Alaska Snail Trails ✉ Box 210894, Anchorage 99521 ☎ 907/337-7517 or 800/348-4532 ⊕ www.aksnailtrails.com. **4th Ave. Theater Trolley Tours** ✉ 612 W. 4th Ave., Downtown, 99501 ☎ 907/276-5603 ⊕ www.fourthavenuetheater.com. **Gray Line of Alaska** ✉ 745 W. 4th Ave., No. 200, Downtown, 99501 ☎ 907/277-5581 or 800/478-6388 ⊕ www.graylineofalaska.com.

WILDLIFE VIEWING Kenai Fjords Tours has day packages to Kenai Fjords National Park April through November.

▶ **Kenai Fjords Tours** ✉ 513 W. 4th Ave., Downtown ☎ 907/276-6249 or 800/468-8068 🖨 907/276-1064 ⊕ www.kenaifjords.com.

TRAIN TRAVEL

The Alaska Railroad runs between Anchorage and Fairbanks via Denali National Park and Preserve daily, mid-May–September, and also south between Anchorage and Seward during the same period. Year-round passenger service is available from Anchorage north to Talkeetna. Call for schedule and fare information.

▶ **Alaska Railroad** ☎ 907/265-2494 or 800/544-0552 🖨 907/265-2323 ⊕ www.akrr.com.

TRANSPORTATION AROUND ANCHORAGE

If, like many visitors to Alaska, you bring your RV or rent one on arrival, you should note that parking an RV downtown on weekdays is challenging. The big parking lot on 3rd Avenue between C and E streets is a good place to park and walk. Parking usually is not a problem in other parts of town, and most of the big discount stores allow free parking in their lots.

VISITOR INFORMATION

▶ **Alaska Public Lands Information Center** ✉ 4th Ave. and F St., Downtown ☎ 907/271-2737 ⊕ www.nps.gov/aplic. **Anchorage Convention and Visitors Bureau (ACVB)** ✉ 524 W. 4th Ave., Downtown, 99501-2212 ☎ 907/276-4118, 800/478-1255 to order visitor guides 🖨 907/278-5559 ⊕ www.anchorage.net. **Daily events** ☎ 907/276-3200. **Log Cabin Visitor Information Center** ✉ 4th Ave. and F St., Downtown ☎ 907/274-3531 ⊕ www.anchorage.net.

VANCOUVER & VICTORIA

4

FODOR'S CHOICE

C Restaurant, *Downtown Vancouver*

Dr. Sun Yat-Sen Garden, *Chinatown, Vancouver*

Granville Island Public Market, *Granville Island, Vancouver*

Liliget Feast House, *West End, Vancouver*

Pan Pacific Hotel, *Downtown Vancouver*

Royal British Columbia Museum, *Downtown Victoria*

Stanley Park, *Vancouver*

HIGHLY RECOMMENDED

RESTAURANTS   Cafe Brio, *Downtown Victoria*

Herald Street Caffé, *Chinatown, Victoria*

HOTELS   Abigail's Hotel, *Downtown Victoria*

Beaconsfield Inn, *Downtown Victoria*

O Canada House, *West End, Vancouver*

SIGHTS   Butchart Gardens, *Brentwood Bay, Victoria*

Parliament Buildings, *Downtown Victoria*

Vancouver Aquarium, *Stanley Park, Vancouver*

By Melissa
Rivers

Updated by
Sue Kernaghan

VANCOUVER AND VICTORIA AREN'T IN ALASKA, but so many Alaska cruises originate or make a stop here that the cities are essential to the Alaska experience. Rich cultural sights and excellent restaurants fill each city, making for a welcome stop to complement your Alaskan adventure.

VANCOUVER

Vancouver is a young city, even by North American standards. Founded in 1886, it was not yet a town in 1871, when British Columbia became part of the Canadian confederation. Still, Vancouver's history, such as it is, remains visible to the naked eye: eras are stacked east to west along the waterfront like some century-old archaeological dig—from cobblestone late-Victorian Gastown to shiny postmodern glass cathedrals of commerce.

Today, Vancouver has a cosmopolitan population of about 2 million. The mild climate, exquisite natural scenery, and relaxed outdoor lifestyle continually attract new residents, and the number of visitors is increasing for the same reasons. People often get their first glimpse of Vancouver when catching an Alaskan cruise, and many return at some point to spend more time here.

Exploring Vancouver

There is much to see and do in Vancouver, but when time is limited (as it usually is for cruise-ship passengers), the most popular options are a walking tour of Gastown and Chinatown, a visit to Granville Island, and a driving or biking tour of Stanley Park, one of two 1,000-acre wilderness parks within the city limits (the other, Pacific Spirit Park, lies near the University of British Columbia). The heart of Vancouver—which includes the downtown area, Stanley Park, and the West End high-rise residential neighborhood—sits on this peninsula hemmed in by English Bay and the Pacific Ocean to the west; by False Creek, the inlet home to Granville Island, to the south; and by Burrard Inlet, the working port of the city, to the north, past which loom the North Shore mountains.

Numbers in the text correspond to numbers in the margin and on the Downtown Vancouver, Stanley Park, and Granville Island maps.

Downtown Vancouver & Gastown

a good
walk

Most cruise ships visiting Vancouver dock at **Canada Place** ❶ ▶, where you can stroll around the cruise-ship-style decks for great ocean and mountain views or catch a film at the IMAX theater. Across Canada Place Way (next to the Fairmont Waterfront Hotel) you'll find the Vancouver Tourist InfoCentre. A short stroll up Howe Street will take you to **Sinclair Centre** ❷, a magnificently restored complex of government buildings that houses offices and retail shops. If you go to Sinclair Centre's upper mall level and leave by the Granville Street exit, you'll come out onto a pedestrian overpass. A left turn will take you to Granville Square, which has great views of the Coast Mountains and Vancouver's working harbor. The redbrick building behind you is **Waterfront Station** ❸, Vancouver's original train terminal. You can enter the station from Granville Square and leave by the main, Cordova Street exit. Across Cordova, between Seymour and Richards streets, is the entrance to the **Vancouver Lookout! Harbour Centre Tower** ❹, where you can take in panoramic views of the city.

From the lookout, return to Cordova Street and continue east along Water Street into Gastown. Named for saloon keeper "Gassy" Jack Deighton, this is Vancouver's oldest neighborhood. The first stop, at the corner of

Water and Richards streets, is the **Landing,** a 1905 warehouse that now houses shops and a brewpub. At the window at the rear of the lobby, you can take in scenic views of Burrard Inlet and the North Shore mountains. A block east, at the corner of Water and Cambie streets, you can see and hear the world's first **steam clock** ❺ (it chimes on the quarter hour). Just past the steam clock is the entrance to **Storyeum** ❻, a multimedia historical attraction set to open in 2004. About 1½ blocks east, you'll pass **Gaoler's Mews** ❼, a courtyard tucked behind 12 Water Street.

Next to Gaoler's Mews at the corner of Water and Carrall streets is the Byrnes Block. Vancouver's oldest brick building, it was built on the site of Gassy Jack Deighton's second saloon after the 1886 Great Fire, which wiped out most of the fledgling settlement of Vancouver. At Powell and Alexander streets is the Hotel Europe, Vancouver's first reinforced concrete structure. Once billed as the best hotel in the city, this 1908 flatiron building is one of the world's best examples of this style of triangular architecture. The glass tiles in the sidewalk on Alexander Street once provided light for an underground saloon. A statue of Gassy Jack stands on the west side of Maple Tree Square, at the intersection of Water, Powell, Alexander, and Carrall streets, where he built his first saloon.

TIMING The walk itself will take less than half an hour each way; allow about 30 minutes for the Vancouver Lookout and at least 90 minutes for Storyeum. Note that the area just to the south of Gastown (roughly east of Cambie and south of Cordova) is one of Vancouver's roughest neighborhoods. Although Gastown itself (along Water Street) is busy with tourists and quite safe during the day, you may want to avoid walking through the area after dark.

What to See

▶ ❶ **Canada Place.** When Vancouver hosted the Expo '86 world's fair, this former cargo pier was transformed into the Canadian pavilion. The complex, which now encompasses the luxurious **Pan Pacific Hotel,** the **Vancouver Convention and Exhibition Centre,** the **World Trade Centre,** and the city's main cruise-ship terminal, mimics the style and size of a luxury ocean liner. You can stroll its exterior promenade and admire views of Burrard Inlet, Stanley Park, and the North Shore mountains. The **CN IMAX Theatre** (☎ 604/682–4629 ✉ C$11) shows films on a five-story-high screen. The roof, shaped like five sails, has become a Vancouver skyline landmark. ✉ *999 Canada Place Way, Downtown* ☎ *604/ 647–7390 or 604/775–7200* ⊕ *www.canadaplace.ca.*

❼ **Gaoler's Mews.** The brick-paved courtyard and the mews leading off it resemble a hidden slice of Victorian England. Once the site of the city's first civic buildings—the constable's cabin, customhouse, and a two-cell log jail—the mews today are home to architectural offices, two courtyard cafés, and an Irish pub. ✉ *Behind 12 Water St., Gastown.*

❷ **Sinclair Centre.** Vancouver architect Richard Henriquez knitted four government office buildings into Sinclair Centre, an office-retail complex that takes up an entire city block between Cordova and Hastings, Howe and Granville streets. Inside are designer clothing shops, federal government offices, and fast-food outlets. The two Hastings Street buildings—the 1910 **Post Office,** which has an elegant clock tower, and the 1911 **Winch Building**—are linked with the 1937 **Post Office Extension** and the 1913 **Customs Examining Warehouse** to the north. In 1986 a meticulous restoration involved moving the post office facade to the Granville Street side of the complex. The original clockwork from the old clock tower is now on display inside on the upper level of the arcade. ✉ *757 W. Hastings St., Downtown.*

KEY

↑ Start of walk

Downtown Vancouver

Roedde House Museum

Nelson Park

Robson Square

Vancouver Art Gallery

Hotel Vancouver

Cathedral Place

HSBC Bank Building

Royal Centre

Vancouver Club

Tourist Info Centre

Royal Bank

The Landing

GASTOWN

Byrnes Block

CHINATOWN

Vancouver Chinatown Millenium Gate

Chinese Freemasons Building

Chinese Times Building

China Gate

International Village

Burrard Inlet

Seabus Route

SKYTRAIN

1/4 mi

400 meters

⑤ **Steam clock.** The world's first steam clock, built by Ray Saunders of **Landmark Clocks** (✉ 123 Cambie St., Gastown ☎ 604/669–3525), is powered by the same underground steam system that heats many Vancouver buildings. On the quarter hour a whistle blows; on the hour a huge cloud of steam spews from the clock. ✉ *Corner of Cambie and Water Sts., Gastown.*

⑥ **Storyeum.** Set to open in spring 2004, this major new attraction will bring western Canada's history to life through multimedia presentations, live theater, and life-size sets. At this writing, the 75- to 80-minute walk-through was slated to start with a two-story descent in a massive cylindrical elevator. Visitors will then move through an interpretation of an aboriginal creation myth; a look at First Nations culture at its artistic peak; and performances about the fur trade, the gold rush, the coming of the railway, and modern-day immigration. Book ahead, as numbers are limited for each show. ✉ *142 Water St., Gastown* ☎ *888/786–7938* ⊕ *www.storyeum.com* ✉ *May–Oct. C$22, Nov.–Apr. C$20* ☉ *May–Oct., daily 9–7, tours every ½ hr; Nov.–Apr., daily 10–6, tours every hr.*

④ **Vancouver Lookout! Harbour Centre Tower.** The lookout looks like a flying saucer stuck atop a high-rise. At 553 feet high, it affords one of the best views of Vancouver. A glass elevator whizzes you up 50 stories to the circular observation deck, where knowledgeable guides point out the sights and give a tour every hour on the hour. On a clear day you can see Vancouver Island and Mount Baker in Washington State. The top-floor restaurant makes one complete revolution per hour; the elevator ride up is free for diners. Tickets are good all day, so you can visit in daytime and return for another look after dark. ✉ *555 W. Hastings St., Downtown* ☎ *604/689–0421* ⊕ *www.vancouverlookout.com* ✉ *C$10* ☉ *May–mid-Oct., daily 8:30 AM–10:30 PM; mid-Oct.–Apr., daily 9–9.*

③ **Waterfront Station.** This former Canadian Pacific Railway passenger terminal was built between 1912 and 1914 as the western terminus for Canada's transcontinental railway. After Canada's railways merged, the station became obsolete, but a 1978 renovation transformed it into an office-retail complex and depot for SkyTrain, SeaBus, and West Coast Express passengers. In the main concourse, panels near the ceiling depict the scenery travelers once saw on journeys across Canada. Here you can catch a 13-minute SeaBus trip across the harbor to the waterfront public market at Lonsdale Quay in North Vancouver. ✉ *601 W. Cordova St., Downtown* ☎ *604/953–3333 SeaBus and SkyTrain, 604/683–7245 West Coast Express.*

Chinatown

a good walk

Vancouver's Chinatown, declared a historic district in 1971, is one of the oldest and largest such areas in North America. Chinese immigrants were among the first to recognize the possibilities of Vancouver's setting and have played an important role here since the 18th century. Many came to British Columbia during the 1850s seeking their fortunes in the Cariboo gold rush. Thousands more arrived in the 1880s, recruited as laborers to build the Canadian Pacific Railway. Though much of Vancouver's Chinese community has now moved to suburban Richmond, Chinatown is still a vital neighborhood. The style of architecture in Vancouver's Chinatown is patterned on that of Guangzhou (Canton).

Although Chinatown is less than a mile from the Canada Place cruise-ship terminal, it's best to get there by cab or bus to avoid walking through the city's rough skid-row neighborhood. You can get a taxi at the stand in front of Canada Place, catch a No. 3 Main or No. 8 Fraser bus from Cordova and Seymour near Waterfront Station, or take the

SkyTrain to Stadium station. Alternatively, you can pick up the Silk Road Walking Tour, a self-guided route marked with banners that starts at the Vancouver Public Library downtown and leads to the main attractions in Chinatown.

At the intersection of West Pender and Taylor streets, the Vancouver Chinatown Millennium Gate marks the western boundary of Chinatown. This four-pillar, three-story-high, brightly painted arch spanning Pender Street was erected in 2002 to mark the millennium and commemorate the Chinese community's role in Vancouver's history. The gate incorporates both Eastern and Western symbols and both traditional and modern Chinese themes.

Just east of the Millennium Gate, a right turn will take you into Shanghai Alley. Also known as Chinatown Heritage Alley, this was the site of the first Chinese settlement in the Vancouver area. By 1890, Shanghai Alley and neighboring Canton Alley were home to about 1,000 Chinese residents. At the end of the alley is a replica of the West Han Dynasty Bell, a gift to Vancouver from the city of Guangzhou, China. Surrounding the bell are a series of panels relaying some of the area's early history.

If you return to Pender Street and turn right, the first building you pass is the **Sam Kee Building** ⑧ ▶, the world's narrowest office building. Across Pender at 3 West Pender Street is the Chinese Freemasons Building, notable for its two completely different facades. The side facing Pender represents a fine example of Cantonese recessed balconies. The Carrall Street side displays the Victorian style common throughout the British Empire. Dr. Sun Yat-Sen hid for months in this building from agents of the Manchu dynasty while he raised funds for its overthrow, which he accomplished in 1911. Directly across Carrall Street is the 1902 Chinese Times Building, at 1 East Pender, where in the early 20th century illicit mah-jongg games were played in the building's hidden mezzanine floor.

On the south side of Pender Street, just east of Carrall Street, is another brightly painted, four-column gate. This one, called the China Gate, was built by a group of Beijing artisans for the Chinese Pavilion at Expo '86; the gate (and some dragons) now guards the entrance to the Chinese Cultural Centre complex. Step through the gate and into the courtyard behind. To your right is the entrance to the **Dr. Sun Yat-Sen Classical Chinese Garden** ⑨, the first authentic classical Chinese garden built outside China. Straight ahead is the entrance to Dr. Sun Yat-Sen Park, a free public park also built in a classical Chinese style. A short path through the park will take you out to Columbia Street, where, to your left, you'll find the entrance to the **Chinese Cultural Centre Museum and Archives** ⑩, a museum and art gallery celebrating Chinese-Canadian culture. Finish up by poking around in the open-front markets and import shops that line several blocks of Pender and Keefer streets (one block south of Pender Street), running east.

TIMING   The walk itself will take about 20 minutes. Allow about an hour each for the garden and the museum and extra time for shopping.

What to See

⑩ **Chinese Cultural Centre Museum and Archives.** This Ming dynasty–style facility is dedicated to promoting an understanding of Chinese-Canadian history and culture. The art gallery on the first floor hosts traveling exhibits by Chinese and Canadian artists. A compelling permanent exhibit traces the history of Chinese Canadians in British Columbia. A Chinese-Canadian military museum is also on-site. ⊠ *555 Columbia St., Chinatown* ☎ *604/658–8880* ⊕ *www.cccvan.com* ✉ *C$4, free Tues.* ☉ *Tues.–Sun. 11–5.*

⑨ Dr. Sun Yat-Sen Classical Chinese Garden. The first authentic Ming dynasty–style garden constructed outside of China, this garden was built in 1986 by 52 artisans from Suzhou, China. It incorporates design elements and traditional materials from several of Suzhou's centuries-old private gardens. As you walk along the paths, remember that no power tools, screws, or nails were used in the construction. Guided tours, which are helpful in understanding the symbolism involved in the garden, are included in the price of admission. They're conducted on the hour between mid-June and the end of August (call for times the rest of the year). A concert series, including classical, Asian, world, jazz, and sacred music, plays on Friday evenings in July and August. The free public Dr. Sun Yat-Sen Park, next door, is also in the style of a traditional Chinese garden. ✉ *578 Carrall St., Chinatown* ☎ *604/662–3207* ⊕ *www. vancouverchinesegarden.com* ✍*C$8.25* ☉ *May–mid-June and Sept., daily 10–6; mid-June–Aug., daily 9:30–7; Oct.–Apr., Tues.–Sun. 10–4:30.*

➤ ⑧ Sam Kee Building. *Ripley's Believe It or Not!* recognizes this structure, dating from about 1913, as the narrowest office building in the world. In 1913, when the city confiscated most of merchant Chang Toy's land to widen Pender Street, he built in protest on what he had left—just 6 feet. These days the building houses an insurance agency whose employees make do with the 4-foot-10-inch-wide interior. ✉ *8 W. Pender St., Chinatown.*

Stanley Park

A morning or afternoon in Stanley Park gives you a capsule tour of Vancouver that includes beaches, the ocean, Douglas fir and cedar forests, and a view of the North Shore mountains. One of the most popular ways to see the park is to walk, rollerblade, or cycle along Vancouver's famous Seawall Walk, a 9-km (5½-mi) seaside pathway around the park's circumference. The seawall extends an additional mile to just west of the cruise-ship terminal at **Canada Place,** so you can start your ride from there. Alternatively, rent a bike on Denman Street near the park entrance and start your ride at the foot of Alberni Street next to Lost Lagoon. Go through the underpass, veer right, and follow the cycle-path markings to the seawall. Cyclists must ride in a counterclockwise direction, wear a helmet, and stay on their side of the path.

It's also possible to see the park by car, entering at the foot of Georgia Street and driving counterclockwise around the one-way Stanley Park Drive. An even better option is to take the free Stanley Park Shuttle, which provides frequent transportation between the park entrance and all the major sights daily from mid-June to mid-September. To get to the park by transit, take any bus marked Stanley Park from the corner of Pender and Granville, downtown. Another option is the Stanley Park Horse-Drawn Tours (➪ *Tours in* Vancouver and Victoria A to Z), which includes a free bus ride from the Canada Place cruise-ship terminal to Stanley Park.Whether you're driving, cycling, or rollerblading, the first sight you'll pass on your right is the Tudor-style Vancouver Rowing Club, a private athletic club established in 1903. Watch for the information booth on the left, and the turnoff to the renowned **Vancouver Aquarium Marine Science Centre ⑪ ➤**, the **Miniature Railway and Children's Farmyard ⑫**, and Painters' Corner, where artists sell their work. Also near the information booth, a salmon demonstration stream has information about the life cycle of this important resource. As you continue along the main road or the seawall, the next thing you'll pass is the Royal Vancouver Yacht Club. About ½ km (¼ mi) farther is the causeway to Deadman's Island, a former burial ground for the local Salish people and now a small naval training base that is not open to the public. The site of the **totem poles ⑬**, a bit farther down the road and on your left,

a good tour

Fodor'sChoice ★

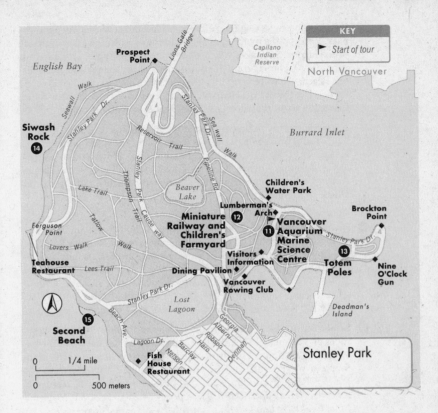

KEY

▶ Start of tour

Stanley Park

is a popular photo stop. Ahead at the water's edge, just past the sign for Hallelujah Point, is the Nine O'Clock Gun. This cannon, originally intended to alert fishermen to the close of the day's fishing, has been fired at the stroke of nine almost every night since 1894. To the north is Brockton Point and its small lighthouse and foghorn.

Inland on your left is Brockton Oval, where you can catch a rugby game in winter or a cricket match in summer. Next, on the water side, watch for the *Girl in a Wetsuit,* a sculpture on a rock just offshore that resembles Copenhagen's *Little Mermaid.* A little farther along the seashore is a replica of the dragon-shape figurehead from the SS *Empress of Japan,* which plied these waters between 1891 and 1922.

At Km 3 (Mi 2) is Lumberman's Arch, a log archway dedicated to workers in Vancouver's first industry. The Children's Water Park across the road is also popular throughout the summer. About 2 km (1 mi) farther is the Lions Gate Bridge—the halfway point of the seawall. Just past the bridge is Prospect Point, at 211 feet the highest point in the park. The top has breathtaking views of the North Shore and Burrard Inlet as well as a snack bar, restaurant, and gift shop. From the seawall you can see where cormorants nest in the cliffs. Continuing around the seawall or the drive, you'll come to the English Bay side and the beginning of sandy beaches. The imposing rock just offshore is **Siwash Rock** ⑭, the focus of a native legend. If you're driving, watch for a sign for the Hollow Tree. This 56-foot-wide stump gives an idea of how large some of the old-growth trees were. Continue along to reach the swimming area and snack bar at Third Beach.

The road and the seawall pass the large, heated pool at **Second Beach** ⑮. If you're walking or cycling, you can take a shortcut from here back to

Lost Lagoon by taking the pathway behind the pool that cuts into the park. Either of the footbridges ahead leads to a path along the south side of the lagoon that takes you back to your starting point at the foot of Alberni or Georgia Street. If you continue along the seawall from Second Beach, you will emerge from the park into a high-rise residential neighborhood, the West End. Here you'll find plenty of places to stop for coffee, ice cream, or a drink along Denman, Davie, or Robson streets.

TIMING A driving tour, with time out for stops and photos, will take about an hour. You'll find pay parking lots near most of the sights in the park; a C$4 ticket (C$3 between October and March) allows you to park all day and to move between lots. A biking tour will take several hours. Add at least two hours to tour the aquarium thoroughly, and you've filled a half- to full-day tour.

What to See

🖐 ⑫ **Miniature Railway and Children's Farmyard.** A child-size steam train takes youngsters and adults on a ride through the woods of Stanley Park. Just next door is a farmyard full of tame, pettable critters, including goats, rabbits, and guinea pigs. ☒ *Off Pipeline Rd., Stanley Park* ☎ *604/ 257–8531* ✆ *Each site C$5, adults accompanying children C$2.50.* ☺ *June–early Sept., daily 11–5; Oct., daily 6 PM–10 PM; Dec., daily 3 PM–10 PM; Sept., and Jan.–May, weekends 11–4 (weather permitting).*

🖐 ⑮ **Second Beach.** In summer the main draw is the 50-meter pool with water slides and lifeguards. The shallow end fills up on hot days, but the lap-swimming section is usually deserted. Nearby you'll also find a sandy beach, a playground, and covered picnic sites. ☒ *Stanley Park Dr., Stanley Park* ☎ *604/257–8371 pool (summer only)* ⊕ *www.city. vancouver.bc.ca/parks* ✆ *Beach free, pool C$4.25* ☺ *Pool mid-May–mid-June, weekdays noon–8:45, weekends 10–8:45; mid-June–Labor Day, daily 10–8:45.*

⑭ **Siwash Rock.** Legend tells of a young First Nations man who, about to become a father, bathed persistently to wash his sins away so that his son could be born pure. For his devotion he was blessed by the gods and immortalized in the shape of Siwash Rock. The rock is visible from the seawall; however, if you're driving you'll need to park and take a short path through the woods. A sign marks the trail.

⑬ **Totem poles.** Totem poles are an important art form among native peoples along British Columbia's coast. These eight poles, all carved in the latter half of the 20th century, include replicas of poles originally brought to the park from the north coast in the 1920s, as well as poles carved specifically for the park by First Nations artists. The several styles of poles represent a cross section of B.C. native groups, including the Kwakwaka'wakw, Haida, and Nisga'a. The combination of carved animals, fish, birds, and mythological creatures represents clan history. An information center near the site has a snack bar, a gift shop, and information about British Columbia's First Nations.

★ 🖐 ⚑ ⑪ **Vancouver Aquarium Marine Science Centre.** Pools with windows below the water level let you come face to face with beluga whales, dolphins, sea otters, sea lions, and harbor seals at this research and educational facility. In the Amazon rain-forest gallery you can walk through a jungle setting populated with piranhas, sloths, tortoises, caimans, and tropical birds and vegetation. Other displays, many with hands-on features for children, show the underwater life of coastal British Columbia, the Canadian Arctic, and the tropics. Whale shows and dive shows (where divers swim with the aquatic life—including the sharks) are held daily. For an extra fee, you can help the trainers feed and train otters, seals, dolphins, belugas, and sea lions. Be prepared for lines on weekends and school holidays. ⊠ *845 Avison Way, Stanley Park* ☎ *604/659–3474* ⊕ *www.vanaqua.org* ☒ *C$15.95* ⊙ *July–Labor Day, daily 9:30–7; Labor Day–June, daily 10–5:30.*

Granville Island

a good
walk

This 35-acre peninsula in False Creek, just south of downtown Vancouver, is home to one of North America's most successful urban-redevelopment schemes. Once a derelict industrial site, Granville Island is now a vibrant urban park, with a bustling public market, several theaters, galleries, crafts shops, and artisans' studios.

To reach Granville Island, make the 15-minute walk from downtown Vancouver to the south end of Hornby Street. Aquabus Ferries depart from here about every five minutes and deliver passengers across False Creek at the **Granville Island Public Market** ⑯ ☞, which has a slew of food and other stalls. False Creek ferries leave every five minutes for Granville Island from a dock behind the Vancouver Aquatic Centre, on Beach Avenue, and deliver passengers between the Bridges pub and the Public Market. Still another option is to take a 20-minute ride on a TransLink bus; from Waterfront Station or stops on Granville Street, take False Creek South Bus 50 to the edge of the island. Buses 4 UBC and 7 Dunbar will also take you within a few minutes' walk of the island. On summer weekend afternoons, you can hop the **Downtown Historic Railway** (⇨ Train Travel in Vancouver and Victoria A to Z), a tram line that runs to the island from stops around False Creek. The market is a short walk from the bus, ferry, or tram stop. If you drive, parking is free for up to three hours, and paid parking is available in garages on the island.

From the market walk south on Johnston Street or take the waterside boardwalk that runs behind the Arts Club Theatre and around the Creekhouse building. Either way, just past the shops of the Creekhouse building is **Ocean Art Works,** an longhouse-style space where you can watch artists at work. Continue south to the **Emily Carr Institute of Art and Design,** the province's leading art college. Just to the right of the main entrance is the **Charles H. Scott Gallery,** which hosts contemporary exhibitions in various media. From the gallery, turn left and follow a covered walkway along the south side of the art school to **Sea Village,** one of the only houseboat communities in Vancouver. Then take the boardwalk that starts at the houseboats and continues partway around the island.

Turn right in front of the Granville Island Hotel (the large white building), right again onto Cartwright Street, and take the right fork into Railspur Alley. This part of the island has a mix of crafts galleries, studios, and workshops and is a great place to watch artisans at work. You can see wooden boats being built at the Alder Bay Boat Company at 1247 Cartwright Street, and you can watch glassblowers at work in the New Small Sterling Glass Studio, which is around the corner at 1440 Old Bridge Street. The Federation of Canadian Artists Gallery, the Crafts Association of B.C. Crafthouse, and the Gallery of B.C. Ceramics all showcase local works.

Back on Cartwright Street, you can pick up maps and find out about special events, including the festivals, outdoor concerts, and dance performances often held on the island at the **Granville Island Information Centre** (open daily 9–5). Just behind the information center the free water slides and sprinklers at the **Granville Island Water Park** are open in the summer. A little farther along the street, the **Kids Market** is full of toy and other kid-focused stores. At **Granville Island Brewing,** across the street from the Kids Market, you can take a brewery tour.

Cross Anderson Street and walk north on Duranleau Street. The **Granville Island Museums** ⑰ are on your left. The sea-oriented shops of the **Maritime Market** are next. The upscale **Net Loft** shopping arcade is the last place to explore. Once you have come full circle, you can either take the ferry back to downtown Vancouver or stay for dinner and catch a play at one of the theaters on the island (⇨ Nightlife and the Arts).

TIMING If your schedule is tight, you can tour Granville Island in three to four hours. If you like to shop or if a festival is in progress, you'll likely need a full day.

What to See

⑰ **Granville Island Museums.** Here you'll find three museums under one roof. The **Sport Fishing Museum** houses the world's largest collection of angling artifacts, including examples of tied flies, and a mounted replica of the largest salmon ever caught with a rod and reel. The collection of the **Model Ships Museum** includes exquisitely detailed replicas of early-20th-century military and working vessels and an excellent collection of model submarines. The **Model Trains Museum** has the world's largest toy-train collection on public display, including a diorama of the Fraser Canyon and the Kettle Valley that involves 1,000 feet of track and some large-scale (3-foot-high) model trains. ✉ *1502 Duranleau St., Granville Island* ☎ *604/683–1939* ⊕ *www.granvilleislandmuseums.com* ✉ *All three museums C$6.50* ☉ *Daily 10–5:30.*

▶ ⑯ **Granville Island Public Market.** Because no chain stores are allowed in this 50,000-square-foot building, each outlet here is unique. Dozens of stalls sell locally grown produce direct from the farm; others sell crafts, chocolates, cheeses, fish, meat, flowers, and exotic foods. In summer, market gardeners sell fruit and vegetables from trucks outside. On the west side

Fodor'sChoice ★

of the market you can pick up a snack, espresso, or fixings for lunch on the wharf. The Market Courtyard, on the water side, is a good place to catch street entertainers. Weekends can get madly busy here. ✉ *1689 Johnston St., Granville Island* ☎ *604/666–6477* ⊕ *www.granvilleisland. com* ☻ *Feb.–Dec., daily 9–6; Jan., Tues.–Sun. 9–6.*

Where to Eat

A diverse gastronomic experience awaits you in cosmopolitan Vancouver. A wave of Asian immigration and tourism has brought a proliferation of upscale Asian eateries. Cutting-edge restaurants currently perfecting and defining Pacific Northwest fare—including such homegrown regional favorites as salmon and oysters, accompanied by British Columbia wines—have become some of the city's leading attractions. A bylaw bans smoking in all Vancouver restaurants.

Vancouver dining is fairly informal. Casual but neat dress is appropriate everywhere. A 15% tip is expected. A 10% liquor tax is charged on wine, beer, and spirits. Some restaurants build the liquor tax into the price of the beverage, but others add it to the bill.

WHAT IT COSTS In Canadian dollars					
	$$$$	**$$$**	**$$**	**$**	**¢**
AT DINNER	over $30	$20–$30	$12–$20	$8–$12	under $8

Prices are per person for a main course. The final tab will include a 7% Goods and Services Tax (GST).

Chinese

$–$$$$ ✕ **Imperial Chinese Seafood.** This elegant Cantonese restaurant in the art-deco Marine Building, two blocks west of the Canada Place cruise-ship terminal, has two-story, floor-to-ceiling windows with spectacular views of Stanley Park and the North Shore mountains across Burrard Inlet. Lobster, crab, or shrimp from the live tanks is recommended, as is the dim sum, served every day from 11 to 2:30. ✉ *355 Burrard St., Downtown* ☎ *604/688–8191* ▤ *DC, MC, V.*

¢–$$ ✕ **Hon's Wun-Tun House.** Mr. Hon has been keeping Vancouverites in Chinese comfort food since the 1970s. The best bets on the 300-item menu (nothing is more than C$15) are the pot stickers (dumplings that come fried, steamed, or in soup), the wonton and noodle dishes, and anything with barbecued meat. The shiny Robson Street location has a separate kitchen for vegetarians and an army of fast-moving waitresses who keep your tea topped up. The older Chinatown outlet is atmospherically steamy and crowded. ✉ *1339 Robson St., Downtown* ☎ *604/685–0871* ✉ *268 Keefer St., Chinatown* ☎ *604/688–0871* ⚲ *Reservations not accepted* ▤ *MC, V at Robson St.; no credit cards at Keefer St.*

Contemporary

$$$–$$$$ ✕ **Five Sails.** A special-occasion restaurant at the Pan Pacific Hotel, Five Sails has a stunning panoramic view of Canada Place, Lions Gate Bridge, and the lights of the North Shore across the inlet. The simple white-tablecloth and candlelight decor doesn't attempt to compete with the view. The broad-reaching, seasonally changing menu takes its inspiration from both Europe and the Pacific Rim. Highlights have included slow-roasted B.C. salmon, date-crusted venison loin, and seared ahi tuna with foie gras and trumpet mushrooms. ✉ *Pan Pacific Hotel, 300–999 Canada Pl., Downtown* ☎ *604/891–2892* ▤ *AE, DC, MC, V* ☻ *No lunch.*

$$–$$$ ✕ **Aqua Riva.** This lofty, lively modern room just yards from the Canada Place cruise-ship terminal affords striking views over the harbor and the

North Shore mountains. Food from the wood-fired oven, rotisserie, and grill includes thin-crust pizzas with innovative toppings, grilled salmon, and spit-roasted chicken. Lunch brings a good selection of salads, sandwiches, and salmon dishes. A microbrew and martini list rounds out the menu. Brunch is served Sundays between May and October. ⊠ *200 Granville St., Downtown* ☎ *604/683–5599* ▭ *AE, DC, MC, V* ⊘ *No lunch weekends.*

$$–$$$ ⤬ **Teahouse Restaurant.** This former officers' mess in Stanley Park is perfectly poised for watching sunsets over the water. The West Coast Continental menu includes such specialties as roasted pear salad and lobster ravioli as well as seasonally changing treatments of duck breast, B.C. salmon, and rack of lamb. In summer you can dine on the patio. Afternoon tapas are served year-round. ⊠ *7501 Stanley Park Dr., at Ferguson Point, Stanley Park* ☎ *604/669–3281* ▭ *AE, MC, V.*

$$–$$$ ⤬ **Water Street Café.** The tables at this popular Gastown café spill out onto the sidewalk for front-row views of the steam clock across the street. Inside, the café is chic but casual, with slate-blue-and-white decor and tall windows overlooking bustling Water Street. It's tempting to pick one of the dozen or so varieties of pasta, but the crab chowder, West Coast crab cakes, and Fanny Bay oysters are also good choices. The breads are baked fresh daily. ⊠ *300 Water St., Gastown* ☎ *604/689–2832* ▭ *AE, MC, V.*

Italian

$$–$$$ ⤬ **Umberto Borgo Antico Al Porto.** Terra-cotta tiles and graceful archways give this spacious room a classical feel; upstairs, tall windows look out toward the harbor. Just a few blocks from the Canada Place cruise-ship dock, Borgo Antico serves such Tuscan dishes as grilled calamari salad, gnocchi with artichokes and sun-dried tomatoes, veal medallions with lemon and capers, and osso buco with risotto. The wine cellar has more than 300 selections. ⊠ *321 Water St., Gastown* ☎ *604/683–8376* ▭ *AE, DC, MC, V* ⊘ *Closed Sun. No lunch Sat.*

Pacific Northwest

$$–$$$ ⤬ **Liliget Feast House.** This intimate downstairs room resembles the interior of a longhouse, with wooden walkways across pebble floors, contemporary First Nations art on the walls, and cedar-plank tables with tatami-style benches. It's one of the few places in the world serving the original Northwest Coast First Nations cuisine. A feast platter lets you try most of the fare, which includes bannock bread, baked sweet potato with hazelnuts, alder-grilled salmon, buffalo smokies, duck breast, venison strips, oysters, mussels, and steamed fern shoots. ⊠ *1724 Davie St., West End* ☎ *604/681–7044* ⊕ *www.liliget.com* ▭ *AE, DC, MC, V* ⊘ *No lunch. Closed Mon. and Tues. Oct.–Feb.*

FodorsChoice ★

Pizza

$ ⤬ **Incendio.** The hand-flipped thin-crust pizzas, with innovative toppings including Asiago cheese, prosciutto, roasted garlic, and sun-dried tomatoes, and the mix-and-match pastas and sauces (try the hot smoked-duck sausage, artichoke, and tomato combination, or the mango-basil-butter sauce) draw crowds to this Gastown eatery. The room, in a circa-1900 heritage building, with exposed brick, local artwork, and big curved windows, has plenty of atmosphere. ⊠ *103 Columbia St., Gastown* ☎ *604/688–8694* ▭ *AE, MC, V* ⊘ *No lunch weekends.*

Seafood

$$$–$$$$ ⤬ **C Restaurant.** Dishes such as lightly smoked Skeena wild salmon and octopus-bacon-wrapped scallops have established C as Vancouver's most innovative seafood restaurant. Start with shucked oysters from the raw bar or try C's Taster Box, in which several morsels are served dramatically on a four-tier display. An eight-course tasting menu highlights

FodorsChoice ★

local and exotic seafood. Both the chic, ultramodern interior and the waterside patio overlook False Creek. ⊠ *2–1600 Howe St., Downtown* ☎ *604/681–1164* ⊕ *www.crestaurant.com* ☰ *AE, DC, MC, V* ⊗ *No lunch weekends or Oct.–mid-Dec. and Jan.–Apr.*

Where to Stay

Accommodations in Vancouver range from luxurious waterfront hotels to neighborhood bed-and-breakfasts and basic European-style pensions. Many of the best choices are in the downtown core, either in the central business district or in the West End near Stanley Park. The chart below shows high-season prices, but from mid-October through May, rates throughout the city can drop as much as 50%.

WHAT IT COSTS In Canadian dollars				
$$$$	**$$$**	**$$**	**$**	**¢**
FOR 2 PEOPLE over $250	$175–$250	$125–$175	$75–$125	under $75

Prices are for two people in a standard double room in high season, excluding 10% provincial accomodations tax, service charge, and 7% Goods and Services Tax (GST).

$$$$ **Pan Pacific Hotel.** Most cruise ships calling at Vancouver arrive at
FodorśChoice Canada Place, a striking waterfront facility shaped like an ocean liner, which
★ is also home to this luxurious 23-story hotel. A dramatic waterfall graces the three-story atrium lobby, and the rooms are spacious and modern, with light woods, travertine vanities, Italian linens, and stunning ocean, mountain, or skyline views. The restaurants and health-club facilities are among the city's finest. ⊠ *300–999 Canada Pl., Downtown, V6C 3B5* ☎ *604/ 662–8111, 800/663–1515 in Canada, 800/937–1515 in U.S.* ☎ *604/ 685–8690* ⊕ *www.panpacific.com* ⇌ *465 rooms, 39 suites* ♢ *3 restaurants, coffee shop, room service, some kitchens, in-room data ports, some in-room faxes, in-room safes, minibars, cable TV with movies and video games, pool, gym, hair salon, hot tub, outdoor hot tub, sauna, spa, steam room, racquetball, squash, lobby lounge, shops, baby-sitting, dry cleaning, laundry service, concierge, Internet, business services, parking (fee), some pets allowed, no-smoking floors* ☰ *AE, DC, MC, V.*

$$$–$$$$ **Fairmont Waterfront.** An underground walkway leads from this striking 23-story glass hotel to Vancouver's cruise-ship terminal. Views from the lobby and from 60% of the guest rooms are of Burrard Inlet, Stanley Park, and the North Shore Mountains. Other rooms look onto the city skyline and a terraced herb garden. The spacious rooms have big picture windows and are attractively furnished with blond-wood furniture and contemporary Canadian artwork. Large corner rooms have the best views. Rooms on the Fairmont Gold floor have extra amenities, including a private lounge and a concierge. ⊠ *900 Canada Place Way, Downtown, V6C 3L5* ☎ *604/691–1991* ☎ *604/691–1828* ⊕ *www. fairmont.com* ⇌ *489 rooms, 29 suites* ♢ *Restaurant, room service, in-room data ports, in-room safes, some kitchenettes, minibars, cable TV with movies and video games, pool, gym, hot tub, massage, steam room, lounge, dry cleaning, laundry service, concierge, concierge floor, Internet, business services, meeting rooms, parking (fee), some pets allowed (fee), no-smoking floors* ☰ *AE, D, DC, MC, V.*

★ **$$$–$$$$** **O Canada House.** This beautifully restored 1897 Victorian, within walking distance of downtown, is where the first version of "O Canada," the national anthem, was written in 1909. Each spacious bedroom is appointed with late-Victorian antiques. The top-floor room is enormous, with two king beds and a private sitting area. A separate one-room coach house in the garden is a romantic option. Breakfast, served in the dining room, is a lavish affair. ⊠ *1114 Barclay St., West End, V6E 1H1* ☎ *604/688–0555 or 877/688–1114* 🖷 *604/488–0556* ⊕ *www. ocanadahouse.com* ⤳ *7 rooms ⟡ Refrigerators, cable TV, in-room VCRs, concierge, free parking; no a/c, no kids under 12, no smoking* ⊟ *MC, V* ¶⊙¶ *BP.*

$$–$$$ 🏨 **Days Inn.** Just two blocks from the Canada Place cruise-ship terminal, this moderately priced hotel operates a free shuttle bus to Vancouver's train and bus station and to both cruise-ship terminals. Rooms in this 1920 six-story building are small but cheerful, with modern pine furniture and floral bedspreads. The two-bedroom, one-bathroom units are a good value for groups and families. ⊠ *921 W. Pender St., Downtown, V6C 1M2* ☎ *604/681–4335 or 877/681–4335* 🖷 *604/681–7808* ⊕ *www. daysinnvancouver.com* ⤳ *80 rooms, 5 suites ⟡ Restaurant, in-room data ports, in-room safes, some microwaves, refrigerators, cable TV with movies, lounge, pub, baby-sitting, dry cleaning, laundry facilities, laundry service, parking (fee), no-smoking floors* ⊟ *AE, D, DC, MC, V.*

$–$$ 🏨 **Sylvia Hotel.** To stay here from June through August you'll need to book six months to a year ahead. This Virginia-creeper-covered 1912 building is so popular because of its low rates and near-perfect location, about 25 feet from the beach on scenic English Bay, 200 feet from Stanley Park, and a 20-minute walk from Robson Street. The rooms and apartment-style suites vary from tiny to spacious. Many are large enough to sleep four and all have windows that open. Contemporary beds, linens, and sofas come in a dark green-and-cream color scheme. ⊠ *1154 Gilford St., West End, V6G 2P6* ☎ *604/681–9321* 🖷 *604/682–3551* ⊕ *www.sylviahotel.com* ⤳ *97 rooms, 22 suites ⟡ Restaurant, room service, in-room data ports, some kitchens, cable TV, lounge, dry cleaning, laundry service, parking (fee), some pets allowed, no-smoking floors; no a/c* ⊟ *AE, DC, MC, V.*

Nightlife & the Arts

For information on events, pick up a free copy of the *Georgia Straight,* available at cafés and bookstores around town, or look in the entertainment section of the *Vancouver Sun* (Thursday's paper has listings in the "Queue" section). For tickets, book through **Ticketmaster** (☎ 604/ 280–4444 ⊕ www.ticketmaster.ca). You can pick up half-price tickets on the day of the event, as well as full-price advance tickets, at **Tickets Tonight** (⊠ 200 Burrard St., Downtown ☎ 604/684–2787 ⊕ www. ticketstonight.ca), at the Vancouver Tourist Info Centre.

Nightlife

BARS, PUBS &
LOUNGES

A massive deck with expansive False Creek views is the big draw at **Bridges** (⊠ 1696 Duranleau St., Granville Island ☎ 604/687–4400), near the Public Market. There's a cozy pub and a restaurant at the same site. Near Stanley Park and attached to Cardero's Restaurant, **Cardero's Pub** (⊠ 1583 Coal Harbour Quay, West End ☎ 604/669–7666) has deep leather couches, marina views, and recycled ship timbers as well as other nautical touches; the pub grub is top-notch. **Cloud 9** (⊠ 1400 Robson St., West End ☎ 604/687–0511), a revolving lounge and restaurant on the 42nd floor of the Empire Landmark Hotel, takes in 360-degree views of Stanley Park, English Bay, and the downtown core.

Dix Barbecue and Brewery (⊠ 871 Beatty St., Downtown ☎ 604/682– 2739) complements its selection of in-house brewed ales and lagers with zesty southern-style barbecue. A seaside patio, casual Pacific Northwest restaurant, and house-brewed German-style beer make the **Dockside Brewing Company** (⊠ Granville Island Hotel, 1253 Johnston St., Granville Island ☎ 604/685–7070) a popular hangout.

For a pint of properly poured Guinness and live traditional Irish music try the **Irish Heather** (✉ 217 Carrall St., Gastown ☎ 604/688–9779). Upstairs is a restaurant, and out back, in an atmospheric coach house, a **Shebeen,** or whiskey house, serves about 130 whiskies.

Though technically a seafood restaurant, the massive three-level **Sand Bar** (✉ 1535 Johnson St., Granville Island ☎ 604/669–9030) has a party atmosphere most nights and dancing on weekends. The sushi bar downstairs is a sedate hideaway, and the covered rooftop patio has dramatic views over False Creek.

Harbor views, pub food, and traditionally brewed beer are the draws at **Steamworks** (✉ 375 Water St., Gastown ☎ 604/689–2739), a multilevel, wood-paneled brewpub on the edge of Gastown. The **Yaletown Brewing Company** (✉ 1111 Mainland St., Yaletown ☎ 604/681–2739) is housed in a renovated warehouse with a glassed-in brewery, turning out eight tasty beers. It also has a lively singles-scene pub, a patio, and a restaurant.

COMEDY   The **Vancouver International Comedy Festival** (☎ 604/683–0883 ⊕ www. comedyfest.com), held in late July and early August, brings an international collection of improv, stand-up, circus, and other acts to Granville Island. The **Vancouver TheatreSports League** (☎ 604/738–7013), a hilarious improv troupe, performs at the New Revue Stage on Granville Island.

DANCE CLUBS   A smartly dressed crowd flocks to dance and celebrity-spot at upscale **Au Bar** (✉ 674 Seymour St., Downtown ☎ 604/648–2227 ⊕ www. aubarnightclub.com).

The **Commodore Ballroom** (✉ 868 Granville St., Downtown ☎ 604/ 739–7469), a 1929 art-deco dance hall with a massive sprung dance floor, hosts bands six nights a week; Tuesday is DJ night. You can dance under the stars at **Skybar** (✉ 670 Smithe St., Downtown ☎ 604/697–9199 ⊕ www.skybarvancouver.com), a chic three-level club with a rooftop patio. The fashionable **Voda** (✉ 783 Homer St., Downtown ☎ 604/684– 3003), in the Westin Grand Hotel, is one of the few places for which Vancouverites dress up. The intimate club draws a thirtysomething professional crowd to its weekend Top 40 and house nights and a younger crowd for midweek hip-hop.

The Arts

THEATRE   The **Arts Club Theatre Company** (✉ 1585 Johnston St., Granville Island ☎ 604/687–1644 ⊕ www.artsclub.com) operates two theaters. The **Arts Club Granville Island Stage** is an intimate venue that showcases works by local playwrights. The **Stanley Theatre** at 2750 Granville Street is a lavish former movie palace staging works by such perennial favorites as William Shakespeare and Noël Coward. Both operate yearround. **Bard on the Beach** (☎ 604/739–0559 or 877/739–0559 ⊕ www. bardonthebeach.org) is a summer series of Shakespeare's plays performed in tents on the beach at Vanier Park. Big international shows, from Broadway musicals to Chinese dance productions, play at the **Centre in Vancouver for the Performing Arts** (✉ 777 Homer St., Downtown ☎ 604/602–0616 ⊕ www.centreinvancouver.com). The **Chan Centre for the Performing Arts** (✉ 6265 Crescent Rd., on University of British Columbia campus ☎ 604/822–2697) contains a 1,200-seat concert hall, a theater, and a cinema. The **Queen Elizabeth Theatre** (✉ 600 Hamilton St., Downtown ☎ 604/665–3050) is a major venue for ballet, opera, and other events. **Theatre Under the Stars** (☎ 604/687–0174) performs such popular family-friendly musicals as *The Sound of Music* and *Kiss Me Kate* at Malkin Bowl, an outdoor amphitheater in Stanley Park, during July and August. Small theater troupes from around the world perform at the **Vancouver Fringe Festival,** (☎ 604/257–0350 ⊕ www.vancouverfringe.com), staged in early September at various venues on and around Granville Island. The **Vancouver Playhouse** (✉ 649 Cambie St., Downtown ☎ 604/665–3050 ⊕ www.vancouverplayhouse. com), in the same complex as the Queen Elizabeth Theatre, is the leading venue in Vancouver for mainstream theatrical shows.

MUSIC   The Jazz Hotline of the **Coastal Jazz and Blues Society** (☎ 604/872–5200 ⊕ www.coastaljazz.ca) has information about concerts and clubs. The society also runs the **Vancouver International Jazz Festival,** which lights up 40 venues around town every June. **Festival Vancouver** (☎ 604/688–1152 ⊕ www.festivalvancouver.bc.ca) is Vancouver's biggest music event, with more than 50 performances of orchestral, chamber, choral, world music, early music, opera, and jazz in venues around the city in early August. The **Vancouver Symphony Orchestra** (☎ 604/876–3434) is the resident company at the **Orpheum Theatre** (✉ 601 Smithe St., Downtown).

Shopping

Unlike many cities where suburban malls have taken over, Vancouver is full of individual boutiques and specialty shops. Store hours are generally 9:30–6 Monday, Tuesday, Wednesday, and Saturday; 9:30–9 Thursday and Friday; and 10–5 Sunday. You'll pay both 7.5% Provincial Sales Tax (PST) and 7% Goods and Services Tax (GST) on most purchases. Non-Canadian residents can reclaim the GST paid on most purchases. You can pick up refund forms at many shops and at the airport. For an instant refund, see **Global Refund** (✉ 900 W. Georgia St. ☎ 604/893–8478) on the lower level of the Fairmont Hotel Vancouver.

Shopping Districts & Malls

About two dozen high-end art galleries, antiques shops, and Oriental-rug emporiums are packed end to end between 5th and 15th avenues on Granville Street, in an area known as **Gallery Row.** As you continue south along Granville Street, **Granville Rise,** between Broadway and 16th Avenue, is lined with chic fashion, home decor, and specialty food shops. **Pacific Centre Mall** (✉ 700 W. Georgia St., Downtown ☎ 604/688–7236), on two levels and mostly underground, takes up three city blocks in the heart of downtown. Midpriced, mainstream clothing shops predominate on the lower level; the upper floor houses designer boutiques. **Robson Street** stretching from Burrard to Bute is the city's main fashion-shopping and people-watching artery. Gap and Banana Republic have their flagship stores here, as do Canadian fashion outlets Club Monaco and Roots. Souvenir shops and cafés, Asian food shops, video outlets, and cheap noodle bars abound. Shops in and near **Sinclair Centre** (✉ 757 W. Hastings St., Downtown) cater to sophisticated and pricey tastes.

Bustling **Chinatown**—centered on Pender and Main streets—is full of restaurants and markets. It's most lively on weekend evenings in summer, when the Chinatown Night Market, an Asian-style outdoor street market, sets up along Keefer and Pender streets. **Commercial Drive,** north of East 1st Avenue, is the heart of Vancouver's Italian and Latin American communities. It's lined with cappuccino bars, Latin cafés, and imported-food shops. **Granville Island** (➪ Exploring Vancouver) has a lively public market and a wealth of galleries, crafts shops, and artisans' studios. In **Little India,** on Main Street around 50th Avenue, curry houses, sweets shops, grocery stores, discount jewelers, and silk shops abound. Treasure hunters enjoy the 300 block of **West Cordova Street,** near Gastown, where offbeat shops sell curios, vintage clothing, and locally designed fashions.

Department Stores

The **Bay** (✉ 674 Granville St., at Georgia St., Downtown ☎ 604/681–6211), founded as part of the fur trade in the 17th century, is now a midprice department store downtown. Modeled on Paris's Colette store, **Bruce** (✉ 1038 Alberni St., Downtown ☎ 604/688–8802) is Vancouver's first "lifestyle" department store, with the latest in designer fashion, home decor, and eyewear. **Sears** (✉ 701 Granville St., Downtown ☎ 604/685–7112) sells a wide range of midprice merchandise. **Holt Renfrew** (✉ 633 Granville St., Downtown ☎ 604/681–3121) focuses on high fashion for men and women.

Specialty Stores

ANTIQUES   Three key antiques-hunting grounds are Gallery Row on Granville Street; the stretch of antiques stores along Main Street from 25th to 30th Avenue; and along Front Street, between 6th and Begbie streets near New Westminster Quay in New Westminster.

The **Vancouver Antique Centre** (✉ 422 Richards St., Downtown ☎ 604/669–7444) has about a dozen antiques and collectibles dealers under one roof.

ART GALLERIES   Gallery Row along Granville Street between 5th and 15th avenues has about a dozen high-end contemporary art galleries. You'll also find a number of notable galleries on the downtown peninsula.

Buschlen Mowatt (✉ 1445 W. Georgia St., West End ☎ 604/682–1234) exhibits the works of contemporary Canadian and international artists. The **Diane Farris Gallery** (✉ 1590 W. 7th Ave., South Granville ☎ 604/737–2629) often showcases new Canadian and international artists. The **Douglas Reynolds Gallery** (✉ 2335 Granville St., South Granville ☎ 604/731–9292) displays one of the city's finest collections of Northwest Coast First Nations art and specializes in woodwork and jewelry. The **Inuit Gallery of Vancouver** (✉ 206 Cambie St., Gastown ☎ 604/688–7323 or 888/615–8399) exhibits Northwest Coast and Inuit art. The **Marion Scott Gallery** (✉ 481 Howe St., Downtown ☎ 604/685–1934) specializes in Inuit art.

BOOKS   The serene **Banyen Books** (✉ 3608 W. 4th Ave. ☎ 604/732–7912) is Vancouver's best source for new age, philosophy, and alternative health titles. Vancouver's two **Chapters** (✉ 788 Robson St., Downtown ☎ 604/682–4066 ✉ 2505 Granville St., at Broadway, South Granville ☎ 604/731–7822) are enormous, with a café in each location. The stores stock a vast selection of popular books and CDs and often discounted bestsellers. **Duthie Books** (✉ 2239 W. 4th Ave., Kitsilano ☎ 604/732–5344) is a long-established homegrown general-interest bookshop. **MacLeod's Books** (✉ 455 W. Pender St., Downtown ☎ 604/681–7654) is one of the city's best antiquarian- and used-book stores. **Sophia Books** (✉ 492 W. Hastings, Downtown ☎ 604/684–0484) specializes in French and other foreign-language titles. **Wanderlust** (✉ 1929 W. 4th Ave., Kitsilano ☎ 604/739–2182) carries thousands of travel books and maps as well as luggage and travel accessories.

CLOTHES   **Dream** (✉ 311 W. Cordova St., Gastown ☎ 604/683–7326) is where up-and-coming local designers sell their wares. Men's and women's fashions by Versace, Yves Saint Laurent Rive Gauche, Dior, Prada, and others are available at **Leone** (✉ 757 W. Hastings St., Downtown ☎ 604/683–1133) in Sinclair Centre. You'll find more affordable, locally made fashions—and an Italian café—at **A-Wear** (✉ 350 Howe St., Downtown ☎ 604/685–9327) on Leone's lower floor.

For outdoorsy clothes that double as souvenirs (many sport maple-leaf logos), check out the sweatshirts, leather jackets, and other cozy casuals at **Roots** (✉ 1001 Robson St., West End ☎ 604/683–4305), outfitter to the Canadian Olympic team. Globe trotters like the practical, hard wearing, Canadian-made travel clothing available at **Tilley Endurables** (✉ 2401 Granville St., South Granville ☎ 604/732–4287).

GIFTS Museum and gallery gift shops are among the best places to buy high-quality souvenirs—West Coast native art, books, music, jewelry, and other items.

The **Clamshell Gift Shop** (✉ Vancouver Aquarium Marine Science Centre, 845 Avison Way, Stanley Park ☎ 604/659–3413 or 800/663–0562) sells souvenir clothing and aquatic-theme toys and gifts. The **Gallery Store** (✉ 750 Hornby St., Downtown ☎ 604/662–4706), in the Vancouver Art Gallery, sells a good selection of art books and locally designed jewelry. **Hill's Native Art** (✉ 165 Water St., Gastown ☎ 604/685–4249) has Vancouver's largest selection of First Nations art. **Lattimer Gallery** (✉ 1590 W. 2nd Ave., False Creek ☎ 604/732–4556), near Granville Island, is full of native arts and crafts in all price ranges.

The **Museum of Anthropology Gift Shop** (✉ 6393 N.W. Marine Dr., University of British Columbia campus ☎ 604/822–5087) stocks Northwest Coast jewelry, carvings, and prints as well as a collection of books on First Nations history and culture. At the **Salmon Shop** (✉ 1689 Johnston St., Granville Island ☎ 604/669–3474), in the Public Market, you can pick up fresh or smoked salmon wrapped for travel. **Salmon Village** (✉ 779 Thurlow St., West End ☎ 604/685–3378), just off Robson Street's main shopping strip, has all manner of travel-ready Canadian delicacies, from maple syrup to salmon.

JEWELRY **Birks** (✉ 698 W. Hastings St., Downtown ☎ 604/669–3333) takes up the grand lower floor of a neoclassical building that was the former headquarters of the Canadian Imperial Bank of Commerce. **Cartier Jewellers** (✉ 408 Howe St., Downtown ☎ 604/683–6878) is the Vancouver outlet of the famous jewelry chain. **Palladio** (✉ 855 W. Hastings St., Downtown ☎ 604/685–3885) carries high-fashion jewelry in gold and platinum.

OUTDOOR EQUIPMENT **Coast Mountain Sports** (✉ 2201 W. 4th Ave., Kitsilano ☎ 604/731–6181 ✉ Park Royal Shopping Centre, Marine Dr., West Vancouver ☎ 604/922–3336 ✉ Metrotown Shopping Centre, Burnaby ☎ 604/434–9397 ✉ Coquitlam Shopping Centre, Coquitlam ☎ 604/945–9511) sells high-performance (and high-fashion) gear.

The massive **Mountain Equipment Co-op** (✉ 130 W. Broadway, Fairview ☎ 604/872–7858) is a local institution with a good selection of high-performance and midprice clothing and equipment. A onetime $5 membership is required. The **Three Vets** (✉ 2200 Yukon St., Fairview ☎ 604/872–5475), near Cambie Street and Broadway, is an army-surplus-style store with budget-price family camping equipment.

VICTORIA

The capital of British Columbia, Victoria is the oldest city (founded 1843) on Canada's west coast and the first European settlement on Vancouver Island. It was chosen to be the westernmost trading outpost of the British-owned Hudson's Bay Company in 1843 and became the capital of British Columbia in 1868. Victoria has since evolved into a walkable, livable seaside town of gardens, waterfront pathways, and restored 19th-century architecture. Often described as the country's most British city, Victoria is these days—except for the odd red phone box, good beer, and well-mannered drivers—working to change that image, preferring to celebrate its combined native, Asian, and European heritage. Though it's quite touristy during the summer, it's also at its prettiest then, with flowers hanging from 19th-century lampposts and strollers enjoying the beauty of Victoria's natural harbor.

Exploring Victoria

Great views, lush gardens, and fine museums are the highlights of a visit to Victoria's walkable downtown. A trip to popular Butchart Gardens is worthwhile if you've got the time.

Numbers in the text correspond to numbers in the margin and on the Downtown Victoria map.

a good tour

For some wonderful views, begin your tour of Victoria on the waterfront at the Tourism Victoria Visitor Information Centre. Just across the way is the **Fairmont Empress Hotel** 18 , a majestic railway hotel that originally opened in 1908 (the public entrance is at the south end, off Belleville Street). A short walk around the harbor along the Inner Harbour Walk (take any of the staircases from Government Street down to the water level) will take you to the **Royal London Wax Museum.** Originally Victoria's steamship terminal, this colonnaded building now houses more than 300 wax figures. Floating in the harbor beside the wax museum are the Pacific Undersea Gardens, an underwater exhibit of local sea life. Across Belleville Street is the **Parliament Buildings** 19 complex, where British Columbia's provincial legislature sits. Cross Government Street to reach the **Royal British Columbia Museum** 20 , where you can explore thousands of years of history. Just behind the museum and bordering Douglas Street are the totem poles and ceremonial longhouse of Thunderbird Park; **Helmcken House** 21 , the oldest house in Victoria; and the tiny 19th-century **St. Ann's Schoolhouse.** A few blocks south on Douglas Street will take you to seaside Beacon Hill Park. A few blocks west of the park on Government Street is the **Emily Carr House,** the birthplace of one of British Columbia's best-known artists. From the park, go north on Blanshard Street to see the grounds and chapel of **St. Ann's Academy** 22 . Then take Belleville Street west to Douglas Street and stop off at the glass-roof **Crystal Garden Conservation Centre** 23 , where you can see endangered tropical birds and animals and hundreds of flowers.

For a different kind of wildlife exhibit, continue two blocks north (uphill) on Douglas and turn left at Courtney Street. Half a block in on your left you'll find the **Victoria Bug Zoo** 24 , a creepy-crawly attraction popular with children. From the Bug Zoo, continue west on Courtney Street to Government Street, Victoria's main shopping thoroughfare. Head north about three blocks to Government and View streets, where you'll find the entrance to the cobblestone **Bastion Square,** the original site of Fort Victoria and the Hudson's Bay Company trading post, which now has restaurants and offices. Just north of Government and View, on the right-hand side of Government Street, is the entrance to Trounce Alley, a pretty pedestrian-only shopping arcade. Back at Bastion Square, you can stop in at the **Maritime Museum of British Columbia** 25 and learn about an important part of the province's history.

North of Bastion Square a few blocks, on Store Street between Johnson Street and Pandora Avenue, is **Market Square** 26 , one of the most picturesque shopping districts in the city. Across Pandora Avenue is the entrance to the narrow, shop-lined Fan Tan Alley, which leads to Fisgard Street, the heart of **Chinatown** 27 . A 15-minute walk or a short drive east on Fort Street will take you to Joan Crescent and lavish **Craigdarroch Castle** 28

Downtown Victoria

and the nearby Art Gallery of Greater Victoria. In summer a ride on Harbour Ferries from the Inner Harbour will take you to **Point Ellice House** ㉙, a 19th-century waterside home and garden.

TIMING Many of the sights are within easy walking distance of one another, and the tour could be covered in half a day. However, allot a full day if you plan on visiting the Royal British Columbia Museum and the other museums.

What to See

㉗ **Chinatown.** Victoria's Chinatown, founded in 1858, is the oldest in Canada. If you enter Chinatown from Government Street, you'll walk under the elaborate **Gate of Harmonious Interest,** made from Taiwanese ceramic tiles and decorative panels. Along the street, merchants display fragile paper lanterns, wicker baskets, and exotic groceries. **Fan Tan Alley,** just off Fisgard Street, holds claim not only to being the narrowest street in Canada but also to having been the gambling and opium center of Chinatown, where games of mah-jongg, fan-tan, and dominoes were played. It's now lined with tiny shops.

㉘ **Craigdarroch Castle.** This lavish mansion was built as the home of British Columbia's first millionaire, coal baron Robert Dunsmuir. He died in 1889, just a few months before the castle's completion. Converted into a museum depicting turn-of-the-20th-century life, the castle has elaborately framed landscape paintings, stained-glass windows, carved woodwork—precut in Chicago for Dunsmuir and sent by rail—and a beautifully restored painted ceiling in the drawing room. From the tower, you can enjoy great views of Victoria and the Olympic Mountains. ⊠ *1050 Joan Crescent, Rockland* ☎ *250/592–5323* ⊕ *www.craigdarrochcastle.com* ✆ *C$10* ⊙ *Mid-June–Labor Day, daily 9–7; Labor Day–mid-June, daily 10–4:30.*

㉓ **Crystal Garden Conservation Centre.** Opened in 1925 as the largest saltwater swimming pool in the British Empire, this glass-roof building now houses exotic flora and a variety of endangered tropical fauna, including flamingos, tortoises, macaws, lemurs, bats, and butterflies. ⊠ *713 Douglas St., Downtown* ☎ *250/953–8815* ⊕ *www.bcpcc.com/crystal* ✆ *C$9* ⊙ *Mid-June–mid-Sept., daily 9–8; mid-Sept.–Oct. and mid-Mar.–mid-June, daily 9–6; Nov.–mid-Mar., daily 9–5.*

⌖ ⑱ **The Fairmont Empress Hotel.** Opened in 1908 by the Canadian Pacific Railway, the Empress is one of the grand château-style hotels you'll find in many Canadian cities. Designed by Francis Rattenbury, who also designed the Parliament Buildings, the Empress, with its solid Edwardian grandeur, has become a symbol of the city. The ingredients that made the 472-room hotel a tourist attraction in the past—old-world architecture and ornate decor, a commanding view of the Inner Harbour—are still here. The archives, a historical photo and cartoon display on the lower level, are open to the public. Nonguests can also stop by the Empress for a traditional afternoon tea (reservations recommended), meet for a curry under the tiger skin in the Bengal Room, enjoy a treatment at the hotel's Willow Stream spa, sample the superb French-influence cuisine in the Empress Room restaurant, or check out the high-end shops and galleries in the hotel's arcade. **Miniature World** (☎ 250/385–9731), a display of doll-size dioramas, including one of the world's longest model railways, is on the Humboldt Street side of the complex. ⊠ *721 Government St. (entrance at Belleville and Government), Downtown* ☎ *250/384–8111, 250/389–2727 tea reservations* ⊕ *www.fairmont.com/empress* ✆ *Afternoon tea C$50 in summer, C$26–C$35 in winter; Miniature World C$9.*

㉑ Helmcken House. The oldest house in British Columbia was erected in 1852 for pioneer doctor and statesman John Sebastian Helmcken. It is a treasure trove of history, from the family's Victorian furnishings to the doctor's intriguing collection of 19th-century medical tools. Audio tours last 20 minutes. Beside Helmcken House is **Thunderbird Park**, with totem poles and a ceremonial longhouse constructed by Kwakiutl chief Mungo Martin. Next door is **St. Ann's Schoolhouse**, one of British Columbia's oldest schools (you can view the interior through the door). ✉ *10 Elliot St., Downtown* ☎ *250/361–0021* ⊕ *www.heritage.gov.bc. ca* ✍ *C$5* ⊙ *May–Oct., daily 10–5; Nov.–Apr., Thurs.–Mon. noon–4; some Christmas and Halloween programs.*

㊙ ㉕ Maritime Museum of British Columbia. In Victoria's original courthouse, model ships, Royal Navy charts, photographs, uniforms, and ships' bells chronicle British Columbia's seafaring history. Among the hand-built boats on display is the Tilikum, a dugout canoe that sailed from Victoria to England between 1901 and 1904. An 1899 hand-operated cage lift, believed to be the oldest continuously operating elevator in North America, ascends to the third floor, where an 1888 Vice-Admiralty courtroom looks set for a court-martial. ✉ *28 Bastion Sq., Old Town* ☎ *250/385–4222* ⊕ *www.mmbc.bc.ca* ✍ *C$6* ⊙ *Daily 9:30–4:30.*

㉖ Market Square. During Victoria's late-19th-century heyday, this three-level square, originally the courtyard of an old inn, provided everything a sailor, miner, or up-country lumberjack could want. Now, beautifully restored to its original architectural, if not commercial, character, it's a traffic-free café- and boutique-lined hangout. ✉ *560 Johnson St., Old Town* ☎ *250/386–2441.*

★ ⑲ Parliament Buildings. Designed by Francis Rattenbury, who also designed the Fairmont Empress Hotel, these massive stone structures, completed in 1898, dominate the Inner Harbour. Two statues flank the main doors: one of Sir James Douglas (1803–77), who chose the site where Victoria was built, and another of Sir Matthew Baille Begbie (1819–94), the man in charge of law and order during the gold rush. Atop the central dome is a gilded statue of Captain George Vancouver (1757–98), the first European to sail around Vancouver Island. A statue of Queen Victoria (1819–1901) stands in front of the complex. More than 3,000 lights outline the buildings at night. The interior is lavishly appointed with stained-glass windows and murals depicting scenes from the province's history. From the public gallery, when the legislature is in session you can watch British Columbian democracy at work; tradition has the opposing parties sitting 2½ sword lengths apart. Informative half-hour tours are free. ✉ *501 Belleville St., Downtown* ☎ *250/387–3046* ⊕ *www. legis.gov.bc.ca* ✍ *Free* ⊙ *Mid-May–Labor Day, daily 8:30–5 (up to 23 tours a day); Sept.–mid-May, weekdays 8:30–5; last tour at 4 PM.*

㉙ Point Ellice House. This restored 1860s Italianate villa overlooking the Upper Harbour has the largest collection of Victorian furnishings in western Canada. Tea with home-baked goodies is served on the lawn. You can also take an audio tour of the house, stroll in the gardens, or try your hand at croquet. To get here, take a Harbour Ferries boat from the dock in front of the Empress Hotel. Reservations are recommended for tea. ✉ *2616 Pleasant St., Upper Harbour* ☎ *250/380–6506* ⊕ *www. heritage.gov.bc.ca* ✍ *C$7, C$20 with tea* ⊙ *Mid-May–mid-Sept., daily noon–5; tea daily noon–4; some Christmas and Halloween programs.*

㊙ ⑳ Royal British Columbia Museum. This excellent museum, one of Victoria's leading attractions, traces several thousand years of British Columbian history. Exhibits include a genuine Kwakwaka'wakw longhouse (the builders retain rights to its ceremonial use) and an extensive collection of First Nations masks and other artifacts. The Natural History Gallery re-creates the sights and sounds of a rain forest, tidal wetlands, and other B.C. natural habitats, and the Open Ocean exhibit mimics a submarine journey. A replica of Captain Vancouver's ship, the HMCS *Discovery*, creaks convincingly, and a re-created frontier town comes complete with cobbled streets, silent movies, and the smells of home baking. Century Hall reviews British Columbia's 20th-century history, and an on-site IMAX theater shows *National Geographic* films on a six-story-high screen. ⊠ *675 Belleville St., Downtown* ☎ *250/356–7226 or 888/ 447–7977* ⊕ *www.royalbcmuseum.bc.ca* ✉ *$10, IMAX theater $9.75, combination ticket $17.75* ◷ *Museum daily 9–5; theater daily 9–8 (call for show times).*

㉒ St. Ann's Academy. This former convent and school, founded in 1858, played a central role in British Columbia's pioneer life. The academy's little chapel, the first Roman Catholic cathedral in Victoria, has been restored to look just as it did in the 1920s. The 6-acre grounds, with fruit trees and herb and flower gardens, are also being restored as historic landscapes. ⊠ *835 Humboldt St., Downtown* ☎ *250/953–8828* ⊕ *www.bcpcc.com/stanns* ✉ *By donation* ◷ *Gardens daily. Chapel mid-May–Labor Day, daily 10–4; Labor Day–mid-May, call for hrs.*

☾ ㉔ Victoria Bug Zoo. Kids of all ages are drawn to this offbeat, two-room mini-zoo. Many of the bugs—mostly large tropical varieties, such as stick insects, scorpions, and centipedes—can be held; staff members are on hand to dispense scientific information. ⊠ *631 Courtney St., Inner Harbour* ☎ *250/384–2847* ⊕ *www.bugzoo.bc.ca* ✉ *C$6* ◷ *July and Aug., daily 9–9; Sept.–June, Mon.–Sat. 9:30–5:30, Sun. 11–5:30.*

off the beaten path	**BUTCHART GARDENS –** This impressive 55-acre garden, 21 km (13 mi) north of downtown Victoria, on the way to the Swartz Bay ferry terminal, grows more than 700 varieties of flowers in its sunken, Italian, Japanese, and rose gardens. In summer, subtle lights illuminate the gardens at night, and fireworks light the sky over the gardens every Saturday night in July and August. Also on the premises are a seed and gift shop, two restaurants, and a coffee shop. Traditional English afternoon tea is served daily in the dining room. To get to the gardens by transit, take Bus 75 from downtown. ⊠ *800 Benvenuto Ave., Brentwood Bay* ☎ *250/652–5256 or 866/652–4422* ⊕ *www.butchartgardens.com* ✉ *Mid-June–late Sept. C$20; discounted rates rest of yr* ◷ *Mid-June–Aug., daily 9 AM–10:30 PM; Sept.–mid-June, daily 9 AM–dusk (call for precise times).*

Where to Eat

"Fresh, local, organic" has become a mantra for many Victoria chefs. Wild salmon, locally made cheeses, Pacific oysters, forest-foraged mushrooms, organic vegetables in season, local microbrews, and even British Columbia wines can all be sampled here. Restaurants in the region generally are casual. A bylaw bans smoking in all Victoria restaurants.

Casual but neat dress is appropriate everywhere. A 15% tip is expected. A 10% liquor tax is charged on wine, beer, and spirits. Some restaurants build the liquor tax into the price of the beverage, but others add it to the bill.

	WHAT IT COSTS In Canadian dollars				
	$$$$	$$$	$$	$	¢
AT DINNER	over $30	$20–$30	$12–$20	$8–$12	under $8

Prices are per person for a main course. The final tab will include a 7% Goods and Service Tax (GST).

Cafés

¢–$ ✕ **Willie's Bakery.** This handsome Victorian building near Market Square is home to a bakery-café, serving wholesome breakfasts, rich soups, delicious sandwiches made with house-baked bread, tasty baked treats, and thin-crust pizzas. The brick patio with an outdoor fireplace and little fountain provides a pleasant spot to watch the world go by. ✉ *537 Johnson St., Old Town* ☎ *250/381–8414* ⌨ *Reservations not accepted* ⊟ *AE, DC, MC, V* ✆ *No dinner Sept.–mid-May.*

Italian

$$–$$$$ ✕ **Il Terrazzo.** A charming redbrick terrace edged by potted greenery, lighted by flickering candles, and warmed by fireplaces and overhead heaters makes Il Terrazzo, tucked away off Waddington Alley and not visible from the street, the locals' choice for romantic alfresco dining in Victoria. Starters include mussels steamed with banana peppers, sun-dried tomatoes, cilantro, garlic, Asiago cheese, and cream. Main courses, such as the Dijon-encrusted rack of lamb and osso buco with porcini mushrooms, come piping hot from the restaurant's wood oven. ✉ *555 Johnson St., off Waddington Alley (call for directions), Old Town* ☎ *250/361–0028* ⊟ *AE, DC, MC, V* ✆ *No lunch Sun., or Sat. Oct.–Apr.*

$$ ✕ **Zambri's.** The setting is a downtown strip mall, but inside is a lively trattoria worthy of a neighborhood in Rome. Lunch is casual. You order at the counter from a daily-changing roster of pastas, soups, and hot hearty sandwiches (such as the hot meatball or Italian sausage). Dinner brings table service and a weekly changing menu of such hearty fare as *tagliolini* (long, thin pasta) with veal, tomato, and artichoke and roasted pork loin with quince butter sauce and polenta. On Saturday night a five-course prix-fixe menu is served to a reservation-only crowd. ✉ *110–911 Yates St., Downtown* ☎ *250/360–1171* ⌨ *Reservations not accepted* ⊟ *AE, MC, V* ✆ *Closed Sun.*

Pacific Northwest

★ **$$–$$$** ✕ **Cafe Brio.** Lush Modigliani nudes and rich gold walls create a warm glow at this Italian-villa-style building. The menu, described by the owners as "West Coast contemporary with a Tuscan hint," changes seasonally and uses a wealth of local, organic ingredients. Appetizers might include smoked sablefish and potato ravioli or seared jumbo scallops with watercress. Main dishes could be Cowichan Bay duck breast; fusilli with roast mushrooms, arugula, and goat cheese; or wild sockeye salmon. The three-course tasting menus, including a vegetarian option, are popular choices. ✉ *944 Fort St., Downtown* ☎ *250/383–0009* ⊟ *AE, MC, V* ✆ *No lunch.*

★ **$$–$$$** ✕ **Herald Street Caffé.** Organic local ingredients—often prepared with Asian touches—good vegetarian selections, and house-made breads, pastas and desserts help make this lively art-filled bistro stand out among Victoria's Pacific Northwest restaurants. Try the steamed mussels in lemon Szechuan peppercorn sauce, the ginger-prawn spinach linguine, or the crab cakes with cilantro-lime pesto. Every evening between 5:30 and 6:30 you can have a three-course menu for less than $20. ✉ *546 Herald St., Chinatown* ☎ *250/381–1441* ⊟ *AE, DC, MC, V* ✆ *No lunch Mon. or Tues.*

Seafood

$$$–$$$$ ✕ **The Blue Crab Bar and Grill.** Fresh seafood and expansive harbor views make this modern, airy restaurant a popular lunch and dinner spot. Signature dishes include Dungeness crab and shrimp cakes, and a scallop and jumbo prawn sautée, though the long list of daily specials is always tempting. In the attached lounge area, open nightly until 1 AM and with equally impressive views, you can choose from the dinner menu or opt for more casual, lower-priced fare. ✉ *146 Kingston St., in Coast Harbourside Hotel and Marina, James Bay* ☎ *250/480–1999* ▤ *AE, D, DC, MC, V.*

¢–$ ✕ **Barb's Place.** This funky, blue-painted take-out shack floats on the quay where the fishing boats dock, west of the Inner Harbour off Erie Street. Cod, lingcod, halibut, oysters, seafood burgers, chowder, and carrot cake are all prepared fresh on the premises. If you eat on the picnic tables on the wharf, you'll have a front-row view of the vessels such as paddle wheelers, houseboats, and vintage fishing boats that moor in the harbor. Ferries sail to Fisherman's Wharf from the Inner Harbor. ✉ *Fisherman's Wharf, Erie St., James Bay* ☎ *250/384–6515* ▤ *MC, V* ⊘ *Closed Nov.–Feb.*

Vegetarian

$–$$ ✕ **Re-Bar Modern Food.** This bright and cheery café in Bastion Square is *the* place for vegetarians in Victoria, though the almond burgers, veggie enchiladas, decadent home-baked goodies, and big breakfasts will keep omnivores happy. An extensive tea and fresh-juice selection shares space with espresso, microbrews, and B.C. wines on the drinks list. ✉ *50 Bastion Sq., Old Town* ☎ *250/361–9223* ⊕ *www.rebarmodernfood.com* ▤ *AE, MC, V* ⊘ *No dinner Sun.*

Afternoon Tea

Perhaps it's the city's British heritage, perhaps it's just a fun thing to do, but the tradition of afternoon tea lives on in Victoria. Many cafés will serve a tea, but the most popular and authentic places are clustered near the Inner Harbour and in the city's very British Oak Bay district, which you may hear described as being "behind the tweed curtain." A note about terminology: afternoon tea is a snack of tea, cakes, and sandwiches taken about 4 PM. High tea is a hot meal eaten at dinnertime. The following places serve afternoon tea.

Victoria's best-known, most elaborate, and most expensive afternoon tea is served, as it has been since 1908, on bone china at antique tables in the airy tea lobby of the **Fairmont Empress Hotel** (✉ 721 Government St., Downtown ☎ 250/389–2727). The tea is, of course, the hotel's own special blend, and the cakes, scones, tarts, and little crustless sandwiches are prepared by some of Victoria's finest pastry chefs. As you face the bill of $C50 per person in high season, remember that tea at the Empress is more than a snack. It was, historically, a way to keep civilization alive in this farthest outpost of the empire. Reservations are recommended.

Long-established and dripping with British memorabilia, the wood-beamed **Blethering Place** (✉ 2250 Oak Bay Ave., Oak Bay ☎ 250/598–1413) serves a tea of scones, Devonshire cream, fruit, sandwiches, cakes, tarts, and more between 11 AM and 7:30 PM. English breakfasts are available in the morning. The cozy, lace-curtained **James Bay Tea Room** (✉ 332 Menzies St. ☎ 250/382–8282) is a short walk from the Inner Harbour and serves full teas all day, starting at 7 AM. Breakfast and lunch are also available here.

Everything, including the jam, is homemade for the Scottish-style teas served at the **White Heather Tea Room** (✉ 1885 Oak Bay Ave., Oak Bay ☎ 250/595–8020), a pretty place with big windows and white table-cloths. Lunch is also served.

Where to Stay

In Victoria you'll find a range of accommodations, from luxury hotels and chains to bed-and-breakfast inns. Most small inns and B&Bs in Victoria ban smoking indoors, and all hotels in the area have nonsmoking rooms.

WHAT IT COSTS In Canadian dollars				
$$$$	$$$	$$	$	¢
FOR 2 PEOPLE over $250	$175–$250	$125–$175	$75–$125	under $75

Prices are for two people in a standard double room in high season, excluding 10% provincial accommodation tax, service charge, and 7% Goods and Service Tax (GST).

$$$$ ⊞ **Delta Victoria Ocean Pointe Resort and Spa.** Across the "blue bridge" (Johnson Street Bridge) from downtown Victoria, the waterfront Delta Victoria has a resort's worth of facilities, including a full spa. You'll find expansive views of the Inner Harbour and the Parliament Buildings across the water from the hotel's striking two-story-high lobby windows and half of the guest rooms. Modern rooms are comfortable and spacious, and the apartment-size suites have separate living and dining areas. An on-site adventure center can arrange fishing, kayaking, whale-watching, and more. ✉ 45 Songhees Rd., V9A 6T3 ☎ 250/360–2999 or 800/667–4677 🖷 250/360–1041 ⊕ www.deltahotels.com ⇥ 240 rooms, 6 suites ♿ 2 restaurants, room service, in-room data ports, minibars, cable TV with movies and video games, 2 tennis courts, indoor pool, health club, hair salon, hot tub, sauna, bicycles, racquetball, squash, lounge, shop, baby-sitting, dry cleaning, laundry service, concierge, concierge floor, Internet, business services, meeting rooms, travel services, parking (fee), some pets allowed, no-smoking floors ▭ AE, DC, MC, V.

★ $$$–$$$$ ⊞ **Abigail's Hotel.** A Tudor-style inn built in 1930, Abigail's is within walking distance of downtown. The guest rooms are attractively furnished in an English Arts and Crafts style, with whirlpool tubs and fireplaces in many rooms. Six large, luxurious rooms in the Coach House have whirlpool tubs, king-size four-poster beds, and wood-burning fireplaces. A lavish hot breakfast is included in the rate. ✉ 906 McClure St., Downtown, V8V 3E7 ☎ 250/388–5363 or 800/561–6565 🖷 250/388–7787 ⊕ www.abigailshotel.com ⇥ 23 rooms ♿ Some fans, in-room data ports, some refrigerators, cable TV, some in-room VCRs, library, shop, dry cleaning, laundry service, free parking; no a/c, no TV in some rooms, no kids under 10, no smoking ▭ AE, MC, V ⦿ BP.

★ $$$–$$$$ ⊞ **Beaconsfield Inn.** This 1905 registered heritage building just four blocks from the Inner Harbour is one of Victoria's most faithfully restored Edwardian mansions. Antique furniture, mahogany floors, fireplaces, stained-glass windows, Ralph Lauren fabrics, and such period details as the Edwardian wooden canopied tub in one room render each room and suite unique. Lavish breakfasts and afternoon tea and sherry in the conservatory or around the library fire complete the Edwardian country-house ambience. ✉ 998 Humboldt St., Downtown, V8V 2Z8 ☎ 250/384–4044 or 888/884–4044 🖷 250/384–4052 ⊕ www.beaconsfieldinn.com ⇥ 5 rooms, 4 suites ♿ Library, free parking; no a/c, no room phones, no room TVs, no smoking ▭ MC, V ⦿ BP.

$$$-$$$$ ⬚ **The Fairmont Empress.** Opened in 1908, this harborside château and city landmark has aged gracefully. Its sympathetically restored Edwardian decor and top-notch service recall a more gracious age. Rooms vary in size and layout, but most are tastefully lush, with rich fabrics, buttery walls, and rosewood furniture. Many of those facing Government Street have front-row views of the Inner Harbour. ✉ *721 Government St., Downtown, V8W 1W5* ☎ *250/384–8111 or 800/441–1414* ⊟ *250/389–2747* ⊕ *www.fairmont.com/empress* ⤺ *436 rooms, 41 suites* ⚫ *3 restaurants, room service, some fans, in-room data ports, some in-room safes, minibars, cable TV with movies and video games, indoor pool, gym, hot tub, sauna, spa, lounge, shops, baby-sitting, dry cleaning, laundry service, concierge, concierge floor, Internet, business services, convention center, meeting rooms, parking (fee), some pets allowed (fee), no-smoking floors; no a/c in some rooms* ⊟ *AE, D, DC, MC, V.*

$$-$$$ ⬚ **Swans Suite Hotel.** Across the road from the waterfront in Victoria's old town, this 1913 former warehouse is one of the city's most attractive boutique hotels. There's a brewery, restaurant, and pub on the first floor and a nightclub in the cellar. High-ceiling, apartmentlike suites, all decorated with Pacific Northwest art, fill the upper floors. The lavish penthouse suite has a private hot tub. ✉ *506 Pandora Ave., Old Town, V8W 1N6* ☎ *250/361–3310 or 800/668–7926* ⊟ *250/361–3491* ⊕ *www.swanshotel.com* ⤺ *30 suites* ⚫ *Room service, fans, in-room data ports, microwaves, kitchens, cable TV, some in-room VCRs, wine shop, dry cleaning, laundry facilities, laundry service, business services, meeting rooms, parking (fee); no a/c, no smoking* ⊟ *AE, DC, MC, V.*

$ ⬚ **Craigmyle Guest House.** This Edwardian manor near Craigdarroch Castle, a mile from the city center, is Victoria's oldest bed-and-breakfast and one of its better values. The four-story guest house houses a variety of rooms, some with original furniture, claw-foot tubs, and offbeat combinations of patterned wallpaper and floral bedspreads. All have private baths, though a few are across the hall from the room. A small garden, a guest kitchen, a big comfy common room, and some units that sleep four make this a good choice for families. ✉ *1037 Craigdarroch Rd., V8S 2A5* ☎ *250/595–5411 or 888/595–5411* ⊟ *250/370–5276* ⊕ *www.bctravel.com/craigmyle* ⤺ *16 rooms, 1 suite* ⚫ *No room phones, no room TVs, no smoking.* ⊟ *AE, MC, V* ⊚ *BP.*

Nightlife & the Arts

For entertainment listings, pick up a free copy of *Monday Magazine* (it comes out every Thursday) or call the Talking Super Pages at 250/953–9000.

Nightlife

BARS & CLUBS The **Snug Pub** (✉ 1175 Beach Dr., Oak Bay ☎ 250/598–4556), about 10 minutes from downtown in the Oak Bay Beach Hotel, is the nearest thing to a traditional English pub in Victoria, with a cozy Tudor ambience and a waterside deck. The **Strathcona Hotel** (✉ 919 Douglas St., Downtown ☎ 250/383–7137) is something of an entertainment complex, with a restaurant, a nightclub, and seven different bars, including a sports bar, a hillbilly-theme bar, and a rooftop patio where patrons play beach volleyball in summer. The **Saltaire Lounge** (✉ 100–407 Swift St., Old Town ☎ 250/383–8439), a chic waterfront cocktail bar near Chinatown with a large patio overlooking the Gorge waterway, hosts live jazz on weekends. Blues, jazz, Top 40, and live bands twice a week draw an over-25 crowd to the big dance floor at the **Upstairs Cabaret** (✉ 15 Bastion Sq., Old Town ☎ 250/385–5483).

BREWPUBS Pub culture is an important part of life in Victoria, and many of the city's most atmospheric pubs brew their own beer. The patio at the **Canoe Brewpub** (⊠ 450 Swift St., Old Town ☎ 250/361–1940) has views over the Gorge waterway. The former power station has been stylishly redone and has a wide range of in-house brews, top-notch bar snacks, and a restaurant.

Chic and arty **Hugo's Brewhouse** (⊠ 625 Courtney St., Downtown ☎ 250/920–4844) serves lunch, dinner, and six of its own brews. This multipurpose nightspot is a pub by day, a lounge in the early evening, and a dance club at night. Across the Johnson Street Bridge, **Spinnakers Brew Pub** (⊠ 308 Catherine St., Vic West ☎ 250/386–2739), with a waterfront deck and cozy rooms filled with pub paraphernalia, pours Victoria's most extensive menu of microbrews. The excellent pub grub and in-house restaurant make this a popular eatery. **Swans Pub** (⊠ 1601 Store St., Downtown ☎ 250/361–3310), in a 1913 heritage building, serves its own microbrews in a room decorated with Pacific Northwest native art and has live music from Sunday through Thursday nights.

The Arts

MUSIC **Pacific Opera Victoria** (☎ 250/385–0222) performs three productions a year in the **Royal Theatre** (⊠ 805 Broughton St., Downtown ☎ 250/386–6121). The **Victoria Symphony** (☎ 250/385–6515) plays in the **Royal Theatre** (⊠ 805 Broughton St. ☎ 250/386–6121) and at the **University Centre Auditorium** (⊠ Finnerty Rd., University of Victoria campus ☎ 250/721–8480). The **TerrifVic Jazz Party** (☎ 250/953–2011) showcases internationally acclaimed musicians every April at seven venues around Victoria. The **Victoria Jazz Society** (☎ 250/388–4423) organizes an annual JazzFest International in late June and the Vancouver Island Blues Bash in Victoria every Labor Day weekend.

THEATER An old church houses the **Belfry Theatre** (⊠ 1291 Gladstone Ave., Fernwood ☎ 250/385–6815), whose resident company specializes in contemporary Canadian dramas. **McPherson Playhouse** (⊠ 3 Centennial Sq., Downtown ☎250/386–6121) hosts touring theater and dance companies.

Shopping

Shopping Districts & Malls

Victoria Eaton Centre (⊠ 1 Victoria Eaton Centre, at Government and Fort Sts., Downtown ☎ 250/952–5680), a department store and mall, holds about 100 boutiques and restaurants. **Antique Row,** on Fort Street between Blanshard and Cook streets, has more than 60 antiques, curio, and collectibles shops. **Market Square** (⊠ 560 Johnson St., Downtown ☎ 250/386–2441) has everything from toys and music to jewelry, local arts, and new-age accoutrements. High-end fashion boutiques, crafts shops, and galleries line **Trounce Alley,** a pedestrian-only lane north of View Street between Broad and Government streets.

Specialty Stores

Most of Victoria's specialty shops are on or near Government Street stretching north from the Empress Hotel.

At **Artina's** (⊠ 1002 Government St., Downtown ☎ 250/386–7000 or 877/386–7700) you can find unusual Canadian art jewelry—mostly handmade, one-of-a-kind pieces. The **Cowichan Trading Co., Ltd.** (⊠ 1328 Government St., Downtown ☎ 250/383–0321) sells First Nations jewelry, art, moccasins, and Cowichan sweaters. The **Fran Willis Gallery** (⊠ 1619 Store St., upstairs, Downtown ☎ 250/381–3422) shows contemporary Canadian paintings and sculpture. **Hill's Native Art** (⊠ 1008 Government St., Downtown ☎ 250/385–3911) sells souvenirs and original West Coast First Nations art. **Irish Linen Stores** (✉ 1019 Government St., Downtown ☎ 250/383–6812) stocks fine linen, lace, and hand-embroidered items. **Munro's Books** (✉ 1108 Government St., Downtown ☎ 250/382–2464), in a restored 1909 building, sells a strong selection of local titles. Forty varieties of tea, plus coffees, tarts, and cakes, are available at **Murchie's** (✉ 1110 Government St., Downtown ☎ 250/383–3112). Handmade chocolates are displayed in antique cases at **Roger's Chocolates** (✉ 913 Government St. ☎ 250/384–7021). At **Starfish Glassworks** (✉ 630 Yates St., Downtown ☎ 250/388–7827) you can watch glassblowers create original works.

VANCOUVER & VICTORIA A TO Z

To research prices, get advice from other travelers, and book travel arrangements, visit www.fodors.com.

AIRPORTS & TRANSFERS

Vancouver International Airport is on an island about 23 km (14 mi) south of downtown. An airport improvement fee is assessed on all flight departures: C$5 for flights within British Columbia, C$10 for flights within North America, and C$15 for overseas flights. Air Canada, Alaska Airlines, American Airlines, Continental Airlines, Northwest, United, and WestJet fly into the airport. Victoria International Airport is served by Air Canada, Horizon Air, Pacific Coastal, and WestJet Airlines.

Air Canada provides frequent airport-to-airport service from Vancouver to Victoria. Flights take about 35 minutes. Kenmore Air Harbor's floatplanes fly daily from Seattle to Victoria's Inner Harbour.

West Coast Air's 35-minute floatplane service flies several times a day between downtown Vancouver, Vancouver International Airport, and Victoria's Inner Harbour. Harbour Air also provides frequent harbor-to-harbor floatplane service. Helijet International has helicopter service from downtown Vancouver, Vancouver International Airport, Abbotsford International Airport, and Boeing Field Seattle to downtown Victoria. The Vancouver heliport is near Vancouver's SeaBus terminal.
🛈 **Abbotsford International Airport** ✉30440 Liberator Ave., Abbotsford V2T 6H5 ☎604/855-1135. **Kenmore Air Harbor** ☎ 425/486-1257 or 800/543-9595 ⊕ www.kenmoreair.com. **Vancouver International Airport** ☎ 604/207-7077 ⊕ www.yvr.ca. **Victoria International Airport** ☎ 250/953-7500 ⊕ www.victoriaairport.com. **Air Canada** ☎ 888/247-2262 ⊕ www.aircanada.ca. **Harbour Air** ☎ 604/274-1277 or 800/665-0212 ⊕ www.harbour-air.com. **Helijet International** ☎ 604/273-1414, 250/382-6222, or 800/665-4354 ⊕ www.helijet.com. **West Coast Air** ☎ 604/606-6888 or 800/347-2222 ⊕ www.westcoastair.com.

AIRPORT TRANSFERS The drive from the airport to downtown Vancouver takes 20–45 minutes, depending on the time of day. The Vancouver Airporter provides service to major downtown hotels for C$12 one-way, C$18 round-trip. Yellow Cab and Black Top cabs serve the whole Vancouver area. Taxi fare to downtown is about C$25. Limousine service from LimoJet Gold costs about C$34 one-way. To travel downtown by public transit, take any TransLink bus marked Airport Station; then transfer at Airport Station to a No. 98 Burrard Station bus. To return to the airport, take a No. 98 Richmond Centre bus and transfer at Airport Station.

Victoria International Airport is about 30 minutes from downtown Victoria. The Airporter bus service drops off passengers at most major hotels. The fare is C$13 one-way, C$23 round-trip. Taxis are available from Empress Taxi and Victoria Taxi. The fare to downtown is about

C$38. There is no public transit available at Victoria Airport, but the Airporter bus will take you to the nearest transit stop for C$2.

🚖 Taxis & Shuttles **Black Top** ☎ 604/681-2181. **Empress Taxi** ☎ 250/381-2222. **Limo-Jet Gold** ☎ 604/273-1331 or 800/278-8742. **Vancouver Airporter Service** ☎ 604/946-8866 or 800/668-3141. **Victoria Airport** ☎ 250/386-2525. **Victoria Taxi** ☎ 250/383-7111. **Yellow Cab** ☎ 604/681-1111.

BOAT & FERRY TRAVEL

B.C. Ferries operates daily service between Vancouver and Victoria (1 hour, 35 minutes' sailing time). The Vancouver terminal is in Tsawwassen, 38 km (24 mi) southwest of downtown. In Victoria, ferries arrive at and depart from the Swartz Bay Terminal at the end of Highway 17, 32 km (20 mi) north of downtown Victoria. Vehicle reservations on Vancouver to Victoria and Nanaimo routes are optional and cost C$15 in addition to the fare. Ferries sail every few hours in each direction. The *Victoria Clipper* operates year-round passenger-only service between Victoria and Seattle (two to three hours' sailing time). Washington State Ferries runs a car ferry daily, year-round, between Sidney, just north of Victoria, and Anacortes, Washington (three hours; one or two sailings a day each way). Black Ball Transport operates car ferries between Victoria and Port Angeles, Washington (1 hour, 35 minutes). Victoria's Oak Bay Beach Hotel & Marine Resort operates a twice-daily, summer-only foot-passenger and bicycle ferry to Roche Harbor on San Juan Island, Washington.

In Vancouver, the SeaBus is a 400-passenger commuter ferry that crosses Burrard Inlet from the foot of Lonsdale (North Vancouver) to downtown. The ride takes 13 minutes and costs the same as the bus (and it's much faster). With a transfer, connection can be made with any TransLink bus or SkyTrain.

Aquabus Ferries connects several stations on False Creek, including Science World, Granville Island, Stamp's Landing, Yaletown, and the Hornby Street dock. Some of the boats can also take bicycles. The company also operates two historic wooden boats on some runs and conducts 45-minute False Creek tours from its Granville Island dock. False Creek Ferries provides foot-passenger service between the Aquatic Centre on Beach Avenue, Granville Island, Science World, Stamps Landing, and Vanier Park as well as 20- and 40-minute tours of False Creek.

In Victoria, Victoria Harbour Ferries operates daily between March and October and on sunny weekends the rest of the year, making eight stops around the Inner Harbour, including the Empress Hotel and Fisherman's Wharf.

🚢 **Aquabus Ferries** ☎ 604/689-5858 ⊕ www.aquabus.bc.ca. **B.C. Ferries** ☎ 250/386-3431, 888/223-3779 in British Columbia outside Victoria; 604/444-2890, 888/724-5223 in B.C. for vehicle reservations ⊕ www.bcferries.com. **Black Ball Transport** ☎ 250/386-2202, 360/457-4491 in U.S. ⊕ www.ferrytovictoria.com. **False Creek Ferries** ☎ 604/684-7781 ⊕ www.granvilleislandferries.bc.ca. **Oak Bay Beach Hotel & Marine Resort** ☎ 250/592-3474 or 800/668-7758 ⊕ www.oakbaybeachhotel.com. **Victoria Clipper** ☎ 250/382-8100 in Victoria, 206/448-5000 in Seattle, 800/888-2535 elsewhere ⊕ www.victoriaclipper.com. **Victoria Harbour Ferries** ☎ 250/708-0201 ⊕ www.harbourferry.com. **Washington State Ferries** ☎ 206/464-6400 or 888/808-7977 ⊕ www.wsdot.wa.gov/ferries.

BUS & RAPID TRANSIT TRAVEL

Vancouver's TransLink system, comprising buses, the SeaBus, and the SkyTrain (an elevated train that runs underground through the downtown core), can get you just about anywhere you need to go. Exact change (C$2 in Vancouver, C$3–C$4 to the suburbs) or a FareSaver ticket (available from convenience stores) is required. Day passes, good for unlimited travel all day, cost C$8. B.C. Transit runs an extensive service in Victoria and the surrounding areas, including service to the B. C. Ferries terminal at Swartz Bay. An all-day pass costs C$5.50. Double-decker buses run on some routes. Pacific Coach Lines operates daily connecting service between Victoria and Vancouver on B.C. Ferries.

🚌 **B.C. Transit** ☎ 250/382-6161 ⊕ www.bctransit.com. **Pacific Coach Lines** ☎ 604/662-8074 or 800/661-1725 ⊕ www.pacificcoach.com. **TransLink** ☎ 604/953-3333 ⊕ www.translink.bc.ca.

CAR TRAVEL

From the south, I–5 from Seattle becomes Highway 99 at the U.S.-Canada border. Vancouver is a three-hour drive (226 km [140 mi]) from Seattle. It's best to avoid border crossings during peak times such as holidays and weekends. Highway 1, the Trans-Canada Highway, enters Vancouver from the east. To avoid traffic, arrive after rush hour (8:30 AM).

Vancouver's rush-hour traffic starts early—about 3 PM on weekdays. The worst bottlenecks outside the city center are the North Shore bridges, the George Massey Tunnel on Highway 99 south of Vancouver, and Highway 1 through Coquitlam and Surrey. Downtown parking costs about C$8 a day, though most lots fill early.

EMERGENCIES

🚑 Doctors **Medicentre** ⊠ Bentall Centre, 1055 Dunsmuir St., lower level, Vancouver ☎ 604/683-8138.

🚑 Emergency Services **Police, fire, ambulance** ☎ 911.

🚑 Hospitals **St. Paul's Hospital** ⊠ 1081 Burrard St., Vancouver ☎ 604/682-2344. **Victoria General Hospital** ⊠ 1 Hospital Way, off Helmcken Rd., Victoria ☎ 250/727-4212.

🚑 Late-Night Pharmacies **Shopper's Drug Mart** ⊠ Town and Country Shopping Centre, 3575 Douglas St. ☎ 250/475-7572. **Shopper's Drug Mart** ⊠ 1125 Davie St. ☎ 604/669-2424.

LODGING

BED & BREAKFASTS **Garden City B&B Reservation Service** can make B&B reservations in Victoria and elsewhere on Vancouver Island. Hello B.C., operated by the provincial Ministry of Tourism, can reserve accommodations anywhere in British Columbia. Town & Country Bed and Breakfast Reservations Service books B&Bs in Vancouver and Victoria.

🏨 Local Agents **Garden City B&B Reservation Service** ⊠ 660 Jones Terr., Victoria V8Z 2L7 ☎ 250/479-1986 or 866/247-2421 ⊕ www.bc-bed-breakfast.com. **Hello B.C.** ☎ 800/435-5622 ⊕ www.hellobc.com. **Town & Country Bed and Breakfast Reservations Service** ⊠ 2803 W. 4th Ave. ⌖ Box 74542, Vancouver V6K 1K2 🖷 604/731-5942 ⊕ www.townandcountrybedandbreakfast.com.

MONEY MATTERS

Most merchants in Vancouver and Victoria will accept U.S. dollars, though if you exchange your money, you'll probably get a better rate at a bank. ATMs are easy to find in both cities: most bank branches and many convenience stores have them.

TOURS

Gray Line, the largest tour operator, leads orientation tours of both cities. The Vancouver Trolley Company runs turn-of-the-20th-century-style trolleys through Vancouver on a two-hour narrated tour of the major sights, including Gastown, Chinatown, Granville Island, and Stanley Park. A day pass (C$25) allows you to complete one full circuit, getting off and on as often as you like. Stanley Park Horse-Drawn Tours runs horse and carriage tours of Stanley Park between March 15 and October 31; the C$20.55 fare includes a shuttle-bus ride to the park from downtown.

With Tally-Ho Sightseeing, you can take a horse-drawn carriage tour of downtown Victoria that includes Beacon Hill Park. Victoria Carriage Tours has horse-drawn tours of the city year-round.

🔲 **Gray Line** ☎ 604/879-3363, 800/667-0882 in Vancouver, 250/388-5248, 800/663-8390 in Victoria ⊕ www.grayline.ca. **Stanley Park Horse-Drawn Tours** ☎ 604/681-5115 ⊕ www.stanleyparktours.com. **Tally-Ho Sightseeing** ☎ 250/383-5067 or 866/383-5067 ⊕ www.tallyhotours.com. **Vancouver Trolley Company** ☎ 604/801-5515 or 888/451-5581 ⊕ www.vancouvertrolley.com. **Victoria Carriage Tours** ☎ 877/663-2207 or 250/383-2207 ⊕ www.victoriacarriage.com.

TRAIN TRAVEL

In Vancouver the Pacific Central Station is the hub for rail and bus service. From here, VIA Rail provides transcontinental service through Jasper to Toronto three times a week. Amtrak has daily service between Seattle and Vancouver. The Downtown Historic Railway operates two restored electric trams (built in 1905 and 1913) between Science World and Granville Island. The trams, which also stop at 1st Avenue and Ontario Street and at Leg-in-Boot Square, near 6th Avenue and Moberly Street, operate 12:30 PM–5 PM weekends and holidays from mid-May to mid-October. The adult fare is C$2.

On Vancouver Island, Via Rail operates the Malahat service, a small-gauge train that runs daily between Victoria, Nanaimo, and Courtenay.

🔲 **Amtrak** ☎ 800/872-7245 ⊕ www.amtrak.com. **Downtown Historic Railway** ☎ 604/665-3903 ⊕ www.trams.bc.ca. **Pacific Central Station** ✉ Main St. and Terminal Ave., near Main St. SkyTrain station, Downtown ☎ No phone. **VIA Rail** ☎ 800/561-8630 in Canada, 800/561-3949 in U.S. ⊕ www.viarail.ca.

VISITOR INFORMATION

Easily spotted on Vancouver streets in their red uniforms, Downtown Ambassadors, sponsored by the Downtown Vancouver Business Improvement Association, provide information, directions, safe walks, and emergency assistance to anyone visiting Vancouver's central business district.

🔲 **Downtown Ambassadors** ☎ 604/689-4357 ⊕ www.downtownvancouver.net. **Hello B.C.** ☎ 800/435-5622 ⊕ www.hellobc.com. **Tourism Victoria** ✉ 812 Wharf St., Inner Harbour, V8W 1T3 ☎ 250/953-2033 or 800/663-3883 🖶 250/382-6539 ⊕ www.tourismvictoria.com. **Vancouver Tourist InfoCentre** ✉ 200 Burrard St., Downtown ☎ 604/683-2000 🖶 604/682-6839 ⊕ www.tourismvancouver.com.

SOUTHEAST ALASKA

INCLUDING KETCHIKAN, JUNEAU, HAINES, SITKA & SKAGWAY

5

FODOR'S CHOICE

Alaska Cruises tour to Misty Fiords National Monument

Alaska's Capital Inn, *Juneau*

The Fiddlehead, *Juneau*

Glacier Bay National Park & Preserve

Gustavus Inn, *Gustavus*

U.S. Forest Service Cabins, *Tongass National Forest*

Waterfall Resort, *Prince of Wales Island*

HIGHLY RECOMMENDED

SIGHTS   Alaska Raptor Center, *Sitka*

Alaska State Museum, *Juneau*

Arctic Brotherhood Hall, *Skagway*

Chief Shakes Island, *Wrangell*

Klondike Gold Rush Park, *Skagway*

Mendenhall Glacier, *Juneau*

Mt. Roberts Tramway, *Juneau*

Pack Creek, *Admiralty Island*

Sheldon Jackson Museum, *Sitka*

Sitka National Historical Park, *Sitka*

Skagway Museum, *Skagway*

St. Michael's Cathedral, *Sitka*

Totem Heritage Center, *Ketchikan*

White Pass & Yukon Route, *Skagway*

ARTS   New Archangel Dancers of Sitka

The Days of '98 with Soapy Smith, *Skagway*

Many other great hotels and restaurants enliven this area. For other favorites, look for the black stars as you read this chapter.

By Mike Miller

Updated by
Don Pitcher

SOUTHEAST ALASKA STRETCHES BELOW THE STATE like the tail of a kite. It is a world of massive glaciers, cliff-rimmed fjords, and snowcapped peaks. The largest concentration of coastal glaciers on Earth can be viewed at spectacular Glacier Bay National Park and Preserve, one of the region's most prized attractions. Lush stands of spruce, hemlock, and cedar blanket thousands of islands. Bays, coves, lakes of all sizes, and swift, icy rivers provide some of the continent's best fishing grounds—and scenery as majestic and unspoiled as any in North America. Many of Southeast Alaska's wildest and most pristine landscapes are within Tongass National Forest, which encompasses nearly 17 million acres—or almost three-quarters of the Panhandle's land.

Like anywhere else, the Southeast has its drawbacks. For one thing, it rains a lot. If you plan to spend a week or more here, you can count on showers during at least a few of those days. Die-hard southeasterners simply throw on a slicker and rubber boots and shrug off the rain. Their attitude is philosophical: without the rain, there would be no forests; no lakes; no streams running with world-class salmon and trout; and no healthy populations of brown and black bears, moose, deer, mountain goats, and wolves. Locals also know that the rain keeps people from moving in; without it in such profusion, Southeast Alaska would probably be as densely populated as Seattle.

Another disadvantage—or advantage, depending on your point of view—is an almost total lack of connecting roads between the area's communities. To fill this void, Alaskans created the Marine Highway System of passenger and vehicle ferries, which have staterooms; observation decks; cafeterias; cocktail lounges; and heated, glass-enclosed solariums.

The Southeast's natural beauty and abundance of wildlife have made it one of the world's fastest-growing cruise destinations. About 20 big cruise ships ply the Inside Passage—once the traditional route to the Klondike goldfields and today the centerpiece of many Alaskan cruises—during the height of the summer. Regular air service to the Southeast is available from the Lower 48 states and other parts of Alaska.

The Native peoples you'll meet in the Southeast coastal region are Tlingit, Haida, and Tsimshian. These peoples, like their coastal neighbors in British Columbia, preserve a culture rich in totemic art forms, including deeply carved poles, masks, baskets, and ceremonial objects. Many live among non-Natives in modern towns and continue their own traditions.

A pioneer spirit dominates the towns of Southeast Alaska. Residents—some from other states, some who can trace their ancestors back to the gold-rush days, and some whose ancestors came over the Bering Land Bridge from Asia thousands of years ago—are an adventurous lot. The rough-and-tumble spirit of the Southeast often combines with a worldly sophistication: those who fish are also artists, Forest Service workers may run a bed-and-breakfast on the side, and homemakers may be Native-dance performers.

Exploring Southeast Alaska

The Southeast Panhandle stretches some 500 mi from Yakutat at its northernmost point to Ketchikan and Metlakatla at its southern end. At its widest the region measures only 140 mi, and in the upper Panhandle just south of Yakutat, it's a skinny 30 mi across. Most of the Panhandle consists of a sliver of mainland buffered by islands.

Like all of Alaska's regions, the Southeast covers a vast area (even though it represents a thin slice of the state), and most of its communities, as well as its parks, national forest lands, and other wildlands, are accessible only by boat or plane. You should therefore allow yourself at least a week here. If you have only a few days, it might be best to fly into one of Southeast Alaska's larger communities—such as Juneau, Sitka, or Ketchikan—and then take a state ferry to one or two nearby Panhandle communities. Or fly to a remote destination. Most visitors explore the Inside Passage on cruise ships, which generate their own schedules. But plenty of adventures await ambitious independent travelers who plan ahead and ride state ferries instead of cruise ships.

If you have 5 days

Spend two or three days in ⊞ **Juneau** ④⑤–⑤⑦. Go south via the state ferry to ⊞ **Sitka** ③⑤–④④, ancestral home of the Tlingits and once the capital of Russian America. Spend the next two days exploring this town and nearby sights, possibly taking in a performance by Russian-style dancers at Centennial Hall. Active travelers can go sea kayaking, hiking, fishing, and wildlife cruising. Instead of going south from Juneau, another option is to travel northwest to ⊞ **Gustavus** ⑥⓪ and nearby **Glacier Bay National Park and Preserve** ⑤⑨, one of America's premier parklands, where tidewater glaciers, rugged mountain scenery, and abundant marine wildlife await.

If you have 7 days

Many cruises to Southeast Alaska last seven days, and a week is also sufficient time for independent travelers to see at least a cross section of the region by traveling aboard state ferries and aircraft. Starting at ⊞ **Ketchikan** ①–⑰, known for its totem poles, the Alaska Marine Highway regularly makes stops at all of the region's larger communities: **Wrangell** ②②–②⑨, with its ancient petroglyphs; ⊞ **Petersburg** ③⓪–③④, which has a strong Norwegian influence; ⊞ **Sitka** ③⑤–④④, former capital of Russian America; ⊞ **Juneau** ④⑤–⑤⑦, the state capital; **Haines** ⑥①–⑥⑥, known for its bald eagles and Native dance troupe; and ⊞ **Skagway** ⑥⑦–⑦②, a gold-rush-era throwback. It also serves several smaller communities such as **Kake, Angoon, Tenakee Springs,** and **Hoonah.** Give yourself time to see local sights and visit one or more out-of-town destinations, such as **Admiralty Island** ⑤⑧, **Glacier Bay National Park and Preserve** ⑤⑨, **Misty Fiords National Monument** ⑬, **Hyder** ⑳, or **Prince of Wales Island** ②①.

More than 1,000 islands line the Inside Passage—most of them mountainous with lush covers of timber (though large clear-cuts are also common). Collectively they constitute the Alexander Archipelago. Most communities are on islands rather than on the mainland. The principal exceptions are Juneau, Haines, and Skagway, plus the hamlets of Gustavus and Hyder. Island outposts include Ketchikan, Wrangell, Petersburg, Sitka, and the villages of Craig, Pelican, Metlakatla, Kake, Angoon, and Hoonah. Bordering Alaska just east of the Panhandle lies the Canadian province of British Columbia.

You can get to and around Southeast Alaska by ship or by plane, but forget arriving by car or RV unless your destination is Haines, Skagway, or Hyder, which are connected by road to the Alaska Highway. Elsewhere in the Southeast, the roadways typically run just a few miles out from towns and villages; then they dead-end. (If you wish to drive up the Alaska Highway and then visit road-isolated communities, you can reserve vehicle space on Alaska's state ferries.)

Numbers in the text correspond to numbers in the margin and on the Ketchikan, Wrangell, Petersburg, Sitka, Juneau, Glacier Bay Park and Preserve, Haines, and Skagway maps.

About the Restaurants

The restaurants we list are the cream of the crop in each price category. Restaurants are indicated in the text by a knife-and-fork icon, ✕ , and establishments denoted by ✕▦ stand out equally for their restaurants and rooms.

WHAT IT COSTS				
$$$$	$$$	$$	$	¢
AT DINNER over $25	$20–$25	$15–$20	$10–$15	under $10

Prices are per person for a main course at dinner.

About the Hotels

The lodgings we list are the cream of the crop in each price category. We always list the facilities that are available—but we don't specify whether they cost extra: when pricing accommodations, always ask what's included and what costs extra.

WHAT IT COSTS				
$$$$	$$$	$$	$	¢
FOR 2 PEOPLE over $225	$175–$225	$125–$175	$75–$125	under $75

Prices are for two people in a standard double room in high season.

Timing

The best time to visit is from May through September, when the weather is mildest, rain is less frequent, daylight hours are longest, wildlife is most abundant, the fishing is best, and festivals and tourist-oriented activities are in full swing.

KETCHIKAN

Ketchikan, which has more totem poles than anywhere else in the world, is perched on a large island at the foot of Deer Mountain (3,000 feet). The site at the mouth of Ketchikan Creek was a summer fish camp of the Tlingit until white miners and fishermen came to settle the town in 1885. Gold discoveries just before the turn of the 20th century brought more immigrants, and valuable timber and commercial-fishing resources spurred new industries. By the 1930s the town bragged it was the "salmon-canning capital of the world." You will still find some of the Southeast's best salmon fishing here.

Exploring Ketchikan

You can see a lot on foot in Ketchikan's compact downtown. For many travelers, the town offers their first taste of Alaska. If this is true for you, you will not be disappointed. Ketchikan rises steeply from the busy fishing docks, with staircases climbing to hillside homes. Downtown's fa-

5

Ferry-Hopping

The Alaska Marine Highway is the primary means of transportation along the Inside Passage, with service to most towns on a daily basis. Most northbound travelers hop aboard the ferry in Bellingham, Washington, or Prince Rupert, British Columbia. Ferries can transport vehicles of all sizes, but reservations are necessary, especially out of Bellingham. A fast catamaran car-and-passenger ferry begins service between Sitka and Juneau in 2004. The Inter-Island Ferry Authority operates daily car-and-passenger ferry service between Ketchikan and Hollis on Prince of Wales Island. It expects to add service from Coffman Cove (also on Prince of Wales) to Wrangell and Petersburg in 2005.

Fishing

Southeast Alaska is an angler's paradise. You'll find salmon and halibut charter boats, fishing lodges (some near the larger communities, others remote and accessible only by floatplane), fly-in mountain-lake lodges where the fishing is for trout and char, and—bargain hunters take special note— more than 150 remote but weather-tight cabins operated by the U.S. Forest Service.

Hiking & Backpacking

Trekking woods, mountains, and beaches is Southeast Alaska's unofficial regional sport. Some of the trails are abandoned mining and logging roads. Others are natural routes—in some sections, even game trails—meandering over ridges, through forests, and alongside streams and glaciers. A few—most notably the Chilkoot Trail out of Skagway—offer historical significance along with grand scenery. The Alaska Division of Parks Southeast regional office in Juneau will send you a list of state-maintained trails and parks in the Panhandle; local visitor bureaus and recreation departments can also help.

Shopping

Southeast Alaska has an abundance of fine artists and artisans, and most towns have galleries exhibiting their works. Tlingit and Haida handicrafts include totem poles of all sizes, wooden masks, paddles, bentwood boxes, and button blankets. You'll find these items at gift shops up and down the coast. If you want to be sure of authenticity, buy items tagged with the state-approved AUTHENTIC NATIVE HANDICRAFT FROM ALASKA label. Virtually every community has at least one canning and/or smoking operation that packs and ships local seafood, smoked and canned salmon included.

Tongass National Forest

America's largest national forest, the **Tongass** (⊠ 648 Mission St., Ketchikan 99901 ☎ 907/225–3101 ⊕ www. fs.fed.us/r10/tongass) stretches the length of Alaska's Panhandle and encompasses nearly 17 million acres, or three-fourths of the Southeast region. Old-growth, temperate rain forest covers much of the area, which includes rugged mountains, steep fjords, glaciers, and ice fields within its boundaries. Its lands and waters teem with animals: black and brown bears, bald eagles, Sitka black-tailed deer, mountain goats, wolves, marine mammals, and dozens of sea- and shorebird species. Two national monuments, Admiralty Island near Juneau and Misty Fiords near Ketchikan, are within its borders.

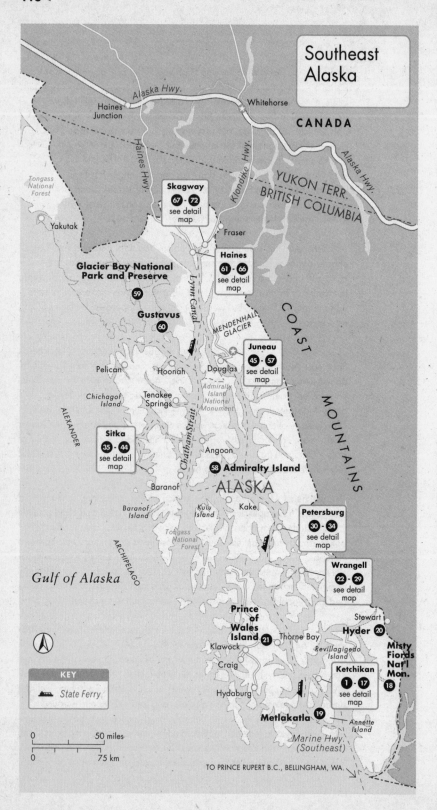

Southeast Alaska

Alaska Hwy.

Haines Junction

Whitehorse

CANADA

Haines Hwy.

Klondike Hwy.

Alaska Hwy.

YUKON TERR.
BRITISH COLUMBIA

Tongass National Forest

Yakutat

Skagway
67 - 72
see detail map

Fraser

Glacier Bay National Park and Preserve

59

Haines
61 - 66
see detail map

Gustavus
60

Lynn Canal

MENDENHALL GLACIER

COAST

Pelican

Hoonah

Douglas

Juneau
45 - 57
see detail map

Chichagof Island

Tenakee Springs

Admiralty Island National Monument

ALEXANDER

Sitka
35 - 44
see detail map

Chatham Strait

Angoon

MOUNTAINS

Baranof

58 **Admiralty Island**

ALASKA

Baranof Island

Kuiu Island

Kake

ARCHIPELAGO

Tongass National Forest

Petersburg
30 - 34
see detail map

Gulf of Alaska

Wrangell
22 - 29
see detail map

Prince of Wales Island
21

Thorne Bay

Stewart

Hyder 20

Klawock

Revillagigedo Island

Misty Fiords Nat'l Mon.

Craig

Ketchikan
1 - 17
see detail map

18

Hydaburg

Metlakatla 19

Annette Island

KEY

State Ferry

Marine Hwy. (Southeast)

0 ___ 50 miles

0 ___ 75 km

TO PRINCE RUPERT B.C., BELLINGHAM, WA.

vorite stops include the Spruce Mill Development shops and Creek Street. A bit farther away you'll find the Totem Heritage Center and Deer Mountain Hatchery. Out of town (but included on most bus tours) are two longtime favorites: Totem Bight State Historical Park and Saxman Native Village.

If you're traveling on the highway in either direction, you won't go far before you run out of road. The North Tongass Highway ends about 18 mi from downtown, at Settler's Cove Campground. The South Tongass Highway terminates at a power plant about 8 mi from town. Side roads soon end at campgrounds and at trailheads, viewing points, lakes, boat-launching ramps, and private property.

a good walk

The best place to begin a walking tour of Ketchikan is from the helpful **Ketchikan Visitors Bureau** ❶ ⏵. Just a few steps up Mill Street is the **Spruce Mill Development** ❷, filled with shops and restaurants. Next door learn about Southeast Alaska's wild places at the **Southeast Alaska Discovery Center** ❸. Continue up Mill Street past minuscule **Whale Park** ❹, with its Chief Kyan totem pole, and turn right on Stedman Street. Cross the bridge to **Thomas Street** ❺, overlooking a busy boat harbor. Continue walking along Stedman to the *Return of the Eagle* ❻ mural before turning left on Deermont Street. Follow it uphill several blocks to the **Totem Heritage Center** ❼ and its collection of ancient totem poles. Just across the footbridge are **Deer Mountain Hatchery and Eagle Center** ❽, where you can see salmon hatchlings and rehabilitated bald eagles and **City Park** ❾. From here, Park Avenue runs parallel to Ketchikan Creek, heading downhill to the fish ladder and Salmon Carving next to **Salmon Falls** ❿. Look uphill to see the historic **Grant Street Trestle** ⓫; it's about a 20-minute walk down Park Avenue, or you can call a cab from the hatchery.

From the fish ladder, a boardwalk path parallels Ketchikan Creek and leads to trendy **Creek Street** ⓬. For a side trip, take the short funicular ($2) to **WestCoast Cape Fox Lodge** ⓭ to get a great view of the harbor, and then take it back before continuing down Creek Street boardwalk to **Dolly's House** ⓮, once a brothel and now a house museum. Retrace your steps up the boardwalk and cross the **Creek Street Footbridge** ⓯, where you can watch salmon heading upstream in the summer. In front of you is the Chief Johnson Totem Pole, and just to your right is the **Tongass Historical Museum** ⓰, with interesting relics from the early days of mining and fishing. Turn left on Bawden Street to pass historic **St. John's Church** ⓱.

TIMING   This walking tour should take around two or three hours, stops included. If you are looking for an easier and shorter version (approximately one hour), omit the leg of the walk that leads to Totem Heritage Center, Deer Mountain Hatchery, and City Park. (Local bus tours typically include these sights as well as Totem Bight State Historical Park and Saxman Native Village.)

What to See

❾ **City Park.** The Deer Mountain Hatchery and Eagle Center lead into this small park, which has picnic tables and paved paths and is bisected by Ketchikan Creek. ✉ *Park and Fair Sts.*

⓬ **Creek Street.** Ketchikan's infamous red-light district once existed here. Today the small, colorful houses, built on stilts over the creek waters, have been restored as trendy shops.

⓯ **Creek Street Footbridge.** Stand over Ketchikan Creek for good salmon viewing when the fish are running in midsummer.

Deer Mountain Hatchery and Eagle Center. Tens of thousands of salmon are raised at this hatchery on Ketchikan Creek. Midsummer visitors can observe both natural spawning in the creek and workers collecting and fertilizing the salmon eggs for the hatchery. Tanks hold young salmon and those old enough to head out to the ocean, and a video details the fascinating life cycle of salmon. Owned by the Ketchikan Indian Corporation, the hatchery has exhibits on traditional Native fishing. Also here is a nesting pair of injured bald eagles. Although both are unable to fly, you may see them catching salmon that swim into their enclosure. ⊠ *429 Deermount St.* ☎ *907/225–6026 or 800/252–5158* ⊕ *www. kictribe.com/hatchery/index.htm* ⊠ *$8* ☉ *Early May–Sept., daily 8–4:30.*

Dolly's House. Once Creek Street's most famous brothel, the house has been preserved as a museum, complete with furnishings, beds, and a short history of the life and times of Ketchikan's best-known madam. ⊠ *Creek St.* ☎ *907/225–6329* ⊠ *$4* ☉ *Daily whenever cruise ships are in port.*

Grant Street Trestle. At one time virtually all of Ketchikan's walkways and streets were made from wooden trestles, but now only one remains, constructed in 1908.

Ketchikan Visitors Bureau. The helpful visitor's bureau is right next to the cruise-ship docks. Half the space is occupied by day-tour, flightseeing, and boat-tour operators. ⊠ *131 Front St., 99901* ☎ *907/225–6166 or 800/770–3300* ⊕ *www.visit-ketchikan.com* ☉ *May–Sept., daily 7–5 (until 6 PM when cruise ships are docked); Oct.–Apr., weekdays 8–5.*

Return of the Eagle. Twenty-one Native students created this colorful mural on a wall of the Robertson Building on the Ketchikan campus of the University of Alaska–Southeast. ⊠ *Stedman St.*

⑰ St. John's Church. Built in 1903, this church is the oldest remaining house of worship in Ketchikan. Its interior is formed from red cedar cut in the Native-operated sawmill in nearby Saxman. ⊠ *Bawden St.*

⑩ Salmon Falls. Get out your camera and set it for fast speed at the fish ladder, a series of pools arranged like steps that allow fish to travel upstream over a dam or falls. When the salmon start running in midsummer, from June onward, thousands leap the falls (or take the easier fish-ladder route) to spawn in Ketchikan Creek's waters farther upstream. Many can also be seen in the creek below the falls. The falls, fish ladder, and wooden Salmon Carving are just off Park Avenue on Married Man's Trail. (The trail was once used by married men for discrete access to the red-light district on Creek Street.) ⊠ *Married Man's Trail, off Park Ave.*

🖑 ③ Southeast Alaska Discovery Center. Museum-quality exhibits, including one on the rain forest, focus on the resources, Native cultures, and ecosystems of Southeast Alaska at this impressive visitor center. The U.S. Forest Service and other federal agencies provide information on Alaska's public lands. Especially helpful for independent travelers is the inviting "trip-planning room," where you can relax on Mission-style furniture while consulting books, maps, and videos about the sights in Ketchikan and the Southeast. The multimedia show "Mystical Southeast Alaska" is shown every half hour during the summer in the center's theater. ⊠ *50 Main St.* ☎ *907/228–6220* ⊕ *www.nps.gov/aplic* ⊠ *$5 May–Sept., free Oct.–Apr.* ☉ *May–Sept., daily 8:30–5; Oct.–Apr., Tues.–Sat. 10–4:30.*

② Spruce Mill Development. The attractive Mill Street complex is modeled after 1920s-style cannery architecture. Spread over 6½ acres along the waterfront, five buildings contain a mix of retail stores, souvenir shops, galleries, and restaurants. Cruise ships moor just a few steps away, filling the shops with tourists all summer long. ⊠ *Spruce Mill and Front Sts.*

⑤ Thomas Street. From this street you can see Thomas Basin, one of four harbors in Ketchikan and home port to pleasure and commercial-fishing boats.

⑯ Tongass Historical Museum. Native artifacts and pioneer relics revisit the mining and fishing eras at this small museum in the same building as the library. Exhibits include a big, brilliantly polished lens from Tree Point Lighthouse and the bullet-riddled skull of a notorious brown bear called Old Groaner. Other exhibits change periodically but always include Tlingit Native items. ⊠ *629 Dock St.* ☎ *907/225–5600* ⊠ *$2* ☉ *May–Sept., daily 8–5; Oct.–Apr., Wed.–Fri. 1–5, Sat. 10–4, Sun. 1–4.*

★ ⑦ Totem Heritage Center. You can get a close-up view at this rare collection of authentic Native totems dating from almost two centuries ago. You can also watch a video about the preservation efforts and take a guided tour. Outside are several more poles carved in the last two decades. ⊠ *Deermount St.* ☎ *907/225–5900* ⊠ *$5* ☉ *May–Sept., daily 8–5; Oct.–Apr., weekdays 1–5.*

⑬ WestCoast Cape Fox Lodge. For a stunning view of the harbor and fine dining, walk to the top of steep Venetia Avenue or take the funicular ($2) up from Creek Street. ⊠ *800 Venetia Way* ☎ *907/225–8001 or 800/426–0670* ⊕ *www.westcoasthotels.com.*

④ Whale Park. This park, catercorner from St. John's Church, is the site of the **Chief Kyan Totem Pole,** now in its third incarnation. The original was carved in the 1890s, but over the decades it deteriorated and was replaced in the 1960s. The current replica was erected in 1993 with the 1960s version now housed in the Totem Heritage Center.

<table>
<tr><td>

off the
beaten
path

</td></tr>
</table>

TOTEM BIGHT STATE HISTORICAL PARK – The 14 poles at Ketchikan's two most famous totem-pole parks (the other is at Saxman Native Village) are, for the most part, 60-year-old replicas of older totem poles brought in from outlying villages as part of a federal works–cultural project during the late 1930s. Totem Bight has many totem poles and a hand-hewn Native tribal house and sits on a scenic spit of land facing the waters of Tongass Narrows. The clan house here is open daily in the summer. Most bus tours of Ketchikan include Totem Bight in their itinerary, but there is no public transportation to the site. ✉ *N. Tongass Hwy., 10 mi north of town* ☎ *907/247–8574* ⊕ *www.dnr.state.ak.us/parks.*

SAXMAN NATIVE VILLAGE – A 2½-mi paved walking path–bike trail parallels the road from Ketchikan to the village of Saxman, named for a missionary who helped Native Alaskans settle here before 1900. A totem park dominates the center of Saxman, with poles moved here in the 1930s from abandoned village sites. Saxman's Beaver Clan tribal house is said to be the largest in the world. Carvers create totem poles and totemic art objects in the adjacent carver's shed (free and open whenever the carvers are working), and signs along a nature trail identify local plants. You can get to the park on foot, by taxi, or by city bus, and you can visit the totem park on your own, but to visit the tribal house and theater you must take a tour. Tickets are sold at the gift shop across from the totems; these two-hour tours include a video about Southeast Alaska's Native peoples, along with dancing, totem stories, local legends, and a visit to the carving shed. Call ahead for tour schedules. ✉ *S. Tongass Hwy., 2 mi south of town* ☎ *907/225–4846* ⊕ *www.capefoxtours.com.*

Where to Stay & Eat

$$$–$$$$ ✕ **Salmon Falls Resort.** This huge, octagonal restaurant is a half-hour drive from town, but the local seafood and steaks make the trip more than worthwhile. The restaurant is built of pine logs, and at the center of the dining room a 40-foot section of 48-inch pipe manufactured to be part of the Alaska pipeline rises to support the roof. The dining area overlooks the waters of Clover Passage, where sunsets can be vivid red. Specialties include blackened salmon or halibut. ✉ *Mile 17, N. Tongass Hwy.* ☎ *907/225–2752, 800/247–9059 outside Alaska* ⊟ *AE, MC, V* ⊘ *Closed mid-Sept.–Apr.*

$$–$$$$ ✕ **Annabelle's Keg and Chowder House.** Housed within the historic Gilmore Hotel, this Victorian-style restaurant serves a tempting choice of seafood and pastas, including five kinds of chowder and steamer clams. Prime rib on Friday and Saturday evenings is a favorite, and an espresso bar and semiformal lounge with a jukebox add a friendly vibe. ✉ *326 Front St.* ☎ *907/225–6009* 🖨 *907/225–7442* ⊟ *AE, D, DC, MC, V.*

★ $$–$$$$ ✕ **Steamers.** Anchoring Ketchikan's Spruce Mill Mall, this lively and spacious restaurant has an extensive menu of fresh seafood (including king crab), pasta, and steaks. Vegetarian choices are also available, and the servings are certain to fill you up. The bar pours 19 draft beers, including a number of Alaskan brews, along with a substantial wine list and 300 different liquors. Tall windows face Ketchikan's busy waterfront, where cruise ships and floatplanes vie for your attention. ✉ *76 Front St.* ☎ *907/225–1600* 🖨 *907/225–0100* ⊟ *AE, D, DC, MC, V* ⊘ *Closed mid-Oct.–Mar.*

$$–$$$$ ✕▣ **WestCoast Cape Fox Lodge.** One of Ketchikan's poshest properties offers scenic views of the town and harbor from 135 feet above the village. The setting is cozy and luxurious, with an open lobby ac-

cented by Tlingit and Haida artwork and a roaring fire. The spacious rooms are attractively decorated with traditional tribal colors and watercolors of Alaskan birds. All rooms have views of either Tongass Narrows or Deer Mountain. Heen Kahidi Restaurant serves seafood, pasta, chicken, and steaks. Be sure to reserve one of the window tables that overlook Ketchikan. ⊠ *800 Venetia Way, 99901* ☎ *907/225–8001, 866/225–8001 reservations* 🖷 *907/225–8286* ⊕ *www. westcoasthotels.com* 🖘 *70 rooms, 2 suites* ⚲ *Restaurant, room service, cable TV with movies and video games, lounge, meeting room; no a/c* ⊟ *AE, D, DC, MC, V.*

★ **$-$$** ✕🖾 **New York Hotel and Cafe.** Now more than a century old, this quaint little hotel has a one of the nicest eateries in Ketchikan. The menu includes breakfasts and lunches, plus dinners on Friday and Saturday nights that always include steak and fresh seafood. Three of the rooms are a short distance away along picturesque Creek Street. Each of these includes a full kitchen, Jacuzzi bath, loft bedroom (with spiral staircase), and deck overlooking the water. ⊠ *207 Stedman St., 99901* ☎ *907/225–0246 or 866/225-0246* ⊕ *www.thenewyorkhotel.com* 🖘 *11 rooms* ⚲ *Restaurant, cable TV, some kitchens, some in-room hot tubs; no a/c* ⊟ *AE, D, MC, V.*

$$-$$$ 🖾 **The Landing.** This Best Western property is named for the state ferry landing directly across the road. Rooms are modern with Mission-style furniture; a two-bedroom apartment is available for families. The Landing Restaurant is always packed with a hungry breakfast clientele and with families. Upstairs, Jeremiah's Fine Food and Spirits offers upscale dining in cozy digs and a relaxing no-smoking lounge built around a stone fireplace. No need for a car; the free shuttle provides transport around town. ⊠ *3434 Tongass Ave., 99901* ☎ *907/225–5166 or 800/428–8304* 🖷 *907/225–6900* ⊕ *www.bestwestern.com* 🖘 *75 rooms, 1 apartment* ⚲ *2 restaurants, microwaves, refrigerators, cable TV, exercise equipment, meeting rooms, airport shuttle, some pets allowed (fee); no a/c* ⊟ *AE, D, DC, MC, V.*

$$-$$$ 🖾 **The Narrows Inn.** Four miles from town, the Narrows is a modern lodge where rustic wood trim and themed prints on the walls brighten the small hotel rooms. Waterside rooms, including three spacious suites, have balconies overlooking Tongass Narrows—a good place to watch seals, otters, and eagles. There is a van with scheduled runs into Ketchikan for dining and shopping and a delicious on-the-premises steak-and-seafood restaurant with a waterfront bar. ⬧ *Box 8296, 99901* ☎ *907/247–2600 or 888/686–2600* 🖷 *907/247–2602* ⊕ *www.narrowsinn.com* 🖘 *44 rooms, 3 suites* ⚲ *Restaurant, microwaves, refrigerators, cable TV, bar, Internet, airport shuttle; no a/c* ⊟ *AE, D, MC, V.*

$-$$$ 🖾 **Cedars Lodge.** This small lodge has a mix of motel-style accommodations on the street side along with deluxe suites whose large windows face Tongass Narrows. The latter are great for a front-row view of the floatplanes, boats, and cruise ships that parade past all summer. All rooms have Jacuzzi baths, and suites also include full kitchens. Various fishing and lodging packages are available, including four nights' lodging and three days of fishing for $1,615–$1,840 per person. These rates include lodging, guided fishing, and meals. Lodging-only rates apply if space is available. ⊠ *1471 Tongass Ave.* ⬧ *Box 8331, 99901* ☎ *907/225–1900 or 800/813–4363* 🖷 *907/225–8604* ⊕ *www.cedarslodge.com* 🖘 *8 rooms, 5 suites* ⚲ *Restaurant, in-room hot tubs, some kitchens, cable TV; no a/c* ⊟ *AE, D, DC, MC, V* ☾ *Closed Oct.–Mid-May.*

$ 🖾 **Gilmore Hotel.** Think of the Gilmore as a boutique hotel without boutique prices. The 1930s-era lobby has a European feel, and rooms, though not large, blend old-fashioned comfort with modern furnishings. The lack of elevator may be a problem for some travelers, but all the other amenities are here, including a courtesy van to shuttle you around town. Downstairs, Annabelle's Keg and Chowder House serves seafood, pasta, and prime rib. ⊠ *326 Front St., 99901* ☎ *907/225–9423 or 800/275–9423* 🖷 *907/225–7442* ⊕ *www.gilmorehotel.com* ⤴ *38 rooms, 2 suites* ⚭ *Restaurant, café, cable TV, bar, some pets allowed; no a/c* ⊟ *AE, D, DC, MC, V.*

Guided Tours

Owned by Goldbelt Native corporation, **Alaska Cruises** (☎ 907/225–6044 or 800/228–1905 🖷 907/225–8636 ⊕ www.mistyfjord.net) runs harbor tours of the Ketchikan waterfront and also provides speedy catamaran excursions from downtown Ketchikan to Misty Fiords National Monument. A Native-owned company, **Cape Fox Tours** (☎ 907/225–4846 🖷 907/225–3137 ⊕ www.capefoxtours.com) leads tours of Saxman Native Village and the historic George Inlet Cannery. You can book most of these tours aboard the cruise ships or at Ketchikan Visitors Bureau.

Nightlife & the Arts

Bars
Ketchikan is a party town, so you won't have any trouble finding something going on at several downtown bars. **First City Saloon** (⊠ 830 Water St. ☎ 907/225–1494) is the main dance spot, with live rock, blues, or jazz Wednesday–Saturday. The **Potlatch Bar** (⊠ Thomas Basin ☎ 907/225–4855) delivers up music most weekends.

Sports & the Outdoors

Fishing
Sportfishing for salmon and trout is excellent in the Ketchikan area, in either saltwater or freshwater lakes and streams. Contact the **Ketchikan Visitors Bureau** for information on guide services and locations.

Spectator Sports
The **Great Alaskan Lumberjack Show** is a 90-minute lumberjack contest providing a taste of old-time woodsman skills, including ax throwing, bucksawing, springboard chopping, log-rolling duels, and a 50-foot tree climb that ends in a free fall. Shows take place in a covered grandstand directly behind the Spruce Mill Development and go on rain or shine all summer. ⊠ *50 Main St.* ☎ *907/225–9050 or 888/320–9049* ⊕ *www.lumberjackshows.com* ▨ *$31* ⊙ *May–Sept., 3 times daily; hrs vary.*

Hiking
If you're an avid hiker, the 3-mi trail from downtown to the top of **Deer Mountain** will repay your efforts with a spectacular panorama of the city below and the wilderness behind. The trail begins at the corner of Fair and Deermount streets. **Ward Cove Recreation Area,** about 6 mi north of town, provides easier hiking next to lakes and streams and beneath towering spruce and hemlock trees; it also has several designated picnic spots.

Scuba Diving
Alaska Diving Service (⊠ 4845 N. Tongass Ave. ☎ 907/225–4667) rents tanks and equipment and guides you to the best places to dive.

Sea Kayaking
Southeast Exposure (☎ 907/225–8829 ⊕ www.southeastexposure.com) gives kayaking classes, guides trips, and rents canoes, kayaks, and mountain bikes. **Southeast Sea Kayaks** (☎ 907/225–1258 or 800/287–1607 ⊕ www.kayakketchikan.com) leads kayak tours of Ketchikan's

historic waterfront and provides kayak lessons and rentals, along with guided trips to Misty Fiords.

Shopping

Art Galleries

AlaskaMade Gallery (✉ 123 Stedman St. ☎ 907/225–5404 or 888/877–9706 ⊕ www.alaskamade.com) is a small creekside gallery with art, ulus (a curved Eskimo knife), cards, gifts, and even Alaskan-roasted coffees.

Scanlon Gallery (✉ 318 Mission St. ☎ 907/247–4730 or 800/690–4730 ⊕ www.scanlongallery.com) displays prints from a number of well-known Alaska artists, including Byron Birdsall, Rie Muñoz, John Fehringer, Barbara Lavalle, and Jon Van Zyle.

Design, art, and clothing converge in the stylish **Soho Coho Contemporary Art and Craft Gallery** (✉ 5 Creek St. ☎ 907/225–5954 or 800/888–4070 ⊕ www.trollart.com), where you'll find an eclectic collection of art and T-shirts featuring the work of owner Ray Troll—best known for his wacky fish art—as well as that of other Southeast Alaskan artists.

Books

Upstairs from the Soho Coho Gallery, **Parnassus** (✉ 5 Creek St. ☎ 907/225–7690) is a book lover's bookstore, with many Alaskan titles and a knowledgeable staff.

Seafood

For some of the Southeast's best canned, smoked, or frozen salmon and halibut, along with crab, clams, and all kinds of other seafood, try either of the two locations of **Salmon Etc.** (✉ 10 Creek St. ☎ 907/225–6008, 800/354–7256 outside Alaska ✉ 322 Mission St. ☎ 907/225–6008 ⊕ www.salmonetc.com).

AROUND KETCHIKAN

Misty Fiords National Monument

18 *40 mi east of Ketchikan by air.*

Misty Fiords National Monument is a wilderness of cliff-faced fjords (or fiords, if you follow the monument's spelling), mountains, and islands with an abundance of spectacular coastal scenery, wildlife, and recreation. Small boats enable close-up views of breathtaking vistas. Travel on these waters can be an almost mystical experience, with the greens of the forest reflected in waters as still as black mirrors. You may find yourself in the company of a whale, see a bear fishing for salmon along the shore, or even pull in your own salmon for an evening meal. Note, however, that the name Misty refers to the weather you're likely to encounter in this rainy part of Alaska.

Most visitors to Misty Fiords arrive on day trips via floatplane from Fodor'sChoice Ketchikan or on board a catamaran run by **Alaska Cruises** (☎ 907/225–6044 or 800/228–1905 ⊕ www.mistyfjord.net).

✉ *3031 Tongass Ave., Ketchikan 99901* ☎ *907/225–2148* ⊕ *www.fs.fed.us/r10/tongass.*

Metlakatla

19 *12 mi south of Ketchikan.*

The village of Metlakatla is on Annette Island, just a dozen miles from busy Ketchikan but a world away culturally. A visit to this quiet and conservative place offers the chance to learn about life in a small Inside Passage Native community. Local taxis can take you to other sights around the island, including Yellow Hill and the old air force base.

In most Southeast Native villages, the people are Tlingit or Haida in heritage. Metlakatla is the exception; here most folks are Tsimshian (*shim-she-an*). They moved to the island from British Columbia in 1887, led by William Duncan, an Anglican missionary from England. The town grew rapidly and soon included dozens of buildings laid out on a grid of streets—a cannery, a sawmill, and a church that could seat a thousand people. Congress declared Annette Island a federal Indian reservation in 1891, and it remains the only reservation in Alaska today. Father Duncan continued to control life in Metlakatla for decades, until the government finally stepped in shortly before his death in 1918.

During World War II the U.S. Army built a major air base 7 mi from Metlakatla that included observation towers for Japanese subs, airplane hangars, gun emplacements, and housing for 10,000 soldiers. After the war, it served as Ketchikan's airport for many years, but today the long runways are virtually abandoned save for a few private flights.

Metlakatla's religious heritage still shows through today. The clapboard **William Duncan Memorial Church,** topped with two steeples, burned in 1948 but was rebuilt several years later. It is one of nine churches in tiny Metlakatla. **Father Duncan's Cottage** is maintained as it was when he was alive and includes numerous artifacts, personal items, and historic photographs. ⊠ *Corner of 4th Ave. and Church St.* ☎ *907/886–4441 or 888/886–8687* ⊠ *$2* ☉ *Weekdays when cruise ships are in port, or by appointment.*

Father Duncan worked hard to eliminate traditional Tsimshian beliefs and dances, so he would probably not approve of recent efforts to relearn the old ways. Today the people of Metlakatla proudly perform these old dances and stories. The best place to see this is at the traditional **long-house,** which faces Metlakatla's boat harbor. Three totem poles stand on the back side of the building, and the front is covered with a Tsimshian design. Inside are displays of Native crafts and a model of the fish traps that were once common throughout the Inside Passage. Native dance groups perform here on Wednesday and Friday in summer. Just down from the longhouse is an **Artists' Village** where booths display locally made arts and crafts. The village and longhouse open when groups and tours are present.

Two miles from town is a boardwalk path that leads up the 540-foot **Yellow Hill.** Distinctive yellow sandstone rocks and panoramic vistas make this a worthwhile detour on clear days.

Where to Stay & Eat

$ ▣ **Metlakatla Hotel and Restaurant.** This two-story building offers standard motel accommodations with private decks off the upstairs rooms. The restaurant has the usual American favorites such as burgers and steak, but the fresh halibut and shrimp are the real attractions. Breakfast is available only for hotel guests. ⊠ *3rd Ave. and Lower Milton St., 99926* ☎ *907/886–3456* ⊠ *907/886–3455* ⊴ *6 rooms* ⚹ *Restaurant, microwaves, refrigerators, cable TV, in-room VCRs; no a/c, no smoking* ⊟ *AE, D, MC, V.*

Guided Tours

You can catch a ferry operated by the **Alaska Marine Highway System** to Metlakatla from Ketchikan. Run by the Metlakatla community, **Metlakatla Tours** (☎ 907/886–4441 or 877/886–8687 ⊕ tours.metlakatla.net) leads local tours that include visits to Duncan Cottage, the cannery, and the longhouse, along with a Tsimshian dance performance. **ProMech Air** (☎ 907/886–3845 or 800/860–3845 ⊕ www.promechair.com) has scheduled floatplane flights between Ketchikan and Metlakatla.

Hyder

⑳ *90 mi northeast of Ketchikan.*

The tiny town of Hyder sits at the head of narrow Portland Canal, a 70-mi-long fjord northeast of Ketchikan. The fjord marks the border between Canada and the United States, and Hyder sits just 2 mi from the larger town of Stewart, British Columbia. Highway 37A continues over spectacular Bear Pass from Stewart, connecting these towns with the rest of Canada.

The 1898 discovery of gold and silver in the surrounding mountains brought a flood of miners to the Hyder area, and the town eventually became a major shipping port. Mining remained important for decades, but a devastating 1948 fire destroyed much of the town, which had been built on pilings over the water. Mining still takes place here, but the beauty of the area now attracts increasing numbers of tourists. Today, quiet Hyder calls itself "the friendliest ghost town in Alaska."

The town of Hyder is small and has only a handful of tourist-oriented businesses, a post office, and library. Nearby Stewart has more to offer, including a bank, museum, hotels, restaurants, and camping. You will need to check in at Canadian customs (open 24 hours) before crossing the border from Hyder into Stewart. Canadian money is primarily used in Hyder, but greenbacks are certainly accepted.

The **Stewart Historical Society Museum** contains wildlife displays and exhibits on the region's mining history. ⊠ *6th and Columbia Sts.* ☎ *250/ 636–2568* ⊕ *www.stewartmuseum.homestead.com* ☞ *$2* ☉ *May–Sept., weekdays 1–4.*

An **old stone storehouse** stands along the road as you enter Hyder. Built in 1896, this is the oldest masonry building in Alaska.

Six miles north of Hyder on Salmon River Road is the **Fish Creek Wildlife Observation Site.** From late July to early September, a large run of salmon attract black and brown bears here, which, in turn, attract more than a few photographers. The creek produces some of the largest chum salmon anywhere. Twenty-five miles east of Stewart on Highway 37A is the imposing **Bear Glacier.** The glacier sits across a small lake that is often crowded with icebergs. A dirt road from Hyder leads 17 mi to remote **Salmon Glacier,** one of few glaciers accessible by road in Southeast Alaska.

Getting "Hyderized" (which involves drinking and drinking-related silliness) is a term that you will hear upon arrival in the area. You can get Hyderized at **Glacier Inn** (⊠ Main St. ☎ 250/636–9243) where the walls are papered with thousands of signed bills, including those of countless tourists. The tradition supposedly began when prospectors would tack a dollar bill on the wall in case they were broke when they returned.

Where to Stay & Eat

¢–$ ✕ **Bitter Creek Cafe.** This bustling Stewart café serves a variety of cuisine, including gourmet pizza, lasagna, burgers, seafood, and even Mexican dishes. The quirky interior is adorned with a fun collection of antiques as well as a 1930 Pontiac. The outside deck is a fine place to relax on a summer afternoon. ⊠ *5th Ave., Stewart* ☎ *250/636–2166* ▤ *AE, MC, V* ☉ *Closed Oct.–Apr.*

$ ⊡ **Ripley Creek Inn.** Stewart's best lodging option has large rooms, classy Mission-style furnishings, sofa beds, and windows fronting the inlet. Some rooms also have decks. The entry houses the little Toastworks Museum, a repository of antique toasters and other kitchen items, where a toast-based Continental breakfast for inn guests is served. ☎ *250/636–2344* ☎ *250/636–2623* ⊕ *www.ripleycreekinn.homestead.com* ⊸ *12 rooms* ○ *Refrigerators, gym, sauna; no a/c* ⊟ *AE, DC, MC, V.*

Guided Tours

Seaport Limousine (☎ 250/636–2622 ⊕ www.tkp-biz.com/ seaportlimousine) leads guided tours of the Hyder area, including Fish Creek and Salmon Glacier. **Taquan Air** (☎ 907/225–8800, 800/770– 8800, or 250/636–9150 ⊕ www.taquanair.com) has year-round service between Ketchikan and Hyder every Monday and Thursday.

Prince of Wales Island

㉑ *15 mi east of Ketchikan.*

Prince of Wales Island stretches more than 130 mi from north to south, making it the largest island in Southeast Alaska. Only two American islands—Kodiak in Alaska and Hawaii in the Hawaiian chain—are larger. Prince of Wales (or "P.O.W." as locals call it) has a diversity of landforms, a plethora of wildlife, and world-class sportfishing. The island has long been a major source of timber, both on Tongass National Forest lands and those owned by Native corporations. Much of the Native land has been cut over, and environmental restrictions on public lands have greatly reduced logging activity. The island's economy is now supported by small-scale logging operations, tourism, sportfishing, and commercial fishing.

Approximately 7,000 people live on Prince of Wales Island, scattered in small villages and towns around the island. A network of 1,500 mi of roads—nearly all built to access clear-cuts—crisscrosses the island, providing connections to even the smallest settlement. Paved roads now link Craig, Hollis, Thorne Bay, and Hydaburg, and the road will be completed to Coffman Cove by 2005. The prevalence of roads, combined with ferry and air access from Ketchikan, makes it easy to explore this island.

The primary commercial center for Prince of Wales is **Craig,** on the island's western shore. This town of 2,000 retains a hard-edged aura fast disappearing in Inside Passage towns, where tourism now holds sway. Commercial fishing, sportfishing, and logging and government jobs support this community. Although sightseeing attractions are slim, the town exudes a frontier spirit, and its small-boat harbors buzz with activity. ⌕ *Prince of Wales Chamber of Commerce, Box 497, Craig 99921* ☎ *907/826–3870* ⊕ *www.princeofwalescoc.org.*

The **Inter-Island Ferry Authority** (☎ 907/826–4848 or 866/308–4848 ☎ 907/826–2829 ⊕ www.interislandferry.com) operates a daily vehicle and passenger ferry between Ketchikan and Prince of Wales Island. The ferry terminal is in the tiny settlement of Hollis, 31 mi from Craig on a paved road. In 2005, a separate ferry service connecting Coffman Cove on the north end of Prince of Wales with the towns of Wrangell and Petersburg is scheduled to begin.

A half-dozen miles from Craig is the Tlingit village of **Klawock,** with a sawmill, cannery, hatchery, and the island's only airport. The town is best known for its striking display of 21 totem poles in **Totem Park.** Several of these colorful poles were moved here in the 1930s when an old village site was abandoned; others are more recent carvings. You can watch carvers restoring old totems at the carving shed, across the road from the grocery store. Klawock is also home to **Prince of Wales Hatchery** (☎ 907/755–2231 ⊕ www.powhasalmon.org ☉ Tours June–Aug., Mon.–Sat. 1–5), where salmon are raised in a canal adjacent to Klawock Lake. It's open for free summertime tours, and it also has a small visitor center with an aquarium full of young coho salmon. Along the bay, you'll find **St. John's by the Sea Catholic Church,** with stained-glass windows picturing Native Alaskans.

The Haida village of **Hydaburg,** approximately 40 mi south of Klawock (via chip-sealed road), lies along scenic Sukkwan Strait. A small collection of **totem poles** occupies the center of this Haida settlement, the only one in Alaska. Originally from British Columbia's Queen Charlotte Islands, the Haida settled here around 1700.

A number of large natural caverns pockmark northern Prince of Wales Island. The best-known of these, **El Capitan Cave,** has one of the deepest pits in the United States and is open to the public. Paleontologists have found a wealth of black bear, brown bear, and other mammal fossils in the cave, including some that date back more than 12,000 years. The Forest Service leads free two-hour El Capitan tours several times a week in the summer. Reservations are required, and no children under age seven are permitted. ⊠ *Mile 51 along North Prince of Wales Rd.* ☎ *907/828–3304 (Forest Service).*

Where to Stay & Eat

$$–$$$ ✕ **Shelter Cove Lodge.** Tall windows front the water at this modern restaurant and lodge along the South Boat Harbor in Craig. Fresh seafood tops the menu, along with steaks, delectable desserts, and nightly specials. Prime rib attracts the locals on Friday and Saturday nights. The lodge here runs all-inclusive three-day fishing packages. ⊠ *703 Hamilton Dr., Craig 99921* ☎ *907/826–2939 or 888/826–3474* 🖷 *907/826–2941* ⊕ *www.sheltercovelodge.com* 🖃 *AE, MC, V* ☉ *Restaurant closed Oct.–May.*

$$$$ 🛏 **McFarland's Floatel.** Across the bay from the logging town of Thorne Bay on the eastern side of Prince of Wales sits this quiet resort, accessible only by boat or floatplane. Each of the four beachfront log cabins sleeps up to six people and includes a loft, woodstove, full kitchen, and private bath. A 200-foot walkway leads to the floating main lodge, which serves hearty home-cooked seafood dinners for $25 (reservations required). Co-owner Jeannie McFarland teaches basketry workshops and sells her pine-needle raffia baskets here. Charter-fishing trips are available, or you can rent a skiff and fishing gear and head out on your own. 🖂 *Box 19149, Thorne Bay 99919* ☎ *907/828–3335 or 888/828–3335* ⊕ *www.mcfarlandsfloatel.com* ⇨ *4 cabins* ⚓ *Boating, fishing, car rental; no a/c, no room phones, no room TVs, no smoking* 🖃 *MC, V.*

$$$$ 🛏 **Waterfall Resort.** At this upscale fishing lodge, you sleep in Cape
Fodor's Choice Cod–style cottages from the 1930s, eat bountiful meals with all the trim-
★ mings, and fish from custom-built cabin cruisers under the care of a fishing guide. You can also have the fish you catch processed, packaged, and shipped. A three-night minimum stay with all meals, including floatplane fare from Ketchikan, comes to around $3,200 per person. This former commercial salmon cannery is a popular retreat for business groups. 🖂 *Box 6440, Ketchikan 99901* ☎ *907/225–9461, 800/544–5125 outside Alaska* 🖷 *907/225–8530* ⊕ *www.waterfallresort.com* ⇨ *10 lodge rooms, 4 suites, 26 cabins* ⚓ *Restaurant, boating, fishing, meeting rooms; no a/c, no room phones, no room TVs, no kids under 10* 🖃 *AE, D, MC, V* ⎡◯⎤ *FAP* ☉ *Closed early Sept.–late May.*

$ 🖫 **Ruth Ann's Motel.** Victorian-style furnishings and details flavor this classy motel. The honeymoon suite includes a large hot tub and kitchenette. Across the street, the popular Ruth Ann's Restaurant serves home-style food with seafood and steaks at dinner and burgers, sandwiches, and fish-and-chips at lunch. Ask for a table in the back room, where picture windows face the harbor; a tiny bar at the front of the restaurant fills up most nights. ⊠ *300 Water St., Craig 99921* ☎ *907/ 826–3378* 🖷 *907/826–3293* 🛏 *14 rooms, 1 suite* 🍴 *Restaurant, some microwaves, refrigerators, cable TV; no a/c* 🖃 *AE, D, DC, MC, V.*

WRANGELL

㉒–㉙ *50 mi northwest of Thorne Bay on Prince of Wales Island.*

The town of Wrangell is on an island near the mouth of the fast-flowing Stikine River. A small, unassuming timber and fishing community, Wrangell has existed under three flags. Russia established Redoubt St. Dionysius here in 1834. Five years later, the Hudson's Bay Company leased the southern Alaska coastline, renaming the settlement Fort Stikine. It became Wrangell when the Americans took over in 1867; the name came from Baron Ferdinand Petrovich von Wrangel, governor of the Russian-American Company.

Exploring Wrangell

The rough-around-the-edges town of Wrangell is off the track of the larger cruise ships, so it does not suffer from tourist invasions to the degree that Ketchikan and Juneau do. The town is fairly compact, and most sights are within walking distance of the city dock or ferry terminal.

a good walk

A good place to start your tour is at the stalls selling local goods and souvenirs outside the **Wrangell Visitor Center** ㉒ ▶, close to the city docks in the Stikine Inn. Head through town along Front Street, stopping at **Kiksetti Totem Park** ㉓ before turning onto Shakes Street to see Wrangell's most interesting sight, **Chief Shakes Island** ㉔. You will probably want to spend time here just soaking in the harbor view and examining the old totem poles. **Chief Shakes's grave site** ㉕ is on the hill overlooking Wrangell Harbor. Get there from Chief Shakes Island by turning right on Case Avenue. From the grave site, head up Church Street to the **Wrangell Museum** ㉖ for another taste of the past. Get to the **Irene Ingle Public Library** ㉗ by continuing up Church Street and turning right on 2nd Street. Head ⅔ mi north of the ferry terminal along Evergreen Avenue to **Petroglyph Beach** ㉘, where ancient etchings are visible along the shore. For a woodsy hike, climb **Mount Dewey** ㉙, the hill right behind town.

TIMING It is a 1½-mi walk between Petroglyph Beach and Chief Shakes Island, so you should plan at least three hours to complete the walk and sightseeing around town.

What to See

★ ㉔ **Chief Shakes Island.** Some of the finest totem poles in Alaska are preserved here. Walk over the footbridge off the harbor dock to see a tribal house constructed in the 1930s as a replica of one that was home to many of the various Shakes and their peoples. ⊠ *Off Shakes St.* ☎ *907/ 874–3747* 🖃 *$2* ☉ *Daily when cruise ships are in port (ask at Wrangell Visitor Center) or by appointment.*

㉕ **Chief Shakes's grave site.** Buried here is Shakes V, who led the local Tlingit during the first half of the 19th century. The site is on Case Avenue, marked by two killer-whale totem poles. ⊠ *Case Ave.*

⑳ **Irene Ingle Public Library.** The library, behind the post office, has two ancient petroglyphs out front. ✉ *124 2nd St.* ☎ *907/874–3535.*

㉓ **Kiksetti Totem Park.** You'll find impressive totem poles at this pocket-size park of Alaska greenery. ✉ *Front St.*

㉙ **Mount Dewey.** Despite the name, this is actually just a small hill right behind Wrangell. It's a steep 15-minute climb to the top through a second-growth forest. The trail begins from 3rd Street behind the high school, and a viewpoint on top provides an obscured vista across protected waterways and forested islands.

㉘ **Petroglyph Beach.** Scattered among other rocks at this public beach are three dozen or more large stones bearing designs and pictures chiseled by unknown, ancient artists. No one knows why the rocks at this curious site were etched the way they were; perhaps they were boundary markers or messages. You can access the beach via a boardwalk, where you'll find signs describing the site along with carved replicas of the petroglyphs. You are welcome to use these replicas to make a rubbing from rice paper and charcoal or crayons (available in local stores). Because the original petroglyphs can be damaged by physical contact, the state discourages visitors from creating a rubbing off the rocks. ✉ ⅔ *mi north of ferry terminal off Evergreen Ave.*

㉖ **Wrangell Museum.** Wrangell's museum moved into spacious new quarters in 2004. Professionally produced exhibits provide a window on the town's rich history. Featured pieces include decorative posts from Chief Shakes's clan house (carved in the late 1700s), petroglyphs, century-old spruce-root and cedar-bark baskets, masks, items from Russian and English settlers, gold-rush memorabilia, and a fascinating photo collection.

✉ *296 Outer Dr.* ☎ *907/874–3770* 🖷 *$4* ◴ *May–Sept., Tues.–Sat. 10–5, and when ferry or cruise ships are in port; Oct.–Apr., Tues.–Sat. 1–5.*

▶ **㉒** **Wrangell Visitor Center.** This tourist office is in the Stikine Inn, close to the city docks. ✉ *107 Stikine Ave.* ☎ *907/874–3901 or 800/367–9745* 🖷 *907/874–3905* ⊕ *www.wrangellchamber.org* ◴ *Weekdays 10–4 and when cruise ships are in port.*

> **off the beaten path**
>
> ANAN CREEK WILDLIFE OBSERVATORY – About 30 mi southeast of Wrangell in the Tongass National Forest, Anan is one of Alaska's premier black- and brown-bear viewing areas. Each summer, from early July to mid-August, as many as 30 to 40 black bears gather at this Southeast stream to feed on pink salmon. On an average visit of about two hours, you might spot two to four bears. Forest Service interpreters are on hand to answer questions. The site is accessible only by boat or floatplane. For details, contact the **Tongass National Forest Wrangell Ranger District** (☎ 907/874–2323 ⊕ www.fs.fed. us/r10/tongass).

Where to Stay & Eat

$–$$$ 🖾 **Harding's Old Sourdough Lodge.** This lodge made of hand-milled cedar sits on the docks in a beautifully converted construction camp. Guest rooms have modest country-style furnishings, and a private suite (large enough for six people) has a luxuriously large bathroom with a heated floor and a hot tub. Home-style meals ($16–20 for dinner), including home-baked sourdough breads and fresh seafood, are also available for lodge guests only. ✉ *1104 Peninsula St.* ⌖ *Box 1062, 99929* ☎ *907/874–3613 or 800/874–3613* 🖷 *907/874–3455* ⊕ *www.akgetaway. com* ➦ *16 rooms* ♨ *Dining room, sauna, steam room, boating, Internet, meeting room, airport shuttle, some pets allowed; no a/c, no room TVs, no smoking* ═ *AE, D, DC, MC, V.*

$ 🖾 **Grand View Bed & Breakfast.** Two miles from town, this contemporary hillside home provides spectacular views across Zimovia Strait. Rooms, some with antiques and some decorated Alaskan style, have private baths and entrances. The friendly owners, John and Judy Baker, prepare delectable breakfast specials, including freshly baked rolls. ⌖ *Box 927, 99929* ☎🖷 *907/874–3225* ⊕ *www.grandviewbnb.com* ➦ *3 rooms* ♨ *Cable TV; no a/c* ═ *No credit cards* ⌾ *CP.*

$ 🖾 **Rooney's Roost Bed & Breakfast.** This century-old home just a block from downtown has been lovingly remodeled and filled with modern collectibles. Six guest rooms are available, three of which have private baths. Friendly owners, a large-screen television, and a filling breakfast add to its homey appeal. ✉ *206 McKinnon St., 99929* ☎ *907/874–2026* ⊕ *www.rooneysroost.com* ➦ *6 rooms, 3 with bath* ♨ *Airport shuttle; no TV in some rooms* ═ *MC, V* ⌾ *CP.*

$ ✕🖾 **Stikine Inn.** On the dock in the main part of town, this inn has great views of Wrangell's harbor. Rooms are basic with aging furnishings, although some have harbor views. The food at the Waterfront Grill, where large windows overlook the harbor, is the real draw here. Staples include burgers, cross-cut waffle fries, pasta, and homemade pizzas. ✉ *107 Stikine Ave., 2 blocks from ferry terminal* ⌖ *Box 990, 99929* ☎ *907/874–3388 or 888/874–3388* 🖷 *907/874–3923* ⊕ *www.stikine. com* ➦ *31 rooms, 3 suites* ♨ *Restaurant, cable TV, some pets allowed; no a/c* ═ *AE, D, MC, V.*

¢ 🖾 **Shakes Slough Cabins.** If you're a hot-springs or hot-tub enthusiast, these Forest Service cabins on the Stikine River, accessible from Wrangell, are worth checking out. Shakes Slough Hot Springs are a short boat ride away from the cabins. Here you can soak in both an open-air hot tub and an enclosed version. Reservations are required for the cabins; request details from the Forest Service office in Wrangell or make reservations by calling **ReserveUSA** (☎ 877/444–6777). *Forest Service,* ✉ *525 Bennett St., Wrangell 99929* ☎ *907/874–2323* 🖶 *907/874–7595* ⊕ *www. reserveusa.com* 🛏 *2 cabins* ♨ *Hot tub* 🚊 *AE, D, MC, V.*

Guided Tours

Alaska Tugboat Tours (☎ 907/874–3101 or 888/488–4386 ⊕ www. alaskatugtours.com) takes groups of four to six through the Inside Passage aboard a vintage 1967 tugboat that's been transformed into a comfortable floating resort. Cruises may be a single day or several days in length and include whale-watching, mountain biking, and sightseeing. **Alaska Vistas** (☎ 907/874–3006 or 866/874–3006 ⊕ www.alaskavistas. com) has jet-boat trips to Anan Creek Wildlife Observatory that depart from Wrangell, plus a variety of guided sea-kayak adventures. **Breakaway Adventures** (☎ 907/874–2488 or 888/385–2488 ⊕ www. breakawayadventures.com) leads day trips up the majestic Stikine River by jet boat, including a visit to Chief Shakes Glacier, along with time to take a dip at Chief Shakes Hot Springs. **Rain Walker Expeditions** leads excellent bus tours of the Wrangell area. **Sunrise Aviation** (☎ 907/874–2319 or 800/874–2311 🖶 907/874–2546 ⊕ www.sunriseflights.com) is a charter-only air carrier that offers trips to the Anan Creek Wildlife Observatory, LeConte Glacier, or Forest Service cabins.

Sports & the Outdoors

Fishing

Numerous companies schedule salmon- and trout-fishing excursions ranging in length from an afternoon to a week. Contact the **Wrangell Visitor Center** for information on guide services and locations.

Golf

Muskeg Meadows Golf Course (☎ 907/874–4653 🖶 907/874–4654 ⊕ www.wrangellalaskagolf.com), in a wooded area ½ mi from town, is a well-maintained 9-hole course with a driving range. Golf clubs and pull carts can be rented.

Hiking

Rain Walker Expeditions (☎ 907/874–2549 ⊕ www.rainwalkerexpeditions. com) leads two-hour, half-day, and full-day guided natural-history, botany, wildlife, and bird-watching tours of wild places near Wrangell.

Shopping

You'll find vendors selling local crafts, including children selling garnets from a nearby quarry, at covered shelters near the Wrangell city dock. **River's Edge Fine Arts and Gifts** (✉ 107 Stikine Ave. ☎ 907/874–3593), just off the lobby of the Stikine Inn, carries a selection of prints, hand-sewn clothing, carved wooden bowls, furniture, jewelry, and pottery. A local marine artist, Brenda Schwartz, often works in her studio inside this shop.

PETERSBURG

㉚–㉞ *22 mi north of Wrangell.*

Getting to Petersburg is an experience, whether you take the "high road" by air or the "low road" by sea. Alaska Airlines claims the shortest jet flight in the world, from takeoff at Wrangell to landing at Petersburg.

The schedule calls for 20 minutes of flying, but it's usually more like 15. At sea level only ferries and smaller cruisers can squeak through Wrangell Narrows with the aid of more than 50 buoys and range markers along the 22-mi crossing, which takes almost four hours. The inaccessibility of Petersburg is part of its off-the-beaten-path charm. Unlike in several other Southeast communities, you'll never be overwhelmed here by hordes of cruise passengers; only the smaller ships can reach the town.

At first sight Petersburg invokes the spirit of Norway: tidy white homes and storefronts line the streets, bright-color swirls of leaf and flower designs (called rosemaling) decorate a few older homes, and row upon row of sturdy fishing vessels pack the harbor. No wonder—this prosperous fishing community was founded by Norwegian Peter Buschmann in 1897.

The Scandinavian heritage is gradually being submerged by the larger American culture, but you may still occasionally hear Norwegian spoken, especially during the Little Norway Festival, held here each year on the weekend closest to May 17. If you're in town during the festival, be sure to partake in one of the fish feeds that highlight the Norwegian Independence Day celebration. You won't find better folk dancing and beer-batter halibut outside Norway.

One of the most pleasant things to do in Petersburg is to roam among the fishing vessels tied up at dockside in the town's expanding harbor. This is one of Alaska's busiest, most prosperous fishing communities, and the variety of seacraft is enormous. You'll see small trollers, big halibut vessels, and sleek pleasure craft. Wander, too, around the fish-processing structures (though be prepared for the pungent aroma). By watching shrimp, salmon, or halibut catches being brought ashore, you can get a real appreciation for this industry and the people who engage in it.

Exploring Petersburg

Although Petersburg is a pretty enough town to explore, here commercial fishing is more important than tourism. The main attractions are the town's Norwegian heritage and its magnificent mountain-backed setting. The country around Petersburg provides a wide array of outdoor fun, from whale-watching and glacier-gazing to brown-bear viewing, hiking, and fishing.

a good walk

The **Petersburg Visitor Information Center** ③⓪ ☞ at 1st and Fram streets is a logical spot to begin any walking (or biking) tour of Petersburg. Just a block up the hill, the **Clausen Memorial Museum** ③① is a testimony to life in Petersburg. From here, head back downhill to Nordic Drive (Main Street), turning left and then right onto historic Sing Lee Alley. Follow it to the **Sons of Norway Hall** ③② along scenic **Hammer Slough** ③③. Walk back through the center of town on Nordic Drive. On the north side of downtown, steps lead down to the water at scenic **Eagle's Roost Park** ③④.

TIMING   Petersburg is small enough to walk around in an hour, but you may want to spend more time biking around the back roads farther from town.

What to See

③① **Clausen Memorial Museum.** The museum has exhibits exploring commercial fishing and the cannery industry, the era of fish traps, the social life of Petersburg, and Tlingit culture. Don't miss the 126½-pound king salmon, the largest ever caught, as well as the Tlingit dugout canoe; two fish-trap anchors; the Cape Decision lighthouse station lens; and *Earth, Sea and Sky,* a 3-D sculptured wall mural outside. ⊠ *203 Fram St., 99833* ☎ *907/772–3598* ⊕ *www.clausenmuseum.alaska.net* ☜ *$2* ⊙ *May–mid-Sept., Mon.–Sat. 10:30–4:30; mid-Sept.–Apr., call for hrs.*

Petersburg

Sandy Beach

Wrangell Narrows

Nordic Dr.

34

1st St.

Dolphin St.

Main St.

Excel St.

31

Fram St.

30

Gjoa St.

Haugen Dr.

Floatplane Base

32

33

2nd St.

3rd St.

4th St.

5th St.

Indian St.

Ferry Terminal

Nordic Dr.

Mitkof Hwy.

Crystal Lake Hatchery/
Blind Slough Recreation Area/
Fall's Creek Fish Ladder

KEY
▶ *Start of walk*

---

34 **Eagle's Roost Park.** Just north of the Petersburg Fisheries cannery, this park is a great place to spot eagles, especially at low tide. On a clear day you will also discover dramatic views of the sharp-edged Coast Range, including the 9,077-foot summit of Devils Thumb.

33 **Hammer Slough.** Stop along this pool for a vision of houses and buildings on high stilts reflected perfectly in still waters; it's best seen at high tide.

▶ **30** **Petersburg Visitor Information Center.** This office is a good source for local information. ⊠ *1st and Fram Sts.* ☎ *907/772–4636* 🖶 *907/772–3646* ⊕ *www.petersburg.org* ⊙ *May–Sept., Mon.–Sat. 9–5, Sun. noon–4; Oct.–Apr., weekdays 10–2.*

32 **Sons of Norway Hall.** The large, white barnlike structure that stands just south of the Hammer Slough is the headquarters of an organization devoted to keeping alive the traditions and culture of Norway. Outside sits a replica of a Viking ship, and south of the building is **Fisherman's Memorial Park,** where local fishermen lost at sea are memorialized with a bronze statue of a working fisherman. ⊠ *Sing Lee Alley* ☎ *907/ 772–4575.*

---

off the beaten path

FALLS CREEK FISH LADDER – Coho and pink salmon migrate upstream in late summer and fall at this fish ladder. ⊠ *Mile 10.8, Mitkof Hwy.*

BLIND SLOUGH RECREATION AREA – This recreation area includes a number of sites scattered along the Mitkof Highway 15–20 mi south of Petersburg. **Blind River Rapids Trail** is a wheelchair-accessible 1-mi path that leads to a three-side shelter overlooking the river before it loops back through the muskeg. Not far away is a bird-viewing area where several dozen trumpeter swans winter. In the summer you're likely to see many ducks and other waterfowl here. At Mile 18, the state-run **Crystal Lake Hatchery** (☎ 907/772–4772) releases thousands of king and coho salmon each year. The kings return in June and July, the coho in August and September. Nearby is a popular picnic area. Four miles south of the hatchery is a Forest Service campground.

LECONTE GLACIER – Petersburg's biggest draw lies about 25 mi east of town and is accessible only by water or air. LeConte Glacier is the continent's southernmost tidewater glacier and one of its most active, often calving off so many icebergs that the tidewater bay at its face is carpeted shore to shore with floating bergs. Ferries and cruise ships pass it at a distance.

Where to Stay & Eat

$$ ✕ **Alaskafe.** This comfortable lunch spot in downtown Petersburg, above Coastal Cold Storage, serves fresh-baked pastries, along with panini sandwiches, pasta, salads, and the best espresso in town. The café is open weekdays for breakfast and lunch and Saturday for brunch, with seafood dinners on Friday and Saturday evenings. ✉ *306-B Nordic Dr.* ☎ *907/ 772–5282* ▤ *No credit cards.*

$ ✕ **Pellerito's Pizza.** Although it has a few tables, this always-crowded pizza joint primarily specializes in take-out pizzas, pizza by the slice, and giant calzones. It also serves ice cream. ✉ *1105 S. Nordic Dr., across from ferry terminal* ☎ *907/772–3727* ▤ *MC, V.*

¢ ✕ **Coastal Cold Storage.** This busy little shop in the heart of Petersburg serves daily lunch seafood specials, including fish chowders and halibut beer bits, along with grilled chicken wraps, steak sandwiches, and breakfast omelets and waffles. Live or cooked crab is here for takeout, and the shop can process your sport-caught fish. ✉ *306 N. Nordic Dr.* ☎ *907/772–4171* ▤ *AE, D, MC, V.*

$–$$$ ▥ **Scandia House.** Exuding an old Norwegian flavor, this hotel on Petersburg's main street, a fixture since 1910, was rebuilt following a 1995 fire. Rosemaling designs adorn the exterior. The interior is squeaky clean, with contemporary oak furniture; some rooms have kitchenettes, king-size beds, or in-room hot tubs and a view of the harbor. Homemade muffins and coffee warm the small but relaxing lobby in the morning. ✉ *110 Nordic Dr.* ✉ *Box 689, 99833* ☎ *907/772–4281 or 800/722–5006* ▤ *907/772–4301* ◆ *30 rooms, 3 suites* ○ *Some kitchenettes, cable TV, boat and car rentals; no a/c* ▤ *AE, D, DC, MC, V* ⦿ *CP.*

$ ▥ **Tides Inn.** This is the largest hotel in town, a block uphill from Petersburg's main thoroughfare. Rooms have comfortable furnishings; some have kitchenettes. Rooms in the newer wing have views of the boat harbor. The coffee is always on in the small lobby, and in the morning there are complimentary juices, muffins, and pastries. ✉ *307 N. 1st St.* ✉ *Box 1048, 99833* ☎ *907/772–4288 or 800/665–8433* ▤ *907/772– 4286* ⊕ *www.tidesinnalaska.com* ◆ *48 rooms* ○ *Some kitchenettes, cable TV, Internet, car rental; no a/c* ▤ *AE, D, DC, MC, V* ⦿ *CP.*

$ ▥ **Water's Edge Bed & Breakfast.** Along the shore of Frederick Sound 1½ mi north of Petersburg, this family-run B&B offers either creekside or waterside rooms. Seals, eagles, and whales are often seen just outside the door. A deluxe Continental breakfast is served, and the library is stocked with books on Alaska and natural history. Take advantage of the owners' Kaleidoscope Cruises or borrow the bikes or canoe to explore on your own. Lodging-cruise packages are offered. ✉ *705 Sandy*

Beach Rd. ✆ *Box 1201, 99833* ☎ *907/772–3736 or 800/868–4373*
⊕ *www.alaska.net/~bbsea* ⇘ *2 rooms* ♿ *Bicycles, library, airport shuttle; no a/c, no smoking* ▭ *No credit cards* ⦿ *CP.*

Guided Tours

Stop by the visitor center for a complete listing of local tour companies.
Kaleidoscope Cruises (☎ 907/772–3736 or 800/868–4373 ⊕ www.
alaska.net/~bbsea) conducts whale-watching and glacier-ecology boat
tours led by professional biologists and naturalists. **Pacific Wing** (✉ 1500
Hagen Dr. ☎ 907/772–9258 ⊕ www.pacificwing.com) is an air-taxi operator that gets high marks from locals for its flightseeing tours over
the Stikine River and LeConte Glacier. **Tongass Kayak Adventures** (☎ 907/
772–4600 ⊕ www.tongasskayak.com) leads multiday sea-kayak trips
to the Stikine River, LeConte Glacier, and elsewhere in the area. **Viking
Travel** (✉ 101 Nordic Dr. ☎ 907/772–3818 or 800/327–2571 🖷 907/
772–3940 ⊕ www.alaska-ala-carte.com) books whale-watching, glacier,
sea-kayaking, and other charters with local operators.

Nightlife & the Arts

Bars & Nightclubs

The **Harbor Bar** (✉ Nordic Dr. ☎ 907/772–4526), with ships' wheels,
ship pictures, and a mounted red snapper, is true to the town's seafaring spirit. Sample the brew and blasting sounds at the smoky **Kito's
Kave** (✉ Sing Lee Alley ☎ 907/772–3207) and examine the odd collection of wall hangings—a Mexican painting on black velvet, a
mounted Alaska king salmon, and two stuffed sailfish from a tropical fishing expedition.

Shopping

Seafood

At **Tonka Seafoods,** across the street from the Sons of Norway Hall, you
can tour the plant and sample smoked or canned halibut and salmon.
It will also ship. ✉ *Sing Lee Alley* ☎ *907/772–3662 or 888/560–3662*
▤ *Free* ◷ *Mon.–Sat. 8–5; tours at 1 PM (minimum 6 people).*

Bookstore

Sing Lee Alley Books (✉ Sing Lee Alley ☎ 907/772–4440), set back off
the alley in a beautiful big white house that served as a boardinghouse
to fishermen and schoolteachers, stocks books on Alaska, best-sellers,
cards, and gifts.

Norwegian Crafts

The appropriately named **CubbyHole** sells Norwegian-style rosemaling.
✉ *102 South 2nd St., two blocks south of museum* ☎ *907/772–2717.*

SITKA

35–**44** *110 mi west of Petersburg.*

Sitka was the home to Tlingit people for centuries prior to the 18th-century arrival of the Russians. In canoes up to 60 feet long, the Tlingits
fished and traded throughout the Alaskan Panhandle and even as far
south as California. Unfortunately for them, Russian territorial governor Alexander Baranof coveted the Sitka site for its beauty, mild climate,
and economic potential. In the island's massive timber forests he saw
raw materials for shipbuilding. Its location offered trading routes as far
west as Asia and as far south as California and Hawaii. In 1799 Baranof negotiated with the local chief to build a wooden fort and trading

post some 6 mi north of the present town. He called the outpost St. Michael Archangel and moved a large number of his Russian and Aleut fur hunters there from their former base on Kodiak Island.

The Tlingits soon took exception to the ambitions of their new neighbors. Reluctant to pledge allegiance to the czar and provide free labor, in 1802 they attacked Baranof's people and burned his buildings. Baranof, however, was away on Kodiak at the time. He returned in 1804 with a formidable force, including shipboard cannons. He attacked the Tlingits at their fort near Indian River, site of the present-day 105-acre Sitka National Historical Park, and forced them to flee north to Chichagof Island.

In 1821 the Tlingits returned to Sitka to trade with the Russians, who were happy to benefit from the tribe's hunting skills. Under Baranof and succeeding managers, the Russian-American Company and the town prospered, becoming known as the Paris of the Pacific. Besides engaging in the fur trade, the community built a major shipbuilding and repair facility, sawmills, and forges and even initiated an ice industry. The Russians shipped blocks of ice from nearby Swan Lake to the booming San Francisco market.

The town declined after its 1867 transfer from Russia to the United States but became prosperous again during World War II, when it served as a base for the U.S. effort to drive the Japanese from the Aleutian Islands. Today its most important industries are fishing, government, and tourism.

Exploring Sitka

It is hard not to like Sitka, with its eclectic blending of Native, Russian, and American history and its dramatic and beautiful setting. This is one of the best Inside Passage towns to explore on foot, with such sights as St. Michael's Cathedral, Sheldon Jackson Museum, Sitka National Historical Park, and the Alaska Raptor Center topping the town's must-see list.

a good walk

A good place to begin a tour of Sitka is the distinctive onion-dome **St. Michael's Cathedral** 35 ▶, right in town center. Next head to **Harrigan Centennial Hall** 36, a block behind the cathedral along Harbor Drive. Inside are the interesting Isabel Miller Museum and an information desk that opens when cruise ships are in port. From Harrigan Centennial Hall, turn right on Lincoln Street and continue a block to the **Russian Bishop's House** 37, one of the symbols of Russian rule, dating from 1842. Continue out Lincoln Street along the harbor to Sheldon Jackson College, where the **Sheldon Jackson Museum** 38 is packed with Native cultural artifacts. Another ½ mi up is the **Sitka National Historical Park** 39, where you can watch Native artisans craft carvings and silver jewelry. Behind the main building, paths take you through the rain forest past tall totem poles and to the site of a Tlingit fort from the battle of 1804. A signed trail crosses the Indian River (watch for spawning salmon in late summer) and heads to the **Alaska Raptor Center** 40, for an up-close look at bald eagles.

Return to town along Sawmill Creek Road to the small Sitka National Cemetery, where you turn left on Jeff Davis Street. Continue downhill to Lincoln Street and turn right, following it back to Harrigan Centennial Hall. From here, walk along Harbor Drive for two blocks and take the path to the summit of **Castle Hill** 41, where Russia transferred Alaska to American hands. Follow the path down the other side of the hill to view the impressive **Sitka State Pioneers' Home** 42, with the statue of pi-

Sitka

oneer "Skagway Bill" Fonda. Across the street is **Totem Square** 43, with its tall totem pole and three ancient anchors. Adjacent to the Pioneers' Home is the **Sheet'ka Kwaan Naa Kahidi Community House** cultural center. Native dances take place here in the summer. Turn right at the center and pass the reconstructed Russian blockhouse that tops a nearby hill. End your walk at the **Russian and Lutheran cemeteries** 44, along Marine Street a block from the blockhouse. The grave of Princess Maksoutoff, a member of the Russian royal family, is here.

TIMING   Sitka has many attractions, and you can easily spend a full day exploring this culturally rich area. You can accomplish the walk in two to three hours if you do not spend much time at each stop.

What to See

★ ☺ 40 **Alaska Raptor Center.** You have the unique experience of viewing American bald eagles and other wild Alaskan raptors up close at this nonprofit center set on a beautifully wooded tract of land just a 20-minute walk from downtown. There's a short video, and guides provide an introduction to the rehabilitation center. In this enormous enclosed space, injured eagles relearn survival skills, including flying and catching salmon. A large deck out back faces an open-air enclosure for eagles whose injuries prevent them from returning to the wild. ☎ *907/747–8662 or 800/643–9425* ⊕ *www.alaskaraptor.org* ✉ *$12* ⊙ *Mid-May–Sept., Sun.–Fri. 8–4.*

41 **Castle Hill.** On this hill Alaska was formally handed over to the United States on October 18, 1867, and the first 49-star U.S. flag was flown on January 3, 1959, signifying Alaska's statehood. To reach the hill and get one of Sitka's best views, take the first right off Harbor Drive just before the O'Connell Bridge; then go into the **Baranof Castle Hill State**

Historic Site entrance. A paved path takes you to the top of the hill, overlooking Crescent Harbor. Several Russian residences on the hill, including Baranof's castle, burned down in 1894.

36 Harrigan Centennial Hall. Out front of this contemporary brick building a block from St. Michael's Cathedral sits a replica of a Tlingit war canoe. Inside you'll find a volunteer-staffed information desk provided by the Sitka Convention and Visitors Bureau; the **Isabel Miller Museum,** with its collection of Russian and American historical artifacts; and an auditorium for New Archangel Dancers performances, which take place when cruise ships are in port. ✉ *Harbor Dr.* ☎ *907/747–6455 museum, 907/747–5940 Visitors Bureau* ⊕ *www.sitka.org/historicalmuseum* ✉ *Free* ⊘ *Museum May–Sept., daily 8–5; Oct.–Apr., Tues.–Sat. 10–4. Information Desk May–Sept., daily 8–5.*

44 Russian and Lutheran cemeteries. Most of Sitka's Russian dignitaries are buried in these sites off Marine Street. The most distinctive grave belongs to Princess Maksoutoff (died 1862), wife of the last Russian governor and one of the most illustrious members of the Russian royal family to be buried on Alaskan soil.

37 Russian Bishop's House. A registered historic landmark, this house facing the harbor was constructed by the Russian-American Company for Bishop Innocent Veniaminov in 1842. Inside the house, one of the few remaining Russian-built log structures in Alaska, are exhibits on the history of Russian America, including a room where a portion of the house's structure is peeled away to expose Russian building techniques. Guided tours are given of the second floor. ✉ *501 Lincoln St.* ☎ *907/747–6281* ⊕*www.nps.gov/sitk* ✉*$3* ⊘ *May–Sept., daily 9–5; Oct.–Apr. by appointment.*

☛ ★ 35 St. Michael's Cathedral. One of Southeast Alaska's best-known national landmarks had its origins in a log structure erected between 1844 and 1848. In 1966 the church was destroyed in a fire that swept through the downtown business district. As the fire engulfed the building, townspeople risked their lives and rushed inside to rescue the cathedral's precious icons, religious objects, vestments, and other treasures brought to the church from Russia. Using original measurements and blueprints, an almost exact replica of onion-dome St. Michael's was built and dedicated in 1976. Today you can see what could possibly be the largest collection of Russian icons in the United States, among them the much-prized *Our Lady of Sitka* (also known as the *Sitka Madonna*) and the *Christ Pantocrator* (*Christ the Judge*) on either side of the doors of the interior altar screen. Other objects include ornate Gospel books, chalices, crucifixes, much-used silver-gilt wedding crowns dating to 1866, and an altar cloth made by Princess Maksoutoff. ✉ *Lincoln St.* ☎ *907/747–8120* ✉ *$2* ⊘ *May–Sept., when large cruise ships are in port; Oct.–Apr., hrs vary.*

★ 38 Sheldon Jackson Museum. At **Sheldon Jackson College,** this octagonal museum, which dates from 1895, contains priceless Aleut and Eskimo items collected by Dr. Sheldon Jackson (1834–1909), who traveled the remote regions of Alaska as an educator and missionary. Carved masks, Chilkat blankets, dog sleds, kayaks—even the impressive helmet worn by Chief Katlean during the 1804 battle against the Russians—are displayed. Native artisans are here all summer, creating baskets, carvings, or masks. ✉ *801 Lincoln St.* ☎ *907/747–8981* ⊕ *www.museums.state. ak.us* ✉ *$4* ⊘ *Mid-May–mid-Sept., daily 9–5; mid-Sept.–mid-May, Tues.–Sat. 10–4.*

★ ➌➒ **Sitka National Historical Park.** The main building at this park has a small museum with historical exhibits and a number of old totem poles, some more than a century old. You can watch a video about 19th-century conflicts between Tlingits and Russians. Also here is the **Southeast Alaska Indian Cultural Center,** where Native artists and artisans demonstrate silversmithing, weaving, wood carving, and basketry. Behind the center, a wide 1-mi path takes you through the forest and along the shore of Sitka Sound. Scattered along the way are some of the most skillfully carved Native totem poles in Alaska, including several from the 1904 St. Louis World's Fair. The trail passes a grassy meadow that once contained a sturdy Tlingit fort; the 1804 battle between the Russians and Tlingits was fought here. Keep going on the trail to see spawning salmon from the footbridge over Indian River. Park Service rangers lead historical walks in the summer. ⊠ *106 Metlakatla St.* ☎ *907/747–6281* ⊕ *www.nps.gov/sitk* ⊠ *$3* ☉ *Mid-May–Sept., daily 8–5; Oct.–mid-May, weekdays 8–5.*

➍➋ **Sitka State Pioneers' Home.** The large, four-level, red-roof structure with the imposing 14-foot statue in front is the first of several state-run retirement homes for Alaska's senior citizens. The statue, symbolizing Alaska's frontier sourdough spirit (a "sourdough" generally refers to Alaska's American pioneers), was modeled by an authentic pioneer, William "Skagway Bill" Fonda. It portrays a determined prospector with pack, pick, rifle, and supplies on his back heading for the gold country. Adjacent to the Pioneers' Home is **Sheet'ka Kwaan Naa Kahidi Community House,** where you can watch Native dance performances throughout the summer. A re-created Russian blockhouse caps the small hill directly behind the community center. ⊠ *Lincoln and Katlian Sts.* ☎ *907/747–7290 or 888/270–8687.*

➍➌ **Totem Square.** On this square directly across the street from the Pioneers' Home are three anchors discovered in local waters believed to be of 19th-century British origin. Look for the double-headed eagle of czarist Russia carved into the cedar of the totem pole in the park.

Where to Stay & Eat

$$–$$$$ ✕ **Channel Club.** Once you've surveyed the dozens of salads arrayed on the salad bar, you might not even make it to the steak and seafood for which this restaurant, festooned with fishnet, floats, and whalebone carvings, is known. A courtesy van provides door-to-door service if you're without transportation. ⊠ *Mile 3.5, 2906 Halibut Point Rd.* ☎ *907/747–9916* ⊟ *AE, DC, MC, V.*

$$–$$$$ ▥ **Westmark Shee Atika.** Conveniently in the heart of town, Sitka's nicest hotel has large rooms and a lobby decorated with Tlingit art. Many rooms overlook Crescent Harbor; the best rooms are the corner suites. Downstairs, the Raven Dining Room serves seafood, pasta, and steak as well as such specials as beer-batter halibut or a homemade bread bowl with clam chowder. Top it off with a slice of ultrarich Mississippi mud pie. ⊠ *330 Seward St., 99835* ☎ *907/747–6241, 800/544–0970 in U.S., 800/999–2570 in Canada* ᐸ *907/747–5486* ⊕ *www.westmarkhotels.com* ↪ *98 rooms, 3 suites* ↻ *Restaurant, room service, cable TV, bar; no a/c* ⊟ *AE, D, DC, MC, V.*

★ $$ ▥ **Rockwell Lighthouse.** On an island ¾ mi from town, Burgess Bauder (a local veterinarian) rents out his 1,600-square-foot four-story lighthouse, hand-built in the 1980s with coastal woods and brass lights. The light at the top is built to Coast Guard specifications. The lighthouse can accommodate eight people in four rooms—you must rent the whole property. A curving staircase wraps up the inside of the lighthouse, amid its nautical decor. The price includes transportation to and from the lighthouse; it's $35 per day extra for use of the hot tub. In summer, you can use a small motorboat to reach the island, but when it's stormy the owner runs a shuttle service. Call up to a year ahead for midsummer reservations. ☐ *Box 277, 99835* 🖃🖃 *907/747–3056* ☖ *Dining room, kitchen, hot tub* 🖃 *No credit cards.*

$ 🖼 **Cascade Inn.** A few miles out of town, this motel is conveniently attached to a grocery, video, and liquor store. The large rooms have simple furnishings and balconies facing the water and Mt. Edgecumbe volcano. Some include kitchenettes. A deck with a cedar sauna and a barbecue pit sits just above the water. ⊠ *2035 Halibut Point Rd., 99835* ☎ *907/747–6804 or 800/532–0908* 🖶 *907/747–6572* ⊕ *www.cascadeinnsitka.com* ➹ *10 rooms* ☖ *Grocery, some kitchenettes, cable TV, in-room VCRs, sauna, bicycle rentals; no a/c, no smoking* 🖃 *AE, MC, V.*

¢–$ 🖼 **Sitka Hotel.** Right in downtown, this friendly, old-fashioned hotel with a Victorian-style lobby was built in 1939. The rooms mix Victorian-style brass beds and wallpaper with contemporary furniture. A cozy lounge provides a comfy place to relax, and convenient off-street parking is available. ⊠ *118 Lincoln St., 99835* ☎ *907/747–3288* 🖶 *907/747–8499* ⊕ *www.sitkahotel.com* ➹ *57 rooms* ☖ *Some refrigerators, cable TV; no a/c* 🖃 *AE, MC, V.*

¢–$ 🖼 **White Sulphur Springs Cabin.** This Tongass National Forest public-use cabin 65 mi outside Sitka has nearby hot springs. Like many other Forest Service cabins, this cabin sleeps four (bring your own sleeping bags) and has bunk beds, woodstove, table, and outhouse. No mattresses, cooking utensils, or any services are provided, so you must bring all of your own supplies. The cabin faces the Pacific Ocean and has a nearby hotsprings bathhouse. Access is by boat (you'll need to walk in from a nearby cove) or helicopter. ☎ *907/747–6671 information, 877/444–6777 reservations* ⊕ *www.reserveusa.com* ➹ *1 cabin* 🖃 *AE, D, MC, V.*

Guided Tours

Sitka Tours (☎ 907/747–8443 🖶 907/747–7510) meets ferries and cruise ships and leads both bus tours and historical walks. In addition, it transports ferry passengers into Sitka. **Tribal Tours** (☎ 907/747–7290 or 888/270–8687 🖶 907/747–3770 ⊕ www.sitkatribal.com) emphasizes Sitka's rich Native culture, with bus or walking tours and with dance performances at the Tribal Community House.

Allen Marine Tours (☎ 907/747–8100 or 888/747–8101 ⊕ www.allenmarine.com) leads boat-based wildlife tours four times a week in the summer. These tours are a good opportunity to view marine mammals (including humpback whales) and seabirds. **Sea Life Discovery Tours** (☎ 907/966–2301 or 877/966–2301 ⊕ www.sealifediscoverytours.com) operates the only semi-submersible tour vessel in Alaska. Large underwater windows provide views of kelp forests, fish, crab, sea urchins, anemones, starfish, and other creatures, and an underwater camera zooms in for close-up views via the video monitor.

Nightlife & the Arts

Bars

As far as the locals are concerned, a spot in one of the green-and-white vinyl booths at **Pioneer Bar** (⊠ 212 Katlian St. ☎ 907/747–3456), across from the harbor, is a destination unto itself. It's vintage Alaska, with hundreds of pictures of local fishing boats, occasional live music, and pickup pool games.

Dance

★ The **New Archangel Dancers of Sitka** performs authentic Russian Cossack–type dances whenever cruise ships are in port. This all-female troupe tours extensively, with a mix of traditional dance styles. Tickets are sold a half hour before performances; a recorded message (☎ 907/ 747–5516 ⊕ www.newarchangeldancers.com) gives the schedule a week in advance. Performances take place in Harrigan Centennial Hall. **Sheet'ka Kwaan Naa Kahidi Dancers** (☎ 907/747–7290 or 888/270– 8687 ⊕ www.sitkatribal.com) performs Tlingit dances in full Native regalia at the Sheet'ka Kwaan Naa Kahidi Community House on Katlian Street. The dance schedule is listed on the board at Harrigan Centennial Hall.

Festivals

Southeast Alaska's major classical chamber-music festival is the annual **Sitka Summer Music Festival** (✉ Box 3333, 99835 ☎ 907/747–6774 ⊕ www.sitkamusicfestival.org), a three-week June celebration of concerts and special events held in Harrigan Centennial Hall. The **Sitka Whale-Fest** (✉ Box 6004, 99835 ☎ 907/747–7964 ⊕ www.sitkawhalefest.org) is held around town the first weekend of November when the whales are plentiful (as many as 80) and tourists are not.

Sports & the Outdoors

Bird-Watching & Hiking

Seven miles north of Sitka along Halibut Point Road are two bird-watching and hiking trails. The **Starrigavan Estuary Life Interpretive Trail** provides views of spawning salmon and waterfowl and has a platform for bird-watchers. The **Starrigavan Forest & Muskeg Interpretive Trail** has great views of the valley along Starrigavan Creek.

Kayaking

Alaska Travel Adventures (☎ 907/789–0052 or 800/478–0052 ⊕ www. alaskaadventures.com) leads a three-hour kayaking tour in protected waters south of Sitka and has a remote cabin on the water. **Baidarka Boats** (✉ 320 Seward St. ☎ 907/747–8996 🖷 907/747–4801 ⊕ www. kayaksite.com) guides excellent half-day and all-day sea-kayaking trips in the Sitka area and also rents kayaks for those who want to head out on their own. Instruction is provided and no experience is necessary.

Shopping

Art Galleries

Fairweather Prints (✉ 209 Lincoln St. ☎ 907/747–8677 ⊕ www. fairweatherprints.com) consists of "wearable art," with hand-printed Alaskan designs on shirts, dresses, and other clothing. **Impressions** (✉ 239 Lincoln St. ☎ 907/747–5502 or 888/747–5502) is a fine downtown gallery with art prints and limited editions from Southeast Alaskan artists, including Evon Zerbetz and Rie Muñoz. Housed within an 1895 home next to the Bishop's House, **Sitka Rose Gallery** (✉ 419 Lincoln St. ☎ 907/ 747–3030 or 888/236–1536) has two small galleries with Alaskan paintings, sculptures, Native art, and jewelry.

Bookstore

Old Harbor Books (✉ 201 Lincoln St. ☎ 907/747–8808 ⊕ www. oldharborbooks.com) has an impressive collection of Alaskan titles, along with a knowledgeable staff. It's a book lovers' bookstore. Directly behind the bookstore is the ever-popular **Backdoor Cafe** (☎ 907/747–8856), with espresso and pastries.

JUNEAU

45 – 57 *100 mi northeast of Sitka.*

Juneau, Alaska's capital and third-largest city, is on the North American mainland but can't be reached by road. The city owes its origins to two colorful sourdoughs (Alaskan pioneers), Joe Juneau and Dick Harris, and to a Tlingit chief named Kowee. The chief led the two men to rich reserves of gold in the outwash of the stream that now runs through the middle of town and in quartz formations back in the gulches and valleys. That was in 1880, and shortly after the discovery a modest stampede resulted in the formation of first a camp, then a town, then finally the Alaska district government capital in 1906.

For 60 years or so after Juneau's founding, gold was the mainstay of the economy. In its heyday the AJ (for Alaska Juneau) Gold Mine was the biggest low-grade ore mine in the world. It was not until World War II, when the government decided it needed Juneau's manpower for the war effort, that the AJ and other mines in the area ceased operations. After the war, mining failed to start up again, and government became the city's principal employer.

Juneau is full of contrasts. The historic downtown buildings and dramatic hillside position provide a frontier feeling, but the city's cosmopolitan nature comes through in fine museums, noteworthy restaurants, and a literate and outdoorsy populace. In addition to enjoying the city itself, you will discover a tramway to alpine trails atop Mt. Roberts, densely forested wilderness areas, quiet bays for sea kayaking, and even a famous drive-up glacier. Surrounded by beautiful wilderness and glaciers in its backyard, Juneau is the cultural center of Alaska.

Exploring Juneau

Juneau is an obligatory stop on the Inside Passage cruise and ferry circuit and enjoys an overabundance of visitors in midsummer. Downtown Juneau is compact enough so that most of its main attractions are within walking distance of one another. Note, however, that the city is very hilly, so your legs will get a real workout. Along with the Alaska State Museum and Mt. Roberts Tramway, be sure to make time for a tour to Mendenhall Glacier and the Gastineau Salmon Hatchery.

a good walk

A good starting point is **Marine Park** 45 ▶, right along the cruise-ship dock. For an introduction to public lands in the area, walk up Marine Way and turn right on Whittier Street to reach the engaging **Alaska State Museum** 46, filled with artifacts and art from around the state. From here, circle back along Willoughby Avenue to the **State Office Building** 47. Catch the elevator to the eighth-floor atrium and head out onto the observation deck for vistas across Gastineau Channel. Then continue out the east side of the building onto 4th Street. The small but informative **Juneau-Douglas City Museum** 48 sits a short distance away at 4th and Calhoun streets. The unimpressive banklike building across the street is the **Alaska State Capitol** 49. Next stop is the **Governor's Mansion** 50, a few minutes uphill on Calhoun Street. If you have the time and energy, you may want to continue along Calhoun, across the Gold Creek Bridge, and then down along 12th Street to the quiet **Evergreen Cemetery** 51, where town fathers Joe Juneau and Dick Harris are buried.

Backtrack to the Governor's Mansion and retrace your steps down Calhoun Street to the overpass. Climb the steps and cross the footbridge to 5th Street; then turn left up Main Street, followed by a right on 7th

Juneau

Street. Next stop is the artifacts-filled old home of Judge Wicker-sham, the **Wickersham State Historical Site** 52, on 7th and Seward streets. From here on you will be working your way back downhill, so the walking gets easier. The **St. Nicholas Russian Orthodox Church** 53 occupies the corner of 5th and Gold streets, and the **Centennial Hall Visitor Center** 54 is just a couple of blocks away, at 3rd and Seward streets. By now you probably have a good taste of Juneau; step inside for the complete details.

Now it's time to explore the historic buildings and busy shops of downtown Juneau, particularly those along **South Franklin Street** 55. Check out the Alaskan Hotel, the Alaska Steam Laundry Building, and the Senate Building before dipping inside the always crowded **Red Dog Saloon** 56 at the intersection of South Franklin Street and Admiral Way. A few more minutes' walking will take you to the **Mt. Roberts Tramway** 57, a great way to reach alpine country for a hike overlooking Juneau and Gastineau Channel.

TIMING   To cover downtown Juneau's many interesting sights, you should allow at least three or four hours for exploring. Add more time to ride the Mt. Roberts Tramway or for the side trip to Evergreen Cemetery.

What to See

49 **Alaska State Capitol.** Built in 1930, this building with southeastern Alaskan marble pillars houses the governor's office and hosts state legislature meetings during the winter months. Historic photos line the upstairs walls. You can pick up a self-guided tour brochure as you enter. ⊠ *Corner of Seward and 4th Sts.* ☎ *907/465–2479* ⊗ *Weekdays 8–5.*

★ 46 **Alaska State Museum.** Alaska's finest museum appeals to all tastes. Native Alaskan buffs will enjoy examining the 38-foot walrus-hide umiak (an open, skin-covered Eskimo boat) built by Eskimos and a re-created interior of a Tlingit tribal house. Natural-history exhibits include stuffed brown bears and a two-story-high eagle nesting tree. Russian-American displays and contemporary art complete the collection. ⊠ *395 Whittier St.* ☎ *907/465–2901* ⊕ *www.museums.state.ak.us* ☜ *$5* ⊘ *Mid-May–mid-Sept., daily 8:30–5:30; mid-Sept.–mid-May, Tues.–Sat. 10–4.*

⑤④ Centennial Hall Visitor Center. Here you can get complete details on Juneau sights and activities, plus walking-tour maps. You can also make ferry reservations and find out about hiking trails and other activities on nearby Tongass National Forest lands. ⊠ *101 Egan Dr.* ☎ *907/586–2201 or 888/581–2201* ⊕ *www.traveljuneau.com* ⊘ *May–Sept., weekdays 8:30–5, weekends 9–5; Oct.–Apr., weekdays 9–4.*

⑤① Evergreen Cemetery. Many Juneau pioneers, including Joe Juneau and Dick Harris, are buried here. A meandering gravel path leads through the graveyard, and at the end of it is the monument commemorating the cremation spot of Chief Kowee.

⑤⓪ Governor's Mansion. The three-level colonial-style home was completed in 1912. Tours of the residence are, unfortunately, not permitted. ⊠ *716 Calhoun Ave.*

⑤ ④⑧ Juneau-Douglas City Museum. Among the exhibits interpreting local mining and Tlingit history are old mining equipment, historic photos, and pioneer artifacts, including a century-old store and kitchen. Also of interest are a Juneau time line, exhibits on commercial fishing and steamships, historic paintings, a hands-on area for children, and a half-hour video of Juneau's history. ⊠ *114 4th St.* ☎ *907/586–3572* ⊕ *www.juneau.org/parksrec/museum* ☜ *$3* ⊘ *Mid-May–Sept., weekdays 9–5; weekends 10–5; Oct.–mid-May, Tues.–Sat. noon–4.*

▶ ④⑤ Marine Park. On the dock where the cruise ships tie up is a little urban oasis with benches, shade trees, and shelter. It's a great place to enjoy an outdoor meal purchased from one of Juneau's many street vendors. A visitor kiosk is staffed according to cruise-ship schedules.

★ ⑤ ⑤⑦ Mt. Roberts Tramway. The tram whisks you from the cruise terminal 1,800 feet up the side of Mt. Roberts. After the six-minute ride, you can take in a film on the history and legends of the Tlingits, visit the nature center, go for an alpine walk on hiking trails, purchase Native crafts, or experience fine mountain-view dining from the decks. The smoke-free bar serves locally brewed beers. ☎ *907/463–3412 or 888/461–8726* ⊕ *www.alaska.net/~junotram* ☜ *$22* ⊘ *May–Sept., daily 9–9.*

⑤⑥ Red Dog Saloon. The frontierish quarters of the Red Dog have housed an infamous Juneau watering hole since 1890. Every conceivable surface in this two-story bar is cluttered with life preservers, business cards, and college banners, and when tourist season hits, a little atmospheric sawdust covers the floor as well. Bands pump out dance tunes when cruise ships are docked. ⊠ *278 S. Franklin St.* ☎ *907/463–9954.*

⑤③ St. Nicholas Russian Orthodox Church. Quaint, onion-domed, and built in 1894, St. Nicholas is the oldest Russian church building in Southeast Alaska. A small gift shop is adjacent. ⊠ *326 5th St.* ☎ *907/780–6320* ☜ *$2 requested donation* ⊘ *Tours mid-May–Sept., Mon.–Sat. noon–6.*

⑤⑤ South Franklin Street. The buildings on South Franklin Street (and Front as well), among the oldest and most interesting structures in the city, house curio and crafts shops, snack shops, and two salmon shops. Many reflect the architecture of the 1920s and '30s, and some are even older. The small **Alaskan Hotel** opened in 1913 and retains its period trappings. The barroom's massive, mirrored oak back bar is accented by Tiffany lights and panels. The 1901 **Alaska Steam Laundry Building**, with a windowed turret, now houses a coffeehouse and other stores. The **Senate Building** is across the street.

47 **State Office Building.** At this government building you can have a picnic lunch with the state workers on the eighth-floor patio. On most Fridays at noon, concerts are played inside the four-story atrium on a grand old theater pipe organ, a veteran of the silent-movie era. ⊠ *4th St. and Calhoun Sts.*

52 **Wickersham State Historical Site.** At the top of the hill behind the capitol stands the former residence of James Wickersham, pioneer judge and delegate to Congress. The home, constructed in 1898, contains memorabilia from the judge's travels throughout Alaska—from rare Native basketry and ivory carvings to historic photos and a Chickering grand piano that came " 'round the Horn" to Alaska in the 1870s. The tour provides a glimpse into the life of this dynamic man and also includes tea and sourdough cookies. ⊠ *213 7th St.* ☎ *907/586–9001* ⊕ *www.dnr.state.ak.us/parks* ⊠ *$2* ⊘ *Mid-May–Sept., Thurs.–Tues. 10–noon and 1–5, additional hrs when cruise ships are in port; Oct.–Apr., by appointment.*

---

off the beaten path

GLACIER GARDENS RAINFOREST ADVENTURE – Spread over 50 acres of rain forest 8 mi north of Juneau are ponds, waterfalls, hiking paths, a large atrium, and gardens. The roots of fallen trees, turned upside down and buried in the ground, act as bowls to hold planters that overflow with begonias, fuchsias, and petunias. Guided tours (on covered golf carts) lead you along the 4 mi of paved paths, and a 580-foot-high overlook provides dramatic views across Mendenhall Glacier. A café and gift shop are here, and the conservatory is a popular wedding spot. The city bus stops right in front of Glacier Gardens. ⊠ *7600 Glacier Hwy.* ☎ *907/790–3377* ⊕ *www.glaciergardens.com* ⊠ *$15 including guided tour* ⊘ *May–Sept., daily 9–6.*

LAST CHANCE MINING MUSEUM – A 1½-mi hike or taxi ride behind town, this small museum is housed in one of the buildings from Juneau's historic AJ Gold Mine. The collection includes old mining tools and equipment, minerals, and a 3-D map of the ore body. ⊠ *1001 Basin Rd.* ☎ *907/586–5338* ⊠ *$3* ⊘ *Mid-May–mid-Sept., daily 9:30–12:30 and 3:30–6:30.*

MACAULAY SALMON HATCHERY – Watch through an underwater window as salmon fight their way up a fish ladder, from mid-June to mid-October. Inside the hatchery you will learn about commercial fishing and the lives of salmon. A retail shop sells gifts and salmon products, and you can fish off the adjacent dock in midsummer. Fishing poles are available for rent. ⊠ *2697 Channel Dr.* ☎ *907/463–4810 or 877/463–2486* ⊕ *www.dipac.net* ⊠ *$3 including short tour* ⊘ *Mid-May–mid-Sept., weekdays 10–6, weekends 10–5; Oct.–Apr. by appointment.*

MENDENHALL GLACIER – Juneau's famous drive-up glacier, 13 mi north of downtown, spans 12 mi and is fed by the massive Juneau Icefield. Like many other Alaskan glaciers, it is slowly retreating up the valley, losing 100 feet a year as massive chunks of ice calve into the small lake separating Mendenhall from the **Mendenhall Visitor Center.** The center has exhibits on the glacier, a theater and bookstore, educational exhibits, and panoramic views. Nature trails lead along Mendenhall Lake and into the mountains overlooking Mendenhall Glacier. Several companies lead bus tours to the glacier. ⊠ *End of Glacier Spur Rd., off Mendenhall Loop Rd.* ☎ *907/789–0097* ⊕ *www.fs.fed.us/r10/tongass* ☜ *Visitor center $3* ☉ *May–Sept., daily 8–6:30; Oct.–Apr., Thurs. and Fri. 10–4, weekends 9–4.*

NATIVE VILLAGES – If you're interested in knowing how the Native Alaskan village peoples of Southeast Alaska live today, you can fly or take the state ferry *LeConte* to **Kake, Angoon,** or **Hoonah.** You won't find much organized touring in any of these communities, but you will find hotels (advance reservations are strongly suggested), and guided fishing, natural-history, and wildlife-watching trips can be arranged by asking around. In Kake, contact the **Waterfront Lodge** (⊘ Box 222, Kake 99830 ☎ 907/785–3472). In Angoon, try the **Whalers' Cove Lodge** (⊘ Box 101, Angoon 99820 ☎ 907/788–3123 or 800/423–3123 ⊕ www.whalerscovelodge.com). In Hoonah is the **Keex' Kwaan Lodge** (⊘ Box 320, Hoonah 99829 ☎ 907/945–3434 ⊕ www.kakealaska.com).

SHRINE OF ST. THERESE – A self-guided pilgrimage to the shrine is well worth the 23-mi journey from downtown Juneau (a taxi should cost at least $45). Built in the 1930s, this stone church and its 14 stations of the cross are the only inhabitants of a serene tiny island that is accessible via a 400-foot-long pedestrian causeway. Sunday services are held at 1 PM from June through August. The "honesty-box" gift shop sells crucifixes, books, T-shirts, and souvenirs. ⊠ *5933 Lund St.* ☎ *907/780–6112* ⊕ *www.shrineofsainttherese.org* ☉ *Daily.*

Where to Stay & Eat

$$$$ ✕ **Gold Creek Salmon Bake.** Trees, mountains, and the rushing water of Salmon Creek surround the comfortable, canopy-covered benches and tables at this authentic salmon bake. Fresh-caught salmon is cooked over an alder fire and served with a succulent sauce of brown sugar, margarine, and lemon juice. For $29 there's all-you-can-eat salmon, pork spareribs, and chicken along with baked beans, rice pilaf, salad, corn bread, and blueberry cake. Wine and beer are extra. After dinner you can pan for gold in the stream or wander up the hill to explore the remains of the Wagner gold mine. A round-trip bus ride from downtown is included. ⊠ *1061 Salmon Lane Rd.* ☎ *907/789–0052 or 800/323–5757* ▤ *MC, V* ☉ *Closed Oct.–Apr.*

$$–$$$$ ✕ **Dragon Inn.** This convenient downtown restaurant serves authentic Chinese meals in stylish surroundings. Chef-owner Peter Lan hails from Hong Kong and skillfully blends Alaskan seafood with Asian sauces and cooking techniques. House specialties include Singapore rice noodles with shredded pork, crispy boneless duck, and a panfried king salmon fillet served over Chinese vegetables with a light black bean sauce. Vegetarian meals are also available. For dessert, try the fried honey banana with almond slices, warm coconut sauce, and caramel. Alcohol isn't served, and you can't bring in your own. ⊠ *213 Front St.* ☎ *907/586–4888* ▤ *MC, V* ☉ *Closed Sun. No lunch Sat.*

$$–$$$$ ✕ **The Fiddlehead.** Juneau's favorite restaurant is actually two dining spots
FodorsChoice in one, both smoke-free. Downstairs you can get a casual breakfast, lunch,
★ or dinner in a bright room accented by stained glass and modern art. The menu includes plenty of vegetarian items and an eclectic assortment

of entrées ranging from fisherman's pie to Black Angus meat loaf. Homemade bread and cookies from the restaurant's bakery are always a hit. Di Sopra, upstairs, is more formal, with a full bar, music on summer weekends, and a heartier menu that includes Sicilian fisherman's stew, pasta, and daily fresh ravioli specials. ✉ *429 Willoughby Ave.* ☎ *907/586–3150* 🖃 *AE, D, DC, MC, V.*

★ **$$–$$$$** ✕ **Summit Restaurant.** Built in 1889, this building served as a brothel until 1958 and now operates as an upscale restaurant. The restaurant, an intimate candlelighted place with a copper-top bar and a dozen tables, serves such specialties as rack of lamb, filet mignon, and pan-seared duck, along with a delectable vanilla crème brûlée. Upstairs, the Inn at the Waterfront provides reasonably priced but cramped lodging, with shared bathrooms down the hall. ✉ *455 S. Franklin St., 99801* ☎ *907/586–2050* 🖶 *907/586–2999* ⌦ *Reservations essential* 🖃 *AE, D, DC, MC, V* ☾ *No lunch in winter.*

$$$ ✕ **Thane Ore House Salmon Bake.** Four miles south of town is this $20 all-you-can-eat restaurant with a waterside setting and indoor dining; it's one of the oldest and most authentic salmon bakes in the state. Your meal includes salmon, halibut, barbecued beef ribs, salad, baked beans, and corn bread. A free round-trip bus ride from downtown hotels is included. ✉ *4400 Thane Rd., 4 mi south of Juneau* ☎ *907/586–3442* 🖃 *MC, V* ☾ *Closed Oct.–Apr.*

$–$$$ ✕ **Hangar on the Wharf.** Crowded with both locals and travelers, the Hangar is in the building where Alaska Airlines started business. The comfortably worn wood, stainless-steel accents, and vintage airplane photos create a casual dining experience. There are expansive views of Gastineau Channel and Douglas Island from every seat. A wide selection of entrées, including locally caught halibut and salmon, jambalaya, filet mignon, and great burgers, makes this a Juneau hot spot. You'll also find two dozen draft beers available. On Friday and Saturday nights, jazz or rock bands take over the Hangar's stage. ✉ *2 Marine Way, Merchants Wharf Mall* ☎ *907/586–5018* 🖃 *AE, D, MC, V.*

¢–$ ✕ **BaCar's.** This is the spot for hearty, inexpensive breakfasts and satisfying lunches. Fluffy omelets are $9 and come with home fries and a big side pancake. Lunches, including the halibut fish-and-chips, prime rib, and French dips, are simple but good. There are also a few interesting variations on diner standards, such as a salmon melt and tempura Spam strips. ✉ *230 Seward St.* ☎ *907/463–4202* 🖃 *AE, MC, V* ☾ *No dinner.*

$$$$ 🏨 **Pearson's Pond Luxury Inn and Adventure Spa.** Built on a small lake facing Mendenhall Glacier, this large home has a three-tier deck with two hot tubs. Rooms vary in size and one is quite small: ask for one of the two large ones with water views, cathedral ceilings, and small lofts. All rooms include either whirlpool tubs or fireplaces, plus kitchenettes stocked for make-it-yourself breakfasts. There's yoga on the deck each morning and wine and cheese in the evening. The owners also have two condos closer to town, which sleep four people each. There's a two-night minimum stay. ✉ *4541 Sawa Cir., 99801* ☎ *907/789–3772 or 888/658–6328* 🖶 *907/789–6722* ⊕ *www.pearsonspond.com* ⬱ *3 suites* ⌂ *Some in-room hot tubs, kitchenettes, cable TV, in-room VCRs, massage, boating, bicycles, Internet, meeting room; no a/c, no smoking* 🖃 *AE, D, DC, MC, V.*

$$–$$$$ 🏨 **Alaska's Capital Inn.** Gold-rush pioneer John Olds built this American foursquare home in 1906, and a major restoration in 2003 transformed it into Juneau's most elegant B&B. Rooms are furnished in Arts and Crafts pieces, blending a nostalgic charm with such modern conveniences as an outdoor hot tub, in-room phones, TV/VCRs, and high-speed Internet access. The Governor's Suite covers the entire fourth floor

Fodor'sChoice
★

and includes a king-size sleigh bed, gas fireplace, and hot tub. Two small rooms on the bottom level have private entrances. Breakfast is a highlight, with a variety of Alaskan seafood dishes. This B&B fills quickly for the summer season. ⊠ *113 W. 5th St., 99801* ☎ *907/586–6507 or 888/588–6507* 🖷 *907/586–6508* ⊕ *www.alaskacapitalinn.com* ⇋ *4 rooms, 3 suites* ♦ *Hot tub, cable TV, in-room VCRs, Internet; no a/c, no kids under 12* ⊟ *AE, D, MC, V* ◯ *CP.*

$$–$$$$ ▨ **Baranof Hotel.** The Baranof has long been Juneau's most prestigious address. Tasteful woods and period lamps in the dark art-deco lobby create an atmosphere reminiscent of 1939, when the hotel first opened. Downstairs dining is available in a casual restaurant as well as in the luxurious Gold Room. Rooms on the front side have the best views, but street noises may keep you awake at the lower levels. The best are spacious corner suites on the upper floors, which overlook Juneau's busy harbor to the forested mountains of Douglas Island. ⊠ *127 N. Franklin St., 99801* ☎ *907/586–2660 or 800/544–0970* 🖷 *907/586–8315* ⊕ *www.westmarkhotels.com* ⇋ *179 rooms, 17 suites* ♦ *Restaurant, coffee shop, some kitchenettes, hair salon, lobby lounge, meeting room, travel services* ⊟ *AE, D, DC, MC, V.*

$$–$$$ ▨ **Goldbelt Hotel Juneau.** A high-rise by local standards, the seven-story Goldbelt is one of Juneau's better lodging places, with well-appointed rooms that include touches such as speaker phones, hair dryers, and irons. Waterside rooms on the upper level have views across Gastineau Channel, and some rooms have king-size beds. A Chilkat blanket and other artifacts are displayed in the lobby, and the adjacent Chinook's restaurant serves three meals a day. ⊠ *51 W. Egan Dr., 99801* ☎ *907/586–6900 or 888/478–6909* 🖷 *907/463–3567* ⊕ *www.goldbelt.com* ⇋ *104 rooms, 1 suite* ♦ *Restaurant, room service, cable TV with movies, lounge, meeting room, airport shuttle; no a/c* ⊟ *AE, D, DC, MC, V.*

$$ ▨ **Aspen Hotel.** This corporate-style inn, within walking distance of the airport and 9 mi from downtown, is perfect for business travelers and families. Rooms are large and clean, with in-room refrigerators and microwaves. This is also one of the few Juneau lodging options with a full-size indoor pool. ⊠ *1800 Shell Simmons Dr., 99801* ☎ *907/790–6435 or 866/483–7848* 🖷 *907/790–6621* ⊕ *www.aspenhotelsak.com* ⇋ *94 rooms* ♦ *Kitchenettes, microwaves, refrigerators, cable TV, indoor pool, exercise equipment, hot tub, Internet, business services, meeting rooms, airport shuttle* ⊟ *AE, D, MC, V* ◯ *CP.*

$$ ▨ **Grandma's Feather Bed.** This small Victorian-style hotel is part of the Best Western chain and is less than a mile from the airport in Mendenhall Valley. Cheerful colors brighten each of the spacious rooms, which come with jetted bathtubs and feather comforters. A complimentary breakfast buffet is included. ⊠ *2348 Mendenhall Loop Rd., 99801* ☎ *907/789–5566 or 888/781–5005* 🖷 *907/789–2818* ⇋ *14 rooms* ♦ *Restaurant, microwaves, refrigerators, cable TV, Internet, business services, airport shuttle, some pets allowed (fee); no smoking* ⊟ *AE, D, DC, MC, V* ◯ *CP.*

$–$$ ▨ **Frontier Suites Airport Hotel.** Near the airport in Mendenhall Valley, 9 mi from Juneau, this rambling hotel is a great option for families. All rooms have modern, functional furniture and full kitchens with a stove, refrigerator, microwave, dishes, silverware, and pans. Suites have separate bedrooms and living rooms (with sleeper sofas) and two televisions. Two bunk rooms include a mini-loft for older children. JR's Cafe, downstairs, serves standard American fare. ⊠ *9400 Glacier Hwy., 99801* ☎ *907/790–6600 or 800/544–2250* 🖷 *907/790–6612* ⊕ *www. frontiersuites.com* ⇋ *104 rooms, 32 suites* ♦ *Restaurant, café, kitchens, microwaves, refrigerators, bar; no a/c* ⊟ *AE, D, DC, MC, V.*

$-$$ ⊞ **The Prospector Hotel.** A short walk west of downtown and next door to the Alaska State Museum, this nicely appointed hotel is frequented by business travelers and legislators (during the winter session). Rooms are spacious and have cherrywood furnishings, refrigerators, and microwaves. T. K. McGuire's dining room and lounge serves prime rib, steaks, and seafood, along with a popular Sunday brunch. ⊠ *375 Whittier St., 99801* ☎ *907/586-3737, 800/331-2711 outside Alaska, 800/478-5866 in Alaska* ⊕ *907/586-1204* ⊕ *www.prospectorhotel.com* ⊸ *14 rooms, 44 suites* ⚭ *Restaurant, kitchenettes, microwaves, refrigerators, cable TV, lobby lounge, meeting rooms, some pets allowed (fee); no a/c* ⊟ *AE, D, DC, MC, V.*

$ ⊞ **Sentinel Island Lighthouse.** A few miles north of Juneau and adjacent to a rock where Steller's sea lions haul out, this operating lighthouse provides a spectacular spot to watch whales and eagles. You have the entire 6-acre island to roam around on. Simple accommodations include bunks in the lighthouse and in an adjacent building; you can also pitch a tent on a platform facing the water. Water and cooking facilities are provided for all accommodations. The lighthouse is managed by Gastineau Channel Historical Society, and access is by charter boat, sea kayak, or helicopter. ✑ *Box 21264, Juneau 99802* ☎ *907/586-5338* ⊸ *6 bunks in 2 buildings* ⊟ *No credit cards.*

★ **¢-$** ⊞ **Alaskan Hotel.** This historic 1913 hotel in the heart of downtown Juneau sits over the popular bar of the same name; rooms can be a bit noisy from Thursday through Saturday nights when bands are playing. The older but well-maintained guest rooms ramble across three floors and include pedestal sinks, old-fashioned radiators, and a smattering of antiques. The flocked wallpaper, red floral carpets, and Tiffany windows are reminiscent of the hotel's original gold rush–era opulence. The least-expensive rooms share a bath down the hall. ⊠ *167 S. Franklin St., 99801* ☎ *907/586-1000 or 800/327-9347* ⊕ *907/463-3775* ⊕ *www.ptialaska.net/~akhotel* ⊸ *42 rooms, 22 with bath* ⚭ *Bar; no a/c, no phones in some rooms, no TV in some rooms* ⊟ *D, DC, MC, V.*

¢ ⊞ **U.S. Forest Service Cabins.** Scattered throughout Tongass National Forest, these rustic cabins offer a charming and cheap escape for just $25–$45 per cabin. Most are fly-in units, accessible by floatplanes from virtually any community in the Southeast. These public-use cabins have bunks for six to eight occupants, tables, stoves, and outdoor privies but no electricity or running water. You provide your own sleeping bag, food, and cooking utensils. Bedside reading in most cabins includes a diary kept by visitors—add your own adventure. ⊠ *Juneau Ranger District, 8465 Old Dairy Rd., Juneau 99801* ☎ *907/586-8800, 877/444-6777 reservations* ⊕ *www.reserveusa.com* ⊸ *150 cabins* ⊟ *AE, D, MC, V.*

Fodor'sChoice
★

¢ ⚠ **U.S. Forest Service Campgrounds.** Eight Forest Service–maintained campgrounds are scattered around Tongass National Forest and are accessible from the communities of Juneau, Sitka, Ketchikan, Petersburg, and Thorne Bay. All have pit toilets and sites for RVs and tents, but not all provide drinking water. Reservations are possible for some of these campgrounds, but space is generally available without a reservation. ⊠ *Juneau Ranger District, 8465 Old Dairy Rd., Juneau 99801* ☎ *907/586-8800, 877/444-6777 reservations* ⊕ *www.reserveusa.com* ⊟ *D, MC, V.*

Guided Tours

Boating & Kayaking

Alaska Travel Adventures (☎ 907/789-0052 or 800/478-0052 ⊕ www.alaskaadventures.com) leads Mendenhall River floats. The Native-owned **Auk Ta Shaa Discovery** (☎ 907/586-8687 or 800/820-2628

⊕ www.goldbelttours.com) also guides rafting trips down the Mendenhall River.

Alaska Fjordlines (☎ 907/766–3395 or 800/320–0146 ⊕ www.alaskafjordlines.com) provides passenger ferry service connecting Juneau with Haines and Skagway on a daily basis in the summer. **Auk Nu Tours** (☎ 907/586–8687 or 800/820–2628 ⊕ www.goldbelttours.com) has all-day catamaran tours to the beautiful glaciers of Tracy Arm Fjord.

Helicopter Flightseeing

Several local companies operate helicopter flightseeing trips that take you to the spectacular glaciers flowing from Juneau Icefield. Most have booths along the downtown cruise-ship dock. All include a touchdown on a glacier, with a chance to romp on these rivers of ice. Some also lead trips that include a dogsled ride on the glacier. Note that though we recommend the best companies, even some of the most experienced pilots have been killed in helicopter accidents; always ask a carrier about their recent safety record before booking a trip. Flightseeing is quite controversial in Juneau, where locals are concerned over noise from the almost constant din of helicopter activity throughout the summer. **Coastal Helicopters** (☎ 907/789–5600 ⊕ www.coastalhelicopters.com) lands on several glaciers within the Juneau Icefield. **ERA Helicopters** (☎ 907/586–2030 or 800/843–1947 ⊕ www.eraaviation.com) has a one-hour trip that includes landing on Norris Glacier. **Northstar Trekking** (☎ 907/790–4530 ⊕ www.glaciertrekking.com) leads an excellent two-hour glacier hike. **Temsco Helicopters** (☎ 907/789–9501 or 877/789–9501 ⊕ www.temscoair.com) lands on Mendenhall Glacier.

Sightseeing

For biologist-guided wheelchair-accessible tours around Juneau, contact **AKcess Eco-Tours** (☎ 907/789–2090 ⊕ www.akess.org). **Juneau Trolley Car Company** (☎ 907/586–7433 ⊕ www.juneautrolley.com) conducts narrated tours, stopping at a dozen or so of Juneau's historic and shopping attractions for $12. **Mendenhall Glacier Tours** (☎ 907/789–5460 ⊕ www.mightygreattrips.com) leads guided bus tours that include a visit to Mendenhall Glacier. The **Juneau Convention and Visitors Bureau** (☎ 907/586–2201 or 888/581–2201 ⊕ www.traveljuneau.com) has a list of other companies that provide tours to Mendenhall Glacier.

Former miners lead three-hour tours of the historic **AJ Gold Mine** (☎ 907/463–5017) south of Juneau. A gold-panning demonstration is included, and approximately 45 minutes of the tour take place inside the old tunnels that lace the mountains. Mine tours depart from downtown by bus.

Taku Glacier Lodge (☎ 907/586–8258 🖷 907/789–6970 ⊕ www.takuglacierlodge.com) is a remote, historic lodge south of Juneau along Taku Inlet. Hole-in-the-Wall Glacier is directly across the inlet from the lodge, and nature trails wind through the surrounding country, where black bears and bald eagles are frequently sighted. Floatplanes fly from Juneau on a scenic trip to the lodge, where you are served a delicious lunch or dinner and then flown back three hours later. No overnight stays are available.

Nightlife & the Arts

Bars

The **Alaskan Hotel bar** (✉ 167 S. Franklin St. ☎ 907/586–1000) is about as funky a place as you'll find in Juneau: flocked-velvet walls, antique chandeliers above the bar, and vintage Alaskan frontier-brothel decor. Sit back and enjoy the live music or take turns with the locals at the open mike. When the ships are in, the music at **Red Dog Saloon** (⊠ 278 S. Franklin St. ☎ 907/463–9954) is live and the crowd gets livelier.

If you're a beer fan, look for **Alaskan Brewing Company**'s (⊠ 5429 Shaune Dr. ☎ 907/780–5866 ⊕ www.alaskanbeer.com) Alaskan Amber, Pale Ale, Stout, ESB, and Smoked Porter beer, brewed and bottled in Juneau. You can also visit the microbrewery and sample various brews while touring the bottling operation May–September, Monday–Saturday 11–5, with tours every half hour; or October–April, Thursday–Saturday 11–4.

Music Festivals

The annual weeklong **Alaska Folk Festival** (✑ Box 21748, 99802 ☎ 907/ 463–3316 ⊕ www.juneau.com/aff) is staged each April in Juneau, drawing singers, banjo masters, fiddlers, and even cloggers from all over the state. During the last week of May, Juneau is the scene of **Juneau Jazz 'n Classics** (✑ Box 22152, 99802 ☎ 907/463–3378 ⊕ www. jazzandclassics.org), which celebrates music from Bach to Brubeck.

Theater

Southeast Alaska's only professional theater company, **Perseverance Theatre** (⊠ 914 3rd St., Douglas ☎ 907/364–2421 ⊕ www. perseverancetheatre.org) presents everything from Broadway and Shakespeare to locally written plays year-round.

Sports & the Outdoors

Climbing Gym

South of Juneau off Thane Road, the **Rock Dump** (⊠ 1310 Eastaugh Way ☎ 907/586–4982 ⊕ www.rockdump.com) is a large indoor climbing facility with something for all abilities.

Cross-Country Skiing

During the winter, the **Parks and Recreation Department** (☎ 907/586– 5226, 907/586–0428 24-hr info ⊕ www.juneau.lib.ak.us/parksrec) sponsors a group ski and snowshoe outing each Wednesday and Saturday when there's sufficient snow. You can rent skis and get advice about touring the trails and ridges around town from **Foggy Mountain Shop** (⊠ 134 N. Franklin St. ☎ 907/586–6780 ⊕ www. foggymountainshop.com).

Downhill Skiing

The only downhill area in Southeast Alaska, **Eaglecrest** (⊠ 155 S. Seward St., Juneau 99801 ☎ 907/790–2000, 907/586–5330 recorded ski information ⊕ www.juneau.org/eaglecrest), on Douglas Island, just 30 minutes from downtown Juneau, offers late-November to mid-April skiing and snowboarding on a well-groomed mountain with two double chairlifts, cross-country trails, a beginner's platter pull, ski school, ski-rental shop, cafeteria, and trilevel day lodge. Enjoy the northern lights while you night-ski from January through mid-March.

Fitness Clubs

The **Juneau Racquet Club/Alaska Club** (⊠ 2841 Riverside Dr. ☎ 907/789– 2181 ⊕ www.thealaskaclub.com), about 10 mi north of downtown, adjacent to Mendenhall Mall, houses first-class indoor tennis and racquetball courts. There's a $9 daily fee for nonmembers. Other facilities include sauna, hot tub, exercise equipment, massage tables, sports shop, and snack bar. **JRC/Alaska Club Downtown** (⊠ W. Willoughby Ave. ☎ 907/ 586–5773) is a smaller version of the JRC on Riverside Drive. It's a $9 charge per day for nonmembers.

Gold Panning

Gold panning is fun, especially for children, and Juneau is one of the Southeast's best-known gold-panning towns. Sometimes you actually uncover a few flecks of the precious metal in the bottom of your pan. You can buy a pan at almost any Alaska hardware or sporting-goods store. **Alaska Travel Adventures** (☎ 907/789–0052 or 800/478–0052 ⊕ www.alaskaadventures.com) has gold-panning tours near the famous Alaska-Juneau Mine.

Golf

Juneau's par-three, 9-hole **Mendenhall Golf Course** (✉ 2101 Industrial Blvd. ☎ 907/789–1221) is pretty modest but does rent clubs and has spectacular views.

Hiking

The **Parks and Recreation Department** (☎ 907/586–5226, 907/586–0428 24-hr info ⊕ www.juneau.lib.ak.us/parksrec) in Juneau sponsors a group hike each Wednesday morning and on Saturday in summer. Hikers can contact the **U.S. Forest Service** (☎ 907/586–8790) for trail books and maps.

Sea Kayaking & Canoeing

Experienced kayakers can rent boats and equipment from **Alaska Boat and Kayak** (☎ 907/586–8220 ⊕ www.juneaukayak.com) in Douglas. **Alaska Travel Adventures** (☎ 907/789–0052 ⊕ www.alaskaadventures. com) conducts sea-kayaking trips to Mendenhall Glacier. **Auk Ta Shaa Discovery** (☎ 907/586–8687 or 800/820–2628 ⊕ www.goldbelttours. com) operates sea-kayaking trips in the Juneau area.

Shopping

Art Galleries

Annie Kaill's Gallery (✉ 244 Front St. ☎ 907/586–2880) displays a mix of playful and whimsical original prints, pottery, jewelry, and other arts and crafts from Alaskan artists. The cooperatively run **Juneau Artists Gallery** (✉ 175 S. Franklin St. ☎ 907/586–9891), on the first floor of the old Senate Building, sells watercolors, jewelry, etchings, photographs, art glass, ceramics, and quilts from more than 20 artists. Head upstairs above Heritage Coffee for **Wm. Spear Designs** (✉ 174 S. Franklin St. ☎ 907/586–2209 ⊕ www.wmspear.com), where this lawyer-turned-artist produces a fun and colorful collection of enameled pins and zipper pulls. The **Raven's Journey** across from the tram (✉ 439 S. Franklin St. ☎ 907/463–4686) specializes in high-quality Native Alaskan masks, grass baskets, carvings, dolls, ivory and silver jewelry, and more.

Rie Muñoz, of the **Rie Muñoz Gallery** (✉ 2101 Jordan Ave. ☎ 907/789–7411 ⊕ www.riemunoz.com) in Mendenhall Valley, is one of Alaska's best-known artists, creator of a stylized, simple, and colorful design technique that is much copied but rarely equaled. Other artists' work is also on sale at the Muñoz Gallery, including wood-block prints by nationally recognized artist Dale DeArmond. Various books illustrated by Rie Muñoz and written by Alaskan children's author Jean Rogers are for sale. In downtown Juneau, see Rie Muñoz's paintings and tapestries at **Decker Gallery** (✉ 233 S. Franklin St. ☎ 907/463–5536 or 800/463–5536).

Clothing

Kodiak Coat (✉ 174 S. Franklin St., Suite 108 ☎ 907/463–2625 ⊕ www. kodiakcoat.com) occupies a small shop inside the Emporium Mall. The owner designs and sews waterproof and breathable coats, hats, and mittens, all made to withstand Alaska's rugged climate. Her kids' coats are especially worth a look.

Seafood

Taku Smokeries (✉ 550 S. Franklin St. ☎ 907/463–5033 or 800/582–5122 ⊕ www.takusmokeries.com), at the south end of town near the cruise-ship docks, processes nearly 6 million pounds of fish, mostly salmon, a year. You can view the smoking procedure through large windows and then purchase the packaged fish in the deli-style gift shop or have some shipped back home.

ADMIRALTY ISLAND, GLACIER BAY NATIONAL PARK & PRESERVE

Admiralty Island

⑤⑧ *10 mi west of Juneau.*

The island is famous for its lush rain forests and abundant wildlife, including one of the largest concentrations of brown bears anywhere on the planet. The island's Tlingit inhabitants called it Kootznoowoo, meaning "fortress of the bears." Ninety-six miles long, with 678 mi of coastline, Admiralty—the second-largest island in Southeast Alaska—is home to an estimated 1,500 bears, or almost one per square mile. **Admiralty Island National Monument** has a system of public-use cabins, a canoe route that crosses the island via a chain of lakes and trails, the world's highest density of nesting bald eagles, large concentrations of humpback whales, and some of the region's best sea kayaking and sportfishing. ✉ *8461 Old Dairy Rd., Juneau 99801* ☎ *907/586–8790.*

★ More than 90% of Admiralty Island is preserved within the Kootznoowoo Wilderness. Its chief attraction is **Pack Creek**, where you can watch brown bears feeding on salmon. One of Alaska's premier bear-viewing sites, Pack Creek is co-managed by the U.S. Forest Service and the Alaska Department of Fish and Game. Permits are required during the main viewing season, from June 1 through September 10, and only 24 people per day are allowed to visit Pack Creek from July 5 through August 25. Reservations can be mailed to the Forest Service beginning February 20. ✉ *8461 Old Dairy Rd., Juneau 99801* ☎ *907/586–8800* ⊕ *www.fs.fed.us/r10/tongass* ✇ *$50.*

Where to Stay

★ **$$$$** 🏠 **Thayer Lake Lodge.** One of Southeast's oldest lodges, Thayer Lake is on the sandy shores of a 9-mi lake within the Admiralty Island National Monument. Built in 1952 by Bob and Edith Nelson and now run by their grandkids, this rustic lodge with cabins houses up to 10 people (5 in each cabin). Borrow a canoe or motorboat for unsurpassed cutthroat and Dolly Varden trout fishing. Simple family-style meals are served. Packages are available, but rates are $700 per person per night for lodging, all meals, bear excursions, fishing, other activities, and guides. ✇ *Box 8897, Ketchikan 99901* ☎ *907/789–5646 in summer, 907/247–8897 in winter* 🖶 *907/247–7053* ⊕ *www.alaskabearviewing.com* ⇌ *2 cabins* ⚭ *Dining room, kitchenettes, boating, fishing, hiking* ⊟ *MC, V* ⊘ *Closed mid-Sept.–late May.*

Guided Tours

Alaska Discovery (✉ 5310 Glacier Hwy., Juneau ☎ 907/780–6226 or 800/586–1911 🖶 907/780–4220 ⊕ www.akdiscovery.com) leads single- and multiday trips to Pack Creek that include a floatplane trip, sea kayaking, and guided bear viewing. **Ward Air** (☎ 907/789–9150 ⊕ www.wardair.com) conducts flightseeing trips to Glacier Bay and the Juneau Icefield. **Wings of Alaska** (☎ 907/789–0790 ⊕ www.wingsofalaska.com) leads flightseeing trips to many areas around Juneau.

Glacier Bay National Park & Preserve

59 *60 mi northwest of Juneau.*

Near the northern end of the Inside Passage, Glacier Bay National Park and Preserve is one of the jewels of the entire national park system. Visiting Glacier Bay is like stepping back into the Little Ice Age—it's one of the few places in the world where you can approach massive tide-water glaciers. With a noise that sounds like cannons firing, bergs the size of 10-story office buildings sometimes come crashing from the "snout" of a glacier. The crash sends tons of water and spray skyward, and it propels mini–tidal waves outward from the point of impact. **Johns Hopkins Glacier** calves so often and with such volume that large cruise ships can seldom come within 2 mi of its face.

Glacier Bay is a still-forming body of water fed by the runoff of the ice fields, glaciers, and mountains that surround it. Captain James Cook and then Captain George Vancouver sailed by Glacier Bay and didn't even know it. At the time of Vancouver's sailing in 1794, the bay was hidden behind and beneath a vast glacial wall of ice. The glacier face was more than 20 mi across and in places more than 4,000 feet in depth. It extended more than 100 mi to its origins in the St. Elias Mountain Range. Since then, due to warming weather and other factors not fully understood, the face of the glacial ice has melted and retreated with amazing speed, exposing 65 mi of fjords, islands, and inlets.

It was Vancouver who named the magnificent snow-clad **Mt. Fairweather,** which towers over the head of the bay. Legend has it that Vancouver named Fairweather on one of the Southeast's most beautiful blue days—and the mountain was not seen again during the following century. That's an exaggeration, to be sure, but overcast, rainy weather is certainly the norm here.

In 1879, about a century after Vancouver's sail-by, one of the earliest white visitors to what is now Glacier Bay National Park and Preserve came calling. Naturalist John Muir was drawn by the flora and fauna that had followed in the wake of glacial withdrawals and fascinated by the vast ice rivers that descended from the mountains to tidewater. Today the naturalist's namesake glacier, like others in the park, continues to retreat dramatically. Its terminus is now scores of miles farther up the bay from the small cabin he built at its face during his time there.

Glacier Bay is a marvelous laboratory for naturalists of all persuasions. Glaciologists, of course, can have a field day. Animal lovers can hope to see the rare glacial "blue" bears of the area, a variation of the black bear, which is here along with the brown bear; whales feasting on krill; mountain goats in late spring and early summer; and seals on floating icebergs. Birders can look for the more than 200 species that have already been spotted in the park, and if you're lucky, you may witness two bald eagles engaging in aerobatics.

A remarkable panorama of plants unfolds from the head of the bay, which is just emerging from the ice, to the mouth, which has been ice-free for more than 200 years. In between, the primitive plants—algae, lichens, and mosses—that are the first to take hold of the bare, wet ground give way to more complex species: flowering plants such as the magenta dwarf fireweed and the creamy dryas, which in turn merge with willows, alders, and cottonwood. As the living plants mature and die, they enrich the soil and prepare it for new species to follow. The climax of the plant community is the lush spruce-and-hemlock rain forest, rich in life

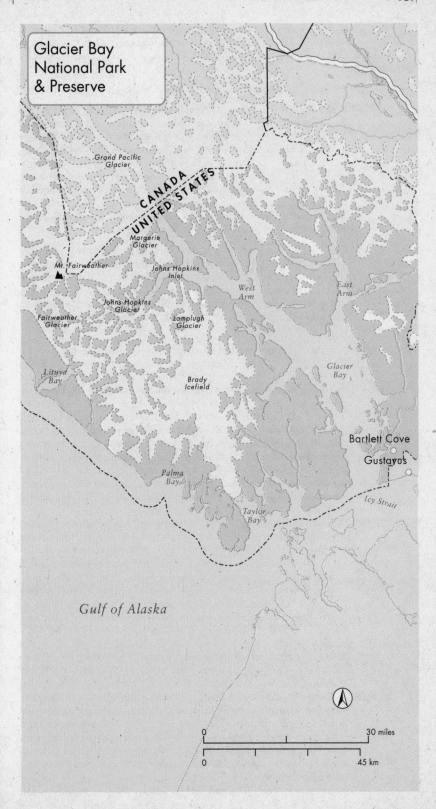

Glacier Bay
National Park
& Preserve

Grand Pacific
Glacier

CANADA
UNITED STATES

Margerie
Glacier

Mt. Fairweather

Johns Hopkins
Inlet

West
Arm

East
Arm

Johns Hopkins
Glacier

Lamplugh
Glacier

Fairweather
Glacier

Lituya
Bay

Brady
Icefield

Glacier
Bay

Bartlett Cove

Gustavus

Palma
Bay

Icy Strait

Taylor
Bay

Gulf of Alaska

0   30 miles

0   45 km

and blanketing the land around **Bartlett Cove.** ✆ *Box 140, Gustavus 99826* ☎ *907/697–2230* ⊕ *www.nps.gov/glba.*

Gustavus

⑥⓪ *50 mi west of Juneau, 75 mi south of Skagway.*

For airborne visitors, Gustavus is the gateway to Glacier Bay National Park. The long, paved jet airport, built as a refueling strip during World War II, is one of the best and longest in Southeast Alaska, all the more impressive because of its limited facilities at the field. Alaska Airlines, which serves Gustavus daily in the summer, has a large, rustic terminal at the site, and from a free telephone on the front porch of the terminal you can call any of the local hostelries for a courtesy pickup. Smaller, light-aircraft companies that serve the community out of Juneau also have on-site shelters. In addition a daily passenger ferry provides service between Juneau and Gustavus throughout the summer.

Gustavus has no downtown. In fact, Gustavus is not a town at all. The 150 or so year-round residents are most emphatic on this point; they regularly vote down incorporation. Instead, Gustavus is a scattering of homes, farmsteads, arts-and-crafts studios, fishing and guiding charters, and other tiny enterprises peopled by hospitable individualists. It is, in many ways, a contemporary example of the frontier spirit in Alaska.

Where to Stay & Eat

$$$$ ✕⊡ **Bear Track Inn.** Built of handcrafted spruce logs, this inn sits on a 57-acre property facing Icy Strait. Soaring ceilings open up the lobby, where a central fireplace, overstuffed couches, rustic wooden tables, and moose-antler chandeliers invite relaxation. Spacious guest rooms are luxuriously furnished, and a full-service restaurant (open to the public for dinner; $32) specializes in seafood but also serves steak, pork chops, and even wild game. Room rates start at $454 per person per night (there are better prices for multiple-night packages), including air transport from Juneau and meals. ⊠ *255 Rink Creek Rd., 99826* ☎ *907/697–3017 or 888/697–2284* 🖷 *907/697–2284* ⊕ *www.beartrackinn.com* 🛏 *14 rooms* ♿ *Restaurant, boating, fishing, hiking, Internet, airport shuttle, some pets allowed; no a/c, no room phones, no room TVs, no smoking* 🚭 *D, MC, V* ⑩ *FAP* ⊘ *Closed Oct.–Apr.*

$$$ ✕⊡ **Glacier Bay Lodge.** Within the national park, this lodge is constructed of massive timbers and blends well into the thick rain forest surrounding it on three sides. The modern yet rustic rooms are accessible by boardwalks. If it swims or crawls in the sea hereabouts, you'll find it on the menu in the rustic dining room, which is open to non-lodge guests as well. One favorite is the halibut baked *aleyeska,* a fillet baked in a rich sauce of sour cream, cheese, and onions. Activities include whale-watching, kayaking, and naturalist-led hikes. ✆ *Box 266, Gustavus 99826* ✆ *226 2nd Ave. W, Seattle, WA 98119* ☎ *907/697–2226 in summer, 800/451–5952* 🖷 *206/623–7809* ⊕ *www. glacierbaytours.com* 🛏 *56 rooms* ♿ *Restaurant, boating, bicycles; no a/c, no room phones, no room TVs* 🚭 *AE, D, DC, MC, V* ⑩ *FAP* ⊘ *Closed mid-Sept.–mid-May.*

★ $$$$ ⊡ **Glacier Bay Country Inn.** Bears and moose might peek into this rambling log structure with its marvelous cupolas, dormers, gables, and porches. Some cabins include antiques and open log-beam ceilings. Innkeepers Ponch and Sandi Marchbanks offer charter-fishing trips (extra charge) and a variety of sightseeing options. Meals are included in the room rate. Among the guests' favorites are steamed Dungeness crab, ale-marinated alder-grilled salmon, and crème brûlée. ✢ *Halfway between airport and Bartlett Cove* ✆ *Box 5, 99826* ☎ *907/697–2288* or 800/628–0912 ⊞ 907/697–2289 ⊕ www.glacierbayalaska.com ⇔ 5 rooms, 5 cabins ⚐ Restaurant, boating, fishing, Internet; no a/c, no room phones, no room TVs, no smoking ⊟ AE, D, MC, V ⎮⊙⎮ FAP ⊙ Closed mid-Sept.–mid-May.

$$$$
Fodor'sChoice
★

⊞ **Gustavus Inn.** Built in 1928 and established as a hotel in 1965, this inn continues a tradition of gracious Alaska rural living. In the remodeled original homestead building, rooms are decorated in New England–farmhouse style. Here you can indulge in Glacier Bay sightseeing trips, fishing expeditions, bicycle rides around the community, and berry picking in season. Hosts David and Jo Ann Lesh heap bountiful servings of seafood and fresh vegetables on the plates of overnight guests (all meals are included in the price) and others who reserve for family-style meals in the cozy farmhouse-style dining room in advance ($30). Dinnertime is 6:30 sharp. ⊠ Mile 1, Gustavus Rd. ⊕ Box 60, 99826 ☎ 907/697–2254 or 800/649–5220 ⊞ 907/697–2255 ⊕ www. gustavusinn.com ⇔ 13 rooms, 11 with bath ⚐ Restaurant, fishing, Internet, airport shuttle; no a/c, no room phones, no room TVs, no smoking ⊟ AE, MC, V ⊙ Closed mid-Sept.–mid-May ⎮⊙⎮ FAP.

$$$–$$$$

⊞ **Annie Mae Lodge.** This quiet two-story lodge, one of the few Gustavus places open year-round, faces the Goode River and is a five-minute walk from the beach. Seven guest rooms have doors that open to a wraparound veranda; one room is entirely wheelchair accessible. Lodging includes three meals a day plus ground transportation. Kayaking, flightseeing, Glacier Bay cruises, and other activities are arranged by the owner. ⊕ Box 55, 99826 ☎ 907/697–2346 or 800/478–2346 ⊕ www.anniemae. com ⇔ 11 rooms, 9 with bath ⚐ Internet; no a/c, no room phones, no room TVs, no smoking ⊟ AE, D, DC, MC, V ⎮⊙⎮ FAP.

Guided Tours

Glacier Bay is best experienced from the water, whether from the deck of a cruise ship, on a tour boat, or from the level of a sea kayak. National Park Service naturalists come aboard to explain the great glaciers; to point out features of the forests, islands, and mountains; and to help spot black bears, brown bears, mountain goats, whales, porpoises, and birds.

Air Excursions (☎ 907/697–2375, 800/354–2479 in Alaska, ⊕ www. airexcursions.com) operates Glacier Bay flightseeing tours from Gustavus, plus flights to Juneau several times a day in the summer. **Glacier Bay Cruiseline** (☎ 907/697–2226 in summer, 800/451–5952 year-round ⊕ www.glacierbaytours.com) provides daily boat tours from the dock at Bartlett Cove, near Glacier Bay Lodge. These all-day trips into Glacier Bay have Park Service naturalists aboard the *Spirit of Adventure*. Campers and sea kayakers heading up the bay ride the same boat. A separate Glacier Bay Cruiseline vessel provides daily passenger ferry service between Juneau and Gustavus in the summer.

Sports & the Outdoors

SEA KAYAKING The most adventurous way to explore Glacier Bay is by paddling your own kayak through the bay's icy waters and inlets. But unless you're an expert, you're better off signing on with the guided tours. You can book a five- or eight-day guided expedition through **Alaska Discovery** (⊠ 5310 Glacier Hwy., Juneau 99801 ☎ 907/780–6226 or 800/586–1911 ⊕ www.akdiscovery.com). Alaska Discovery provides safe, seaworthy kayaks and tents, gear, and food. Its guides are tough, knowledgeable Alaskans, and they've spent enough time in Glacier Bay's wild country to know what's safe and what's not. You can also take a guided one-day kayak trip from Bartlett Cove if you're just looking for a chance to explore the area. **Spirit Walker Expeditions** (⊕ Box 240, 99826 ☎ 907/

697–2266 or 800/529–2537 ☎ 907/697–2701 ⊕ www.seakayakalaska.com) leads 1- to 10-day sea-kayaking trips to various parts of Icy Strait (but not within Glacier Bay itself).

Kayak rentals for unescorted Glacier Bay exploring and camping can be arranged through **Glacier Bay Sea Kayaks** (✉ Bartlett Cove ⛺ Box 26, 99826 ☎ 907/697–2257 ⊕ www.glacierbayseakayaks.com). Prior to going out, you will be given instructions on handling the craft plus camping and routing suggestions. **Sea Otter Kayak** (⛺ Box 228, 99826 ☎ 907/697–3007 in summer, 907/226–2338 in winter ☎ 907/697–2338 ⊕ www.he.net/~seaotter) rents kayaks, gives instructions on their use, and supplies the essentials.

HAINES

61–**66** *75 mi north of Gustavus.*

The town of Haines encompasses an area that has been occupied by Tlingit peoples for centuries. Missionary S. Hall Young and famed naturalist John Muir were intent on establishing a Presbyterian mission in the area, and with the blessing of local chiefs, they chose the site that later became Haines. It's hard to imagine a more beautiful setting—a heavily wooded peninsula with magnificent views of Portage Cove and the snowy Coast Range. Unlike most other cities in Southeast Alaska, Haines, 80 mi northwest of Juneau, can be reached by the 152-mi Haines Highway, which connects at Haines Junction with the Alaska Highway. It's also accessible by the state ferry and by scheduled plane service from Juneau. The Haines ferry terminal is 4½ mi northwest of downtown, and the airport is 4 mi west.

The town has two distinct personalities. On the northern side of the Haines Highway is the portion of Haines that grew up around the Presbyterian mission. In the 1890s, Jack Dalton maintained a toll route from the settlement of Haines into the Yukon, charging $1 for foot passengers and $2.50 per horse. His Dalton Trail later provided access for miners during the 1897 gold rush to the Klondike. The following year, when gold was discovered on the nearby Porcupine River, Haines became a supply center and jumping-off place for those goldfields as well.

South of the highway the town looks like a military post, which is what it was for nearly half a century. In 1903 the U.S. Army established a post—Ft. William Henry Seward—at Portage Cove just south of town. For 17 years (1923–39) the post, renamed Chilkoot Barracks in commemoration of the gold-rush route, was the only military base in the territory. That changed with World War II. Following the war, the post closed down and the buildings were sold to private individuals. They are now part of a National Historic Landmark.

The Haines–Fort Seward community today is recognized for the Native dance and art center at Fort Seward, as well as for the superb fishing, camping, and outdoor recreation to be found at Chilkoot Lake, Portage Cove, Mosquito Lake, and Chilkat State Park on the shores of Chilkat Inlet. Northwest of the city is the Alaska Chilkat Bald Eagle Preserve. Thousands of eagles come here each winter to feed on a late run of chum salmon, making it one of Alaska's premier bird-watching sites.

Exploring Haines

Haines is a delightful place to explore on foot. Local weather is drier than in much of Southeast Alaska, and the town exudes a down-home friendliness. Perhaps this is because Haines sees fewer cruise ships, or maybe it's the grand landscape and ease of access to the mountains and sea.

Start your walking tour of Haines downtown at the helpful **Haines Convention and Visitors Bureau** ⑥ ⌐ on 2nd and Willard streets, where you can pick up a walking-tour brochure. Walk two blocks up 2nd Avenue and turn right on Main Street; the **Sheldon Museum and Cultural Center** ⑥ is just a block away. Step inside for an introduction to the area and its history. From here, head a block downhill to the busy small-boat harbor, filled with commercial-fishing boats and pleasure craft. Turn right on Front Street and follow the shoreline ¼ mi to Lookout Park, a fine place to take in the view on a sunny day. Turn uphill here on steps next to a small cemetery with graves dating from the 1880s. The steps emerge on Mission Street; follow it to 2nd Avenue and turn left for one block to the **American Bald Eagle Foundation** ⑥, a museum and research center for these majestic birds. Continue out 2nd Avenue another ⅓ mi to the most interesting sight in Haines, **Fort William H. Seward National Historic Landmark** ⑥. Turn right as you enter the grounds past **Halsingland Hotel** ⑥, originally the commanding officers' quarters. Circle the parade ground, passing the line of officers' homes along the top, and then proceed back down to **Alaska Indian Arts** ⑥, housed within the old fort hospital. The Chilkat Center for the Arts is just behind, and the central parade ground contains a tribal house and trapper's cabin.

TIMING   Plan to take two hours for this ramble around Haines and longer if you want to explore the various sights in depth. Local companies offer bus tours that include all these sights plus the "Dalton City" buildings at the fairgrounds and the Alaska Chilkat Bald Eagle Preserve (get information at the visitor's bureau).

What to See

🕐 ⑥ **Alaska Indian Arts.** Dedicated to the revival of Tlingit art, this nonprofit organization is housed in the former fort hospital, between the parade ground and the Chilkat Center for the Arts. You can watch Tlingits carving totem poles, metalsmiths working in silver, and other artists doing blanket weaving. ⊠ *Fort Seward* ☎ *907/766–2160* ⊕ *www. alaskaindianarts.com* ⊠ *Free* ⊗ *Weekdays 8–5, Sat. 9–5, and evenings when cruise ships are in port.*

⑥ **American Bald Eagle Foundation.** The main focuses here are bald eagles and the Chilkat Preserve, explored in lectures, displays, and videos. A diorama also shows examples of local animals. The gift shop sells natural-history items. The foundation also sponsors bald-eagle research cooperatively with the University of Alaska. ⊠ *2nd Ave. at Haines Hwy.* ⓓ *Box 49, 99827* ☎ *907/766–3094* 🖶 *907/766–3095* ⊕ *www. baldeagles.org* ⊠ *$3* ⊗ *May–Nov., daily 8–6 or whenever cruise ships are in port.*

⑥ **Fort William H. Seward National Historic Landmark.** Circle the sloping parade ground of Alaska's first army post, where clapboard structures stand against a mountain backdrop. The Haines Convention and Visitors Bureau provides a walking-tour brochure of the fort.

⌐ ⑥ **Haines Convention and Visitors Bureau.** At this helpful tourist office you can pick up walking tours of both Haines and Fort Seward, learn about lodging and attractions, check out menus from local restaurants, or pick up a hiking brochure. ⊠ *2nd Ave. near Willard St.* ⓓ *Box 530, 99827* ☎ *907/766–2234 or 800/458–3579* ⊕ *www.haines.ak.us* ⊗ *Mid-May–mid-Sept., weekdays 8–7, weekends 10–5; mid-Sept.–mid-May, weekdays 8–5; and when cruise ships are in port.*

Haines

TO
ALASKA CHILKAT
BALD EAGLE
PRESERVE

**Southeast Alaska
State Fairgrounds**

Haines Hwy.

6th Ave.

Union St.

4th Ave.

5th Ave.

Dalton St.

Main St.

3rd Ave.

TO
MT. RIPINSKY

2nd Ave.

Willard St.

61

62

TO CHILKOOT LAKE

TO MOSQUITO LAKE

Front St.

3rd Ave.

2nd Ave.

63

Haines Hwy.

Mission

Tlingit
Park

Lookout
Park

Portage Cove

65

Fort
Seward

64

Port Chilkoot
Dock

Lynn Canal

Soapsuds
Alley

66

Mud Bay Rd.

Small Tract Rd.

F.A.A. Rd.

KEY

Start of walk

65 **Halsingland Hotel.** In Fort Seward wander past the huge, stately, white-column former commanding officers' home, now a part of the hotel on Officers' Row.

62 **Sheldon Museum and Cultural Center.** Steve Sheldon began assembling Na-tive artifacts, Russian items, and gold-rush memorabilia, such as Jack Dalton's sawed-off shotgun, in the 1880s and started an exhibit of his finds in 1925. The core of what's here is this Alaskan family's personal collection. Particularly noteworthy are the Chilkat artifacts, including an 18th-century carved ceremonial hat from the Murrelet Clan, Chilkat blankets, and a model of a Tlingit tribal house. The impressive lens came from Eldred Rock Lighthouse, just south along Lynn Canal. ⊠ *11 Main St.* ☎ *907/766–2366* 🖷 *907/766–2368* ⊕ *www.sheldonmuseum.org* 🖾 *$3* ⊙ *Mid-May–mid-Sept., Sat.–Mon. daily 1–5, Tues. and Fri.*

10–noon and 1–5, Wed. and Thurs. 10–noon and 7–9, and when cruise ships are in port; mid.-Sept.–mid-May, Sun., Mon., and Wed. 1–4, Tues. and Thurs.–Fri. 3–5.

off the
beaten
path

HAINES HIGHWAY – Whether you plan to travel its full length or not, you should spend at least a bit of time on this scenic highway, which is paved on both sides of the border. It starts at Mile 0 in Haines and continues 152 mi to Haines Junction, where it joins the Alaska Highway in the Canadian Yukon. At about Mile 6 there's a delightful picnic spot near the Chilkat River. At Mile 9.5 the view of Cathedral Peaks, part of the Chilkat Range, is magnificent. From Mile 19 to Mile 21 you can see the Alaska Chilkat Bald Eagle Preserve. At Mile 33 is a roadside restaurant called, aptly, **Mile 33 Roadhouse,** where you can refill your gas tank and coffee mug, grab a burger, and stock up on home-baked goods. The United States–Canada border lies at Mile 42; stop at Canadian customs and be sure to set your clock ahead one hour.

ALASKA CHILKAT BALD EAGLE PRESERVE – In winter, the preserve harbors the largest concentration of bald eagles in the world. Thousands come to feast on the late run of salmon in the clear, ice-free waters of the Chilkat River, heated by underground warm springs. November and December are the best months for viewing. ⊠ *Mile 19–Mile 21* ☎ *907/766–2292.*

CHILKAT STATE PARK – This park on the Chilkat Inlet has beautiful and accessible viewing of both the Davidson and Rainbow glaciers along with public campgrounds. ☐ *Box 430, Haines 99827* ☎ *907/ 766–2292* ⊕ *www.dnr.state.ak.us/parks.*

DALTON CITY – An 1890s gold-rush town was re-created as a set for the movie *White Fang* and moved to the **Southeast Alaska State Fairgrounds** (☎ 907/766–2476), less than a mile from downtown. The movie-set buildings now house local businesses, including the **Klondike Restaurant and Saloon,** with good Tex-Mex, an old-fashioned bar, a microbrewery, and live music on Friday night. The five-day-long **Southeast Alaska State Fair,** held the second week of August, is one of several official regional blowouts, and in its homegrown, homespun way it's a real winner. In addition to the usual collection of barnyard animals, the fair has live music, rides on a vintage 1920 Herschal-Spillman carousel, local culinary arts, and Native dances, totemic crafts, and fine art and photography. ☎ *907/ 766–2476* ⊕ *www.seakfair.org* ☎ *$7.*

Where to Stay & Eat

$–$$$ ✕ **Bamboo Room.** Pop culture meets greasy spoon in this unassuming coffee shop with red vinyl booths. The menu includes sandwiches, burgers, fried chicken, chili, and halibut fish-and-chips, but the place really is at its best for an all-American breakfast (available until 3 PM). The bar has pool, darts, a big-screen TV, and a jukebox. ⊠ *2nd Ave. near Main St.* ☎ *907/766–2800* ▭ *AE, D, DC, MC, V.*

$–$$$ ✕ **The Wild Strawberry.** Just a few doors down from the visitor center, this café provides a bright escape from a rainy day. Owned by a family of commercial fishermen, the restaurant specializes in fresh salmon and halibut caught on their own boats. Popular lunchtime menu items include smoked-salmon chowder, crab-and-artichoke three-cheese melt (with fresh Dungeness crab), and panini sandwiches. For dinner try the fresh king salmon, shrimp, or halibut. Everything is homemade, and some of the produce is locally grown. The outside deck is a delight on sunny afternoons. ⊠ *138 2nd Ave.* ☏ *907/766–3608* ▤ *MC, V* ◷ *Closed Oct.–Apr.*

¢–$ ✕ **Mountain Market.** Meet the locals over coffee (including espresso in all its variations) and a fresh-baked pastry at this busy corner natural-foods store and deli. Mountain Market is also great for lunchtime sandwiches, wraps, soups, and salads. Friday is pizza night. ⊠ *3rd Ave. and Haines Hwy.* ☏ *907/766–3340* 🖷 *907/766–3339* ▤ *MC, V.*

¢–$ ✕▦ **Ft. Seward Lodge.** This lodge, restaurant, and saloon has, over time, served as the fort's PX, soda fountain, bowling alley, and gymnasium. The raw-wood decor and sparse interior bring the pioneering spirit of Alaska to life. The dining room even comes with a mechanical red-velvet swing left over from wilder times. All-you-can-eat Dungeness crab dinners are $23, or choose beef, chicken, or pasta from the menu. Save room for the "ice screaming" pie. The lodge's rooms are clean but not at all fancy; the least expensive share a bath and lack televisions, and two have well-equipped kitchenettes and ocean views. ⊠ *39 Mud Bay Rd.* ☏ *907/766–2009 or 800/478–7772* 🖷 *907/766–2006* ⊕ *www.ftsewardlodge.com* ⇆ *10 rooms* ☼ *Restaurant, some kitchenettes, cable TV, bar, airport shuttle; no a/c, no room phones, no smoking* ▤ *D, MC, V.*

¢–$ ✕▦ **Halsingland Hotel.** Fort Seward's commanding officers once lived in the big white Victorian building that today houses this hotel. On the National Register of Historic Places, the hotel still has original claw-foot bathtubs and nonworking fireplaces decorated with Belgian tiles. Rooms are charming and nicely maintained. The Commander's Room Restaurant and Lounge prides itself on its seafood and steaks, but burgers and fish-and-chips are also on the menu. In summer, at the Tlingit tribal house nearby, the Halsingland prepares a delicious all-you-can-eat lunchtime salmon bake ($25) when cruise ships are in port. ⊠ *Fort Seward* ♢ *Box 1649, 99827* ☏ *907/766–2000, 800/542–6363 in U.S., 800/478–2525 in Yukon Territory and B.C.* 🖷 *907/766–2060* ⊕ *www.hotelhalsingland.com* ⇆ *58 rooms, 52 with bath* ☼ *Restaurant, cable TV, bar, Internet, meeting rooms, some pets allowed; no a/c* ▤ *AE, D, DC, MC, V.*

$$$$ ▦ **Weeping Trout Sports Resort.** Enjoy wilderness with style at this small resort on Chilkat Lake—reachable only by boat or plane—where you can golf on a 9-hole course, fish, relax, and refresh and *not* be bothered by telephones (the lodge has one for emergencies). All-inclusive package trips are available starting at $270 per person per night, and you stay in clean but simple cabins; showers are in the main lodge. Day trips are available, and the restaurant is open to the public Saturday nights with a set four-course, family-style meal ($48 with transportation from Haines). ♢ *Box 129, 99827* ☏ *907/766–2827 or 877/948–7688* 🖷 *907/766–2824* ⊕ *www.weepingtrout.com* ⇆ *4 cabins* ☼ *Restaurant, 9-hole golf course, fishing; no a/c, no room phones, no room TVs* ▤ *MC, V* ⦿ *FAP* ◷ *Closed Oct.–mid-May.*

$–$$ ▦ **Captain's Choice Motel.** In the summer overflowing flower boxes surround the perimeter of this contemporary motel in downtown Haines. Rooms are standard, but those on the second floor open onto a deck with tables and chairs. A patio down below serves as a nightly meeting place where you can enjoy libations and conversation. The honeymoon suite has a hot tub. ⊠ *108 2nd Ave. N* ♢ *Box 392, 99827* ☏ *907/766–3111 or 800/478–2345* 🖷 *907/766–3332* ⊕ *www.capchoice.com* ⇆ *39 rooms, 3 suites* ☼ *Refrigerators, cable TV, car rental, some pets allowed; no a/c* ▤ *AE, D, DC, MC, V.*

Guided Tours

Adventure

Alaska Nature Tours (☎ 907/766–2876 🖷 907/766–2844 ⊕ www. alaskanaturetours.net) conducts bird-watching and natural-history tours through the Alaska Chilkat Bald Eagle Preserve and leads hiking treks in summer and ski tours in winter. A full-service kayak outfitter in Haines, **Deishu Expeditions** (☎ 907/766–2427 or 800/552–9257 ⊕ www. seakayaks.com) leads guided trips for a day or a week. It also rents kayaks for do-it-yourselfers.

Boating & Fishing

Alaska Fjordlines (☎ 907/766–3395 or 800/320–0146 ⊕ www. alaskafjordlines.com) operates a high-speed catamaran between Haines and Juneau throughout the summer, stopping along the way to watch sea lions and other marine mammals. **Chilkat Cruises** (☎ 907/766–2100 or 888/ 766–2103 ⊕ www.chilkatcruises.com) provides a passenger catamaran ferry between Skagway and Haines, with service several times a day in the summer. **Glacier Valley Wilderness Adventures** (☎☎ 907/767–5522 ⊕ www.glaciervalleyadventures.com) conducts fly-in trips to a remote gold-mine base camp, with a variety of rafting, jetboat, or helicopter options. Overnight accommodations are available in tents at a working gold mine.

For information on numerous sportfishing charter boats in Haines, contact the **Haines Convention and Visitors Bureau** (☎ 907/766–2234 or 800/458–3579 ⊕ www.haines.ak.us).

Flightseeing

Housed a few doors up the street from the visitor center, **Mountain Flying Service** (☎ 907/766–3007 or 800/954–8747 ⊕ www.flyglacierbay. com) leads flightseeing trips to nearby Glacier Bay National Park. **Wings of Alaska** (☎ 907/789–0790 ⊕ www.wingsofalaska.com) flies to Juneau and Skagway.

Nightlife & the Arts

Bars

Locals might rule the pool tables at **Fogcutter Bar** (✉ 122 Main St. ☎ 907/766–2555), but the jukebox is often up for grabs at this lively spot. **Haines Brewing Company** (✉ 108 Whitefang Way ☎ 907/766–3823) is a microbrewery in the Dalton City buildings at the fairgrounds. Commercial fisherfolk gather nightly at **Harbor Bar** (✉ Front St. at the Harbor ☎ 907/766–2444), a bar and restaurant dating from 1907. You might catch some live music here in summer. Inside one of the oldest buildings in town (it was once a brothel), the **Pioneer Bar** (✉ 2nd Ave. near Main St. ☎ 907/766–3443) has historical photographs on the walls, a large-screen television for sports, and occasional bands.

Dance

The **Chilkat Dancers' Storytelling Theater** (☎ 907/766–2540 ⊕ www. tresham.com/show) performs at the Tribal House on the fort's parade grounds during the summer. This unique theatrical production includes elaborate carved masks and impressive costumes as dancers tell ancient Tlingit legends. Performances cost $10 and are held several times a week, typically when cruise-ship passengers are in town.

Sports & the Outdoors

Bicycling

Sockeye Cycle Company (✉ 24 Portage St. ☞ Box 829, 99827 ☎ 907/ 766–2869 ⊕ www.cyclealaska.com) specializes in guided mountain tours in and around the backcountry of Haines; the outfit also rents, services, and sells bikes.

Hiking

Battery Point Trail is a fairly level path that hugs the shoreline for 2 mi, providing fine views across Lynn Canal. The trail begins a mile east of town, and a campsite can be found at Kelgaya Point near the end. For other hikes, pick up a copy of "Haines Is for Hikers" at the Haines Convention and Visitors Bureau.

Shopping

Art Galleries

A surprising number of artists live in the Haines area, and you will find their works in several local galleries. **Form and Function Art Gallery** (⊠211 Willard St. ☎907/766–2539 ⊕www.formnfunction-haines.com) has an impressive collection of handcrafted Native artwork.

One of the nicest galleries in Haines, **Wild Iris Gallery** (⊠ Portage St. just up from cruise-ship dock ☎ 907/766–2300) displays attractive jewelry, prints, and fashion wear created by owners Madeleine and Fred Shields.

SKAGWAY

67–72 *17 mi northeast of Haines.*

Skagway is a short hop (14 mi) north of Haines if you take the Alaska Marine Highway ferry. If you go by road, the distance is 359 mi, as you have to take the Haines Highway up to Haines Junction, Yukon, then take the Alaska Highway 100 mi south to Whitehorse, and then drive a final 100 mi south on the Klondike Highway to Skagway. North-country folk call this well-traveled sightseeing route the Golden Horseshoe or Golden Circle tour, because it takes in a lot of gold-rush country in addition to lake, forest, and mountain scenery.

However you get to Skagway, you'll find the town an amazingly preserved artifact from one of North America's biggest, most storied gold rushes. Most of the downtown district forms part of the Klondike Gold Rush National Historical Park, a unit of the national park system dedicated to commemorating and interpreting the frenzied stampede that extended to Dawson City in Canada's Yukon. Old false-front stores, saloons, and brothels—built to separate gold-rush prospectors from their grubstakes going north or their gold pokes heading south—have been restored, repainted, and refurnished by the federal government and Skagway's citizens. Although the town feels a little like a Disney theme park in spots, when you walk down Broadway today, the scene is not appreciably different from what the prospectors saw in the days of 1898, except the street is now paved to make your exploring easier.

Skagway had only a single cabin still standing when the Yukon gold rush began. At first, the argonauts, as they liked to be called, swarmed to Dyea and the Chilkoot Trail, 9 mi west of Skagway. Skagway and its White Pass Trail didn't seem as attractive until a dock was built in town. Then it mushroomed overnight into the major gateway to the Klondike, supporting a wild mixture of legitimate businesspeople, con artists (among the most cunning was Jefferson "Soapy" Smith), stampeders, and curiosity seekers.

Three months after the first boat landed in July 1897, Skagway numbered perhaps 20,000 persons and had well-laid-out streets, hotels, stores, saloons, gambling houses, and dance halls. By the spring of

1898, the superintendent of the Northwest Royal Mounted Police in neighboring Canada would label the town "little better than a hell on earth."

A lot of the "hell" ended with a shoot-out one pleasant July evening in 1898. Good guy Frank Reid (the surveyor who laid out Skagway's streets so wide and well) faced down bad guy Soapy Smith on a dock downtown near the present ferry terminal. After a classic exchange of gunfire, Smith lay dead and Reid lay dying. The town built a substantial monument at Reid's grave. You can see it in Gold Rush Cemetery and read the inscription on it: HE GAVE HIS LIFE FOR THE HONOR OF SKAGWAY. For Smith, whose tombstone was continually chiseled and stolen by vandals and souvenir seekers, today's grave marker is a simple wooden plank.

When the gold rush played out after a few years, the town of 20,000 dwindled to 700. The White Pass & Yukon Railroad kept the town alive until 1982, when it began to run in summers only. By this time, however, tourism revenue was sufficient to compensate for any economic loss suffered as a result of the railroad's more limited schedule.

Exploring Skagway

Skagway's compact downtown makes it ideal to explore by foot. Nearly all the historic sights are within a few blocks of the cruise-ship and ferry dock, so you can take all the time you want. Skagway runs on tourism, as you will discover the minute you step from a ferry or cruise ship. Unless you're willing to hike into the backcountry on the Chilkoot Trail, you aren't likely to find a quiet Alaskan experience around Skagway.

a good walk

A good starting point is the corner of 1st Avenue and Main Street, where a marker notes the infamous 1898 gun battle between Soapy Smith and Frank Reid. Head two blocks east along 1st Avenue and turn left on Broadway Street into the heart of the town. Be sure to stop by the old White Pass & Yukon Railroad Depot at 2nd Avenue and Broadway, which now houses the **Klondike Gold Rush National Historical Park** 67 ▶ visitor center. Check out the exhibits and films, or join a ranger-led tour to learn more about Skagway's fascinating history. Next door is the White Pass & Yukon Route Depot, a modern structure that blends well with the town's many Victorian-era buildings.

The next block up Broadway contains several of the town's best-known buildings. The two-centuries-old Red Onion Saloon remains a favorite place to imbibe under the watchful eyes of "working girl" mannequins. Next door is the **Arctic Brotherhood Hall** 68, with its driftwood-stick false front. Inside you'll find the helpful **Skagway Convention and Visitors Bureau** for local information. Next up the street is the **Golden North Hotel** 69, with its distinctive golden dome. Across the street sits the old Mascot Saloon, which now houses Park Service historical exhibits and public rest rooms. Back on Broadway, continue two more blocks until you reach **Corrington's Museum of Alaskan History** 70, with its large collection of scrimshaw. Turn right on 5th Avenue to the Park Service's **Moore Cabin** 71, Skagway's oldest structure. The beautifully restored Skagway City Hall sits directly in front of the **Skagway Museum** 72. Return to Broadway and follow it to 6th Avenue, where you can see *The Days of '98 with Soapy Smith* show inside historic Eagles Hall.

If you are up for a longer walk continue 2 mi out of town along Alaska Street to the **Gold Rush Cemetery,** where you'll find the graves of combatants Soapy Smith and Frank Reid. (A city bus takes you most of the way to the cemetery for $2 each direction.) No tour of Skagway is complete without a train ride on the famed **White Pass & Yukon Route.** Trains depart from the corner of 1st Avenue and Broadway several times a day in the summer.

TIMING The six blocks that compose the heart of downtown Skagway can be explored in a half hour, but you will almost certainly want to spend more time learning about the gold rush in the Park Service's historical buildings and the Skagway Museum. (If you include the 4-mi round-trip walk to the Gold Rush Cemetery, plan on three to four hours.) Also, leave time to explore Skagway's many shops, restaurants, and other attractions.

What to See

★ ➏➑ **Arctic Brotherhood Hall.** The Arctic Brotherhood was a fraternal organization of Alaskan and Yukon pioneers. To decorate the exterior false front of their Skagway lodge building, local members created a mosaic out of 20,000 pieces of driftwood and flotsam gathered from local beaches. The AB Hall now houses the **Skagway Convention and Visitors Bureau,** along with public rest rooms. ⊠ *Broadway, between 2nd and 3rd* ✆ *Box 1029, 99840* ☎ *907/983–2854, 888/762–1898 message only* ⊕ *www.skagway.org* ☉ *May–Sept., daily 8–6; Oct.–Apr., weekdays 8–noon and 1–5.*

➐➎ **Corrington's Museum of Alaskan History.** This impressive scrimshaw museum highlights 40 exquisitely carved pieces. There's also a gift shop. ⊠ *5th and Broadway.* ☎ *907/983–2637* ☞ *Free* ☉ *Open when cruise ships are in port.*

➏➒ **Golden North Hotel.** Built during the 1898 gold rush, the Golden North Hotel was—until closing in 2002—Alaska's oldest hotel. It retains its gold rush–era appearance; a golden dome tops the corner cupola. ⊠ *3rd Ave. and Broadway.*

★ ⚑ **67** **Klondike Gold Rush National Historical Park.** In what was once the White Pass & Yukon Route Depot, this park contains exhibits, photos, and artifacts from the White Pass and Chilkoot trails and is of special interest if you plan to take a White Pass train ride, drive the nearby Klondike Highway, or hike the Chilkoot "Trail of '98." Films, ranger talks, and walking tours are offered. Special free Robert Service poetry performances take place two evenings a week at the visitor center. ✉ *2nd Ave. at Broadway* ☎ *907/983–2921 or 907/983–9224* ⊕ *www. nps.gov/klgo* 🖙 *Free* ☉ *June–Aug., daily 8–8; May and Sept., daily 8–6; Oct.–Apr., weekdays 8–5.*

71 **Moore Cabin.** Built in 1887 by Captain William Moore, the tiny cabin marks the birthplace of Skagway. An early homesteader, Moore prospered from the flood of miners, constructing a dock, warehouse, and sawmill to supply them and selling land for other ventures. Its interior walls are covered with turn-of-the-20th-century newspapers. Next door, the larger **Moore House** (1897–98) contains interesting exhibits on the Moore family. Both structures are maintained by the Park Service, and the main house is open daily in the summer. ✉ *Off 5th Ave.* 🖙 *Free* ☉ *Memorial Day–Labor Day, hrs vary.*

★ **72** **Skagway Museum.** This nicely designed museum occupies the ground floor of a historic building that also houses Skagway City Hall. Inside, you'll find gambling paraphernalia from the old Board of Trade Saloon on display along with a 19th-century Tlingit canoe (one of the only two like it on the West Coast), historic photos, gold scales, a red-and-black sleigh, and other gold rush–era artifacts, along with Native baskets, beadwork, and carvings. ✉ *7th and Spring Sts.* ☎ *907/983–2420* ⊕ *www. skagwaymuseum.org* 🖙 *$2* ☉ *Mid-May–Sept., weekdays 9–5, weekends 1–4; Oct.–mid-May., hrs vary.*

---

off the beaten path

KLONDIKE HIGHWAY – The highway, which starts at the foot of State Street, often parallels the older White Pass railway route as it travels northwest to Carcross and Whitehorse in the Canadian Yukon. It meets the Alaska Highway, which you follow northwest into Whitehorse, and then heads on its own again to terminate at Dawson City, on the shores of the Klondike River. From start to finish, it covers 435 mi. Along the way the road climbs steeply through forested coastal mountains with jagged, snow-covered peaks. It passes by deep, fish-filled lakes and streams in the Canadian high country, where you might spot a mountain goat, moose, black bear, or grizzly. If you're driving the Klondike Highway north from Skagway, you must stop at Canadian customs, Mile 22. If you're traveling south to Skagway, check in at U.S. customs, Mile 6. And remember that when it's 1 PM in Canada at the border, it's noon in Skagway.

WHITE PASS & YUKON ROUTE – Visitors to Skagway can travel at least part of the way along the gold-rush route aboard the White Pass & Yukon Route (WP & YR) narrow-gauge railroad. The historic (started in 1898) gold-rush railroad's diesel locomotives tow vintage viewing cars up the steep inclines of the route, hugging the walls of precipitous cliff-sides and providing views of craggy peaks, plummeting waterfalls, lakes, and forests. It's open mid-May to late September only, and reservations are highly recommended.

Several options are available. Twice daily during the season (three times on Tuesday and Wednesday) the WP & YR leaves Skagway for a three-hour round-trip excursion to the White Pass summit. Sights along the way include Bridal Veil Falls, Inspiration Point, and Dead

Horse Gulch. The fare is $82. Through service to Whitehorse, Yukon, is offered daily as well—in the form of a train trip to Fraser, where bus connections are possible on to Whitehorse. The one-way fare to Whitehorse is $95. Special steam excursions (Saturday for $156) and a Chilkoot Trail hikers' service ($65 to Skagway from Lake Bennett) are also offered. ☏ *907/983–2217 or 800/343–7373* ⊕ *www.whitepassrailroad.com.*

CHILKOOT TRAIL – If you're a strong and experienced backpacker who likes a challenge, you might want to hike the highly scenic, historic Chilkoot Trail, route of the 1897–98 gold-rush sourdoughs, from Skagway into Canada. Most hikers will need four to five days for the 33-mi hike. Expect steep slopes and wet weather, along with exhilarating vistas at the summit across the much drier Canadian landscape. Deep snow often covers the pass until late summer. The trail stretches from Dyea (9 mi out a dirt road from Skagway) to Lake Bennett and includes a climb up Chilkoot Pass at the United States–Canada border. The National Park Service maintains the American side of the pass as part of **Klondike Gold Rush National Historical Park**; the Canadian side is part of the **Chilkoot Trail National Historic Park.** A backcountry permit is required.

The trail is generally in good condition (particularly in the lower stretches); the forest, mountain, and lake country is both scenic and richly historic, and primitive campsites are strategically located along the way. The Chilkoot is not, however, an easy walk: you'll encounter lots of ups and downs before you cross the pass and reach the Canadian high country, and rain is likely. To return to Skagway, hikers usually catch the White Pass & Yukon Route train from Lake Bennett. The fare is $65, and these trains run daily in the summer.

For details, maps, and backcountry permits (C$50), contact the Park Service's summer-only **Chilkoot Trail Center** (✉ 1st Ave. and Broadway ☏ 907/983–9234 ⊕ www.nps.gov/klgo) in the historic Martin Itgen House. Trail permits are also available through **Parks Canada** (☏ 907/983–2921, 867/667–3910, or 800/661–0486 ⊕ parkscan.harbour.com/ct).

Where to Stay & Eat

★ **$$–$$$$** ✕ **Stowaway Cafe.** Always crowded, this noisy little harborside café is just a few steps from the cruise-ship dock. Not surprisingly, seafood is the attraction—including prawns with Gorgonzola, seafood lasagna, and a hot scallop-and-bacon salad—but you also can choose tasty steaks, chicken, or smoked ribs. The café is open daily for lunch and dinner. ✉ *Congress Way* ☏ *907/983–3463* ⌖ *Reservations essential* ▭ *AE, MC, V* ☾ *Closed Oct.–Apr.*

$$ ✕ **Skagway Fish Company.** This small, seasonal eatery serves fresh seafood including salmon, oysters, clams, halibut, and prawns for lunch and dinner. Most popular are the halibut fish-and-chips, served with a side of homemade coleslaw. Tables overlooking the harbor surround the central bar. Baby-back ribs, pork chops, and steaks, along with a New York–style cheesecake topped with strawberries, fill out the menu. ✉ *On waterfront* ☏ *907/983–3474* ▭ *MC, V* ☾ *Closed Oct.–Apr.*

$–$$ ✕🖼 **Skagway Inn Bed & Breakfast.** Each room in this downtown Victorian inn is named after a different gold-rush gal. The building, one of Skagway's oldest, was built in 1897. Rooms share a Victorian motif, with antiques and cast-iron beds; some have mountain views. The inn also houses a pair of seasonal eateries: Greg's Bistro for espresso and baked-on-the-premises pastries, and the more upscale Olivia's, with fresh Alaskan seafood dinners. Outdoor seating is available next to the colorful gardens. ⊠ *655 Broadway* ⬠ *Box 500, 99840* ☎ *907/983–2289 or 888/752–4929* 🖷 *907/983–2713* ⊕ *www.skagwayinn.com* ⇲ *10 rooms, 5 with bath* ⚇ *Restaurant, Internet, airport shuttle; no a/c, no room TVs, no smoking* ⊟ *AE, D, MC, V* ⊘ *Closed Oct.–Apr.* ⊧*CP.*

$$ 🛏 **The White House.** About two blocks from downtown Skagway, this B&B is a welcome addition to the roster of housing choices in Skagway. Built in 1902 by Lee Guthrie, a gambler and owner of one of the town's most profitable gold-rush saloons, the white clapboard two-story house is furnished with original Skagway antiques and handmade quilts. The warm dining room and sitting room invite conversation while hearty homemade breakfasts are served up, and later in the day you can unwind with a cup of tea and a movie on the communal VCR. ⊠ *8th Ave. and Main St.* ⬠ *Box 41, 99840* ☎ *907/983–9000* 🖷 *907/983–9010* ⊕ *www.atthewhitehouse.com* ⇲ *10 rooms* ⚇ *Cable TV; no a/c, no smoking* ⊟ *AE, D, MC, V* ⊧*CP.*

$ 🛏 **Mile Zero Bed & Breakfast.** In a quiet residential area a few blocks from downtown, this modern and comfortable B&B contains spacious and well-insulated guest rooms, all with private entrances, phones, and baths. A Continental breakfast is served each morning. Mile Zero is primarily for adults, though well-behaved children are allowed. ⊠ *9th Ave. and Main St., 99840* ☎ *907/983–3045* 🖷 *907/983–3046* ⊕ *www.mile-zero.com* ⇲ *6 rooms* ⚇ *No a/c, no room TVs, no smoking* ⊟ *AE, D, MC, V* ⊧*CP.*

Guided Tours

Alaska Sled Dog Adventures (☎ 907/983–3990 🖷 907/983–3392 ⊕ www.alaskasleddog.com) leads a 2½-hour wheeled (no snow) sled-dog tour that ends at historic Dyea. For an on-the-snow version, **Temsco Helicopters** (☎ 907/789–9501 or 877/789–9501 ⊕ www.temscoair.com) will fly you to Denver Glacier for an hour of learning about mushing and riding on a dogsled.

Alaska Fjordlines (☎ 907/766–3395 or 800/320–0146 ⊕ www.alaskafjordlines.com) operates a high-speed catamaran between Skagway and Juneau throughout the summer, stopping along the way to watch sea lions and other marine mammals.

Chilkat Cruises (☎ 907/766–2100 or 888/766–2103 ⊕ www.chilkatcruises.com) provides a fast passenger catamaran ferry between Skagway and Haines, with service several times a day in the summer.

Packer Expeditions (☎ 907/983–2544 ⊕ www.packerexpeditions.com) guides day trips that include a helicopter flight from Skagway, a 5-mi hike to Laughton Glacier, and a train ride back to town.

Skagway Street Car Co. (☎ 907/983–2908 🖷 907/983–3908 ⊕ www.skagwaystreetcar.com) revisits the gold-rush days in lovingly renovated 1920s sightseeing buses. Costumed conductors lead these popular two-hour tours, but advance reservations are recommended for independent travelers, since most seats are sold aboard the cruise ships. Call one to two weeks ahead in peak season to reserve a space.

Nightlife & the Arts

Bars

Imbibe with the locals at **Moe's Frontier Bar** (⊠ Broadway between 4th and 5th Aves. ☎ 907/983–2238), a longtime fixture on the Skagway scene. At **Red Onion Saloon** (✉ Broadway at 2nd Ave. ☎ 907/983–2222), where upstairs was once a gold-rush brothel, you'll find a convivial crowd of Skagway locals and visitors. An impromptu jam with cruise-ship musicians gets under way almost every afternoon. Thursday night is when local musicians strut their stuff. The saloon closes up shop for winter.

Theater

★ Since 1927, locals have performed a show called *The Days of '98 with Soapy Smith* at Eagles Hall. You'll see cancan dancers, learn a little local history, and watch desperado Soapy Smith being sent to his reward. If you stop in for the evening show, you can enjoy a few warm-up rounds of mock gambling with Soapy's money. Performances of Robert Service poetry start a half hour before each show time. *✉ Broadway and 6th Ave., 96726 ✉ In winter: ✆ Box 695, Honaunau, HI 96726 ☎ 907/983–2545 in summer, 808/328–9132 in winter ⊕ www.alaskan.com/daysof98 ☎ $14 ⊙ Mid-May–mid-Sept., daily at 10:30, 2:30, and 8.*

SOUTHEAST ALASKA A TO Z

To research prices, get advice from other travelers, and book travel arrangements, visit www.fodors.com.

AIR TRAVEL

Alaska Airlines operates several flights daily from Seattle and other Pacific Coast and southwestern cities to Ketchikan, Wrangell, Petersburg, Sitka, Glacier Bay, and Juneau (⇨ Smart Travel Tips for airline numbers). The carrier connects Juneau to the northern Alaskan cities of Yakutat, Cordova, Anchorage, Fairbanks, Nome, Kotzebue, and Prudhoe Bay. Wings of Alaska can connect you from Juneau to several towns, including Haines and Skagway.

Every large community in Southeast Alaska, and many smaller ones, has air-taxi services that fly you from town to town and, if you're seeking backcountry adventures, into remote wilderness cabins. Local chambers of commerce can provide lists of Bush-plane services.

⚑ Wings of Alaska ☎ 907/789-0790 ⊕ www.wingsofalaska.com.

BOAT & FERRY TRAVEL

From the south, the Alaska Marine Highway operates stateroom-equipped vehicle and passenger ferries from Bellingham, Washington, and from Prince Rupert, British Columbia. The vessels call at Ketchikan, Wrangell, Petersburg, Sitka, Juneau, Haines, and Skagway, and they connect with smaller vessels serving Bush communities; in all, 11 Southeast towns are served by state ferries. B.C. Ferries operates similar passenger and vehicle ferries from Vancouver Island, British Columbia, to Prince Rupert. From here, travelers can connect with the Alaska Marine Highway System. A separate ferry, operated by the Inter-Island Ferry Authority, runs between Ketchikan and Prince of Wales Island, with additional service to Wrangell and Petersburg to start in 2005.

In the summer, staterooms on the ferries are always sold out before sailing time; reserve months in advance. If you are planning to take a car on the ferry, early reservations for vehicle space are also highly recommended. This is particularly true for recreational vehicles.

⚑ Alaska Marine Highway ✆ 6858 Glacier Hwy., Juneau 99801-7909 ☎ 907/465-3941 or 800/642-0066 ☎ 907/277-4829 ⊕ www.alaska.gov/ferry. **B.C. Ferries** ✉ 1112 Fort St., Victoria, BC V8V 4V2 ☎ 250/386-3431, 888/223-3779 in B.C. ⊕ www.bcferries.com. **Inter-Island Ferry Authority** ✆ Box 495, Craig 99921 ☎ 907/826-4848 or 866/308-4848 ☎ 907/826-2829 ⊕ www.interislandferry.com.

BUS TRAVEL

Alaska Direct Bus Lines has year-round service connecting Anchorage, Fairbanks, and Skagway. Though it's a long ride, you can travel Greyhound Lines of Canada from Vancouver or Edmonton to Whitehorse and make connections there with Alaska Direct buses to Skagway.

🚍 **Alaska Direct Bus Lines** ✆ Box 100501, Anchorage 99510 ☎ 907/277–6652 or 800/770–6652. **Greyhound Lines of Canada** ☎ 604/482–8747 or 800/661–8747 ⊕ www.greyhound.ca.

CAR TRAVEL

Only Skagway and Haines, in the northern Panhandle, and tiny Hyder, just across the border from Stewart, British Columbia, are accessible by conventional highway. To reach Skagway or Haines, take the Alaska Highway to the Canadian Yukon's Whitehorse or Haines Junction, respectively, and then drive the Klondike Highway or Haines Highway southwest to the Alaska Panhandle. You can reach Hyder on British Columbia's Cassiar Highway, which can be reached, in turn, from Highway 16 just north of Prince Rupert.

EMERGENCIES

🚨 **Police, fire, ambulance** ☎ 911.

HOSPITALS 🚨 **Bartlett Memorial Hospital** ✉ 3260 Hospital Dr., Juneau ☎ 907/586–2611 ⊕ www.bartletthospital.org. **Haines Medical Clinic** ✉ Next to Visitor Information Center ☎ 907/766–2521. **Ketchikan General Hospital** ✉ 3100 Tongass Ave. ☎ 907/225–5171. **Petersburg Medical Center** ✉ 103 Fram St. ☎ 907/772–4291 ⊕ www.hisea.org/psg.html. **Sitka Community Hospital** ✉ 209 Moller Ave. ☎ 907/747–3241 ⊕ www.sitkahospital.org. **Skagway Medical Clinic** ✉ 310 11th Ave., between State St. and Broadway ☎ 907/983–2255. **Wrangell General Hospital** ✉ 310 Bennett St. ☎ 907/874–7000 ⊕ www.wrangellmedicalcenter.com.

PHARMACIES 🚨 Juneau **Juneau Drug Co.** ✉ 202 Front St. ☎ 907/586–1233. **Ron's Apothecary Shoppe** ✉ 9101 Mendenhall Mall Rd., about 10 mi north of downtown in Mendenhall Valley, next to Super Bear market ☎ 907/789–0458, 907/789–9522 after hours for prescription emergencies.
🚨 Ketchikan **Downtown Drugstore** ✉ 300 Front St. ☎ 907/225–3144. **Race Avenue Drugs** ✉ 2300 Tongass Ave., across from Plaza shopping mall ☎ 907/225–4151. After hours, call **Ketchikan General Hospital** ☎ 907/225–5171.
🚨 Petersburg **Rexall Drugs** ✉ 215 N. Nordic Dr. ☎ 907/772–3265. After hours, call **Petersburg Medical Center** ☎ 907/772–4291.
🚨 Sitka **Harry Race Pharmacy** ✉ 106 Lincoln St. ☎ 907/747–8006. **Sitka Community Hospital** ✉ 209 Moller Dr. ☎ 907/747–3241 after hours. **White's Pharmacy** ✉ 705 Halibut Point Rd. ☎ 907/747–8233.
🚨 Wrangell **Stikine Drugs** ✉ 202 Front St. ☎ 907/874–3422. **Wrangell General Hospital** ✉ 310 Bennett St. ☎ 907/874–7000 after hours.

LODGING

BED & BREAKFAST RESERVATION SERVICE The Alaska Bed & Breakfast Association Innside Passage Chapter books B&B accommodations in most Southeast communities.
🚨 Local Agents **Alaska Bed & Breakfast Association Innside Passage Chapter** ✆ Box 22800, Juneau 99802 ☎ 907/789–8822 🖷 907/780–4673 ⊕ www.accommodations-alaska.com.

TOURS

ADVENTURE 🚨 **Alaska Discovery** ✉ 5310 Glacier Hwy., Juneau ☎ 907/780–6226 or 800/586–1911 🖷 907/780–4220 ⊕ www.akdiscovery.com. **Alaska Tugboat Tours** ☎ 907/874–3101 or 888/488–4386 ⊕ www.alaskatugtours.com. **Cape Fox Tours** ☎ 907/225–4846 🖷 907/225–3137 ⊕ www.

capefoxtours.com. **Tongass Kayak Adventures** ☎ 907/772–4600 ⊕ www.
tongasskayak.com.

AIR CHARTERS & **Air Excursions** ☎ 907/697–2375, 800/354–2479 in Alaska, ⊕ www.
FLIGHTSEEING airexcursions.com, in Gustavus. **Mountain Flying Service** ☎ 907/766–
3007 or 800/954–8747 ⊕ www.flyglacierbay.com, in Haines. **Pacific
Airways** ☎ 907/225–3500 or 877/360–3500 ⊕ www.flypacificairways.
com, in Ketchikan. **Pacific Wing** ☎ 907/772–9258 ⊕ www.pacificwing.
com, in Petersburg. **ProMech Air** ☎ 907/886–3845 or 800/860–3845
⊕ www.promechair.com, in Ketchikan. **Sunrise Aviation** ☎ 907/874–
2319 or 800/874–2311 🖶 907/874–2546 ⊕ www.sunriseflights.com,
in Wrangell. **Wings of Alaska** ☎ 907/789–0790 ⊕ www.wingsofalaska.
com, in Juneau.

BICYCLING **Sockeye Cycle Company** ✉ 24 Portage St. ✑ Box 829, Skagway 99827
☎ 907/766–2869 ⊕ www.cyclealaska.com.

BOATING **Alaska Travel Adventures** ☎ 907/789–0052 or 800/478–0052 ⊕ www.
alaskaadventures.com. **Auk Nu Tours** ☎ 907/586–8687 or 800/820–2628
⊕ www.auknutours.com. **Auk Ta Shaa Discovery** ☎ 907/586–8687 or
800/820–2628 ⊕ www.goldbelttours.com. **Glacier Valley Wilderness Adventures** ☎🖶 907/767–5522 ⊕ www.glaciervalleyadventures.com. **Spirit
Walker Expeditions, Inc.** ✑ Box 240, Gustavus 99826 ☎ 907/697–2266
or 800/529–2537 🖶 907/697–2701 ⊕ www.seakayakalaska.com.

HELICOPTER All of the following operators fly from Juneau.
FLIGHTSEEING **Coastal Helicopters** ☎ 907/789–5600 ⊕ www.coastalhelicopters.com. **ERA Helicopters** ☎ 907/586–2030 or 800/843–1947 ⊕ www.eraaviation.com. **Northstar Trekking**
☎ 907/790–4530 ⊕ www.glaciertrekking.com. **Temsco Helicopters** ☎ 907/789–9501
or 877/789–9501 ⊕ www.temscoair.com.

NATURE Alaska Nature Tours runs bird-watching and nature trips, plus hiking
and skiing trips, from Haines. Kaleidoscope Cruises runs whale-watching and glacier-ecology boat tours from Petersburg.
 Alaska Nature Tours ☎ 907/766–2876 🖶 907/766–2844 ⊕ www.alaskanaturetours.
net. **Kaleidoscope Cruises** ☎ 907/772–3736 or 800/868–4373 ⊕ www.alaska.net/~bbsea.

SIGHTSEEING Alaska Cruises has catamaran cruises from Ketchikan to Misty Fiords
National Monument. Juneau Trolley Car Company makes stops at a
dozen or so of Juneau's sights. Metlakatla Tours conducts tours from
Metlakatla. Seaport Limousine leads guided tours of the Hyder area.
Sitka Tours runs sightseeing, historical, and raptor tours in Sitka. Skagway Street Car Co. lets you revisit Skagway's gold-rush days in the
original 1937 White Motor Company streetcars while showing you the
sights.
 Alaska Cruises ☎ 907/225–6044 or 800/228–1905 🖶 907/225–8636 ⊕ www.
mistyfjord.net. **Juneau Trolley Car Company** ☎ 907/586–7433 ⊕ www.juneautrolley.
com. **Metlakatla Tours** ☎ 907/886–4441 or 877/886–8687 ⊕ tours.metlakatla.net.
Seaport Limousine ☎ 250/636–2622 ⊕ www.tkp-biz.com/seaportlimousine. **Sitka
Tours** ☎ 907/747–8443 🖶 907/747–7510. **Skagway Street Car Co.** ☎ 907/983–2908
🖶 907/983–3908 ⊕ www.skagwaystreetcar.com. **Tribal Tours** ☎ 907/747–7290 or
888/270–8687 🖶 907/747–3770 ⊕ www.sitkatribal.com.

TRAIN TRAVEL
Southeast Alaska's only railroad, the White Pass & Yukon Route, operates between Skagway and Fraser, British Columbia. The tracks follow the historic path over the White Pass summit—a mountain-climbing,
cliff-hanging route of 28 mi each way. Bus connections are available at
Fraser to Whitehorse, Yukon.
 White Pass & Yukon Route (WP & YR) ☎ 907/983–2217 or 800/343–7373 ⊕ www.
whitepassrailroad.com.

VISITOR INFORMATION

Hours of operation of the following visitor information centers are generally mid-May–August, daily 8–5, and additional hours when cruise ships are in port; September–mid-May, weekdays 8–5.

Tourist Information **Alaska Department of Fish and Game** ᴆ Box 25526, Juneau 99802-5526 ☏ 907/465-4112, 907/465-4180 sportfishing seasons and regulations, 907/465-2376 license information ⊕ www.state.ak.us/adfg. **Alaska Division of Parks** ⊠ 400 Willoughby Ave., Suite 400, Juneau 99801 ☏ 907/465-4563 ⊕ www.dnr.state.ak.us/parks. **Haines Convention and Visitors Bureau** ⊠ 2nd Ave. near Willard St. ᴆ Box 530, Haines 99827 ☏ 907/766-2234 or 800/458-3579 ⊕ www.haines.ak.us. **Juneau Convention and Visitors Bureau** ⊠ 1 Sealaska Plaza, Suite 305, Juneau ☏ 907/586-2201 or 888/581-2201 ⊕ www.traveljuneau.com. **Ketchikan Visitors Bureau** ⊠ 131 Front St., Ketchikan 99901 ☏ 907/225-6166 or 800/770-3300 ⊕ www.visit-ketchikan.com. **Klondike Gold Rush National Historical Park** visitor center ⊠ 2nd Ave. and Broadway ᴆ Box 517, Skagway 99840 ☏ 907/983-2921 or 907/983-9224 ⊕ www.nps.gov/klgo. **Petersburg Visitor Information Center** ⊠ 1st and Fram Sts. ᴆ Box 649, Petersburg 99833 ☏ 907/772-4636 ⊕ www.petersburg.org. **Prince of Wales Chamber of Commerce** ᴆ Box 497, Craig 99921 ☏ 907/826-3870 ⊕ www.princeofwalescoc.org. **Sitka Convention and Visitors Bureau** ⊠ 303 Lincoln St. ᴆ Box 1226, Sitka 99835 ☏ 907/747-5940 ⊕ www.sitka.org. **Skagway Convention and Visitors Bureau** ᴆ Box 1029, Skagway 99840 ☏ 907/983-2854 or 888/762-1898 ⊕ www.skagway.org. **Southeast Alaska Tourism Council** ⊕ www.alaskainfo.org. **Stewart-Hyder Chamber of Commerce** ᴆ Box 306, Stewart, BC V0T 1W0 ☏ 250/636-9224 ⊟ 250/636-2199 ⊕ www.stewartbchyderak.homestead.com. **U.S. Forest Service** ⊠ 648 Mission St., Ketchikan 99901 ☏ 907/225-3101 ⊕ www.fs.fed.us/r10/tongass. **Wrangell Visitor Center** ⊠ 107 Stikine Ave. ᴆ Box 49, Wrangell 99929 ☏ 907/874-3901 or 800/367-9745 ⊕ www.wrangellchamber.org.

SOUTH CENTRAL ALASKA

INCLUDING PRINCE WILLIAM SOUND, HOMER & THE KENAI PENINSULA

6

FODOR'S CHOICE

Alaska SeaLife Center, *Seward*

Kenai Princess Wilderness Lodge, *Cooper Landing*

Sackett's Kenai Grill, *Cooper Landing*

Saltry in Halibut Cove, *Homer*

Teddy's Inn the Woods, *Seward*

HIGHLY RECOMMENDED

RESTAURANTS   The Duck Inn, *Soldotna*

Homestead Restaurant, *Homer*

Ray's Waterfront, *Seward*

HOTELS   Alaska's Treehouse B&B, *Seward*

Driftwood Inn, *Homer*

Great Alaska Adventure Lodge, *Sterling*

Kachemak Bay Wilderness Lodge, *near Homer*

Kennicott Glacier Lodge, *McCarthy*

Kodiak Buskin River Inn, *Kodiak*

Pioneer Ridge Bed and Breakfast Inn, *Wasilla*

Talkeetna Alaskan Lodge, *Talkeetna*

SIGHTS   Alutiiq Museum and Archaeological Repository, *Kodiak*

Columbia Glacier, *Valdez*

Exit Glacier, *Seward*

Independence Mine, *Palmer*

Kenai Fjords National Park

Kennicott Mine, *McCarthy*

Pratt Museum, *Homer*

NIGHTLIFE   Salty Dawg Saloon, *Homer*

OUTDOORS   Resurrection Pass Trail, between Hope & Cooper Landing

By Robin
Mackey Hill
and Kent
Sturgis

Updated by
Tom Reale

ANCHORAGE MAY DOMINATE THE REGION IN SIZE, recognition, and political clout, but don't let that mislead you into thinking Anchorage *is* South Central Alaska. The city is actually an anomaly—a modern, urban environment amid historic ports, wilderness outposts, and fishing towns. It also functions as the gateway to some of Alaska's most spectacular parks and wilderness areas, most of which are accessible by floatplane, the Alaska Railroad, or car.

The city lies near the convergence of two of Alaska's most magnificent mountain systems. To the east of the city and sweeping on to the southwest are the Chugach Mountains, a young, active, and impressively rugged range notable for its high coastal relief. Near-mile-high valley walls and peaks rise almost directly from the sea. Across Cook Inlet to the southwest march the high volcanic peaks of the Alaska Range, part of the Pacific Ocean's great Ring of Fire, but snowcapped nonetheless. Farther north in the Alaska Range, and visible from Anchorage on clear days, shimmers Mt. McKinley, with Mt. Foraker at its shoulder—the towering granite giants of the North American continent. Also visible from town are the Talkeetna Range, to the northeast, and the Kenai Range, just across Turnagain Arm and forming the spine of Anchorage's playground, the Kenai Peninsula.

South Central starts with the port towns on the Gulf of Alaska, Prince William Sound, and Cook Inlet—Cordova, Valdez, Whittier, Seward, Seldovia, Kodiak, Homer, Kenai—with their harbors, ferries, glaciers, and ocean life. Unlike the towns and cities of Interior Alaska, where the common theme of gold-rush history links most of the communities, South Central towns and cities have very different personalities. Kodiak, for example, is a busy commercial-fishing port, whereas Homer is a funky tourist town and artists' colony on beautiful Kachemak Bay. Then come those mountains, curled like an arm embracing the region. Talkeetna, at the western limits of South Central, is where mountaineers gather to launch their assaults on towering Mt. McKinley. On the eastern border, the defunct copper mine outside McCarthy lies at the foot of the Wrangell Mountains.

Nature lovers can rejoice at the meeting of these mountain ranges, for they bring together a wide sampling of Alaska's flora and fauna. Dall sheep and mountain goats dance their way around the heights of the Chugach and Kenai mountains. Tree species mingle here, too, including three different varieties of spruce—Sitka, black, and white. You'll see larch, birch, cottonwood, and aspen turn golden in the crisp days of late summer and early autumn. South Central is also Alaska's farm country. In the Matanuska-Susitna Valley, under an ever-present summertime sun, 75-pound cabbages are a common occurrence.

Exploring South Central

South Central Alaska can be broken down into three general subregions—the towns and bays of Prince William Sound, communities south of Anchorage on the Kenai Peninsula, and communities north of Anchorage in the Matanuska-Susitna (Mat-Su) Valley and beyond. The region is ideal for exploring by boat, train, car, RV, or plane. All but a couple of the coastal communities are on the road system. For the most part, roads have two lanes and are paved. Traffic, especially on the Kenai Peninsula, can be bumper to bumper on summer weekends, so give yourself plenty of time; better yet, try to travel midweek. Long summer days give you plenty of daylight for exploring.

About the Restaurants

When you leave Anchorage, your menu options in South Central Alaska tend to contract. There are bright spots to be found along the road and in the smaller towns, but exotic cuisines aren't among them. However, the prospects for finding good food prepared well have increased in recent years. Fresh salmon, halibut, crab, and shellfish are readily available even in places far from the seashore. And it's easy to find items like pasta dishes, fresh-baked pastries, and even the occasional vegetarian main course in places where, in past years, you could have your food however you liked it, as long as you liked it fried.

Among the things that haven't changed are the lack of formality in the eating establishments—the folks at the next table just might be wearing hip waders and fishing vests—and the friendliness of the locals. The need for reservations is minimal even during the busy summer season, but you may have the occasional short wait for a table.

About the Hotels

The hotel scene is undergoing the same kind of changes as the restaurants. More properties are being built or remodeled to meet the demands of the growing tourist trade, and the upgrades in facilities and service are a welcome trend. You can find everything from budget-priced hostels to remote deluxe accommodations guaranteed to satisfy even the most jaded sybarite. There's a lot in between, including some national chains, some local and regional chains, and more than a few mom-and-pop operations. Reservations are not always required during the summer but are usually a good idea between Memorial Day and Labor Day. The growing numbers of bed-and-breakfasts means that you can always find someplace to stay, even late at night at the height of the tourist season.

WHAT IT COSTS					
	$$$$	$$$	$$	$	¢
RESTAURANTS	over $25	$20–$25	$15–$20	$10–$15	under $10
HOTELS	over $225	$175–$225	$125–$175	$75–$125	under $75

Restaurant prices are for a main course at dinner. Hotel prices are for two people in a standard double room in high season, excluding service charges and tax.

Timing

The region is most alive with visitors and recreational activities between Memorial Day and Labor Day, which is also when it is the most crowded with people enjoying the spectacular fishing and boating, hiking and backpacking, and wildlife spotting and flightseeing. Fall comes early—in mid- to late August—to South Central but can be a gorgeous time to travel. Trees are painted gold and orange, and mountaintops are dusted with snow. Dining and lodging options outside Anchorage may be limited in winter, as many businesses close during the off-season.

PRINCE WILLIAM SOUND

The sound covers some 15,000 square mi—15 times the size of San Francisco Bay. It receives an average of 150 inches of rain a year and is home to more than 150 glaciers, 20 of them reaching tidewater. Along its shoreline are quiet bays, trickling waterfalls, and hidden coves perfect for camping. In addition to hosting brown bears, gray wolves, and marten, the sound thrives with a variety of birds and all manner of marine life, including salmon, halibut, humpback and killer whales, sea otters, sea lions, and porpoises. Bald eagles often soar overhead or perch

Numbers in the text correspond to numbers in the margin and on the South Central Alaska map.

6

If you have 3 days

Spend them on the Kenai Peninsula. Head south out of Anchorage on the Seward Highway alongside Turnagain Arm and stop in the ski town of Girdwood for a light lunch and a stroll before continuing southeast to **Portage Glacier** ❸ and the Begich-Boggs Visitor Center in the **Chugach National Forest** ❷. Take a day hike out of **Hope** ❻ or a boat trip into **Kenai Fjords National Park** ❽ out of ⛴ **Seward** ❼. After spending the night in Seward, work your way down to ⛴ **Homer** ⓬. There's plenty to see and do along Kachemak Bay, including taking a dinner cruise over to Halibut Cove or trying your luck at landing a huge halibut. On your way back up to Anchorage, stop for a bite to eat in **Soldotna** ⓫ and make any other stops you missed during the trip down.

If you have 5 days

Follow the three-day itinerary above, return to Anchorage, and head north out of town the next day along the Glenn Highway. Wander the back roads between **Palmer** ⓱ and **Wasilla** ⓲, continuing up to Hatcher Pass and the Independence Mine. Visit a couple of area attractions, such as the Musk Ox Farm or the Iditarod Trail Headquarters, before working your way up to ⛴ **Talkeetna** ⓳ for the night. The other option for Day and Night 3 is a backpacking trip into ⛴ **Denali State Park** ⓴. On your way back to Anchorage, stop along the roadside for a short hike or a picnic.

If you have 7 days

Follow the five-day itinerary before cutting over to ⛴ **Valdez** ❹, which you should use as a base. Take a day trip past Columbia Glacier; see the sights, including the Valdez Museum; or take a hike in the surrounding Chugach Mountains. Consider flying or taking the ferry across the sound to **Cordova** ❺, or drive or fly into McCarthy and the nearby Kennicott Mine in **Wrangell–St. Elias National Park and Preserve** ㉒. Adventurers may consider an excursion to ⛴ **Kodiak Island** ⓯ to watch for Kodiak brown bears and to explore the island's Russian origins. If hiking is your passion, you can spend the entire seven days on a guided backcountry trip through the park or venture farther afield to the pristine ⛴ **Lake Clark National Park and Preserve** ⓰. If exploring Prince William Sound is more to your liking, arrange for a kayak trip out of Valdez or Cordova.

in tall trees. The sound was heavily damaged by the *Exxon Valdez* oil spill in 1989. The oil has sunk into the beaches below the surface and is sometimes uncovered after storms and high tides. What lasting effect this lurking oil will have on the area is still being studied and remains the topic of much debate.

Chugach State Park

Bordering Anchorage to the east.

❶ Chugach State Park is Alaska's most accessible wilderness. Nearly half a million acres in size, the park rises from the coast to more than 8,000 feet, with mountains bearing such colorful names as Williwaw Peak, Temp-

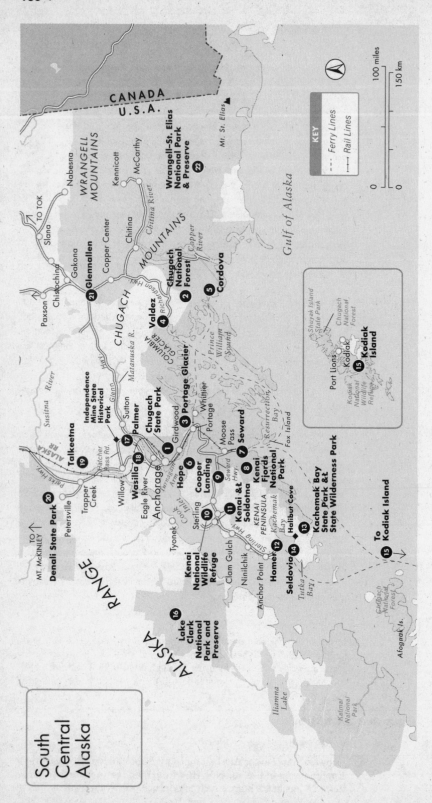

South Central Alaska

CANADA
U.S.A.

WRANGELL MOUNTAINS

Wrangell-St. Elias National Park & Preserve **22**

Mt. St. Elias

Gulf of Alaska

KEY
--- Ferry Lines
— Rail Lines

100 miles
150 km

Nabesna

TO TOK

Slana

Kennicott

McCarthy

Chitina River

Chistochina

Gakona

Copper Center

Chitina

Copper River

CHUGACH MOUNTAINS

Glennallen **21**

Paxson

Chugach National Forest **2**

Cordova **5**

Valdez **4**

Prince William Sound

CHUGACH

Columbia River

Richardson HWY.

Matanuska R.

Independence Mine State Historical Park

Palmer **17**

Chugach State Park

Portage Glacier **3**

Whittier

Portage

Seward **7**

Resurrection Bay

Fox Island

Shuyak Island State Park

Chugach National Forest

Port Lions

Kodiak

Kodiak Island **15**

Kodiak National Wildlife Refuge

Susitna River

Glenn HWY.

Sutton

Girdwood

Hatcher Pass Rd.

Talkeetna **19**

Willow

Wasilla **18**

Eagle River

Anchorage **1**

Hope **6**

Cooper Landing **9**

Moose Pass

Kenai Fjords National Park **8**

Kachemak Bay State Park & State Wilderness Park

ALASKA RR

Trapper Creek

Petersville

Denali State Park **20**

MT. McKINLEY

Parks HWY.

Tyonek

Cook Inlet

Sterling

Kenai & Soldotna **11**

Kenai National Wildlife Refuge

KENAI PENINSULA

10

Seward Hwy.

Sterling Hwy.

Clam Gulch

Ninilchik

Anchor Point

Homer **12**

Halibut Cove **13**

Seldovia **14**

Tutka Bay

Kachemak Bay

To Kodiak Island **15**

Lake Clark National Park and Preserve **16**

Illiamna Lake

ALASKA RANGE

Afognak Is.

Chugach National Forest

Katmai National Park

6

Boating

You'll find abundant opportunities for boating on lakes, rivers, and the ocean in South Central. Canoe and kayak parties in the South Central utilize Prince William Sound, Kachemak Bay, and the Tangle Lakes region. Access to the Tangle Lakes system is off the Denali Highway, 20 mi west of Paxson. This mountainous country on the southern flank of the Alaska Range forms the headwaters of the Delta River. You can spend a few lazy hours paddling near the road or take an extended trip requiring overnight camping and portages.

Boaters should exercise caution, however, because local waters are icy cold and can be deadly. Even a life jacket will not save you if hypothermia sets in. Ask locals about conditions before setting out on any but the smallest, most placid lakes. Also, beware of the exposed land on the mudflats of Turnagain Arm between Anchorage and Portage—the huge expanse of seemingly dry ground can quickly turn into a muddy morass when the incoming tide comes roaring in. Keep off, no matter how safe it appears to be.

Fishing

South Central has Alaska's most accessible fishing. Thousands of tourists flock to the Kenai River and its tributaries for trophy king salmon, which can reach nearly 100 pounds. Saltwater fishing yields huge halibut, cod, and shellfish. Drift boats are a good means of access to the rivers. Boat rentals and guide services are available all along the South Central coastline. Fishing licenses are required for all fresh- and saltwater fishing, including gathering clams and shellfish. Licenses are available at sporting-goods, grocery, and drug stores statewide. Nonresident licenses can be purchased for 1-, 3-, 7-, or 14-day periods or for an entire calendar year. King salmon stamps are also required if you intend to pursue kings. Call the **Alaska Department of Fish and Game** (☎ 907/267–2218) for information.

tation Peak, Mt. Magnificent, and Mt. Rumble. The park has nearly 30 trails—from 2 mi to 30 mi long—totaling more than 150 mi, suitable for shorter hikes, weeklong backpacking, and mountain biking. Easy-to-follow cross-country routes extend from one park entrance to another, allowing multiday excursions and a variety of loop trips. This is not your typical urban park—it's real wilderness, home to Dall sheep, mountain goats, brown bears, and several packs of wolves who reside on the edge of town. Many of the trails were blazed by early miners who usually sought the easiest passes. There are also some comfortable roadside campgrounds for people traveling by car or bicycle. Trailheads are scattered around the park's perimeter from Eklutna Lake, 30 mi north of Anchorage, to the trailhead for the Crow Pass Trail near Girdwood, 37 mi to the south. Some of the more popular trailheads charge a daily parking fee of $5. The Eagle River Nature Center or the park headquarters near Potter Marsh 12 mi south of town has park information. ⊠ *Headquarters, Mile 115, Seward Hwy.* ☎ *HC 52, Box 8999, Indian 99540* ☎ *907/ 345–5014.*

The views from high perches in this park are heady. You can look down on the city of Anchorage, observe the great tides in Cook Inlet, gaze north toward Mt. McKinley, or delineate the grand procession of snowy peaks across the inlet, marching down the Alaska Peninsula. The most frequently climbed alpine perch in Alaska is **Flattop Mountain,** on Chugach Park's western edge, ascended by hikers of all abilities. The trailhead is at the Glen Alps parking lot on the hillside above town.

Eagle River Road leads 12 mi into the mountains from the bedroom community of Eagle River. The **Eagle River Nature Center,** at the end of Eagle River Road, has wildlife displays, telescopes for wildlife spotting, and volunteers to answer questions, lead hikes, and host naturalist programs throughout the year. A cabin that sleeps eight and a pair of yurts (insulated tents) that sleep four and six are available for rental. Cost is $55 per night for nonmembers of the nature center, and a walk-in of about 1½ mi is required. Amenities include woodstoves, firewood, and outdoor latrines. ⊠ *Eagle River Rd.* ☎ *907/694–2108* ⊕ *www.ernc.org* ⊠ *Parking $5* ⊘ *May, Tues.–Sun. 10–5; June–Aug., Sun.–Thurs. 10–5, Fri. and Sat. 10–7; Sept., Tues.–Sun. 10–5; Oct.–Apr., Fri.–Sun. 10–5.*

Where to Stay

¢ △ **Alaska State Park Campgrounds.** You'll find three road-accessible campgrounds in Chugach Park, at Eklutna Lake, Bird Creek, and Eagle River. All are within a short drive from Anchorage. The sites have picnic tables, fire pits, water, and latrines and are available on a first-come, first-served basis. Ⓓ *Alaska State Parks, HC52, Box 8999, Indian 99540* ☎ *907/345–5014* ⊕ *www.dnr.state.ak.us/parks/units/ chugach/facility.htm* ⇋*3 campgrounds, 154 campsites* ⊟*No credit cards* ⊘ *Closed roughly Oct.–Apr.*

Sports & the Outdoors

Main trailheads in the park are at the top of O'Malley, Huffman, and DeArmoun roads; south of Anchorage at Potter Valley, McHugh Creek, and Bird Ridge on the Seward Highway; and to the north of town at Arctic Valley Road (6 mi out) and Eagle River Road (13 mi out). The **Little Rodak Trail** is less than 1 mi long and has a viewing platform that overlooks the Eagle River valley. **Albert Loop Trail** behind the nature center has markers that coordinate with a self-guided hike along its 3-mi route; pick up a brochure at the Eagle River Nature Center.

Chugach National Forest

❷ *40 mi east of Anchorage.*

Sprawling east of Chugach State Park, Chugach National Forest encompasses nearly 6 million acres to embrace a major part of the Kenai Peninsula as well as parts of Prince William Sound. It's the second-largest national forest in the United States, exceeded in size only by the Tongass in Southeast Alaska.

Recreational opportunities here include hiking; camping; backpacking; fishing; boating; mountain biking; horseback riding; hunting; rock climbing; flightseeing; and, in the winter, snowshoeing, cross-country skiing, ice climbing, snowmobiling, and dog mushing. Hiking trails offer easy access into the heart of the forest. You can go for a short walk in the woods, pack a lunch and go for a hike looking for birds and wildlife, or embark on a multiday backpacking excursion. You can also take the opportunity to fish a backcountry lake or just indulge yourself in a part of Alaska that's seldom seen by visitors. At all but the most popular trailheads, a five-minute stroll down a wooded trail leads you to the sights, smells, and tranquility of backcountry Alaska.

The Seward Highway between Anchorage and Seward has a number of trail access points. (Check the highway for mile markers, with the distance measured from Seward.) At Mile 63.7 south of Turnagain Pass is the turnoff to the Johnson Pass Trail, a relatively flat trail to walk. Seven miles farther south, take the Hope Highway 18 mi to its end and find the Porcupine Campground. From there, the Gull Rock Trail follows the shore of Turnagain Arm for 5 mi, offering scenic views across the Arm and the chance to spot beluga whales as they forage for salmon. Farther south on the Seward Highway at Mile 23.1, the Ptarmigan Creek trail starts at the campground and climbs into the mountains, ending next to a placid lake surrounded by snowy peaks.

Be prepared to be self-sufficient when entering Chugach Forest. Trailheads typically offer nothing more than a place to park and perhaps an outhouse. Running water, trail maps, and other amenities that you may have come to expect when visiting national forests in the Lower 48 are not available here. Also, be "bear aware" whenever you travel in bear country—and all of Alaska is bear country (⇨ Bear Facts box *in* Chapter 2). Be aware of your surroundings, and make noise when traveling, especially in areas of reduced visibility. Bears will most likely make themselves scarce as long as they've got some advance warning of your arrival.

For information on recreational opportunities in the forest, call **forest headquarters** (☎ 907/743–9500 Anchorage) or the **Alaska Public Lands Information Center** (☎ 907/271–2737 ⊕ www.nps.gov/aplic/center).

Sports & the Outdoors

★ **Resurrection Pass Trail,** a 38-mi-long backpacking trail through the Chugach National Forest, draws hikers and backpackers from around the world for its colorful wildflowers in spring and summer and the chance to spot wildlife. Moose, caribou, Dall sheep, mountain goats, black and brown bears, wolves, coyotes, and lynx all traverse the forest. Carry binoculars for the best viewing opportunities. Scan every place for movement or anything that doesn't look like a rock, a bush, or a tree, especially whenever you see an open area.

The northern end of the trail starts south of the town of Hope, following an old mining trail through the Kenai Mountains to its end near the town of Cooper Landing. Side trails lead to trailheads along the Seward Highway at Summit Creek and Devil's Pass Creek. The well-maintained trail offers easy access to open country above the tree line. Besides U.S. Forest Service cabins, the Forest Service has provided several "official" campsites along the trail where you'll find a cleared patch of ground and a fire ring; however, you're free to pitch your tent wherever you like.

Where to Stay

¢ 🏠 **U.S. Forest Service Cabins.** Along trails, near wilderness alpine lakes, in coastal forests, and on saltwater beaches, these rustic cabins offer retreats for the solo hiker or a group of friends. Some cabins are built of logs, and some are A-frames. Most have tables, chairs, wood-burning stoves, and bunks but no electricity, running water, or bedding. Many require a fly-in or boat ride, although some can be reached by car and then foot. ☎ *877/444–6777 reservations* ⊕ *www.reserveusa.com* ⟿ *41 cabins* ▭ *D, MC, V.*

¢ ⛺ **U.S. Forest Service Campgrounds.** The Forest Service maintains 18 campgrounds, 14 of them road-accessible, within Chugach National Forest. All of the road-accessible campgrounds have toilet facilities, usually outhouses, and drinking water available from hand pumps. The Russian River Campground has a three-day limit during salmon-fishing season in June and July. Most have sites suitable for RVs as well as tents. Reservations (for a fee) are accepted at only a limited number of sites.

☎ 877/444–6777 *reservations* ⊕ *www.reserveusa.com* 🖙 *18 camp-grounds* ☰ *D, MC, V.*

Portage Glacier

54 mi southeast of Anchorage.

❸ Portage Glacier is one of Alaska's most frequently visited tourist desti-nations. A 6-mi side road off the Seward Highway leads to the **Begich-Boggs Visitor Center** (☎ 907/783–2326 ⊕ www.fs.fed.us/r10/chugach/chugach_pages/bbvc), on the shore of Portage Lake and named after two U.S. congressmen who disappeared on a small-plane journey out of An-chorage in 1972. The center is staffed by Forest Service personnel, who can help plan your trip and explain the natural history of the area. A film on glaciers is shown hourly, and icebergs frequently drift down to the center from Portage Glacier.

The mountains surrounding Portage Glacier are covered with smaller glaciers. A 1-mi hike west brings you to the **Byron Glacier** overlook. The glacier is notable for its accessibility—it's one of the few places where you can hike onto a glacier from the road system. In summer, natural-ists lead free weekly treks in search of microscopic ice worms. Several hiking trails are accessible from the Seward Highway, including the Old Johnson Trail and the path up Bird Ridge. Both offer spectacular views of **Turnagain Arm,** where explorer Captain Cook searched for the North-west Passage. Local lore has it that the arm is so named because Cook entered it repeatedly, only to be forced to turn back by the huge tide. The tide is so powerful it sometimes rushes up the arm as a tidal bore—a wall of water that goes up an inlet. Keep an eye out for black bears in all the Portage side valleys in the summer.

🐾 **Big Game Alaska** is a 144-acre drive-through wildlife center just before the Portage Glacier turnoff. Moose, bison, elk, caribou, Sitka black-tailed deer, musk ox, great horned owls, a brown bear, and a bald eagle, many of them orphaned in the wild, now live in the park. There are also snack and gift shops. ⊠ *Mile 79, Seward Hwy.* ☎ *907/783–2025* 🖷 *907/783–2370* 🖻 *$5* ⊙ *May–Sept., daily 8–8; Oct.–Apr., daily 10–dusk.*

Little remains of the community of **Portage** as a result of the 1964 earth-quake. The ghost forest of dead spruce in the area was created when the land subsided by 6 feet–10 feet after the quake, and salt water pen-etrated inland from Turnagain Arm, killing the trees. A tumbledown build-ing or two still stand along the highway, and there's a café at the turnoff to Portage Glacier.

| en route | The town of **Whittier** primarily serves as access point for those who want to visit Prince William Sound. Access is via a one-way combination highway and railway tunnel with restricted hours, so it's not always possible to just breeze into and back out of Whittier. Tolls through the tunnel are $12 for passenger vehicles and $20–$35 for RVs and trailers; waits of up to an hour, however, are possible, and summer hours are from 6 AM until 11 PM. There's a small-boat harbor, a ferry terminal for trips to Valdez and Cordova, fishing and sightseeing charter companies, and sea-kayak rentals and tours. A few small restaurants and shops surround the harbor, but lodging facilities are limited. Despite the town's limited appeal, the sound and surrounding snowcapped mountains make for fabulous views on a clear day. |

Guided Tours

Gray Line of Alaska (☎ 907/277–5581 or 800/478–6388) leads summer boat tours (from mid-May to mid-September) along the face of Portage Glacier aboard the 200-passenger *Ptarmigan* for $25.

Shopping

On your way to Portage, look for **Indian Valley Meats** (✉ Huot Cir., 23 mi south of Anchorage on Seward Hwy. ☎ 907/653–7511), where workers sell the smoked salmon and musk ox, reindeer, and buffalo sausage made on the premises. They'll also smoke, can, and package the fish you've caught and arrange for shipping anywhere in the world.

Valdez

6 hrs northeast of Whittier by water, 304 mi east of Anchorage.

❹ Valdez (pronounced val-*deez*) is the largest of the Prince William Sound communities. This year-round ice-free port was originally the entry point for people and goods going to the Interior during the gold rush. Today that flow has been reversed, with Valdez harbor being the southern terminus of the trans-Alaska pipeline, which carries crude oil from Prudhoe Bay and surrounding oil fields nearly 800 mi to the north. This region, with its dependence on commercial fishing, is still feeling the aftereffects of 1989's massive oil spill. Much of Valdez looks modern because the business area was relocated and rebuilt after its destruction by the 1964 Good Friday earthquake.

Many Alaskan communities have summer fishing derbies, but Valdez may hold the record for the number of such contests, stretching from late May into September for halibut and various runs of salmon. If you go fishing, by all means enter the appropriate derby. Every summer the newspapers run sob stories about tourists who landed possible prizewinners but couldn't share in the glory because they hadn't forked over the five bucks to officially enter the contest. The **Valdez Silver Salmon Derby** is held the entire month of August. Fishing charters abound in this area of Prince William Sound, and for good reason: these fertile waters provide some of the best saltwater sportfishing in all of Alaska.

A pleasant attraction on a rainy day, if you ever tire of gazing at the 5,000-foot mountain peaks surrounding Valdez, is the **Valdez Museum.** It explores the lives, livelihoods, and events significant to Valdez and surrounding regions. Exhibits include a restored 1880s Gleason & Baily hand-pumped fire engine, a 1907 Ahrens steam fire engine, a 19th-century saloon, information on the local Native peoples, and an exhibit on the 1989 oil spill. Every summer the museum hosts an exhibit of quilts and fiber arts made by local and regional artisans. At a separate site, a 35-foot by 40-foot model of **Historical Old Town Valdez** (✉ 436 Hazlet Ave.) depicts the original town, which was devastated by the 1964 earthquake. There's also an operating seismograph and an exhibit on local seismic activity. ✉ *217 Egan Dr.* ☎ *907/835-2764* ⊕ *www.alaska.net/~vldzmuse/index.html* 🎟 *$3* ⊙ *June–Aug., Mon.–Sat. 9–6, Sun. 8–5; Sept.–May, weekdays 1–5, Sat. noon–4.*

★ A visit to **Columbia Glacier,** which flows from the surrounding Chugach Mountains, certainly should be on the agenda. Its deep aquamarine face is 5 mi across, and it calves icebergs with resounding cannonades. This glacier is one of the largest and most readily accessible of Alaska's coastal glaciers. The state ferry travels past the face of the glacier, and scheduled tours of the glaciers and the rest of the sound are available by boat and aircraft from Valdez and Whittier.

Where to Eat

$–$$$ ✕ **Mike's Palace.** This convivial restaurant with Italian-diner decor is a local favorite. The menu includes veal, terrific pizza, beer-batter halibut, steaks, and Greek gyros. ⊠ *On harbor, 201 N. Harbor Dr.* ☎ *907/835–2365* ▭ *MC, V.*

Guided Tours

Numerous charter operators, including **Alpine Aviation Adventures** (☎ 907/835–4304, 800/478–4304 in Alaska ♨ 907/835–2523), based in Valdez, give aerial tours of Columbia Glacier, Prince William Sound, and the Wrangell Mountains.

Valdez-based **Columbia Glacier Wildlife Cruises/Lu-Lu Belle** (☎ 907/835–5141 or 800/411–0090 ♨ 907/835–5899 in summer ☎☎ 800/411–0090 off-season ⊕ www.lulubelletours.com) leads small-group whale-watching, wildlife-viewing, and Columbia Glacier cruises.

Keystone Raft & Kayak Adventures (☎ 907/835–2606 or 800/328–8460 ♨ 907/835–4638 ⊕ www.alaskawhitewater.com) provides all gear for guided raft and kayak tours on rivers rated up to Class V in the Valdez and Copper River valley areas.

Stan Stephens Glacier & Wildlife Cruises (☎ 907/835–4731 or 866/867–1297 ♨ 907/835–3765 ⊕ www.stanstephenscruises.com), based in Valdez, leads Prince William Sound glacier and wildlife-viewing cruises to Columbia and Meares glaciers from mid-May through mid-September.

Cordova

6 hrs southeast of Valdez by water, 150 mi east of Anchorage by air.

❺ Perched on Orca Inlet in eastern Prince William Sound, Cordova began life early in the 20th century as the port city for the Copper River–Northwestern Railway, which was built to serve the Kennicott copper mines 191 mi away in the Wrangell Mountains. With the mines and the railroad shut down since 1938, Cordova's economy now depends heavily on fishing. Attempts to develop a road along the abandoned railroad line connecting to the state highway system were dashed by the 1964 earthquake, so Cordova remains isolated. Access to the community is limited to airplane or ferry. A small town with the spectacular backdrop of snowy Mt. Eccles, Cordova is the gateway to the Copper River delta—one of the great birding areas of North America.

The **Cordova Museum** emphasizes Native artifacts as well as pioneer, mining, and fishing history. Displays include an 1840s handcrafted lighthouse lens and a stuffed 800-pound leatherback turtle. Afternoon video programs and an informative brochure outline a self-guided walking tour of the town's historical buildings. The gift shop sells masks, pottery, and children's and local history books. ⊠ *622 1st St.* ☎ *907/424–6665* ▭ *$1* ☉ *Memorial Day–Labor Day, Mon.–Sat. 10–6, Sun. 2–4; Labor Day–Memorial Day, Tues.–Fri. 1–5, Sat. 2–4.*

Drive out of town along the Copper River Highway and visit the **Million Dollar Bridge,** at Mile 48, where you can view the **Childs Glacier.** Although there is no visitor center, a covered viewing area right next to the bridge enables you to watch the face of the glacier and read the informational plaques while you wait for a huge chunk of ice to topple into the river. The waves produced by falling ice frequently wash migrating salmon onto the riverbank, and the local brown bears have been known to patrol the river's edge looking for an easy meal, so keep your eyes wide open.

Where to Stay & Eat

$–$$$ ✕ **Powder House Bar & Restaurant.** On clear summer evenings you can relax on the deck overlooking Eyak Lake at this roadside bar and enjoy whatever the cook's in the mood to fix: homemade soups, sandwiches, sushi, and seasonal seafood are all possibilities. If you're lucky or skillful in your fishing endeavors, the kitchen staff will cook your catch. On Friday and Saturday, shrimp and steak are added to the menu. ⊠ *Mile 2.1, Copper River Hwy.* ☎ *907/424–3529* ▤ *AE, D, MC, V.*

¢–$$ ✕ **Ambrosia.** Pastas, hamburgers, and steaks are served behind the storefront, but it's the hearty pizzas that have earned this place its reputation among locals. ⊠ *410 1st St.* ☎ *907/424–7175* ▤ *AE, MC, V.*

¢ ✕ **Killer Whale Café.** Have a breakfast of espresso and baked goods or an omelet at this bookstore café. For lunch you can choose from a deli menu of soups, salads, and sandwiches, followed by a fresh, homemade dessert. On the back balcony, tables overlook the harbor. ⊠ *507 1st St.* ☎ *907/424–7733* ▤ *No credit cards* ◷ *Closed Sun. No dinner.*

$–$$ ▦ **Reluctant Fisherman Inn.** At this waterfront hotel and restaurant, with its collection of Native art and artifacts, you can watch the commercial-fishing fleet and other maritime traffic sail by. Comfortable, nautical-theme rooms overlook the harbor. The restaurant serves local seafood, including a king salmon chili, as well as pastas and espresso. ⊠ *407 Railroad Ave., 99574* ☎ *907/424–3272 or 800/770–3272* 🖷 *907/424–7465* ⊕ *www.cordovaak.com* ⤳ *41 rooms* ⌂ *Restaurant, in-room data ports, cable TV, bar, laundry facilities, meeting rooms, airport shuttle, car rental, travel services, some pets allowed; no a/c* ▤ *AE, D, DC, MC, V.*

¢–$ ▦ **Northern Nights Inn B&B.** Commanding a dramatic view of Orca Inlet just a couple of blocks above downtown Cordova, this bed-and-breakfast has rooms furnished with turn-of-the-20th-century antiques. If owner Becky Chapek doesn't have room for you, she'll serve as a valuable source of information on other B&Bs in town. She also operates bus tours around town and to the Million Dollar Bridge, and she can transport you to and from the airport as well. ⊠ *500 3rd St.* ⌖ *Box 1564, 99574* ☎ *907/424–5356* ⤳ *4 rooms* ▤ *AE, D, MC, V.*

Guided Tours

Cordova Air Service (☎ 907/424–3289, 800/424–7608 in Alaska 🖷 907/424–3495) leads aerial tours of Prince William Sound on planes with wheels or floats. **Alaskan Wilderness Outfitting Co.** (☎ 907/424–5552 🖷 907/424–5564 ⊕ www.alaskawilderness.com) operates an air-taxi service out of Cordova and conducts fresh- and saltwater fly-out fishing experiences, from drop-off to fully outfitted and guided lodge accommodations.

Sports & the Outdoors

BIRD-WATCHING Spring migration to the **Copper River delta** provides some of the finest avian spectacles in the world. Species include the Western sandpiper, American dipper, orange-crowned warbler, and short-billed dowitcher. Trumpeter swans and dusky Canada geese can also be seen. The **Copper River Delta Shorebird Festival** (☎ 907/424–7260 ⊕ www.cordovachamber.com), held the first week of May, includes five days of workshops and guided field trips.

Shopping

Orca Book & Sound Co. (⊠ 507 1st St. ☎ 907/424–5305), closed Sunday, is much more than a bookstore. In addition to books, it sells music, art supplies, children's toys, and locally produced art. The walls often double as a gallery for local works or traveling exhibits, and the store specializes in old, rare, out-of-print, and first-edition books, especially Alaskana. In the back is the Killer Whale Café.

KENAI PENINSULA

The Kenai Peninsula, thrusting into the Gulf of Alaska south of Anchorage, is South Central's playground, offering salmon and halibut fishing, spectacular scenery, and wildlife viewing. Commercial fishing is important to the area's economy; five species of Pacific salmon run up the aqua-color Kenai River every summer. Campgrounds and trailheads for back-woods hiking are strung along the roads. Along the way, you can explore three major federal holdings on the peninsula—the western end of the sprawling Chugach National Forest, Kenai National Wildlife Refuge, and Kenai Fjords National Park.

Hope

39 mi west of Portage, 87 mi south of Anchorage.

❻ The little gold-mining community of Hope is 87 mi south of Anchor-age by road but just across Turnagain Arm. To visit, however, you must drive all the way around, as no ferry service exists. Hope was founded by miners in 1896 but now consists mainly of retirement homes for for-mer Anchorage residents. The old log cabins and weathered frame buildings in the town center are favorite photography subjects. You'll find lots of gold panning, fishing, and hiking opportunities here, and the northern trailhead for the 38-mi-long Resurrection Pass Trail is nearby. Contact the U.S. Forest Service for information on campgrounds, cabin rentals, and hikes in this area.

Where to Stay

$ 🏠 **Bear Creek Lodge.** Of the five cabins here, four are around a pond and one is down by the creek. Each is carpeted and has both a wood-stove and an electric heater. Interior walls are chinked logs, beds are cov-ered with colorful quilts, and the lighting fixtures are modeled after gold rush–era styles. The cabins vary in size, with the largest sleeping up to six. A central bathhouse has hot showers and toilets. The lodge café serves breakfast, lunch, and dinner year-round. ⊠ *Mile 15.9, Hope Hwy.* ✉️ *Box 147, Hope 99605* ☎ *907/782–3141* ⊕ *www.bearcreeklodgencafe. com* ➠ *5 cabins without bath* ⚪ *Café; no room phones* ☰ *MC, V.*

Seward

74 mi south of Hope, 127 mi south of Anchorage.

❼ Seward, at the head of Resurrection Bay, was founded in 1903 when survey crews arrived at this ice-free port to begin planning for a rail-road to the Interior. Since then the town has relied heavily on tourism and commercial fishing, and its harbor is important for loading coal bound for Asia. One of the peninsula's major communities, it lies at the south end of the Seward Highway, which connects with Anchorage and is the southern terminus of the Alaska Railroad. Seward also is the launching point for excursions into Kenai Fjords National Park, where you can spy calving glaciers, sea lions, whales, and otters.

Seward, like Valdez, was badly damaged by the 1964 earthquake. A movie illustrating the upheaval caused by the disaster is shown from Memo-rial Day until Labor Day, Monday through Saturday at 2 PM in the **Se-ward Community Library.** Russian icons and paintings by prominent Alaskan artists are on exhibit. ⊠ *5th Ave. and Adams St.* ☎ *907/224–3646* 🎞 *Movie $3* ⊙ *Weekdays 11–8, Sat. 11–6.*

The **Seward Museum** displays photographs of the quake's damage, model rooms and artifacts from the early pioneers, and historical up to current information on the Seward area. ⊠ *336 3rd Ave., at Jefferson St.* ☎ *907/224–3902* ⊠ *$3* ⊙ *Mid-May–Sept., daily 9–5; Oct.–mid-May, weekends noon–4. Hrs may vary seasonally; call for recorded information.*

The first mile of the historic original **Iditarod Trail** runs along the beach and makes for a nice, easy stroll, as does the city's printed walking tour—available at the visitor's bureau, the converted railcar at the corner of 3rd Avenue and Jefferson Street, or the Seward Chamber of Commerce Visitor Center at Mile 2 on the Seward Highway. For a different view of the town, drive out **Nash Road**, around Resurrection Bay, and see Seward as it appears nestled at the base of the surrounding mountains.

The **Alaska SeaLife Center** is a world-class research and visitor facility complete with massive cold-water tanks and outdoor viewing decks. Housing some of Alaska's abundant marine life, including harbor seals and sea lions, as well as films, hands-on activities, and a gift shop, the center was partially funded with reparations money from the *Exxon Valdez* oil spill. The center performs cold-water research on fish, seabirds, and marine mammals; provides educational experiences for the general public and school groups; and rehabilitates injured marine wildlife. ⊠ *301 Railway Ave.* ☎ *907/224–6300 or 800/224–2525* 🖷 *907/224–6320* 🌐 *www.alaskasealife.org* ⊠ *$12.50* ⊙ *May–Aug., daily 8–8; Sept. daily 9–6; Oct.–April, daily 10–5.*

A short walk from the parking lot along a paved path will bring you face to face with **Exit Glacier** (⇨ Kenai Fjords National Park), just outside Seward. Look for the marked turnoff at Mile 3.7 as you enter town or ask locals for directions.

Where to Stay & Eat

$–$$$$ ✕ **Chinooks Waterfront Restaurant.** On the waterfront in the small-boat harbor, Chinooks has a dazzling selection of fresh seafood items, an extensive wine list, and a great view from the upstairs window seats. The theme is marine, with fish photos and carvings, antique fishing tackle, and mounted fish on the walls. Pasta dishes and a few beef specialties round out the menu. ⊠ *1404 4th Ave.* ☎ *907/224–2207* ⊙ *Mid-Sept.–late May.*

★ **$$–$$$** ✕ **Ray's Waterfront.** True to its name, this dining spot has views of the bay and a small-boat harbor. Sea otters and sea lions have occasionally been known to swim right past the large picture windows. Seafood is the specialty here; the seafood chowder is a must-try. The walls are lined with stuffed and mounted fish so you can point to the kind you'd like to eat. ⊠ *Small-boat harbor* ☎ *907/224–5606* 🖩 *AE, D, DC, MC, V* ⊙ *Closed Nov.–mid-Mar.*

¢–$$$ ✕ **Legends Restaurant.** In downtown Seward close to the SeaLife Center, Legends delivers an extensive and varied menu, from seafood and barbecue chicken to burgers and salads, all augmented with homemade sauces, desserts, and mashed potatoes. An extensive beer and wine list round out the experience. Windows on two walls of the open dining room provide lots of summertime light as well as great views of Resurrection Bay from every seat in the place. ⊠ *5th and Washington St.* ☎ *907/224–3912* 🖩 *MC, V* ⊙ *Closed Sept.–May. No dinner Sun.–Thurs.*

$$$$ 🏨 **Kenai Fjords Wilderness Lodge.** An hour's boat ride from Seward, this wilderness lodge sits within a quiet, forest-lined cove on Fox Island in Resurrection Bay. Built of local wood with natural finish on interior walls, each cabin has expansive views of the bay and surrounding mountains, as well as private baths with shower, two beds, and woodstoves. Lodging rates include meals, boat transportation to the island, and a cruise of Kenai Fjords National Park. Meals are served family style in the main lodge. Hiking trails make it possible to explore the island. Guided kayak trips and coastal wildlife tours can also be arranged. ⬧ *Box 1889, 99664* ☎ *907/224–8068 or 800/478–8068* 🖷 *907/224–8934* 🌐 *www. kenaifjords.com* 🖙 *8 cabins* ⬧ *Dining room, hiking, travel services; no a/c, no room phones, no room TVs, no smoking* ⊟ *AE, D, MC, V* ❄ *AI* ☾ *Sept.–May.*

$$$–$$$$ 🏨 **Hotel Seward.** Decorated in resplendent gold-rush style, this downtown hotel is convenient to restaurants, shopping, and the Alaska SeaLife Center. In each of its elegant rooms, you'll find a king- or queen-size pillow-top bed, and a phone in the bathroom as well as the bedroom; some rooms have bay views. The hotel runs a shuttle to the harbor and is close to the ferry. ✉ *221 5th Ave.* ⬧ *Box 670, 99664* ☎ *907/224–2378 or 800/478–4050* 🖷 *907/224–3112* 🌐 *www.alaskaone.com/ hotelseward* 🖙 *38 rooms* ⬧ *In-room data ports, refrigerators, cable TV, outdoor hot tub* ⊟ *AE, D, DC, MC, V.*

$$$ 🏨 **Seward Windsong Lodge.** The Seward Windsong rests in a forested setting near the banks of the Resurrection River. Rooms are decorated in warm plaids, pine furniture, and Alaskan prints and include coffeemakers, data ports, and TVs. The lodge is just down the road from Exit Glacier. A full-service restaurant is on the premises. ✉ *Mile 0.6, exit Glacier Rd., about 2 mi north of Seward* ⬧ *2525 C St., Anchorage 99503* ☎ *907/ 265–4501 or 888/959–9590* 🖷 *907/263–5559* 🌐 *www.sewardwindsong. com* 🖙 *98 rooms, 10 suites* ⬧ *Restaurant, in-room data ports, cable TV, bar, shop, meeting rooms; no smoking* ⊟ *AE, D, MC, V.*

★ **$** 🏨 **Alaska's Treehouse B&B.** Enjoy spectacular views of the Chugach Mountains from the solarium and from the hot tub on the tiered deck at this quiet, rustic retreat. The house has vaulted cedar ceilings and skylights, and the suite has a skylight, too. Custom floral tilework complements the view of the national forest right outside the window. The hand-built wood-fired sauna is perfect for relaxing in after a hike or ski along nearby trails. Breakfast includes sourdough pancakes with homemade wild-berry sauces. A two-bedroom suite sleeps five comfortably. ✉ *Mile 7, ½ mi off Seward Hwy.* ⬧ *Box 861, 99664* ☎ *907/224–3867* 🖷 *907/224–3978* 🌐 *www.virtualcities.com/ak/treehouse.htm* 🖙 *1 room, 1 suite* ⬧ *Dining room, outdoor hot tub, sauna* ⊟ *No credit cards* ❄ *BP.*

$ 🏨 **Breeze Inn.** A mile or so from downtown and across the street from the small-boat harbor, this modern hotel is convenient—very convenient if you're planning an early morning fishing or sightseeing trip. Shops and restaurants are all within easy strolling distance. The rooms are bright and airy, with custom-made wooden furnishings and Alaskan wildlife photos on the walls. Some rooms in the annex building overlook the harbor. ⬧ *Box 2147, 99664* ☎ *907/224–5237 or 888/224–5237* 🖷 *907/224–7024* 🌐 *www.breezeinn.com* 🖙 *86 rooms* ⬧ *Restaurant, refrigerators, cable TV, Internet, some pets allowed, no-smoking rooms* ⊟ *AE, D, MC, V.*

$ 🏨 **Teddy's Inn the Woods.** Set back from the road in a forest of spruce
Fodor's Choice   trees in parklike surroundings, this bed-and-breakfast has room for up
★   to six in an outbuilding. The furnishings are impeccable, with lots of natural wood accents, comfortable seating, local artwork, and flower arrangements. Two cubbyhole bunks are especially child-friendly, and the two decks are prime sun-lounging spots. The breakfast of fresh homemade pastries just might be complemented with freshly smoked salmon. ✉ *Mile 23, Seward Hwy. in Moose Pass* ⬧ *29792 Seward Hwy., Seward 99664* ☎ *907/288–3126* 🌐 *www.seward.net/teddys* 🖙 *1 room* ⊟ *MC, V* ❄ *BP.*

Guided Tours

Alaska Heritage Tours (☎ 907/265–4500 or 877/258–6877 ☎ 907/263–5559 ⊕ www.ahtours.com) conducts a variety of tours that cover itineraries from Seward to Anchorage, Talkeetna, Denali, Prince William Sound, and Kenai Fjords National Park. **Alaska Wildland Adventures** (☎ 907/783–2928 or 800/478–4100), in Cooper Landing, operates a tidy, pleasant resort and outdoor adventure center on the Kenai River at Mile 50.1 of the Sterling Highway. It arranges a large variety of adventure travel packages all over the state, from 2-day fishing trips and 12-day exploration safaris to small-ship cruising trips, bear-viewing adventures, and trips to backcountry lodges in several locations. **Fish House** (✉ Small-boat harbor ☎ 907/224–3674 or 800/257–7760) is Seward's oldest booking agency for deep-sea fishing.

Sports & the Outdoors

RUNNING The footrace best known among Alaskans is Seward's annual **Mt. Marathon Race,** run on July 4 since 1915. It doesn't take the winners very long—44 minutes or so—but the route is straight up the mountain (3,022 feet) and back down to the center of town. The field is limited, past participants have priority, and early registration is required—applications go out February 1. For more information, contact the **Seward Chamber of Commerce** (✉ Box 749, Seward 99664 ☎ 907/224–8051 ☎ 907/224–5353).

Shopping

Bardarson Studio (✉ Across from small-boat harbor ☎ 907/224–5448), selling everything from prints and watercolors to sculpture and beaded earrings, is a browser's dream. There's a kiddie cave for children and a video-viewing area for nonshoppers. At **I.R.B.I. Custom Alaska Knives** (✉ Mile 20, Seward Hwy. ☎ 907/288–3616) father-and-son craftsmen Irvin and Virgil Campbell handcraft beautiful, functional knives and *ulus* (Alaska Native "women's knives"), with local and exotic antler ivory and horn for handles. The **Ranting Raven** (✉ 224 4th Ave. ☎ 907/224–2228) is a combination gift shop, bakery, and lunch spot, adorned with raven murals on the side of the building. You can indulge in fresh baked goods, espresso drinks, and daily lunch specials such as quiche, focaccia, and homemade soups while perusing the packed shelves of Russian handicrafts and artwork, Native crafts, and jewelry.

Kenai Fjords National Park

125 mi south of Anchorage.

★ ❽ Photogenic Seward is the gateway to the 670,000-acre Kenai Fjords National Park. This is spectacular coastal parkland incised with sheer, dark slate cliffs rising from the sea, ribboned with white waterfalls, and tufted with deep-green spruce. Kenai Fjords presents a rare opportunity for an up-close view of blue tidewater glaciers as well as some remarkable ocean wildlife. If you take a day trip on a tour boat out of Seward, you can be pretty sure of seeing sea otters, crowds of Steller's sea lions lazing on the rocky shelves along the shore, a porpoise or two, bald eagles soaring overhead, and tens of thousands of seabirds. Humpback whales and orcas are also sighted occasionally. Tours range in length from 4 hours to 10 hours. The park's coastal fjords are also a favorite of sea kayakers, who can camp or stay in public-use cabins reserved through headquarters. Backcountry travelers should be aware, however, that much of the park's coastline has been claimed by local Native organizations and is now private property. Be sure to check with park headquarters to avoid trespassing.

One of the park's chief attractions is **Exit Glacier,** which can be reached by the one road that passes into Kenai Fjords. Trails inside the park lead to an overlook of the vast **Harding Icefield.** ⬠ *Box 1727, Seward 99664* ☎ *907/224–3175* ⊕ *www.nps.gov/kefj.*

Guided Tours

Kenai Coastal Tours (☎ 907/277–2131 or 800/478–8068) leads day trips into Kenai Fjords National Park. It also conducts combination train–cruise–motor-coach trips from Anchorage. **Kenai Fjords Tours** (☎ 907/276–6249, 800/478–8068, 907/224–8068 in Seward ☎ 907/276–1064 ⊕ www.kenaifjords.com) is the oldest and largest company running tours through the park. From March through November, it leads 3- to 10-hour cruises, which include lunch. Transportation and overnight options are also available. **Mariah Tours** (☎ 907/224–8068 or 800/270–1238 ☎ 907/224–8625 ⊕ www.kenaifjords.com) operates smaller boats through the park and into the Chiswell Islands, with a maximum of 16 passengers per boat mid-May through mid-September. This is a great option for birders or groups.

Where to Stay

¢ ⚠ **National Park Service Cabins.** The Kenai Fjords National Park manages four cabins, including three along the coast, favored by sea kayakers and for summer use only. Accessible only by boat or floatplane, they must be reserved in advance. The cabins cost $35 per night: three have a three-night limit, and the North Arm cabin can be reserved for up to nine nights, since it's considerably farther out than the others. The park's lone winter cabin is at Exit Glacier and is a stopping place for many skiers, mushers, and snow machiners (the local name for snowmobilers). Cabins have wooden bunks, heating stoves and tables. There's no electricity, running water, indoor plumbing, or bedding. ✉ *1212 4th Ave.* ⬠ *Box 1727, Seward 99664* ☎ *907/224–3175 to reserve winter cabin, 907/271–2737 in Anchorage for summer rentals* ⬟ *4 cabins* ⊟ *MC, V.*

Cooper Landing

100 mi south of Anchorage.

❾ Centrally located on the Kenai Peninsula, Cooper Landing is within striking distance of some of Alaska's most popular fishing locations. The Russian River flows into the Kenai River here, and spectacular fishing opportunities abound. Solid lines of traffic head south from Anchorage every summer weekend, and the confluence of the two rivers can get very crowded with enthusiastic anglers, to the point where the pursuit of salmon is often referred to as "combat fishing." However, a short walk upstream will separate you from the crowds and afford a chance to enjoy this gorgeous little river.

The Russian River supports two runs of red (sockeye) salmon every summer, and it's known as the most popular fishery in the state. The Kenai River is famous for its runs of king, red, and silver (coho) salmon, as well as the resident populations of large rainbow trout and Dolly Varden char. Several guide services operate out of Cooper Landing, and the travel services at Gwin's Lodge and the Kenai Princess can recommend competent and trustworthy fishing guides. A number of nearby freshwater lakes, accessible only by hiking trail, also provide excellent fishing for rainbow trout and Dolly Varden.

Cooper Landing serves as a trailhead for the 38-mi-long Resurrection Pass trail, which connects to the village of Hope, and the Russian Lakes/Resurrection River trails, which run south to Exit Glacier near Seward.

The town's central location also affords easy access to saltwater recreation in Seward and Homer.

Where to Stay & Eat

$–$$$$ ✕ **Sackett's Kenai Grill.** At a wide spot in the road on the shore of Kenai
Fodor'sChoice Lake, the Kenai Grill is a real find. The food is a welcome change from
★ most Alaska roadside eateries—try the specialty of the house, the smoked
prime rib, or one of the fresh seafood or creative pasta dishes accompanied by a generous Caesar salad. Even the burgers are a treat. The
interior is decorated with such items as a traditional fish trap made of
willow branches and an upside-down rowboat used as a rack for glasses
in the bar. Outside seating is available for sunny days. The owners and
staff are friendly and helpful, and the view of the lake and the surrounding
Kenai Mountains makes for a memorable dining experience. ⊠ *Mile 47.4,
Sterling Hwy. 99572* ☎ *907/595–1827* ▭ *MC, V.*

$–$$ ✕ **Sunrise Inn.** On the shore of Kenai Lake, this restaurant serves breakfast, lunch, and dinner, dishing up homemade soups, chowders, and salsas. The eclectic and very reasonably priced menu includes wraps and
vegetarian items. Fish feature prominently in what the owners describe
as a "backwoods bistro" environment. There's even a spotting scope in
the parking lot for spying on the Dall sheep and mountain goats in the
surrounding peaks. The bar hosts live music on Saturday in summer.
⊠ *Mile 45, Sterling Hwy., 99572* ☎ *907/595–1222* 📠 *907/595–1570*
⊕ *www.alaskasunriseinn.com* ▭ *AE, D, MC, V.*

$–$$ ✕⬚ **Gwin's Lodge.** If Cooper Landing is the heart of Kenai Peninsula
summer-recreation action, then Gwin's is surely the epicenter of much
of the activity. This roadside establishment is a one-stop-shop for visitors and locals alike, providing food, lodging, shopping, and fishing tackle
around the clock in the summer. The lodge is the fishing headquarters
of prospective anglers during the annual salmon runs on the nearby Russian and Kenai rivers. Cabins vary in configuration from standard log
cabin with beds and private baths to deluxe chalets with lofts, vaulted
ceilings, and full kitchens. The restaurant serves a full menu, including
fresh fish when available, as well as sandwiches, steaks, and very hearty
breakfasts. The travel agency can book fishing, hiking, rafting, and
other adventure travel anywhere on the peninsula. ⊠ *Mile 52, Sterling
Hwy., 99572* ☎ *907/595–1266* 📠 *907/595–1681* ⊕ *www.gwinslodge.
com* ⬚ *13 rooms* △ *Restaurant, bar, shop, travel services, no-smoking rooms; no a/c, no room phones, no room TVs* ▭ *D, MC, V* ⊙ *Restaurant closed Oct.–Mar.*

★ **$$$$** ⬚ **Great Alaska Adventure Lodge.** Midway between Seward and Homer,
this lodge lives up to its name. Activities include natural history, soft-adventure options, and a remote bear-viewing camp. If you're here to
fish, you've come to the right place: the guides are top-notch, and seven
world records have been set along the camp's riverbanks. Rates include
lodging, meals, and most activities, and the basic fishing package—two
days and one night, all expenses covered, including a fishing guide—
runs $950 per person. Rooms, which are in the main lodge or in riverside cabins, have fireplaces, painted walls, artwork, and comfortable
seating. Some of the cabins are two story, complete with spiral staircases.
⊠ *Mile 82.5, 33881 Sterling Hwy., Sterling 99672* ⬚ *Box 2670,
Poulsbo, WA 98370* ☎ *907/262–4515, 800/544–2261, 360/697–6454
in winter* 📠 *907/262–8797, 360/697–7850 in winter* ⊕ *www.greatalaska.
com* ⬚ *23 rooms* △ *Dining room, boating, fishing, hiking* ▭ *AE, MC,
V* �‖ *FAP* ⊙ *Closed Oct.–mid-May.*

$$$$ ⬚ **Kenai Princess Wilderness Lodge.** "Elegantly rustic" might best describe
Fodor'sChoice this sprawling complex approximately 45 mi from Seward, on a bluff
★ overlooking the Kenai River. Paths lead from the main lodge to charm-

ing bungalows, each containing four spacious units. Buildings higher on the bluff house eight units. Each has a king or two double beds, a wood-burning fireplace, a comfortable sitting area, and a porch. Vaulted ceilings of natural-finish wood complement the Alaskan art prints on the walls. Staff can arrange for fishing, flightseeing, horseback riding, and river rafting. There's also a nature trail. The Eagle's Crest Restaurant serves a variety of Alaska fare, including local seafood. ⊠ *Mile 47.7, Sterling Hwy.* ⬧ *Box 676, Cooper Landing 99572* ☎ *907/595–1425 or 800/426–0500* 🖷 *907/595–1424* ⊕ *www.princessalaskalodges.com* ⇒ *86 rooms* ♨ *Restaurant, cable TV, exercise equipment, 2 outdoor hot tubs, bar, shop* ⊟ *AE, DC, MC, V.*

$$$$ 🏠 **Kenai River Sportfishing Lodge.** This lodge is actually a collection of buildings on the bank of the Kenai River. Guests stay in clean, comfortable cabins and share a bathhouse. Cabins, with two double beds or a double and single, have heat and electricity but no running water. Meals are served family-style in the log-cabin dining room. Fishing expeditions ranging from two to five days can be arranged, along with transportation to and from Anchorage, Kenai Fjords sightseeing trips, and Alaska Railroad travel options. The lodge can also arrange half- and full-day rafting trips on the Kenai River, as well as trips to its Kenai Backcountry Lodge downstream on Skilak Lake. ⊠ *Milepost 50.1, Sterling Hwy.* ⬧ *Box 389, Girdwood 99587* ☎ *907/783–2928, 800/478–4100* 🖷 *907/783–2130* ⊕ *www.alaskarivertrips.com* ⇒ *16 cabins* ♨ *Dining room, sauna; no room phones, no room TVs, no smoking* ⊟ *D, MC, V* ⊙ *Closed Oct.–mid-May* ⦿ *FAP.*

Kenai National Wildlife Refuge

95 mi northwest of Kenai Fjords National Park, 150 mi southwest of Anchorage.

🔟 The U.S. Fish and Wildlife Service administers nearly 2 million acres on the Kenai Peninsula in one of its prime wildlife refuges. The **Kenai National Wildlife Refuge** takes in a portion of the Harding Icefield as well as two large and scenic lakes, Skilak and Tustumena. The refuge is not only the finest moose habitat in the region, but its waterways are great for canoeing and kayaking. The U.S. Fish and Wildlife Service maintains a canoe system, campgrounds, and four free cabin shelters, available on a first-come, first-served basis. Two of the cabin shelters are fly-ins; you can hike or canoe to the other two. For information (including canoe rentals), contact the Alaska Public Lands Information Center in Anchorage.

Where to Stay

¢ ⛺ **Kenai National Wildlife Refuge Campgrounds.** The U.S. Fish and Wildlife Service maintains 14 road-accessible campgrounds in the Kenai refuge, with a total of 130 sites, 110 of which are suitable for RVs, though there are no hookups. Only two of the campgrounds (Hidden Lake and Upper Skilak Lake) charge fees for camping. All have toilet facilities, and all but three have drinking water. The campgrounds also have picnic tables, fire pits, nearby hiking trails, and fishing. The maximum length of stay is 14 consecutive days, with a few exceptions—Russian River ferry site limit is 3 days, and Hidden Lake and Upper Skilak limit is 7. ⬧ *Kenai National Wildlife Refuge, Box 2139, Soldotna 99669-2139* ☎ *907/262–7021* ⊕ *www.kenai.fws.gov* ⇒ *14 campgrounds* ♨ *Reservations not accepted* ⊟ *No credit cards.*

Kenai & Soldotna

116 mi northwest of Seward, 148 mi southwest of Anchorage.

⑪ The towns of Kenai and Soldotna are often mentioned almost interchangeably due to their physical proximity. Soldotna, with its strategic location on the peninsula's northwest coast, takes its name from a nearby stream; it's a corruption of the Russian word for "soldier," although some say the name came from a Native American word meaning "stream fork." Today this city of 3,900 residents is the commercial and sport-fishing hub of the Kenai Peninsula. Along with its sister city, Kenai, whose onion-dome Holy Assumption Russian Orthodox Church highlights the city's old town, it is home to Cook Inlet oil-field workers and their families. Soldotna's commercial center stretches along the Sterling Highway, making this a stopping point for those traveling up and down the peninsula. The town of Kenai lies near the end of the road that branches off the Sterling Highway in Soldotna. Near Kenai is Captain Cook State Park, one of the least-visited state parks on the road system. This portion of the peninsula is level and forested, with numerous lakes and streams pocking and crisscrossing the area. Trumpeter swans return here in the spring, and sightings of moose and caribou are common.

♻ In addition to fishing, clam digging is also popular at **Clam Gulch,** 24 mi south of Soldotna on the Sterling Highway. This is a favorite of local children, who love any excuse to dig in the muddy, sloppy goo. Ask locals on the beach how to find the giant razor clams (recognized by their dimples in the sand). The clam digging is best when tides are minus 4 or 5 feet. A sportfishing license, available at grocery, sporting-goods, and drug stores, is required.

Where to Stay & Eat

★ **$-$$$** ✕ **The Duck Inn.** The Duck Inn serves pizzas, burgers, chicken, steaks, and seafood. Portions are generous, pricing is reasonable, and the variety of items on the menu guarantees something for everyone. Locally caught halibut is a specialty, prepared in enough different ways to stave off feelings of halibut overload. Muted lighting, soft background music, hanging plants, and lots of artwork featuring ducks create an enjoyable dining experience. ✉ *43187 Kalifornsky Beach Rd., 99669* ☎ *907/262–1849* ▭ *AE, D, MC, V.*

$$ ▦ **Aspen Hotel Soldotna.** You'll find Aspen Hotels in five Alaska cities; the Soldotna facility opened in spring of 2002. It sits on a bluff overlooking the Kenai River, a world-famous fishing destination drawing hopeful anglers from all over the world. The contemporary decor is open and airy, with bright wood accents throughout. ✉ *326 Binkley Cir., 99669* ☎ *907/260–7736 or 888/308–7848* 🖷 *907/260–7786* ⊕ *www.aspenhotelsak.com* ⮒ *63 rooms* ⚭ *In-room data ports, microwaves, refrigerators, pool, exercise equipment, spa, laundry facilities, Internet, business services, meeting room* ▭ *AE, D, DC, MC, V.*

$-$$ ▦ **Best Western King Salmon Motel.** This member of the reliable Best Western franchise has large, airy rooms, including some with kitchenettes. If you're traveling by RV, you'll find a park complete with full hookups available for $20 per night. ✉ *35546 Kenai Spur Hwy., 99669* ☎ *907/262–5857 or 888/262–5857* 🖷 *907/262–9441* ⊕ *www.bestwestern.com* ⮒ *49 rooms* ⚭ *Restaurant, in-room data ports, some kitchenettes, some microwaves, cable TV, laundry facilities, meeting room* ▭ *AE, D, DC, MC, V.*

Sports & the Outdoors

FISHING Anglers from around the world come for the salmon-choked streams and rivers, most notably the **Kenai River** and its companion, the **Russian**

River. Deep-sea fishing for salmon and halibut out of **Deep Creek** is challenging Homer's position as the preeminent fishing destination on the southern Kenai Peninsula. This fishery is unusual in that tractors launch boats off the beach and into the Cook Inlet surf. The local campground and RV lot is packed on summer weekends.

Area phone books list some 300 fishing charters and guides, all of whom stay busy during the hectic summer fishing season. **Hi Lo Charters** (☎ 907/283–9691 or 800/757–9333 ⊕ www.hilofishing.com) runs salmon-fishing trips on the world-famous Kenai River. The **Sports Den** (☎ 907/262–7491 ⊕ www.alaskasportsden.com) arranges fishing trips on the river, on the saltwater, or to a remote fly-in location for salmon, trout, or halibut.

Homer

⑫ *77 mi south of Soldotna, 226 mi south of Anchorage.*

At the southern end of the Sterling Highway lies the city of Homer, on the head of a narrow spit that juts into beautiful Kachemak Bay. Founded just before the turn of the 20th century as a gold-prospecting camp, this community was later used as a coal-mining headquarters. Today the town of Homer is an eclectic community filled with tacky tourist paraphernalia, commercial-fishing facilities—including boats, canneries, and repair yards—and a thriving group of local artists, sculptors, actors, and writers. An annual influx of college kids referred to locally as "spit rats" works the slime lines in the processing factories while living in tents on the spit. They mix freely with foreign tourists and Alaskans who make annual pilgrimages to the Halibut Capital of the World. The local architecture includes everything from homes that are little more than assemblages of driftwood, flotsam, and jetsam to featureless steel commercial buildings and magnificent homes on the hillside overlooking the surrounding bay, mountains, forests, and glaciers. In addition to highway and air access, Homer also has regular ferry service to Seldovia.

★ ☾ The **Pratt Museum** has a saltwater aquarium; an exhibit on the 1989 Prince William Sound oil spill; a wildflower garden; a gift shop; and pioneer, Russian, and Alaska Native displays. You can spy on wildlife with a robotic video camera set up on a seabird rookery. There's also a refurbished homestead cabin and outdoor summer exhibits along the trail out back. ⊠ *Bartlett St. off Pioneer Ave.* ☎ *907/235–8635* ⊕ *www. prattmuseum.org* ⊠ *$6* ☾ *May–Sept., daily 10–6; Oct.–Dec. and Feb.–Apr., Tues.–Sun. noon–5.*

Kachemak Bay abounds in wildlife, including a large population of puffins and eagles. Tour operators take you past bird rookeries or across the bay to gravel beaches for clam digging. Most fishing charters include an opportunity to view whales, seals, porpoises, and birds close up. At the end of the day, walk along the docks on Homer Spit and watch commercial-fishing boats and charter boats unload their catch.

Directly across from the end of the Homer Spit is **Halibut Cove,** a small community of people who make their living on the bay or by selling handicrafts. Spend a relaxing afternoon or evening meandering along the boardwalk and visiting galleries. The cove itself is lovely, especially during salmon runs, when fish leap and splash in the clear water. You'll find several lodges on this side of the bay, on pristine coves away from summer crowds. The *Danny J* ferries people across from Homer Spit, with a stop at the rookery at Gull Island and two or three hours to walk around Halibut Cove, for $45. The ferry makes two trips daily: the first leaves Homer at noon and returns at 5 PM, and the second leaves at 5 PM and returns at 10 PM. Central Charters handles all booking.

Where to Stay & Eat

★ **$$–$$$$** ✕ **Homestead Restaurant.** This former log roadhouse 8 mi from town is a favorite of locals who appreciate artfully presented food served amid contemporary art. The Homestead specializes in seasonal fish and shellfish prepared with garlic, citrus fruits, or spicy ethnic sauces, as well as steak, rack of lamb, and prime rib. Epic views of the bay, mountains, and hanging glaciers are yours for the looking. An extensive wine list and locally brewed beer on tap are available. ⊠ *Mile 8.2, East End Rd.* ☎ *907/235–8723* ▤ *AE, MC, V* ☾ *Closed Jan.–Feb.*

$$–$$$ ✕ **Café Cups.** It's hard to miss this place as you drive down Pioneer Avenue—look for the huge namesake cups on the building's facade. One of Homer's oldest restaurants, this café serves lunches and dinners that make the most of the locally abundant seafood, complemented by a terrific wine list. It's one of the few small restaurants in Alaska where the menu includes vegetarian dishes. ⊠ *162 W. Pioneer Ave.* ☎ *907/235–8330* ▤ *MC, V* ☾ *Closed Sun.*

$–$$$ ✕ **Saltry in Halibut Cove.** This restaurant serves local seafood as sushi
Fodor'sChoice or prepares it with curries and pastas. For libations, you can choose
★ from a wide selection of imported beers. The restaurant is small, and although the tables aren't exactly crowded together, it's definitely intimate. The deck overlooks the boat dock and the cove. Dinner seatings are at 6 and 7:30; before or after dinner, you can stroll around the boardwalks at Halibut Cove and visit the art shops and soak up the view. Reservations are essential for the ferry (at a reduced $22 round-trip), which leaves Homer Spit at 5 PM. A noon ferry ($45) will take you to Halibut Cove for lunch ($5–$17), stopping along the way for wildlife viewing. ⊠ *Halibut Cove* ☎ *907/235–7847 or 800/478–7847 Central Charters* ⌂ *Reservations essential* ▤ *D, MC, V* ☾ *Closed Labor Day–Memorial Day.*

$–$$$ ✕▦ **Land's End.** This sprawling blue-and-white complex at the end of the spit has wide-open views of the bay. Most of the rooms face the bay; some have nautical decor, and others are in floral. Some are perfect for a couple, some big enough for a family—five rooms have lofts. Its restaurant ($$–$$$$) specializes in seafood, including halibut, scallops, oysters, and clams; burgers and steak are also served. ⊠ *4786 Homer Spit Rd., 99603* ☎ *907/235–0400, 800/478–0400* ▤ *907/235–0420* ⊕ *www.lands-end-resort.com* ↝ *80 rooms* ⌂ *Restaurant, in-room data ports, cable TV, hot tub, spa, bar, meeting rooms, travel services* ▤ *AE, D, DC, MC, V.*

$$$$ ▦ **Land's End Lodges.** Adjacent to the Land's End hotel, this group of fully furnished luxury condos sits at the end of the 4-mi-long Homer Spit, with decks and windows fronting on Kachemak Bay. Commercial and charter-fishing boats, Alaska Marine Highway ferries, and pleasure boats parade past your front door day and night, against a stunning view of snow-capped mountains, spruce forest, and glaciers. The price is for two people, but with a mere additional $10 per-person charge per night, these places can be surprisingly economical for a small group traveling together. ⊠ *4786 Homer Spit Rd., 99603* ☎ *907/235–0400 or 800/478–0400* ▤ *907/235–0420* ⊕ *www.lands-end-resort.com* ↝ *6 condos* ⌂ *Kitchens, microwaves, refrigerators, cable TV, laundry facilities* ▤ *AE, D, DC, MC, V.*

★ **¢–$$** ▦ **Driftwood Inn.** Rooms here are bright, with large windows, expansive views of the bay, and light pastel walls and bedspreads. Various room configurations include standard hotel-type bedrooms and a "ship's quarters," with cedar walls and a pull-down bed. The suite is family-friendly, with queen-size beds, dining room table, microwave, refrigerator, full private bath, and private outside entrance. Downstairs has a comfortable sitting room with fireplace, TV, books, and videos. A small eating area has serve-yourself coffee, tea, pastries, and hot and cold cereal. A microwave, refrigerator, barbecue, and fish-cooking and -cleaning area are also available. An on-site camping area and full-hookup RV park have full access to the inn's facilities. ⊠ *135 W. Bunnell St., 99603* ☎ *907/235–8019 or 800/478–8019* 🖷 *907/235–8019* ⊕ *www.thedriftwoodinn.com* 🖙 *20 rooms, 11 with bath* ↻ *Dining room, cable TV, laundry facilities, some pets allowed; no phones in some rooms, no smoking* 🖃 *D, MC, V.*

$ 🖫 **Old Town Bed & Breakfast.** Housed in a former trading post, the Old Town B&B is on its second floor, above the Bunnell Street art gallery and the Little Luna Deli. Rooms are elegantly appointed with period furnishings and fixtures, and the second-story setting provides sweeping views of the bay and mountains. One room has a private bath, and the other two share a bath. You have easy access to evening programs in the art gallery, and breakfast is served in the deli downstairs. ⊠ *106 W. Bunnell St., 99603* ☎ *907/235–7558* ⊕ *www.xyz.net/~oldtown* 🖙 *3* ↻ *No room phones, no TVs, no smoking* 🖃 *MC, V* 🍴 *BP.*

Guided Tours

Central Charters (⊠ 4241 Homer Spit Rd., 99603 ☎ 907/235–7847 or 800/478–7847 ⊕ www.centralcharter.com) arranges fishing and ferry trips to Halibut Cove, around Kachemak Bay, and across to Seldovia. **Homer Ocean Charters** (☎ 907/235–6212 or 800/426–6212) on the Spit conducts fishing, hunting, and sightseeing trips, as well as ocean kayaking and water-taxi services and remote cabin rentals. Cruises go to the Rookery Restaurant—the narrated lunch cruise leaves at noon ($55), and dinner trips to the restaurant leave at 4:30 and 7; the ferry trip is $20, and dinner main courses run $9–$30.

Nightlife & the Arts

Dance to lively bands at **Alice's** (⊠ 195 E. Pioneer Ave. ☎ 907/235–7650).
★ The Spit's **Salty Dawg Saloon** (☎ 907/235–9990) is a tumbledown lighthouse, sure to be frequented by a carousing fisherman or two.

Shopping

ART & GIFTS   A variety of art by the town's residents can be found in the galleries on and around Pioneer Avenue. The gift shop at the **Pratt Museum** stocks natural-history books, locally crafted or inspired jewelry, note cards, and gifts for children. The **Bunnell Street Gallery** (⊠ Corner of Main and Bunnell Sts. ☎ 907/235–2662) displays innovative contemporary art primarily produced in Alaska. The gallery, which occupies the first floor of a historic trading post, also hosts workshops, lectures, musical performances, and other community events.

FOODSTUFFS   **Alaska Wild Berry Products** (⊠ 528 E. Pioneer Ave. ☎ 907/235–8858) sells chocolate-covered candies, jams, jellies, sauces, and syrups made from wild berries handpicked on the Kenai Peninsula, as well as Alaskan-theme gifts and clothing. **Two Sisters Bakery** (⊠ 233 E. Bunnell St. ☎ 907/235–2280) serves fresh bread baked on the premises as well as coffee, muffins, soup, and pizza. **Fritz Creek Store** (⊠ 55770 East End Rd. ☎ 907/235–6753), across the street from the Homestead Restaurant, sells gas and groceries. The real attraction here, however, is the fresh, homemade food served in the café. They have sandwiches, hoagies, pizza, soups, and some surprisingly exotic items like duck and sausage gumbo and handmade tamales.

Kachemak Bay State Park & State Wilderness Park

10 mi southeast of Homer.

⑬ Kachemak Bay State Park and State Wilderness Park, accessible by boat or Bush plane, protects more than 350,000 acres of coast, mountains, glaciers, forests, and wildlife on the lower Kenai Peninsula. Recreational opportunities include boating, sea kayaking, fishing, hiking, and beach-combing. Facilities are minimal but include 20 primitive campsites, five public-use cabins, and a system of trails accessible from Kachemak Bay. ⬨ *Kenai State Parks Office, Box 1247, Soldotna 99669* ☎ *907/262–5581 or 907/235–7024* ⊕ *www.dnr.state.ak.us/parks/units/kbay/kbay.htm.*

Where to Stay

★ **$$$$** ⊠ **Kachemak Bay Wilderness Lodge.** Across Kachemak Bay from Homer, this luxurious lodge provides wildlife-viewing opportunities and panoramic mountain and bay vistas in an intimate setting for up to 12 guests. The main log building has a piano and a big stone fireplace to warm you after a day of hiking, fishing, kayaking, or touring in one of the lodge's five guided boats (some of the guided fly-out trips may cost extra). Scattered throughout the woods, the rustic cabins, all with electricity, full baths, and decks, are decorated with antiques, original artworks, and homemade quilts. Cabin layouts differ slightly; some are suited for couples, some for groups or families. Dinners spotlight seafood—clams, mussels, and fish—caught in the bay. The price is per person for a five-day, four-night all-inclusive package. ⬨ *Box 956, Homer 99603* ☎ *907/235–8910* ⊟ *907/235–8911* ⊕ *www.alaskawildernesslodge. com* ⬥ *4 cabins, 1 room in lodge* ♨ *Dining room, hot tub, sauna, boating, fishing, hiking; no room phones, no room TVs, no smoking* ⭗ *FAP* ⊟ *No credit cards* ☉ *Closed Oct.–Apr.*

¢ ⊠ **Alaska State Parks Cabins.** Three public-use cabins are within Kachemak Bay's Halibut Cove Lagoon area, another is near Tutka Bay Lagoon, and a fifth is at China Poot Lake. All but the lakeside cabin are accessible by boat; China Poot can be reached only by foot from the boat landing on the beach or by floatplane to the lake. The spartan cabin furnishings consist of wooden bunks and sleeping platforms, table, and chairs but no running water or electricity. Four of the five cabins sleep up to six people (the other, the Overlook cabin at Halibut Cove, sleeps eight), and all must be reserved up to six months in advance. ⊠ *Alaska State Parks Information Center, 550 W. 7th Ave., Suite 1260, Anchorage 99501-3557* ☎ *907/269–8400* ⊕ *nutmeg.state.ak.us/ixpress/dnr/parks/kenai. dml* ⬥ *5 cabins* ⊟ *No credit cards.*

¢ ⛰ **Alaska State Parks Campsites.** Twenty primitive, free campsites with pit toilets and fire rings are scattered along the shores of Kachemak Bay across from Homer and are accessible by boat (water taxis operate here daily in summer). The sites are available on a first-come, first-served basis, and camping is allowed nearly everywhere in the park, not restricted to developed sites. ⬨ *Alaska State Parks, Kenai Area Office, Box 1247, Soldotna 99669* ☎ *907/235–7024 or 907/262–5581* ⊕ *www.dnr.state. ak.us/parks/units/kbay/kbay.htm* ⬥ *6 campgrounds* ♨ *Reservations not accepted* ⊟ *No credit cards.*

Seldovia

16 mi south of Homer.

⑭ Seldovia, isolated across the bay from Homer, retains the charm of an earlier Alaska. The town's Russian bloodline shows in its onion-dome church and its name, meaning "herring bay." Those who fish use plenty of herring for bait, catching record-size salmon, halibut, and king or Dungeness crab. You'll find excellent fishing whether you drop your line into the deep waters of Kachemak Bay or cast into the surf for silver salmon on the shore of Outside Beach, near town. Stroll through town and along the slough, where frame houses rest on pilings.

Where to Stay & Eat

¢ × **The Buzz.** This coffee shop sells espresso, monster-size baked goods, breakfast burritos, quiche, and granola—all of it homemade. For lunch, try pasta, chili, or soup with homemade bread. ⊠ *231 Main St., next to harbormaster's office* ☎907/234–7479 ▤*MC, V* ⊘ *Closed Oct.–Mar.*

$$–$$$ ▥ **Across the Bay Tent & Breakfast Adventure Co.** A step up the comfort ladder from camping, this beachfront compound is reachable via water taxi from Homer. You stay in sturdy canvas-wall tents with carpeted floors and twin beds, and a large common room has hardwood floors and a piano. Prices vary depending on whether you do your own cooking or eat meals prepared by the staff. A propane stove and grill, as well as pots, pans, and picnic tables, are provided. Otherwise, host-prepared meals are hearty and served family style. A beach is great for walking and beachcombing; escorted kayak trips and mountain bikes are available for an extra charge. ⊠ *Mile 8, Jakalof Bay Rd., 8 mi from Seldovia* ✉ *Box 81, Seldovia 99663* ☎ *907/235–3633 in summer, 907/345–2571 in winter* ⊕ *www.tentandbreakfastalaska.com* ➳ *5 tents* ♨ *Dining room, sauna, boating, bicycles* ▤ *MC, V* ⊘ *Closed late Sept.–late May.*

$ ▥ **Seldovia Boardwalk Hotel.** This hotel with a fabulous view of the harbor has immaculate modern rooms, half of which face the water. The rooms are bright, with white walls and ceilings, lots of plants, and old photos of local interest. A large, sunlit parlor downstairs has a woodstove and coffee service. The proprietors can also arrange charter-fishing or sea-kayaking trips. ✉ *Box 72, 99663* ☎ *907/234–7816 or 800/238–7862* ⊕ *www.alaskaone.com/boardwalkhotel* ➳ *14 rooms* ♨ *No room TVs, no smoking* ▤ *MC, V.*

Kodiak Island

🅕 *248 mi southwest of Anchorage by air.*

Alaska's largest island is accessible only by air from Anchorage and by ferry from Homer and Seward. Russian explorers discovered the island in 1763, and Kodiak served as Alaska's first capital until 1804, when the government was moved to Sitka. Situated as it is in the northwestern Gulf of Alaska, Kodiak has been subjected to several natural disasters. In 1912 a volcanic eruption on the nearby Alaska Peninsula covered the town site in knee-deep drifts of ash and pumice. A tidal wave resulting from the 1964 earthquake destroyed the island's large fishing fleet and smashed Kodiak's low-lying downtown area.

Today, commercial fishing is king in Kodiak. Despite its small population—about 15,000 people scattered among the several islands in the Kodiak group—the city is among the busiest fishing ports in the United States. The harbor is also an important supply point for small communities on the Aleutian Islands and the Alaska Peninsula.

Floatplane and boat charters are available from Kodiak to numerous remote attractions not served by roads. Chief among these areas is the 1.6-million-acre **Kodiak National Wildlife Refuge,** lying partly on Kodiak Island and partly on Afognak Island to the north, where spotting the enormous Kodiak brown bears is the main goal of a trip. Seeing the Kodiak brown bears, which weigh a pound at birth but up to 1,500 pounds when fully grown, is worth the trip to this rugged country. The bears are spotted easily in July and August, feeding along salmon-spawning streams. Charter flightseeing trips are available to the area, and exaggerated tales of encounters with these impressive beasts are frequently heard. ⊠ *1390 Buskin River Rd., Kodiak 99615* ☎ *907/487–2600* ⊕ *www.r7.fws.gov/nwr/kodiak.*

As part of America's North Pacific defense in World War II, Kodiak was the site of an important naval station, now occupied by the Coast Guard fleet that patrols the surrounding fishing grounds. Part of the old military installation has been incorporated into **Abercrombie State Park and Campground,** 3½ mi north of Kodiak on Rezanof Drive. Self-guided tours take you past concrete bunkers and gun emplacements.

The **Baranov Museum** presents artifacts from the area's Russian origins. On the National Register of Historic Places, the building was built in 1808 by Alexander Baranov to warehouse precious sea-otter pelts. W. J. Erskine made it his home in 1911. On display are samovars, Russian Easter eggs, Native baskets, and other relics from the early Native Koniags and the later Russian settlers. A collection of 40 albums of archival photography portrays various aspects of the island's history. ⊠ *101 Marine Way* ☎ *907/486–5920* 🖷 *907/486–3166* ⊕ *www.ptialaska. net/~baranov* 🖾 *$2* ☉ *May–Sept., daily 10–4; Oct.–Apr., Mon.–Wed., Fri., and Sat. 10–3.*

The ornate **Holy Resurrection Russian Orthodox Church** is a visual feast, both inside and out. The cross-shape building is topped by two onion-shape blue domes, and the interior contains brass candle stands, distinctive chandeliers, and numerous icons representing Orthodox saints. Three different churches have stood on this site since 1794. Built in 1945, the present structure is on the National Register of Historic Places. ⊠ *Corner of Mission and Kashevaroff Rds.* ☎ *907/486–3854 (parish priest)* ☉ *By appointment* 🖾 *Donations accepted.*

★ The **Alutiiq Museum and Archaeological Repository** is home to one of the largest collections of Eskimo materials in the world and contains archaeological and ethnographic items dating back 7,500 years. The museum displays only a fraction of its more than 100,000 artifacts, including harpoons, masks, dolls, stone tools, seal-gut parkas, grass baskets, and pottery fragments. The museum store sells Native arts and educational materials. ⊠ *215 Mission Rd., Suite 101* ☎ *907/486–7004* ⊕ *www. alutiiqmuseum.com* 🖾 *$2 donation requested* ☉ *Memorial Day–Labor Day, weekdays 9–5, Sat. 10–5, Sun. by appointment; Labor Day–Memorial Day, Tues.–Fri. 9–5, Sat. 10:30–4:30.*

Where to Stay & Eat

¢–$$$$ ✕ **Henry's Great Alaskan Restaurant.** Henry's is a big, boisterous, friendly place at the mall near the small-boat harbor. The menu is equally big, ranging from fresh local seafood and barbecue to pastas and even some Cajun dishes. Dinner specials, a long list of appetizers, salads, rack of lamb, and a tasty dessert list round out the choices. ⊠ *512 Marine Way* ☎ *907/486–8844* 🖃 *AE, MC, V.*

¢ ✕ **Mill Bay Coffee & Pastries.** Serving soups, sandwiches, and fabulous pastries, this charming little shop is well worth the trip. Inside, elegant antique furnishings are complemented by local artwork and handicrafts. ⊠ *3833 Rezanof Dr. E* ☎ *907/486–4411* 🖷 *907/486–4416* ⊕ *www.millbaycoffee.com* 🖃 *MC, V* ☉ *Closed Sun. No dinner.*

★ $$ ✕🛏 **Kodiak Buskin River Inn.** This modern lodge is a five-minute walk from the main terminal at the airport, about 4½ mi from downtown. Dark woods and bedspreads offset the light-colored walls in the large, well-kept rooms. You can fish for salmon in the river out back. The Eagle's Nest ($$–$$$$) serves local seafood, including king crab, scallops, and a chilled seafood sampler. It also serves Cajun prawns, tempura vegetables, pasta, and steaks. The atmosphere is semiformal (in Alaska that means hip waders would be a bit out of place), with candlelike lamps on each table. ☒ *1395 Airport Way, 99615* ☎ *907/487–2700 or 800/544–2202* 🖶 *907/487–4447* ⊕ *www.kodiakadventure.com* ⇨ *50 rooms* ⟁ *Restaurant, some in-room data ports, cable TV, fishing, bar, meeting room, airport shuttle, some pets allowed (fee)* ▤ *AE, D, DC, MC, V.*

$$ 🏨 **Best Western Kodiak Inn.** Rooms here have soothing floral decor, and some overlook the harbor. However, the rooms with harbor views are on the street, so if a quiet room is a priority, take one in the back. The Chartroom Restaurant has harbor views and serves local seafood and American fare, including steak and pasta. The bar hosts live music on Friday. ☒ *236 Rezanof St. W, 99615* ☎ *907/486–5712 or 888/563–4254* 🖶 *907/486–3430* ⊕ *www.kodiakinn.com* ⇨ *81 rooms* ⟁ *Restaurant, in-room data ports, microwaves, refrigerators, cable TV, hot tub, bar, some pets allowed (fee)* ▤ *AE, D, DC, MC, V.*

$ 🏨 **Kodiak B&B.** Kodiak's first bed-and-breakfast commands a view of the St. Paul harbor and the waterways beyond. It's within a short walk of downtown and easily accessible to most of the town's businesses. Owner Mary Monroe is a gracious and knowledgeable host and can help you make the most of your Kodiak stay with plenty of helpful local information. The bedrooms share a bath and common sitting area, and bookshelves contain loads of local history. ☒ *308 Cope St., 99615* ☎ *907/486–5367* 🖶 *907/486–6567* ⊕ *www.ptialaska.net/~monroe* ⇨ *2 rooms share 1 bath* ▤ *MC, V* ⊘ *Closed Dec.–Jan.* ⧈ *BP.*

Guided Tours

Dig Afognak (⌂ Box 968, Kodiak 99615 ☎ 907/486–2993 🖶 907/486–6529 ⊕ www.afognak.org/dig) gives would-be archaeologists a chance to work alongside professionals during a seven-day dig and to learn about the island's natural history. **Kodiak Island Charters** (🛥 907/486–5380 or 800/575–5380) operates boat tours for fishing, hunting, and sightseeing aboard the 43-foot *U-Rascal*. They'll take you on a combined halibut and salmon trip, with sightseeing and whale-watching thrown in as well.

MATANUSKA-SUSITNA VALLEY & BEYOND

Giant homegrown vegetables and the headquarters of the best-known dogsled race in the world are among the most prominent attractions of the Matanuska-Susitna (Mat-Su) Valley. The valley, lying an hour north of Anchorage by road, draws its name from its two largest rivers, the Matanuska and the Susitna, and is bisected by the Parks and Glenn highways. Major cities are Wasilla on the Parks Highway and Palmer on the Glenn Highway. To the east, the Glenn Highway connects to the Richardson Highway by way of several high mountain passes sandwiched between the Chugach Mountains to the south and the Talkeetnas to the north. At Mile 103 of the Glenn Highway, the massive Matanuska Glacier comes almost to the road.

Lake Clark National Park & Preserve

🟢 *100 mi west of Anchorage by air.*

When the weather is good, an idyllic choice beyond the Mat-Su Valley is the 3.4-million-acre Lake Clark National Park and Preserve, on the Alaska Peninsula and a short flight from Anchorage. The parklands stretch from the coast to the heights of two grand volcanoes: **Mt. Iliamna** and

Mt. Redoubt, both topping out above 10,000 feet. The country in between holds glaciers, waterfalls, and turquoise-tinted lakes. The 50-mi-long **Lake Clark,** filled by runoff waters from the mountains that surround it, is an important spawning ground for thousands of red, or sockeye, salmon.

The river running is superb in this park. You can make your way through dark forests of spruce and balsam poplars or you can hike over the high, easy-to-travel tundra. The animal life is profuse: look for bears, moose, Dall sheep, wolves, wolverines, foxes, beavers, and minks on land; seals, sea otters, and white (or beluga) whales offshore. Wildflowers embroider the meadows and tundra in spring, and wild roses bloom in the shadows of the forests. Plan your trip to Lake Clark for the end of June or early July, when the insects may be less plentiful. Or consider late August or early September, when the tundra glows with fall colors. ⊠ *4230 University Dr., Suite 311, Anchorage 99508* ☎ *907/ 271–3751* ⊕ *www.nps.gov/lacl/index.htm.*

Where to Stay

$$$$ 🏨 **Farm Lodge.** Near park headquarters in Port Alsworth, the farm was built as a homestead back in the 1940s and has been a lodge since 1977. Two modern duplexes house as many as 20 guests in private rooms that have either bunk or double beds. A large, manicured, and fenced lawn with flower and vegetable gardens surrounds the main lodge, where home-cooked meals including fresh vegetables, salmon, wild game, and domestic meats are served. The lodge also provides flight services and guided trips. ⌂ *Box 1, Port Alsworth 99653* ☎ *907/781–2208 or 888/440– 2281* 🖷 *907/781–2215* ⊕ *www.lakeclarkair.com/lodge.htm* 🛏 *10 rooms* ⚘ *Dining room, some microwaves, fishing, meeting room; no smoking* ▭ *AE, D, MC, V.*

Palmer

⑰ *40 mi north of Anchorage.*

In 1935 the federal government relocated about 200 farm families from the Depression-ridden Midwest to the Mat-Su Valley, and some elements of these early farms remain around Palmer. The valley has developed into the state's major agricultural region. Good growing conditions result in some outsize vegetables—such as 100-pound cabbages.

🕃 You'll find a variety of outsize vegetables at the **Alaska State Fair,** which runs 11 days, ending on Labor Day (it will be held August 26–September 6, 2004). Locals whoop it up with midway rides, livestock and 4-H shows, bake-offs, home-preserved produce contests, food, and live music. ⊠ *Alaska State Fairgrounds, Mile 40.2, Glenn Hwy.* ⌂ *2075 Glenn Hwy., Palmer 99645* ☎ *907/745–4827 or 800/850–3247* 🖷 *907/ 746–2699* ⊕ *www.alaskastatefair.org* 🎫 *$8.*

On a sunny day the town of Palmer looks like a Swiss calendar photo, with its old barns and log houses silhouetted against craggy Pioneer Peak. On nearby farms (on the Bodenburg Loop off the old Palmer Highway) you can pay to pick your own raspberries and other fruits and vegeta-

🕃 bles. At **Pyrah's Pioneer Peak Farm** (⊠ Mile 2.8, Bodenburg Loop ☎ 907/ 745–4511), which cultivates 35 kinds of fruits and vegetables and begins harvesting in mid-June, the peak picking time occurs around mid-July.

🕃 The **Musk Ox Farm** conducts 30-minute guided tours from May to September. In addition to the 40-some animals roaming outside, there's a hands-on museum and a gift shop. ⊠ *Mile 50.1, Glenn Hwy.* ☎ *907/745–4151* 🎫 *$8.50* ☉ *May–Sept., daily 10–6; Oct.–Apr., by appointment.*

Gold mining was an early mainstay of the Mat-Su Valley's economy.
★ You can tour the long-dormant **Independence Mine** on the Hatcher Pass
Road, a loop that in summer connects the Parks Highway just north
of Willow to the Glenn Highway near Palmer. (The gravel roads leading to the gold mine are rough and full of potholes, even under the best
of conditions.) In the 1940s as many as 200 workers were employed
by the mine. Today it is a 271-acre state park and a cross-country ski
area in winter. Only the wooden buildings remain; one of them, the
red-roof manager's house, is now used as a visitor center. Guided tours
are given on weekdays at 1:30 and 3:30 PM. ⊠ *Independence Mine State
Historical Park, 19 mi from Glenn Hwy. on Hatcher Pass Rd.* ☎ *907/
745–3975* ⊕ *www.dnr.state.ak.us/parks/units/indmine.htm* 🖾 *$5 per
vehicle, tours $3* ⊙ *Visitor center early June–Labor Day, daily 11–7;
grounds year-round.*

Where to Stay & Eat

$ ╳🍴 **Colony Inn.** All guest rooms in this lovingly restored historic build-
ing are tastefully decorated with antiques and quilts. The building was
used as a women's dormitory during the farm colonization of the 1930s.
The small café ($–$$) serves light breakfasts, lunches, and Friday- and
Saturday-night dinners. Be sure to try one of the homemade pies; the
recipes have won blue ribbons at the Alaska State Fair. Inn reservations
and check-in are handled at the Valley Hotel. ⊠ *325 E. Elmwood Ave.,
99645* ☎ *907/745–3330, 800/478–7666 in Alaska* 🖨 *907/746–3330*
⊕ *www.colonyinnalaska.com* 🖙 *12 rooms* ♿ *Restaurant, in-room
data ports, cable TV; no smoking* ⊟ *AE, D, MC, V.*

$ 🏨 **Hatcher Pass Lodge.** This lodge has spectacular views and can serve
as base camp for hiking, berry picking, and—in fall and winter—skiing. Most rooms and cabins have queen-size beds. Three dormer-style
rooms provide cozy accommodations for one or two guests. The cabins, some with lofts, are carpeted and have large picture windows with
views of Hatcher Pass Valley. The cabins' half baths have chemical toilets and water coolers; showers are in the lodge. The restaurant's Continental menu ($$–$$$) includes fondues, halibut, and pizzas. The bar
serves cappuccinos and hot buttered rum for chilly nights. 🕭 *Box 763,
99645* ☎ *907/745–5897 or 907/745–1200* ⊕ *www.hatcherpasslodge.
com* 🖙 *3 rooms, 9 cabins without shower* ♿ *Restaurant, sauna, bar,
some pets allowed (fee); no room phones, no room TVs, no smoking*
⊟ *AE, D, MC, V.*

$ 🏨 **Valley Hotel.** Built in 1948, this three-story budget hotel was remod-
eled in 2003. Small, well-kept rooms have quilts and carpets. The hotel
is close to shopping, the library, and the local tourist information center. All desserts in the restaurant, the only 24-hour operation in the area,
are homemade. ⊠ *606 S. Alaska St., 99645* ☎ *907/745–3330, 800/478–
7666 in Alaska* 🖨 *907/746–3330* ⊕ *www.valleyhotelalaska.com* 🖙 *43
rooms* ♿ *Restaurant, in-room data ports, cable TV, bar, no-smoking rooms*
⊟ *AE, D, MC, V.*

Wasilla

⑱ *42 mi north of Anchorage, 10 mi west of Palmer.*

Wasilla is one of the valley's original pioneer communities and over time
has served as a supply center for farmers, gold miners, and mushers. Today,
fast-food restaurants and strip malls line the Parks Highway. Rolling hills
and more scenic vistas can be found by wandering the area's back roads.

The **Museum of Alaska Transportation and Industry,** on a 20-acre site, exhibits some of the machines that helped develop Alaska, from dogsleds

to jet aircraft, and everything in between. The Don Sheldon Building houses aviation artifacts as well as antique autos and photographic displays. A snow-machine exhibit also is on display. ✛ *Take Parks Hwy., turn south onto Neuser Rd. at Mile 47, follow road ¼ mi to end* ☎ *907/ 376–1211* 🖷 *907/376–3082* ⊕ *www.alaska.net/~rmorris/mati1.htm* 🎫 *$8* ☉ *May–Sept., daily 10–6.*

Wasilla is the headquarters and official starting point for the Iditarod Trail Sled Dog Race, run each March from here to Nome, more than 1,000 mi to the northwest. A ceremonial start is held on Anchorage's 4th Avenue the first Saturday in March, then continues from Wasilla the following day. The **Iditarod Trail Headquarters** displays dogsleds, mushers' clothing, and trail gear, and you can catch video highlights of past races. The gift shop sells Iditarod items. During the summer, dogsled rides on wheels are available for $5. ⊠ *Mile 2.2, Knik Rd.* ☎ *907/376– 5155* ⊕ *www.iditarod.com* 🎫 *Free* ☉ *Memorial Day–mid-Sept., daily 8–7; mid-Sept.–Memorial Day, weekdays 8–5.*

Where to Stay & Eat

$–$$$ ✕ **Evangelo's Trattoria.** The food is good and the servings ample at this spacious local favorite on the Parks Highway. Try the garlic-sautéed shrimp in a white-wine butter sauce or a mammoth calzone. The pizzas are loaded with goodies, and a salad bar provides a fresh selection. ⊠ *Mile 40, Parks Hwy.* ☎ *907/376–1212* ▭ *AE, MC, V.*

$–$$ ✕ **Cadillac Café.** Hearty fare fills the menu at this diner-style café, including homemade pies; big, hand-pressed burgers; exotic pizzas turned out of a stone, wood-fired oven; and southwestern-style Mexican food. The decor is described by the owner as "Alaska minimalist," but the booths are plush and comfortable, and hand-rubbed wood is much in evidence. Breakfast is served only on weekends. ⊠ *Mile 49, Parks Hwy., at Pittman St.* ☎ *907/357–5533* ▭ *AE, D, MC, V.*

$$ 🏨 **Best Western Lake Lucille Inn.** This well-maintained resort on Lake Lucille provides easy access to several recreational activities, including boating in summer and ice-skating and snowmobiling in winter. Half of the inn's bright and cheery rooms have private balconies overlooking the lake. Room decor includes art prints and quilts. ✛ *Mile 43.5 on the Parks Highway* ⊠ *1300 W. Lake Lucille Dr., 99654* ☎ *907/373– 1776 or 800/528–1234* 🖷 *907/376–6199* ⊕ *www.bestwestern.com/ lakelucilleinn* ⇆ *50 rooms, 4 suites* ⚑ *Restaurant, in-room data ports, cable TV, health club, hot tub, sauna, boating, lobby lounge, meeting room, some pets allowed* ▭ *AE, D, DC, MC, V.*

★ $–$$ 🏨 **Pioneer Ridge Bed and Breakfast Inn.** Each of the spacious, log-partitioned rooms in this converted barn is decorated according to a theme. The Denali Room has posters of the mountain, snowshoes, crampons, and other climbing gear. A dogsled and other race paraphernalia mark the Iditarod Room. A rooftop room has a spectacular 360° panorama of the mountains and river valleys. ⊠ *2221 Yukon Cir.* ⚐ *HC31, Box 5083K, 99654* ☎ *907/376–7472 or 800/478–7472* 🖷 *907/376–7470* ⊕ *www.pioneerridge.net* ⇆ *4 rooms share 2 baths, 3 suites, 1 cabin* ⚑ *Gym, sauna* ▭ *AE, D, MC, V.*

Talkeetna

⑲ *56 mi north of Wasilla, 112 mi north of Anchorage.*

Talkeetna lies at the end of a spur road near Mile 99 of the Parks Highway. Mountaineers congregate here to begin their assaults on Mt. McKinley in Denali National Park. The Denali mountain rangers have their climbing headquarters here, as do most glacier pilots who fly

CloseUp

A PRIVILEGED COMMUNION

BETWEEN 1903 AND 1912, eight expeditions walked the slopes of 20,320-foot Mt. McKinley. But none had reached the absolute top of North America's highest peak (also commonly known by the Native name Denali, meaning "the high one"). Among those who failed were some of North America's premier explorers and climbers. Thus the stage was set for Hudson Stuck, a self-described American amateur mountaineer who had previously climbed in Great Britain, the western United States, and Canada.

Stuck came to Alaska in 1904, drawn not by mountains but by a missionary calling. As the Episcopal Church's archdeacon for the Yukon River region, he visited Native villages year-round. His passion for climbing was unexpectedly rekindled in 1906, when he saw from afar the "glorious, broad, massive uplift" of McKinley, the "father of mountains." Five years after that wondrous view, Stuck pledged to reach McKinley's summit—or at least try. For his climbing party he picked three Alaskans experienced in snow and ice travel, though not in mountaineering: Harry Karstens, a well-known explorer and backcountry guide who would later become the first superintendent of Mt. McKinley National Park; Robert Tatum, Stuck's missionary assistant; and Walter Harper, part Native, who served as Stuck's interpreter and dog-team driver.

Assisted by two sled-dog teams, the group began its expedition on St. Patrick's Day, 1913, at Nenana, a village 90 mi northeast of McKinley. A month later, they began their actual ascent of the great peak's northern side, via the Muldrow Glacier. The glacier's surface proved to be a maze of crevasses, some of them wide chasms with no apparent bottom. Carefully working their way up-glacier, the climbers established a camp at 11,500 feet. From there they had to ascend a steep and jumbled ridgeline. Moving slowly, the team chopped a staircase up several miles—and 3,000 vertical feet—of rock, snow, and ice. Their progress was delayed several times by high winds, heavy snow, and near-zero visibility.

By May 30, the climbers had reached the top of the ridge (later named in Karstens's honor) and moved into a high glacial basin. Despite temperatures ranging from subzero to 21°F, they kept warm at night by sleeping on sheep and caribou skins and covering themselves with down quilts, camel's-hair blankets, and a wolf robe.

On June 6, the team established its high camp at 18,000 feet. The following morning was bright, cloudless, and windy. Three of the climbers suffered headaches and stomach pains, but given the clear weather everyone agreed to make an attempt. They left camp at 5 AM and by 1:30 PM stood within a few yards of McKinley's summit. Harper, who had been leading all day, was the first to reach the top, soon followed by the others. After catching their breath, the teammates shook hands, said a prayer of thanks, made some scientific measurements, and reveled in their magnificent surroundings. In his classic book The Ascent of Denali, Hudson Stuck later reflected, "There was no pride of conquest, no trace of that exultation of victory some enjoy upon the first ascent of a lofty peak, no gloating over good fortune that had hoisted us a few hundred feet higher than others who had struggled and been discomfited. Rather, was the feeling that a privileged communion with the high places of the earth had been granted."

climbing parties to the mountain. The **Talkeetna Historical Society Museum,** across from the Fairview Inn, explores the history of Mt. McKinley climbs. A carved pole at the town cemetery honors deceased mountaineers.

Where to Stay & Eat

$ ✕▦ **Swiss-Alaska Inn.** Family-run since 1976, this rustic-style property is well known among those who come to fish in the Talkeetna, Susitna, and Chulitna rivers. Floral decor embellishes the bright rooms. Menu selections at the restaurant ($$) include halibut, salmon, buffalo burgers, and the owner's secret-recipe Swiss-style French toast. ✉ *East Talkeetna, by boat launch* ⌖ *Box 565, 99676* ☎ *907/733–2424* 🖷 *907/ 733–2425* ⊕ *www.swissalaska.com* ⇆ *20 rooms* ⚘ *Restaurant, in-room VCRs, Internet; no room phones, no room TVs, no smoking* ▭ *AE, D, MC, V.*

¢–$ ✕▦ **Talkeetna Roadhouse.** This log roadhouse has a common sitting area and rooms in a variety of sizes, including a bunk room with four beds ($21). Rooms are very basic—bed, table, window, period. Sizable breakfasts are the order of the day at the restaurant (¢–$), along with soup-and-salad combos, sandwiches, desserts, and pies, all made from scratch. It's a popular place with locals and with climbers who use Talkeetna's air taxis to reach nearby Mt. McKinley. In the winter, the café is open only on weekends, but rooms are available year-around. ✉ *Main St.* ⌖ *Box 604, 99676* ☎ *907/733–1351* 🖷 *907/733–1353* ⊕ *www. talkeetnaroadhouse.com* ⇆ *8 rooms share 4 baths* ⚘ *Restaurant, Internet, some pets allowed; no room phones, no room TVs, no smoking* ▭ *MC, V* ☺ *No dinner. Restaurant closed Oct.–Nov. and weekdays Dec.–mid-Apr.*

★ $$$$ ▦ **Talkeetna Alaskan Lodge.** This luxury hotel has excellent views of Mt. McKinley as well as access to nature trails. Rooms are modern, in the style of an Alaska hunting lodge, and mountainside upgrades are available. The Great Room has comfortable seating, a 45-foot river-rock fireplace in the center of the room, and an espresso bar. The tour desk can arrange flightseeing, river trips, or any other Alaska adventure you can imagine. ⌖ *2525 C St., Suite 405, Anchorage 99503* ☎ *907/265–4501 or 888/959–9590* 🖷 *907/263–5559* ⊕ *www.talkeetnalodge.com* ⇆ *201 rooms, 3 suites* ⚘ *Restaurant, in-room data ports, some microwaves, cable TV, hiking, bar, meeting room; no smoking* ▭ *AE, D, MC, V.*

¢ ▦ **Fairview Inn.** Built in 1923, the Fairview is listed on the National Register of Historic Places. It oozes local color, from the bear rug nailed to the ceiling over the bar to photographs of local characters and former owners on the wall. You're likely to meet members of Mt. McKinley climbing expeditions during the early-summer climbing season. You'll also hear lots of good, local music, but be forewarned: you'll hear it even if you don't want to, so if a good night's sleep is important, check first to see if the band will be playing. The inn is open year-round, but food is served only from Memorial Day to Labor Day in the outdoor beer garden. ✉ *101 Main St.* ⌖ *Box 1109, Talkeetna 99676* ☎ *907/733–2423* 🖷 *907/733–1067* ⊕ *www.denali-fairview.com* ⇆ *5 rooms, shared baths* ⚘ *Restaurant, bar; no room phones, no room TVs* ▭ *AE, MC, V.*

Guided Tours

Hudson Air Service (☎ 907/733–2321 or 800/478–2321 🖷 907/733–2333 ⊕ www.alaskan.com/hudsonair) has a fleet of four airplanes to take you on flightseeing trips, glacier landings, and remote drop-offs. **K2 Aviation** (☎ 907/733–2291 or 800/764–2291 🖷 907/733–1221 ⊕ www.flyk2. com) lands you on a glacier and also leads overnight trips to Denali National Park. **Talkeetna Air Taxi** (☎ 907/733–2218 or 800/533–2219 🖷 907/733–1434 ⊕ www.talkeetnaair.com) conducts a breathtaking exploration flight close to massive Mt. McKinley, as well as fly-in hiking trips and glacier landings.

Mahay's Riverboat Service (☎ 907/733–2223 or 800/736–2210 ⊕ www. mahaysriverboat.com) conducts guided jet-boat tours, scenic cruises, and fishing on the Susitna and Talkeetna rivers. **Denali Floats** (☎ 907/733– 2384 or 800/651–5221) leads scenic raft trips on the Susitna River, complete with shore lunch and occasional musical accompaniment, and can arrange wilderness expeditions to suit your schedule. **Tri-River Charters** (✉ Box 312, Talkeetna 99676 ☎ 907/733–2400 ⊕ www. tririvercharters.com) operates fishing trips out of Talkeetna and on the nearby Deshka River and can provide all the necessary tackle and gear.

Denali State Park

㉑ *34 mi north of Talkeetna, 132 mi north of Anchorage.*

Overshadowed by the larger and more charismatic Denali National Park and Preserve in the Interior, "Little Denali" offers excellent access (it's bisected by the Parks Highway), beautiful views of Mt. McKinley, scenic campgrounds, and prime wilderness hiking and backpacking opportunities within a few miles of the road system. Between the Talkeetna Mountains and the Alaska Range, Denali State Park combines wooded lowlands and forested foothills topped by alpine tundra. ✉ *Alaska State Parks, Mat-Su Area Office, HC 32, Box 6706, Wasilla 99687* ☎ *907/ 745–3975.*

The park's chief attraction, other than McKinley views, is the 35-mi-long **Curry-Kesugi Ridge**, which forms a rugged spine through the heart of the park that is ideal backpacking terrain. Another destination favored by backcountry travelers is the **Peters Hills**, accessible from Petersville Road in Trapper Creek.

Where to Stay

$$$ 🏨 **McKinley Princess Wilderness Lodge.** When the sky is clear and Mt. McKinley is visible, this lodge has excellent views of North America's highest peak, especially from the lobby, with its large stone fireplace. On private land inside Denali State Park, this hillside lodge is surrounded by forest and overlooks the Chulitna River. You stay in bungalow-style guest rooms with separate sitting rooms. The tour desk can arrange horseback rides, river-rafting trips, naturalist walks, flightseeing excursions, fishing trips, mountain-bike rentals, and alpine hikes. ✉ *Mile 133, Parks Hwy.* ☎ *907/733–2900 or 800/426–0500* 🖶 *907/ 733–2922* ⊕ *www.princessalaskalodges.com* ⬤ *238 rooms, 4 suites* ⬧ *Restaurant, café, some in-room hot tubs, gym, hiking, shop, meeting rooms, travel services* ▱ *AE, D, DC, MC, V* ⊙ *Closed mid-Sept.–mid-May.*

¢ 🏨 **Alaska State Parks Cabins.** Two public-use cabins are in Denali State Park, along the shores of Byers Lake. One cabin is on a gravel road, 1 mi from the highway, and the other is accessible by canoe or by a ½-mi walk-in trail. Both are equipped with bunks, wood-burning stove, table, and benches, but they have no running water or electricity. ✚ *Mile 147.1 of the Parks Highway* ✉ *Alaska State Parks Information Center, 550 W. 7th Ave., Suite 1260, Anchorage 99501-3557* ☎ *907/269–8400* ⬤ *2 cabins without bath* ▱ *No credit cards.*

¢ ⚠ **Alaska State Parks Campgrounds.** Three roadside campgrounds are within Denali State Park—Byers Lake, Lower Troublesome Creek, and Denali View North. All are easily accessible from the Parks Highway and have picnic tables, fire pits, drinking water, and latrines. The Byers Lake campground also has a boat launch and nearby hiking trails. Sites are available on a first-come, first-served basis. ⓓ *Alaska State Parks, HC 32, Box 6706, Wasilla 99654* ☎ *907/745–3975* ⊕ *www.dnr.state. ak.us/parks/units/denali2.htm* ▭ *No credit cards* ◷ *Closed Oct.–May.*

Glennallen

㉑ *187 mi northeast of Anchorage.*

This community of 900 residents is the gateway to Wrangell–St. Elias National Park and Preserve. It's 124 mi from Glennallen to McCarthy, the last 58 mi on unpaved gravel. This town is also the service center for the Copper River basin and is a fly-in base for several wilderness outfitters.

Where to Stay & Eat

¢–$$ ✕ **Caribou Restaurant.** This convivial place serves such typical roadside fare as burgers, hot sandwiches, meat loaf, pancakes, and charbroiled steak. Sweet rolls, pies, and other treats are baked fresh daily. If you haven't managed to spy any of the local wildlife on your trip, just check out the walls here for numerous taxidermied examples. ⊠ *Mile 186.5, Glenn Hwy.* ☎ *907/822–4222* ▭ *AE, D, MC, V.*

$$ ▥ **Caribou Hotel.** Rooms decorated in mauve and sea green fill this modern hotel. Unless you're on a strict budget, ask for a room in the main building and not in the trailerlike annex out front, where rooms are spartan and share a bath. Several rooms in the main building have hot tubs. The owners operate a nearby B&B and a property with three two-bedroom apartments and a one-bedroom apartment. ⓓ *Box 329, 99588* ☎ *907/822–3302, 800/478–3302* 🖷 *907/822–3711* ⊕ *www. alaskan.com/caribouhotel* ⇗ *83 rooms, 63 with bath; 3 suites* ⚒ *In-room data ports, some in-room hot tubs, some kitchens, some microwaves, some refrigerators, cable TV, meeting room, some pets allowed* ▭ *AE, D, DC, MC, V.*

Wrangell–St. Elias National Park & Preserve

㉒ *77 mi southeast of Glennallen, 264 mi east of Anchorage.*

In a land of many grand and spectacularly beautiful mountains, those in the 9.2-million-acre Wrangell–St. Elias National Park and Preserve have been singled out by many Alaskans as the finest of them all. This extraordinarily compact cluster of immense peaks toward the southeastern part of Alaska belongs to four different mountain ranges. ⊠ *Mile 106.8, Richardson Hwy.* ⓓ *Box 439, Copper Center 99573* ☎ *907/822–5234* ⊕ *www.nps.gov/wrst/index.htm.*

Covering an area some 100 mi by 70 mi, the **Wrangells** tower above the 2,500-foot-high Copper River Plateau, and the peaks of Mts. Jarvis, Drum, Blackburn, Sanford, and Wrangell rise 15,000 feet–16,000 feet from sea level. The white-iced spire of **Mt. St. Elias,** in the St. Elias Range, reaches more than 18,000 feet. It's the fourth-tallest mountain on the North American continent and the crown of the planet's highest coastal range.

The park's coastal mountains are frequently wreathed in snow-filled clouds, their massive height making a giant wall that contains the great storms brewed in the Gulf of Alaska. As a consequence, they bear some of the continent's largest ice fields, with more than 100 glaciers radiating from them. One of these, the **Malaspina Glacier,** is 1,500 square mi— larger than the state of Rhode Island. This tidewater glacier has an incredible pattern of black-and-white stripes made by the other glaciers that coalesced to form it. Look for it on the coast north of Yakutat if you fly between Juneau and Anchorage.

Rising through many life zones, the Wrangell–St. Elias Park and Preserve is largely undeveloped wilderness parkland on a grand scale. The area is perfect mountain-biking and hiking terrain, and the rivers invite rafting for those with expedition experience. The mountains attract climbers from around the world; most of them fly in from Glennallen or Yakutat. The nearby abandoned **Kennicott Mine** is one of the park's main visitor attractions. Limited services are available in the end-of-the-road town of **McCarthy.** Facilities include guest lodges, a B&B, and a restaurant. There's no gas station or post office.

The park is accessible from Alaska's highway system, via one of two gravel roads. The unpaved **Nabesna Road** leaves the Glenn Highway–Tok Cutoff at the village of Slana and takes you 45 mi into the park's northern foothills. The better-known route is the **McCarthy Road,** which stretches 60 mi as it follows an old railroad bed from Chitina to the Kennicott River. At the end of the road you must park and cross the river via a footbridge.

Before setting out make sure both you and your car are prepared. Your car should be equipped with a working jack and a properly inflated spare tire, or else potholes, old railroad ties, and occasional railroad spikes may leave you stranded.

Where to Stay

$$$$ ⊡ **Ultima Thule Outfitters.** This remote fly-in-only lodge on the Chitina River in Wrangell–St. Elias National Park and Preserve provides a wonderful chance to experience an "air-safari adventure." The cost is $990 per person per day, with a four-day minimum. Included in your stay are breathtaking flightseeing, rafting, climbing, hiking, fishing, mushing, and skiing excursions, among others. The family-style meals include local foods such as fish, game, and vegetables from the garden as well as homemade bread, pies, and cakes. Oak floors, wallpaper, wood-burning stoves, and brass beds provide the comforts of home Bavarian style. ⌂ *Box 109, Chitina 99566 or Box 770361, Eagle River 99577* ☎ *907/688–1200* ⊕ *www.ultimathulelodge.com* ⌁ *6 cabins* ⌂ *Dining room, sauna, boating, fishing, hiking, cross-country skiing* ⊟ *No credit cards* ⏀ *AI.*

$$$ ⊡ **Copper River Princess Wilderness Lodge.** At the gateway to the park, this lodge has views of the Wrangell–St. Elias mountain range and the Copper and Klutina rivers. A wall of windows two stories high provides dramatic views of towering peaks and the Copper River. Dark-wood accents and Alaska wildlife and scenery prints, conveying the ambience of a well-appointed hunting lodge, adorn each room. ⊠ *Brenwick Craig Rd., Mile 102 Richardson Hwy. Copper Center 99573* ☎ *907/822–4000, 800/426–0500 reservations* 🖷 *907/822–4480* ⊕ *www.princesslodges. com* ⌁ *85 rooms* ⌂ *Restaurant, coffee shop, bar, shop, meeting room, airport shuttle; no smoking* ⊟ *AE, DC, MC, V* ⊘ *Closed mid Sept.-mid-May.*

★ $$$ ⊡ **Kennicott Glacier Lodge.** Artifacts and photos of the era when mining was the main order of business in the ghost town of Kennicot adorn the small rooms in this modern, wooden lodge. Rooms have cold-water sinks and share bath and shower facilities. Dinner is a "wilderness gourmet" of breads and desserts served family style. Breakfast and lunch are served restaurant style, with the same exceptional attention to detail and freshness. Afterward, you can relax in the spacious living room or on the front porch. The front desk can arrange glacier trekking, flightseeing, rafting, and alpine hiking for additional fees, and an evening tour of Kennicott is included in the room rate. A vacation package that includes room and all meals is available. ⌂ *Box 103940, Anchorage 99510*

☎ *907/258–2350 or 800/582–5128* 🖷 *907/248–7975* ⊕ *www. kennicottlodge.com* ↻ *25 rooms* ♿ *Dining room, hiking, meeting room; no room phones, no room TVs, no smoking* ⊟ *AE, D, MC, V* ⊘ *Closed mid-Sept.–mid-May.*

¢ ⚠ **Alaska State Parks Campgrounds.** The state maintains 23 road-accessible campgrounds in the Matanuska-Susitna–Copper River region. Most can accommodate RVs up to 35 feet long, though electrical hookups are not available. Length of stay varies from 4 to 15 days. All have toilet facilities, and most have drinking water, picnic sites, fire pits, fishing, and nearby hiking trails. ⊡ *Alaska State Parks, Mat-Su Area Office, HC 32, Box 6706, Wasilla 99654* ☎ *907/745–3975* ⚲ *Reservations not accepted* ↻ *23 campgrounds* ⊟ *No credit cards* ⊘ *Closed Oct.–May.*

Sports & the Outdoors

St. Elias Alpine Guides (☎ 907/345–9048, 888/933–5427, or 907/554–4445 mid-May–mid-Sept. ⊕ www.steliasguides.com) gives introductory mountaineering lessons, leads excursions ranging from half-day glacier walks to monthlong backpacking trips, and conducts guided tours of historic Kennicott buildings and day raft trips from Kennicott. This service, which is owned by experienced mountaineer Bob Jacobs, has been in business more than 20 years.

SOUTH CENTRAL ALASKA A TO Z

To research prices, get advice from other travelers, and book travel arrangements, visit www.fodors.com.

AIR TRAVEL

Anchorage is the air hub of the South Central region, served by major national and international airlines and well stocked with smaller carriers and local air-taxi operators. ERA Aviation flies to Homer, Kenai, Valdez, Cordova, and Kodiak. Reservations are handled by Alaska Airlines. For flights to the Alaska Peninsula, the Aleutians, and western Alaska Bush villages, call PenAir. Frontier Flying Service flies to Fairbanks, Deadhorse, Barrow, and several western Alaska Bush villages.

🛪 **ERA Aviation** ☎ 907/243-3300 or 800/866-8394. **Frontier Flying Service** (800/478-6779 in Alaska; 907/474-0014 reservations). **PenAir** ☎ 907/243-2323 or 800/448-4226.

BOAT & FERRY TRAVEL

Ferries are a great way to explore the South Central coast, with its glaciers, mountains, fjords, and sea mammals. The ferries between Valdez and Whittier run by way of Columbia Glacier in summer, where it is not unusual to witness giant fragments of ice calving from the face of the glacier into Prince William Sound.

The Alaska Marine Highway, the state-run ferry operator, has scheduled service to Valdez, Cordova, Whittier, Seward, Homer, and Seldovia on the mainland; to Kodiak and Port Lions on Kodiak Island; and to the port of Dutch Harbor in the Aleutian Islands. The same agency runs the ferries that operate in Southeast Alaska, but the two systems connect only on once-a-month sailings. The system operates on two schedules; summer (May–September) sailings are considerably more frequent than fall and winter service. Check your schedules carefully: ferries do not stop at all ports every day. Reservations are required on all routes; they should be made as far in advance as possible, particularly in summer.

🛥 **Alaska Marine Highway** ⊡ Box 25535, Juneau 99802-5535 ☎ 907/465-3941 or 800/642-0066 🖷 907/277-4829 ⊕ www.state.ak.us/ferry.

BUS TRAVEL

Year-round service runs between Fairbanks and Anchorage by way of Denali National Park and also down to Homer, at the very tip of the Kenai Peninsula. Alaska Direct Bus Lines provides service between Anchorage and Fairbanks and also to Whitehorse and Skagway. The Park Connection has regularly scheduled shuttle service between Seward, Anchorage, and Denali National Park mid-May to mid-September. Seward Bus Line serves Anchorage, Portage, and Seward. A subsidiary offers service between Anchorage and Homer.

Alaska Direct Bus Lines ☎ 907/277-6652 or 800/770-6652 ⎙ 907/338-1951. **Park Connection** ☎ 800/208-0200, 907/224-7116 for Seward same-day bookings, 907/683-1240 for Denali same-day bookings. **Seward Bus Line** ☎ 907/563-0800 or 907/224-3608 ⎙ 907/224-7237.

CAR TRAVEL

Keep in mind that all but a few miles of the road system consist of two-lane highways, not all of which are paved. Two highway routes offer a choice for travel by car between Fairbanks and Anchorage. Heading north from Anchorage, the Parks Highway (turn left off Glenn Highway near Palmer) passes through Wasilla, up the Susitna River drainage area and through a low pass in the Alaska Range, then down into the Tanana Valley and Fairbanks. This route passes the entrance to Denali National Park and roughly parallels the Alaska Railroad. A longer route (436 mi) follows the Glenn Highway to the Richardson Highway, then heads north to Fairbanks through the Copper River valley. This route makes possible a side trip to Valdez, and it's the most direct connection to the Alaska Highway, joining it at Tok.

You can also link the two routes by using the Denali Highway, which, despite its name, doesn't run through Denali National Park. Rather, it connects the Richardson Highway with the Parks Highway between the towns of Paxson and Cantwell. You can make a huge figure eight by using the Denali, but be advised that this 135-mi-long road isn't paved except for relatively short sections at either end, and services are limited. Don't start the trip without a full tank of gas and at least one real spare tire, just to be on the safe side.

State Department of Transportation ☎ 907/243-7675 in Anchorage for hot-line reports on highways during snow season.

EMERGENCIES

Police, ambulance, emergency ☎ 911. **Alaska State Troopers** ☎ 907/269-5722 in Anchorage, 907/822-3263 in Glennallen, 907/235-8239 in Homer, 907/486-4121 in Kodiak, 907/745-2131 in Palmer, 907/224-3346 in Seward, 907/262-4052 in Soldotna, 907/835-4359 in Valdez.

Hospitals Cordova: **Cordova Medical Center** ✉ 602 Chase Ave. ☎ 907/424-8000. Glennallen: **Crossroads Medical Center** ✉ Mile 187.5, Glenn Hwy. ☎ 907/822-3203. Homer: **South Peninsula Hospital** ✉ 4300 Bartlett St. ☎ 907/235-8101. Kodiak: **Providence Kodiak Island Medical Center** ✉ 1915 E. Rezanof Dr. ☎ 907/486-3281. Palmer: **Valley Hospital** ✉ 515 E. Dahlia St. ☎ 907/746-8600. Seldovia: **Seldovia Medical Clinic** ✉ 252 Seldovia St. ☎ 907/234-7825. Seward: **Providence Seward Medical Center** ✉ 417 1st Ave. ☎ 907/224-5205. Soldotna: **Central Peninsula General Hospital** ✉ 250 Hospital Pl. ☎ 907/262-4404. Valdez: **Community Hospital** ✉ 911 Meals St. ☎ 907/835-2249.

LODGING

BED & BREAKFASTS **Local Agents** **Accommodations on the Kenai** ✎ Box 2956-F, Soldotna 99669 ☎ 907/262-2139 ⊕ www.aokreservations.com. **Alaska Private Lodgings/Stay with a Friend** ✉ 704 W. 2nd Ave., Anchorage 99501 ☎ 907/258-1717 ⎙ 907/258-6613 ⊕ www.alaskabandb.com. **Alaska Sourdough Bed and Breakfast Association** ✉ 889 Cardi-

gan Cir., Anchorage 99501 ☎ 907/563-6244 🖷 907/563-6073 ⊕ www.alaskan.com/
aksourdoughbba.

TOURS

ARCHAEOLOGY   📌 Tour Operators **Dig Afognak** 🕮 Box 1277, Kodiak 99615 ☎ 907/486-6014 or 800/
770-6014 🖷 907/486-2514.

BOATING &   📌 Tour Operators **Alaskan Wilderness Sailing & Kayaking** 🕮 Box 1313, Valdez
GLACIERS   99686 ☎ 907/835-5175 🖷 907/835-3765. **Columbia Glacier Wildlife Cruises/Lu-Lu
Belle** ☎ 907/835-5141 or 800/411-0090 🖷 907/835-5899 in summer ☎☎ 800/411-0090
off-season. **Homer Ocean Charters** ☎ 907/235-6212 or 800/426-6212. **Kenai Coastal
Tours** ☎ 907/277-2131 or 800/770-9119. **Kenai Fjords Tours** ☎ 907/224-8068 in Seward, 907/276-6249, 800/478-8068 🖷 907/276-1064. **Keystone Raft & Kayak Adventures, Inc.** ☎ 907/835-2606 or 800/328-8460 🖷 907/835-4638. **Kodiak Island Charters**
☎☎ 907/486-5380 or 800/575-5380. **Mariah Tours** ☎ 907/224-8623 or 800/270-1238
🖷 907/224-8625. **Prince William Sound Cruises and Tours** ☎ 907/835-4731 or 800/
992-1297 🖷 907/835-3765. **26 Glacier Cruise** ✉ Phillips' Cruises & Tours, 519 W. 4th
Ave., Suite 100, Anchorage 99510.

FISHING   📌 Tour Operators **Central Charters** ✉ 4241 Homer Spit Rd., Homer 99603 ☎ 907/
235-7847 or 800/478-7847. **Fish House** ✉ Small-boat harbor, Seward ☎ 907/224-3674
or 800/257-7760. **U-Rascal** ☎ 907/486-5380.

FLIGHTSEEING   📌 Tour Operators **Alpine Aviation Adventures** ✉ Valdez ☎ 907/835-4304, 800/478-
4304 in Alaska 🖷 907/835-2523. **Cordova Air Service** ☎ 907/424-3289, 800/424-7608
in Alaska 🖷 907/424-3495. **Prince William Sound Adventures** ☎ 907/424-3350.

GENERAL   📌 Tour Operators **Alaska Heritage Tours** ☎ 907/265-4500 or 877/258-6877 🖷 907/
INTEREST   263-5559. **Alaska Wildland Adventures** ☎ 907/783-2928 or 800/334-8730. **Gray Line
of Alaska** ☎ 907/277-5581 or 800/478-6388.

HIKING   Information on locations and difficulty of trails is available at the Alaska
Public Lands Information Center at 4th and F streets in Anchorage. Another good resource is *55 Ways to the Wilderness in South Central Alaska,*
published by the Mountaineers and available at most local bookstores.

TRAIN TRAVEL

The Alaska Railroad Corporation operates the Alaska Railroad, which
is said to be the last railroad in North America that still makes flag stops
to accommodate the homesteaders, hikers, fishing parties, and other travelers who get on and off in remote places. The 470-mi main line runs
up Alaska's rail belt between Seward and Fairbanks via Anchorage. There's
daily service between Anchorage and Fairbanks in summer, and in winter there's one round-trip per week (Anchorage to Fairbanks on Saturday, Fairbanks to Anchorage on Sunday). Service to Seward from
Anchorage runs mid-May to September 1 only. Adults are allowed two
pieces of luggage to a maximum of 50 pounds. There's a $20 charge
for bicycles; camping equipment is allowed on a space-available basis.

For information on the luxury-class Ultradome service between Anchorage
and Fairbanks, contact Princess Tours about its *Midnight Sun Express.*
Westours/Gray Line of Alaska operates the *McKinley Explorer* on
Alaska Railroad trains as well.
📌 **Alaska Railroad Corporation** 🕮 Box 107500, Anchorage 99510 ☎ 907/265-2494
or 800/544-0552 🖷 907/265-2323 ⊕ www.akrr.com. **Princess Tours** ☎ 206/728-4202
or 800/835-8907. **Westours/Gray Line of Alaska** ☎ 907/277-5581 or 800/478-6388.

TRANSPORTATION AROUND SOUTH CENTRAL ALASKA

Anchorage is the central hub, connected by rail and road to Seward and
Whittier. Valdez can be reached by a rather indirect but interesting road
route (the Glenn Highway to the Richardson Highway) out of Anchorage. The Seward and Sterling highways connect to most of the places you'll

want to see on the Kenai Peninsula, including the small towns of Hope, Soldotna, and Homer. South Central's other "highway," the ferry-driven Alaska Marine Highway, connects with Kodiak, Whittier, Seward, Valdez, Dutch Harbor, Homer, Seldovia, and Cordova via the gulf. Air taxis are also a viable means of transportation around South Central.

VISITOR INFORMATION

🖪 Alaska Public Lands Information Center ⊠ 605 W. 4th Ave., Anchorage 99501 ☏ 907/271-2737. **Bureau of Land Management** ✑ Box 147, Glennallen 99588 ☏ 907/822-3217. **Cordova Chamber of Commerce** ✑ Box 99, Cordova 99574 ☏ 907/424-7260. **Homer Chamber of Commerce** ⊠ 135 Sterling Hwy. ✑ Box 541, Homer 99603 ☏ 907/235-5300. **Kenai Peninsula Visitor Information Center** ⊠ 44790 Sterling Hwy., Soldotna 99669 ☏ 907/262-1337. **Kodiak Island Convention and Visitors Bureau** ⊠ 100 Marine Way, Kodiak 99615 ☏ 907/486-4782. **Palmer Chamber of Commerce** ✑ Box 45, Palmer 99645 ☏ 907/745-2880. **Seward Visitors Bureau** ⊠ Mile 2, Seward Hwy. ✑ Box 749, Seward 99664 ☏ 907/224-8051. **U.S. Fish and Wildlife Service** ⊠ Alaska Regional Office, 1011 E. Tudor Rd., Anchorage 99503 ☏ 907/786-3487. **U.S. Forest Service** ⊠ 3301 C St., Room 300, Anchorage 99503 ☏ 907/271-2500. **Valdez Convention and Visitors Bureau** ⊠ 200 Chenega St. ✑ Box 1603, Valdez 99686 ☏ 907/835-2984. **Wasilla Chamber of Commerce** ⊠ 1830 E. Parks Hwy., A-116, Wasilla 99654 ☏ 907/376-1299.

THE INTERIOR
WITH FAIRBANKS, DENALI NATIONAL PARK & THE YUKON

FODOR'S CHOICE

Chena Hot Springs Resort, *Chena Hot Springs*

Denali Backcountry Lodge, *Kantishna*

Denali National Park & Preserve

Lynx Creek Pizza, *near Denali National Park*

Pump House Restaurant, *Fairbanks*

University of Alaska Museum, *Fairbanks*

Wedgewood Resort, *Fairbanks*

HIGHLY RECOMMENDED

RESTAURANTS   Alaska Salmon Bake, *Fairbanks*

The Chocolate Claim, *Whitehorse*

The Cookie Jar, *Fairbanks*

Gambardella's Pasta Bella, *Fairbanks*

Pike's Landing, *Fairbanks*

Rika's Roadhouse, *Delta Junction*

Sam's Sourdough Cafe, *Fairbanks*

Two Rivers Lodge, *Chena Hot Springs*

HOTELS   Camp Denali and North Face Lodge, *Denali National Park*

Fairbanks Princess Riverside Lodge, *Fairbanks*

Pike's Waterfront Lodge, *Fairbanks*

SIGHTS   Fairbanks Ice Museum, *Fairbanks*

Pioneer Park, *Fairbanks*

SS *Klondike*, *Whitehorse*

Silver Gulch Brewing and Bottling Co., *Fairbanks*

University of Alaska Fairbanks

NIGHTLIFE   Blue Loon, *Fairbanks*

Midnight Mine, *Fairbanks*

By Kent Sturgis

Updated by
Tom Reale

THE IMAGE OF 1890 ALASKA, with its heady gold rushes set to the jangling sounds of countless honky-tonk saloons, has its roots in the Interior. Gold fever struck in Circle and Eagle in the 1890s, spread into Canada's Yukon Territory in the big Klondike gold rush of 1898, then came back to Alaska's Interior when Fairbanks hit pay dirt in the 1900s. The broad, swift Yukon River was the rush's main highway. Flowing almost 2,300 mi from Canada to the Bering Sea, just below the Arctic Circle, it carried prospectors across the border in search of instant fortune.

Although Fairbanks has grown up into a small city, many towns and communities in the Interior seem little changed. While soaking in the water of the Chena Hot Springs Resort, you can almost hear the whispers of gold seekers exaggerating their finds and claims, ever alert for the newest strike. When early missionaries set up schools in the Bush, the nomadic Native Alaskan peoples were herded to these regional centers for schooling and "salvation," but Interior Alaska is still flecked with Native villages. Fort Yukon, on the Arctic Circle, is the largest Athabascan village in the state.

Alaska's current gold rush—the pipeline carrying black gold from the oil fields in Prudhoe Bay south to the port of Valdez—snakes its way through the heart of the Interior. The pipeline itself is something of an enigma: it's a symbol of commercial interests against the environment yet also a monumental construction that hugs the land like a giant necklace. The Richardson Highway, which started as a gold stampeders' trail, parallels the trans-Alaska pipeline on its route south of Fairbanks.

Gold glitters anew in the Interior. Fairbanks, the site of the largest gold production in Alaska in pre–World War II days, is the location of the Fort Knox Gold Mine, which is expected to double Alaska's gold production. The mine is starting up more than a century after the discovery of gold in the Klondike in 1896 and the massive stampede of prospectors to Dawson City in 1898.

The Alaska Range—the "great wall" dividing the Interior from the South Central region—rises more than 20,000 feet. Its grandest member, Mt. McKinley (known among Athabascan-speaking Native people as *Denali,* or "the high one"), rises 18,000 sky-filling feet from base to peak (one of the highest uplifts in the world); and at 20,320 feet above sea level, it is the highest peak in North America. (Although Mt. Everest reaches more than 29,000 feet above sea level, it rises only 11,000 feet above the Tibetan Plateau.)

This tumultuous landscape was formed by the head-on collision of two tectonic plates. Between them, in the Denali fault system, lies the largest crack in the Earth's crust on the North American continent. This barrier between South Central and the Interior Plateau gathers colder weather and bears a fine glacial system because of its high altitude. These ice-capped mountains resemble the way a large part of the continent looked during the Ice Age. Flying in a small plane over the black-striped glaciers of the Alaska Range can be a dazzling experience.

Exploring the Interior

Interior Alaska is neatly sandwiched between two monumental mountain ranges—the Brooks Range to the north and the Alaska Range to the south. Important cities and towns are spread along two major transportation routes. The Yukon River flows east–west in the northern half of the region. Interior Alaskans often define their area by the road system. A few highways cut through this great land, and only one connects Alaska to the rest of the world. The Alaska Highway, still often referred

7

Numbers in the text correspond to numbers in the margin and on the Interior and the Yukon, Fairbanks, Denali National Park and Preserve, and Dawson City maps.

If you have 3 days

Spend a day in ⬚ **Fairbanks** ①–⑦, taking in the trans-Alaska pipeline, University of Alaska Museum, and the Riverboat Discovery tour. Try to end your day at Pioneer Park so that you can have dinner at the Alaska Salmon Bake. The next day head to ⬚ **Denali National Park and Preserve** ⑭ and do some hiking or take a white-water rafting trip down the nearby Nenana River. Spend the night in the park area, but be sure to call ahead for room or campsite reservations and for seats on the bus—the park area is very crowded in the summer. The next morning get up early to take a shuttle bus to Eielson Visitor Center at the park entrance, and start the third day exploring the national park. Stay in Fairbanks the last night, catching dinner and a show at the Ester Gold Camp.

If you have 5 days

Follow the three-day itinerary; then spend the fourth day in ⬚ **Fairbanks** ①–⑦, taking the tour of El Dorado Gold Mine, where you can pan for gold, and visiting the **Fairbanks Ice Museum** ② if you missed it earlier. That afternoon head out to the scenic Chena Hot Springs Road for a relaxing soak at Chena Hot Springs Resort in ⬚ **Chena Hot Springs** ⑧. Spend the night at the resort or head back to town and consider stopping for dinner at Two Rivers Lodge.

If you have 10 days

Follow the five-day itinerary; then head east to the Fortymile and Klondike gold-rush areas, visiting some of the unique attractions along the Richardson and Alaska highways, such as the Santa Claus House in **North Pole** ⑮, the Knotty Shop just south of North Pole, and Rika's Roadhouse in **Delta Junction** ⑯. Spend the night in ⬚ **Tok** ⑰. The next day take the gravel Taylor Highway up to ⬚ **Eagle** ⑲ and the Yukon River. Take the walking tour of Eagle in the morning, and then drive to ⬚ **Dawson City** ⑳–㉔, spending a day or two there. From Dawson you can go back to Fairbanks the way you came, or—if you're up for the 337-mi drive—you can continue on to **Whitehorse** ㉕, on the Alaska Highway. If a long drive doesn't suit you, on Day 6 hop a flight to Dawson, spend a couple of days there, and then return for more Fairbanks attractions.

---

to as the Alcan (Alaska-Canada Highway), enters Alaska by way of Yukon Territory, Canada.

On the eastern edge of the state lies Fortymile Country and, just across the border, the Yukon Territory. In Alaska the Taylor Highway cuts through Fortymile Country, connecting Eagle, a gold-rush town, to the Alaska Highway. A cutoff connects the Taylor to the Top of the World Highway, which runs through Dawson City, a town that's a celebration of mining history. Both highways are gravel. The Alaska Highway officially ends in Delta Junction, where the Richardson Highway leads to Fairbanks. The highways run through fairly flat land, by Alaska standards, though they do get close to some mountains. The George Parks Highway connects Fairbanks to Anchorage, passing right by Denali Na-

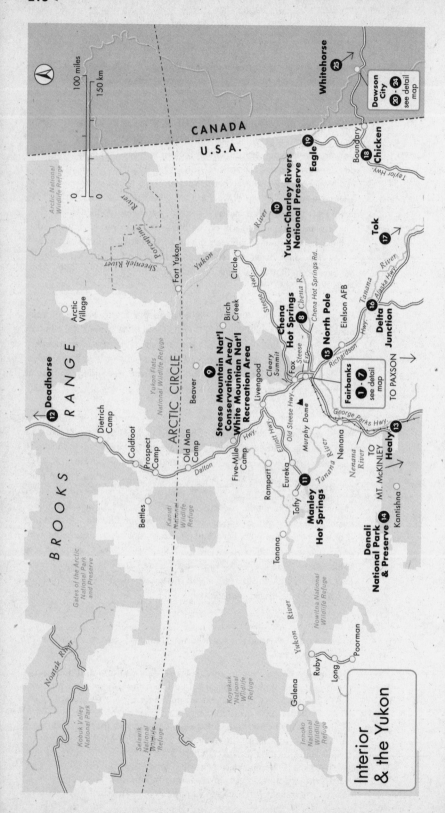

Interior
& the Yukon

100 miles

150 km

CANADA
U.S.A.

Whitehorse ➜

Dawson
City
20 - 24
see detail
map

Eagle 19

Chicken 18
Boundary
Taylor Hwy

Tok 17 ➜

Yukon-Charley Rivers
National Preserve

10

Arctic National
Wildlife Refuge

River

Porcupine

River

Sheenjek River

Fort Yukon

Yukon River

Circle

Chena Hot Springs Rd.

Chena R.

Chena
Hot Springs 8

Delta 16
Junction

Tanana River

Hwy

Alaska Hwy

Arctic
Village

Birch
Creek

Steese Hwy

Eielson AFB

North Pole 15

Richardson Hwy

TO PAXSON ➜

Deadhorse 12 ←

BROOKS RANGE

Arctic National Wildlife Refuge

Yukon Flats
National Wildlife Refuge

Beaver

ARCTIC CIRCLE

Old Man
Camp

Steese Mountain Nat'l
Conservation Area/
White Mountain Nat'l
Recreation Area

9

Cleary
Summit

Fox

Steese

Livengood

Murphy Dome

Fairbanks
1 - 7
see detail
map

Dietrich
Camp

Coldfoot

Prospect
Camp

Dalton Hwy

Five-Mile
Camp

Elliott Hwy

Old Steese Hwy

George Parks Hwy

Healy 13 ➜

Gates of the Arctic
National Park
and Preserve

Kanuti
National
Wildlife
Refuge

Rampart

Eureka

Tofty

Manley 11
Hot Springs

Tanana River

Nenana

Nenana River

TO
MT. McKINLEY

Bettles

Denali
National Park
& Preserve 14

MT. McKINLEY

Kantishna

Noatak River

Kobuk Valley
National Park

Selawik
National
Wildlife
Refuge

Koyukuk
National
Wildlife
Refuge

Tanana

Yukon River

River

Nowitna National
Wildlife Refuge

Long

Poorman

Ruby

Galena

Innoko
National
Wildlife
Refuge

7

Dogsledding

Alaska is to dog mushing what Kentucky is to horse racing, and the Interior is arguably the prime mushing spot in Alaska. A number of dog-mushing races are held here, ranging from short sprint races with small teams to the Yukon Quest International, the second-longest sled-dog race in the world next to the Iditarod. But this isn't a sport solely for racers. Many people live in the Interior just so they can spend their free time in winter mushing their dogs. Skijoring—being pulled on skis by dogs—is also a pastime. A web of trails surrounds many communities. You can find out more information at the Alaska Public Lands Information Center.

Flora & Fauna

This part of Alaska has, through many millennia, escaped the onset of glaciers and thus formed a refuge for the Ice Age flora and fauna that were crowded out of other areas by ice and intense cold. Many species of plants and animals survived only in this refugium. Certain species of birds notably follow age-old patterns of migration and spend summers in the Interior's vast, prodigiously rich wetlands.

Below the tundra of the Alaska Range, the trees of the taiga take over: dark, spiky spruce; paper birch; aspen; and, in the wetter places, cottonwood. The soft green leaves of the deciduous trees shine golden in autumn. Among and around the trees, fireweed paints the landscape soft magenta. Spring paints the meadows blue with lupine, summer brings succulent berries, and fall splashes the berry leaves with crimson. Winter turns the region frigid, white, and crisp with ice.

As it stretches farther to the north, the Interior's near-vertical terrain near the Alaska Range flattens out into low, rounded hills. Tundra and taiga persist, with soft greens spiked by dark spruce trees, and deep green-gold mossy muskegs squish like soggy trampolines underfoot. Lakes gleam like black mirrors.

Hiking

Below the high, snowy reaches of the Alaska Range, the lower foothills are often stained with color, evidence of their ancient, restless past. Polychrome Pass in Denali National Park is aptly named: it commands a vista of rose-, orange-, gray-, and soft brown–shaded slopes fingered by swards of green alpine tundra. This high tundra is fine hiking country, but in other areas, the ground is tufted with slippery tussocks, and even the most nimble-footed will be forced into balancing acts.

Several developed trails offer hikers everything from an afternoon outing to an expedition of several days. Water is often scarce along the trails, so make sure you pack enough. Those adventurous souls interested in forging their own paths off the developed trails will find lots of space to explore. Alaska's beauty, however, is still mostly wild and can be dangerous if you're not well informed, and trespassing on private property is illegal. The Alaska Public Lands Information Center in Fairbanks is a crucial stop for all hikers. The staff is helpful and knowledgeable, and in many cases, they can tell you about areas from personal experience.

Hot-Springs Retreats

Forty below zero isn't a temperature that inspires thoughts of swimming, but that's what visitors have done for many years at the three hot-springs resorts in the Interior. Early miners discovered natural hot springs in the frozen wilderness just north of Fairbanks and scrambled to build communities around this heaven-sent phenomenon. The areas around the hot springs also make excellent bases for fishing, hiking, snowshoeing, or cross-country skiing. Each of the resorts is accessible by road and air from Fairbanks.

Wild & Scenic Rivers

Great rivers travel through this landscape: the Tanana, the Nenana, the Kuskokwim, and one of the world's most powerful—the mighty Yukon. (Only four rivers in the Americas have a greater capacity of water than the Yukon: the Amazon, the St. Lawrence, the Mississippi, and the Missouri.) Twenty miles wide in places, the Yukon travels for 2,300 mi, from Canada to the Bering Sea, and runs through some of the most beautiful country of the Interior Plateau. Countless people traversed this pathway as they moved through the North American continent, and many people still travel the river by boat in the summer and by snowmobile across its frozen surface in the winter.

The Bureau of Land Management is in charge of three Wild and Scenic Rivers, each of which has a special draw. Beaver Creek threads through the White Mountain National Recreation Area north to the Yukon and offers good fishing—arctic grayling, northern pike, and burbot—and spectacular vistas. Along the rapid-ripped Birch Creek, moose, caribou, and birds are easily spotted. The beautiful Fortymile River provides a range of canoeing terrain, from Class I to IV rapids.

---

tional Park. If you're fortunate enough to make the drive on a clear day, Mt. McKinley seems to loom over the highway as you approach Talkeetna. There are a couple of marked viewpoints along the road so you don't have to risk your life in traffic to get some good photos. Then as you near the town of Cantwell, the road passes through high taiga forest and is flanked by the Talkeetna Mountains to the east and the Alaska Range to the west.

North of Fairbanks are three highways, one of which stretches into the Arctic. All three wind through wild, wooded country. The Steese Highway heads northeast through alpine landscapes and dead-ends in Circle at the Yukon River. The Elliott Highway takes you northwest to the beginning of the Dalton Highway and then turns south to a dead-end at Manley Hot Springs on the Tanana River. The final main highway in the Interior, the Dalton, splits from the Elliott Highway at Livengood. It cuts through the Brooks Range, an imposing collection of rocky Arctic peaks, and spills out onto the tundra coast of the North Slope.

The Denali Highway, oddly enough, isn't in Denali National Park. It connects the towns of Paxson and Cantwell, running for 135 mi through tundra and spruce forests. Most of the road is unpaved, and services are few and far between, so make sure you've got a full tank of gas and at least one real spare tire.

About the Restaurants

Although Alaska's Interior isn't on a lot of gourmet must-visit lists, there are some pleasant surprises to be found. Travelers and locals expect fresh seafood, and even though the salmon streams and saltwater are hundreds of miles away, most restaurants oblige by flying in salmon and halibut regularly. Meat-and-potatoes main courses and the occasional pasta dish fill out the menus. Vegetarians might have a tough time, but there's usually something on the bill of fare that will suffice. Most restaurants stay open late during the summer, and attire is definitely casual—wear a coat and tie to most places and you'll draw puzzled stares. National chains are almost nonexistent, so local ownership and knowledge prevail.

About the Hotels

Lodging choices range from hostels and intimate B&Bs to national chain hotels and stop just short of ultraluxury spots. However, options exist to please even the most discriminating travelers. Swimming pools are a rarity, but most other amenities that you've come to expect in the Lower 48 are available. Reservations for summer dates at the more popular places need to be made months in advance, but even at the last minute comfortable choices can usually be found.

WHAT IT COSTS					
	$$$$	**$$$**	**$$**	**$**	**¢**
RESTAURANTS	over $25	$20–$25	$15–$20	$10–$15	under $10
HOTELS	over $225	$175–$225	$125–$175	$75–$125	under $75

Restaurant prices are per person for a main course at dinner. Hotel prices are for two people in a standard double room in high season.

Timing

Among the warmest in Alaska, Interior summers have a few days each month with temperatures in the high 80s or 90s. From the first week of May to the middle of August, it's bright enough at midnight to read a newspaper outdoors. Sunny days or partly cloudy ones, sometimes punctuated with afternoon cloudbursts, are the norm. In the winter it gets so cold (−50°F or below) that a glass of boiling water flung out a window will explode. Parking meters in Fairbanks routinely have electrical outlets for heaters to keep cars from freezing solid. Dry snow glitters in the air, and smog freezes in the Fairbanks bowl.

Tourism is big business in Alaska, but many of the attractions shut down after tourist season, which generally runs from Memorial Day to Labor Day. Consider coming early or late in the season to avoid the rush. But be forewarned—it's been known to snow in Fairbanks in May, and higher elevations and northern areas could have snow as early as mid-August. Late August brings fall colors, ripening berries, and active wildlife, but it also brings more chance of rain. If you are a sports enthusiast, come to Interior Alaska in March, when the dark days of winter are over, snow blankets the ground, and there's lots of radiant sun.

FAIRBANKS

Its nickname, the Golden Heart, reflects Fairbanks's geographical location (it's the gateway to the Far North—the Arctic and the Bering Coast—and to Canada's Yukon Territory) as well as its economic history. The city lies between the rugged Alaska and Brooks mountain ranges and serves as the Interior's hub. Here the Parks and Richardson highways end and several Bush commuter air services base their operations. But Fairbanks got its start as a gold-mining town in 1901 by a merchant and a prospector who struck it rich, and residents have celebrated this beginning ever since. Many of the old homes and commercial buildings trace their history to the early days of the city, especially in the downtown area, with its narrow, winding streets following the contours of the Chena River.

Exploring Fairbanks

Combining a walking tour with some driving is the best way to see Fairbanks. After getting an overview of the area's highlights, you may want to revisit those spots that encourage more extensive and detailed examination.

a good
tour

Start downtown by parking in the two-hour lot on Cushman Street between 1st and 2nd avenues. Stop at the **Fairbanks Convention and Visitors Bureau** ❶ ⌐, in the log cabin on 1st Avenue, for information and brochures from the helpful local staff. Turn right on 1st Avenue, and then take another right to cross the Cushman Street Bridge. Try to visualize all of downtown under 8 feet of water as it was in 1967. The Chena River flood-control project was initiated shortly thereafter, making future recurrences highly unlikely. Stroll across the bridge to the river overlook on the right.

Recross the bridge and head south on Cushman Street, then left on 2nd Avenue, and walk for a block to the Lacey Street Theater, home of the **Fairbanks Ice Museum** ❷. Cool off and take in the artfully carved ice sculptures. Turn north (left) on Lacey Street, left again on 1st Avenue, and stop at the Golden Heart Plaza, on the far side of 1st Avenue, with beautiful floral displays in summer and the *Unknown First Family* statue dedicated to Interior Alaska families. Retrace your steps to pick up your car. Turn right on Cushman Street, take a left on 1st Avenue, and drive parallel to the river to Cowles Street, the third left. Follow Cowles Street to Airport Way, and turn right, then right again on Peger Road. Take an immediate right into the **Pioneer Park** ❸ parking lot. Visiting a Native village and viewing mining artifacts at the outdoor museum Mining Valley are just a couple of the attractions at this 44-acre park.

Take the Avenue of the Flags exit as you drive out of the park. Turn right onto Wilbur Street and right again on Airport Way. Take Airport Way to University Avenue and turn right. Cross the Chena River and stay on University Avenue until you get to Taku Drive. Turn left onto the **University of Alaska Fairbanks** ❹ campus. Take the first right on Tanana Drive, and then go left at the stop sign at Yukon Drive. Take Yukon Drive for ½ mi to the **Alaska Range overlook** ❺. If it's a clear day, and it usually is, you can see the Alaska Range and Mt. McKinley far to the south. Continue on Yukon Drive to Sheenjek Street and the **University of Alaska Museum** ❻ on the right. No trip to Fairbanks is complete without a visit to this museum. A fascinating series of informative displays presents Alaska history, anthropology, natural history, and geography. When you leave the museum, continue on Yukon Drive to Kantishna Drive and turn right, then left on Sheep Creek Road to the Georgeson Botanical Garden, where researchers study the unique growing environment of the Far North. Continue on Sheep Creek Road for 1 mi and turn right on Miller Hill Road, then right again on Yankovich Road for just under ½ mi to the Large Animal Research Station, where scientists study the habits of musk ox, caribou, and reindeer.

Retrace your route back to Sheep Creek Road, and follow it past the intersection with Kantishna Drive, where the road turns into Tanana Drive. After the sharp left curve, turn right on Taku Drive, right again

Fairbanks

Gold Dredge Number 8 ◆
Silver Gulch ◆
Trans-Alaska Pipeline ◆

TO CHENA HOT SPRINGS

Clay Street Cemetery ◆

Noble St.
Lacey St.
Cushman St.

❶ ❷

Odd Fellows Hall ◆
Falson Joslin Home ◆
Railroad Depot ◆
Immaculate Conception Church

Golden Heart Plaza
The Line
Empress Theater

Minnie St.
Illinois St.
Expwy.
Johansen
1st Ave.
Chena R.
Kellum St.
Barnette St.
Hilton St.
Cowles St.
Wilbur St.
2nd Ave.
Lathrop St.

College Rd.
Aurora Dr.

Phillips Field Rd.

Ave. of the Flags
Peger Rd.
❸

Davis Rd.

Sophie Station ◆

Sam's Sourdough ◆

University Ave.

Large Animal Research Station ◆
Georgeson Botanical Gardens ◆

❹
❺
❻
Yukon Dr.
Taku Dr.
Tanana Dr.
Sheenjek St.
Kanishna Dr.
George Parks Hwy.

Slough
Noyes
ALASKA RAILROAD

Geist Rd.

Airport Way

Riverboat Discovery Cruise ◆

TO IVORY JACK'S

Parks Hwy.
Sheep Creek Rd.
Gold Hill Rd.

TO ESTER GOLD CAMP

Chena Pump Rd.
Chena Ridge
Chena R.

Pump House Restaurant and Bar ◆

Richardson Hwy.

Stiese Expy.
Steese
Airport Way

0   1 mile
0   1.5 km

KEY

▶ Start of tour

Alaska Range overlook 5
Creamer's Field Migratory Waterfowl Refuge 7
Fairbanks Convention and Visitors Bureau 1
Fairbanks Ice Museum 2
Pioneer Park 3
University of Alaska Fairbanks 4
University of Alaska Museum 6

on Farmers Loop Road, then left on College Road. Turn left on Danby and follow the road straight ahead to the bird-watching area at **Creamer's Field Migratory Waterfowl Refuge** ❼.

TIMING The walking and driving parts of the tour can be done in an hour to an hour and a half, but you can extend that time considerably by exploring the various spots. Lingering over the University Museum exhibits alone can extend the tour to nearly an entire day. Let your interests and the weather determine your schedule.

What to See

❺ **Alaska Range Overlook.** The entire north side of the Alaska Range is visible at this overlook, a favorite spot for time-lapse photography of the midwinter sun just peeking over the southern horizon on a low arc. The three major peaks, called the Three Sisters because of their similar appearance, are nearly always distinguishable on a clear day. From your left are **Mt. Hayes**, 13,832 feet; **Mt. Hess**, 11,940 feet; and **Mt. Deborah**, 12,339 feet. Much farther to the right, toward the southwest, hulks **Mt. McKinley**, the highest peak in North America. On some seemingly clear days it's not visible at all. At other times the base is easy to see but the peak is lost in cloud cover. When Mt. McKinley is entirely visible, **Mt. Foraker** can often be seen just to the right of Mt. McKinley's base— at 75 mi away from Mt. McKinley, it appears as a small pyramid, but it's actually the second-highest peak in the Alaska Range. ⊹ *West Ridge, University of Alaska Fairbanks campus, Yukon Dr.; look for parking area just east of University of Alaska Museum.*

❼ **Creamer's Field Migratory Waterfowl Refuge.** Three pleasant nature trails lead through fields, forest, and wetlands. This is a great place to view waterfowl, cranes, songbirds, and moose. The barns and buildings of **Creamer's Dairy** are also still standing here. Now on the National Register of Historic Places, Creamer's Dairy was the farthest-north dairy in North America from 1910 to 1966. The farmhouse is now a nature and visitor center. ✉ *1300 College Rd., Lemeta* ☎ *907/459–7307 or 907/459–7301* ⊕ *www.state.ak.us/adfg/wildlife/region3/refuge3/creamers.htm.*

▶ ❶ **Fairbanks Convention and Visitors Bureau.** At this visitor center on the river at the Cushman Street Bridge you can pick up a map for a self-guided 1½-hour walking tour through the historic downtown area. The bureau also has maps for a two-hour do-it-yourself driving tour. Points of interest on the tours include **Golden Heart Park,** home of the *Unknown First Family* statue; the **Clay Street Cemetery,** with its marked and unmarked graves of early pioneers; the **Empress Theater,** the first concrete structure in Interior Alaska; the stately **Falcon Joslin Home,** the oldest frame house in Fairbanks still at its original location; the **Line,** home of the red-light district until the mid-1950s; **Odd Fellows Hall,** a bathhouse for gold miners until the pipes froze in the winter of 1910–11; and the historic **Immaculate Conception Church,** which was raised off its foundation in 1911 and rolled across the frozen Chena River on logs pulled by horses. ✉ *550 1st Ave., Downtown* ☎ *907/456–5774, 800/327–5774 recording* 🖷 *907/452–2867* ⊕ *www.explorefairbanks.com.*

★ ❷ **Fairbanks Ice Museum.** The ice carvings showcased around Fairbanks in winter, especially the Ice Art competition held in March, are on display. The Ice Showcase, a large glass-wall display, is kept at 20°F. The chilly environment allows ice sculptors to demonstrate their skills and sculptures throughout the summer. "Freeze Frame" is a large-screen film demonstrating the techniques of ice sculpture. The museum is in the historic Lacey Street Theater, on the corner of 2nd Avenue and Lacey Street. ✉ *500*

2nd Ave., Downtown ☎ *907/451–8222* 🖷 *907/456–1951* ⊕ *fairbanks-alaska.com/fairbanks-ice-museum.htm* 🖾 *$6* ☽ *Late May–mid-Oct., daily 10–9.*

★ ☺ ❸ **Pioneer Park.** The 44-acre park, formerly known as Alaskaland, is set along the Chena River near downtown Fairbanks and has several museums, an art gallery, theater, civic center, Native village, large children's playground, miniature-golf course, antique merry-go-round, restaurants, and a gold-rush town consisting of historic buildings saved from urban renewal. The complex has log-cabin gift shops and **Mining Valley,** an outdoor museum of mining artifacts surrounding an indoor-outdoor Alaska salmon bake restaurant. President Warren Harding traveled in the plush *Denali* railcar when he came north in 1923 to hammer the golden spike on the Alaska Railroad. The 227-foot stern-wheeler *Nenana* is the second-largest wooden vessel in existence and a national historic landmark. The railroad built the *Nenana* in 1933 to serve the rivers of the Interior. A diorama inside the stern-wheeler details the course the riverboat took on the Yukon and Tanana rivers around the turn of the 20th century. The **Crooked Creek and Whiskey Island Railroad,** a small-gauge train, circles the park. No-frills RV camping is available for $10 a night in the west end of the large parking lot on Airport Way. ⊠ *Pioneer Park, Airport Way, and Peger Rd.* ☎ *907/459–1087* 🖷 *907/459–1199* 🖾 *Free* ☽ *Daily 11–9.*

★ ❹ **University of Alaska Fairbanks.** The university has earned an international reputation for its Arctic research, including a study of the aurora borealis, or northern lights. A free two-hour student-guided campus walking tour is offered weekdays throughout the summer. Tours of the following campus facilities are also conducted from June through August (hours and admission fees vary): the **Large Animal Research Station** (⊠ Yankovich Rd. off Ballaine Rd. behind university ☎ 907/474–7207 tour information), which houses caribou, musk ox, and reindeer; the **Arctic Region Supercomputing Center** (⊠ Butrovitch Bldg.), where researchers use high-performance supercomputers to solve problems in science and engineering for the high latitudes and the Arctic; the **Geophysical Institute** (⊠ West Ridge, about 1 mi from campus center ☎ 907/474–7588 tour information), a center of atmospheric and earthquake research; the **Poker Flat Research Range** (⊠ Steese Hwy., 33 mi northeast of Fairbanks ☎ 907/474–7558 tour information), where the university launches rockets studying the aurora borealis; and the **Georgeson Botanical Garden of the Agricultural and Forestry Experiment Station Farm** (⊠ West end of campus), where researchers study Interior Alaska's unique, short, but intense midnight-sun growing season. ⊠ *Office of University Relations, 202 Eielson Bldg.* ☎ *907/474–7581* ⊕ *www.uaf.edu* ☽ *Tour schedule varies; call for details or inquire at Fairbanks Convention and Visitors Bureau.*

❻ **University of Alaska Museum.** A stuffed grizzly bear—8 feet, 9 inches tall—guards the entrance to the ethnographic, historic, and fine arts collection, divided into five Alaska regions: Southeast, Interior, South Central, Southwest, and the western Arctic coast. Blue Babe, a mummified steppe bison that lived 38,000 years ago during the Pleistocene, was preserved in permafrost (permanently frozen ground), complete with claw marks indicating attack by a saber-toothed tiger. The bison's remains were found by gold miners in 1979. Besides the usual "don't touch" exhibits, the museum has several "please touch" items, including the molars of a mammoth and a mastodon, a gray-whale skull, and a 5,495-pound copper nugget. Audio guides are available for an additional $3. ⊠ *907 Yukon Dr., West Ridge, University of Alaska Fairbanks campus,* ☎ *907/474–*

Fodor'sChoice ★

7505 🖶 907/474–5469 ⊕ *www.uaf.edu/museum* 🖂 $5 ⊘ *Mid-May–mid-Sept., daily 9–7; mid-Sept.–mid-May, weekdays 9–5, weekends noon–5.*

off the beaten path

GOLD DREDGE NUMBER 8 – Imagine a giant gold dredge making its own waterway as it chews through the gold pay dirt, crawling along at a snail's pace and processing tons of rock and gravel. Built by Bethlehem Shipbuilders in 1928, the dredge was operated by the Fairbanks Exploration Company until its retirement in 1959. The five-deck ship is more than 250 feet long and took millions of dollars' worth of gold out of the Goldstream and Engineer creeks north of Fairbanks. *Gold Dredge Number 8* has been declared a National Historic District by the National Park Service, one of the few privately owned districts in the nation. This mining vessel came to rest at Mile 9, Old Steese Highway. The price of admission entitles you to the necessary tools, some gold-panning instructions, and a chance to find "colors" at the sluice or to seek gold independently in old tailings from the mining days. A sit-down, family-style miner's pot-roast stew is served from 11 AM to 3 PM for an additional $9.50. The dredge (and the miner's stew) is a featured stop on Gray Line of Alaska's tours. 🖂 *1755 Old Steese Hwy. N, Fox, Fairbanks 99712* 🕾 *907/457–6058* ⊕ *www.golddredgeno8.com* 🖂 *$23* ⊘ *Mid-May–mid-Sept., daily 9–5.*

TRANS-ALASKA PIPELINE – Just north of Fairbanks you can see and touch the famous trans-Alaska pipeline. The parking lot is right off the Steese Highway and has a sign loaded with information. Informative guides staff a small visitor center, and there's a gift shop with pipeline-company memorabilia. 🖂 *Mile 7.5, Steese Hwy.,* 🕾 *907/456–9391* 🖶 *907/456–9392* 🖂 *Free* ⊘ *Visitor center mid-May–Sept., daily 8–5.*

SILVER GULCH BREWING AND BOTTLING CO – You'll find some unique souvenirs and an interesting collection of Fairbanks citizens at North America's farthest-north brewery. Brewing a variety of styles since 1998, Silver Gulch is probably best known for its Pilsner. Fairbanks and Anchorage are the major markets, but a few spots on the Kenai carry Silver Gulch as well. Stop by for free tours and beer tastings every Friday evening from 5 to 7 PM or by appointment. The brewery is in the Fox Roadhouse building (around the right and through the side door). 🖂 *2195 Old Steese Hwy., Fox* 🕾 *907/452–2739* ⊕ *www.silvergulch.com* 🖂 *Free* ⊘ *Fri. 5–7 PM.*

Where to Stay & Eat

★ **$$–$$$$** ✕ **Pike's Landing.** Enjoy lunch on a huge outside deck (it seats 420) overlooking the Chena River, or dine inside in the elegant dining room of an extended log cabin. The meals run in price up to $38 for steak and lobster and rank with the best in the Interior. For a dinner in the $10 range, relax in the sports bar and catch a view of the river. The palate-pleasing Sunday brunch delivers tempting dishes and an irresistible dessert table. 🖂 *4438 Airport Way* 🕾 907/479–7113 ▭ *AE, D, DC, MC, V.*

$–$$$$ ✕ **Ivory Jack's.** Jack "Ivory" O'Brien used to deal in Alaskan ivory and whalebone out of this small restaurant tucked into the gold-rich hills of the Goldstream Valley on the outskirts of Fairbanks. New York Yankees, Elvis, Dartmouth University, and dog-mushing paraphernalia adorns the large, open, and airy bar-restaurant. You can choose from more than 15 appetizers as well as burgers, pizza, and entrées such as halibut Dijon and Alaskan king crab. You'll catch some live local music on some weekends; cover charge depends on the band. ☒ *2581 Goldstream Rd., Goldstream* ☎ *907/455–6666* ☰ *AE, D, DC, MC, V.*

$–$$$$ ✕ **Pump House Restaurant.** Alongside the Chena River sits this mining
Fodor'sChoice pump station turned restaurant, with American and specifically Alaskan
★ seafood dishes. Alaskan reindeer stew and seafood chowder are house specialties. The furnishings and floor are rich, polished wood, and an Alaskan grizzly bear in a glass case is on sentry next to the hostess station. Wednesday night is karaoke night in the bar. ☒ *Mile 2.0, Chena Pump Rd.,* ☎ *907/479–8452* ☰ *AE, D, MC, V* ☉ *No lunch mid-Sept.–mid-May.*

★ **$$$** ✕ **Alaska Salmon Bake.** Mouthwatering salmon cooked over an open fire with a special lemon and brown-sugar sauce is a favorite at this indoor-outdoor restaurant in Pioneer Park's Mining Valley. Halibut, cod, a single serving of prime rib, a salad bar, and homemade blueberry cake are also available at the all-you-can-eat dinner. ☒ *Airport Way and Peger Rd., Pioneer Park* ☎ *907/452–7274 or 800/354–7274* ☰ *MC, V* ☉ *Closed mid-Sept.–mid-May. No lunch.*

★ **$–$$** ✕ **The Cookie Jar.** Tucked away in a nondescript neighborhood on a street not found on most Fairbanks maps, this gorgeous little restaurant is well worth tracking down. The open, airy space predictably features lots of cookie jars, along with just enough plants and artwork to complete the picture. Spanning breakfast, lunch, and dinner, the huge menu includes scads of homemade items, an extensive kids' menu, and vegetarian selections. Entrées range from steak and shrimp to coq au vin. For dessert, try the homemade tortes or a variety of cookies to match anything your grandma ever produced. Weekend breakfasts are especially popular, so allow extra time. Take Danby Street off the Johansen Expressway, and the restaurant is behind Aurora Motors. ☒ *1006 Cadillac Court* ☎ *907/479–8319* ⊕ *frb-biz.com/cookiejarrestaurant* ☰ *AE, D, MC, V.*

★ **$–$$** ✕ **Gambardella's Pasta Bella.** Locals crowd the family-run Italian restaurant at the edge of downtown known simply as Gambardella's. The place is small but cozy, with covered outside seating in the summer. The menu includes salads, pasta, pizza, vegetarian entrées, and submarine sandwiches on homemade bread. Its specialties, however, are lasagna, which the *Seattle Times* described as "the mother of all lasagnas"; the seafood *fra diavolo*; and the tiramisu. ☒ *706 2nd Ave., Downtown* ☎ *907/456–3417* 🖷 *907/456–3425* ☰ *AE, MC, V* ☉ *No lunch Sun.*

★ **¢–$$** ✕ **Sam's Sourdough Cafe.** Although Sam's serves meals all day, knowledgeable Fairbanksans know it as the best breakfast place in town. Sourdough recipes are a kind of minor religion in Alaska, and Sam's serves an extensive menu of sourdough specialties including hotcakes and French toast, as well as standard meat-and-eggs items, all at very reasonable prices. On weekends get here early or be prepared for a wait. The address is Cameron Street, but it's really fronted on University, just over the railroad tracks. ☒ *3702 Cameron St.* ☎ *907/479–0523* ☰ *MC, V.*

★ **$$$** 🛏 **Fairbanks Princess Riverside Lodge.** An expansive wooden deck facing a scenic section of the Chena River draws a crowd at this luxury lodge in summer. Gold, russet, green, and burgundy accents warm the rustic decor. You can stop by the tour desk to book additional excursions around Fairbanks. The Edgewater Restaurant welcomes diners in suits and evening gowns or duct-tape-patched Carhartt's work clothes, and there's a daily breakfast buffet during the high season. You'll find the lodge just off the road to Fairbanks International Airport. ☒ *4477 Pikes Landing Rd., 99709* ☎ *907/455–4477 or 800/426–0500* 🖷 *907/455–4476* ⊕ *www.princessalaskalodges.com* ⟿ *326 rooms* ♧ *2 restaurants, in-room data ports, cable TV, health club, steam room, bar, shop, laundry*

facilities, business services, meeting rooms, airport shuttle, travel ser-
vices ⊟ *AE, D, DC, MC, V.*

★ **$$$** 🏨 **Pike's Waterfront Lodge.** Log columns and beams support the high-ceiling lobby of this hotel and conference center on the banks of the Chena River. Rustic decorations include two scenic Alaskan murals and numerous taxidermy pieces. Rooms have either a king or two queen beds, desk and armoire, and coffeemakers; microwaves and refrigerators can be added for a fee. Rooms with a river view are worth the extra $15 per night. The restaurant serves a buffet breakfast in the summer, lunch, and a casual dinner. A free shuttle to the Great Alaska Railroad depot leaves daily at 7:05 AM; call for pickup if you're arriving. ⊠ *1850 Hoselton Rd., 99709,* ☎ *877/774–2400 or 907/456–4500* 📠 *907/456–4515* ⊕ *www.pikeslodge.com* ➫ *179 rooms* ♻ *Restaurant, cable TV with movies and video games, gym, sauna, spa, steam room, concierge, Internet, business services, meeting rooms, airport shuttle* ⊟ *AE, D, MC, V.*

$$$ 🏨 **Sophie Station Hotel.** Its quiet location and helpful staff make this spacious hotel near the airport one of Fairbanks's best. It has comfy furniture, rich upholstery, and Alaskan artwork throughout. Rooms are suites with kitchens that include a full-size range and refrigerator. You can try a buffalo burger at Zach's, the hotel restaurant, which serves breakfast, lunch, and dinner. Both the lobby and restaurant were completely remodeled in 2002. ⊠ *1717 University Ave., 99709* ☎ *907/479–3650 or 800/528–4916* 📠 *907/479–7951* ⊕ *www.fountainheadhotels. com* ➫ *148 suites* ♻ *Restaurant, kitchenettes, microwaves, refrigerators, cable TV, bar, Internet, meeting room, airport shuttle* ⊟ *AE, D, DC, MC, V.*

$–$$$ 🏨 **Cranberry Ridge B&B.** The proprietors, Mike and Floss Caskey, a fifth-generation Alaskan family, designed and built this small B&B, north of Fairbanks off Farmers Loop Road. The contemporary house's position affords magnificent views of the Alaska Range. The two guest rooms share a bath and a large sitting and family area and can be taken together as a suite. Each morning you can expect fresh-baked pastries (possibly peach cobbler), a full breakfast with smoked salmon quiche, a large fruit tray, and coffee. Mike Caskey leads Arctic Circle and Mt. McKinley flightseeing tours in his Cessna 185 for up to three passengers for $250 an hour. Special room rates are available for extended stays. ⊠ *705 Cranberry Ridge Dr., Farmers Loop, 99712* ☎ *907/457–4424 or 888/326–4424* ⊕ *www.alaskaflyingtours.com* ➫ *2 rooms with shared bath* ⊟ *AE, D, DC, MC, V* ⦿ *BP.*

$$ 🏨 **Comfort Inn–Chena River.** Its location on a wooded bank of the Chena River directly across the water from Pioneer Park makes this hotel a popular choice. It also has a full-length, glass-enclosed indoor pool and hot tub. Rooms are done in green and dark wood and punctuated with artwork, and all were renovated in 2002 with new bedding, furniture, and window treatments. The room rate includes Continental breakfast. ⊠ *1908 Chena Landings Loop, 99701,* ☎ *907/479–8080 or 800/228–5150* 📠 *907/479–8063* ⊕ *www.choicehotels.com* ➫ *74 rooms* ♻ *In-room data ports, some microwaves, some refrigerators, cable TV with movies and video games, indoor pool, hot tub, airport shuttle, some pets allowed, no-smoking rooms* ⊟ *AE, D, DC, MC, V* ⦿ *CP.*

$$ 🏨 **The Villages.** Though close to downtown, this establishment is tucked away in a wooded area. Two studios and one- and two-bedroom suites are available. Dining tables in the full kitchens seat four, and the sitting rooms have living-room-size sofas, comfortable easy chairs, and 25-inch stereo TVs. The contrast of off-white wallpaper and dark burgundy carpeting provides a pleasant warmth to some of the rooms. ⊠ *205 Palace Cir., 99701, Downtown* ☎ *907/456–7612 or 800/770–7612* 📠 *907/*

456–8358 ↩*24 suites* ⚬ *Kitchens, microwaves, cable TV, in-room VCRs, laundry service, some pets allowed* ⊟ *AE, D, DC, MC, V.*

$$ ⊞ **Wedgewood Resort.** Both wild and cultivated flowers adorn the landscaped grounds of the Wedgewood Resort. This garden spot borders on the Creamer's Field Migratory Waterfowl Refuge, and the Alaska Bird Observatory, a local nonprofit that researches and promotes the conservation of Alaska's birds, is headquartered on the resort grounds. You'll also find a replica miner's cabin, a Bush plane, courtyards, and gazebos. All rooms are suites, decorated with local artwork that's available for purchase. The Bear Lodge hotel—also part of the resort—has 157 large rooms available in summer. Shuttles make the run to downtown Fairbanks and the Great Alaska Railroad station. ⊠ *212 Wedgewood Dr., 99701* ☎ *800/528–4916, 907/456–3642* 🖷 *907/451–8184* ⊕ *www.fountainheadhotels.com* ↩ *297 rooms* ⚬ *2 restaurants, in-room data ports, kitchens, microwaves, refrigerators, cable TV, shops, dry cleaning, business services, meeting rooms, airport shuttle* ⊟ *AE, D, DC, MC, V.*

Fodor's Choice
★

$$ ⊞ **Westmark Fairbanks Hotel and Conference Center.** Built on a courtyard on a quiet street, this full-service, snazzy complex remains close to downtown. All rooms, done in rose and burgundy, have a writing desk; some have a StairMaster or stationary bike. A conference center and personal voice mail make it a good choice for business travelers. The Bear 'n Seal serves steaks and seafood. ⊠ *813 Noble St., 99701,* ☎ *907/456–7722 or 800/544–0970* 🖷 *907/451–7478* ⊕ *www.westmarkhotels.com* ↩ *400 rooms* ⚬ *Restaurant, cable TV with movies, bar, laundry service, Internet, meeting room, airport shuttle, no-smoking floor* ⊟ *AE, D, DC, MC, V.*

$ ⊞ **Crestmont Manor B&B.** Handmade quilts and furnishings and antique fixtures accent this elegant colonial-style B&B. The rooms provide privacy, and comfort is a top priority of the house. You can relax on the deck while contemplating the sweeping view of the Chena River valley and the Alaska Range. Breakfast, with quiche, fresh pastries, juice, and coffee, is a pleasant affair. ⊠ *510 Crestmont Dr., Chena Ridge, 99709* ☎ *907/456–3831* 🖷 *907/456–3841* ↩ *5 rooms* ⚬ *Laundry service, business services; no smoking* ⊟ *AE, MC, V* ⊚⊪ *BP.*

Guided Tours

Adventure

Northern Alaska Tour Company (🖃 Box 82991, Fairbanks 99708 ☎ 907/474–8600 or 800/474–1986 🖷 907/474–4767 ⊕ www.northernalaska.com) leads half- and full-day excursions to the Arctic Circle and the Yukon River and two- and three-day fly-drive tours to Prudhoe Bay, Barrow, and the Brooks Range.

Cruising & Canoeing

The excitement and color of the city's riverboat history and the Interior's cultural heritage are relived each summer aboard the **Riverboat Discovery** (⊠ 1975 Discovery Dr. ☎ 907/479–6673 or 866/479–6673 ⊕ www.riverboatdiscovery.com), a 3½-hour narrated trip by sternwheeler along the Chena and Tanana rivers to a rustic Native village on the Tanana River. The cruise provides a glimpse of the lifestyle of the dog mushers, subsistence fishermen, traders, and Native Alaskans who populate the Yukon River drainage. Sights along the way include operating fish wheels, a Bush airfield, floatplanes, a smokehouse and cache, log cabins, and Iditarod champion Susan Butcher's dog kennels. Captain Jim Binkley, his wife, Mary, and their children have operated the Discovery cruises for more than 50 years. Their family, with its four generations of river pilots, has run the great rivers of the north for more than 100 years. The cruise costs $44.95, and two cruises run daily (8:45 and 2) mid-May to mid-September.

Sightseeing

Gray Line of Alaska (☎ 800/478–6388 ⊕ www.graylinealaska.com) runs several scenic and informative trips through the Fairbanks area, including a four-hour Discover the Gold sightseeing tour of the city that features the *Gold Dredge Number 8* and a lunch of miner's stew for $60.

Nightlife & the Arts

Fairbanks supports a year-round arts program that rivals that of many larger communities. In summer you will find that the lack of a true "night"—thanks to the midnight sun—doesn't seem to hinder nightlife at all. Check the "Kaleidoscope" section in the Thursday *Fairbanks Daily News–Miner* for current nightspots, plays, concerts, and art shows.

The Arts

FESTIVALS The **Fairbanks Summer Arts Festival** (✉ Box 80845, Fairbanks 99708 ☎ 907/474–8869 🖷 907/479–4329 ⊕ www.fsaf.org) has grown from a small jazz festival for adults to a major University of Alaska Fairbanks–affiliated annual event attracting students worldwide. The festival presents music, dance, theater, opera, ice-skating, and visual-arts instruction and performances spread over two weeks in late July.

Every July Fairbanks hosts the **World Eskimo-Indian Olympics** (⊕ www. weio.org), when northern peoples from Alaska and Canada gather to compete in traditional Native athletic competitions and dances. The **World Ice Art Championships** (⊕ www.icealaska.com) in March draws ice artists from around the world for the carving competition. The annual **Winter Carnival** (⊕ www.fairbankswintercarnival.com) held in mid-March, hosts dog-mushing and skijoring competitions, basketball tournaments, a craft fair, fur auctions, and various winter events in Fairbanks and in outlying areas.

Nightlife

CABARET For an evening of varied and high-quality entertainment head to **Ester**
THEATER **Gold Camp** (✉ Ester ☎ 907/479–2500 or 800/676–6925 🖷 907/474–1780 ⊕ www.akvisit.com/ester.html), a former gold-mining town about 5 mi west of Fairbanks on the Parks Highway. Its 11 historical structures date to the early 1900s and include the rustic Malemute Saloon, which is open daily from 2 PM to midnight. The camp, which is on the National Register of Historic Places, comes alive at night with a show in the saloon ($15) featuring gold rush–era songs, stories, and Robert Service poetry; a beautiful northern-lights photography show ($8) in the Firehouse Theatre; and a dinner buffet ($17.95) serving halibut and reindeer stew in yet another building. Plan your evening to catch dinner and all the shows. The camp has a hotel with semiprivate bathrooms, RV parking, a gift shop, and evening bus service to and from Fairbanks. The camp is open late May to early September.

The **Palace Theatre and Saloon** (☎ 907/456–5960 or 800/354–7274 ⊕ www.akvisit.com/palace.html) at Pioneer Park is one of the livelier summer spots. The Palace's *Golden Heart Revue* ($15), a musical-comedy show about the founding and building of Fairbanks, begins at 8:15 nightly.

SALOONS The **Blue Loon** (☎ 907/457–5666 ⊕ www.theblueloon.com), at Mile ★ 353.5, Parks Highway, between Ester and Fairbanks, presents year-round rock and roll and folk music, concerts, DJ events, and dance events and sells microbrews to complement its full-service menu. The head chef formerly worked at the Chena Pump House, and the menu is steps above standard bar fare. There's a volleyball court, a campfire area, RV parking, and movies every evening at 7 (except Monday).

The **Senator's Saloon** (☎ 907/479–8452) at the Pump House Restaurant is the place to hear easy-listening music alongside the Chena River on a warm summer evening. Don't be alarmed by the exterior appearance
★ of the **Midnight Mine** (☎ 907/456–5348), within walking distance of downtown at 308 Wendell Street. It's a friendly, *Cheers*-like neighborhood bar with darts, Foosball, pool, and a big-screen TV. Sam the dog is likely to greet you as you come in—be sure to ask to see his trick. It'll cost you a buck, but it's well worth it.

SQUARE   There are square-dancing clubs in Fairbanks, North Pole, Delta Junc-
DANCING   tion, and Tok. The groups are affiliated with the **Northern Lights Council of Dancers** (☎ 907/452–5699 ⊕ www.fairnet.org/agencies/dance/farnofed.html), which holds frequent dances.

Sports & the Outdoors

BASEBALL   Scores of baseball players, including Tom Seaver, Dave Winfield, and Jason Giambi, have passed through Fairbanks on their way to the major leagues. The Interior city is home to the **Alaska Goldpanners** (☎ 907/451–0095 ⊕ www.goldpanners.com), a member of the Alaska Baseball League, a string of amateur baseball organizations throughout the state. Players are recruited from college teams nationwide, and the summer season (mid-June–early August) generates top-caliber competition. Home games are played at Growden Field, along Lower 2nd Avenue at Wilbur Street, not far from Pioneer Park. The baseball park hosts the **Midnight Sun Baseball Game,** a Fairbanks tradition in which the Goldpanners play baseball at midnight of the summer solstice without benefit of artificial lights. This is thrilling (and possibly chilly) to watch on a clear, sunny night when the daylight never ends.

BICYCLING   Bicyclists in Fairbanks use the paved paths from the University of Alaska campus around Farmers Loop to the Steese Highway. Another path follows Geist and Chena Pump roads into downtown Fairbanks. A shorter, less strenuous route is the bike path between downtown and Pioneer Park along the south side of the Chena River. Maps showing all the bike paths are available at the **Fairbanks Convention and Visitors Bureau** (⇨ Exploring Fairbanks). Mountain bikers can test their skills during the summer on the ski trails of the University of Alaska Fairbanks and the Birch Hill Recreation Area or on many of the trails and dirt roads around Fairbanks. Stop by the **Alaska Public Lands Information Center** for mountain-biking information.

BOATING   For relaxing boating in or near Fairbanks, use Chena River access points at Nordale Road east of the city, the Cushman and Wendell Street bridges near downtown, Pioneer Park above the Peger River Bridge, the state campground, and the University Avenue Bridge.

The Tanana is riverboat country. On this river and others in the Yukon River drainage, Alaskans use long, wide, flat-bottom boats powered by one or two large outboard engines. The boats include a lift to raise the engine a few inches, allowing passage through the shallows, and some of the engines come equipped with a jet unit instead of a propeller to allow more bottom clearance. Arrangements for riverboat charters can be made in almost any river community. Ask at the **Fairbanks Convention and Visitors Bureau** (⇨ Exploring Fairbanks).

CURLING   Hundreds of Fairbanksans participate each year in curling, a game in which people with brooms play a giant version of shuffleboard on ice. Curlers have an almost fanatical devotion to their sport, and they're eager to explain its finer points to the uninitiated. This ancient Scottish game was brought to Alaska and the Yukon during the Klondike gold rush. The **Fairbanks Curling Club** (✉ 1962 2nd Ave., 99701 ☎ 907/452–2875 ⊕ www.curlfairbanks.org) hosts an annual international bonspiel (match) on the first weekend of April. The club season runs from early October through the middle of April.

DOGSLEDDING   At **Tivi Haus** (✉ Mile 2, Kallenberg Rd., off Cripple Creek Rd. at Mile 349, Parks Hwy., call first for directions ☎ 907/474–8702 ⊟ 907/479–7601) learn about the official state sport from a family of dog mushers who offer dinner and then a ride with the dogs. In summer (mid-June–Labor Day) ride on the dog-powered Arfmobile. In winter (December–March) take a dogsled ride and possibly see the northern lights. Overnight lodging and cross-country skiing are available.

FISHING   Although a few fish can be caught right in town from the Chena River, avid fishermen can find outstanding angling by hopping a plane or riverboat. Fishing trips include air charters to **Lake Minchumina** (an hour's flight from Fairbanks), known for good pike fishing and a rare view of the north sides of Mt. McKinley and Mt. Foraker. Another charter trip by riverboat or floatplane will take you pike fishing in the **Minto Flats**, west of Fairbanks off the Tanana River, where the mouth of the Chatanika River spreads through miles of marsh and sloughs.

Salmon run up the **Tanana River** most of the summer, but they're not usually caught on hook-and-line gear. Residents take them from the river with gill nets and fish wheels, using special commercial and subsistence permits. Check the "Outdoors" section in the Friday *Fairbanks Daily News–Miner* for weekly updates on fishing in the Interior.

GOLD PANNING   You can pan for gold in several places without fear of jumping a claim. **Alaskan Prospectors** (✉ 504 College Rd., Lemeta ☎ 907/452–7398 ⊕ www.mosquitonet.com/~lmadonna) is the oldest mining and prospecting supply store in the state. In addition to maintaining a rocks and minerals museum, it sells gold pans and books and videos on mining. The employees can offer lots of valuable advice for the neophyte gold bug, even though the store's outward appearance may put you off—once you get inside, you'll find enough interesting material to keep you occupied for hours.

El Dorado Gold Mine (✉ 1975 Discovery Dr. ☎ 907/479–6673 or 866/479–6673 ⊕ www.eldoradogoldmine.com) conducts two-hour tours of a seasonal mining operation that include a ride on a narrow-gauge railroad. The tours cost $27.95.

Chatanika Gold Camp (✉ Mile 27.9, Steese Hwy. ☎ 907/389–2414 ⊕ www.fegoldcamp.com) provides a water trough for panners at an authentic gold camp.

GOLF   **Chena Bend** (☎ 907/353–6223), a well-maintained army course open to civilians, is an 18-hole spread on nearby Ft. Wainwright. The 9-hole course at the **Fairbanks Golf and Country Club** (☎ 907/479–6555) straddles Farmers Loop just north of the university. The 18-hole course at the **North Star Golf Club** (✉ 330 Golf Club Dr. ☎ 907/457–4653, 907/455–8362 in winter ⊟ 907/457–3945) is on the Old Steese Highway, ⁷⁄₁₀ mi past Chena Hot Springs Road.

HIKING   **Creamer's Field Migratory Waterfowl Refuge** (⇨ Exploring Fairbanks) has three nature trails within its 1,800 acres on the edge of Fairbanks.

CELESTIAL RAYS OF LIGHT

THE LIGHT SHOW often begins simply, as a pale yellow-green luminous band that arches across Alaska's night sky. Sometimes the band will quickly fade and disappear. Other nights, however, it may begin to waver, flicker, and pulsate. Or the quiescent band may suddenly explode and fill the sky with curtains of celestial light that ripple wildly above the northern landscape. Growing more intense, these dancing lights take on other colors: pink, red, blue, or purple. At times they appear to be heavenly flames, leaping across the sky. Or perhaps they're exploding fireworks or cannon fire.

Known to scientists as the aurora borealis, the dazzling nighttime bands and ribbons that appear in Alaska's skies are also commonly called the northern lights. As you watch them, it is sometimes possible to see a rhythm in their movements—or at least imagine one. It's also easy to imagine why many northern cultures, including Alaska's Native peoples, have created myths to explain auroral displays. If you watch closely, what started out as patches, arcs, or bands can be magically transformed into vaporous, humanlike figures. Some of Alaska's Native groups have traditionally believed the lights to be spirits of their ancestors. According to one belief, the spirits are celebrating with dance and drumming; another says they're playing games. Yet another tradition says the lights are torches, carried by spirits who lead the souls of recently deceased people to life in the "afterworld."

Non-Natives, too, have occasionally created stories around the brightly flashing lights. During Alaska's gold-rush era, for instance, some stampeders supposed the aurora to be reflections of ore deposits. Even renowned wilderness explorer John Muir allowed the northern lights to spark his imagination. Once while traveling through Southeast Alaska in 1890, Muir stayed up all night to watch a gigantic, glowing auroral bridge and bands of "restless electric auroral fairies" who danced to music "too fine for mortal ears."

Scientists have a more technical explanation for these heavenly apparitions. They explain that the aurora borealis is an atmospheric phenomenon that's tied to explosive events on the sun's surface, known as solar flares. Those flares produce a stream of charged particles, the "solar wind," which goes shooting off into space. When such a wind intersects Earth's magnetic field, most of the particles are deflected; some, however, are sent into the upper atmosphere, where they collide with gas molecules such as nitrogen and oxygen. The resulting reactions produce glowing colors. The aurora is most commonly a pale yellowish green, but its borders are sometimes tinged with pink, purple, or blue. Especially rare is the all-red aurora, which appears when charged solar particles collide with oxygen molecules up to 150 mi high.

Although the science may seem complex and difficult to comprehend, the results are pure beauty. Alaska has some of the world's brightest auroras, with the best light shows occurring in a band that stretches from the Alaska Range into the Arctic. In Fairbanks, northern lights may appear more than 200 nights per year (they're much less common in Anchorage, partly because of urban glare). Alaska's long hours of daylight hide the aurora in summer, so the best viewing is from September through April. **Chena Hot Springs Resort** (✉ Chena Hot Springs ☎ 907/452–7867) has a glassed-in and heated hut set up on a hillside for gazing at the northern lights. **North Star Tours** (✆ Box 71677, Fairbanks ☎ 907/451–1125) runs aurora tours to Mt. Aurora/ Skiland from December into April. It'll arrange pickup and delivery to your hotel, supply warm clothes if needed, and offer an "aurora insurance" plan if you're the gambling type.

The longest trail is 2 mi, and one is accessible to people who use wheelchairs.

HOCKEY At the nearby University of Alaska Fairbanks, the **Nanooks** (☎ 907/474–6868) play NCAA Division I hockey.

RIVERBOAT. RACING Another summer highlight is riverboat racing sanctioned by the **Fairbanks Outboard Association** (☎ 907/459–2023). These specially built 24-foot racing boats are powered by 50-horsepower engines and reach speeds of 75 mph. Weekend races throughout the summer and fall begin and end either at the Pump House Restaurant or at Pike's Landing, just off Airport Way near Fairbanks International Airport. The season's big event in late June is the **Yukon 800 Marathon,** a two-day, 800-mi race between Fairbanks and Galena by way of the Chena, Tanana, and Yukon rivers. The **Roland Lord Memorial Race,** from Fairbanks to Nenana and back, is held in early August, and the **Tanana 440** is held in late July.

RUNNING Two of Fairbanks's best runs are the **Midnight Sun Run** each June on the weekend nearest the summer solstice and the September **Equinox Marathon,** a tough run up and down the large Ester Dome, northwest of the city. Check with local sporting-goods stores for race schedules.

SKIING The Interior has some of the best weather and terrain in the nation for cross-country skiing, especially during the late fall and early spring. Among the developed trails in the Fairbanks area, the ones at the **Birch Hill Recreation Area,** on the city's north side, and the **University of Alaska Fairbanks** are lighted to extend their use into the winter nights. Cross-country ski racing is a staple at several courses on winter weekends. The season stretches from October to late March or early April. Other developed trails can be found at **Chena Hot Springs Resort, White Mountain National Recreation Area,** the **Chena Lakes Recreation Area,** and the **Two Rivers Recreation Area.** For more information check with the **Alaska Public Lands Information Center.**

For downhill skiing, **Mt. Aurora/Skiland** (☎ 907/456–7669 or 907/389–2314 ⊕ home.att.net/~Skiland), on the Steese Highway about 20 mi from Fairbanks at Cleary Summit, has a chairlift, 20-plus runs ranked intermediate to expert, and a 1,100-foot vertical drop. There's lodging in an old gold-camp bunkhouse, dog mushing, snowmobile rides, and aurora viewing. It's open weekends from December to mid-April. **Moose Mountain** (☎ 907/479–8362 ⊕ www.shredthemoose.com), off Murphy Dome Road, has beginner, intermediate, and a few advanced slopes; it's open November–April, Thursday–Sunday. **Birch Hill** (☎ 907/353–7053), in Ft. Wainwright, has a chairlift and beginner and intermediate runs; it's open November–April, Thursday–Sunday.

SLED-DOG RACES From November to March, a constant string of sled-dog races is held throughout the region, culminating in the **North American Open Sled-Dog Championship,** which attracts international competition to Fairbanks. Throughout Alaska, sprint races, freight hauling, and long-distance endurance runs are held in late February and March, during the Alaska season when longer days afford enjoyment of the remaining winter snow. Men and women often compete in the same classes in the major races. For children, various racing classes are based on age, starting with the one-dog category for the youngest.

In Fairbanks many of the sprint races are organized by the **Alaska Dog Mushers Association** (☎ 907/457–6874 ⊕ www.sleddog.org), one of the oldest organizations of its kind in Alaska, and held at its Jeff Studdert Sled Dog Racegrounds at Mile 4, Farmers Loop. The **Yukon Quest International Sled-Dog Race** (☎ 907/452–7954 ⊕ www.yukonquest.org) is an endurance race held in February that covers more than 1,000 mi between Fairbanks and Whitehorse, Yukon Territory, via Dawson and the Yukon River. You can get more details from the visitor center in either city or by calling the Yukon Quest office in Fairbanks.

Shopping

Crafts

The **Arctic Travelers Gift Shop** (✉ 201 Cushman St., Downtown ☎ 907/456–7080) has a wide selection of Athabascan beadwork. **Beads and Things** (✉ 537 2nd Ave., Downtown ☎ 907/456–2323) sells Native handicrafts from around the state. The **Great Alaskan Bowl Company** (✉ 4630 Old Airport Rd. ☎ 907/474–9663 ⊕ www.woodbowl.com) sells lathe-turned bowls made out of Alaskan birch.

Jewelry

In her small, eponymous shop, **Judie Gumm Designs** (✉ 3600 Main St., Ester 99725 ☎ 907/479–4568 ⊕ www.judiegumm.com), Ms. Gumm fashions stunning silver and gold designs best described as sculptural interpretations of northern images. Moderately priced and easy to pack, her jewelry makes a nice memento of your trip north. Ester is 6 mi south of Fairbanks off the George Parks Highway—follow the signs.

Outerwear & Outdoor Gear

Simon Rakower, the owner of the Far North bike shop **All Weather Sports** (✉ 4001 Geist Rd., No. 12 ☎ 907/474–8184 ✉ 927 Old Steese Hwy. ☎ 907/474–2811 ⊕ www.allweathersports.com), invented the double-wide mountain-bike rim—the Snow-Cat—so that competitors in IditaSport, a mountain-bike, snowshoe, and ski version of the Iditarod Trail Sled Dog Race, would be able to pedal their bikes on snow-packed trails. His shop carries a full line of extra-wide rim wheels, studded bicycle tires, and other items hard to find anywhere else. He also sells bikes, and the shop specializes in repairs of bikes damaged in transit to Alaska.

Apocalypse Design (✉ 101 College Rd. ☎ 907/451–7555 or 866/451–7555 ⊕ www.akgear.com) makes its own specialized cold-weather clothing for dog mushers and other winter adventurers. Travelers from colder sections of the Lower 48 will appreciate the double-layer fleece mittens, among other items.

AROUND FAIRBANKS

The three roads north of Fairbanks head straight out of civilization. They all dead-end at water—two at rivers and one on the Arctic Ocean. If you want to see untamed Alaska and cross paths with some rugged, independent people, head in this direction.

Chena Hot Springs

❽ *62 mi northeast of Fairbanks.*

The 57-mi paved Chena Hot Springs Road, which starts 5 mi outside Fairbanks, leads to Chena Hot Springs, a favorite playground of many Fairbanks residents. Several attractions lie along the road, including Tack's General Store and Greenhouse Café, Chena River State Recreation Area, and Chena Hot Springs Resort.

Where to Stay & Eat

★ **$–$$$$** ✕ **Two Rivers Lodge.** Fairbanksans are known to make the 40-mi round-trip for the delicious dinners here, including hand-cut, aged filet mignon;

prime rib; and frequent crab specials and other Alaskan seafood dishes. Don't be discouraged by the outward appearance of the building. Rustic logs belie the elegance of the menu. For a study in contrasts, Alaskan style, stop in the Trapline Lounge first for a predinner refreshment. ✉ *Mile 16, Chena Hot Springs Rd.* ☎ *907/488–6815* 🖷 *907/488–9761* ⊕ *www. tworiverslodge.com* ▭ *AE, D, MC, V* ⊘ *No lunch.*

$$ 🖾 ⚠ **Chena Hot Springs Resort.** Fairbanksans come in droves to this re-
Fodor'sChoice sort to soak in the hot-springs-warmed hot tubs or swimming pool and
★ to engage in various outdoor sports. Summer activities include gold panning, flightseeing, and mountain biking. In winter you can go snowmobiling, dogsledding, and Snow-Cat touring. ATV tours are given year-round. The Aurorarium is a large, glassed-in room for viewing the northern lights in the winter. There are sports-equipment rentals, camping sites, and heated cabins without running water. Cabins rent for $65–$200. ✑ *Box 58740, Fairbanks 99711* ☎ *907/451–8104 or 800/ 478–4681* 🖷 *907/456–3122* ⊕ *www.chenahotsprings.com* ⤳ *80 rooms, 10 cabins* ⚷ *Restaurant, cable TV, massage, fishing, mountain bikes, horseback riding, cross-country skiing, sleigh rides, snowmobiling, bar, laundry facilities, Internet, meeting room, some pets allowed (fee); no phones in some rooms* ▭ *AE, D, DC, MC, V.*

Sports & the Outdoors

BOATING The **Chena River State Recreation Area,** along Chena Hot Springs Road from Mile 26 to Mile 51, has numerous well-marked river-access points. The lower sections of the river area are placid, but the area above the third bridge, at Mile 44.1, can be hazardous for inexperienced boaters.

HIKING The **Chena River State Recreation Area,** which straddles Chena Hot Springs Road from Mile 26 to Mile 51, has a few hiking trails. The Granite Tors Trail, a 15-mi loop, can be done in a day and offers a view of the upper Chena Valley and an opportunity to see these dramatic "tors" (fingers of rock protruding through grassy meadow). Carry plenty of drinking water on this trip because of limited water sources. A shorter hike is the 3½-mi Angel Rocks Trail, near the eastern boundary of the area. This area is managed by the **Alaska Division of Parks** (☎ 907/451–2695), which also maintains five area public-use cabins, although only one is reachable by car.

Steese Highway

From Fairbanks: 128 mi northeast to Central, 162 mi to Circle.

The Steese Highway follows the Chatanika River and several other creeks along the southern part of the White Mountains. It eventually climbs into weatherworn alpine mountains, peaking at Eagle Summit (3,624 feet), about 100 mi from Fairbanks, and drops back down into forested creek beds en route to Central. At Central you can drive the 30-plus mi on a winding gravel road to Circle, a small town on the Yukon River. The highway is paved to Mile 44 and usually in good shape. A possible exception is during winter, when Eagle Summit is sometimes closed due to drifting snow.

Where to Stay

¢–$ 🖾 ⚠ **Historic Chatanika Gold Camp.** Miners working the dredges for the F. E. Gold Co. in the early 1900s bunked at this 55-acre site, formerly known as the Old F. E. Gold Camp. The grounds are on the National Register of Historic Places, and the world's largest coal cookstove is still operating in the dining room. The rooms in the hotel share bathrooms. Additionally, there are two four-room log cabins that share four complete baths. The area is a wonderland for local winter-sports enthusiasts, summertime hikers, and aurora viewers. ⊠ *Mile 27.9, 5550 Steese Hwy., Fairbanks 99712* ☎ *907/389–2414* 🖷 *907/457–6463* ⊕ *www. fegoldcamp.com* ⇩ *26 rooms share 6 baths, 2 four-unit cabins share 4 baths* ⚐ *Restaurant, bar, meeting room* ▤ *AE, MC, V.*

¢ ▥**Chatanika Lodge.** Rocket scientists from the nearby Poker Flat Research Range gather at this cedar lodge, as do mushers (guests can take dogsled rides), snowmobilers, and local families. The eclecticism of the clientele is matched by that of the furnishings: diamond willow lamps and a variety of wild-animal trophy heads and skins, including bear, lynx, and wolf. The rooms generally have a double and single bed, sink, and TV. The bathrooms and showers are down the hall. ⊠ *Mile 28.6, 5760 Steese Hwy., Fairbanks 99712* ☎ *907/389–2164* 🖷 *907/389–2166* ⇩ *10 rooms share 4 baths* ⚐ *Restaurant, cable TV, snowmobiling, bar, some pets allowed; no room phones* ▤ *MC, V.*

Sports & the Outdoors

BOATING The **Chatanika River,** a choice spot for canoeists and kayakers, has a wilderness feel to it yet it's still fairly close to Fairbanks. The most northerly access point is at Cripple Creek campground, near Mile 60 of the Steese Highway. Other commonly used access points are at Long Creek (Mile 45, Steese Highway); at the state campground, where the Chatanika River crosses the Steese Highway at Mile 39; and at the state's Whitefish Campground, where the river crosses the Elliott Highway at Mile 11. The stream flows into the Minto Flats below this point, and river access is more difficult.

Water in the Chatanika River may or may not be clear, depending on mining activities along its upper tributaries. In times of very low water, the upper Chatanika River is shallow and difficult to navigate. Avoid the river in times of high water, especially after heavy rains, because of the danger of sweepers, floating debris, and hidden gravel bars. Contact the Alaska Public Lands Information Center to find out the status of the river.

Steese Mountain National Conservation Area & White Mountain National Recreation Area

❾ *About 31 mi northeast of Fairbanks.*

The **Bureau of Land Management** (⊠ BLM Headquarters, 1150 University Ave., Fairbanks 99709 ☎ 907/474–2200) administers the Steese Mountain National Conservation Area and the White Mountain National Recreation Area. Both preserves are accessible by car. The White Mountain Recreation Area has limited camping facilities from June to November. The BLM also has three campsites on the Taylor Highway between Tok and Eagle at Miles 48.5, 82, and 160.

In the Steese National Conservation Area you can take a four- to five-day float trip on the lively, clear-water **Birch Creek,** a challenge with its several rapids along its 126 mi. Moose, caribou, and birds are easily spotted. Access is at Mile 94 of the Steese Highway. This stream winds its way north through the historic mining country of the Circle District. The take-out point is at the Steese Highway Bridge, 15 mi from Circle. From there Birch Creek meanders on to the Yukon River well below the town.

Rising out of the White Mountain National Recreation Area, **Beaver Creek** makes its easy way north. If you have enough time, it's possible to run its entire 268-mi length to the Yukon (if you make a shorter run, you will have to go out by small plane).

Where to Stay

¢ 🏠 **BLM Public-Use Cabins.** The BLM manages 11 public-use cabins in
the White Mountain NRA, with 300 mi of interconnecting trails. Designed primarily for winter use by dog mushers, snow machiners
(snowmobilers), and cross-country skiers, cabins provide shelter for
summer backpackers, although summer access is limited by mountainous
and boggy terrain. The cabins have bunk beds, woodstoves, tables, and
chairs. Permits are required and available up to 30 days in advance.
⊠ *BLM Headquarters, 1150 University Ave., Fairbanks 99709* ☎ *907/*
474–2200 or 800/437–7021 ⊕ *aurora.ak.blm.gov/whitemtns* ⇱ *11*
cabins ⊟ *MC, V.*

¢ 🏕 **BLM Campgrounds.** The BLM manages three road-accessible campgrounds in the Steese Highway area and another along the Dalton Highway. They all have picnic tables, fire pits, latrines, and well water.
They're available on a first-come, first-served basis. In addition, you'll
find several undeveloped campsites along the Dalton—old gravel pits
with no facilities, available free of charge. ⊠ *BLM Headquarters, 1150*
University Ave., Fairbanks 99709 ☎ *907/474–2200 or 800/437–7021*
⊕ *aurora.ak.blm.gov* ⇱ *4 campsites* ⊟ *No credit cards.*

Sports & the Outdoors

HIKING The BLM maintains the moderately difficult 20-mi **Summit Trail,** from
the Elliott Highway, near Wickersham Dome, north into the White
Mountain National Recreation Area. This hiking trail can be done as
a day hike or overnight backpacking trip. It quickly rises into alpine country with 360° vistas that include lots of wildland, the trans-Alaska
pipeline, and a pipeline pump station. You can see many wildflowers in
early summer. Look for the parking lot at Mile 28.

Yukon–Charley Rivers National Preserve

🔟 *20 mi north of Eagle, 100 mi east of Fairbanks.*

The 126-mi stretch of the Yukon River running between the small towns
of Eagle and Circle—former gold-rush metropolises—is protected in the
2.5-million-acre **Yukon–Charley Rivers National Preserve** (⊠ National
Park Service, 201 1st Ave., Doyon Bldg., Fairbanks 99701 ☎ 907/456–
0281 ⊕ www.nps.gov/yuch/index.htm).As its name suggests, this parkland also covers the pristine watershed of the Charley River, a crystalline
white-water stream flowing out of the Yukon-Tanana uplands that provides fine river running. You can put in a raft or a kayak (with a small
plane) at the headwaters of the Charley River and travel 88 mi down
this joyful, bouncing waterway.

In great contrast to the Charley River, the Yukon River is an inexorably
powerful stream, dark with mud and glacial silt. The only bridge built
across it holds the trans-Alaska pipeline, north of Fairbanks. The river
surges deep, and to travel on it in a small boat is a humbling, if magnificent, experience. You can drive from Fairbanks to Eagle (via the Taylor Highway off the Alaska Highway) and to Circle (via the Steese
Highway) and from either of these arrange for a ground-transportation
shuttle back to your starting city at the end of your Yukon River trip.
Weeklong float trips down the river from Eagle to Circle, 150 mi away,
are possible. For information contact the **National Park Service** (☎ 907/
547–2233) in Eagle. Note that no developed campgrounds or other visitor facilities exist within the preserve itself, though low-impact backcountry camping is permitted.

Sports & the Outdoors

CROSS-COUNTRY SKIING, SNOWMOBILING & SNOWSHOEING
Once past Mile 20 of the Steese Highway you enter a countryside that seems to have changed little in 100 years, even though you're only an hour from downtown Fairbanks. Mountains loom in the distance, and in winter, a solid snowpack of 4–5 feet makes the area great for snowshoeing, backcountry skiing, and riding snowmobiles—Alaskans refer to them as snowmachines, and calling them snowmobiles automatically brands you as someone from "Outside."

Snow-RV (✉ 5760 Old Steese Hwy., off Steese Hwy. at Mile 28.5, at Chatanika Lodge ☐ Box 10804, Fairbanks 99710 ☎ 907/389–7669 📠 907/389–5665) rents Arctic Cat snowmobiles. Rentals are available by the hour or for several days. Guided rides are required for those from out of state.

HIKING
The Alaska Public Lands Information Center (⇨ Interior A to Z, *below*) has detailed information about the trails in the Yukon–Charley Rivers National Preserve.

The BLM maintains the **Pinnell Mountain National Recreation Trail,** connecting Twelve-Mile Summit and Eagle Summit on the Steese Highway. This 27-mi-long trail passes through alpine meadows and along mountain ridges, all above the tree line. It has two emergency shelters. No dependable water supply is available in the immediate vicinity. Most hikers spend three days making the trip.

The **Circle-Fairbanks Historic Trail** stretches 58 mi from the vicinity of Cleary Summit to Twelve-Mile Summit. This route, which is not for novices, follows the old summer trail used by gold miners; in winter they generally used the frozen Chatanika River to make this journey. The trail has been roughly marked and cleared, but there are no facilities and water is scarce along much of it. Most of the trail is on state land, but it does cross valid mining claims, which must be respected. Although you'll find rock cairns and mileposts while hiking, no well-defined tread exists, so it's easy to become disoriented. The State Department of Natural Resources strongly recommends that backpackers on this trail equip themselves with the following USGS topographical maps: Livengood (A-1), Circle (A-6), Circle (A-5), and Circle (B-4).

Elliott Highway

From Fairbanks: 28 mi north to Wickersham Dome, north 73 mi to Dalton Hwy. junction, 152 mi northwest to Manley.

The Elliott Highway, which starts in Fox, takes you to the Tanana River
⑪ and the small community of **Manley Hot Springs.** A colorful, close-knit "end-of-the-road" place, this town originally was a trading center for placer miners who worked the nearby creeks. Residents maintain a small public campground, across from Manley Roadhouse. Northern pike are caught in the nearby slough, and a dirt road leads to the Tanana River with its summer runs of salmon. The Manley Hot Springs Resort has closed, but the hot springs are only a short walk from the campground. The highway is paved for 28 mi outside Fairbanks.

Where to Stay

$ 🛏 **Manley Roadhouse.** Built in 1906 in the midst of the gold rush into the Interior, this roadhouse is among the oldest in Alaska. Today it caters to a diverse crowd of vacationers, miners, and road maintenance crews. Not only is the roadhouse known for the food and the rooms, which occupy the original roadhouse and several cabins, but the bar earns bragging rights for its 250 brands of liquor and 20 varieties of beer. The restau-

rant serves breakfast, lunch, and dinner. ⊠ *Mile 152, Elliott Hwy.,*
Manley Hot Springs ⏪ *Box 1, Manley Hot Springs 99756* ☎ *907/672–*
3161 ⤴ *13 rooms, 6 with bath; 3 cabins* ⚒ *Restaurant, bar, some pets*
allowed; no room phones, no TV in some rooms ➦ *AE, MC, V.*

Sports & the Outdoors

HIKING   The BLM maintains the 22-mi **Summit Trail** from the Elliott Highway,
near Wickersham Dome, north into the White Mountain National
Recreation Area. Water is scarce on the trail, so be sure to carry plenty
with you.

Dalton Highway

From Fairbanks: 140 mi north to the Yukon River, 199 mi to the Arc-
tic Circle, 259 mi to Coldfoot, 329 mi to Atigun Pass, 499 mi to Dead-
horse.

The Dalton Highway is a road of "onlys." It's the only road that goes
to the Beaufort Sea, it's the only Alaskan road to cross the Arctic Circle, and it has the state's only bridge across the Yukon River. The 414-
mi gravel road starts 84 mi from Fairbanks on the Elliott Highway and
runs northwest of Fairbanks to the North Slope oil fields at Prudhoe
Bay. It was built in 1974 and 1975 to open a truck route necessary to
build the facilities at Prudhoe and the northern half of the trans-Alaska
pipeline. For a few months a ferry was used to carry loads across the
Yukon River, until the present bridge was completed in late 1975.

The road is named for James Dalton, a pioneer Alaskan engineer who recognized early the potential of oil on the North Slope. If you are planning
to drive the Dalton Highway, remember these tips: slow down and move
to the side of the road for trucks; leave your headlights on at all times;
yield on one-lane bridges; pull to the side of the road when stopping for
pictures or the view; carry at least one spare tire; and consider bringing
extra gas and purchasing a citizen's band radio. Remember there are no
services between Coldfoot and Prudhoe Bay, a distance of nearly 250 mi.

The Dalton Highway has two **visitor centers** open in the summer. One
is just north of the Yukon River bridge and has no phone. The other is
in **Coldfoot** (☎ 907/678–5209). The centers are operated by the Fish
and Wildlife Service, the National Park Service, and the BLM. A picnic
area and a large, colorful sign mark the spot where the road crosses the
Arctic Circle.

The **Wiseman Trading Co.**, a museum and general store 12 mi north of
Coldfoot, is run by Coldfoot Services–Slate Creek Inn.

⓬   Today the road is still used to carry oil-field supplies and is now open
all the way to **Deadhorse**, just shy of the Arctic coast. This town exists
mainly to service the oil fields of Prudhoe Bay, so while scenery isn't in
great supply, it does have important facilities for travelers, including fuel,
vehicle maintenance, a general store, an airport, a post office, hotels,
and restaurants.Oil-field tours and shuttles to the Arctic Ocean leave
daily from the three hotels in Deadhorse. The two tours include a one-
hour tour to the ocean for $25 and a 2½-hour tour and video screen-
ing ($50) of the trans-Alaska pipeline. For tour reservations call the **Arctic**
Caribou Inn (☎ 907/659–2368) or the ➪ **Prudhoe Bay Hotel.**

Where to Stay

Five camping areas plus many scenic turnouts are along the road. Only
one of the camping areas (Marion Creek, at Mile 180) is developed. Most
of the rest are gravel pads, sometimes with outhouses. Call the **Alaska**
Public Lands Information Center for more information.

¢–$$ ⊡ ⚠ **Coldfoot Camp.** Fuel, tire repairs, and towing are available here in Coldfoot. Basic and clean rooms are built from surplus pipeline-worker housing. The 24-hour restaurant serves generous portions of truck-stop fare. The complex has a 20-space RV hookup and post office. Although the place looks more than a little offbeat, bear in mind that it's the only facility of any sort within 100 mi or more, so you may have to adjust your standards accordingly. ⊠ *Mile 175, Dalton Hwy.* ⊙ *Box 9041, Coldfoot 99701* ☏ *907/474–3400 or 866/474–3400* ⊟ *907/474–4767* ⊕ *www.coldfootcamp.com* ⇗ *81 rooms, 52 with bath* ♢ *Restaurant, shop; no room phones, no room TVs* ⊟ *MC, V.*

$$ ⊡ **Prudhoe Bay Hotel.** Like most of Deadhorse, this hotel was originally built to house mining workers. Spartan but comfortable guest rooms are the result. There is a TV room with a big-screen TV. The restaurant (all meals are included in the room rate) serves pizza and American fare in an all-you-can-eat buffet. ⊠ *Airport Rd., across from airport* ⊙ *Pouch 340004, Prudhoe Bay 99734* ☏ *907/659–2449* ⊟ *907/659–2752* ⊕ *www.prudhoebayhotel.com* ⇗ *180 rooms, 15 with bath* ♢ *Restaurant, gym; no phones in some rooms, no TV in some rooms* ⊟ *MC, V* ⦿ *FAP.*

$ ⊡ **Arctic Caribou Inn.** This hotel is made up of trailer-type units, with basic rooms. The restaurant serves American fare in an all-you-can-eat buffet. ⊠ *Airport Rd.* ⊙ *Box 340111, Deadhorse 99734* ☏ *907/659–2368 or 877/659–2368* ⊟ *907/659–2692* ⊕ *www.arcticcaribouinn.com* ⇗ *45 rooms* ♢ *Restaurant* ⊟ *MC, V* ⊗ *Closed Labor Day–Memorial Day.*

$ ⊡ **Yukon Ventures Alaska.** You'll find a motel, a tire repair shop, and gasoline, diesel fuel, and propane on this property on the Yukon River. The motel is basic and clean, built from surplus pipeline-worker housing. None of the rooms have private baths, but two (one for men, one for women) have showers and are centrally located. The restaurant serves large portions of diner fare. ⊠ *Mile 56, Dalton Hwy.* ⊙ *Box 60947, Fairbanks 99706* ☏ *907/655–9001* ⇗ *40 rooms share 3 baths* ♢ *Restaurant* ⊟ *MC, V.*

Guided Tours

Northern Alaska Tour Company (☏ 907/474–8600) conducts van tours and boat tours of the Yukon River with Yukon River Tours. **Princess Tours** (☏ 907/479–9660 or 800/426–0442) runs tour buses on the Dalton from Fairbanks all the way to Prudhoe Bay, with a variety of services, including an overnight at Coldfoot, a tour of the oil field, and air service from Prudhoe Bay back to Fairbanks or Anchorage. Tours operate once a week from June through August. **Trans Arctic Circle Treks** (☏ 907/479–5451 or 800/336–8735 ⊟ 800/479–8908 ⊕ www.arctictreks.com) has an extensive menu of guided trips ranging in duration from 1 day to 11 days, covering areas from Anchorage and Southwest Alaska to Barrow and Prudhoe Bay. It is the only tour company with a winter "Adventures to the North Slope" trip.

Sports & the Outdoors

FISHING Although this is not a prime fishing area, fish, mostly grayling, populate the streams along the Dalton. You'll do better if you are willing to hike more than ¼ mi from the road, where fishing pressure is the heaviest. Lakes along the road have grayling, and some have lake trout and arctic char. The Alaska Department of Fish and Game puts out a pamphlet titled "Sport Fishing Along the Dalton Highway," which is also available at the **Alaska Public Lands Information Center.**

HIKING No trails have been officially established along the road, but hikers willing to pick their own route can explore much of the area. The road passes near the **Yukon Flats National Wildlife Refuge,** the **Kanuti National Wildlife Refuge,** the **Arctic National Wildlife Refuge,** and just east of **Gates of the Arctic National Park and Preserve.** Check with the **Alaska Public Lands Information Center.** Chances of seeing wildlife are fairly good, as this is grizzly bear and caribou habitat.

Healy

13 *11 mi north of Denali National Park, 109 mi south of Fairbanks, 248 mi north of Anchorage.*

Coal mining fuels the economy of Healy, which is home to the **Usibelli Coal Mine,** the largest mine of its kind in the state and Alaska's only commercially viable coal mining operation. Each summer overflow crowds from Denali National Park and Preserve stream into this small community of 500 people on the George Parks Highway, north of the entrance, to park. However, more and more frequently, Fairbanks-area residents and visitors from the Lower 48 and other countries are seeking out Healy's year-round lodging and the magnificent views.

Healy is close to the **Stampede Trail,** which offers those interested in snow-mobiling, mushing, cross-country skiing, and mountain biking a way to enter the northern expanse of Denali National Park and Preserve. This wide, well-traveled path begins where Stampede Road ends and leads to the former gold-rush boomtown of Kantishna, 90 mi inside the park. Take the George Parks Highway 2 mi north of Healy to Mile 251.1, where Stampede Road intersects the highway. Eight miles west on Stampede Road is a parking lot and the start of the Stampede Trail.

Where to Stay & Eat

¢–$$ ✕ **Totem Inn.** Travelers from along the George Parks Highway, Healy, and Denali National Park come here for standard American food at reasonable prices. Pizzas, steaks, sandwiches, and a Sunday lunch buffet are served all year-round. The kitchen is open daily 7 AM–11 PM. ⊠ *Mile 248.7, George Parks Hwy.* ☎ *907/683–2420* ⊟ *D, MC, V.*

$$$$ 🏨 **Denali Wilderness Lodge.** This backcountry, fly-in-only lodge is on the banks of the Wood River in a vast wilderness expanse adjacent to Denali National Park. Guests stay in cozy private cabins, complete with electricity and running water, a rarity in such remote circumstances. Room price includes all meals, served family style in a large, airy dining room. Fresh ingredients are flown in daily, and most food is homegrown or homemade. Activities include hiking, either on your own or accompanied by a staff naturalist, horseback riding (fee), canoeing, gold panning, and evening nature programs. The flight in from Healy costs an additional $100 per person, each way. ⌂ *4 10 Denali St., Anchorage 99501* ☎ *907/644–9980 or 800/541–9779* 🖷 *907/644–9981* ⊕ *www.denaliwildernesslodge.com* ⬐ *22 rooms* ⚇ *Restaurant, boating, hiking, horseback riding, bar, airstrip; no room phones, no room TVs, no smoking* ⊟ *MC, V* ⫶⊙⫶ *FAP.*

$–$$ 🏨 **Motel Nord Haven.** Five wooded acres protect this motel from the road, providing a secluded feeling other lodgings along the George Parks Highway lack. There's wood trim throughout, and rooms have one or two queen-size beds, a telephone, television, and a private bath. Rooms with two queen beds can accommodate up to five people at no additional charge. A Continental breakfast is served, and box lunches will be prepared for clients to carry along on their explorations. ⊠ *Mile 249.5, George Parks Hwy.* ⌂ *Box 458, Healy 99743* ☎ *907/683–4500 or 800/683–4501* 🖷 *907/683–4503* ⊕ *www.motelnordhaven.com* ⬐ *28 rooms* ⚇ *Some kitchenettes, cable TV, meeting room; no smoking* ⊟ *AE, MC, V* ⫶⊙⫶ *CP.*

$ ⓋDenali Dome Home. A huge, 7,200-square-foot, modified geodesic dome houses this all-year B&B. Each guest room has a private bath, TV, VCR, and phone; one has a sauna and two rooms have jetted tubs. A common room has a TV, fireplace, and Alaska-related books and videos. The fireplace fits 5-foot-long logs, and the high ceiling is enhanced by tall windows that provide spectacular views of nearby mountains. There's an extensive videotape and DVD collection at your disposal as well as DSL Internet access. ⊠ 137 Healy Spur Rd. ⬠ Box 262, Healy 99743 ☎ 907/683–1239 or 800/683–1239 ⊕ www.denalidomehome. com ⪡ 7 rooms ⬠ In-room hot tubs, in-room VCRs, Internet; no smoking ⊟ AE, D, MC, V.

DENALI NATIONAL PARK & PRESERVE

⓮ *11 mi south of Healy, 120 mi south of Fairbanks, 240 mi north of An-*
FodorśChoice *chorage.*
★

The most accessible of Alaska's national parks and one of only three connected to the state's highway system, 6-million-acre Denali National Park and Preserve is one of North America's finest and easiest places to see wildlife in its natural environment. Nowhere in the world is there more spectacular background scenery to these wildlife riches, with 20,320-foot Mt. McKinley looming above forested valleys, tundra-topped hills, and the glacier-covered peaks of the Alaska Range.

Also commonly known by its Athabascan Indian name, *Denali*, meaning "the high one," North America's highest mountain is also the world's tallest when measured from base to top: the great mountain rises more than 18,000 feet above surrounding lowlands. Unfortunately for visitors with little time to spend in the area, McKinley is wreathed in clouds an average of two days of every three during the summer. However, if you plan ahead and venture far enough into the park, you'll have a better chance of seeing the mountain in all its glacier-capped magnificence.

Although most Denali visitors are content to watch Mt. McKinley from afar, more than 1,000 adventurers walk the mountain's slopes each summer. About half of them succeed in "summiting" the peak during the May-to-July climbing season. The great majority of McKinley mountaineers fly to the mountain's base camp on the Kahiltna Glacier at 7,200 feet, then follow the West Buttress Route, generally considered the safest and easiest path to the top. Whatever route they take, climbers must deal with avalanches, glacial crevasses, high altitude, and extreme cold. Even in summer, temperatures high on McKinley can fall to –30°F or –40°F. The mountain is so large it creates its own weather, and storms frequently batter its upper slopes with winds of 100 mph or more. If you feel you must attempt the peak, talk to the Park Service people about procuring a guide. The hazards of climbing Denali are frequently underestimated, and prospective adventurers must be aware of the dangers. Fatalities are unfortunately an occasional occurrence.

You need not climb Mt. McKinley to appreciate Denali; the park is both a hiker's and wildlife-watcher's paradise. The one 88-mi road into the heart of the park is unpaved after the first 14¾ mi, and in summer you can travel on shuttle buses, from which you can see grizzly bears, wolves, caribou, and moose. The bulk of the parkland, however, is accessible only on foot in summer or by dog team or cross-country skis in winter.

For all the challenges of access and planning, those who explore Denali are certain to reap many rewards: wilderness solitude, a sense of discovery, wildlife encounters, and a greater appreciation of the landscape's immensity and the rigors of the sub-Arctic climate.

Geology & Terrain

Several of Denali's most spectacular landforms are deep in the park. The multicolor volcanic rocks at Cathedral Mountain and Polychrome Pass remind many travelers of the vivid hues of the desert Southwest. The braided channels of glacially fed streams such as the Teklanika, Toklat, and McKinley rivers serve as "highway routes" for both animals and hikers. The debris- and tundra-covered ice of the Muldrow Glacier, one of the largest glaciers to flow out of Denali National Park's high mountains, is visible from Eielson Visitor Center, at Mile 66 of the park road. Wonder Lake, a dark and narrow "kettle pond" that's a remnant from Alaska's Ice Ages, lies at the end of the park road near Kantishna.

The most prominent geological feature of the park is the Alaska Range, a 600-mi-long crescent of summits that separates South Central Alaska from the Interior. These peaks are all immense, but the truly towering ones are Mt. Hunter (14,573 feet), Mt. Foraker (17,400 feet), and Mt. McKinley (20,320 feet). Mt. McKinley's granite heart is covered with glacial ice, which is hundreds of feet thick in places. Glaciers, in fact, are abundant along the entire Alaska Range, and a few are visible from the park road. Muldrow Glacier is only 5 mi from the road, near Mile 67.

Flora

Vegetation in the park consists largely of taiga and tundra. Taiga is coniferous forest that exists in moist areas below a tree line of 2,000 feet and consists mainly of spruce trees. These trees have very shallow root systems due to the layer of permafrost that lies just under the surface of the land, and they are subject to the vagaries of wind and land movements. A turnoff and informational sign on the road near the park entrance points out an area of "drunken forest," where the uppermost layer of soil has shifted on the permafrost, moving the trees around and leaving them in a disheveled state that suggests some sort of arboreal inebriation. Ground cover in the taiga forest includes such shrubs as dwarf birch, blueberry, and willows. From the road the taiga looks open, with wide views and very few trees, but the dense bushes make it difficult for inexperienced travelers.

The rest of the land mass that isn't permanently covered by ice and snow is overlaid by tundra, which consists of a variety of plant types including lichens, berries, and woody plants—all in miniature. This complex carpet of low-lying vegetation generates brilliant color, especially in August, when the subtle variations of green begin to turn into the colors similar to those sought out by "leaf peepers" in the Lower 48. By the time the autumn colors max out in September, the tundra is ablaze with brilliant swaths of deep red among more restrained hues of yellows and greens. Most tundra areas enable easy hiking, but there are exceptions. After a while you may learn to evaluate tundra "walkability" from a distance, distinguishing by color and texture which areas are like a springy carpet and delightful to walk on and which are too moist for comfort and can turn an enjoyable hike into a boot-sucking slog.

Fauna

Nearly every wild creature that walks or flies in South Central and Interior Alaska inhabits the park. Thirty-eight species of mammals reside here, from wolves and bears to little brown bats and pygmy shrews that weigh a fraction of an ounce. The park also has a surprisingly large avian population in the summer, when some 160 species have been identified. Most of the birds migrate in fall, leaving only two dozen year-round resident species, including ravens, boreal chickadees, and hawk owls. Some of the summer birds travel thousands of miles to nest and breed in sub-Arctic valleys, hills, and ponds. The northern wheatear comes here from southern Asia, warblers fly here from Central and South America, and the arctic tern annually travels 24,000 mi while seasonally commuting between Denali and Antarctica.

The most sought-after species among visitors are the large mammals: grizzlies, wolves, Dall sheep, moose, and caribou. All inhabit the forest or tundra landscape that surrounds Denali Park Road. While traveling the park road you can expect to see Dall sheep finding their way across high meadows, grizzlies and caribou frequenting stream bottoms and tundra, moose in the forested areas both near the park entrance and deep in the park, and the occasional wolf or fox that may dart across the road. Keep in mind that, as one park lover put it, "this ain't no zoo." You might hit an off day and have few viewings—enjoy the surroundings anyway. Under no circumstances should you feed the animals or birds (a mew gull or ground squirrel may try to share your lunch).

Exploring Denali

To spend a full day in Denali, plan to stay in or near the park entrance the night before and the night of your bus trip. This way you can get an early start on a morning bus, get far enough into the interior to increase your wildlife-viewing opportunities, and maybe catch a glimpse of Mt. McKinley. The animals are most active early in the morning and in the evening. If you're willing to catch one of the first buses out before 6 AM, you'll have less competition for seats.

The real wilderness experience in Denali is reserved for those who get off the buses and walk. There are excellent day hikes near the entrance, and overnight options are unlimited, since there are no formal trails. Many hikers follow riverbeds or ridges. To avoid potentially dangerous encounters with wildlife, follow the advice of park rangers about routes and safety.

The **visitor center** near the park's entrance (at Milepost 237.3 of the Parks Highway) can fill all your information needs, from campground registration to bus reservations, backcountry permits, and daily schedules for naturalist presentations and sled-dog demonstrations by the park ranger. A video kiosk provides park information, including flora, fauna, and bear avoidance. A bookstore stocks titles on Denali's animals, wildflowers, and geology. The Backcountry Reservations desk has hiking information, including current data on animal sightings, river-crossing conditions, weather, and closed areas. ✆ *Box 9, Denali National Park 99755* ☎ *907/683–2294 year-round, 907/683–1266 in summer* ✉ *$5, $10 family* ✉ *Shuttle bus:* ☎ *800/622–7275, 907/272–7275 in Alaska* 🖨 *907/264–4684* ⊕ *www.nps.gov/dena* ✉ *Shuttle bus $17.50–$33.75.*

You can reach the park by bus or by car along the George Parks Highway. The Alaska Railroad line runs through Denali and stops at the park on its runs between Anchorage and Fairbanks. When you arrive at the park entrance, stop at the visitor center to pick up your camping permit and your bus passes. Only one road penetrates Denali's expansive wilderness: the 90-mi Denali Park Road, which winds from the park entrance to Wonder Lake and Kantishna, the historic mining community in the heart of the park. The first 14 mi of the road are open to all vehicles, but beyond the checkpoint at the Savage River only tour and shuttle buses and vehicles with permits are allowed to travel. Bicycles are currently allowed on the park road. The road, however, is suitable only for mountain bikes.

Shuttle buses travel as far as Wonder Lake, nearly 90 mi from the park entrance; seats can be reserved in advance, with reservations accepted beginning in late February. Making the entire trip to Wonder Lake and back will take 10 hours or more, but you can get off along the route and catch another bus in either direction.

The shuttle-bus system is designed to minimize disturbances to the park's wildlife. Large, potentially dangerous animals roam the park at will, and the park's primary mission is to protect the animals that live here and to keep conflicts between humans and animals at a minimum. It's quite common to see large sections of the park declared off-limits to visitors, including sensitive denning or nesting areas important to wildlife.

Seeing the park at its best requires time. The road is unpaved beyond the 14-mi checkpoint, and the speed limit is 35 mph. Add in frequent stops to view wildlife, rest stops, and the time it takes to negotiate the hills and turns. The general rule, however, is the farther in you go, the better the views of McKinley and the more likely you are to see wildlife.

Nature Trails & Short Walks

Both day hiking and backpacking can be supreme in Denali. The park's entrance area has a system of forest and tundra trails. These range from easy to challenging and are therefore suitable for all ages and hiking abilities. Along these paths you may see beavers working on their lodges in Horseshoe Lake; red squirrels chattering in trees; red foxes hunting squirrels and other rodents; sheep grazing on tundra plants; golden eagles soaring above high alpine ridges; and moose feeding on willow, one of their favorite foods. You should be cautious around moose and enjoy them from a distance; weighing 1,000 pounds or more, they can cause severe injuries despite their harmless appearance. If you encounter a moose at close range acting aggressively, run from it immediately to leave its "personal space." Just the opposite is true for Denali's grizzlies. Most important, **never** run from a bear. You may trigger its predatory chase instincts and have the bear respond to you as prey (⇨ Bear Facts box *in* Chapter 2). A little caution and a large dose of common sense will assure you a safe trip in the park. A summary of bear-safety tips is available at the visitor center.

Longer Hikes

The only relatively long, marked trail for hiking in the park, Mt. Healy Overlook Trail gains 1,700 feet in 2½ mi and takes about four hours round-trip, with outstanding views of the Nenana River below and the Alaska Range above. It's also a great starting point for backcountry hiking. You'll find few trails in the backcountry, however. In tundra areas, you set your own routes, and in forested and brushy areas, you have to bushwhack. The one exception is to find game trails through thick brush, but be advised that these trails were pioneered by bears, moose, and caribou. Whenever you're in an area of restricted visibility, make plenty of noise to announce your presence, and allow the resident critters to move away ahead of you. Because this is bear country, the Park Service provides backpackers with bearproof food containers. Use of these containers is mandatory. You can plan your itinerary with park rangers and use the shuttle bus for transportation to and from your starting point. No firearms are permitted.

Denali National
Park & Preserve

KEY
— Rail Line
····· Trail
--- Unpaved Road
⛺ Campground
🏠 Lodge
🪧 Picnic Area
🏚 Ranger Station
🍴 Restaurant

20 miles

20 km

Nenana River

Denali Hwy.

Cantwell
Denali

Alaska Railroad

George Parks Hwy. 3

Chulitna River

TO ANCHORAGE

Riley Creek

River

Igloo Creek

Sable Pass

Tokla River

Polychrome Pass

Toklat

Eielson Visitor Center

Park Rd.

West Fork Gl.

Eldridge Gl.

Buckskin Gl.

Alaska Range

Range

Alaska

Range

Sheldon Amphitheater

Muldrow Glacier

Mt. McKinley

Mount Hunter

Tokositna

WILDERNESS

Wonder Lake

Moose Creek

Kantishna

Wonder Lake

NATIONAL PARK

McKinley River

Straightaway Gl.

Foraker Gl.

Mount Foraker

Scenic Drives & Views

You can disembark at any point along the road in the park for hiking and sightseeing, then catch the next bus in either direction to continue your trip. Buses run continuously, and you'll seldom have to wait more than a half hour to catch a ride. Polychrome Pass, at Mile 46 of the park road, is a popular place to disembark, walk around, and take in the wide views of the stream valleys and tundra below. Many visitors turn around at Eielson Visitor Center, at Mile 66 of the park road. But on blue-sky days you might wish to go the distance to Wonder Lake, which has one of the grandest views of Denali. The Eielson–Wonder Lake stretch is particularly beautiful from mid-August to early September, when the tundra is ablaze with autumn's yellows, reds, and oranges. If you can't get a spot on one of the buses into the park, you can drive to the parking lot next to the Savage River at Mile 14. From there you can hike on nearby trails, climb the rock that gives the river its name, or head up onto one of the nearby ridge tops.

When to Go

Summer is the prime visiting time for Denali—the area is loosed from winter's icy grip and the animals are awake, active, and cruising for food and/or companionship. Most of the park lies above the tree line and gets 16 to 20 hours of daylight—which means you'll have plenty of time to enjoy the expansive view of unspoiled landscape and catch a few glimpses of Alaskan wildlife in the open spaces. However, late spring and early autumn also provide opportunities to see the area when visitor traffic is lessened, but be advised that the onset of winter and the appearance of spring are far different from those in the Lower 48 and even from the seasonal changes in Anchorage. In early summer trails may be muddy and all the trees won't be fully leafed out, but young animals may be more readily visible. The park is open all winter, although services are curtailed and the road into the park is blocked by snow. Intrepid travelers can visit the park on dogsleds, snowshoes, or cross-country skis and get a glimpse of Denali that's seldom enjoyed by outsiders.

What to Pack

Whether hiking in the high mountains or driving the park road, you should always come prepared for the park's highly variable summer weather. At lower elevations the weather can vary from hot and sunny to near freezing and drizzly, and those changes can sometimes occur within a few hours, so you'll want to bring along appropriate clothing and gear. Dress in layers. If you'll be hiking, carry polypropylene long underwear followed by layers of wool or synthetic materials such as fleece. Even if you're not planning on taking a long hike, you should carry durable rain gear, preferably made of a breathable material. In the Far North, cotton is not your friend—once it gets wet, it stays wet for too long, drawing warmth away from your body. Remember to bring binoculars and a camera, as Denali is one of the country's premier outdoor photography locations.

Where to Eat

$$–$$$$ ✕ **The Perch.** The bay windows of this fine-dining restaurant atop a forested hillside present a panoramic view of the surrounding Alaska Range foothills. The Perch serves breakfast, lunch, and dinner, offering home-baked breads and desserts along with steak and seafood. Cabin rentals are available year-round (summer rates are $95 with a private bath, $65 shared; call for winter rates). ⊠ *Mile 224, Parks Hwy., Denali Park* ☎ *907/683–2523 or 888/322–2523* ⊕ *www.alaskaone.com/perchrest* ⊟ *D, MC, V.*

$$–$$$$ ✕ **Tamarack Inn.** Dine on American cuisine by the light of a fireplace at this inn, which houses one of the best-known restaurants on the road from Anchorage to Fairbanks. It serves breakfast, lunch, and dinner in summer and dinner only in winter. ⊠ *Mile 298, Parks Hwy., 6 mi south of Nenana* ☎ *907/832–5455* ▤ *AE, MC, V* ⊗ *Closed Mon.–Tues. in Jan.*

¢–$$$ ✕ **Lynx Creek Pizza.** Locals hang out here for pizza, sandwiches, salads, ice cream, and some Mexican entrées. You order at the front and grab a seat at picnic-table benches. It's 1 mi north of the park entrance. ⊠ *Mile 238.6, Parks Hwy.* ☎ *907/683–2547* ▤ *AE, D, DC, MC, V* ⊗ *Closed in winter.*

FodorsChoice
★

$–$$ ✕ **McKinley/Denali Salmon Bake.** Baked fresh salmon tops the menu at this rustic building, which looks as if it might blow away in a stiff wind. Steaks, burgers, and chicken are also available, and breakfast, lunch, and dinner are served. It's 1 mi north of the park entrance, and shuttle service is provided to area hotels. ⊠ *Mile 238.5, Parks Hwy.* ☎ *907/683–2733 in summer* ▤ *AE, D, DC, MC, V* ⊗ *Closed Oct.–Apr.*

Where to Stay

Hotels, motels, RV parks, B&Bs, and campgrounds are clustered along the highway near the park entrance and in the town of Healy, 10 mi north.

★ **$$$$** ▦ **Camp Denali and North Face Lodge.** Camp Denali is in the heart of the park near the end of the park road. Camp guests stay in cabins that are comfortable and rustic, and the communal buildings have electricity and running water. Just a mile away, the North Face Lodge has hotel-style rooms with private baths. Each property has its own kitchen and dining room. The knowledgeable staff leads evening natural-history programs and guided outings. Packages include stays of either three or four nights, and all meals are included. A bus navigates the 85-mi road from the park entrance to the property, picking up and dropping off guests twice a week. ⌂ *Box 67, Denali Park 99755* ☎ *907/683–2290* 🖷 *907/683–1568* ⊕ *www.campdenali.com* ➪ *17 cabins (Camp Denali), 15 rooms (North Face Lodge)* ⚐ *Dining room, boating, fishing, mountain bikes, hiking; no room phones, no room TVs* ▤ *No credit cards* ⊗ *Closed mid-Sept.–early June* ⦿ *FAP.*

$$$$ ▦ **Denali Backcountry Lodge.** These cabins in the community of Kantishna at the end of the park road have private baths and individual climate controls, a rarity in such remote parts. Activities include naturalist programs; hiking; fishing; gold panning; mountain biking; and, for an extra fee, flightseeing when weather permits. Family-style meals emphasizing Alaskan fare are included in the room rate. Access to the lodge by van along the park road is the same system used by Camp Denali, and it takes a good part of a day to travel either way, so staying for at least two nights is necessary if you want to participate in any activities. ⌂ *410 Denali St., Anchorage 99501* ☎ *907/644–9980 or 800/541–9779* 🖷 *907/644–9981* ⊕ *www.denalilodge.com* ➪ *30 cabins* ⚐ *Restaurant, fishing, mountain bikes, hiking, bar; no room phones, no room TVs, no smoking* ▤ *MC, V* ⦿ *FAP* ⊗ *Closed mid-Sept.–early June.*

FodorsChoice
★

$$$ ▦ **Denali Princess Wilderness Lodge.** Views from this hotel take in the Nenana River, and rich forest colors in rooms mimic the surroundings. Complimentary shuttle service is provided to the park and railroad station. The large Summit Dining Room offers an estimable view and fine dining. Burgers and more casual fare are available at the Cruiser's Café, which can also supply picnic lunches. ⊠ *Mile 238.5, Parks Hwy., 1 mi north of park entrance* ⌂ *Box 110, Denali Park 99755* ☎ *907/683–2282, 800/426–0500 reservations* 🖷 *907/683–2545* ⊕ *www.*

princessalaskalodges.com ⌨ *353 rooms* ☆ *Restaurant, café, cable TV, outdoor hot tub, bar, meeting room; no smoking* ▤ *AE, DC, MC, V* ☺ *Closed mid-Sept.–mid-May.*

\$\$–\$\$\$ ▦ **Denali River Cabins and Cedars Lodge.** The cabins, clustered along the Nenana River, are next to McKinley Village Lodge and 6 mi south of the park entrance. A boardwalk connects the cedar-sided cabins, all with double beds, and leads down to the river. Cedars Lodge has standard hotel rooms. The management operates park excursions and a courtesy shuttle service to and from the train depot. ⌧ *Mile 231.1, Parks Hwy.* ⌂ *Box 210, Denali Park 99755* ☏ *907/683–8000 in summer, 907/459–2121 in winter, 800/230–7275 year-round* ⎙ *907/683–8040 in summer, 907/459–2160 in winter* ⊕ *www.denalirivercabins.com* ⌨ *48 rooms, 54 cabins* ☆ *Restaurant, cable TV, sauna, bar; no smoking* ▤ *AE, D, MC, V* ☺ *Closed in winter.*

\$\$ ▦ **Denali Crow's Nest Log Cabins.** These spartan, cantilevered log cabins 1 mi north of the park entrance are on a forested hillside with river and mountain views. Each has its own bath. ⌧ *Mile 238.5, Parks Hwy.* ⌂ *Box 70, Denali Park 99755* ☏ *907/683–2723 or 888/917–8130* ⎙ *907/683–2323* ⊕ *www.denalicrowsnest.com* ⌨ *39 rooms* ☆ *Restaurant, hot tub, bar, travel services; no room phones, no TV* ▤ *MC, V* ☺ *Closed Oct.–mid-May.*

\$\$ ▦ **Denali River View Inn.** This hotel sits atop a bluff overlooking the Nenana River, just north of the park entrance. Modern rooms—with a blue-and-beige color scheme, private baths, and a no-smoking policy—set above the highway rather than along it, offer a quiet experience. ⌧ *Mile 238.4, Parks Hwy.* ⌂ *Box 49, Denali Park 99755* ☏ *907/683–2663 or 866/683–2663* ⎙ *907/683–7433* ⊕ *www.denaliriverviewinn.com* ⌨ *12 rooms* ☆ *Cable TV; no room phones, no smoking* ▤ *D, MC, V* ☺ *Closed mid-Sept.–mid-May.*

\$–\$\$ ▦ **Denali Cabins.** Cabins share hot tubs and barbecue grills at this complex near the highway and 8 mi south of the park entrance. All units have private baths. Complimentary shuttle service to the park visitor center is provided. A four-day, three-night package links the cabins with the Denali Backcountry Lodge in the park. For \$875 per person (all inclusive), room and meals at the Backcountry Lodge and wildlife drives offer a more leisurely experience than the more hiking-intensive lodge visit. ⌧ *Mile 229, Parks Hwy.* ⌂ *410 Denali St., Anchorage 99701* ☏ *907/644–9980 or 800/541–9779* ⎙ *907/644–9981* ⊕ *www.denali-cabins.com* ⌨ *43 cabins* ▤ *MC, V* ☆ *Cable TV, 2 outdoor hot tubs, travel services; no smoking* ☺ *Closed mid-Sept.–mid-May.*

Camping

If you want to camp in the park, either in a tent or an RV, six campgrounds are available with varying levels of access and facilities. Three of the campgrounds—Riley Creek (near the park entrance), Savage River (Mile 12.8), and Teklanika (Mile 29)—have spaces that accommodate tents, RVs, and campers. Sanctuary River (Mile 22), Igloo Creek (Mile 34), and Wonder Lake (Mile 85) have tent spaces only. Access to these three camping areas is by shuttle bus only. The bus service runs special camper buses with extra storage space for campers with gear.

If you're camping overnight in Denali's wilderness, you must obtain a special permit (free of charge) from rangers at the visitor center. You must also choose an area to camp in. Denali's backcountry is divided into 43 units, and only a limited number of campers are allowed each night in most units. The most desirable units are near the middle of the park, in areas with open tundra and wide-open vistas. These fill up faster than the low-lying areas, many of which are moist and have high mosquito populations. The best strategy for securing good backpacking areas is to arrive a couple of days early, stay at one of the facilities near the park entrance, and check in at the backcountry desk early each morning until you can get the unit you desire.

¢ △**McKinley RV Park and Campground.** A variety of RV sites, from "basic" to those with full electricity, water, and sewer, as well as two-person tent sites are available at this campground, about 10 mi outside the park. A dump station, public showers, laundry facilities, deli, espresso bar, ice, and gasoline, diesel, and propane are also available. ⊠ *Mile 248.5, Parks Hwy., Healy 99743* ☎ *907/683–2379 or 800/478–2562* ⊕ *www. mtaonline.net/~rvcampak.*

¢ △**National Park Service Campgrounds.** Six campgrounds are inside the park: three are open to private vehicles for tent and RV camping, three are reached by shuttle bus only and are restricted to tent camping. All have toilet facilities, most have drinking water, and a couple have nearby hiking trails. All are open from late May to September, depending on snow conditions, and one is open year-round. There is a one time $4 reservation fee, in addition to the nightly rate. You can apply for a site at the visitor center, but it's wise to reserve in advance. ⌂ *Denali National Park Headquarters, Box 9, Denali Park 99755* ☎ *907/683–2294 information, 907/272–7275, 800/622–7275 reservations* ⊕ *www.nps. gov* ⊟ *AE, D, MC, V* ⊘ *All but Riley Creek (no visitor facilities) closed Oct.–late May.*

Guided Tours

Privately operated bus trips are available through **Denali Park Resorts** (☎ 907/276–7234 or 800/276–7234). The Tundra Wildlife Tour costs $75.50 and includes a boxed snack, and the shorter Natural History Tour costs $41. **Alaska Mountaineering School** (☎ 907/733–1016 ☎ 907/ 733–1362 ⊕ www.climbalaska.org) leads backpacking trips in Denali National Park and elsewhere in the state, including the Brooks Range. It also conducts 6- and 12-day mountaineering courses, mountaineering expeditions to Denali and other peaks in the Alaska Range, and climbs for all levels of climbing expertise. **Mountain Trip** (☎ 907/345–6499) guides climbing expeditions on Mt. McKinley and other Alaska Range peaks (experience required).

Besides exploring the park on your own, you can take free ranger-guided "discovery hikes" and learn more about the park's natural and human history. Rangers lead daily hikes throughout the summer. Ask about them at the visitor center.

Sports & the Outdoors

Kayaking & Rafting

Several privately owned raft and tour companies operate along the Parks Highway near the entrance to Denali, and they schedule daily rafting, both in the fairly placid areas on the Nenana and through the 10-mi-long Nenana River canyon, which contains some of the roughest white water in North America.

Alaska Raft Adventures books white-water and scenic raft trips along Nenana River through **Denali Park Resorts** (☎ 907/276–7234 or 800/ 276–7234 ☎ 907/258–3668 ⊕ www.denaliparkresorts.com). **Denali Outdoor Center** (⊠ Mile 238.5, Parks Hwy. ⌂ Box 170, Denali Park 99755 ☎ 907/683–1925 or 888/303–1925 ⊕ www.denalioutdoorcenter.com) takes visitors of all ages and abilities on rafting trips on the Nenana River. It also leads more adventurous trips down the Nenana River rapids in inflatable kayaks. No river experience is necessary. The kayaks, called Duckies, are easy to get out of, stable, and self-bailing. The company also leads a variety of rafting trips and teaches white-water kayaking. All gear is provided, including full dry suits. Mountain-bike tours and rentals are also available.

Denali Raft Adventures (☎ 907/683–2234 or 888/683–2234 🖷 907/683–1281 ⊕ www.denaliraft.com) launches its rafts several times daily on two- or four-hour, all-day, and overnight scenic and white-water raft trips on the Nenana River. Dry suits are provided. Courtesy pickup at hotels and the train depot is available. **Nenana Raft Adventures** (☎ 907/683–7238 or 800/789–7238 🖷 907/683–1618 ⊕ www.raftdenali.com) runs four- and six-hour rafting trips along Nenana River and puts all its rafters in dry suits.

Mountain Biking

Mountain biking is allowed on the park's dirt road, and no permit is required for day trips. The first 14 mi of the road is paved. Beyond the Savage River checkpoint the road is dirt and gravel and during the day is traversed by the park buses, which can make for a very dust-intensive experience. Late night, when the midnight sun is shining and buses have ceased shuttling passengers for the day, can be a rewarding time to bike and view the park's wildlife.

RICHARDSON HIGHWAY

The Richardson Highway stretches 364 mi, from Fairbanks to the all-year, ice-free port of Valdez. The Richardson takes travelers the final 98 mi from the official end of the Alaska Highway in Delta Junction to Fairbanks, but it's more than a mere connecting route. The first road built in Alaska offers fantastic mountain views while also providing excellent river and lake fishing. Named after General Wilds P. Richardson, first president of the Alaska Road Commission, the highway evolved from a pack-train trail and dogsled route that mail carriers and gold seekers followed in the early 1900s to a two-lane asphalt highway in 1957. It's a four-lane, divided highway from Fairbanks to North Pole, home of the Santa Claus House gift shop, with its towering Santa silhouette, and the North Pole Coffee Roasting Company, which provides many Fairbanks-area restaurants with fresh-roasted coffee. The Richardson also links Fairbanks with Delta's farm country and the winter and summer recreation areas near Summit Lake in the Alaska Range. At Paxson, the Richardson takes travelers to the Denali Highway, a gravel road leading west through the Alaska Range to campgrounds and fishing in the Tangle Lakes area and, later, to Denali National Park and Preserve. Fifty-six miles south of the Denali Highway, the Richardson borders Wrangell–St. Elias National Park, the largest U.S. national park.

North Pole

⑮ *15 mi southeast of Fairbanks, 85 mi northwest of Delta Junction.*

Christmas lives in North Pole all year long. Many of the street names maintain the theme, including Santa Claus Lane and St. Nicholas Drive. The prime attraction here is the **Santa Claus House Gift Shop** (⇨ Shopping, *below*), a must-see if you have young children.

Off the Richardson Highway just south of North Pole, **Chena Lakes Recreation Area** (✉ Mile 346.8 Richardson Highway) offers hiking, swimming, boating, camping, picnicking, dog mushing, and cross-country skiing. Created by the Army Corps of Engineers as part of the Chena River Flood-

Control Project, it is now operated by the local government, the **Fairbanks North Star Borough** (☎ 907/488–1655 Parks and Recreation Department).

Sports & the Outdoors

FISHING Rainbow trout are not native to the Interior, but they are stocked in some lakes. **Birch Lake** (Mile 303.5), **Harding Lake** (Mile 321.4), and **Quartz Lake** (Mile 277.8), easily accessible from the Richardson Highway between Fairbanks and Delta Junction, are good trout-fishing spots. All have campgrounds and boat-launching areas. To catch migrating salmon in the fall, head to **Salcha River**, 40 mi below Fairbanks on the Richardson Highway.

Shopping

The **Knotty Shop** (✉ Mile 332, 6565 Richardson Hwy., 32 mi south of Fairbanks, ☎ 907/488–3014 ☉ Closed Jan.–Feb. 15) has a large selection of Alaskan handicrafts as well as a mounted wildlife display and a yard full of spruce burl sculptures, including a 6-foot mosquito. It also serves soft drinks and ice cream over a counter carved from spruce burl.

The **Santa Claus House Gift Shop** (✉ Mile 349, 101 St. Nicholas Dr., 14 mi south of Fairbanks ☎ 907/488–2200 or 800/588–4078 ⊕ www. santaclaushouse.com) is hard to miss. Look for the giant Santa statue and the Christmas mural on the side of the building. The store has a variety of toys, gifts, and Alaskan handicrafts. Santa is often on duty to talk to children, and two reindeer are kept in a pen outside the store.

Delta Junction

16 *100 mi southeast of Fairbanks, 106 mi northwest of Tok, 266 mi north of Valdez.*

As the hub of the state Delta Agricultural Project, Delta Junction has the manner of a small farming town. Although the project has had many difficulties, grain and dairy farms still define the area. In summer Delta becomes a bustling rest stop for road-weary tourists traveling the Alaska and Richardson highways. Delta is also known for its access to good fishing and its proximity to the Delta Bison Range. However, don't expect to see the elusive bison, as they roam free and generally avoid people.

Where to Stay & Eat

$–$$$ ✕ **Pizza Bella.** Delicious pizzas and other Italian and American entrées compose the menu here. Italian scenic paintings and maps bring a slice of Italy to Alaska. ✉ *Mile 265* ☎ *907/895–4841 or 907/895–4524* ▭ *MC, V.*

★ ¢ ✕ **Rika's Roadhouse.** This historic landmark, part of Big Delta State Historical Park, is well worth a detour if you're nearby. There are free tours of the beautifully restored and meticulously maintained grounds, gardens, and historic buildings. The restaurant serves breakfast and lunch. The home-baked goods, including pies, muffins, cookies, sweet rolls, and breads, are delectable. ✉ *Mile 275 Alaska Hwy.* ☎ *907/895–4201* 🖷 *907/895–4787* ⊕ *www.rikas.com* ▭ *AE, D, MC, V* ☉ *Closed mid-Sept.–mid-May. No dinner.*

$ 🏨 **Alaska 7 Motel.** Cheap and clean accommodations right off the highway are what you get here—small refrigerators and color televisions with satellite service in each room. Some units have kitchenettes, and some have phones. ✉ *Mile 270.3* 🕮 *Box 1115, 99737* ☎ *907/895–4848* 🖷 *907/895–4193* ⊕ *www.alaska7motel.com* ▭ *16 rooms* △ *Some kitchenettes, refrigerators, cable TV* ▭ *AE, D, DC, MC, V.*

$ 🏨 **Kelly's Country Inn Motel.** Delta residents most often put visitors up at this downtown motel. It has clean, modern rooms, including some with kitchenettes, decorated in neutral colors. ⊠ *Mile 266.5* ⌂ *Box 849, 99737* ☎ *907/895–4667* 🖨 *907/895–4481* ⊕ *www. kellysalaskacountryinn.com* ⇨ *20 rooms* ⌂ *Some kitchenettes, some microwaves, cable TV* ⊟ *AE, D, MC, V.*

¢ ▦**Black Spruce Lodge.** Park at a nearby campground and take a 10-minute pontoon-boat shuttle ride to this comfortable, rustic lodge with 10 cabins. The lodge sits on the shore of Quartz Lake, rife with rainbow trout, arctic char, and landlocked silver salmon. If you're visiting in winter, you can rent ice houses as shelter when fishing through the ice. ⊠ *10 mi northwest of Delta Junction* ⌂ *Box 265, 99737* ☎ *907/388–2409* ⇨ *10 cabins* ⌂ *Boating, fishing, bar* ⊟ *MC, V* ⊘ *Closed Oct., Nov., and Apr.*

FORTYMILE COUNTRY

A trip through the Fortymile Country up the Taylor Highway will take you back in time more than a century—when gold was the lure that drew hardy travelers to Interior Alaska. It's still one of the few places to see active mining without leaving the road system.

The 160-mi Taylor Highway runs north from the Alaska Highway at Tetlin Junction, 12½ mi south of Delta Junction. It's a narrow rough-gravel road that winds along mountain ridges and through valleys of the Fortymile River. The road passes the tiny community of Chicken and ends in Eagle at the Yukon River. This is one of only three places in Alaska where the river can be reached by road. A cutoff just south of Eagle connects to the Canadian Top of the World Highway leading to Dawson City in the Yukon Territory. This is the route many Alaskans take to Dawson City. The highway is not plowed in winter, so it is snowed shut from fall to spring. Watch for road reconstruction.

Tok

⓱ *12 mi west of Tetlin Junction, 175 mi southwest of Dawson City.*

Loggers, miners, and hunting guides who live and work along Tok's surrounding streams or in the millions of acres of spruce forest nearby come here for supplies, at the junction of the Glenn Highway and the Alaska Highway. Each summer the city, with a resident population of fewer than 1,500, becomes temporary home to thousands of travelers, including those journeying up the Alaska Highway from the Lower 48.

If you can't travel into the Fortymile Country itself, you can catch the flavor of the region at the **Tok Main Street Visitors Center** (⊠ Mile 1314, Alaska Hwy., 99780 ☎ 907/883–5775).

Where to Stay & Eat

$–$$$$ ╳**Fast Eddy's Restaurant and Young's Motel.** It's much better than the name would indicate: the chef makes his own noodles for chicken noodle soup, and the homemade hoagies and pizza are a welcome relief from the road-house hamburgers served by most Alaska Highway restaurants. It's open 6 AM–midnight (but no soup after 5). The summer rate for the motel rooms is $79 for a double. ⊠ *Mile 1313.3 Alaska Hwy.* ☎ *907/883–4411* ⊕ *www.tokalaska.com* ⊟ *AE, D, MC, V.*

$$ ▦**Westmark Tok.** The spacious dining room of this reliable, comfortable, and well-appointed hotel is a welcome respite when you are traveling the long stretches between civilization outposts along the Alaska Highway. ⊠ *Junction of Alaska and Glenn Hwys.* ⌂ *Box 130, 99780* ☎ *907/883–5174 or 800/544–0970* 🖨 *907/883–5178* ⊕ *www. westmarkhotels.com* ⇨ *92 rooms* ⌂ *Restaurant, cable TV, bar, shop, some pets allowed* ⊟ *AE, D, DC, MC, V* ⊘ *Closed Oct.–May.*

Shopping

The **Burnt Paw** (✉ Junction of Alaska and Glenn Hwys. ☎ 907/883–4121 🖷 907/883–5680 🌐 www.burntpawcabins.com) sells jade and ivory, Alaskan ceramics, crafts, paintings, smoked salmon—even sled-dog puppies. There's also a B&B on the premises and log cabins with traditional Alaska sod roofs. In Northway, south of Tok, **Naabia Niign** (✉ Mile 1264, Alaska Hwy. ☎ 907/778–2297 🖷 907/778–2334 🌐 www.birchbaskets.com/html/northway_ak.html) is a Native-owned crafts gallery with an excellent selection of authentic, locally made birch baskets, beadwork items, and fur moccasins and gloves. The Web site tells about the Northway Athabascan people.

Chicken

18 *78 mi north of Tok, 109 mi west of Dawson City.*

Chicken was once in the heart of major gold-mining operations, and the remains of many of these works are visible along the highway. Here you'll find a country store, bar, liquor store, café, and gas station. Ask about tours of the old mining operations ($5) at the café, which hosts a salmon barbecue every afternoon from 4 PM to 8 PM. Be careful not to trespass on private property. Miners rarely have a sense of humor about trespassing.

Sports & the Outdoors

CANOEING The beautiful **Fortymile River** offers everything from a 38-mi run to a lengthy journey to the Yukon and then down to Eagle. Its waters range from easy Class I to serious Class IV (possibly Class V) stretches. Only experienced canoeists should attempt boating on this river, and rapids should be scouted beforehand. Several access points can be found off the Taylor Highway.

CanoeAlaska (✉ Box 735, Tok 99780 ☎ 907/883–2628 🌐 canoealaska.net/) has been conducting guided canoe and raft trips on Interior Alaska rivers for 25 years. Trips begin in mid-May and continue through Labor Day and range from two to eight days on rivers that vary in difficulty and remoteness. It also leads multiday Voyager trips—16 people in a 34-foot Voyager canoe—and offers weekend canoe instructional programs by ACA-certified instructors.

Eagle

19 *95 mi north of Chicken, 144 mi northwest of Dawson City.*

Eagle was once a seat of government and commerce for the Interior. An army post (Ft. Egbert) operated here until 1911, and territorial judge James Wickersham had his headquarters in Eagle until Fairbanks began to grow from its gold strike. The population peaked at 1,700 in 1898. Today it is fewer than 200.

The **Eagle Historical Society** (☎ 907/547–2325 🌐 www.eagleak.org) has a two-hour walking tour ($5) that visits seven museum buildings while regaling participants with tales of the famous people who have passed through this historic Yukon River border town. One daily tour begins at the courthouse at 9 each morning, from Memorial Day to Labor Day.

YUKON TERRITORY

Gold! That's what called Canada's Yukon Territory to the world's attention with the Klondike gold rush of 1897–98. Although Yukon gold mining today is mainly in the hands of a few large companies that go almost unnoticed by the visitor, the territory's history is alive and thriving.

Though the international border divides Alaska from Yukon Territory, the Yukon River tends to unify the region. Early prospectors, miners, traders, and camp followers moved readily up and down the river with little regard to national boundaries. An earlier Alaska strike preceded the Klondike find by years, yet Circle was all but abandoned in the stampede to the creeks around Dawson City. Later gold discoveries in the Alaskan Fortymile Country, Nome, and Fairbanks reversed that flow across the border into Alaska.

Dawson City

109 mi east of Chicken.

Dawson City today forms the heart of the Yukon's gold-rush remembrances. Since the first swell of the gold rush more than 100 years ago, many of the original buildings have disappeared, victims of fire, flood, and weathering. But enough of them have been preserved and restored to give more than a glimpse of the city's onetime grandeur. In a period of three years up to the turn of the 20th century, Dawson was transformed into the largest, most refined city north of San Francisco and west of Winnipeg. It had grand buildings with running water, telephones, and electricity. The city's population, only about 1,500 now, numbered almost 30,000 in 1899.

Regular air service to Dawson is available from Fairbanks. You can also drive the Taylor Highway route, leaving the Alaska Highway at Tetlin Junction and winding through the Fortymile Country past the little communities of Chicken and Jack Wade Camp into Canada. The border is open 8 AM to 8 PM in summer. The Canadian section of the Taylor Highway is called Top of the World Highway. Broad views of range after range of tundra-covered mountains stretch in every direction. Travelers heading north on the Alaska Highway can turn north at Whitehorse to Dawson City, then rejoin the Alaska Highway by taking the Taylor Highway south. This adds about 100 mi to the trip.

② Recapture some of Dawson City's former magnificence at the reconstructed **Palace Grand Revue** (⊠ King St. between 2nd and 3rd Aves. ☎ 867/993–6217). Performances of the Gaslight Follies are staged every night from mid-May to mid-September. The show starts at 8:30, and reservations are recommended. Admission is C$15 or C$17, depending on where you choose to sit.

② **Diamond Tooth Gertie's Gambling Hall** (⊠ Arctic Brotherhood Hall, Queen St. ☎ 867/993–5525), for adults 19 and over only, presents live entertainment and three different cancan shows three times a night, seven days a week. It is the only authentic, legal gambling establishment operating in all of the North. Yes, there really was a Diamond Tooth Gertie—Gertie Lovejoy, a prominent dance-hall queen who had a diamond between her two front teeth.

② The **Dawson City Museum** houses a variety of gold-rush exhibits. You'll also find numerous relics in the Train Shelter next door, including trains from the Klondike Road Railroad that operated along the gold creeks. ⊠ *Territorial Administration Bldg., 5th Ave.* ☎ *867/993–5291* ✆ *C$7* ⊙ *Mid-May–Labor Day, daily 10–6.*

Parks Canada leads tours of **Bonanza Creek and *Gold Dredge Number 4,*** a wooden-hull gold dredge about 10 minutes outside town. Exit the Klondike Highway at kilometer marker 74. ✛ *Mile 7.8 of Bonanza Creek*

Dawson City

Rd. ⓘ *Parks Canada National Office, 25 Eddy St., Hull, Québec K1A 0M5* ☎ *888/773–8888* ⊕ *www.parkscanada.gc.ca* ☒ *C$5* ◷ *June–mid-Sept., daily 10–4.*

Scholars still argue the precise details of the tenure of writers Robert Service and Jack London in Dawson City, but no one disputes that between Service's poems and London's short stories, the two did more than anyone else to popularize and romanticize the Yukon. **Robert Service's cabin** (☒ 8th Ave. and Hanson St. ☎ 867/993–5566 ☒ C$5) has been restored and is open for visitors from June through mid-September. **Jack London's cabin** (☒ 8th Ave. and Firth St. ☎ 867/993–6317 ◷ mid-May–mid-Sept., daily 10–1 and 2–6 ☒ C$2) is literally a stone's throw from the Service cabin. The small museum contains photos, documents, and letters from London's life and the gold-rush era. Half-hour talks are given at 11 and 2:15.

Where to Stay & Eat

$$–$$$$ ✕ **Amica's.** The menu here includes fresh thick-crust pizzas, salads, and classic southern Italian dishes modified in some instances to include local salmon and Alaskan halibut, as well as steaks and dinner salads. The restaurant has a sweeping view of the Yukon and Klondike rivers. ☒ *401 Craig St.* ☎ *867/993–6800* ☱ *MC, V.*

$$ ✕▫ **Downtown Hotel.** A large collection of artwork from area artists, including mushing scenes, accents the hotel's early-1900s decorations, and all the rooms were renovated in 2002. The Jack London Grill ($$–$$$$) is a best bet: go for the Canadian and American regional specialties, including daily appetizer, pasta, and prime rib specials. The restaurant serves three meals a day and has an outside deck for summer dining. ☒ *2nd Ave. and Queen St.* ⓘ *Box 780, Y0B 1G0* ☎ *867/993–5346, 800/661–*

0514 reservations ☒ 867/993–5076 ⊕ www.downtown.yk.net ➴ 59 rooms ⚭ Restaurant, cable TV, hot tub, bar, Internet, meeting room, airport shuttle ⊟ AE, D, DC, MC, V.

$$ ⊡ **Eldorado Hotel.** The lobby of this hotel has gold rush–era decor. During the summer tourist season, the staff dresses up in 1898-era garb. However, the modern rooms, some with kitchenettes, are outfitted with decidedly non-1898 amenities such as cable TV and remote controls. ☒ 3rd Ave. and Princess St. ☐ Box 338, Y0B 1G0 ☎ 867/993–5451, 800/764–3536 from Alaska ☒ 867/993–5256 ⊕ www.eldoradohotel. ca ➴ 52 rooms ⚭ Dining room, some kitchenettes, cable TV, bar, laundry service, Internet, meeting room, airport shuttle ⊟ AE, D, DC, MC, V.

$ ⊡ **Triple "J" Hotel.** Log cabins with kitchenettes, a central hotel, and a detached annex make up this clean, quiet compound next to Diamond Tooth Gertie's. All rooms have TVs, coffeemakers, phones, and private baths. ☒ 5th Ave. and Queen St. ☐ Box 359, Y0B 1G0 ☎ 867/993–5323 or 800/764–3555 ☒ 867/993–5030 ⊕ www.triplejhotel.com ➴ 29 rooms, 18 cabins ⚭ Restaurant, some kitchenettes, bar, meeting room, airport shuttle, some pets allowed ⊟ AE, DC, MC, V.

$ ⊡ **Westmark Dawson City.** This downtown two-story hotel is built around a central courtyard and is convenient to the sights. With its flocked wallpaper and lace curtains, the lobby recalls the days of the gold rush. While staying at the hotel enjoy a rare opportunity to have your photo taken with a genuine RCMP Mountie in Red Serge dress uniform. Rooms are decorated in soft blues and greens. ☒ 5th Ave. and Harper St. ☐ Box 420, Y0B 1G0 ☎ 867/993–5542 or 800/544–0970 ☒ 867/993–5623 ⊕ www.westmarkhotels.com ➴ 133 rooms ⚭ Dining room, bar, shop, laundry facilities, some pets allowed ⊟ AE, DC, MC, V ⊘ Closed mid-Sept.–mid-May.

Whitehorse

㉕ 337 mi southeast of Dawson City, 600 mi southeast of Fairbanks.

Near the White Horse Rapids of the Yukon River, Whitehorse began as an encampment in the late 1890s. It was a logical layover point for gold rushers heading north along the Chilkoot Trail toward Dawson to seek their fortune. The next great population boom came during World War II with the building of the Alcan—the Alaska-Canada Highway. Today this city of more than 22,000 residents is Yukon's center of commerce, communication, and transportation and the seat of the territorial government.

Besides being a great starting point for explorations of other areas of the Yukon, the town itself has plenty of diversions and recreational opportunities. You can easily spend a day exploring its museums and cultural displays—research the Yukon's mining and development history, look into the backgrounds of the town's founders, learn about its indigenous First Nations people, and gain an appreciation of the Yukon Territory from prehistoric times up to the present. You can obtain a free three-day parking permit at **City Hall** (☒ 2121 2nd Ave. ☎ 867/668–8687).

The logical place to start touring Whitehorse is the **Yukon Visitor Reception Centre,** housed in the block-long, pine-sided headquarters for Yukon Tourism. Anything to do with the Yukon can be found in the reception center. ☒ 100 Hanson St. ☎ 867/667–3084 ☒ 867/667–3546 ⊕ www. touryukon.com ⊘ May–Sept., daily 8–8; Oct.–Apr., weekdays 9–noon and 1–4:30.

The Yukon Territorial Government Building houses the **Yukon Permanent Art Collection,** a display of works by Yukon artists depicting northern people and their culture. In addition to the collection on the premises, a brochure available at the visitor center leads you on a neighborhood art walk, giving locations of galleries and art shops. ✉ *2071 2nd Ave.* ☎ *867/667–5811* ⊕ *www.yukoninfo.com/whitehorse/ytg-tour* ✉ *Free* ⊙ *Weekdays 8:30–5.*

The **MacBride Museum** is your best general introduction to the spirit and heritage of the Yukon. More than 5,000 square feet of exhibits display natural history, geology, archaeology, First Nations, Mounties in the North, the gold rush, and the city of Whitehorse. Outdoor artifacts include Sam McGee's cabin—the same Sam McGee immortalized in Robert Service's famous poem "The Cremation of Sam McGee"—the Whitehorse telegraph office, and various transportation vehicles. ✉ *1124 1st Ave. and Wood St.* ☎ *867/667–2709* 🖷 *867/633–6607* ⊕ *www. macbridemuseum.com* ✉ *C$5* ⊙ *Mid-May–Labor Day, daily 10–6; Labor Day–mid-May, Thurs.–Sat. noon–5; and by appointment.*

The **Waterfront Walkway** along the Yukon River will take you past a few stops of interest. Your walk starts on the path along the river just east of the MacBride Museum entrance on 1st Avenue. Traveling upstream (south), you'll go by the old White Pass & Yukon Route Building, on Main Street.

The former Yukon Visitor Reception Centre at the Whitehorse Airport is the home of the **Yukon Beringia Interpretive Centre,** which presents the story of the Yukon during the Ice Age. Beringia is the name given to the large subcontinental landmass of eastern Siberia and Interior Alaska and the Yukon, which were linked by the Bering Land Bridge during the Ice Age. The center unfolds extensive information on the area's prehistoric origins and pays tribute to the First Nations people and the miners who have contributed information and exhibits to the museum. The center displays large dioramas depicting the lives of animals in Ice Age Beringia and replicas of skeletons of the animals who lived there. ✉ *Mile 914, Alaska Hwy.* ☎ *867/667–8855* ⊕ *www.beringia.com* ✉ *C$6* ⊙ *May and Sept., daily 9–6; June–Aug., daily 8:30–7 and by appointment.*

★ The **SS *Klondike*,** a national historic site, is dry-docked in Rotary Park. The 210-foot stern-wheeler was built in 1929, sank in 1936, and was rebuilt in 1937. In the days when the Yukon River was the transportation link between Whitehorse and Dawson City, the *Klondike* was the largest boat plying the river. ✉ *S. Access Rd. and 2nd Ave.* ☎ *867/667–4511* ✉ *C$3* ⊙ *May–Sept., daily 9–6:30.*

If you're in Whitehorse during late summer, it's possible to see the chinook (king) salmon, which hold one of nature's great endurance records: longest fish migration in the world. The **Whitehorse Rapids Dam and Fish Ladder** has interpretive exhibits, display tanks of freshwater fish, and a platform for viewing the fish ladder. The best time to visit is August, when between 150 and 2,100 salmon (average count is 800) use the ladder to bypass the dam. ✉ *End of Nisutlin Dr.* ☎ *867/633–5965* ✉ *Free* ⊙ *June–Labor Day, daily; hrs vary, so call ahead.*

Miles Canyon, a 10-minute drive south of Whitehorse, is both scenic and historic. Although the dam below it makes the canyon seem relatively tame, it was this perilous stretch of the Yukon River that determined the location of Whitehorse as the starting point for river travel north. In 1897 Jack London won the admiration—and cash—of fellow stampeders headed north to the Klondike goldfields because of his steady hand as pilot of hand-hewn wooden boats here. You can hike on trails along the canyon or take a two-hour cruise aboard the MV *Schwatka* and experience the canyon from the waters of Lake Schwatka, which obliterated the White-horse Rapids when the dam creating the lake was built in 1959. ⊠ *Miles Canyon Rd., 2 mi south of Whitehorse* ⌖ *68 Miles Canyon Rd., White-horse, Yukon Territory Y1A 6L4* ☎ *867/668–4716* 🖷 *867/633–5574* ⊕ *www.yukon-wings.com* ⊠ *C$25* ⊘ *Cruises depart early to mid-June at 2 PM, mid-June to mid.-Aug. 2 and 4 PM, late Aug.–Sept. 2 PM.*

At **Takhini Hot Springs,** off the Klondike Highway, there's swimming in the spring-warmed water (suits and towels are available for rent), horse-back riding, areas for camping and picnicking, and a "licensed" (beer and wine) restaurant. ⊠ *Kilometer 10, Takhini Hot Springs Rd., 17 mi north of Whitehorse* ☎ *867/633–2706* ⊕ *www.takhinihotsprings.yk. ca* ⊠ *C$6.50* ⊘ *May–Sept., daily 8 AM–10 PM; call for winter hrs.*

The **Canyon City Archaeological Dig** provides a glimpse into the past of the local First Nations people. Long before the area was developed by Western civilizations, the First Nations people used the Miles Canyon area as a seasonal fish camp. The Yukon Conservation Society conducts free tours of the area twice a day in summer; it also leads walks and hikes from short, child-friendly tours to challenging five- to six-hour scram-bles on the nearby mountains. All the hikes are free and provide a great way to see the surrounding countryside with local naturalists. The so-ciety office houses a bookstore on Yukon history and wilderness and sells souvenirs, maps, and posters. ⊠ *302 Hawkins St.* ☎ *867/668–5678* ⊕ *www.yukonconservation.org* ⊠ *Free* ⊘ *Tours July–late-Aug., week-days at 10 and 2.*

The **Yukon Wildlife Preserve** provides a fail-safe way of photographing rarely spotted animals in a natural setting. Animals roaming freely here include elk, caribou, mountain goats, musk ox, bison, mule deer, and Dall and Stone sheep. Two-hour tours can be arranged through Gray Line Yukon. ⊠ *Gray Line Yukon, 208G Steele St.* ☎ *867/668–3225* 🖷 *867/667–4494* ⊕ *www.yukonweb.com/tourism/westours* ⊠ *C$21* ⊘ *Tours mid-May–mid-Sept., daily.*

Where to Stay & Eat

★ ¢–$ ✕**The Chocolate Claim.** Choose from fresh-baked breads and pastries, homemade soups and sandwiches, salads, and quiches at this charming little deli. Artwork—ranging from paintings and pottery to rugs and quilts by local artists and artisans—is on display and for sale. On sunny days you can sit outside. ⊠ *305 Strickland St.* ☎ *867/667–2202* 🖃 *MC, V* ⊘ *Closed Sun.*

$$ ✕▥**Westmark Whitehorse Hotel and Conference Center.** You can catch a nightly Klondike vaudeville show, the Frantic Follies, in summer at this full-service, comfortable hotel in the heart of downtown. The car-peted lobby has low tables and plush chairs, an espresso bar, and a beau-tiful model of the Klondike riverboat. The restaurant serves pork chops, filet mignon, salmon, and low-calorie selections. ⊠ *2nd Ave. and Wood St.* ⌖ *Box 4250, Y1A 3T3* ☎ *867/393–9700 or 800/544–0970* 🖷 *867/668–2789* ⊕ *www.westmarkhotels.com* ⇗ *176 rooms, 5 suites* ⚘ *Restaurant, in-room data ports, microwaves, cable TV with movies, hair salon, bar, shop, meeting rooms, travel services, some pets allowed* 🖃 *AE, MC, V.*

$–$$$ ▦**High Country Inn.** At this mountainside inn, you'll find tastefully ap-pointed modern rooms. Deluxe suites come with kitchenettes. Public areas are cozy, and the location is close to the SS *Klondike* and the public swim-ming pool. ⊠ *4051 4th Ave., Y1A 1H1* ☎ *867/667–4471 or 800/554–4471* 🖷 *867/667–6457* ⊕ *www.highcountryinn.yk.ca* ⇗ *95 rooms, 5* suites ☼ Restaurant, some kitchenettes, cable TV, bar, Internet, meeting room, some pets allowed ☰ AE, DC, MC, V.

Sports & the Outdoors

SLED-DOG RACE   Whitehorse and Fairbanks organize the **Yukon Quest International Sled-Dog Race** (☎ 867/668–4711) in February. The race's starting line alternates yearly between the two cities, and in 2004 it will be in Fairbanks. This is one of the longest and toughest races in the North.

HIKING   The **Kluane National Park and Reserve** (✉ Visitor Center, 119 Logan St., Haines Junction ☎ 867/634–7207), west of Whitehorse, has millions of acres for hiking. The **Yukon Conservation Society** (☎ 867/668–5678) leads hiking expeditions of varying lengths and degrees of difficulty.

INTERIOR A TO Z

To research prices, get advice from other travelers, and book travel arrangements, visit www.fodors.com.

AIR TRAVEL

Alaska Airlines and Delta Airlines fly the Anchorage–Fairbanks route. Both have connecting routes to the Lower 48 states (⇨ Air Travel *in* Smart Travel Tips A to Z for airline numbers). Air North, based in Whitehorse, has direct, scheduled air service between Alaska and Canada, flying regular runs from Fairbanks and Juneau to the Yukon Territory towns of Dawson City and Whitehorse.

In much of the Bush, federally subsidized mail runs make regular air schedules possible. From Fairbanks, you can easily catch a ride on the mail run to small, predominantly Native villages along the Yukon River or to Eskimo settlements on the Arctic coast. Frontier Flying Service has an extensive roster of scheduled flights that includes Anchorage, as well as many of the Bush villages in northwest Alaska, the Interior, and the North Slope of the Brooks Range. Larry's Flying Service has scheduled flights to more than a dozen Bush villages as well as charter service and flightseeing tours. Tanana Air Service flies freight and passengers to almost 30 villages along the Yukon and in the Interior and western Alaska. Wright Air Service flies from its Fairbanks base to Interior and Brooks Range villages. For commuter flights out of Anchorage, ERA Aviation flies to Cordova, Whitehorse, Homer, Iliamna, Kenai, Kodiak, and Valdez. Peninsula Airways serves the Aleutian and Pribilof Island groups and communities in Southwest Alaska from its base in Anchorage.

🛪 **Air North** ☎ 867/668-2228 or 800/764-0407. **ERA Aviation** ☎ 907/243-6633 or 800/866-8394 ⊕ www.era-aviation.com. **Frontier Flying Service** ☎ 907/474-0014, 800/478-6779 in Alaska ⊕ www.frontierflying.com. **Larry's Flying Service** ☎ 907/474-9169 ⊕ www.larrysflying.com. **Peninsula Airways** ☎ 907/243-2323 or 800/448-4226 ⊕ www.penair.com. **Tanana Air Service** ☎ 907/474-0301. **Wright Air Service** ☎ 907/474-0502, 800/478-0502 in Alaska.

BUS TRAVEL

The most common run is between Fairbanks and Anchorage by way of Denali National Park and Preserve. However, you can take side trips by bus or van into the Yukon Territory. For more information about bus service throughout the Interior, contact Princess Tours. Alaska Direct Bus Lines has year-round service. The Alaskon Express provides scheduled service between Whitehorse, Fairbanks, Valdez, Skagway, Denali National Park, Anchorage, and other communities en route. Haines is accessible from Skagway via water taxi.

The Park Connection provides regularly scheduled shuttle service between Seward, Anchorage, and Denali National Park mid-May to mid-September. Denali Overland Transportation serves Anchorage, Talkeetna, and Denali National Park with charter-bus and van service. Fairbanks has a city bus system. For information about schedules ask at the **Fairbanks Convention and Visitors Bureau** (⇨ Visitor Information).

🚌 **Alaska Direct Bus Lines** ☎ 907/277-6652 or 800/770-6652 has year-round service. **Alaskon Express** ☎ 907/277-5581 or 800/478-6388 ⊕ www.graylineofalaska.com. **Denali Overland Transportation** ☎ 907/733-2384 🖶 907/733-2385. **Park Connection** ☎ 907/245-0200 or 800/208-0200 ⊕ www.alaska-tour.com. **Princess Tours** ☎ 800/426-0442.

CAR RENTAL

People flying into Anchorage and renting a car can reach the Interior on the Parks Highway or the Glenn and Richardson highways. All are paved, are in good condition, and offer spectacular views. The Parks Highway route is shorter by a few miles and passes by Denali National Park and Preserve, but traffic is busier.

🚗 **National Agencies** **Avis** ☎ 907/474-0900, 800/478-2847 in Alaska, 800/331-1212. **Budget Car and Truck Rental** ☎ 907/474-0855, 800/248-0150 in Alaska. **Hertz** ☎ 907/452-4444, 907/456-4004, or 800/654-3131. **Payless Car Rental** ☎ 907/474-0177.

CAR TRAVEL

In the Interior your choices of side trips by road from Fairbanks include the Steese Highway to historic Circle on the Yukon River, with its legacy of gold mining; the Dalton Highway, across the Yukon River and along the trans-Alaska pipeline; and the Taylor Highway (closed in winter), connecting the Alaska Highway near Tok with the historic towns of Eagle on the Alaska side of the border and Dawson City, Yukon Territory, in Canada. These are mainly well-maintained gravel roads. However, summer rain can make them slick and dangerous.

Only one road connects Alaska to the Outside—the Alaska Highway. The highway starts in Dawson Creek, British Columbia, in Canada. It is paved but long, almost 1,500 mi to Fairbanks. Lots of people make this trek in the summer, so there are ample restaurants and motels along the way. Winter driving takes more planning, as many businesses and service stations shut down for the season. An alternative route through part of Canada is the Cassiar Highway, which leaves the Yellowhead Highway several miles northwest of Prince Rupert and connects to the Alaska Highway just outside Watson Lake. The Cassiar is a more scenic drive but may have long sections of gravel road. Summer road construction somewhere along the Alaska Highway is a given.

For road reports in Alaska call the State Department of Transportation in Fairbanks. For conditions in the Yukon Territory, call the Department of Community and Transportation Services.

🚧 **Department of Community and Transportation Services** ☎ 867/667-8215. **State Department of Transportation** ☎ 907/456-7623 in Fairbanks.

EMERGENCIES

🏥 **Doctors & Dentists** Dawson City (Yukon Territory): **Dawson City Nursing Station** ☎ 867/993-4444. Fairbanks: **Bassett Army Hospital** ☎ 907/353-5172 or 800/478-5172; **Fairbanks Memorial Hospital** ☎ 907/452-8181; **Medical Dental Arts Building** ☎ 907/452-1866 or 907/452-7007. Tok: **Public Health Clinic** ☎ 907/883-4101. Whitehorse (Yukon Territory): **General Hospital** ☎ 867/668-9444.

🚑 **Emergency Services** **Police, emergency assistance** ☎ 911. **Alaska State Troopers** ✉ Delta Junction ☎ 907/895-4344 ✉ Fairbanks ☎ 907/451-5100 ✉ Nenana ☎ 907/832-5554 ✉ Tok ☎ 907/883-5111. **Royal Canadian Mounted Police** ✉ Dawson Creek ☎ 250/782-5211 ✉ Whitehorse ☎ 867/667-5555.

TOURS

ADVENTURE TOURS ⬛ Tour Operators **Northern Alaska Tour Company** ✉ Box 82991, Fairbanks 99708 ☎ 907/474-8600 🖷 907/474-4767.

CANOEING ⬛ Tour Operators **CanoeAlaska** ✉ Box 735, Tok 99780 ☎ 907/883-2628.

CLIMBING ⬛ Tour Operators **Alaska-Denali Guiding** ☎ 907/733-2649. **Mountain Trip** ☎ 907/345-6499.

CRUISING ⬛ Tour Operators **Riverboat Discovery** ✉ Alaska Riverways, Dale Rd. Landing, near Fairbanks International Airport ☎ 907/479-6673 or 866/479-6673. **Yukon River Tours** ✉ 214 2nd Ave., Fairbanks 99701-4811 ☎ 907/452-7162 🖷 907/452-5063.

SIGHTSEEING ⬛ Tour Operators **Denali Park Resorts** ☎ 907/276-7234, 800/276-7234 information. **Gray Line of Alaska** ☎ 800/478-6388. **Northern Alaska Tour Company** ☎ 907/474-8600. **Princess Tours** ☎ 907/479-9660 or 800/426-0442. **Trans Arctic Circle Treks** ☎ 907/479-5451. **Westours** ☎ 907/456-7741 or 800/478-6388.

TRAIN TRAVEL

Between late May and early September, daily passenger service runs between Anchorage and Fairbanks by way of Talkeetna and Denali National Park and Preserve. You can choose more conventional and considerably less expensive seating in reconditioned coach cars with access to dining, lounge, and dome cars, operated by the Alaska Railroad. Because of the scenery, there is no such thing as a poor seat. A panorama will unfold beyond your window, with scenes of alpine meadows and snowcapped peaks and the muddy rivers and taiga forests of the Interior. If you're looking for a bit more luxury in your rail experience, passengers may ride in one of the window-dome cars with luxury seating, an outdoor viewing platform, and fine dining operated by Princess Tours. Holland America/Westours also runs rail trips in special cars that cater to their clients with a bit more personal attention and a more sumptuous menu than you'll find on the Alaska Railroad cars. However, all the Princess and Holland America cars are part of the same train and are pulled by the same engines as the "standard" AKRR cars.

⬛ **Alaska Railroad** ☎ 907/456-4155 or 800/544-0552. **Holland America/Westours** ☎ 907/456-7741 or 800/478-6388. **Princess Tours** ☎ 206/336-6000 or 800/426-0442.

VISITOR INFORMATION

⬛ Tourist Information **Alaska Public Lands Information Center** ✉ 250 Cushman St., Suite 1A, Fairbanks 99701 ☎ 907/456-0527 🖷 907/456-0514. **Alaska Department of Fish and Game** ✉ 1300 College Rd., Fairbanks 99701 ☎ 907/459-7207. **Delta Chamber of Commerce** ✉ Mile 1422, Alaska Hwy., 99737 ☎ 907/895-5068. **Fairbanks Convention and Visitors Bureau** ✉ 550 1st Ave., 99701 ☎ 907/456-5774 or 800/327-5774 🖷 907/452-4190. **Klondike Visitors Association** ✉ Front and King Sts. ✉ Box 389F, Dawson City, Yukon Territory, Canada Y0B 1G0 ☎ 867/993-5575. **Nenana Visitor Center** ✉ A and 4th Sts., 99760 ☎ 907/832-9953. **Tok Main Street Visitors Center** ✉ Mile 1314, Alaska Hwy., 99780 ☎ 907/883-5775. **Whitehorse Visitor Reception Centre** ✉ 100 Hanson St. ✉ Box 2703, Whitehorse, Yukon Territory, Canada Y1A 2C6 ☎ 867/667-3084.

THE BUSH

INCLUDING NOME, BARROW, PRUDHOE BAY & THE ALEUTIAN ISLANDS

8

FODOR'S CHOICE

Brooks Lodge, *Katmai*

Iditarod Trail Sled Dog Race, *Nome*

Living Museum of the Arctic, *Kotzebue*

McNeil River State Game Sanctuary, *near Anchorage*

St. Paul Island, *Pribilof Islands*

HIGHLY RECOMMENDED

RESTAURANTS   Fat Freddie's, *Nome*

Pepe's North of the Border, *Barrow*

HOTELS   Grand Aleutian Hotel, *Dutch Harbor*

Katmai Wilderness Lodge, *Katmai*

Peace of Selby Wilderness, *Gates of the Arctic*

Top of the World Hotel, *Barrow*

SIGHTS   Arctic National Wildlife Refuge

Becharof & Alaska Peninsula National Wildlife Refuges

Gates of the Arctic National Park & Preserve

Katmai National Park & Preserve

Wood-Tikchik State Park

Yupiit Piciryarait Cultural Center, *Bethel*

By Stanton
H. Patty

Updated by
Bill Sherwonit

ALASKANS CALL IT THE BUSH—those wild and lonely bands of territory beyond cities, towns, highways, and railroad corridors stretching from the Kodiak Archipelago, Alaska Peninsula, and Aleutian Islands in the south through the Yukon-Kuskokwim Delta and into the northern High Arctic. It is a land where caribou roam and, in its northern regions, the sun really does shine at midnight. It is a land that knows the soft footsteps of the Eskimos and the Aleuts, the scratchings of those who search for oil and gold, and the ghosts of almost-forgotten battlefields of World War II.

It is a vast, misunderstood wonderland—bleak yet beautiful, harsh yet bountiful. A look across the Arctic tundra in summer yields the miracle of bright wildflowers growing from a sponge of permafrost ice water. In the long, dark Arctic winter, a painter's-blue kind of twilight rises from the ice and snowscapes at midday. Spring and fall are fleeting moments when the tundra awakens from its winter slumber or turns briefly brilliant with autumn colors.

The Arctic is separated by the Brooks Range from the rest of the state, and the Brooks Range itself is so grand that it contains several mountain systems. Each has its own particular character, ranging from pale, softly rounded limestone mountains in the east and west to the towering granite spires and faces of the Arrigetch Peaks in the heart of the range. Large portions of the Brooks Range's middle and western sections are preserved within Gates of the Arctic National Park and neighboring Noatak National Preserve and its eastern reaches within the Arctic National Wildlife Refuge.

North of the Brooks Range, a great apron of land called the North Slope tilts gently until it slides under the Beaufort Sea and the Arctic Ocean. The vast sweep of this frozen tundra brightens each summer with yellow Arctic poppies and dozens of other wildflower species that seem to stretch into infinite distances. Permafrost has worked over this land for centuries and fragmented it into giant polygons that make a fascinating pattern when viewed from the sky.

Great herds of caribou—hundreds of thousands of them—move in slow waves across the tundra, feeding and fattening for the next winter and attempting to stay clear of wolves and grizzlies. And out on the Arctic Ocean's Beaufort Sea, polar bears, stained a light gold from the oil of seals they have killed, pose like monarchs on ice floes, swinging their heads as if warning humans to keep their distance. One of Alaska's premier wildlands, the Arctic National Wildlife Refuge protects mountain and tundra landscape important to caribou, polar bears, grizzlies, wolves, musk ox, and other Arctic wildlife.

The rivers that drain the Brooks Range have names such as Kongakut, Kobuk, and Sheenjek. These speak of the Native peoples who have lived here for thousands of years. The great Noatak River defies the Arctic's northerly drainage pattern and runs east–west, making a right-angle turn before emptying into Kotzebue (*kots*-eh-bew) Sound.

The colorful Eskimo town of Kotzebue is the jumping-off point to much of this area; it is the largest Native village in the state. Eskimo ceremonial dances are demonstrated at Kotzebue's Living Museum of the Arctic, as is the Eskimo blanket toss, a sport dating to ancient times, when Eskimo hunters were bounced high in the air so they could see across ice ridges in their search for seals and other wildlife.

Another coastal community, this one first settled by prospectors, is the former gold-rush boomtown of Nome, where you can still pan for gold.

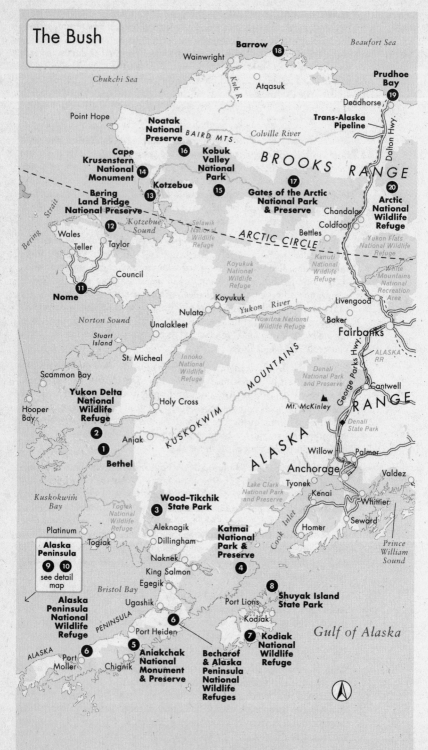

The Bush

Beaufort Sea

Chukchi Sea

Barrow 18
Wainwright
Atqasuk
Prudhoe Bay 19
Deadhorse
Point Hope
Trans-Alaska Pipeline
Noatak National Preserve
BAIRD MTS.
Colville River
BROOKS RANGE
Dalton Hwy.
16 **Kobuk Valley National Park**
Cape Krusenstern National Monument 14
Kotzebue 13
15
17 **Gates of the Arctic National Park & Preserve**
Chandalar
20 **Arctic National Wildlife Refuge**
Bering Land Bridge National Preserve
12
Kotzebue Sound
Selawik National Wildlife Refuge
ARCTIC CIRCLE
Coldfoot
Bettles
Yukon Flats National Wildlife Refuge
Wales
Teller
Taylor
Council
Koyukuk National Wildlife Refuge
Kanuti National Wildlife Refuge
White Mountains National Recreation Area
Bering Strait
11 **Nome**
Norton Sound
Koyukuk
Nulata
Yukon River
Livengood
Baker
Fairbanks
Unalakleet
Nowitna National Wildlife Refuge
Stuart Island
St. Micheal
Innoko National Wildlife Refuge
ALASKA RR
Scammon Bay
Holy Cross
MOUNTAINS
Denali National Park and Preserve
Cantwell
Hooper Bay
Yukon Delta National Wildlife Refuge
KUSKOKWIM
Mt. McKinley
RANGE
George Parks Hwy.
2
Anjak
Denali State Park
1 **Bethel**
Willow
Palmer
Kuskokwim Bay
Togiak National Wildlife Refuge
ALASKA
Anchorage
Valdez
Wood–Tikchik State Park
3
Lake Clark National Park and Preserve
Tyonek
Whittier
Platinum
Aleknagik
Kenai
Seward
Togiak
Dillingham
Katmai National Park & Preserve
Cook Inlet
Homer
Prince William Sound
Alaska Peninsula 9 10 see detail map
Naknek
King Salmon
4
Gulf of Alaska
Alaska Peninsula National Wildlife Refuge
Egegik
8 **Shuyak Island State Park**
Bristol Bay
Ugashik
Port Lions
6
Kodiak
ALASKA
Port Moller
6
5
Port Heiden
7 **Kodiak National Wildlife Refuge**
Chignik
PENINSULA
Aniakchak National Monument & Preserve
Becharof & Alaska Peninsula National Wildlife Refuges

PACIFIC OCEAN

In the spring, the going gets wild when Nome hosts a zany golf tournament with "greens" painted on the ice of the Bering Sea coast. Nome also serves as the end of the 1,049-mi Iditarod Trail Sled Dog Race, which begins in Anchorage the first Saturday in March.

Within Southwest Alaska are the highly productive wetlands of the Yukon-Kuskokwim Delta. Sloughs, ponds, marshes, mud, streams, and puddles in these flat regions near sea level can slow water travel to a standstill. Birds thrive here, and the waters teem with life. Farther south, Bristol Bay is the site of the largest salmon runs in the world. Nearby Wood-Tikchik encompasses huge lake systems within the nation's largest state park. And on the upper Alaska Peninsula, the brown bears of Katmai rule a vast national park, sharing salmon and trout streams with wary sportfishermen and always receiving the right-of-way. Also in the Southwest, the lower Alaska Peninsula and the Aleutian Islands reach well into the Pacific Ocean toward Alaska's closest point to Japan. This chain beckoned Russian explorers to Alaska in the 18th century. Along the islands, weathered onion-dome Russian Orthodox churches in Aleut villages brace against the fierce Pacific winds.

Dutch Harbor, in the Aleutians, a former U.S. Navy base pounded by Japanese bombs in 1942, is one of America's busiest commercial-fishing ports. Deep-sea trawlers and factory ships venture from here into the stormy north Pacific Ocean and the Bering Sea for harvests of bottom fish, crab, and other catches. Unalaska, an ancient Aleut village, is Dutch Harbor's across-the-bay neighbor and home to one of the oldest Russian Orthodox churches in Alaska. North of the Aleutian chain in the Bering Sea, the remote volcanic islands called the Pribilofs support immense populations of birds and sea mammals as well as two small Aleut communities, St. George and St. Paul.

The Bush also is where America's largest oil field, Prudhoe Bay, was discovered in 1968. At its peak, more than 2 million barrels a day of North Slope crude from Prudhoe and neighboring lesser basins flowed southward via the 800-mi pipeline to the port of Valdez, on Prince William Sound in South Central Alaska, to help fuel the Lower 48 states. Now the flow has diminished to about 1 million barrels per day.

As roads in the Bush are few, airplanes—from jetliners to small Bush planes—are the lifelines. Throughout Alaska you'll hear about the legendary pilots of the Far North—Noel and Sig Wien, Bob Reeve, Ben Eielson, Harold Gillam, Joe Crosson, Jack Jefford, and the others—who won their wings in the early years. They are Alaska's counterparts to the cowboy heroes of the Wild West. The Bush is where America's favorite humorist, Will Rogers, died in a crash with famed aviator Wiley Post in 1935.

Be aware that many of the Bush communities have voted to be dry areas in order to fight alcohol-abuse problems affecting Alaska's Native people. The sale and possession of alcohol is prohibited. Enforcement is strict, and bootlegging is a felony. Nome, of course, remains wet, with numerous lively saloons.

Bush Alaskans have a deep affection for their often-raw land, which is difficult to explain to strangers. They talk of living "close to nature," a cliché, perhaps, until you realize that these Alaskans reside in the Bush all year long, adapting to brutal winter weather and isolation. They have accepted the Bush for what it is: dramatic and unforgiving.

Exploring the Bush

Philosophically speaking, the Bush is more of a lifestyle than a location. Technically, it's a place in Alaska that can't be reached by road. Beginning in the southwestern part of the state, a tour of the Bush can begin in Bethel, an important Bush outpost on the Yukon-Kuskokwim Delta, surrounded by the Yukon Delta National Wildlife Refuge; off the mainland coast is the undeveloped wilderness of Nunivak Island. Next is the Alaska Peninsula, which juts out between the Pacific Ocean and the Bering Sea; here are Katmai National Park and Preserve, Aniakchak National Monument and Preserve, and the Becharof and Alaska Peninsula National Wildlife refuges. To the south of the Alaska Peninsula is the Kodiak Archipelago, where you'll find the Kodiak National Wildlife Refuge and Shuyak Island State Park; the Aleutian Islands start where the peninsula ends and sweep southwest toward Japan.

The Pribilof Islands lie north of the Aleutians, 200 mi off Alaska's coast. Head north along the Bering Sea coast and you come to Nome, just below the Arctic Circle. North of Nome is the Bering Land Bridge National Preserve. Kotzebue, just above the circle, is a coastal Eskimo town surrounded by sea and tundra and a jumping-off place for several parklands: Kobuk Valley, Noatak, Cape Krusenstern, and Gates of the Arctic (though the last is more easily reached from the town of Bettles). Barrow, another Eskimo community, sits at the very top of the state, the northernmost town in the United States. Follow the Arctic coastline eastward and you reach Deadhorse, on Prudhoe Bay, the custodian to the region's important oil and gas reserves. And east of Prudhoe Bay is the Arctic National Wildlife Refuge.

About the Restaurants

The dining options are few when traveling through Alaska's Bush; smaller communities may have only one or two eateries. Some have no restaurants at all, so be sure to check ahead of time. Restaurants are busiest during the summer peak, from June through August, but in most cases, reservations are not needed. Many places serve Alaskan seafood and locally-grown vegetables, but you can find Mexican and Asian fare in Alaska's remotest corners—from Barrow in the far north to the Aleutian Island chain in the North Pacific.

About the Hotels

As with the restaurants, lodging choices in the Bush are few. Some communities have a single hotel; the smallest have none. Others have a mix of hotels and B&Bs. As a rule, rooms are simply furnished, with few of the "extras" that you expect in urban hotels. You may have to share bathroom or kitchen facilities. Rooms go fast during the summer season, so be sure to book several months in advance. Seasoned Alaska travelers sometimes make reservations up to a year in advance.

WHAT IT COSTS					
	$$$$	**$$$**	**$$**	**$**	**¢**
RESTAURANTS	over $25	$20–$25	$15–$20	$10–$15	under $10
HOTELS	over $225	$175–$225	$125–$175	$75–$125	under $75

Restaurant prices are for a main course at dinner. Hotel prices are for two people in a standard double room in high season, excluding service charges and tax.

8

Because of its immense size—the Bush encompasses a third of the state—and the expense of transportation, it's best to give yourself at least a week and preferably more when exploring Alaska's rural regions. But even with a week or two, you'll see no more than a small slice of Alaska's wildest and most remote parts. The easiest way to go, of course, is through a package tour. For those with shorter amounts of time, many companies offer one-, two-, or three-day tours to Arctic communities.

Numbers in the text correspond to numbers in the margin and on the Bush and Alaska Peninsula, Aleutians, and Pribilof Islands maps.

If you have
3 days

Visit ⬚ **Katmai National Park and Preserve**'s ➍ Brooks Falls and Camp, where brown bears can be seen fishing for salmon, and take the bus tour to the Valley of Ten Thousand Smokes, formed in 1912 by a giant volcanic eruption. Or visit ⬚ **Dutch Harbor** ➒ and Unalaska in the Aleutian Islands, where guided fishing and wildlife-watching trips can be arranged. If you're visiting in winter, consider ⬚ **Bethel** ➊, which hosts one of the state's premier dogsled races, the Kuskokwim 300, each January and the Camai Dance Festival in late March.

If you have
5 days

On guided wildlife tours, visit ⬚ **St. Paul Island** ➓, one of the Pribilof Islands in the Bering Sea. Or if fishing is your thing, stay at one of the region's many lodges; you'll find several in and around ⬚ **Katmai National Park and Preserve** ➍ and **Wood-Tikchik State Park** ➌.

If you have
7 days
or
more

Take a kayaking trip on ⬚ **Shuyak Island State Park** ➑ while staying in comfortable public-use cabins; or go with guides on a river-floating trip through the **Arctic National Wildlife Refuge** ⓴, where you're likely to see caribou, grizzlies, lots of birds, and perhaps even musk ox or wolves. In late winter or early spring, consider a mushing expedition through ⬚ **Gates of the Arctic National Park and Preserve** ⓱, but be prepared for harsh weather and rustic tent camping.

Timing

The best time to visit is from June through August, when the weather is mildest (though you should still anticipate cool, wet, and sometimes stormy weather), daylight hours are longest, and the wildlife is most abundant.

SOUTHWEST

The Southwest region encompasses some of Alaska's most remote, inaccessible, and rugged land- and seascapes. Ranging from the Alaska Peninsula down through the Aleutian chain, it also includes many islands within the Bering Sea, among them the Pribilof Islands, as well as the Bristol Bay watershed, the Kodiak Archipelago, and the Yukon-Kuskokwim Delta. A place of enormous biologic richness, it harbors many of North America's largest breeding populations of seabirds and waterfowl and also supports the world's densest population of brown bears and the world's greatest salmon runs. Given all this richness, it's no surprise to learn that Southwest Alaska has some of Alaska's premier parklands and refuges, from Katmai National Park to Aniakchak National Monument and the Kodiak National Wildlife Refuge. Here, too, are dozens of rural communities, most of them small, remote Native villages whose residents continue to lead subsistence-gathering lifestyles.

Bethel

❶ *400 mi west of Anchorage.*

Spread out on the tundra along the Kuskokwim River, Bethel is a frontier town with 6,000 or so residents, originally established by Moravian missionaries in the late 1800s. One of rural Alaska's most important trading centers, it is a hub for more than 50 Native villages in a region roughly the size of the state of Oregon. The surrounding lowland tundra is a rich green in summer and turns fiery shades of red, orange, and yellow in autumn, when plants burst with blueberries, cranberries, blackberries, and salmonberries. Salmon, arctic grayling, and Dolly Varden trout fill the area's many lakes, ponds, and streams, providing excellent fishing just a few miles outside town. The wetlands are also important breeding grounds for many varieties of birds.

The town is also the northernmost freshwater port for oceangoing vessels. Among its businesses are radio and television stations, a theater, a hotel, two banks, a credit union, a newspaper, two colleges (including a newly founded tribal college), and the largest Alaska Native Health Service field hospital in the state, which is contracted to the tribally owned Yukon-Kuskokwim Health Corporation.

Each year, on the last weekend in March, Bethel hosts a regional celebration called the Camai Dance Festival (in Yup'ik, *camai* means "hello"). Held in the high school gym, which is filled to capacity for the three-day event, this festival draws dance groups from dozens of villages.

★ The **Yupiit Piciryarait Cultural Center** showcases artifacts and artwork of three Native cultures: Athabascan, Cup'ik, and Yup'ik. In its three galleries you'll find historic and prehistoric treasures: masks, statues, and carvings in ivory, baleen, and whalebone. Two permanent collections include numerous implements and tools used in traditional subsistence-gathering lifestyles. A small gift shop has locally made artwork for sale, including water-grass baskets, wooden spirit masks, ivory-handle knives, grass and reindeer-beard dance fans, yo-yos, dolls, and seal-gut raincoats. ⊠ *Cultural Center, 420 Eddie Hoffman Hwy.* ☎ *907/543–1819* ⊕ *www. avcp.org* ✉ *Free (donations requested)* ☉ *Tues.–Fri. 1:30–4:30.*

Where to Stay & Eat

$–$$ ✕ **Shogun.** This rural café-style restaurant specializes in Chinese food, with daily lunch and dinner specials. It also serves Japanese and Italian dishes, plus American-style steaks and seafood. ⊠ *473 Ridgecrest St.* ☎ *907/543–2272* ▭ *MC, V.*

$$ ▣ **Bentley's Porter House B&B.** Hospitality is never in short supply at this two-story bed-and-breakfast in downtown Bethel. Rooms are decorated according to theme, including African, Southwestern U.S., and English Countryside. Several overlook the Kuskokwim River. Besides those in the main inn, rooms are available in a nearby duplex and cottage. ⊠ *624 1st Ave.* ✆ *Box 529, 99559* ☎ *907/543–3552* 🖨 *907/543–3230* 🛏 *30 rooms share 14 baths* ♿ *Cable TV, Internet, some pets allowed; no a/c, no smoking* ▭ *AE, D, DC, MC, V* ⦿*BP.*

$–$$ ▣ **Pacifica Guest House.** Three detached buildings make up this inn, which provides a quiet stay and Bush-savvy owners who provide insightful tips. Alaskan crafts and artwork adorn the modern rooms, some of which

8

Fishing

Alaska's Bush regions offer some of the state's premier sportfishing. Southwest Alaska is especially well known around the world for its remarkable salmon migrations and healthy populations of native rainbow trout. The easiest way to find the fish is to arrange for a guided trip—many sportfishing guides combine fishing and river-floating adventures—or visit a lodge. The Alaska Department of Fish and Game, National Park Service, and U.S. Fish and Wildlife Service can provide lists of guides and outfitters who operate in the region's parks and refuges.

Native Culture

More and more, Native communities throughout Alaska are reconnecting with and celebrating their cultural traditions. Nowhere is this movement stronger than in the Bush. At the same time, many rural communities are recognizing the value of tourism to local economies, and a growing number of cultural tours and activities are being offered in rural villages—from drumming and dancing to arts-and-crafts exhibits and potlatches, which are traditional Native gatherings with songs, food, and gift-giving.

Shopping

Alaska's Arctic is known for Eskimo arts, and Southwest communities such as Bethel feature the artwork of the Athabascan, Cup'ik, Yup'ik Eskimo cultures. Artwork ranges from wildlife or human figures carved from walrus ivory, baleen, and whale bone to grass baskets and bracelets and other jewelry fashioned from ivory, gold, Alaska jade, and other local materials. The Marine Mammals Protection Act permits the purchase of walrus-ivory goods from Native Alaskans. Bethel, Nome, Kotzebue, and Barrow all have reputable gift shops. Prices range from under $20 for tiny earrings to hundreds of dollars for ceremonial masks and other major pieces.

Wildlife Viewing

From the brown bears of Katmai National Park to the seals and seabirds of the Pribilofs and the caribou herds and wolf packs of the Arctic, the Bush in spring and summer is a place of great activity. The Alaska Peninsula has Alaska's—and the world's—largest gathering of brown bears, which congregate at clear-water streams to feed on the huge runs of salmon that return each summer. Millions of sea- and shorebirds breed in the Aleutian and Pribilof islands annually, and all sorts of marine mammals—sea lions, seals, sea otters, porpoises, and whales—inhabit coastal waters. Two of the continent's largest caribou herds, the Western Arctic and Porcupine, roam across the Arctic's mountains, valleys, and coastal plains. By far the easiest way for most travelers to see wildlife is to participate in guided tours, though independent travelers can also expect to see abundant animals if they do their homework before visiting Alaska and plan trips well in advance.

---

share a bath. Next door in a solarium, Diane's Café serves Alaska salmon, halibut, steaks, roasts, and a variety of vegetarian and heart-healthy meals. ⊠ 1220 Hoffman Hwy. ⌖ Box 1208, 99559 ☎ 907/543-4305 🖷 907/543-3403 or 907/543-5715 ⇨ 30 rooms, 14 with bath ⌂ Restaurant, cable TV, library, meeting room; no a/c, no pets, no smoking ▭ AE, D, DC, MC, V.

Shopping

The **Moravian Bookstore** (✉ 301 3rd Ave. ☎ 907/543–2474) stocks arts and crafts as well as books about religion and Eskimo culture. It is open Monday–Saturday 11–5:30.

> **off the beaten path**
>
> **NUNIVAK ISLAND –** Due west of Bethel, and separated from the Yukon-Kuskokwim Delta by Etolin Strait, Nunivak Island is an important wildlife refuge. Part of the **Yukon Delta National Wildlife Refuge,** this site is noted for its large herd of reindeer, a transplanted herd of musk ox, and the Eskimo settlement of Mekoryuk.
>
> For information on the island, contact the **U.S. Fish and Wildlife Service** (☎ 907/543–3151 ⊕ www.r7.fws.gov) in Bethel. Visitors, lured by fine ivory carvings, masks, and items knit from qiviut (musk ox) wool, should check with **ERA Aviation** (☎ 800/866–8394 ⊕ www.eraaviation.com) about accommodations, which are limited and far from deluxe.

Yukon Delta National Wildlife Refuge

② *Surrounds Bethel.*

At 20 million acres, Yukon Delta is the nation's largest wildlife refuge; nearly one-third of that acreage is water, in the form of lakes, sloughs, bogs, creeks, and rivers. The two most significant of these waters are the **Yukon** and **Kuskokwim** rivers, Alaska's two largest. As they flow toward the Bering Sea, these rivers carry huge amounts of sediment; over the millennia, the sediments have formed an immense delta that serves as critical breeding and rearing grounds for an estimated 100 million shorebirds and waterfowl. More than 50 species of birds nest here, traveling from nearly every state and province in North America and from all of the continents that border the Pacific Ocean. All of North America's cackling Canada geese and more than half the continent's population of black brant are born here. Other birds making the annual pilgrimage to the Yukon Delta refuge include emperor geese, tundra swans, gulls, jaegers, cranes, loons, snipe, sandpipers, and the rare bristle-thighed curlew.

Not all of the refuge is flat wetlands. North of the Yukon River are the Nulato Hills, site of the 1.3-million-acre **Andreafsky Wilderness area,** which includes both forks of the Andreafsky River, one of Alaska's specially designated Wild and Scenic Rivers. Rainbow trout, arctic char, and grayling flourish in upland rivers and creeks; pike, sheefish, and burbot thrive in lowland waters. These abundant waters are also spawning grounds to five species of Pacific salmon. Several species of mammals, ranging from black and grizzly bears to moose, beaver, mink, and arctic foxes, inhabit the refuge's lands. Occasionally, wolves venture into the delta's flats from neighboring uplands.

Given the abundance of fish and wildlife, it's not surprising that the delta holds special importance to residents of Bethel and other villages in the region. Yup'ik Eskimos have lived here for thousands of years; despite modern encroachment, the Eskimos continue their centuries-old subsistence-gathering lifestyle.

Recreational use of the refuge includes observing wildlife, hiking, boating, and fishing. Access is by boat or aircraft only, and, as in most of Alaska's other remote wildlands, visitor facilities are minimal. Refuge staff can provide tips on recreational opportunities and guides and outfitters who operate in the refuge. ☐ *Box 346, Bethel 99559* ☎ *907/ 543–3151* ⊕ *www.r7.fws.gov.*

Wood-Tikchik State Park

★ ❸ *150 mi southeast of Bethel, 300 mi southwest of Anchorage.*

In the Bristol Bay region, Wood-Tikchik State Park—the nation's largest state park—is a water-based wildland despite its inland setting. Two separate groups of large, idyllic, interconnected lakes, as much as 45 mi long, dominate the park. Besides the many large lakes and clear-water streams that fill its 1.55 million acres, the park's landscape includes rugged mountains, remnant glaciers, forested foothills, and vast expanses of lowland tundra. Everything from grizzlies and caribou to porcupines, eagles, and loons inhabits the park's forests and tundra, but Wood-Tikchik is best known for its fish. Its lakes and streams are critical spawning habitat for five species of Pacific salmon; they also support healthy populations of rainbow trout, arctic char, arctic grayling, and northern pike. The abundance of fish attracts anglers from around the world. Boaters, including rafters and kayakers, also come to explore its expansive and pristine waterways.

Managed as a wild area, Wood-Tikchik has no maintained trails and few other visitor amenities. Most of its campsites are primitive, and those who plan to explore the park should be experienced in backcountry travel and camping. Access is by either boat or air. *Mid-May–Sept.* ⬦ *Box 3022, Dillingham 99576* ☎ *907/842-2375* ✉ *Oct.–mid-May* ⬦ *550 W. 7th Ave., Suite 1380, Anchorage 99501* ☎ *907/269-8698* ⊕ *www.alaskastateparks.org.*

You can also travel from Dillingham, the town closest to Wood-Tikchik, by boat or by air to view the walruses offshore on Round Island within **Walrus Islands State Game Sanctuary.** ⬦ *Box 1030, Dillingham 99576-1030* ☎ *907/842-2334* ▤ *907/842-5514* ⊕ *www.state.ak.us/adfg/wildlife/region2/refuge2/rnd-isl.htm.*

Katmai National Park & Preserve

★ ❹ *100 mi southeast of Wood-Tikchik, 290 mi southwest of Anchorage.*

For an extraordinary perspective on the awesome power of volcanoes, visit the 4-million-acre Katmai National Park and Preserve. In this wild, remote area at the northern end of the Alaska Peninsula, moose and almost 30 other species of mammals, including foxes, lynx, and wolves, share the landscape with bears fishing for salmon from stream banks, rivers, and along the coast. At the immensely popular **Brooks Falls and Camp,** you can be sure of seeing brown bears when the salmon are running in July. No special permits are required here, though there is a $10 day-use fee at Brooks. Ducks are common along the park's rivers, lakes, and outer coast; so are whistling swans, loons, grebes, gulls, and shorebirds. Bald eagles perch on rocky pinnacles by the sea. More than 40 species of songbirds alone can be seen during the short spring and summer season. Marine life abounds in the coastal area, with Steller's sea lions and hair seals often observed on rock outcroppings.

Compared with Denali National Park, Katmai is much more remote and primitive, but therein lies part of the park's appeal. The first visitors to the Katmai area arrived more than 4,000 years ago. Some evidence exists, in fact, that Native Alaskan people inhabited Katmai's eastern edge for at least 6,000 years. On the morning of June 1, 1912, a 2,700-foot mountain called **Novarupta** erupted. The earth shook in violent tremors for five straight days. When the quakes subsided, rivers of white-hot ash poured into the valley. A foot of ash fell on Kodiak Island, 100 mi away. Winds carried the ash to eastern Canada and as far as Texas. While Novarupta was belching pumice and scorching ash, another explosion occurred 6 mi east. The mountaintop peak of **Mt. Katmai** collapsed, creating a chasm almost 3 mi long and 2 mi wide. The molten andesite that held up Mt. Katmai had rushed through newly created fissures to Novarupta and was spewed out. Sixty hours after the first thunderous blast, more than 7 cubic mi of volcanic material had been ejected, and the green valley lay under 700 feet of ash. Everyone fled from Katmai and other villages; no one was killed.

By 1916 things had cooled off. A National Geographic expedition led by Dr. Robert F. Griggs reached the valley and found it full of steaming fumaroles, creating a moonlike landscape. The report on what Griggs dubbed the **Valley of Ten Thousand Smokes** inspired Congress in 1918 to set it and the surrounding wilderness aside as a national monument. Steam spouted in thousands of fountains from the smothered streams and springs beneath the ash and gave the valley its name. Although the steam has virtually stopped, an eerie sense of earth forces at work remains, and several nearby volcanoes still smolder.

The Native peoples never returned to their traditional village sites, but many now live in other nearby communities. They are joined by sightseers, anglers, hikers, and other outdoors enthusiasts who migrate to the Katmai region each summer. Fish and wildlife are plentiful, and a few "smokes" still drift through the volcano-sculpted valley.

No roads lead to the national park, at the base of the Alaska Peninsula. Planes wing from Anchorage along Cook Inlet, rimmed by the lofty, snowy peaks of the Alaska Range. They land at **King Salmon,** near fish-famous Bristol Bay, where passengers transfer to smaller floatplanes for the 20-minute hop to **Naknek Lake** and Brooks Camp. Travel to Brooks from King Salmon is also possible by boat. You are required to check into the park ranger station, next to Brooks Lodge, for a mandatory bear talk.

From Brooks Lodge, a daily tour bus with a naturalist aboard makes the 23-mi trip through the park to the **Valley Overlook.** Hikers can walk the 1½-mi trail for a closer look at the pumice-covered valley floor. (Some consider the return climb strenuous.)

The Katmai area is one of Alaska's premier sportfishing regions. It's possible to fish for rainbow trout and salmon at the **Brooks River,** though seasonal closures have been put in place to prevent conflicts with bears, and only fly-fishing is permitted. For those who would like to venture farther into the park, seek out the two other backcountry lodges, Grosvenor and Kulik, set in prime sportfishing territory, or contact fishing-guide services based in King Salmon. A short walk up the Brooks River brings you to Brooks Falls, where salmon can be seen from a viewing platform (on a trail and boardwalk separated from the river to avoid confrontations with bears) as they leap a 6-foot barrier. ⊘ *National Park Service, Box 7, King Salmon 99613* ☎ *907/246–3305* ⊕ *www.nps.gov/katm.*

At the northern end of the Alaska Peninsula, 200 mi southwest of Anchorage, **McNeil River State Game Sanctuary** was established in 1967 to protect the world's largest gathering of brown bears. The main focus is McNeil Falls, where bears come to feed on chum salmon returning to spawn. During the peak of the chum run (July to mid-August) dozens of brown bears congregate at the falls. As many as 30 to 70 bears, including cubs, have been observed along the river in a single day. No more than 10 people a day, always accompanied by one or two state biologists, are allowed to visit bear-viewing sites from June 7 through August 25. Because demand is so high, an annual drawing is held in mid-March to determine permit winners. Applications must be received by March 1 to be eligible. Nearly all visitors fly into McNeil sanctuary on floatplanes. Most arrange for air-taxi flights out of Homer, on the Kenai Peninsula. Once you are in the sanctuary, all travel is on foot. ⊠ *Alaska Department of Fish and Game, Division of Wildlife Conservation, 333 Raspberry Rd., Anchorage 99518-1599* ☎ *907/267–2182* ⊕ *www.wc.adfg.state.ak.us/mcneil.*

Where to Stay

All of the four lodges below are on inholdings within Katmai National Park. Three are inland, and Katmai Wilderness Lodge is on the remote outer coast.

$$$$
FodorsChoice ★
Brooks Lodge. All the attractions of Katmai National Park are at this lodge's doorstep: world-class fly-fishing for rainbow trout, lake trout, arctic grayling, and salmon; brown-bear viewing; and tours to the Valley of Ten Thousand Smokes. Accommodations are in detached modern cabins adorned with Alaskan artwork; they accommodate two to four people. The cabins surround the main lodge, which has a spectacular view of aquamarine Naknek Lake; it has a circular stone fireplace and dining area where buffet-style meals are served three times daily. ⊠ *Katmailand, 4125 Aircraft Dr., Anchorage 99502* ☎ *907/243–5448 or 800/544–0551* 🖷 *907/243–0649* ⊕ *www.katmainationalpark.com* 🛏 *16 cabins* ⚐ *Dining room, lake, boating, fishing, hiking, bar; no a/c, no room phones, no room TVs, no pets* ☰ *MC, V* ☉ *Closed mid-Sept.–May.*

$$$$
Grosvenor Lodge. Once you've arrived at this remote Katmai National Park lodge, reachable only by floatplane, you have access by motorboat to numerous rivers and streams filled with sport fish. The lodge can accommodate six people in three cabins, which share a separate bathhouse. The main lodge houses a kitchen, lounging area, and bar and has an excellent view of Grosvenor Lake. Three-, four-, and seven-night price packages include airfare from Anchorage, meals, lodging, and guiding. ⊠ *Katmailand, 4125 Aircraft Dr., Anchorage 99502* ☎ *907/243–5448 or 800/544–0551* 🖷 *907/243–0649* ⊕ *www.katmailand.com* 🛏 *3 cabins with shared baths* ⚐ *Dining room, lake, boating, fishing, bar, travel services; no a/c, no room TVs, no room phones, no pets* ☰ *MC, V* ☉ *Closed Oct.–May* ⋈ *FAP.*

★ **$$$$**
Katmai Wilderness Lodge. Built on land owned by the Russian Orthodox Church, this rustic lodge straddles the rugged outer coast of Katmai National Park, along the shores of Kukak Bay. Mountains, coastal flats, and the waters of Shelikof Strait surround the log cabin–style lodge. The primary recreational activities include bear viewing, sea kayaking, and fishing for halibut and salmon. You may stay from three nights to a week or more. Price includes a round-trip flight from Kodiak, meals, lodging, and guide services. ⚐ *Box 4332, Kodiak 99615* ☎ *800/488–8767* 🖷 *907/486–6798* ⊕ *www.katmai-wilderness.com* 🛏 *7 rooms* ⚐ *Dining room, boating, fishing, travel services; no a/c, no room phones, no room TVs, no pets* ☰ *No credit cards* ☉ *Closed Oct.–mid-May* ⋈ *FAP.*

$$$$
Kulik Lodge. Positioned along the gin-clear Kulik River, between Nonvianuk and Kulik lakes, this remote wilderness lodge is reachable only by floatplane. It accommodates up to 28 anglers and is popular as a base for fly-out fishing to hot spots in the surrounding Katmai wilderness. Guests stay in two- or four-person cabins with electricity and private baths. In the evening, when fishing's done for the day, you gather in the spruce lodge, which has a large stone fireplace, dining area, and bar. Three-, four-, or seven-night packages include airfare from Anchorage, meals, lodging, and guiding. ⊠ *Katmailand, 4125 Aircraft Dr., Anchorage 99502* ☎ *907/243–5448 or 800/544–0551* 🖷 *907/243–0649* ⊕ *www.kuliklodge.com* 🛏 *12 cabins* ⚐ *Dining room, lake, boating, fishing, bar,*

travel services; no a/c, no room phones, no room TVs, no pets ⊟ *MC,*
V ⊙ *Closed mid-Oct.–May* ⏐⊙⏐ *FAP.*

¢ ⚠ **Brooks Campground.** This National Park Service campground is a short
walk from Brooks Lodge, where campers can pay to eat and shower.
There are designated cooking and eating shelters, latrines, well water,
and a storage cache to protect food from the ever-present brown bears.
Reservations are required. ⓘ *Katmai National Park, Box 7, King*
Salmon 99613 ☎ *907/246–3305, 800/365–2267 reservations* ⊕ *www.*
nps.gov/katm ⊟ *D, MC, V* ⊙ *Closed mid-Sept.–May.*

Guided Tours

Katmai Air Services (☎ 907/246–3079 in King Salmon summer only, 800/
544–0551 in Anchorage ⊕ www.katmailand.com) can arrange flightseeing tours of the park. **Katmailand** (✉ 4125 Aircraft Dr., Anchorage
99502 ☎ 907/243–5448 or 800/544–0551 🖷 907/243–0649 ⊕ www.
katmailand.com) assembles packages to Katmai National Park.

Aniakchak National Monument & Preserve

⑤ *100 mi southwest of Katmai National Park.*

Aniakchak, an extraordinary living volcano, rises to the south of Katmai. It has one of the largest calderas in the world, with a diameter av-
eraging 6 mi across and the small **Surprise Lake** within it. Although
Aniakchak last erupted in 1931, the explosion that formed the enormous crater occurred before history was written. Because the area is not
glaciated, geologists place the blowup after the last Ice Age. It was literally a world-shaking event. Marking the volcano's significance, Congress in 1980 established the 586,000-acre Aniakchak National
Monument and Preserve.

This is wild and forbidding country, with a climate that brews mist, clouds,
and winds of great force much of the year. Although the **Aniakchak River**
(which drains Surprise Lake) is floatable, it has stretches of Class III and
IV white water navigable only by expert river runners, and you must
travel through open ocean waters to reach the nearest community, Chignik Bay (or get picked up by plane, along the coast); this makes the run
an ambitious undertaking. An alternative way to enjoy Aniakchak is to
wait for a clear day and fly to it in a small plane able to land you on
the caldera floor or on Surprise Lake. However you choose to see it, it's
an unforgettable experience. But be aware that there are no trails, campgrounds, ranger stations, or other visitor facilities here; you must be prepared to be self-sufficient.

Aniakchak is both remote and expensive to reach. The only easy access
is by air, usually from the town of King Salmon. Thus few people visit
this spectacular place—and those who do are likely to have the caldera
all to themselves. ⓘ *Aniakchak National Monument and Preserve,*
Box 7, King Salmon 99613 ☎ *907/246–3305* ⊕ *www.nps.gov/ania.*

Becharof & Alaska Peninsula National Wildlife Refuges

★ ⑥ *Adjacent to Aniakchak National Monument and Preserve, 250 to 450*
mi southwest of Anchorage.

Stretching along the southern edge of the Alaska Peninsula, these two
refuges encompass nearly 6 million acres of towering mountains, glacial
lakes, broad tundra valleys, and coastal fjords. Volcanoes dominate the
landscape—14 in all, including 9 considered active. **Mt. Veniaminov** last
erupted in 1993. Other glimpses of volcanic activity include **Gas Rocks,**

where gases continually seep through cracks in granitic rocks, and **Ukrinek Marrs,** a crater that bears the marks of a violent eruption in 1977.

Besides being known for their rugged volcanic landscape, these two refuges are best known for abundant wildlife. More than 220 species of resident and migratory wildlife seasonally inhabit the region, including 30 land and 11 marine mammals, nearly 150 varieties of birds, and 35 species of fish. Caribou, wolves, and moose roam the region's tundra; sea lions, seals, seabirds, and waterfowl thrive along the rocky shores; and bald eagles and falcons nest on craggy cliffs above the coast. You'll find brown bears nearly everywhere, from coastal lowlands to high mountain ridges.

Becharof Lake, at 35 mi long and up to 15 mi wide, is the second-largest lake in Alaska (behind Lake Iliamna). Fed by two rivers and 14 major creeks, it serves as a nursery to the world's second-biggest run of salmon. **Ugashik Lakes** are known for their salmon and trophy grayling. The world-record grayling, nearly 5 pounds (most grayling weigh a pound or less), was caught at Ugashik Narrows in 1981.

Remote and rugged, with weather that is frequently stormy, the Becharof and Alaska Peninsula refuges draw mostly anglers and hunters; however, backpackers, river runners, and mountain climbers also occasionally visit. No visitor facilities are available here, and the only access is by boat or plane. Most visitors begin their trips in King Salmon and use guides or outfitters. *Box 277, King Salmon 99613* ☎ *907/246–3339* ⊕ *www.r7.fws.gov.*

Kodiak National Wildlife Refuge

❼ *50 mi south of Katmai National Park, 300 mi southwest of Anchorage.*

The 1.9-million-acre Kodiak National Wildlife Refuge lies mostly on Kodiak Island and partly on neighboring Afognak and Uganik islands, in the Gulf of Alaska. All are part of the Kodiak Archipelago, separated from Alaska's mainland by the often stormy Shelikof Strait. Within the refuge are rugged mountains, tundra meadows and lowlands, thickly forested hills, lakes, marshes, and hundreds of miles of pristine coastland. No place in the refuge is more than 15 mi from the ocean. The weather here is generally wet and cool, and storms born in the North Pacific often bring heavy rains.

Dozens of species of birds inhabit the refuge each spring and summer, including Aleutian terns, horned puffins, black oystercatchers, ravens, ptarmigan, and chickadees. At least 200 pairs of bald eagles live on the islands year-round, nesting on shoreline cliffs and in tall trees. Seeing the Kodiak brown bears—the world's largest carnivores, along with polar bears—weighing only 1 pound at birth but up to 1,500 pounds when full grown, is worth the trip to this rugged country. When they emerge from their dens in spring, the bears feed on sedges and grasses but become fish eaters when salmon return in early summer. In fall, the bears depend heavily on Kodiak's berries. Kodiak's brown bears share the refuge with only a few other land mammals native to the archipelago: red fox, river otter, short-tailed weasel, and tundra vole.

Kodiak's waters are valuable spawning grounds for five species of Pacific salmon, which return to the refuge in a series of runs that begin in May and last into October. Other resident species include rainbow trout, steelhead, Dolly Varden, and arctic char. The abundance of fish—and bears—makes the refuge popular with anglers, hunters, and wildlife watchers. The only access here is by boat or plane. Refuge staff will provide lists of guides, outfitters, and air taxis. ⊠ *1390 Buskin River Rd., Kodiak 99615* ☎ *907/487–2600* ⊕ *www.r7.fws.gov.*

¢ ⊞ **Kodiak Refuge Public-Use Cabins.** It's possible to rent one of seven recreation cabins (accessible by floatplane or boat) within the refuge for up to seven days (longer in the off-season). Set along the coast and on inland lakes, the cabins include bunks with mattresses, kerosene heaters, tables, and benches. Reservations are awarded through quarterly lotteries, held on the first of January, April, July, and October. The cabins on inland lakes are usually not accessible in winter. ✉ *1390 Buskin River Rd., Kodiak 99615* ☎ *907/487–2600* ⊕ *www.r7.fws.gov* ⤙ *7 cabins* ⚠ *Reservations essential* ⊟ *No credit cards.*

Shuyak Island State Park

❽ *50 mi north of Kodiak Island.*

The 46,000-acre Shuyak Island State Park is one of the newest—and most overlooked—units in the state parks system. At the northern end of the Kodiak Archipelago, it's accessible only by plane or boat. Its rugged outer coastline is balanced by a more protected system of interconnected bays, channels, and passages that make the park a favorite with sea kayakers. It also offers excellent wildlife viewing, especially for seabirds and sea mammals, and top-notch sportfishing for salmon. Wildlife ranges from Sitka black-tailed deer and brown bears to sea otters, sea lions, bald eagles, puffins, and whales. The park has four public-use cabins but no developed campgrounds; limited hiking trails pass through old-growth coastal rain forest. ✉ *Alaska State Parks, Kodiak District Office, 1400 Abercrombie Dr., Kodiak 99615* ☎ *907/486–6339* ⊕ *www.alaskastateparks.org.*

¢ ⊞ **Alaska State Parks Cabins.** Alaska State Parks maintains four recreational public-use cabins on Shuyak Island. All are accessible by boat or plane only. The cabins may be rented for up to seven days and hold up to eight people. Each has a woodstove, propane lights, hot plate, four bunks, outside shower and wash area, cooking utensils, and pit toilets. You can make reservations up to six months in advance. ✉ *Alaska State Parks, Kodiak District Office, 1400 Abercrombie Dr., Kodiak 99615* ☎ *907/486–6339* ▤ *907/486–3320* ⊚ *DNR Public Information Center, 550 W. 7th Ave., Suite 1260, Anchorage 99501* ☎ *907/269–8400* ⊕ *www.alaskastateparks.org* ⤙ *4 cabins* ⊟ *MC, V.*

¢ ⚠ **Alaska State Parks Campgrounds.** The state has three road-accessible campgrounds (Ft. Abercrombie, Buskin River, and Pasagshak) on Kodiak Island, with a total of 35 tent sites. All have toilets, drinking water, and fishing, and two have nearby hiking trails. Camping at Pasagshak is free; the campgrounds at Fort Abercrombie and Buskin River charge $10 a night. ⊚ *Alaska State Parks, Kodiak District Office, 1400 Abercrombie Dr., Kodiak 99615* ☎ *907/486–6339* ▤ *907/486–3320* ⚠ *Reservations not accepted* ⊟ *No credit cards.*

KAYAKING Contact Alaska State Parks in Kodiak for the names of companies leading guided trips in Shuyak State Park.

Aleutian Islands

The Aleutians begin 540 mi southwest of Anchorage and stretch more than 1,000 mi.

Separating the North Pacific Ocean from the Bering Sea, the Aleutian Islands (also called the Chain) stretch from the Alaska Peninsula in a southwesterly arc toward Japan. The distance from the point nearest

Alaska Peninsula, Aleutians & Pribilofs

the Alaska mainland, Unimak Island, to the most distant island, Attu, is more than 1,000 mi. This volcanic, treeless archipelago consists of about 20 large islands and several hundred smaller ones. The Aleutian Islands and surrounding coastal waters make up one of the most biologically rich areas in Alaska, with abundant seabird, marine mammal, and fish populations.

Before the Russians came, the islands were dotted with Aleut villages. Today's communities include **Nikolski,** on Umnak Island; **Unalaska,** on Unalaska Island; **Atka,** on Atka Island; and **Cold Bay,** at the peninsula's tip. The hardy Aleuts work at commercial fishing or in canneries and as expert guides for those who hunt and fish. The settlements are quite small, and accommodations are scarce.

You are not allowed to visit Shemya Island, which has a remote U.S. Air Force base, without special permission. Because of downsizing, the military has closed its Adak operation, and the base's infrastructure provides the core for what now is a small coastal community and commercial-fishing port.

⑨ **Dutch Harbor,** on Unalaska Island, is by far the most populous destination in the Aleutian Islands. Traditionally a fishing port, it is also the region's tourism center. The Japanese bombed Dutch Harbor during World War II, and you can still see concrete bunkers, gun batteries, and a partially sunken ship left over from the war. In addition to military history, you'll find a hotel and restaurants that rival those on Alaska's mainland, and guided adventure tours.

Where to Stay & Eat

★ **$$$** ✕⊡ **Grand Aleutian Hotel.** A three-story atrium lobby with a stone fireplace unfolds as you enter this chaletlike hotel. Rooms have views of

Margaret Bay or Unalaska Bay. Each lushly carpeted, brightly-lit room is decorated with Alaskan artwork and is equipped with full bath, built-in hair dryer, extra vanity and sink, and in-room coffeemaker. The Chart Room Restaurant and Lounge ($$–$$$$) specializes in Pacific Rim cuisine with locally caught seafood. Guided activities include bird-watching, cultural tours, archaeological digs, marine wildlife tours, photography, and halibut and salmon fishing. ⊠ *498 Salmon Way* ⌂ *Box 921169, Dutch Harbor 99692-1169* ☎ *907/581–3844 or 866/ 581–3844* 🖷 *907/581–7150* ⊕ *www.grandaleutian.com* ⊷ *112 rooms, 2 suites* ⌂ *2 restaurants, cable TV, fishing, 2 bars, Internet, meeting rooms, airport shuttle, travel services, no-smoking rooms, some pets allowed; no a/c* ⊟ *AE, D, DC, MC, V.*

$ ✕⊡ **Unisea Inn.** For travelers on a budget, this hotel on the water has clean, spartan rooms; try to book a room with a view of the small-boat harbor. Mexican fare, burgers, and sandwiches are served in the Unisea Inn Sports Bar and Grill ($–$$). Sit back and watch satellite broadcasts of spectator sports or try your hand at darts, pool, or video games. Bands play Top 40 or country music six nights a week. ⊠ *185 Gilman Rd.* ⌂ *Box 921169, Dutch Harbor 99692* ☎ *907/581–1325, 866/581–3844 reservations* 🖷 *907/581–1633* ⊷ *25 rooms* ⌂ *Restaurant, cable TV, hair salon, sports bar, Internet, airport shuttle, travel services, no-smoking rooms; no a/c* ⊟ *AE, D, DC, MC, V.*

Pribilof Islands

200 mi north of the Aleutian Islands, 800 mi southwest of Anchorage.

The Pribilof Islands are misty, fog-bound breeding grounds of seabirds and northern fur seals. Five islets make up the Pribilof group—a tiny, green, treeless oasis, with rippling belts of lush grass contrasting with red volcanic soil. In early summer seals come home from far Pacific waters to mate, and the larger islands, St. Paul and St. George, are overwhelmed with scenes of frenzied activity. The seals' sounds can roll out several miles to sea.

The islands are a 1,600-mi round-trip from Anchorage, over the massive snowy peaks of the Alaska Peninsula and past the rocky islands of the Aleutian chain. This was the supply route for U.S. forces during World War II, when Japan invaded Attu and Kiska islands toward the tip of the chain. During the Bering Sea leg, a playful pod of whales may be lurking below.

Wildlife watching is what brings nearly all visitors to the Pribilof Islands. Together, St. Paul and St. George islands are seasonal homes to nearly 1 million fur seals (about 80% of them on St. Paul) and 200 species of birds. Some birds migrate here from as far away as Argentina, whereas others are year-round residents. Of special interest to birders are the rare Asian vagrants sometimes blown here by strong western winds. Most spectacular of all is the islands' seabird population: each summer more than 2 million seabirds gather at traditional Pribilof nesting grounds; about 90% of them breed on St. George. The Pribilofs are also home to foxes, and sea lions and whales are occasionally spotted off their shores.

For most travelers, it is much easier and more cost-efficient to participate in package tours that arrange air travel from Anchorage, lodging, ground transportation on the islands, and guided activities. If you are planning to visit here, be aware that guest accommodations in the Pribilofs are very limited.

⑩ At **St. Paul Island,** nature lovers can watch members of the largest north-
FodorśChoice ern fur-seal herd in the world and more than 180 varieties of birds. In
★ town, you can visit with local residents; about 500 descendants of Aleut-
Russians live here now, in the shadow of the old Russian Orthodox church
and the vestiges of Aleut culture. **St. George Island** is home to nearly 2
million nesting seabirds, but it is much less frequently visited, because
no organized tours go there and accommodations are limited.

Where to Stay & Eat

$$ ✕ **Trident Sea Foods.** This cafeteria-style eatery—the island's only restau-
rant—serves fish processors as well as visitors to St. Paul Island. Plan your
day carefully, because meals are served according to a strict schedule: break-
fast 5–6:30, lunch noon–1, and dinner 5–6. ⊠ *Downtown St. Paul, 2
blocks from King Eider Hotel* ☎ 907/546–2377 ▤ *No credit cards.*

$$$$ ▥ **King Eider Hotel.** More functional than luxurious, this rustic three-story
clapboard hotel is filled in summer by tour groups. The original part of
this historic landmark dates to the late 1800s; it's been expanded four
times since. The hotel has simply furnished rooms, a TV room, reading
lounge, and gift shop. If you are traveling on your own, make reserva-
tions months in advance. ⊠ *523 Tolstoi St.* ⊕ *Box 88, St. Paul 99660*
☎ *907/546–2477 or 907/278–2312* ⊕ *907/546–5026* ⊕ *www.
alaskabirding.com* ⇨ *25 rooms, 5 shared baths* ⬙ *Travel services; no
a/c, no room phones, no room TVs, no smoking* ▤ *AE, MC, V.*

$$$$ ▥ **St. George Tanaq Hotel.** A national historic landmark, St. George Is-
land's only hotel is a small, rustic building with a dark-wood interior
and a mix of modern and vintage furniture. Rooms are sparsely furnished
with shared baths. The hotel's shared kitchen includes a stove, a re-
frigerator, and cooking utensils—necessary, since the island has no
restaurant. ⊠ *Downtown* ⊕ *Box 939, St. George 99591* ☎ *907/272–
9886 or 907/859–2255* ⊕ *907/859–2230* ⊕ *www.stgeorgetanaq.com*
⇨ *10 rooms, 4 shared baths* ⬙ *Cable TV, dining room; no a/c, no smok-
ing* ▤ *MC, V.*

Guided Tours

Contact **Tanadgusix Village Corporation of St. Paul Island** (⊠ 4300 B St.,
Suite 402, Anchorage 99503 ☎ 907/278–2312 or 877/424–5637
⊕ www.alaskabirding.com) for St. Paul Island tour information.

NORTHWEST & THE ARCTIC

This is a largely roadless region of long, dark, sunless winters and short,
bright summers, when the sun remains in the sky around the clock for
up to nearly three months. It's the land of Eskimos and huge caribou herds
and polar bears, a place where people still lead subsistence lifestyles and
where traditional Native culture is making a strong comeback. It's also
a place of gold rushes and America's largest oil field as well as a region
with many of Alaska's wildest and most remote parklands as well as one
of the country's premier refuges, the Arctic National Wildlife Refuge.

Nome

⑪ *540 mi northwest of Anchorage.*

More than a century has passed since a great stampede for gold put a
speck of wilderness called Nome on the Alaska map, but gold mining
and noisy saloons are still mainstays in this frontier community on the
icy Bering Sea. Mainly a collection of ramshackle houses and low-slung
commercial buildings, Nome looks like a vintage gold-mining camp or
the neglected set of a western movie—rawboned, rugged, and somewhat

shabby. What the town lacks in appearance is made up for with a cheerful hospitality and colorful history.

Only 165 mi from the coast of Siberia, Nome is considerably closer to Russia than either Anchorage or Fairbanks. And though you'll find a local road system, to get to Nome you must either fly or mush a team of sled dogs.

Nome's golden years began in 1898, when three prospectors—known as the Lucky Swedes—struck rich deposits on Anvil Creek, about 4 mi from what became Nome. The news spread quickly. When the Bering Sea ice parted the next spring, ships from Puget Sound, down by Seattle, arrived in Nome with eager stampeders. An estimated 15,000 people landed in Nome between June and October of 1900. Among the gold-rush luminaries were Wyatt Earp, the old gunfighter from the O. K. Corral, who mined the gold of Nome by opening a posh saloon; Tex Rickard, the boxing promoter, who operated another Nome saloon; and Rex Beach, the novelist.

Nome is also proud to be the hometown of General James H. Doolittle, the Tokyo raider of World War II. When Doolittle's bombers hit Japan in a daring raid in 1942, the headline in the *Nome Nugget* proudly announced: "NOME TOWN BOY MAKES GOOD!"

A network of 250 mi or so of gravel roads around the town leads to creeks and rivers for gold panning or fishing for trout, salmon, and arctic grayling. You can also see reindeer, bears, foxes, and moose in the wild on the back roads that once connected early mining camps and hamlets. Independent travelers with hardy vehicles should go exploring. **Alaska Cab Garage** (☎ 907/443–2335) rents pickup trucks, suburbans, minibuses, and vans, both two- and four-wheel drive. **Stampede Car Rentals** (☎ 907/443–5598 ⊕ www.aurorainnome.com) rents vans, pickup trucks, and SUVs. Because the sun stays up late in the summer months, drive to the top of **Anvil Mountain**, near Nome, for a panoramic view of the old gold town and the Bering Sea. Be sure to carry mosquito repellent.

For exploring downtown, stop at the **Nome Convention and Visitors Bureau** (⊠ 301 Front St. ☎ 907/443–6624, 800/478–1901 in Alaska 🖷 907/443–5832 ⊕ www.nomealaska.org/vc) for a historic-walking-tour map, a city map, and information on local activities from flight-seeing to bird-watching.

Where to Stay & Eat

$$–$$$$ ✕ **Fort Davis Roadhouse.** The Roadhouse, which specializes in prime rib and seafood, is a favorite spot for locals. Above the dining area is a lounge with live music and room for dancing on Friday and Saturday nights. Some visitors fall for the Bering Ball, a infamously potent cocktail that most locals seem to avoid. Taxis serve the area. ⊠ *Nome-Council Rd., 1½ mi east of town* ☎ 907/443–2660 ▤ MC, V ☺ *Closed Sun.–Tues. No lunch.*

★ $–$$$ ✕ **Fat Freddie's.** This popular café-style eatery overlooking the Bering Sea serves New York steak and prime rib, plus its notable burgers and seafood. During the Iditarod, many mushers hang out here after their grueling trip across Alaska. If you're staying at the Nome Nugget Inn, you can enter directly from the hotel. ⊠ *50 Front St.* ☎ 907/443–5899 ▤ AE, D, MC, V.

$–$$$ ✕ **Polar Cub.** American diner food, from omelets to steak, fills the menu here. Locals like to linger over coffee, making it a good place to eaves-drop on residents discussing area issues, or just gaze out at the Bering Sea. With its sea views, good prices, and friendly service, the Cub is a great place for early-morning breakfast. ⊠ *Next to seawall, off Front St., downtown* ☎ *907/443–5191* ⊟ *AE, MC, V.*

$$$$ ⌕ **Camp Bendeleben.** At the site of an early 1900s gold-mining camp, this lodge sits along the clear-water Niukluk River, about 75 mi northeast of Nome. You can fish for arctic char, grayling, and four species of salmon; other outdoor activities include bird-watching and wildlife photography. Packages include transportation between the lodge and Nome. Prices vary considerably, depending on whether you stay at the lodge or remote tent camps, cook your own meals, or choose to be guided when fishing. There is a three-night minimum. *In summer:* ⬠ *Box 1045, Nome 99762* ⊠ *in winter:* ⬠ *12110 Woodward Dr., Anchorage 99516* ☎☎ *907/522–6663* ⊕ *www.campbendeleben.com* ⇲ *3 rooms* ⚭ *Dining room, fishing; no a/c, no room phones, no room TVs* ⊟ *No credit cards* ⊘ *Closed Oct.–May.*

$ ⌕ **Nome Nugget Inn.** The architecture and decor of the Nugget Inn combine every cliché of the Victorian gold-rush era. Authentic it's not, but fun it is. Outside, a signpost marks the mileage to various points, serious and silly, around the globe. Inside, frontier memorabilia abounds in the lobby and lounge. Rooms are small and clean but not nearly as atmospheric. Arctic tour groups stay here. ⊠ *Front St.* ⬠ *Box 1470, 99762* ☎ *907/ 443–2323 or 877/443–2323* ⎙ *907/443–5966* ⊕ *www.nomenuggetinn. com* ⇲ *47 rooms* ⚭ *Restaurant, cable TV, bar, Internet, no-smoking rooms, some pets allowed; no a/c* ⊟ *AE, D, DC, MC, V.*

¢ ⚠ **Bureau of Land Management Campground.** BLM manages a free campground at Mile 40 of the Nome-Taylor Highway. The campground, which is a short walk from the highway, has six tent sites, toilet facilities, and nearby fishing. The maximum length of stay is 14 days. The campground has a pit toilet and fire rings for cooking, but the only water is in nearby Salmon Lake and Pilgrim River; it must be boiled or otherwise treated. ⬠ *Bureau of Land Management, Nome Field Office, Box 925, 99762* ☎ *907/443–2177 in Nome, 907/474–2231 in Fairbanks, 800/437– 7021* ⊕ *aurora.ak.blm.gov* ⇲ *6 tent sites* ⚭ *Fishing* ⚑ *Reservations not accepted* ⊟ *No credit cards* ⊘ *Closed Oct.–Apr.*

Sports & the Outdoors

FodorsChoice The famed 1,049-mi **Iditarod Trail Sled Dog Race**—the Olympics of sled-
★ dog racing—reaches its culmination in Nome in mid-March. Racers start in Anchorage for a trip of nine days to two weeks. The arrival of the mushers heralds a winter carnival. For dates, starting times, and other information, contact the **Iditarod Trail Committee** (⬠ Box 870800, Wasilla 99687 ☎ 907/376–5155 ⊕ www.iditarod.com).

Shopping

Nome is one of the best places to buy ivory, because many of the Eskimo carvers from outlying villages come to Nome first to sell their wares to dealers. The **Arctic Trading Post** (⊠ Bering and Front Sts. ☎ 907/443–2686 ⊕ www.arctictradingpost.com) has an extensive stock of authentic Eskimo ivory carvings and other Alaskan artwork, jewelry, and books. The **Board of Trade Ivory Shop** (☎ 907/443–2611) on Front Street specializes in ivory carvings but also sells Native Alaskan artwork and handicrafts. **Chukotka–Alaska** (⊠ 514 Lomen ☎ 907/443–4128) sells both Native Alaskan and Russian artwork and handicrafts as well as books, beads, and furs.

Bering Land Bridge National Preserve

⑫ *100 mi north of Nome.*

The frozen ash and lava of the 2.8-million-acre Bering Land Bridge National Preserve lie between Nome and Kotzebue immediately south of the Arctic Circle. The Imuruk lava flow is the northernmost flow of major size in the United States, and the paired *maars* (clear volcanic lakes) are a geological rarity.

Of equal interest are the paleontological features of this preserve. Sealed into the permafrost are flora and fauna—bits of twigs and leaves, tiny insects, small mammals, even remnants of woolly mammoths—that flourished here when the Bering Land Bridge linked North America to what is now Russia. Early peoples wandered through this treeless landscape, perhaps following the musk ox, whose descendants still occupy this terrain. A remarkable 250 species of flowering plants thrive in this seemingly barren region, and there are tens of thousands of migrating birds. More than 100 species, including ducks, geese, swans, sandhill cranes, and various shorebirds and songbirds, come here from around the world each spring. You may hear the haunting call of loons on the many clear lakes and lagoons.

The Bering Land Bridge National Preserve has no trails, campgrounds, or other visitor facilities. Access is largely by air taxi, although there is a road north of Nome that passes within walking distance. ⌂ *National Park Service, Box 220, Nome 99762 ☎ 907/443–2522. ✉ Box 1029, Kotzebue 99752 ☎ 907/442–3890 ⊕ www.nps.gov/bela.*

Kotzebue

🔞 *170 mi northeast of Nome.*

Kotzebue, Alaska's largest Eskimo community, is home to around 3,100 residents. It lies 26 mi above the Arctic Circle, on Alaska's northwestern coast. "We have four seasons—June, July, August, and winter," a tour guide jests. But don't worry about the sometimes chilly weather—the local sightseeing company has snug, bright loaner parkas for visitors on package tours.

Strung out in clusters of weather-bleached little houses and a few public buildings on the gravelly shore of Kotzebue Sound, Kotzebue provides you with a glimpse of the way Alaska's Eskimos live today. It was an ancient Eskimo trading center; now it is an example of the modern spirit nudging Alaska's Natives into the state's mainstream culture without leaving their traditions behind.

The **NANA Regional Corporation** (Northwest Alaska Native Association; ☎ 907/442–3301 or 800/478–3301 ⊕ www.nana.com), one of the 13 Native corporations formed when Congress settled the Alaskan Natives' aboriginal land claims in 1971, has its headquarters in Kotzebue. It was NANA that built the **Living Museum of the Arctic** (☎ 907/ 265–4100 or 907/442–3301 ⊕ www.nana.com) in 1977 and turned it into one of Alaska's top-rated museums. Bleachers face a stage where stories are told, and after the storytelling, a cultural slide show relates the wisdom of the elders, followed by traditional Eskimo singing and dancing and blanket tossing, in which audience members are invited to participate. It may look like a game, but the blanket toss was serious business in the early days, when Eskimo hunters were launched high in the air from blankets of walrus or seal hide to scan the seas for game. You may even be urged to take a turn on the bouncing blanket. The museum is open when tour groups are in town or by special arrangement. Admission to the museum is free, but a fee is charged for cultural programs. After attending programs at the museum, stop at the **InuCraft Gift Shop** (☎ 907/442–3331) in the Nullagvik Hotel. It stocks a good selection of Native arts and crafts as well as T-shirts, sweatshirts, and postcards.

FodorśChoice
★

Tours of the museum can be arranged through NANA's **Tour Arctic** program (☎ 907/265–4100 or 907/442–3301 ⊕ www.nana.com), in which you may participate in a guided "Kotzebue Tour" or a "Native Village Excursion." Prices vary, depending on the tour.

If you're hiking the wildflower-carpeted tundra around Kotzebue, you are entering a "living museum" dedicated to **permafrost,** the permanently frozen ground that lies just a few inches below the spongy tundra. Even Kotzebue's 6,000-foot airport runway is built on permafrost—with a 6-inch insulating layer between the frozen ground and the airfield surface to ensure that landings are smooth, not slippery.

Kotzebue serves as a gateway for three exceptional national **wilderness areas:** Cape Krusenstern National Monument, Kobuk Valley National Park, and Noatak National Preserve. North and east of Kotzebue is the **Brooks Range,** one of Alaska's great mountain ranges. Stretching across the state, much of the range is protected by Gates of the Arctic National Park and Preserve and the Arctic National Wildlife Refuge.

Where to Stay & Eat

¢–$$ ╳ **Kotzebue Pizza House.** Although this cozy pizza parlor serves pizza and Chinese food, locals especially tout the burgers, which are among the best in the state. ⊠ *2nd Ave. and Bison St., Downtown* ☎ *907/442–3432* ▤ *MC, V.*

$$ ╳▣ **Nullagvik Hotel.** This hotel overlooking Kotzebue Sound is built on pilings driven into the ground because the heat of the building would melt the underlying permafrost and cause the hotel to sink. Images of Eskimo life adorn the spacious, modern rooms. Public areas on the second and third floors provide picture-window views of the bay. Open only during the summer season, the hotel's coffee shop–restaurant ($–$$$) serves American fare and occasionally local specialties, such as reindeer and fresh Arctic fish. ⊠ *308 Shore Ave.* ⌂ *Box 336, 99752* ☎ *907/442–3331* 🖷 *907/442–3340* ⊕ *www.nullagvik.com* ⥅ *73 rooms* ⌂ *Restaurant, cable TV, meeting room, travel services, no-smoking rooms, some pets allowed; no a/c* ▤ *AE, D, DC, MC, V.*

Cape Krusenstern National Monument

⑭ *10 mi north of Kotzebue.*

Just north of Kotzebue, the 560,000-acre Cape Krusenstern National Monument has important cultural and archaeological value. This is a coastal parkland, with an extraordinary series of beach ridges built up by storms over a period of at least 5,000 years. Almost every ridge—more than 100 in all—contains artifacts of different human occupants, representing every known Arctic Eskimo culture in North America. The present Eskimo occupants, whose culture dates back some 1,400 years, use the fish, seals, caribou, and birds of this region for food and raw materials much as their ancestors did. They are also closely involved in the archaeological digs in the park that are unearthing part of their own history.

Cape Krusenstern is a starkly beautiful Arctic land shaped by ice, wind, and sea. Its low, rolling gray-white hills scalloped with light-green tundra attract hikers and backpackers, and kayakers sometimes paddle its coastline. The monument is valuable also for human and historical reasons, and it should be experienced as something like a marvelous living museum. It's possible to camp in the park, but be mindful, as are the Native people when they rig their big white canvas tents for summer fishing, that any tent pitched along the shore is subject to fierce winds.

Further, both grizzlies and polar bears patrol the beaches in search of food, so clean camping is a must.

Check with the National Park Service in Kotzebue about hiring a local guide to interpret this unusual scene. The monument, which has no visitor facilities, is accessible by air taxi and by boat from Kotzebue. ⌂ *National Park Service, Box 1029, Kotzebue 99752* ☏ *907/442–3890* ⊕ *www.nps.gov/cakr.*

Kobuk Valley National Park

⑮ *65 mi east of Kotzebue.*

Kobuk Valley National Park lies entirely north of the Arctic Circle, along the southern edge of the Brooks Range. Its 1.14 million acres contain remarkable inland deserts and the **Great Kobuk Sand Dunes** and are home to interesting relict (or remnants of otherwise extinct) flora. In addition to housing the **Kobuk River,** this park contains two smaller streams that provide delightful river running, the Ambler and the Salmon. These brilliantly clear rivers are accessible by wheeled plane, and each provides a good week's worth of pleasure (if the weather cooperates).

Another place of special interest is the **Onion Portage.** Human occupation here dates back 12,500 years; herds of caribou that once fed the Woodland Eskimo centuries ago are still hunted at Onion Portage by present-day Eskimo residents of the region.

Kobuk Valley National Park is, like most other Alaska parks, undeveloped wilderness with no visitor facilities. It's a good place for backpacking and river trips. In nearby Kotzebue, the National Park Service has a visitor center where staff can provide tips for travel into the park. The villages of Kobuk and Kiana both provide immediate takeoff points and have air service. ⌂ *National Park Service, Box 1029, Kotzebue 99752* ☏ *907/442–3890* ⊕ *www.nps.gov/kova.*

Noatak National Preserve

⑯ *20 mi northeast of Kotzebue.*

Adjacent to Gates of the Arctic National Park and Preserve, the 6.5-million-acre Noatak National Preserve takes in much of the basin of the **Noatak River.** This is the largest mountain-ringed river basin in the United States that is still relatively wild (part of it is designated a Wild and Scenic River). Along its 425-mi course, this river carves out the "Grand Canyon of the Noatak," which serves as a migration route between Arctic and sub-Arctic ecosystems. Its importance to wildlife and plants has resulted in this parkland's designation as an International Biosphere Reserve.

The Noatak River also serves as a natural highway for humans and offers particular pleasures to river runners, with inviting tundra to camp on and the Poktovik Mountains and the Igichuk Hills nearby for good hiking. Birding can be exceptional: horned grebes, gyrfalcons, golden eagles, parasitic jaegers, owls, terns, and loons are among the species you may see. You may also observe grizzly bears, Dall sheep, wolves, caribou, or lynx. As with other parks and preserves in this northwest corner of Alaska, no facilities are available and you are expected to be self-sufficient. ⌂ *National Park Service, Box 1029, Kotzebue 99752* ☏ *907/442–3890* ⊕ *www.nps.gov/noat.*

Gates of the Arctic National Park & Preserve

★ **⑰** *180 mi east of Kotzebue.*

Gates of the Arctic National Park and Preserve is entirely north of the Arctic Circle, in the center of the Brooks Range; at 8.2 million acres, it's the size of four Yellowstones. This is parkland on a scale suitable to the country. It includes the **Endicott Mountains** to the east and the **Schwatka Mountains** to the southwest, with the **Arrigetch Peaks** in between. *Arrigetch* is an Eskimo word meaning "fingers of a hand outstretched," which aptly describes the immensely steep and smooth granite peaks that have attracted many mountaineers and backcountry explorers, past and present. To the north lies a sampling of the Arctic foothills, with their colorful tilted sediments and pale green tundra. Lovely lakes are cupped in the mountains and in the tundra.

The ultimate wilderness, this landscape captured the heart of Arctic explorer and conservationist Robert Marshall in the 1930s. Accompanied by local residents, Marshall explored much of the region now included within Gates and named many of its features, including Frigid Crag and Boreal Mountain, two peaks on either side of the North Fork Koyukuk River. These were the original "gates" for which the park is named.

Wildlife known to inhabit the park include barren-ground caribou, grizzlies, wolves, moose, Dall sheep, wolverines, and smaller mammals and birds. The communities of Bettles and Anaktuvuk Pass are access points for Gates of the Arctic, which has no developed trails, campgrounds, or other visitor facilities (though there is a wilderness lodge on private land within the park). You can fly into Bettles commercially and charter an air taxi into the park or hike directly out of Anaktuvuk Pass. ⊠ *National Park Service, 201 1st Ave., Fairbanks 99701* ☎ *907/457–5752* ⊕ *www.nps.gov/gaar.*

Where to Stay

★ **$$$$** 🖼 **Peace of Selby Wilderness.** On Selby/Narvak Lake within Gates of the Arctic National Park, Peace of Selby is perfectly situated for wilderness adventures. Crafted from white spruce, the main lodge includes a kitchen, small library, bathroom, and loft. Meals are cooked with fresh vegetables, fruits, and meats. If you want to rough it, you can stay in sleeping bags and cook your own meals in a rustic log cabin or a large canvas "wall" tent. Activities include hiking, fishing, wildlife viewing and photographing, river floating, and flightseeing. ⊲ *Box 86, Manley Hot Springs 99756* ☎☎ *907/672–3206* ⊕ *www.alaskawilderness. net* ⟿ *1 room in lodge, 4 cabins, wall tents* ⟃ *Dining room, boating, fishing, hiking, cross-country skiing, library; no a/c, no room phones, no room TVs* ⊟ *No credit cards* ⊙ *Closed mid-Sept.–mid-June, except for specially arranged expeditions Mar.–Apr.*

Sports & the Outdoors

Contact **Sourdough Outfitters** (⊲ Box 26066, Bettles Field 99726 ☎ 907/ 692–5252 🖷 907/692–5557 ⊕ www.sourdoughoutfitters.com) for summer backpacking and river trips (from family float trips to wild-rapid running and fishing expeditions) and winter dogsled trips in the Brooks Range.

Barrow

⑱ *330 mi northeast of Kotzebue.*

The northernmost community in the United States, Barrow sits just 1,300 mi from the North Pole on the Beaufort Sea. For 82 days, from May to August, the sun stays above the horizon. It is the best place in Alaska to catch the legendary midnight sun. An umiak (Eskimo skin boat), a fish-drying rack, and drifting Arctic pack ice, often close to shore, complete the scene. Barrow's 4,000 residents, many of them Natives (only Kotzebue has a larger Eskimo population), live in a modern village but maintain traditional Eskimo activities such as whale hunting. The Barrow airport is the site of the **Will Rogers and Wiley Post Monument,** commemorating the 1935 crash of the American humorist and the pilot 15 mi south of town.

Visitors arriving in Barrow usually come on a one- or two-day tour from Alaska Airlines. Packages include a bus tour of the town's dusty roads and major sights. A highlight is **Mound 44,** where the frozen body of a 500-year-old Eskimo was discovered. Scientists have been studying her remains to learn more about pre-Outside-contact Eskimo life and culture. An **early warning radar installation** once watched for incoming Soviet missiles. The air force has since mothballed its big dishes, but Barrow duty must have given special meaning to the term "cold war." Without a doubt, the best part about visiting the top of the world is walking along the sandy beach and seeing the pack ice stretching across the horizon, even in the middle of summer.

Where to Stay & Eat

★ **$$–$$$$** ✕ **Pepe's North of the Border.** The warmth of Pepe's will make you forget that you're in the middle of the Arctic tundra. Murals depicting Mexican village scenes highlight the Mission-style decor, and an extensive selection of Mexican dishes, from soft tacos to burritos and fajitas, makes this restaurant a favorite of locals and visitors alike. Dinner at Pepe's is surprisingly refined for being on the very fringe of civilization. ⊠ *Next to Top of the World Hotel* ☎ *907/852–8200* ⊟ *DC, MC, V.*

$$–$$$ ✕ **Ken's Restaurant.** Burgers, steaks, and Chinese food are the staples at this family restaurant, which has daily specials and the best prices in town. Breakfast is served throughout the day. ⊠ *Above airport terminal building* ☎ *907/852–8888* ⊟ *MC, V.*

★ **$$$$** ▦ **Top of the World Hotel.** Frontier touches at this popular hotel on the shore of the Arctic Ocean include one complete stuffed polar bear and the mounted head of another. You can mingle in the lobby or in front of the community television. Modern, spacious rooms have sitting areas; ask for a room with an ocean view. ⊠ *1200 Agviq St.* ⊡ *Box 189, 99723* ☎ *907/852–3900, 800/882–8478, or 800/478–8520 in Alaska* ⊟ *907/852–6752* ⊕ *www.topoftheworldhotel.com* ⊅ *43 rooms* ♺ *Some in-room data ports, some refrigerators, cable TV, Internet, no-smoking; no a/c* ⊟ *AE, D, DC, MC, V.*

$ ▦ **Barrow Airport Inn.** As the name says, this modern and well-appointed property is convenient to the airport. ⊠ *1815 Momegana St.* ⊡ *Box 933, 99723* ☎ *907/852–2525 or 800/375–2527* ⊟ *907/852–2528* ⊅ *16 rooms* ♺ *Some kitchenettes, some microwaves, some refrigerators, cable TV, Internet, travel services, no-smoking rooms; no a/c* ⊟ *AE, D, DC, MC, V* ▯◯▯ *CP.*

THE PIPELINE HIGHWAY

STRETCHING 800 MI ACROSS the 49th state, the trans-Alaska pipeline is both an engineering marvel and a reminder of Alaska's economic dependence on oil and gas production. It begins at Prudhoe Bay, along the Arctic Ocean, and snakes its way south to the port town of Valdez, on the shores of Prince William Sound. Along the way, the pipeline carries crude oil across three mountain ranges, 34 major rivers—including the mighty Yukon—and hundreds of smaller creeks. Though much of it is buried, more than half of the pipeline runs aboveground, where it is held aloft by 78,000 vertical supports. You can see sections of it along some of Alaska's major roadways, most notably the Dalton Highway.

Alaska's northernmost highway, the Dalton parallels the pipeline for more than 400 mi while connecting Interior Alaska to North Slope oil fields. It was built so that trucks could haul supplies to Prudhoe Bay and pipeline construction camps in Alaska's northern reaches, hence its other name: the Haul Road.

Thousands of 18-wheelers continue to drive the Dalton Highway each year, but they now share the 414-mi route with recreational travelers. This doesn't mean the Dalton has become an easy drive. It's narrow as highways go, often winding, and has several steep grades, and sections may be heavily potholed or washboarded. Besides being tough on vehicles, the road has few visitor facilities. Public access ends at Deadhorse, the support town for Prudhoe Bay's industrial operations; the only way to visit the oil fields or reach the ocean is by group tour (scheduled daily in summer).

The origins of the Haul Road and trans-Alaska pipeline can be traced to 1968, when oil companies announced the discovery of a major field at Prudhoe Bay. A lawsuit by environmental groups temporarily halted work on the proposed pipeline across Alaska, but congressional legislation authorizing its construction was signed into law in November 1973. Things moved quickly after that. Work on the Haul Road began the following April

and was finished in five months. Forty-eight inches wide and up to 60 feet long, the first pipes were installed in March 1975; 27 months later, oil began moving down the pipeline and reached Valdez on July 28, 1977. Four days later, the ARCO Juneau headed south with the first tanker load of Prudhoe Bay crude.

Since it began operation, the pipeline has transported approximately 14 billion barrels (nearly 600 billion gallons) of oil across Alaska. At its peak in 1988, 2.14 million barrels of oil flowed through the pipeline in a day's time. Nowadays the daily flow is closer to 1 million barrels.

The trans-Alaska pipeline was designed and built and continues to be operated by the Alyeska Pipeline Service Company, a consortium of seven oil companies. Concerns about spills and corrosion led to the formation of a Joint Pipeline Office, composed of nine state and federal regulatory agencies. Although the pipline has had a number of temporary shutdowns and spills, the only catastrophic event connected to the trans-Alaska pipeline project was the 1989 Exxon Valdez oil spill, in which 270,000 barrels of oil oozed from the damaged tanker into Prince William Sound.

Shopping

Shopping

The AC Value Center, or, as it's known locally, **Stuaqpak** ("Big Store"; ✉ 4725 Ahkovak St. ☎ 907/852–6711 ⊕ www.alaskacommercial. com), is the largest store in town. Though it mainly sells groceries, the store also stocks Eskimo crafts made by locals, including furs, parkas, mukluks, and ceremonial masks.

Prudhoe Bay

⑲ *250 mi southeast of Barrow.*

Most towns have museums that chronicle local history and achievements. Deadhorse is the town anchoring life along Prudhoe Bay, but it could also serve as a museum dedicated to humankind's hunt for energy and its ability to adapt to harsh conditions.

The costly, much-publicized Arctic oil and gas project is complex and varied. One-day tours explore the tundra terrain from oil pipes to sandpipers. Along with spotting caribou, wildflowers, and an unusual stand of willow trees at the edge of the Arctic Ocean, the field tour surveys oil wells, stations, and oil-company residential complexes—small cities themselves. Your guide will discuss the multimillion-dollar research programs aimed at preserving the region's ecology and point out special tundra vehicles known as Rollagons, whose great weight is distributed to diminish their impact on delicate terrain.

In the past, individual travelers rarely turned up in Deadhorse and Prudhoe Bay. But now that the Dalton Highway has been opened as far north as Deadhorse, adventurous independent travelers are finding their way north. Still, most people traveling to Deadhorse either work here or come on a tour with one of Alaska's airlines or bus-tour operators. And even those who travel here on their own must join a guided tour (arranged through the Arctic Caribou Inn) if they wish to cross the oil fields to get to the Arctic Ocean. Keep in mind, you'll find no restaurants here, though meals can sometimes be arranged through the hotel.

Arctic National Wildlife Refuge

★ **⑳** *70 mi southeast of Prudhoe Bay.*

The 18-million-acre Arctic National Wildlife Refuge, lying wholly above the Arctic Circle, is administered by the U.S. Fish and Wildlife Service and contains the only protected Arctic coastal lands in the United States (and some of the very few protected in the world), as well as millions of acres of mountains and alpine tundra, in the easternmost portion of the Brooks Range.

This is the home of one of the greatest remaining groups of caribou in the world, the **Porcupine Caribou Herd.** The herd, numbering around 130,000, is unmindful of international boundaries and migrates back and forth across Arctic lands into Canada, flowing like a wide river across the expansive coastal plain, through U-shape valleys and alpine meadows, and over high mountain passes. The refuge's coastal areas also serve as critical denning grounds for polar bears, which spend most of their year on the Arctic Ocean's pack ice. Other residents here are grizzly bears, Dall sheep, wolves, musk ox, and dozens of varieties of birds, from snowy owls to geese and tiny songbirds. The refuge's northern areas host legions of breeding waterfowl and shorebirds each summer. As in many of Alaska's more remote parks and refuges, there are no roads here, no developed trails, campgrounds, or other visitor facilities. This is a place to experience true wilderness—and to walk with care, for the plants are fragile and the ground can be soft and wet in summer. You can expect snow to sift over the land in almost any season and should anticipate subfreezing temperatures even in summer, particularly in the mountains. Many of the refuge's clear-flowing rivers are runnable, and tundra lakes are suitable for base camps (a Kaktovik or Fort Yukon air taxi can drop you off and pick you up). The hiking, too, can be invigorating. It can also be extremely challenging for those not used to crossing wet, tussocky tundra or slippery scree deposits of rocks. But the effort is worth it; upon scrambling up a ridge, you'll look out upon wave after wave of mountains, in a wilderness that seems to stretch forever. ✆ *Refuge Manager, Arctic National Wildlife Refuge, 101 12th Ave., Room 236, Box 20, Fairbanks 99701* ☎ *907/456–0250 or 800/362–4546* ⊕ *arctic.fws.gov.*

THE BUSH A TO Z

To research prices, get advice from other travelers, and book travel arrangements, visit www.fodors.com.

AIR TRAVEL

Alaska Airlines is among the major carriers serving Alaska from Seattle, and it flies within Alaska to most major communities (⇨ Smart Travel Tips A to Z for airline numbers). Peninsula Airways serves the communities on the Alaskan Peninsula, the Aleutian and Pribilof islands, and parts of the Interior and Northwest.

Many Anchorage and Fairbanks air taxis serve the Bush in addition to Bush-based carriers such as Bering Air, which also offers local flightseeing tours and, weather and politics permitting, flights to Provideniya, on the Siberian coast across the Bering Strait. Cape Smythe Air Service serves the communities of the North Slope plus Kotzebue. Frontier Flying Service serves the Interior and the Bering and Arctic coasts. Wright Air Service flies throughout the Interior and Arctic Alaska.

Besides flights on those carriers, information about certified air-taxi operations is available from the Federal Aviation Administration. Individual parks and Alaska Public Lands Information centers also can supply lists of reputable air-taxi services. Make your reservations in advance, and plan for the unexpected; weather can delay a scheduled pickup for days.
🛫 Airlines & Contacts **Alaska Airlines** ☎ 800/426-0333 ⊕ www.alaskaair.com. **Alaska Public Lands Information Center** ✉ 250 Cushman St., Suite 1A, Fairbanks 99701 ☎ 907/456-0527 ⊕ www.nps.gov/aplic. **Bering Air** ✆ Box 1650, Nome 99762 ☎ 907/443-5464, 800/478-5422 in Alaska, 907/443-5620 Russian desk ☐ 907/443-5919 ⊕ www.beringair.com. **Cape Smythe Air Service** ✉ 1707 Ahkovak St. ✆ Box 549, Barrow 99723 ☎ 907/852-8333 or 800/478-8333 ☐ 907/852-2509 ⊕ www.capesmythe.com. **Federal Aviation Administration** ✉ Flight Standards District Office, 4510 W. International Airport Rd., Anchorage 99502-1088 ☎ 907/271-2000 ☐ 907/271-4777 ⊕ www.faa.gov. **Frontier Flying Service** ✉ 5245 Airport Industrial Way, Fairbanks 99709 ☎ 907/474-0014, 800/478-6779 in Alaska ☐ 907/474-0774 ⊕ www.frontierflying.com. **Peninsula Airways** ✉ 6100 Boeing Ave., Anchorage 99502 ☎ 907/243-2323 or 800/448-4226 ☐ 907/243-6848 ⊕ www.penair.com. **Wright Air Service** ✉ 3842 University Ave. ✆ Box 60142, Fairbanks 99706 ☎ 907/474-0502, 800/478-0502 in Alaska ☐ 907/474-0375.

BOAT & FERRY TRAVEL

The Alaska State Ferry makes monthly trips April through October to Kodiak, Dutch Harbor/Unalaska, and several other Bush communities in southwestern Alaska.
🚢 Boat & Ferry Information **Alaska State Ferry** ✉ Alaska Marine Highway System, 6858 Glacier Hwy., Juneau 99801 ☎ 800/382-9229 or 800/642-0066 ☐ 907/277-4829 ⊕ www.alaska.gov/ferry.

CAR TRAVEL

The James W. Dalton Highway—formerly the construction road for the trans-Alaska pipeline—is Alaska's only highway to the High Arctic. Popularly known as the Haul Road, this 414-mi, all-gravel road begins about 73 mi north of Fairbanks, connecting with the Steese and Elliott highways to points south. Private vehicles may travel the entire length of the highway to Deadhorse. However, access to oil-company facilities and the shore of the Arctic Ocean is limited to commercial operators.

Vehicle services are limited along the highway. Plans are to add new facilities, but currently fuel, repairs, food, and lodging are available at only three places: the Yukon River crossing (Mile 56), Coldfoot (Mile 175), and Deadhorse (Mile 414). Motorists are cautioned not to expect assistance from truckers shuttling between Prudhoe Bay and Fairbanks. For Dalton Highway information, contact the Fairbanks office of the Alaska Public Lands Information Center.

Neither the Arctic and near-Arctic communities of Nome, Kotzebue, and Barrow nor Bethel, the Aleutian chain, nor the Pribilof Islands have highway connections to the rest of Alaska.
🔳 **Alaska Public Lands Information Center** ✉ 250 Cushman St., Suite 1A, Fairbanks 99701 ☎ 907/456-0527 ⊕ www.nps.gov/aplic.

EMERGENCIES

DOCTORS & DENTISTS A statewide air-ambulance service operates through Alaska Regional Lifeflight in Anchorage.
🔳 **Alaska Regional Lifeflight** ☎ 800/478-9111 ⊕ www.alaskaregional.com. **Maniilaq Health Center** ✉ Kotzebue ☎ 907/442-3321 ⊕ www.maniilaq.org.

EMERGENCY SERVICES 🔳 **Police** ☎ 907/852-0311 in Barrow, 907/442-3351 in Kotzebue, 907/443-7766 in Nome ⊕ www.kotzebuepolice.com in Kotzebue, www.nomealaska.org in Nome. **State troopers** ☎ 907/852-3783 in Barrow, 800/789-3222 in Kotzebue, 907/443-5525 in Nome ⊕ www.dps.state.ak.us/ast.

HOSPITALS 🔳 **Norton Sound Regional Hospital** ✉ Nome ☎ 907/443-3311 ⊕ www.nortonsoundhealthcorporation.org. **Samuel Simmonds Memorial Hospital** ✉ Barrow ☎ 907/852-4611.

SPORTS & THE OUTDOORS

For information about camping, hiking, and fishing, contact the following:
🔳 **Alaska Department of Fish and Game** 🖃 Box 25526, Juneau 99802-5526 ☎ 907/465-4100 general information about fish and wildlife, 907/465-4180 sportfishing seasons and regulations, 907/465-2376 licenses ⊕ www.state.ak.us. **Alaska State Parks Information** ✉ 550 W. 7th Ave., Suite 1260, Anchorage 99501 ☎ 907/269-8400 🖶 907/269-8401 ⊕ www.alaskastateparks.org. **Anchorage Alaska Public Lands Information Center** ✉ 605 W. 4th Ave., Suite 105, Anchorage 99501 ☎ 907/271-2737 🖶 907/271-2744 ⊕ www.nps.gov/aplic. **Fairbanks Alaska Public Lands Information Center** ✉ 250 Cushman St., Suite 1A, Fairbanks 99701 ☎ 907/456-0527 🖶 907/456-0514 ⊕ www.nps.gov/aplic. **National Park Service Alaska Regional Office** ✉ 240 W. 5th Ave., Anchorage 99501 ☎ 907/257-2696 ⊕ www.nps.gov. **U.S. Fish and Wildlife Service** ✉ 1011 E. Tudor Rd., Anchorage 99503 ☎ 907/786-3309 🖶 907/786-3495 ⊕ www.r7.fws.gov.

TOURS

Package tours are the most common way of traveling to Bush communities, where making your flight connections and having a room to sleep in at the end of the line are no small feats. Guided trips, or stays in wilderness lodges, can be arranged in many of the Bush's remote parklands and wildlife refuges. Independent travel, particularly for campers and hikers, can be highly rewarding, but it takes careful planning. During peak season—late May through Labor Day—planes, state ferries, hotels, and sportfishing lodges are likely to be crowded with travelers on organized tours. Booking well ahead is recommended; many Alaska travelers make their reservations a year in advance.

The type of tour you choose will determine how you get there. On air tours—which include travel to most Bush communities—you will fly to and from your destination. On bus tours to Deadhorse and Prudhoe Bay, you will travel at least one way by bus. Each type of tour has its own advantages: air travel is faster and gives you an aerial perspective of the Arctic; bus tours travel at a more leisurely pace and give you a ground-level view of sweeping tundra vistas. However, most Bush locales can be reached only by plane.

Most tours to Arctic towns and villages are short—one, two, or three days. These often can be combined with visits to other regions of the state. Packages may include stays at wilderness lodges.

The Bush is home to many Native Alaskan groups, many of which are active in tourism. Often, local Native corporations act as your hosts—running the tours, hotels, and attractions. Nome Tour and Marketing in Nome (book through Alaska Airlines Vacations) provides ground transportation, accommodations, and other services for visitors. The NANA Development Corporation provides ground transportation and accommodations in Kotzebue as well as at Prudhoe Bay in conjunction with bus tours. If you visit Barrow and stay at the Top of the World Hotel, Tundra Tours (book through Alaska Airlines Vacations), another Native operation, will be your host. On Gambell Island (book through Alaska Village Tours), local residents also run all the ground operations.
🚩 **Alaska Airlines Vacations** ✈ Box 68900, SEARV, Seattle, WA 98168 ☎ 800/468-2248 🌐 alaskaair.com. **NANA Development Corporation** ☎ 800/478-3301 🌐 www.nana.com, or book through Princess Tours or Gray Line of Alaska.

BUS In the summer tourist season, tour operators run trips up the Dalton Highway out of Fairbanks and Anchorage. Travelers go one way by air, the other by motor coach. The route crosses the rugged Brooks Range, the Arctic Circle, and the Yukon River. It also brushes the edges of Gates of the Arctic National Park and the Arctic National Wildlife Refuge. Holland America Tours/Gray Line of Alaska operates package tours that travel the Dalton Highway to Deadhorse. Princess Tours runs tours along the Dalton Highway.

The Northern Alaska Tour Company conducts ecotours to the Arctic Circle, the Brooks Range, and Prudhoe Bay that emphasize natural and cultural history, wildlife, and geology. Groups are limited to 25 people on Arctic day tours and to 10 on Prudhoe Bay overnight trips. Some tours are completely ground-based; others include a mix of ground and air travel.
🚩 **Holland American Tours/Gray Line of Alaska** ✉ 1980 S. Cushman, Fairbanks 99701 ☎ 907/451-6835, 800/887-7741 in Alaska 🌐 www.graylineofalaska.com. **Northern Alaska Tour Company** ✈ Box 82991, Fairbanks 99708 ☎ 907/474-8600 or 800/474-1986 🖷 907/474-4767 🌐 www.northernalaska.com. **Princess Tours** ✉ 2815 2nd Ave., Suite 400, Seattle, WA 98121 ☎ 206/336-6000 in Seattle, 907/479-9660 in Fairbanks, 800/426-0442 reservations 🌐 www.princess.com.

PLANE Alaska Airlines Vacations packages air tours to Barrow, Nome, and Kotzebue. Local arrangements are taken care of by Native ground operators. These trips are especially good for travelers who would otherwise move about independently. The Alaska Travel Industry Association can give tips on air travel and flightseeing opportunities throughout the Bush.
🚩 **Alaska Airlines Vacations** ✈ Box 68900, SEARV, Seattle, WA 98168 ☎ 800/468-2248 🌐 alaskaair.com. **Alaska Travel Industry Association** ✉ 2600 Cordova St., Suite

201, Anchorage 99503 ☎ 907/929-2200, 800/862-5275 for vacation planner 📠 907/561-5727 ⊕ www.travelalaska.com.

VISITOR INFORMATION

🖪 **Alaska Travel Industry Association** ✉ 2600 Cordova St., Suite 201, Anchorage 99503 ☎ 907/929-2200, 800/862-5275 for vacation planner 📠 907/561-5727 ⊕ www.travelalaska.com. **Bethel Chamber of Commerce** 🖃 Box 329, Bethel 99559 ☎ 907/543-2911 📠 907/543-2255 ⊕ www.bethelakchamber.org. **Nome Convention and Visitors Bureau** 🖃 Box 240, Nome 99762 ☎ 907/443-5535, 800/478-1901 in Alaska 📠 907/443-5832 ⊕ www.nomealaska.org. **Southwest Alaska Municipal Conference** ✉ 3300 Arctic Blvd., Suite 203, Anchorage 99503 ☎ 907/562-7380 📠 907/562-0438 ⊕ www.swamc.org. **Unalaska-Dutch Harbor Convention and Visitors Bureau** 🖃 Box 545, Unalaska 99685 ☎ 907/581-2612 or 877/581-2612 📠 907/581-2613 ⊕ www.unalaska.info.

UNDERSTANDING ALASKA

NATIVE ALASKANS

ALASKA: A GEOLOGICAL STORY

NATIVE ALASKANS

THE HISTORY OF ALASKA'S NATIVE peoples—Eskimos, Indians, and Aleuts—is not unlike that of aboriginal people throughout Central and North America. After they had held domain over their land for thousands of years, their elaborate societies were besieged by a rapid onslaught of white settlers. Unable to stem the tide, the Native peoples were forced into retreat.

The first European to visit Alaska—in 1728—was Vitus Bering, a Dane serving in the Russian navy. Bering died on his journey home, but survivors returned to Russia with a rich booty of sea-otter furs, sparking a stampede that would crush the traditional lifestyles of Alaska's Native peoples. The way was open for eager Russian fur traders who plundered Aleut territory along the Aleutian Islands.

Records indicate that the Native population of the Aleutian chain dropped from perhaps 20,000 to about 2,500 in the first 50 years of Russian rule. Diseases took a heavy toll, but the more ruthless among the Russian frontiersmen were also responsible—killing Aleut leaders to discourage uprisings. Stories of brutality are common. One trader, Feodor Solovief, reportedly tied together 12 Aleuts and fired a musket ball through them to see how far it would penetrate. It stopped in the body of the ninth man.

In 1867, when the United States purchased Alaska, the Natives were classified in the Treaty of Cession as "uncivilized tribes." To early tourists, they were little more than "those charming folk you take pictures of in their quaint villages."

Early missionaries and government teachers in Southeast Alaska ordered Indian totem poles destroyed, mistakenly believing them to be pagan symbols. Important works of art were lost. The totem poles of the Tlingit and Haida Indians were—and still are—simply the decorative record of outstanding events in the life of a family or clan.

The plight of the Natives improved little as Alaska grew more prosperous by exploiting its great natural resources. A painful split between traditional and modern living developed—public health experts call it "a syndrome of grief." Under increasing pressure from this clash of cultures, alcoholism grew to epidemic levels, and the suicide rate of Alaskan Natives climbed to twice that of Native Americans living on reservations in the continental United States. Still, by the 1960s, Native groups were making major strides toward claiming overdue political clout. In 1966, Native leaders from across the state gathered and organized the present Alaska Foundation of Natives. It was a fragile coalition of differing cultures, but the meeting was a significant move. With 16% of the state's population, a unified Native voice was suddenly a political force to be reckoned with.

At the same time, Eskimo leaders founded the *Tundra Times* and selected Howard Rock, a quiet, articulate man from Point Hope village, as its editor. Rock, whose background was in art rather than journalism, quickly prodded Natives to press their aboriginal land claims.

"The natives are reticent by nature, and time was passing them by," the Eskimo editor said. "At first, it was kind of discouraging. Nothing happened. And then, one by one, the Native leaders started speaking up."

The *Tundra Times* helped file the first suit for Native land claims. More lawsuits followed, and soon the whole state was tied up in litigation. Oil companies, hungry to build a pipeline from the newly discovered giant oil field at Prudhoe Bay to Valdez, on Alaska's southern coast, soon realized they could not get federal construction permits until the Native land claims were settled.

In 1971 the Natives won a spectacular settlement in Congress: 40 million acres of land and almost $1 billion in cash. The settlement has not been a cure-all for the many problems of Alaska's Natives. Poverty is still widespread, as little of the land-claims money (allocated mostly to 13 regional, for-profit Native corporations by Congress) has trickled down to the village level. But the settlement has given many a sense of dignity and purpose. Several villages in the Arctic have voted themselves "dry" (prohibiting alcohol) to combat drinking problems.

Today, the fundamental issue is whether the Natives will be allowed by the larger Alaskan society to pursue their own future, says Byron Mallott, former chief operating officer of Sealaska Corp., the regional Native corporation for Southeast Alaska.

"In one way, Alaska is truly the last frontier," Mallott says. "Will the final chapter of the total and unremitting decimation of our nation's Native American people be written in Alaska—or will, with the benefit of the lesson of history, Alaska be the place where Native peoples finally are able to become a part of the overall society with their pride, strength, and ethnicity intact?" There are, he adds, few guideposts to suggest the answer.

Most of Alaska's Natives still reside in widely scattered communities spread across the ½-million square mi of Alaska. Unlike the Native Americans of the Lower 48 states, the Alaskan Natives have never been restricted to reservations. Many villages remain isolated, the preference of traditional villagers; others have plunged into modern life with mixed results. Recently, Alaska's Native peoples have become more enterprising in the tourist business. No longer content to let out-of-state tour operators have all the business, they are now starting to take charge of tours in their communities.

The various Native peoples tend to group in well-defined regions. Here is a brief look at the different Native cultures and their locations.

Eskimos. Most of Alaska's more than 40,000 Eskimos are found in scattered settlements along the Bering Sea and Arctic Ocean coasts, the deltas of the lower Yukon and Kuskokwim rivers in western Alaska, and on remote islands in the Bering Sea such as St. Lawrence, Nunivak, and Little Diomede. The principal Arctic and sub-Arctic Eskimo communities include Barrow, Kotzebue, Nome, Gambell, Savoonga, Point Hope, Wainwright, and Shishmaref.

The Eskimos are divided into two linguistic groups: the Inupiat of the Far North and the Yup'ik, who reside mostly along the coastal regions of the west. The Yup'ik share the same dialect as the Eskimos of Siberia. Both groups are famed for their hunting and fishing skills. They are also noted craftspeople, carving animals and creating jewelry from Native materials.

Indians. Alaska has four major Indian cultures: Tlingit, Haida, Athabascan, and Tsimshian.

Once among North America's most powerful tribes, the **Tlingits** (pronounced *klink*-its) are found mostly throughout coastal Southeast Alaska. They number about 13,000 and live in cities such as Juneau, Ketchikan, and Sitka and in villages from Hoonah, near Juneau, to Klukwan, near Haines.

The Tlingits developed a highly sophisticated culture and fought hard against Russian incursions. Social status among early Tlingits depended on elaborate feasts called potlatches. Heads of families and clans vied in giving away vast quantities of valuable goods, their generosity so extravagant at times that the hosts fell into a form of ancient bankruptcy. There are still potlatches for important occasions, such as funerals, but they are greatly scaled down from earlier times.

Haidas are also found mainly in Southeast Alaska, as well as in British Columbia. They number only about 1,000 in Alaska. Their principal community is Hydaburg on Prince of Wales Island, near Ketchikan. The Queen Charlotte Islands of British Columbia are another Haida center. Historically, the Haidas were far-ranging voyagers and traders. Some historians credit the artistic Haidas with originating totem carving among Alaska's Natives.

Most of Alaska's 7,000 or so **Athabascan** Indians are found in the villages of Alaska's vast Interior, including Fort Yukon, Stevens Village, Beaver, Chalkyitsik, and Minto, near Fairbanks. Other Athabascans are scattered from the Kenai Peninsula–Cook Inlet area, near Anchorage, to the Copper River area near Cordova. Linguistically, the Athabascans are related to the Navajo and Apache of the American Southwest. They were driven out of Canada by Cree tribes more than 700 years ago.

The ancestral home of the **Tsimshian** (pronounced *simp*-shee-ann) Indians was British Columbia, but Tsimshian historians say their forebears roamed through much of southeastern Alaska fishing, hunting, and trading long before the arrival of the white man. The 1,000 or so Tsimshians of Alaska settled in 1887 on Annette Island, near Ketchikan, when a dissident Church of England lay missionary, William Duncan, led them out of British Columbia to escape religious persecution. The town of Metlakatla on Annette Island is their principal community. Their artwork includes wood carvings, from totem poles to ceremonial masks.

Aleuts. With their villages on the Aleutian Islands, curving between Siberia and Alaska like broken beads, the Aleuts (pronounced al-ee-*oots*) were first in the path of early explorers and ruthless fur traders. There are about 7,000 Aleuts in Alaska today, their principal communities being Dutch Harbor/Unalaska, Akutan, Nikolski, and Atka in the Aleutians and St. Paul and St. George in the Pribilof Islands. Grass basketry, classed by museums as some of the best in the world, is the principal art of the Aleuts. Finely woven baskets from Attu, at the tip of the Aleutian chain—where villages were destroyed in American-Japanese combat during World War II and never rebuilt—are difficult-to-obtain treasures.

— Stanton H. Patty

ALASKA: A GEOLOGICAL STORY

MOST PEOPLE know about Alaska's oil and gold. But did you know that the state has a desert? That camels once roamed here? That there's a fault line nearly twice as long as the San Andreas Fault? That the largest earthquake ever to hit North America struck Alaska in 1964 and affected the entire planet? That the state has 80 potentially active volcanoes and approximately 100,000 glaciers?

All these physical wonders are geological in origin and are in addition to a North Slope oil supply that accounts for 25% of U.S. production and more than 10% of U.S. consumption as well as caches of gold that fueled more than 20 rushes.

Nearly all visitors will have at least one encounter with a glacier (with 29,000 square mi of them, they're hard to miss). Courtesy of the Pleistocene Ice Age, high-latitude location, and abundant moisture from the North Pacific, Alaska has approximately 100,000 of these large sheets of ice. The vast majority are in the southern and southeastern parts of the state, as these are the areas with the most moisture. How much moisture? Portions of the Chugach Mountains can gather 600 inches of snow each year, an amount that is comparable, in rain, to the annual precipitation in Seattle. In north-central Alaska, the Brooks Range contains a glacial field of approximately 280 square mi. Although small by Alaskan standards, it is larger than all the glacial fields in the rest of the United States combined, which comprise approximately 230 square mi.

There are alpine or valley glaciers, those that form high in mountain valleys and travel to lower elevations. Alaska harbors several of the great alpine glaciers in the world, found in the high country of the Alaska Range, the Talkeetna, Wrangell, Chugach, St. Elias, and Coast mountains. Some, such as the Bering Glacier, come tantalizingly close to the water. At more than 100 mi in length, and with an area of more than 2,250 square mi, the Bering is the longest and largest Alaskan glacier, its seclusion guarded by Cape St. Elias and the stormy waters of the Gulf of Alaska. Also impressive are the Hubbard, its imposing terminus dominating the head of isolated Yakutat Bay; and the Columbia, foreboding and threatening, calving icebergs that tack in line like Nelson's fleet across the mouth of Valdez Arm.

The Malaspina Glacier is an unusual piedmont glacier. Formed by the coalescence of several glaciers, this 850-square-mi mass is lobate, or fan-shape, and occupies a benchland on the northwest side of Yakutat Bay. So much of the Alaska Range, Wrangell, Chugach, St. Elias, and Coast mountains are covered by glacial ice that it is often more appropriate to talk about ice fields than individual glaciers.

Then there are the great tidewater glaciers of Prince William Sound and southeastern Alaska. Alpine glaciers that come right to the water's edge, they creak, moan, thunder, and calve off great bergs and little bergeys. The world's longest is the previously mentioned Hubbard Glacier, which, because it stretches more than 70 mi from its head in Canada to its terminus in Yakutat Bay, is both an alpine and a tidewater glacier. Sixteen tidewater glaciers can be found in Glacier Bay National Park, 20 in Prince William Sound. Some are advancing, some retreating. Hubbard has not only advanced in recent years but has surged. In 1986, a surge by Hubbard blocked the Russell Fjord at the upper end of Yakutat Bay, turning it into Russell Lake. Later that year, the portion of the glacier acting as a dam in front of Russell Lake gave way, violently releasing the backed-up water to an elevation of 83 feet above sea level. That's pretty impressive when you stop to think that the Russell Fjord is normally at sea level. Surging glaciers can move downhill hundreds of feet per day. The Hubbard's greatest surge was in September 1899, when it advanced ½ mi into the bay in just five minutes, courtesy of an earthquake.

Glaciologists are interested in knowing more about how glaciers, especially tidewater glaciers, advance and retreat. The Columbia Glacier, both an alpine and a tidewater glacier like the Hubbard, in Prince William Sound is approximately

40 mi long, covers more than 400 square mi, and flows to sea level from 10,000- to 12,000-foot peaks in the Chugach Range. Its width at the terminus can be as much as 4 mi; its ice thickness can reach 900 feet (on average 300 feet above the water and 600 feet below). It is also only 8 mi from the shipping lanes traveled by oil tankers leaving the Alaska pipeline terminal at Valdez. Columbia has been receding since the early 1980s, sending berg after berg into Prince William Sound and into the shipping lanes to Valdez, and now that it's receding, it has the potential to calve even more bergs. Although a shallow sill, or shoal, of underwater glacial deposits keeps icebergs more than 100 feet thick from entering Prince William Sound, some big bergs still make it to the shipping lanes. Columbia's calving took its toll just after midnight on March 29, 1989, when Captain Hazlewood of the *Exxon Valdez* steered too far east while trying to avoid bergs in Valdez Arm and ran aground on Bligh Reef.

You can see many glaciers from the Alaska Marine Highway. The tidewater glaciers of Glacier Bay and the Malaspina and Hubbard glaciers in Yakutat Bay are best seen by boat or ship. Sailing into Valdez Arm, you may see more of the Columbia Glacier than you want—it's often coming to see you in the form of scores of bergs and bergeys, forcing you east toward Bligh Reef. Once you are safely ashore in Valdez it's time to look at valley glaciers. You can access either the Valdez or Worthington Glacier by road. If in the Matanuska Valley, go see the Matanuska Glacier. If on the Kenai Peninsula, try either the Exit or Portage Glacier. If you are visiting Juneau, the Mendenhall Glacier is on the outskirts of town.

More than 80 volcanoes in Alaska are potentially active. Novarupta, Pavlof, Augustine, Redoubt, and Spurr are Alaskan volcanoes that are part of the "Ring of Fire," the volcanic rim of the Pacific. From Mt. Wrangell at 144 degrees west longitude in Southeast Alaska to Cape Wrangell at 173 degrees east longitude at the tip of the Aleutian archipelago, southern Alaska exists, to paraphrase historian Will Durant, by volcanic decree . . . subject to change.

Anchorage (and the greater Cook Inlet area) is a great place to watch volcanoes erupt. Augustine, Redoubt, and Spurr volcanoes have put on shows up and down the Cook Inlet; the Mt. Spurr eruption of August 1992 temporarily stopped air travel into and out of Anchorage. The most violent Alaskan eruption? The 2½-day eruption of Novarupta in 1912 in what is now Katmai National Park. The 2½ cubic mi of ash deposited there has left an Alaskan legacy: the surreal Valley of Ten Thousand Smokes.

The length of a fault system and whether or not the fault is straight over great distances are of interest to geologists. Fault length is related to earthquake magnitude. Generally speaking, the longer a fault, the greater the potential magnitude. Impressed by the 600-mi length of California's San Andreas? The onshore portion of the Denali Fault System is more than 1,000 mi long. Numerous long faults around the world move horizontally. This produces some interesting results if the fault trace is not straight. A fault system such as the Denali has a large component of horizontal movement (called strike-slip motion): crustal blocks on either side move past each other, rather than up or down. If a strike-slip fault bends, one of two situations results: a gap or hole in the crust (usually filled by volcanic outbreaks and/ or sediments sloughing into the hole) or a compression of the bend, resulting in vertical uplift (mountains). Which condition occurs is a function of fault motion, whether into or out of the bend. South of Fairbanks, the Denali Fault System changes trend, from northwest–southeast to northeast–southwest. The sense of horizontal motion is into the bend, resulting in vertical uplift. What mountain just happens to be in the vicinity? Mt. McKinley, at 20,320 feet the tallest mountain in North America. Moreover, its relief (difference in elevation between the base and top of the mountain), at 18,000 feet, is unsurpassed. Mt. Everest is more than 29,000 feet, but "only" 11,000 feet above the Tibetan Plateau, which forms its base.

With such big faults, it's no wonder geologists look at Alaska as big earthquake country. Seward, Valdez, Whittier, and Anchorage are just some of the more prominent names associated with the Good Friday Earthquake of 1964. Upgraded in 1977 to magnitude 9.2, the Good Friday quake is the largest on record for North

America. Fifteen to thirty seconds is not unusual for ground motion in a big, destructive earthquake; Alaskans shook for three to four minutes during the Good Friday quake. The epicenter was about 6 mi east of College Fjord in Prince William Sound, some 70 mi east of Anchorage. Vertical deformation (uplift or down-dropping of the land) affected an area of 100,000 square mi. By the time the shaking had stopped, the area of Latouche Island had moved 60 feet to the southeast and portions of the Montague Island area were uplifted by as much as 30 feet. The area of Portage was down-dropped by approximately 10 feet. The largest tsunami (often misnamed a tidal wave) that hit Hilo, Hawaii, checked in at 12½ feet; the largest at Crescent City, California, was 13 feet; and in Chenega, Alaska, Native residents were never sure what rose from the sea to smite them . . . just that it was 90 feet tall. The entire planet was affected: the area in which the quake was felt by people is estimated at 500,000 square mi—South Africa checked in to report that groundwater was sloshing around in wells.

Geologists generally describe tsunamis with respect to displacement on a fault underwater. They use the more general term "seismic sea wave" when other things, such as submarine landslides, cause enormous waves. The 90-foot seismic sea wave that hit Chenega was topped by the 220-foot wave reported from the Valdez Arm area. But a few years earlier in southeastern Alaska, on the evening of July 9, 1958, an earthquake in the Yakutat area dumped an enormous landslide into the head of Lituya Bay. The result was a seiche, or splash wave, that traveled 1,740 feet up the opposite mountainside.

Impressed yet? In the last century the average recurrence interval for Alaskan earthquakes in excess of 8.0 on the Richter Scale was 10 years. The recurrence interval for earthquakes over 7.0 is just over a year. Never mind California—Alaska is the most seismically active state in the Union. Volcanic hazard? Well, Pavlof has averaged an eruption every 6 years over the last 240.

Earthquakes, volcanoes—it's not called the Ring of Fire for nothing. The North American and Pacific tectonic plates are battling all the way from California to Japan. The two battle awfully hard in Alaska.

And now about that desert. The North Slope of Alaska is 80,000 square mi of frozen, windswept desert where Inupiat Eskimos live. It's a desert from the climatological perspective that the North Slope receives less than 10 inches of precipitation each year. If you go around the west end of the Brooks Range, you can even find sand dunes—Great Kobuk, Little Kobuk, and Hunt River sand-dune fields. Temperatures during the short, cool summers are usually between 30°F and 40°F. Temperatures during the winter can average –20°F. In winter, the Arctic Ocean moderates temperatures on the North Slope . . . but there is nothing to moderate the wind.

The first people to "come into the country" came across the Bering Land Bridge from Asia, between 10,000 and 40,000 years ago. The Bering Land Bridge was a product of the Pleistocene epoch—the "Great Ice Age"—which lowered the sea level enough for the bridge to form. At the start of the Mesozoic era (beginning about 245 million years before the present), sandstones and conglomerates deposited in a warm, shallow sea marked the beginning of Prudhoe Bay. That abundant organic matter is now abundant oil under the North Slope. Also during the Mesozoic era, oil-bearing shales were deposited in the Cook Inlet, home of Alaska's first oil boom; copper and silver deposits were formed in what is now the Copper River country; Cretaceous swamps in South Central Alaska became the Matanuska coalfield; and gold was emplaced around present-day Fairbanks and near Nome on the Seward Peninsula.

The oldest rocks in Alaska are of Precambrian age (the "Time Before Life") and are in southwestern Alaska. They have been dated at 2 billion years of age, nearly half the age of the earth. Rocks 1 billion years old have been identified in the area of the Brooks Range south to the Yukon River. Interestingly, the 1-billion-year-old rocks are native; the 2-billion-year-old rocks are expatriates. In fact, southern and southeastern Alaska are composed of a mosaic or quilt of microplates, all much smaller than continent size. Some terranes (blocks or fragments of the Earth's crust that may vary in age, geologic character, or site of origin) arrived in Alaska from as far south as the equator.

Certain Alaskan rocks tell a tale of warm climates and seas. Evidence? Hike the Holitna River basin in Southwest Alaska and look for fossil remains of the many trilobites (those now-extinct three-lobed marine arthropods that scavenged the bottoms of warm, shallow, Cambrian seas—parents, if you don't know what they look like, ask your children). The central interior of Alaska evidently was never covered by ice but was instead a cool steppe land roamed by mammoths, bison, horses, saber-toothed cats, and camels. Yes, camels.

Alaska's stunning expanse incorporates fire and ice, wind and rain, volcano, glacier, windswept tundra, towering rain forest, and mist-shrouded island. Its geologic story covers a great deal of time and distance and has produced (and is producing) some of the most exquisite land anywhere. In the north, the rocks tell a story of relative stability—geological homebodies born and raised. In the south, the patchwork terrains tell a tale of far-traveled immigrants coming into the country. Geological processes that have produced, and are still producing, both homebodies and expatriates create a land in constant flux. But the majesty of the land . . . that is the unchanging legacy of Alaska.

— Dr. Charles Lane

INDEX

NOTES

FODOR'S KEY TO THE GUIDES

America's guidebook leader publishes guides for every kind of traveler. Check out our many series and find your perfect match.

FODOR'S GOLD GUIDES
America's favorite travel-guide series offers the most detailed insider reviews of hotels, restaurants, and attractions in all price ranges, plus great background information, smart tips, and useful maps.

COMPASS AMERICAN GUIDES
Stunning guides from top local writers and photographers, with gorgeous photos, literary excerpts, and colorful anecdotes. A must-have for culture mavens, history buffs, and new residents.

FODOR'S CITYPACKS
Concise city coverage in a guide plus a foldout map. The right choice for urban travelers who want everything under one cover.

FODOR'S EXPLORING GUIDES
Hundreds of color photos bring your destination to life. Lively stories lend insight into the culture, history, and people.

FODOR'S TRAVEL HISTORIC AMERICA
For travelers who want to experience history firsthand, this series gives in-depth coverage of historic sights, plus nearby restaurants and hotels. Themes include the Thirteen Colonies, the Old West, and the Lewis and Clark Trail.

FODOR'S POCKET GUIDES
For travelers who need only the essentials. The best of Fodor's in pocket-size packages for just $9.95.

FODOR'S FLASHMAPS
Every resident's map guide, with dozens of easy-to-follow maps of public transit, restaurants, shopping, museums, and more.

FODOR'S CITYGUIDES
Sourcebooks for living in the city: thousands of in-the-know listings for restaurants, shops, sports, nightlife, and other city resources.

FODOR'S AROUND THE CITY WITH KIDS
Up to 68 great ideas for family days, recommended by resident parents. Perfect for exploring in your own backyard or on the road.

FODOR'S HOW TO GUIDES
Get tips from the pros on planning the perfect trip. Learn how to pack, fly hassle-free, plan a honeymoon or cruise, stay healthy on the road, and travel with your baby.

FODOR'S LANGUAGES FOR TRAVELERS
Practice the local language before you hit the road. Available in phrase books, cassette sets, and CD sets.

KAREN BROWN'S GUIDES
Engaging guides—many with easy-to-follow inn-to-inn itineraries—to the most charming inns and B&Bs in the U.S.A. and Europe.

BAEDEKER'S GUIDES
Comprehensive guides, trusted since 1829, packed with A–Z reviews and star ratings.

OTHER GREAT TITLES FROM FODOR'S
Baseball Vacations, The Complete Guide to the National Parks, Family Vacations, Golf Digest's Places to Play, Great American Drives of the East, Great American Drives of the West, Great American Vacations, Healthy Escapes, National Parks of the West, Skiing USA.
